MATHPOWER™
Eight

Authors

George Knill, B.Sc., M.S.Ed.
Hamilton, Ontario

Dino Dottori, B.Sc., M.S.Ed.
North Bay, Ontario

Eileen Collins, B.A., M.Ed.
Hamilton, Ontario

Mary Lou Forest, B.Ed., M.Ed.
Edmonton, Alberta

Mary Lou Kestell, B.Math.
Ancaster, Ontario

Archie Macdonald, B.A., B.Ed.
Dartmouth, Nova Scotia

Reviewers

Terry Clifford
Winnipeg, Manitoba

Denys Kornuta
Saskatoon, Saskatchewan

Kate Le Maistre
Montreal, Quebec

Brian Outerbridge
Delta, British Columbia

McGraw-Hill Ryerson Limited

Toronto   Montreal   New York   Auckland   Bogotá   Caracas
Lisbon   London   Madrid   Mexico   Milan   New Delhi   Paris
San Juan   Singapore   Sydney   Tokyo

MATHPOWER™ 8

ISBN 0-07-549889-8
ISBN 0-07-552509-7 (includes answers)

7 8 9 10   TRI   4 3 2 1 0

Printed and bound in Canada

Care has been taken to trace ownership of copyright material contained in this text. The publishers will gladly accept any information that will enable them to rectify any reference or credit in subsequent editions.

Canadian Cataloguing in Publication Data

Main entry under title:

Mathpower eight

Includes index.
ISBN 0-07-549889-8

1. Mathematics.   2. Mathematics — Problems,
exercises, etc.   I. Knill, George, date—   .

QA107.M37 1994   510   C94-931714-4

Executive Editor: Michael Webb
Editors: Sheila Bassett, Julia Keeler, Susan Marshall, Jean Ford
Senior Supervising Editor: Carol Altilia
Permissions Editor: Jacqueline Donovan
Cover and Interior Design: Pronk&Associates
Electronic Assembly: Pronk&Associates
Art Direction: Pronk&Associates/Joe Lepiano
Production: Pronk&Associates/ Technical Art and Page Assembly,
    Linda Stephenson; Production Coordinator, Nelly Toomey;
    Production Assistant, Nancy Cook; Art Assistant, Caren Thomas;
    Typesetting, Stanley Tran
Cover Illustration: Doug Martin
Photo Researcher: Lois Browne/In a Word Communications Services

This book was manufactured in Canada using acid-free and recycled paper.

CONTENTS

CHAPTER 3
Geometry

CHAPTER 4
Perimeter and Area

CHAPTER 5
Fractions

CHAPTER 8
Three-Dimensional Geometry

CHAPTER 9
Statistics and Probability

USING MATHPOWER™ 8

Each chapter contains a number of sections.
In a typical section, you find the following features.

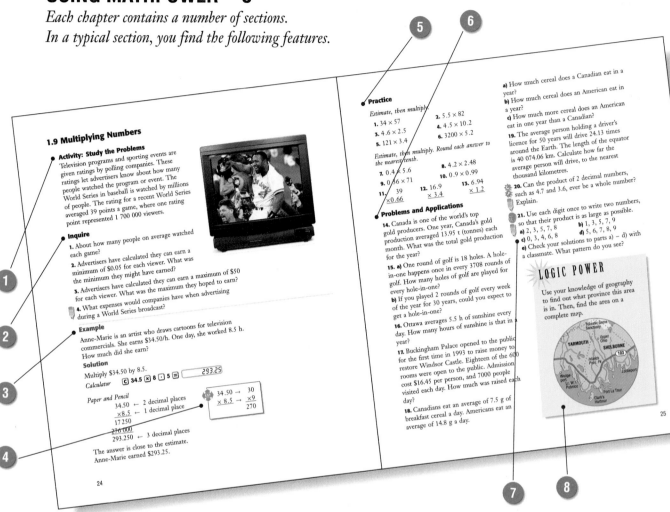

1.9 Multiplying Numbers

Activity: Study the Problems

Television programs and sporting events are given ratings by polling companies. These ratings let advertisers know about how many people watched the program or event. The World Series in baseball is watched by millions of people. The rating for a recent World Series averaged 39 points a game, where one rating point represented 1 700 000 viewers.

Inquire

1. About how many people on average watched each game?

2. Advertisers have calculated they can earn a minimum of $0.05 for each viewer. What was the minimum they might have earned?

3. Advertisers have calculated they can earn a maximum of $50 for each viewer. What was the maximum they hoped to earn?

4. What expenses would companies have when advertising during a World Series broadcast?

Example

Anne-Marie is an artist who draws cartoons for television commercials. She earns $34.50/h. One day, she worked 8.5 h. How much did she earn?

Solution

Multiply $34.50 by 8.5.

Calculator C 34.5 × 8 . 5 =   293.25

Paper and Pencil

```
34.50  ← 2 decimal places          34.50 → 30
 ×8.5  ← 1 decimal place           × 8.5 → ×9
17 250                                     270
276 000
293.250  ← 3 decimal places
```

The answer is close to the estimate.
Anne-Marie earned $293.25.

24

Practice

Estimate, then multiply.

1. 34×57
2. 5.5×82
3. 4.6×2.5
4. 4.5×10.2
5. 121×3.4
6. 3200×5.2

Estimate, then multiply. Round each answer to the nearest tenth.

7. 0.4×5.6
8. 4.2×2.48
9. 0.86×71
10. 0.9×0.99
11. 39×0.66
12. 16.9×3.4
13. 6.94×1.2

Problems and Applications

14. Canada is one of the world's top gold producers. One year, Canada's gold production averaged 13.95 t (tonnes) each month. What was the total gold production for the year?

15. a) One round of golf is 18 holes. A hole-in-one happens once in every 3708 rounds of golf. How many holes of golf are played for every hole-in-one?
b) If you played 2 rounds of golf every week of the year for 30 years, could you expect to get a hole-in-one?

16. Ottawa averages 5.5 h of sunshine every day. How many hours of sunshine is that in a year?

17. Buckingham Palace opened to the public for the first time in 1993 to raise money to restore Windsor Castle. Eighteen of the 600 rooms were open to the public. Admission cost $16.45 per person, and 7000 people visited each day. How much was raised each day?

18. Canadians eat an average of 7.5 g of breakfast cereal a day. Americans eat an average of 14.8 g a day.

a) How much cereal does a Canadian eat in a year?
b) How much cereal does an American eat in a year?
c) How much more cereal does an American eat in one year than a Canadian?

19. The average person holding a driver's licence for 50 years will drive 24.13 times around the Earth. The length of the equator is 40 074.06 km. Calculate how far the average person will drive, to the nearest thousand kilometres.

20. Can the product of 2 decimal numbers, such as 4.7 and 3.6, ever be a whole number? Explain.

21. Use each digit once to write two numbers, so that their product is as large as possible.
a) 2, 3, 5, 7, 8
b) 1, 3, 5, 7, 9
c) 0, 3, 4, 6, 8
d) 5, 6, 7, 8, 9
e) Check your solutions to parts a) – d) with a classmate. What pattern do you see?

LOGIC POWER

Use your knowledge of geography to find out what province this area is in. Then, find the area on a complete map.

25

---

1 You start with an activity to generate your own learning.

2 The inquire questions help you learn from the activity.

3 The example shows you how to use what you have learned.

4 The EST logo in a solution indicates an estimate.

5 These questions let you practise what you have learned.

6 These questions let you apply and extend what you have learned.

7 These logos indicate special kinds of questions.

The pencil logo tells you that you will be writing about math.

The critical thinking logo indicates that you will need to think carefully before you answer a question.

The working together logo shows you opportunities for working with a class-mate or in a larger group.

8 The power questions are challenging and fun. They encourage you to reason mathematically.

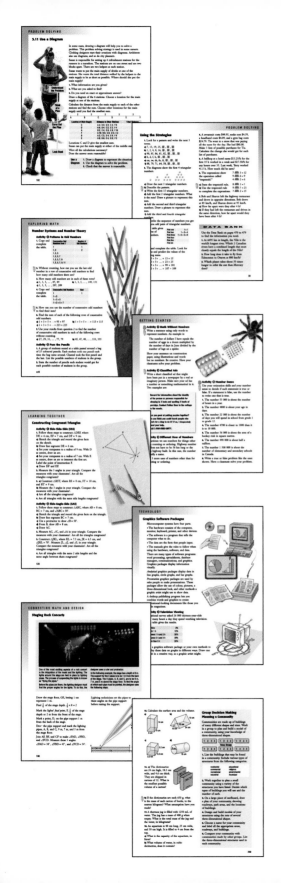

In the first 4 chapters of the book, there are 12 PROBLEM SOLVING sections that help you to use different problem solving strategies.

At or near the end of each chapter is a page headed PROBLEM SOLVING: Using the Strategies. To solve the problems on this page, you use the strategies you have studied. In each chapter, this page ends with DATA BANK questions. To solve them, you need to look up information in the Data Bank on pages 470 to 479.

There are 13 EXPLORING MATH pages before Chapter 1. The activities on these pages let you explore 13 mathematical standards that will be essential for citizens of the twenty-first century.

A GETTING STARTED section begins each chapter. This section reviews, in a fun way, what you should know before you work on the chapter. Each GETTING STARTED section includes a set of Mental Math questions.

In LEARNING TOGETHER sections, you learn by completing activities with your classmates.

The TECHNOLOGY sections show you some uses of technology and how you can apply technology to solve problems.

Some sections are headed CONNECTING MATH AND.... In these sections, you apply math to other subject areas, such as art, language, science, and the environment.

Each chapter includes sets of questions called REVIEW and CHAPTER CHECK, so that you can test your progress.

At the end of each review is a column headed GROUP DECISION MAKING. Here, you work with your classmates to research careers and do other projects.

Chapters 4, 8, and 12 end with sets of questions headed CUMULATIVE REVIEW. These three reviews cover the work you did in Chapters 1–4, 5–8, and 9–12.

The GLOSSARY on pages 481 to 487 helps you to understand mathematical terms.

A Problem Solving Model

The world is full of mathematical problems. A problem exists when you are presented with a situation and are at first unable to make sense of it. To solve any problem, you must make decisions.

MATHPOWER™ 8 will help you to become actively involved in problem solving by providing the experiences and strategies you need.

George Polya was one of the world's best problem solvers. The problem solving model used in this book has been adapted from a model developed by George Polya.

The problem solving model includes the following 4 stages.

Understand the Problem

First, read the problem and make sure that you understand it. Ask yourself these questions.
- Do I understand all the words?
- What information am I given?
- What am I asked to find?
- Can I state the problem in my own words?
- Am I given enough information?
- Am I given too much information?
- Have I solved a similar problem?

Think of a Plan

Organize the information you need. Decide whether you need an exact or approximate answer. Plan how to use the information. The following list includes some of the problem solving strategies that may help.
- Act out the problem.
- Manipulate materials.
- Work backward.
- Account for all possibilities.
- Change your point of view.
- Draw a diagram.
- Look for a pattern.
- Make a table.
- Use a formula.
- Guess and check.
- Solve a simpler problem.
- Use logical reasoning.

Carry Out the Plan

Choose the calculation method you will use to carry out your plan. Estimate the answer to the problem.
Carry out your plan, using paper and pencil, a calculator, a computer, or manipulatives.
Write a final statement that gives the solution to the problem.

Look Back

Check all your calculations.
Check your answer against the original problem. Is your answer reasonable? Does it agree with your estimate?
Look for an easier way to solve the problem.

Problem Solving

The ability to solve problems is an important skill that can be learned.

Solve the following problems. Compare your solutions with your classmates'.

1. Suppose June 1 is a Monday. If you start counting days on June 1, how many days will you count to reach the first Monday in October?

2. Divide the numbers from 1 to 12 into 2 groups. One group must have twice as many numbers as the other. The sum of the numbers in the larger group must be twice the sum of the numbers in the smaller group.

3. Draw a 3-by-3 grid. Colour 3 of the small squares red, 3 of them blue, and 3 of them green to meet these conditions.
- Every red square touches at least one green square along a complete side.
- Every green square touches at least one blue square along a complete side.
- Every blue square touches at least one red square along a complete side.

4. Professional basketball, hockey, and baseball championships are decided on the best 4 out of 7 games. The first team to win 4 games wins the championship. One way in which a team could win the first game and then go on to win a best-of-7 championship series is as follows.

Game	1	2	3	4	5	6	7
Result	W	L	L	W	W	W	

In how many other possible ways could the team win the championship series after winning the first game?

5. Two cars are travelling along a highway in the same direction toward a service centre. Car A is travelling at 20 m/s and is 100 m from the service centre. Car B is travelling at 25 m/s and is 125 m from the service centre.

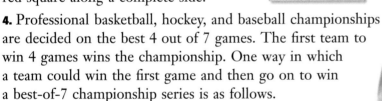

Will car B draw level with car A before, at, or after the service centre?

Communication

Activity ❶ Communicating Information

Ideas can be represented and communicated in many ways.
Here are 4 ways of communicating information about 3 dogs.

A

60 cm   39 cm   25 cm

B

Age | Height

• CS
CT •
• GR

C

Age: CS > CT > GR
Height: CT < CS < GR

D

The golden retriever is 60 cm high at the shoulder and is 10 months old.
The cocker spaniel is 39 cm high at the shoulder and is 3 years old.
The cairn terrier is 25 cm high at the shoulder and is 2 years old.

 1. a) Which communication method gives the most complete
information?
b) Which method is the most efficient way to present
a lot of information?
c) What mathematical symbols are used in the
algebraic method? What do these symbols mean?
d) When would each method of communication
be the most helpful?

2. Gather information about the pets owned by some
classmates. Communicate the information in 4 different
ways.

Activity ❷ Interpreting Conditions

List as many answers as possible that satisfy each condition.

1. even numbers between 30 and 50 that are multiples of 5

2. plane figures with 4 sides and at least 2 right angles

3. square numbers greater than 40 and less than 150

4. solid figures with exactly 4 flat faces

5. ways to represent $\frac{1}{2}$, other than with equivalent fractions

6. pairs of whole-number factors whose product is 36

Reasoning

Reasoning is the process of drawing conclusions from given facts or pieces of information. Reasoning often involves looking for a pattern.

Activity ❶ A Number Pattern

1. Start with 5×5, 15×15, and so on, until you think you have found the pattern in the products.

5×5	15×15	25×25	35×35	45×45
55×55	65×65	75×75	85×85	95×95

2. Predict the rest of the products and check them with a calculator.

3. Describe the pattern in words.

4. Use the pattern to predict each of the following products. Check your answers with a calculator.

a) 150×150 **b)** 450×450
c) 125×125 **d)** 195×195

Activity ❷ A Tile Pattern

The floor of a rectangular room is covered with square tiles. The tiles around the outside are red, and the tiles in the middle are white. In the diagram, the room is 6 tiles by 5 tiles. There are 18 red tiles and 12 white tiles.

Find the dimensions of a rectangular room in which the number of red tiles equals the number of white tiles.

Activity ❸ Dividing a Grid

Here are 2 ways to divide a 4-by-4 grid into 2 identical halves, with 8 small squares in each half.

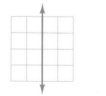

There are 4 other ways of dividing the grid into 2 identical halves, so that each half contains only complete squares. Find these 4 other ways.

EXPLORING MATH

Connections

Mathematics is used in many fields, including sports, music, and design. What other fields can you think of?

Activity ❶ Strike Zones in Baseball

In baseball, a player's official strike zone is a rectangle. The width is 43 cm, the width of home plate. The length is the distance from the knees to the armpits when the player is in a batting stance.

1. Find the distance from the knees to the armpits for players in a batting stance, if they have these official strike zones.

a) 3440 cm² **b)** 3655 cm² **c)** 3827 cm²

 2. With a classmate, find the area of your official strike zone.

3. In major league baseball, the length of the strike zone used by umpires is the distance from the player's knees to the waist. If you played major league baseball, what would be the area of your strike zone?

4. Find the difference in the areas of your 2 strike zones.

Activity ❷ Musical Notes

Music is written in notes that have different values.

Whole note	$\frac{1}{2}$ note	$\frac{1}{4}$ note	$\frac{1}{8}$ note	$\frac{1}{16}$ note

1. Write one note that has the equivalent value to each group of notes.

a) **b)** **c)**

2. Each group of notes is equivalent to one whole note. Write the missing note.

a) **b)**

3. What is the total value, in whole notes, of all the notes in this piece of music?

Activity ❸ Flag Designs

Geometric figures are used to design flags.

1. Name the figures used in the flag of each country.

a)

Bangladesh

b)

St. Vincent

c)

Kuwait

d)

Sudan

2. Design a rectangular flag that includes the following.

a) at least 4 triangles

b) a hexagon and a circle

c) a kite, a square, and at least 2 rectangles

Number and Number Relationships

Numbers can be expressed in a variety of forms, including fractions, decimals, integers, and percents.

Activity ❶ Using a Floor Plan

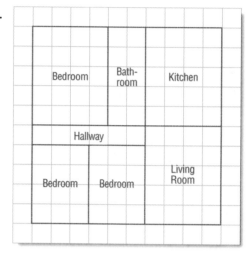

Scale drawings are often used to shrink or enlarge diagrams. This scale drawing shows the floor plan of a 3-bedroom apartment.

1. What fraction of the apartment does each room occupy?

2. What percent of the apartment does each room occupy?

3. Express your answers to question 2 as decimals.

4. Which form of the numbers you found in questions 1, 2, and 3 is most helpful in describing the plan? Explain.

5. If the actual dimensions of the apartment are 12 m by 12 m, does the fraction occupied by each room change?

6. Decide on the fraction of an apartment you think each of the following should occupy. Then, draw a floor plan.

Living Room   Kitchen   2 Bedrooms   Laundry Room

Bathroom   Hallway   Dining Room

Activity ❷ Interpreting a Graph

Larisa sells books to bookstores. On one sales trip, she drove from Ancaster to Evergreen through the towns of Blinky, Chad, and Devon. The graph shows the time of day and the distance she was from Ancaster every hour. Write a description of her trip using the information on the graph. Your description should give the following facts, plus any others you wish to provide.

a) the time she started, the times at which she stopped, and the time she arrived in Evergreen

b) the total distance she travelled

c) her speed at various times during the trip

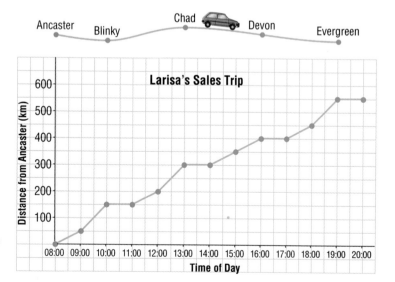

Number Systems and Number Theory

Activity ❶ Patterns in Odd Numbers

1. Copy and complete the table.

Consecutive Odd Numbers from 1	Number of Odd Numbers
1	1
1, 3	2
1, 3, 5	
1, 3, 5, 7	
1, 3, 5, 7, 9	
1, 3, 5, 7, 9, 11	

2. Without counting, how can you use the last odd number in a row of consecutive odd numbers to find how many odd numbers there are?

3. How many odd numbers are in each of these rows?
a) 1, 3, 5, ... , 87, 89   **b)** 1, 3, 5, ... , 149, 151
c) 1, 3, 5, ... , 207, 209

4. Copy and complete the table.

Consecutive Odd Numbers	Sum
1	1
1 + 3	
1 + 3 + 5	
1 + 3 + 5 + 7	

5. How can you use the number of consecutive odd numbers to find their sum?

6. Find the sum of each of the following rows of consecutive odd numbers.
a) 1 + 3 + 5 + ⋯ + 95 + 97   **b)** 1 + 3 + 5 + ⋯ + 113 + 115
c) 1 + 3 + 5 + ⋯ + 223 + 225

7. Use your results from question 2 to find the number of consecutive odd numbers in each of the following rows without counting.
a) 27, 29, 31, ... , 77, 79   **b)** 45, 47, 49, ... , 333, 335

Activity ❷ Pass the Pencils

1. A group of students seated at a table passed around a bag of 25 coloured pencils. Each student took one pencil each time the bag came around. Chantal took the first pencil and the last. List the possible numbers of students in the group.

2. State the number of pencils each student would get for each possible number of students in the group.

Computation and Estimation

You estimate to check or to make sense of an answer
you have computed. Practising mental math helps you
to make good estimates.

Activity ❶ Adding from the Left

One way to add mentally is to *add from the left*.

To add 45 + 38, think: "40 + 30 is 70,
5 + 8 is 13,
70 + 13 is 83."

Add mentally.

1. 24 + 63   **2.** 56 + 32   **3.** 64 + 87

4. 93 + 68   **5.** 426 + 339   **6.** 135 + 826

7. 7.3 + 8.2   **8.** 61.7 + 85.2

Activity ❷ Adding in Expanded Form

Another way to add mentally is to break up
numbers into expanded form. This method
can be called *bridging*.

To add 247 + 78, you can add 247 + 70 + 8.

Think: "247 + 70 is 317,
317 + 8 is 325."

To add 8.5 + 5.6, you can add 8.5 + 5 + 0.6.

Think: "8.5 + 5 is 13.5,
13.5 + 0.6 is 14.1."

Add mentally.

1. 120 + 75   **2.** 846 + 92   **3.** 634 + 95

4. 460 + 135   **5.** 309 + 168   **6.** 123 + 159

7. 2.5 + 2.6   **8.** $0.25 + $0.58

Activity ❸ Checking Your Change

After you buy something, it is a good idea
to check your change. You can decide how
much change you should have by subtraction.
Another way is to use *adding on*.

Suppose you spend $3.68 and hand over a
$10 bill.

To check the change,
you think: "$3.68 + $0.02 gives $3.70,
$3.70 + $0.30 gives $4.00,
$4.00 + $6.00 gives $10.00.
So, the change is $6.32."

Calculate the change from $20.00.

1. $12.50   **2.** $15.75   **3.** $16.97

4. $14.32   **5.** $17.69   **6.** $13.52

7. $7.55   **8.** $4.74

Patterns and Functions

In mathematics, we often study patterns and use them to make predictions.

Activity ❶

1. A small village had 3 roads passing through it, one going north–south (N–S) and 2 going east–west (E–W).

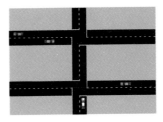

There was a stop sign at each corner of each intersection. How many stop signs were there?

2. As the village grew larger, new roads were built. Each time a new intersection was created, a stop sign was placed at each corner. How many stop signs were needed for the following numbers of roads?

a) 2 N–S, 2 E–W   **b)** 2 N–S, 3 E–W
c) 3 N–S, 3 E–W   **d)** 3 N–S, 4 E–W

3. Assume that the next street added will run N–S, the one after that E–W, and so on. Use your results from question 2 to predict how many streets there will be when the total number of stop signs is 120.

Activity ❷

1. Look for patterns. Copy and complete the table.

Large Cube	Number of Small Cubes	Dimensions of Each Face of Large Cube	Number of Small Cube Faces Showing
	1	1 × 1	6
	8	2 × 2	24
	27	3 × 3	
	64		
	125		
	216		

 2. Describe the patterns in words.

3. Predict the number of small cube faces showing on a large cube with the dimensions of each face 10 × 10.

Algebra

Algebra uses numbers and symbols to communicate ideas.
Algebra is the language of mathematics.

Activity ❶

The first diagram shows how you can use 16 toothpicks to make
a square with a perimeter of 16. Call the perimeter p. The
second diagram shows 16 toothpicks arranged as 5 identical
squares connected along entire sides. The perimeter is 12 or
$p - 4$. Draw diagrams to show how you can use 16 toothpicks
to make the following.

1. three different rectangles with a perimeter of p

2. two rectangles connected along entire sides to give a
perimeter of $p - 4$

3. three rectangles connected along entire sides to give a
perimeter of $p - 2$

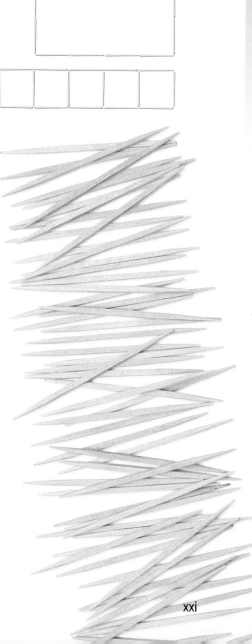

Activity ❷

1. The statement $+$ ▲ $=$ ▲ $+$ ■ $+$ ■ is not true for
▲ $= 1$ and ■ $= 2$, because $1 + 1$ does not equal $1 + 2 + 2$.
The statement is true for ▲ $= 4$ and ■ $= 2$, because $4 + 4$
does equal $4 + 2 + 2$. Find 3 other pairs of whole numbers
that make the statement true.

2. Find 3 pairs of whole numbers that make each of these
statements true.

a) ▲ $+$ ▲ $=$ ■

b) ■ $+$ ■ $+$ ■ $=$ ▲

c) ▲ $+$ ▲ $=$ ■ $+ 2$

d) ▲ $+$ ▲ $-$ ■ $= 1$

e) ▲ $+$ ■ $+$ ■ $=$ ■ $+ 4$

Activity ❸

1. Find a value of ■ to make each number sentence true.

a) ■ $+ 3 = 7$ **b)** ■ $+$ ■ $= 10$ **c)** ■ $+$ ■ $+ 3 = 19$

2. Find a value of n to make each number sentence true.

a) $n - 3 = 6$ **b)** $2 \times n = 8$ **c)** $3 \times n - 1 = 8$

3. Write each of the following as a number sentence,
using n to represent the unknown number. Then, find
the value of n.

a) A number plus three equals eight.

b) Four times a number equals twelve.

c) A number decreased by seven equals 4.

Statistics

Statistics is the science of collecting facts and making predictions based on the facts.

Activity ❶ A Sampling Experiment

Work in pairs.

1. Student A places 20 cubes in a paper bag, without showing them to student B. The cubes are of 2 different colours. Student B must predict the number of cubes of each colour by sampling.

2. Student A mixes the cubes. Student B takes a sample of 5 cubes from the bag and records the number of each colour in a table. Student B then returns the cubes to the bag.

3. Student A again mixes the cubes, and student B draws 5 more. The students carry out the process a total of 10 times. If the colours are red and blue, the table looks like this.

Trial	1	2	3	4	5	6	7	8	9	10	Totals
Number of Red Cubes											
Number of Blue Cubes											

4. Student B uses the totals to predict the number of cubes of each colour in the bag. The students compare the prediction to the actual number of each colour. They then switch roles and repeat the experiment.

Activity ❷ Phone Book Statistics

Each of the last 2 digits of a telephone number can be any digit from 0 to 9. If you add the last 2 digits, the sum can be any number from 0 (the last two digits are 0 and 0) to 18 (the last two digits are 9 and 9).

1. Without looking in a phone book, predict whether certain sums occur more often than others.

2. Test your prediction for one column of numbers from a phone book. Find the sum of the last 2 digits in each number, make a tally, and record the results on a bar graph.

3. Compare your graph with the graphs of other students. Explain the results.

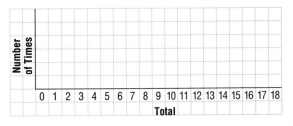

Probability

Probability is the mathematics of chance. Probabilities do not give you the exact answers to questions, but they tell you what you can expect to happen, on the average. When you think of tossing a coin 10 times, you might expect it to land "heads" 5 times, but you will not know how it will land until you actually toss it.

Activity ❶ Number Tiles

There are 10 number tiles, numbered from 1 to 10, in a paper bag.

1. You pick one tile from the bag without looking. The probability, or chance, of getting the tile with the 3 on it is $\frac{1}{10}$. Why?

2. What is the probability of picking an odd number?

3. What is the probability of picking an even number?

4. What is the probability of picking a number greater than 6?

Activity ❷ Birthdays

Do you think there is a good chance that two students in a grade 8 class have the same birthday?

1. If there are 30 students and 365 possible birthdays, you might think the chance is about 1 in 10. Why?

2. In fact, if there are 23 students, the chance is about 1 out of 2, or 50%, that two students have the same birthday. For 42 students, the chance is about 9 out of 10, or 90%, that two students have the same birthday. For 57 students, there is a 99% chance that two have the same birthday.

Divide 57 slips of paper among the members of your class. Have each person secretly write a different birthday on each of the slips he or she has. Collect the slips of paper and see if 2 birthdays are the same.

3. Canada has 104 senators. The probability that two of them have the same birthday is almost 100%. Use an almanac to find out how many senators have the same birthday.

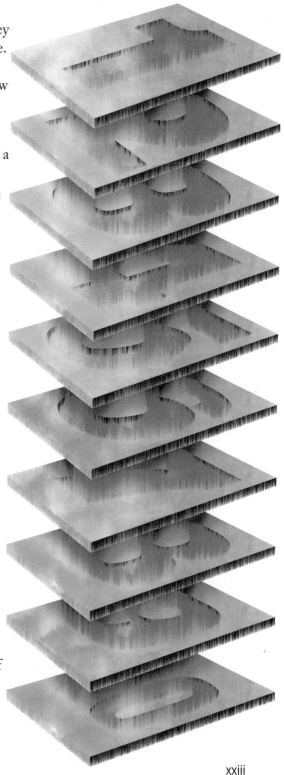

Geometry

A knot design is one way of making pictures on a flat page look three-dimensional. The woodcut *Snakes*, by M.C. Escher, is a knot design.

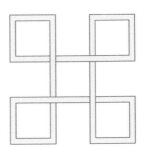

Activity ❶

Draw a knot design with squares by following these steps.

1. Start with 9 squares. Make the sides of the squares double lines.

2. Erase the 4 centre sections on the outside of the design.

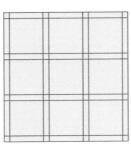

3. Erase the parts of doubles lines that overlap with other double lines.

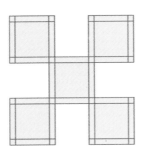

Now, start with 16 squares and make a knot design.

Activity ❷

Knot designs can be made from circles. The logo for the Olympic Games has 5 circles in a knot design.

1. Draw the Olympic logo.

2. Make 2 different knot designs with 4 circles in each.

Measurement

Measurement is all around us.

Activity ❶ Using Measurements

1. List as many situations as possible in which each of the following types of measurement is required.

a) speed   **b)** depth   **c)** height

d) mass   **e)** volume   **f)** temperature

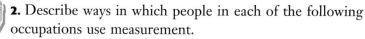

2. Describe ways in which people in each of the following occupations use measurement.

a) police officer   **b)** mail carrier

c) disc jockey   **d)** meteorologist

e) nurse   **f)** truck driver

3. Sports coaches must deal with many measurements. Choose a sport and list the types of measurement that the coach must be aware of.

Activity ❷ Designing a Room

An interior designer decorates rooms in homes and businesses.

1. List all the measurements an interior designer must know in order to decorate a room.

2. What units of measurement are used to measure each of the following?

a) carpeting   **b)** floor tiles   **c)** wallpaper

d) window blinds   **e)** curtains   **f)** paint

3. Using catalogues, magazines, and advertising flyers, choose materials to furnish and decorate a room used by your family. Write a report in which you describe your plan and estimate the cost of decorating the room.

Activity ❸ Earth Measurements

Through the ages, humans have explored and measured the highest, widest, longest, and deepest features of the Earth. Use an almanac or other reference source to name these features of the Earth and find their dimensions.

a) longest river   **b)** largest desert

c) highest mountain   **d)** deepest ocean

e) coldest continent   **f)** largest lake

CHAPTER 1

Number Connections

The object is to spell out a word on a telephone keypad according to these rules:

1. Start on any button with letters and choose one of the letters on that button. This is the first letter of your word.

2. Move horizontally, vertically, or diagonally to a second button that is next to your first button. Choose one of the letters on the second button. This is the second letter in your word.

3. Continue moving to the buttons that are next to each other until you have spelled a word.

4. You cannot stay on a button and take 2 letters from it, but you can come back to a button as often as you like.

5. If you use the same button more than once, you can choose the same letter each time, if you wish.

6. The score of your word is found by adding the numbers on the buttons for the letters that you use. The best word has the highest score.

Activity ❶ Math Without Numbers

Write a sentence using only words to represent numbers. An example is:

> The number of dollars I have equals the number of eggs in a dozen multiplied by the number of days in June divided by the number of legs on a spider.

Show your sentence on construction paper, using illustrations and words but no numbers. Be creative. Have your classmates solve your problem.

Activity ❷ Classified Ads

Write a short classified ad that might have been put in a newspaper by a real or imaginary person. Make sure your ad has a number or something mathematical in it. Two examples are:

> **Reward for information about the identity of the person or persons responsible for sleeping in 3 beds and spoiling 3 bowls of porridge. Contact Father Bear in the cottage in the woods.**
>
> **Are you good at putting puzzles together? Do you think you could teach people who work for a king to do it? If so, I desperately need your help.**
> **Call 1-800-HMD-DMTY.**

Activity ❸ Different Uses of Numbers

Sometimes we use numbers for things other than counting or ordering. Highway number 56 does not have to be 56 km long or the 56th highway built. In this case, the number is really a name.

List 3 more uses of numbers other than for counting or ordering.

Activity ❹ Number Sense

Use your estimation skills and your number sense to decide if each statement is true or false. If a statement is false, use the number to write one that is true.

1. The number 53 000 is about the number of hours in a year.

2. The number 4800 is about your age in days.

3. The number 22 000 is about the number of days you will spend in school from grade 1 to grade 12.

4. The number 4700 is closer to 1000 than it is to 10 000.

5. The number 56 000 is about the area of a hockey rink in square metres.

6. The number 490 000 is about half a million.

7. The number 1 500 000 is about the number of elementary and secondary schools in Canada.

8. Write a true or false problem like the ones shown. Have a classmate solve your problem.

Keeping Time

Activity ❶ Time

1. a) Work in pairs. You will need a digital watch or a watch with a second hand.

Person 1: Tap your finger for what you think is 10 s.

Person 2: Use the watch to time Person 1. Then, calculate how close Person 1 was to 10 s. If Person 1 did not tap close to 10 s, have him or her try the experiment again until he or she can tap between 9 s and 11 s. Switch roles and repeat the experiment.

b) Repeat the experiment, but this time try to tap for 100 s. Compare your results with your classmates'.

2. Calculate.

a) How many minutes are there in 1000 s?

b) How many hours are there in 10 000 s?

c) How many days and hours are there in 100 000 s?

d) How long is 1 000 000 s in days, hours, and minutes?

Activity ❷ "Sun Time" and "Official Time"

1. a) Do some library research to find out when railroad officials finally came to an agreement about "official times" and time zones.

b) What role did a famous Canadian, Sir Sandford Fleming, play in the development of time zones?

2. Write a short description about how time was organized before "official time." When people worked on "sun time," by how much did neighbouring towns disagree over a specific time, such as noon?

3. How many time zones are there in Canada? How many are there in the United States? (Do not forget Hawaii and Alaska.)

4. Approximately how many degrees of longitude are there in one time zone?

5. Write a funny story about the confusion there would be in your family if a time zone line went through the middle of your house.

Mental Math

Calculate. Add the tens and then the ones.

1. 54 + 32   **2.** 77 + 81   **3.** 19 + 99

4. 44 + 88   **5.** 127 + 73   **6.** 238 + 85

7. 15 + 65 + 45   **8.** 109 + 56 + 22

9. 34 + 56 + 73   **10.** 182 + 40 + 34

11. 71 + 13 + 42   **12.** 88 + 13 + 54

Calculate. Subtract the tens and then the ones.

13. 369 − 42   **14.** 48 − 26   **15.** 173 − 64

16. 81 − 37   **17.** 600 − 58   **18.** 129 − 38

19. 528 − 65   **20.** 733 − 46   **21.** 366 − 27

22. 208 − 19   **23.** 188 − 96   **24.** 500 − 68

Calculate.

25. 6 × 12   **26.** 3 × 80   **27.** 4 × 90

28. 9 × 90   **29.** 12 × 50   **30.** 12 × 600

31. 15 × 7   **32.** 11 × 29   **33.** 8 × 55

34. 49 × 3   **35.** 99 × 2   **36.** 16 × 12

Calculate.

37. 720 ÷ 9   **38.** 8100 ÷ 9   **39.** 240 ÷ 6

40. 720 ÷ 80   **41.** 360 ÷ 6   **42.** 150 ÷ 10

43. 560 000 ÷ 700   **44.** 150 ÷ 15

45. 15 000 ÷ 300   **46.** 960 ÷ 80

47. 1080 ÷ 12   **48.** 840 ÷ 70

Number Sequences

0 1 2 3 4 5 6 7 8 9 . . . .

Activity ❶ Adding Digits

A number sequence starts as follows:
0, 1, 2, 3, 4, 5, 6, 7, 8, 9, ...
After 9, the number is replaced by the sum of its digits. So, 10 becomes 1, 11 becomes 2, and so on. Because you add the digits only once, 19 becomes 10.

The numbers from 20 to 30 become

20 → 2	21 → 3	22 → 4	23 → 5
24 → 6	25 → 7	26 → 8	27 → 9
28 → 10	29 → 11	30 → 3	

1. Write the digit totals for the numbers from 30 to 40.

2. Write the digit totals for the numbers from 100 to 110.

3. Write the digit totals for the numbers from 1230 to 1240.

4. What is the first number that gives you a digit total of 17?

5. What is the largest digit total for a 2-digit number?

6. What is the first 3-digit number that gives the highest digit total you found in question 3?

7. What is the first number that gives you a digit total of 21?

8. What is the largest digit total for a 3-digit number?

9. If you do not count 0, what is the smallest digit total? When does this total happen?

10. How often does the digit total 2 happen between 0 and 1200?

Activity ❷ Constant Addition

1. Share one calculator with your partner. Find out how your calculator does "constant addition." This means that pressing *only* the equal key will allow you to count by any number you choose. For example, many calculators work as follows:

Press	C	2	+	=	=	=	=	=
Display	0	2		2	4	6	8	10	12

or

Press	C	2	+	2	=	=	=	=	=
Display	0	2		2	2	4	6	8	10	12

2. Try the sequence that lets you count by threes. One person should press the keys. The other person should quietly read the calculator display. Stop when you pass 100.

3. Trade jobs and count out the sequence of sevens. Again, stop when you pass 100.

4. Repeat steps 2 and 3 for some numbers of your choice.

5. Which sequences will contain the number 100? How do you know?

6. Which sequences will contain the number 48? How do you know?

7. Which sequences will contain the number 60? How do you know?

8. Write a rule for finding which sequences contain a specific number that you or someone else chooses.

Activity ❸ Adding Decimals

1. *Person 1:* Press [C] 0 [.] 1 [+] [=] [=] [=]
or Press [C] 0 [.] 1 [+] 0 [.] 1 [=] [=] [=]
and so on.
Person 2: Read the calculator displays.

2. Start again, and both of you write the sequence of decimals. Write the decimals in standard form from 0.1 to 1.2.

3. Write, in words, the numbers from one tenth to one and two tenths.

4. Explain what happens after you pass 0.9 or nine tenths. Write a sentence or two to explain to a younger student why it happens.

Activity ❺ More Place Values

1. Again, trade responsibilities.
The person with the calculator should press
[C] 0 [.] 01 [+] [=] [=] [=]
or [C] 0 [.] 01 [+] 0 [.] 01 [=] [=] [=]
and so on.

2. Record what happens when you pass 0.09, 0.19, 0.29, and so on. Use "..." to represent "and so on" and to show you left some numbers out of your sequence. It should look like this: 0.01, 0.02, 0.03, ..., 0.09, 0.1, 0.11, ..., 0.19, ...

3. When did you first use an extra place value to record your numbers?

4. After how many numbers will you have to use yet another place value?

5. Race with another team on calculators.
One team counts
[C] 1 [+] [=] [=] [=] or [C] 1 [+] 1 [=] [=] [=]
and so on to 100. The other counts
[C] 0 [.] 01 [+] [=] [=] [=] or
[C] 0 [.] 01 [+] 0 [.] 01 [=] [=] [=]
and so on to 1.
Which team should win? Why?

Activity ❹ Exploring Place Values

1. Trade responsibilities with your partner. The person with the calculator should press
[C] 0 [.] 01 [+] [=] [=] [=]
or [C] 0 [.] 01 [+] 0 [.] 01 [=] [=] [=]
and so on.

2. Write the numbers that you see. Stop when you get to 0.15.

3. Explain what happens when you pass 0.09. Why does this happen?

4. Look at the section numbers in this chapter.
a) Which section number follows section 1.9?
b) If the section numbers behaved like decimal numbers, which section number should follow section 1.9?
c) If the section numbers were decimals, how should we have numbered the sections in the chapter?

5

1.1 Choosing a Calculation Method

When you are given a mathematical problem, the first thing you should decide is whether you need an exact answer or an approximate answer. Then, decide what calculation method to use: estimation, mental math, paper and pencil, calculator, or computer.

Approximate answers are found by **estimation.** Estimation also lets you check that the answers you get from other calculation methods are reasonable. Some computations can be done in your head using **mental math.**

When a calculation looks simple and the numbers do not have many digits, **paper and pencil** may be the most efficient way to calculate.

A **calculator** is best for harder computations involving numbers with many digits.

A **computer** is useful for calculations that must be made over and over again.

Activity: Study the Problems

Jennifer Wilson works in the office of the Rainforest Protection Foundation. These are some of the problems she has to solve.

1. *The Rainforest* magazine subscription is $19.95 a year. She has to calculate the bill for a school board that ordered 34 subscriptions.

2. A newspaper reporter asks her how many hectares of rain forest are being lost each year.

3. The foundation has 11 567 members, and the dues are increasing by $5.00. The foundation director asks Jennifer, "About how much more money is that a year?"

4. Memberships cost $35.00 each. Someone phones and asks how much it would cost for a family of 3 to join.

5. The foundation operates from an old house, which the foundation bought. The director wants to know how many years it will take to pay off the mortgage.

Inquire

1. Which problems require an exact answer? Explain.

2. Which problems require an approximate answer? Explain.

3. Which method would you use for each problem? Give a reason for your answer.

4. Write 5 problems, one for each of the 5 methods.

6

Practice

Explain how you would use mental math to make each calculation. Then, calculate.

1. $18 + 12$
2. $613 + 5$
3. 33×3
4. $80 \div 8$
5. $345 - 112$
6. $234 + 111$
7. 101×2
8. $999 \div 9$

Explain which calculation method—mental math, paper and pencil, or a calculator—might be most efficient to make each calculation. Then, calculate.

9. 387×56
10. $44 + 23$
11. $234 - 127$
12. $2045 \div 5$
13. 247×10
14. $903 \div 43$
15. $35\ 645 - 31\ 234$
16. $101 + 202$

Problems and Applications

State whether you would need an exact answer or an approximate answer.

17. You are a player in a computer game competition: "What are your points at the end of level 5?"

18. You are a front desk attendant in a large hotel: "How long does it take to get to the airport?"

19. You are preparing an advertisement for Banff National Park: "How many people visited the park last year?"

20. You are a commercial airline pilot: "What is the plane's altitude?"

21. You are planning an athletic banquet: "How much money will we need to run the event?"

22. You work for Environment Canada. "What amount of chemical waste was dumped into the Great Lakes last year?"

23. You are a veterinarian: "When do you expect the wolf pup to be born?"

 Choose a calculation method for each of the following problems. Explain your choice and compare your choice with a classmate's.

24. You want to decorate the tops of your bedroom walls. What length of border will you need?

25. You are the lifeguard at the beach on a hot, sunny day. A newspaper reporter asks how many people are on the beach.

26. You are responsible for ticket sales for the Summer Olympics. Ticket prices vary, depending on the event. The organizers of the games want to know how much money will be made if all the tickets are sold.

27. You work in a pet store. The cash register is out of order. You have to calculate the total bill for several items, including taxes.

28. You need to calculate 15% of the bill to leave a tip in a restaurant.

29. You are the statistician for a hockey team. You need to keep track of the number of goals and assists for each player for a season.

 30. The costs for admission to the Water Slide are: $4.75 per child under 12, $8.25 per adult. Children under 5 are admitted free but must be accompanied at all times by an adult. The attendance figures for a few hot days are given.

Day	Number of Adults	Number of Children (6–11)	Number of Small Fries (under 5)
Friday	478	804	241
Saturday	1294	3862	712
Sunday	1643	2948	992

Write two questions using these data. One should need an exact answer, and the other an approximate answer. Have a classmate answer your questions.

1.2 Place Value and Ordering

Activity: Review Our Number System

There are about 4 500 000 km² of trees in Canada. Each year, every person in Canada uses a lot of wood and paper products. A person uses the equivalent of one tree with a 45-cm diameter and a height of 30.54 m. There are about 25.4 trees planted per person in Canada every year.

Trillions			Billions			Millions			Thousands			Ones			Tenths	Hundredths	Thousandths
Hundred	Ten	One	Hundred	Ten	One	Hundred	Ten	One	Hundred	Ten	One	Hundred	Ten	One			
								4	5	0	0	0	0	0			
													4	5			
													3	0	. 5	4	
													2	5	. 4		

The digit **4** has a **different value** in each number, as shown in the place value chart.

4 500 000	45	30.54	25.4
4 millions	**4 tens**	**4 hundredths**	**4 tenths**
or 4 000 000	or 40	or 0.04	or 0.4

Inquire

1. How many times greater than 40 is 4 000 000?

2. How many times greater than 0.04 is 0.4?

3. How many times greater than 0.04 is 40?

4. How many times greater than 0.4 is 4 000 000?

5. How many times less than 40 is 0.4?

Most people take 300 000 000 steps in their lifetime. This is about 185 000 km. The length of the equator is 40 074.06 km, so most people will walk about 4.6 times around the Earth.

Read 300 000 000 as **three hundred million.**

Read 185 000 as **one hundred eighty-five thousand.**

Notice that the digits of numbers are grouped in threes, with a space between each group. You begin at the decimal point and move outward to the left and the right. The groups of three digits are called **periods.**

Read 4.6 as **four and six tenths.**

Read 40 074.06 as **forty thousand seventy-four and six hundredths.**

In decimal numbers, the word **and** replaces the decimal point.

The number 4.6 is in **standard form.** In **expanded form,** the number is written as a sum.

$$4 + 0.6$$
$$= 4 \times 1 + 6 \times 0.1$$

The **expanded form** of the number 40 074.06 is

$$40\ 000 \qquad\qquad + 70 + 4 \qquad\qquad + 0.06$$
$$= 4 \times 10\ 000 + 0 \times 1000 + 0 \times 100 + 7 \times 10 + 4 \times 1 + 0 \times 0.1 + 6 \times 0.01$$

Practice

Write each number in words.

1. 809   **2.** 92 567

3. 67.21   **4.** 45.097

5. 2 347 812   **6.** 45 000 000 000

Write the total value of the underlined digit in each number.

7. 82<u>3</u> 719   **8.** <u>9</u>1 666 502.9

9. 8 723 <u>6</u>01.901   **10.** 192 452.76<u>3</u>

Write in standard form.

11. six thousand four hundred fifty-three

12. two hundred seventy-six thousand

13. sixty million twenty-four

14. eighty-one thousand and four tenths

Write in standard form.

15. 200 000 + 5000 + 300 + 10 + 4

16. 3 000 000 + 6000 + 5

17. $1 \times 10 + 4 \times 1 + 6 \times 0.1 + 2 \times 0.01$

18. $3 \times 0.1 + 4 \times 0.01 + 7 \times 0.001$

Write each number in expanded form.

19. 5706   **20.** 98.47

21. 150 000   **22.** 1.023

23. 1 760 000   **24.** 120.003

The symbols < and > are used to compare two different numbers. Read 7 > 6 as "7 is greater than 6." Read 7 < 8 as "7 is less than 8." Replace each ◆ with < or > to make each statement true.

25. 47.53 ◆ 47.52   **26.** 3543 ◆ 3643

27. 19.101 ◆ 19.11   **28.** 82.300 ◆ 82.030

List the numbers in order from greatest to least.

29. 6349, 6348, 6483, 6439, 6493

30. 23.52, 23.51, 23.53, 23.511, 23.519

Problems and Applications

Write two numbers, in order, between each of the following pairs of numbers.

31. 8 and 9   **32.** 3.5 and 3.9

33. 4.6 and 4.7   **34.** 0.05 and 0.06

Write the number that is

35. seven tenths less than 8.89

36. two hundred more than 34 566

37. five thousand less than 657 900

38. three hundredths more than 0.456

In almanacs, some data are recorded as shown below. Write each number in standard form.

39. One year, 798 thousand cars were sold in Canada.

40. The Earth's average distance from the sun is 149.6 million kilometres.

 41. The computerized sign at the Bagel Bin reads **3671890 BAGELS SOLD!**

a) How many times would the number in the units place change for a count of 1000 sales?

b) How many times would the number in the tens place change for a count of 1000 sales?

c) How many times would the number in the tens place change for a count of 100 000 sales? 1 000 000 sales?

d) How many times would the number in the hundreds place change for a count of 100 000 sales? 1 000 000 sales?

 e) What kind of sign would not require as much attention? Explain.

 42. With a classmate, take numbers from page 8 to create a news release about the use of wood by Canadians or about walking distances. As you create the story, do some calculations that involve such data as the total volume of wood used in a specific time period or the total distance walked by all the people in the world.

1.3 Rounding Numbers: Mental Math

Activity: Study the Numbers

A female monarch butterfly lays her eggs on the leaves of milkweed plants. She lays 100 eggs, with 1 egg on each plant. Each egg is 1 mm in diameter.

The caterpillar hatches after a few days. After 2 weeks, it has moulted 4 times and is 3000 times heavier than when it hatched. If a human grew this fast, a 3-kg baby would have a mass of 9000 kg after 2 weeks.

The caterpillar then moults 1 more time, forming a chrysalis, and then transforms into a butterfly.

About 100 000 000 monarch butterflies migrate from Canada and the United States each year. They winter on *oyamel* trees in the Transvolcanic Range in Mexico. The longest migration is 4000 km. During the trip, monarchs cruise at 18 km/h. They have been clocked at speeds as high as 35 km/h.

 Inquire

1. Which of the above numbers are exact? Explain.

2. Which of the numbers have been rounded to an approximate value? Explain.

To round a number, think about where it is on a number line.

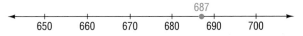

687 is closer to 690 than to 680.

687 rounds to 690.

The digit to the right of the place value to which you are rounding is called the **key digit.** If the key digit is 5 or more, round up.

Example

Round 267.539 to these place values.

a) the nearest 1　　　　**b)** the nearest tenth　　　　**c)** the nearest hundredth

Solution

a) In 267.539, the ones digit is 7, the key digit is 5. So, round up.
267.539 → 268

b) In 267.539, the tenths digit is 5, the key digit is 3. So, round down.
267.539 → 267.5

c) In 267.539, the hundredths digit is 3, the key digit is 9. So, round up.
267.539 → 267.54

Practice

Round each red number to one end of the line.

1.

26.7
26   26.5   27

2.

18.32
18   18.5   19

3.

905.382
905.300   905.350   905.400

4.

6.825
6.820   6.825   6.830

Write the key digit and round each decimal to the stated place value.

5. 18.403; nearest tenth

6. 82.91; nearest one

7. 127.542; nearest tenth

8. 0.9857; nearest thousandth

9. 327.294; nearest hundred

10. 43.008; nearest hundredth

11. 8349.52; nearest one

State the place value to which each decimal has been rounded.

12. $73.98 \to 70$

13. $108.438 \to 108.4$

14. $9273.006 \to 9273.01$

15. $0.3728 \to 0.373$

16. $3796 \to 3800$

17. $7381 \to 7000$

18. $82.076 \to 82.1$

19. $6027.999 \to 6028$

20. $9.455 \to 9.46$

Problems and Applications

Round to the stated place value.

21. Winnipeg Arena seats 15 393 people. (nearest thousand)

22. When the Canadian women's 3000-m speed skating team broke the world record, the average speed of the skaters was 10.853 m/s. (nearest hundredth)

23. Mercury has the lowest boiling point of any metal, at 356.62°C. (nearest one)

24. When Yuri Gagarin became the first astronaut in space, his rocket flew 40 868.6 km. (nearest hundred)

25. Edmonton's City Centre building is 124.7 m tall. (nearest ten)

26. Pluto takes 6.38 days to spin once around its axis. (nearest tenth)

27. Rounding a whole number to the nearest hundred gives 700, and to the nearest ten gives 750. What are the possible values of the whole number?

28. Baseball batting averages are rounded to the nearest thousandth. Why are they not rounded to the nearest hundredth or the nearest tenth?

Newspaper headlines often use rounded numbers. Write a headline based on each of the following pieces of information. Include a rounded number in each headline. Compare your headlines with your classmates'.

29. Theresa Brick of Manitoba became a double Canadian champion by throwing the hammer 51.8 m and the discus 51.7 m.

30. The Toronto Blue Jays' total home game attendance for the season was 4 057 947.

31. The grounding of the oil tanker *Exxon Valdez* in Prince William Sound, Alaska, dumped 38 150 000 L of oil into the water.

1.4 Look for a Pattern

It has been said that *mathematics is a search for patterns.*
Patterns are used in many kinds of work. Astronomers look for
patterns in signals from outer space and in the way comets
move. Managers of fast-food restaurants use patterns to decide
how many employees they need at certain times. Patterns help
you make predictions.

Sue works at the Dunlop Horse Stables. She must buy
brass numbers for the 99 horse stalls. The stalls are to
be numbered from 1 to 99. How many brass numbers
should she buy for each digit from 0 to 9?

Understand the Problem

1. What information are you given?

2. What are you asked to find?

3. Do you need an exact or approximate answer?

Think of a Plan

Use a table to organize the information.
Then, look for a pattern in the first few rows.

Carry Out the Plan

Stall Numbers	Brass Digits Needed									
	0	1	2	3	4	5	6	7	8	9
1 – 9		1	1	1	1	1	1	1	1	1
10 – 19	1	11	1	1	1	1	1	1	1	1
20 – 29	1	1	11	1	1	1	1	1	1	1
30 – 39	1	1	1	11	1	1	1	1	1	1
40 – 49										
50 – 59										
60 – 69										
70 – 79										
80 – 89										
90 – 99										

There are 10 rows in the table.
The zeros column will show 9 brass zeros.
The ones column will show 9 + 11 or 20 brass ones.
The twos column will show 9 + 11 or 20 brass twos.

Sue should buy 9 brass zeros and 20 brass numbers for
each digit from one to nine.

Look Back

Does the answer seem reasonable?
Can you think of another way to solve the problem?

Look for a Pattern	1. Use the given information to find a pattern.
	2. Use the pattern to solve the problem.
	3. Check that the answer is reasonable.

Problems and Applications

Look for a pattern, then write the next 3 terms in each sequence.

1. 5, 9, 13, 17, ■ , ■ , ■

2. 81, 74, 67, 60, ■ , ■ , ■

3. 40, 39, 37, 34, ■ , ■ , ■

4. 3, 6, 12, 24, ■ , ■ , ■

5. a, d, g, j, ■ , ■ , ■

6. a, c, f, j, ■ , ■ , ■

Find the pattern, then copy and complete each table.

7.

4	10
6	12
9	15
11	
	33

8.

8	5
12	9
17	14
21	
	26

9.

4	8
5	10
7	
9	
	26

10.

21	7
9	3
24	
33	
	15

11. Find the pattern in the first 5 rows of Pascal's triangle. Then, write the next 4 rows.

First row				1				
Second row			1		1			
Third row		1		2		1		
Fourth row	1		3		3		1	
Fifth row	1	4		6		4	1	

12. The figures show the acute angles formed by 2, 3, 4, and 5 rays.

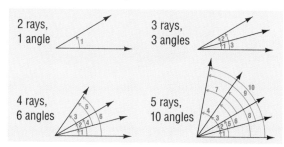

2 rays, 1 angle
3 rays, 3 angles
4 rays, 6 angles
5 rays, 10 angles

a) How many acute angles will be formed by 6 rays? 7 rays?

b) Describe the pattern in words.

13. a) How many small triangles are in the 8th figure? the 12th figure? the 25th figure?

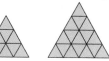

b) Describe the pattern in words.

14. The table gives the sums of even numbers.

First two	$2 + 4 = 6$
First three	$2 + 4 + 6 = 12$
First four	$2 + 4 + 6 + 8 = 20$
First five	$2 + 4 + 6 + 8 + 10 = 30$

a) What is the sum of the first 6 even numbers? the first 20? the first 100?

b) Describe the pattern in words.

15. The following expressions show the operation called "triangle."

$$2 \triangle 3 = 7$$
$$3 \triangle 2 = 8$$
$$5 \triangle 4 = 14$$

a) State the "triangle rule."

b) Copy the following. Use the triangle rule to complete them.

$$4 \triangle 5 = ■$$
$$6 \triangle ■ = 14$$
$$■ \triangle 3 = 17$$

16. The following expressions show the operation called "rectangle."

$$3 \square 5 = 16$$
$$4 \square 2 = 12$$
$$6 \square 1 = 14$$

a) State the "rectangle rule."

b) Copy the following. Use the rectangle rule to complete them.

$$7 \square 5 = ■$$
$$2 \square ■ = 22$$
$$■ \square 5 = 20$$

17. Write a problem similar to question 15 or question 16. Have a classmate solve your problem.

1.5 Estimating Sums and Differences: Mental Math

Activity: Study the Methods

The local newspaper in Des Moines, Iowa, is called the *Register*. Every year the *Register* sponsors the RAGBRAI, the *Register's* Annual Great Bicycle Ride Across Iowa. It is the longest and oldest touring bicycle ride in the world. The ride is held in July and is limited to 7500 riders. Cyclists from around the world, including many from Canada, participate in the ride. One year, the ride started in Sioux City and ended in Dubuque. The diagram shows the route.

	125.5 km		257.4 km		270.4 km		248.7 km	
Sioux City		Sheldon		Clarion		Decorah		Dubuque

Here are four ways to estimate the total distance the cyclists rode.

Method 1: Rounding	Method 2: Compatible Numbers	Method 3: Front-End Estimation	Method 4: Clustering
125.5 → 100 257.4 → 300 270.4 → 300 248.7 → 200 —— 900	125.5 → about 125 + 275 257.4 ⟍⟋ or 400 270.4 ⟋⟍ about 250 + 250 248.7 → or 500 400 + 500 = 900	125.5 → 100 257.4 → 200 270.4 → 200 248.7 → 200 —— 700	125.5 257.4 ⎫ These 3 cluster 270.4 ⎬ around 250. 248.7 ⎭ 250 × 3 = 750 750 + 125 = 875

Inquire

1. To what place value were the numbers rounded in Method 1?

2. Method 2 used compatible numbers. Describe this method of estimating.

3. Describe how to use front-end estimation.

4. Describe how to use clustering to estimate.

Example

Estimate 23.19 − 0.572.

Solution

Round each number and subtract mentally.
Your estimate will vary with the place value you choose for rounding.

Round to the greatest place value of the greater number.	Round to the greatest place value of the smaller number.	Round to the greatest place value of each number.	Use front-end estimation.
23.19 → 20 −0.572 → −0 —— 20	23.19 → 23.2 −0.572 → −0.6 —— 22.6	23.19 → 20 −0.572 → −0.6 —— 19.4	23.19 → 20 −0.572 → −0.5 —— 19.5

Practice

1. Four movie theatres sold these numbers of tickets: 309, 296, 284, and 420. Estimate the total attendance using rounding, compatible numbers, front-end estimation, and clustering.

2. Estimate the difference $256.1 - 49.6$, using four methods.

Estimate by rounding each number to its highest place value.

3. $836 + 341 + 194 + 724$ **4.** $8415 - 5926$

5. $26.9 + 5.01 + 3.82 + 1.41$

6. $45.9 + 24.3 + 82.78$

7. $82.769 - 33.953$

Estimate using clustering.

8. $19 + 27 + 24 + 30$

9. $\$17.59 + \$22.19 + \$19.89 + \$23.15$

10. $\$219 + \$349 + \$279 + \$319 + \$295$

11. $36.175 + 45.028 + 39 + 46.912 + 37.1 + 40.472$

Estimate using compatible numbers.

12. $12 + 78 + 33 + 66$

13. $\$1.29 + \$4.69 + \$3.45 + \$1.59$

14. $\$4.98 + \$2.22 + \$3.39 + \$1.58 + \$0.79$

Find only those sums greater than 1000.

15. $291 + 485 + 485$ **16.** $372 + 821$

17. $76.01 + 592.5 + 41.93$ **18.** $498.7 + 501.9$

Find only the differences less than 400.

19. $872 - 327$ **20.** $3762.92 - 3401.57$

21. $525.97 - 292.11$ **22.** $92\ 075 - 91\ 775$

Copy the question and the answer. Estimate to locate the decimal point.

23. $36.82 + 91.6$ Answer 12842

24. $17.463 + 21.74 + 42$ Answer 81203

25. $1245 - 634$ Answer 611

26. $980.433 - 721.673$ Answer 25876

27. $67.43 + 35.801 - 9.1134$ Answer 941176

28. $52.892 - 52.422$ Answer 47

Problems and Applications

29. Steven Spielberg directed four movies that were among the top money-makers of the 1980s. The income from *E.T. The Extra-Terrestrial* was $228 620 000, and from the three Raiders films was $115 598 000, $115 500 000, and $109 000 000. Estimate the total income from these movies.

30. The mass of an African elephant is about 4615 kg. The mass of a giraffe is about 1175 kg. Estimate the difference in these masses.

*Estimate the total for each of the following grocery store receipts. In each case, state whether your total is an **overestimate** (more than the total) or an **underestimate** (less than the total).*

31.	**32.**
4.82	1.49
0.99	11.18
3.29	5.75
6.95	3.36

33. Of the 4 methods shown on the opposite page for estimating a sum, which method always gives an underestimate? Explain.

34. Every airplane is allowed to carry loads up to a certain maximum. Do you think that the maximum load is an overestimate or an underestimate of the load that the plane can carry safely? Explain.

35. Estimate the total number of people who live in capital cities in Canada. Include the national, provincial, and territorial capitals. Compare your estimate with your classmates', and describe how you found it.

1.6 Adding and Subtracting

Activity: Study the Information

Swimmer Alex Baumann of Canada won 2 gold medals at the Los Angeles Summer Olympics. He broke the world records in the 200-m and the 400-m individual medley finals. The tables give his times, in seconds, for each stroke.

Inquire

1. What was Alex's fastest stroke in each event?

2. Estimate his time for the 200-m event.

3. Calculate his time for the 200-m event.

4. Estimate his time for the 400-m event.

5. Calculate his time for the 400-m event.

6. Estimate, then calculate the difference between his fastest time and his slowest time in each event.

	Time (s)	
Stroke	**200–m Medley**	**400–m Medley**
Butterfly	27.81	60.01
Backstroke	30.44	64.62
Breaststroke	35.03	73.36
Freestyle	28.14	59.42

Example

The Canadian women's team won a bronze medal in the 400-m medley relay at the Los Angeles Olympics. The table shows the team members, their strokes, and their times.

a) Calculate their total time for the event.

b) Calculate the difference between Reema's time and Pamela's time.

Swimmer	Stroke	Time (s)
Reema Abdo	Backstroke	64.19
Anne Ottenbrite	Breaststroke	70.87
Michelle MacPherson	Butterfly	61.28
Pamela Rai	Freestyle	56.64

Solution

a) Add to find the total time. Estimate to check for reasonableness.

Paper and Pencil   *Estimate by rounding to the nearest 10.*

```
    64.19          64.19 →  60
    70.87          70.87 →  70
    61.28          61.28 →  60
  +56.64          +56.64 → +60
  252.98                   250
```

The total time was 252.98 s or 4 min 12.98 s.

b) Subtract to find the difference. Estimate to check for reasonableness.

Calculator   *Estimate by rounding to the nearest 1.*

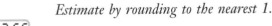

```
                                 64.19 →   64
                               −56.64 →  −57
                                           7
```

The difference between Reema's time and Pamela's time was 7.55 s.

Practice

Estimate, then add.

1. $486 + 813$ **2.** $4.57 + 81.333$

3. $0.3812 + 4610.3$ **4.** $23 + 56 + 81$

5. $992.5 + 291 + 516.3$

Estimate, then subtract.

6. $817 - 402$ **7.** $6198 - 4914$

8. $56.2 - 9.12$ **9.** $135\ 671 - 89\ 532$

Problems and Applications

Find the missing term.

10. ■ $+ 321 = 807$ **11.** ■ $= 921 - 375$

12. $67 - ■ = 19$ **13.** $9782 + ■ = 15\ 721$

The following questions refer to the Oaktown Ball Tournament. Use the map of Oaktown when necessary.

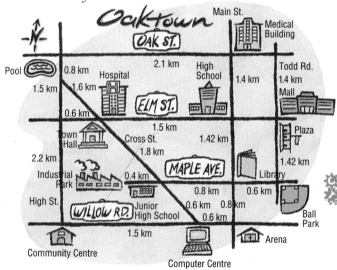

14. Write directions to go from Oaktown Arena to the industrial park. Calculate the distance.

15. What is the difference in distance from the community centre to the pool and the community centre to the medical building? Write your routes.

16. Write directions from the ball park to the junior high school to the community centre and back to the ball park. Calculate the total distance to follow your route.

17. In how many ways can you go from the library to the hospital if you can go only north and west? Assume Cross St. runs north and south. Find each total distance and compare.

18. In how many ways can you go from the arena to the pool if you can go only north and west? Find each total distance and compare.

The booth menu looked like this. Use it to answer questions 19 to 21.

Hot Dog	$1.25	Juice	$1.00	Mineral Water	$1.30
Sandwich	$1.50	Soda	$0.80		
Pizza Slice	$2.60	Apple	$0.75	Frozen Dessert	$1.10
Popcorn	$1.45	Peanuts	$0.90		

19. Calculate the total cost of this order.
7 hot dogs, 5 sandwiches, 8 pizza slices, 20 sodas, 15 frozen desserts

20. a) In how many ways can you order one item from each of the two left columns?

Make a list of the combinations.
For example: hot dog   juice
                 hot dog   soda

b) Calculate the cost of each combination.

21. a) Without listing all the possibilities, how many choices would you have if you chose 1 item from each column of the menu?
b) List the items and calculate the cost of the cheapest combination.
c) List the items and calculate the cost of the most expensive combination.

22. a) Make a grid map of the community around your house. Include at least four streets in each direction: north, south, east, and west. Label parks, arenas, malls, and so on.
b) Write two problems based on your map. Have a classmate solve your problems.

Designing for the Future: The Multi-Purpose Vehicle

Some people prefer cars in two- or four-door models. Other people drive vans or pickup trucks. If you lived on Moose Factory Island, you would travel to the mainland by boat. Some wilderness camps can be reached only by aircraft.

There are many examples of technology in the above modes of transportation. These range from the speedometer in a car to the depth finder in a boat to the altimeter in an airplane, as well as the engine in each type of vehicle.

Today, some people own several vehicles. Will this situation be possible in the future? Will environmental and cost concerns lead to the development of multi-purpose vehicles (MPVs)?

Activity ❶

1. Design an MPV to run on land and on water.

2. What changes would you make so that the MPV could also run under water?

3. Change your design so that the MPV could fly.

4. Would you steer the vehicle with a steering wheel, joystick, or trackball, or would you design something new?

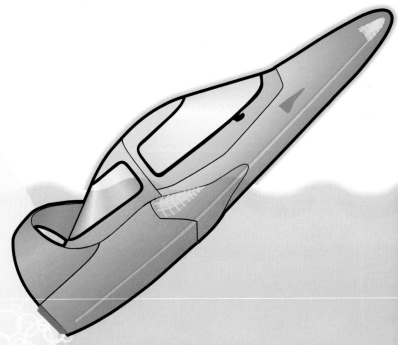

Activity ❷

The personal vehicle of the future may be equipped as a mobile office.

1. List the equipment to be included.

2. Design the interior of an MPV as an office, showing where you would place the equipment.

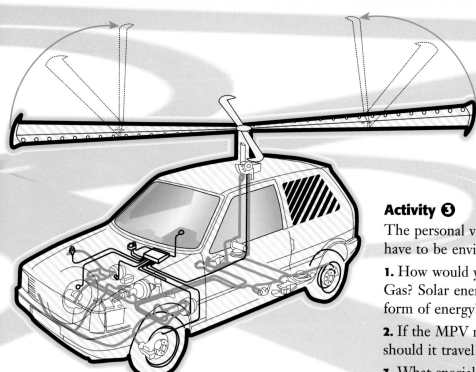

Activity ❸

The personal vehicle of the future will have to be environmentally friendly.

1. How would you power the MPV? Gas? Solar energy? Batteries? Another form of energy?

2. If the MPV needs to refuel, how far should it travel before refuelling?

3. What special parts should the MPV have to protect the environment?

Activity ❹

The personal vehicle of the future will need to be equipped with an onboard computer, as well as a communication system.

1. What jobs will the onboard computer have?

2. Should the communication system use an antenna, a dish, or some other kind of technology?

19

1.7 Multiplying and Dividing by Powers of Ten: Mental Math

The table shows the relationship in the powers of ten, written in standard form and with exponents.

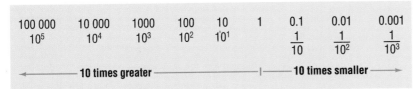

100 000	10 000	1000	100	10	1	0.1	0.01	0.001
10^5	10^4	10^3	10^2	10^1		$\dfrac{1}{10}$	$\dfrac{1}{10^2}$	$\dfrac{1}{10^3}$

$\longleftarrow$————— 10 times greater —————|—— 10 times smaller ——$\longrightarrow$

Activity: Find a Pattern
Copy the chart. Complete each calculation with pencil and paper.

Number	Instruction	Calculation	Result
74.2	Multiply by 10.	$74.2 \times 10 = 742$	
74.2	Multiply by 100.		
74.2	Multiply by 1000.		
74.2	Multiply by 0.1.		
74.2	Multiply by 0.01.		
74.2	Multiply by 0.001.		
74.2	Divide by 10.		
74.2	Divide by 100.		
74.2	Divide by 1000.		
74.2	Divide by 0.1.		
74.2	Divide by 0.01.		
74.2	Divide by 0.001.		

Inquire

1. Describe the pattern you see when you
a) multiply by a power of 10 greater than 1
b) multiply by a power of 10 less than 1
c) divide by a power of 10 greater than 1
d) divide by a power of 10 less than 1

2. Write a rule for
a) multiplying by a power of 10 greater than 1
b) multiplying by a power of 10 less than 1
c) dividing by a power of 10 greater than 1
d) dividing by a power of 10 less than 1

3. Compare your 4 rules and describe any similarities.

Practice

Multiply by 10.

1. 45.65　　**2.** 0.034　　**3.** 600

Multiply by 100.

4. 85.575　　**5.** 4.1　　**6.** 800

Multiply by 1000.

7. 3600　　**8.** 1.453　　**9.** 0.0141

Multiply by 0.1.

10. 772.1　　**11.** 12 155　　**12.** 0.56

Multiply by 0.01.

13. 0.19　　**14.** 500　　**15.** 32.8

Multiply by 0.001.

16. 0.83　　**17.** 300　　**18.** 35 681.03

Multiply mentally.

19. 896.27×1000　　**20.** $660\ 273 \times 0.01$

21. 1.364×10　　**22.** 225.43×100

23. 80.01×0.1　　**24.** 5.300×0.001

25. 0.292×0.01　　**26.** 10.8001×100

Divide by 10.

27. 456　　**28.** 67.98　　**29.** 102.87　　**30.** 1.895

Divide by 100.

31. 345　　**32.** 9187　　**33.** 23.87　　**34.** 4.0196

Divide by 1000.

35. 4491　　**36.** 103.2　　**37.** 1.5　　**38.** 26 553

Divide by 0.1.

39. 1.58　　**40.** 65.22　　**41.** 0.03　　**42.** 200

Divide by 0.01.

43. 250.1　　**44.** 0.0039　　**45.** 1.6　　**46.** 100

Divide by 0.001.

47. 0.25　　**48.** 17.5　　**49.** 400　　**50.** 1765.2

Divide mentally.

51. $362 \div 100$　　**52.** $5.34 \div 10$

53. $99.9 \div 0.1$　　**54.** $1.8 \div 1000$

55. $0.536 \div 0.01$　　**56.** $3562 \div 0.001$

57. $\dfrac{3.71}{1000}$　　**58.** $\dfrac{3.71}{10}$

59. $\dfrac{36}{0.01}$　　**60.** $\dfrac{3.71}{100}$

61. $\dfrac{3.71}{0.1}$　　**62.** $\dfrac{3422}{0.001}$

Problems and Applications

63. Express each length in kilometres.
a) 3000 m　**b)** 458 m　**c)** 1.58 m　**d)** 59.12 m

64. Express each length in centimetres.
a) 1.1 m　　　　　　**b)** 0.0251 m
c) 35 m　　　　　　**d)** 0.955 m

65. Scientists sometimes measure time in milliseconds (ms).

1 ms = 0.001 s

a) Express 47 ms in seconds.
b) Express 1 s in milliseconds.
c) Express 1 min in milliseconds.

66. At the Winter Olympics in Albertville, France, Frédéric Blackburn of Canada won a silver medal in the 1000-m short track speed skating event. He completed the race in 91.11 s. About how many seconds did he take to complete each of the following distances?
a) 100 m　　**b)** 10 m　　**c)** 1 m

67. The average mass of a pygmy shrew is only 4.5 g. The average mass of a porpoise is about 10 000 times greater.
a) What is the average mass, in grams, of a porpoise?
b) How many grams equal 1 kg?
c) Express the average mass of a porpoise in kilograms.

1.8 Estimating Products and Quotients: Mental Math

To estimate products and quotients, use either rounded or compatible numbers.

Activity: Use the Information

In the early days of Confederation, Canadian coinage came from the Royal Mint in London, England. The Royal Mint in Ottawa was not established until 1908.

The list shows the amounts of coinage sent on two different dates.

20 December, 1858
107 boxes of silver containing a total of:
480 392   twenty-cent pieces
1 116 402   ten-cent pieces
1 160 389   five-cent pieces

22 May, 1860
485 boxes of bronze containing a total of:
9 690 388   one-cent pieces

Inquire

1. What operation(s) will you use to estimate the value of the twenty-cent pieces in dollars?

2. Estimate the value of the twenty-cent pieces.

3. Estimate the value of the
a) ten-cent pieces   **b)** five-cent pieces   **c)** one-cent pieces

4. a) What operation will you use to estimate the number of one-cent pieces in each box of bronze?
b) Estimate the number.

 5. Estimate the average number of pieces of silver in a box of silver.

Example 1

Light travels through space at a speed of 299 800 km/s. The average distance of the Earth from the sun is 149 600 000 km. Estimate how many seconds it takes for sunlight to reach the Earth.

Solution

To find the time, in seconds, divide the distance by the speed of light. Estimate using compatible numbers.

$$\frac{149\ 600\ 000}{299\ 800} \to \frac{150\ 000\ 000}{300\ 000}$$
$$= \frac{1500}{3}$$
$$= 500$$

Sunlight takes about 500 s to reach the Earth.

Example 2

Estimate. **a)** 21.7×0.86 **b)** $0.649 \div 10.9$

Solution

a) $21.7 \times 0.86 \doteq 20 \times 1$
$= 20$

b) $0.649 \div 10.9 \doteq 0.6 \div 10$
$= 0.06$

$\doteq$ means approximately equals

Practice

Estimate each product.

1. 47×92 **2.** 16.7×8

3. 28×31 **4.** 91.4×64.5

5. 162.98×5.821 **6.** 902.67×82.91

Estimate each product.

7. 68×0.502 **8.** 764×0.899

9. 1984×0.48 **10.** 386×0.39

Round the numerator to be compatible with the denominator. Then, estimate the quotient.

11. $\dfrac{56.7}{7}$ **12.** $\dfrac{80.42}{9}$ **13.** $\dfrac{198.4}{3}$ **14.** $\dfrac{93.2}{11}$

15. $347.6 \div 6$ **16.** $219.78 \div 7$

Estimate each quotient.

17. $\dfrac{1.98}{0.928}$ **18.** $\dfrac{5.98}{2.01}$

19. $\dfrac{208}{29}$ **20.** $\dfrac{615.76}{6.18}$

21. $44.723 \div 6.89$ **22.** $756.9 \div 5.09$

Problems and Applications

The answers to each calculation in questions 23-28 are written without the decimal point. Estimate each answer. Then, write the exact answer with the decimal point.

23. 14.1×88 12408

24. 0.095×350 3325

25. 22.2×22.2 49284

26. $602.5 \div 25$ 241

27. $5.6 \div 11.2$ 5

28. $6.84 \div 0.4$ 171

29. Kelly bought popcorn for $3.49 a box. About how much did she pay for 15 boxes?

30. Kaveh bought 2.65 kg of chicken for a family dinner. If the chicken sold for $6.39/kg, and he had $20.00 in his pocket, did he have enough money to pay for the food? Explain.

31. Malek earned $362.72 for working 24 h. About how much did he earn each hour?

32. Claudia paid $25.84 to take a taxi to the airport. If the fare was quoted as $4.28, plus $0.89 per kilometre, about how far did she travel to the airport?

33. The Earth orbits the sun at 29.8 km/s. Estimate the Earth's orbital speed in kilometres per hour.

34. The population of Canada grew by 23 834 000 in the first 124 years after Confederation. Estimate the average population increase per year.

35. In your group, compare estimates from questions 29 to 34. For each question, also compare estimation methods. If they are different, decide which method you prefer and explain why.

LOGIC POWER

How many cubes are there? Assume that no cubes are missing from the back of the stack.

1.9 Multiplying Numbers

Activity: Study the Problems

Television programs and sporting events are given ratings by polling companies. These ratings let advertisers know about how many people watched the program or event. The World Series in baseball is watched by millions of people. The rating for a recent World Series averaged 39 points a game, where one rating point represented 1 700 000 viewers.

Inquire

1. About how many people on average watched each game?

2. Advertisers have calculated they can earn a minimum of $0.05 for each viewer. What was the minimum they might have earned?

3. Advertisers have calculated they can earn a maximum of $50 for each viewer. What was the maximum they hoped to earn?

 4. What expenses would companies have when advertising during a World Series broadcast?

Example

Anne-Marie is an artist who draws cartoons for television commercials. She earns $34.50/h. One day, she worked 8.5 h. How much did she earn?

Solution

Multiply $34.50 by 8.5.

Calculator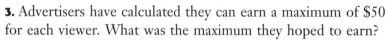

Paper and Pencil

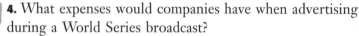

```
    34.50  ← 2 decimal places        EST   34.50 →   30
   ×8.5    ← 1 decimal place               × 8.5 →   ×9
   17250                                             270
  276 000
  293.250  ← 3 decimal places
```

The answer is close to the estimate.
Anne-Marie earned $293.25.

Practice

Estimate, then multiply.

1. 34×57 **2.** 5.5×82

3. 4.6×2.5 **4.** 4.5×10.2

5. 121×3.4 **6.** 3200×5.2

Estimate, then multiply. Round each answer to the nearest tenth.

7. 0.4×5.6 **8.** 4.2×2.48

9. 0.36×71 **10.** 0.9×0.99

11. $\begin{array}{r} 39 \\ \times 0.66 \\ \hline \end{array}$ **12.** $\begin{array}{r} 16.9 \\ \times 3.4 \\ \hline \end{array}$ **13.** $\begin{array}{r} 6.94 \\ \times 1.2 \\ \hline \end{array}$

Problems and Applications

14. Canada is one of the world's top gold producers. One year, Canada's gold production averaged 13.95 t (tonnes) each month. What was the total gold production for the year?

15. a) One round of golf is 18 holes. A hole-in-one happens once in every 3708 rounds of golf. How many holes of golf are played for every hole-in-one?
b) If you played 2 rounds of golf every week of the year for 30 years, could you expect to get a hole-in-one?

16. Ottawa averages 5.5 h of sunshine every day. How many hours of sunshine is that in a year?

17. Buckingham Palace opened to the public for the first time in 1993 to raise money to restore Windsor Castle. Eighteen of the 600 rooms were open to the public. Admission cost $16.45 per person, and 7000 people visited each day. How much was raised each day?

18. Canadians eat an average of 7.5 g of breakfast cereal a day. Americans eat an average of 14.8 g a day.

a) How much cereal does a Canadian eat in a year?
b) How much cereal does an American eat in a year?
c) How much more cereal does an American eat in one year than a Canadian?

19. The average person holding a driver's licence for 50 years will drive 24.13 times around the Earth. The length of the equator is 40 074.06 km. Calculate how far the average person will drive, to the nearest thousand kilometres.

20. Can the product of 2 decimal numbers, such as 4.7 and 3.6, ever be a whole number? Explain.

21. Use each digit once to write two numbers, so that their product is as large as possible.
a) 2, 3, 5, 7, 8   **b)** 1, 3, 5, 7, 9
c) 0, 3, 4, 6, 8   **d)** 5, 6, 7, 8, 9
e) Check your solutions to parts a) – d) with a classmate. What pattern do you see?

LOGIC POWER

Use your knowledge of geography to find out what province this area is in. Then, find the area on a complete map.

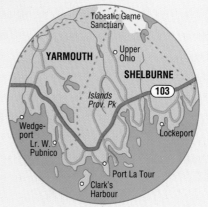

1.10 Dividing Numbers

Activity: Study the Information

A half-hour cartoon show has 21 min of cartoons and 9 min of commercials. The cartoon includes 30 240 drawings for the 21 min. Because you blink, you do not see all of the drawings.

Inquire

1. Estimate how many drawings are needed for each minute of a cartoon.

2. Calculate how many drawings are needed for each minute.

3. Estimate how many drawings are needed for each second of a cartoon.

4. Calculate how many drawings are needed for each second.

5. You blink 25 times a minute, and your eyes are closed for 0.2 s every time you blink. For how long are your eyes closed every minute?

6. How many drawings do you fail to see in a minute?

7. How many drawings do you fail to see in a half-hour show?

 **8.** The movie *E.T. The Extra-Terrestrial* is 1 h 55 min long and uses 207 000 pictures. If you watch *E.T. The Extra-Terrestrial*, how many pictures do you fail to see because you blink?

Example

Evaluate $4.59 \div 0.3$.

Solution

Paper and Pencil

Multiply the divisor by a power of 10 to make it a whole number. $\qquad$ $0.3 \times 10 = 3$

Multiply the dividend by the same power of 10. $\qquad$ $4.59 \times 10 = 45.9$
Then, divide.

$$\begin{array}{r} 15.3 \\ 3\overline{)45.9} \end{array}$$

 EST $45 \div 3 = 15$

Calculator

[C] 4 [.] 59 [÷] 0 [.] 3 [=] [15.3]

So, $4.59 \div 0.3 = 15.3$.

Notice that when we divide on a calculator, there is no need to make the divisor a whole number.

Practice

Rewrite each question so that the divisor is a whole number. Then, divide using short division.

1. $\dfrac{3.5}{0.7}$ **2.** $\dfrac{7.2}{0.8}$

3. $\dfrac{460}{0.02}$ **4.** $\dfrac{120}{0.03}$

5. $\dfrac{6.3}{0.09}$ **6.** $\dfrac{0.75}{0.005}$

7. $0.18 \div 0.3$ **8.** $0.012 \div 0.06$

9. $4500 \div 0.5$ **10.** $1.458 \div 0.03$

Estimate, then calculate.

11. $972 \div 54$ **12.** $12.22 \div 2.6$

13. $22.26 \div 5.3$ **14.** $0.72 \overline{)10.8}$

15. $3.5 \overline{)1.68}$ **16.** $41 \overline{)90.2}$

Estimate, then calculate. Round each answer to the nearest tenth.

17. $956 \div 17$ **18.** $60.4 \div 43$

19. $11.2 \div 2.3$ **20.** $0.84 \overline{)6.8}$

Problems and Applications

21. Waterton Lakes Park, Alberta, gets 1074 mm of precipitation in a year. What is the average amount of precipitation each month?

22. Each pony express rider rode a total of 133 km on 6 different horses before being replaced by another rider. If each horse was ridden the same distance, how far was each horse ridden, to the nearest tenth of a kilometre?

23. The most tickets ever sold for a movie in Canada and the United States happened in 1939, when 198 500 000 were sold for *Gone With the Wind*. The total income from the sales was $79 375 000. What was the average cost of a movie ticket in 1939?

24. The Place Ville-Marie building in Montreal is 189 m tall and has 45 storeys. The storeys are all the same height. What is the height of each storey?

25. About how many laps of a 50-m pool would you have to swim to complete each of these distances?
a) Lake Erie, which is 388 km long
b) the Mackenzie River, which is 4241 km long
c) the Pacific Ocean, which is 17 230 km wide

26. Sandpipers, in flocks of up to 2 million, feed on the Bay of Fundy's mudflats before their 4200-km, 89-h, non-stop migration over open water to South America. Find their average speed, to the nearest tenth of a kilometre per hour.

27. Canada's area includes 9 215 430 km² of land and 755 180 km² of fresh water. To the nearest tenth, how many times greater is the area of land than the area of fresh water?

28. Write a problem that requires the division of numbers. Have a classmate solve your problem.

WORD POWER

The word CANADA contains an equal number of consonants and vowels. List the names of other countries with equal numbers of consonants and vowels. Compare your list with a classmate's.

1.11 Use a Data Bank

A data bank is a collection of information organized so that the information can be easily retrieved. A telephone book is one example of a data bank. A data bank can provide you with the information you need to solve a problem.

A plane leaves Vancouver for Montreal at 08:00 and flies at 820 km/h. At about what time will the plane land in Montreal, Montreal time?

Understand the Problem

1. What information are you given?

2. What are you asked to find?

3. What information do you need?

4. Where could you find the missing information?

5. Do you need an exact or approximate answer?

Think of a Plan

Find the flying distance from Vancouver to Montreal and the time zone each city is in. An atlas or an almanac gives this information. You can also use the Data Bank on pages 470 to 479 of this book.

Divide the flying distance by 820 to determine how long the flight will take. Find the time the plane will land in Montreal, Vancouver time. Then, allow for the change in time zones.

Carry Out the Plan

The flying distance from Vancouver to Montreal is 3679 km. The time the flight will take is

$$\frac{3679}{820} \doteq 4.49$$

EST $4000 \div 800 = 5$

The flight will take about 4.5 h.
The plane will land in Montreal at about 12:30, Vancouver time. Montreal is 3 h ahead of Vancouver, so the plane will land in Montreal at about 15:30, Montreal time.

Look Back

Does the answer seem reasonable?

Use a	1. Find the missing information.
Data	2. Use the information to solve the problem.
Bank	3. Check that the answer is reasonable.

Problems and Applications

Use the Data Bank on pages 470 to 479 of this book to solve these problems.

1. Which distance is longer, the driving distance from Regina to Saint John or the length of the Mackenzie River?

2. Which feels colder —an outside temperature of −29°C with a wind speed of 48 km/h, or an outside temperature of −32°C with a wind speed of 40 km/h?

3. About how long does it take to fly from Winnipeg to Ottawa at a speed of 800 km/h?

4. What is the difference between the flying distance and the driving distance from Toronto to Halifax?

5. What is the total number of known moons in the solar system?

6. A plane flies from Ottawa to Edmonton at 850 km/h. If it leaves Ottawa at 15:00, at about time will it land in Edmonton, Edmonton time?

7. The area of Alberta is 661 190 km². How many of the world's islands have a bigger area than Alberta?

8. One year on Earth is how many years on Mercury? Round your answer to the nearest one hundredth.

9. Wei phoned her friend in Victoria from Hong Kong on Saturday at 11:00, Hong Kong time. What was the day and the time in Victoria?

10. The Alaska Highway runs for 2400 km from Dawson Creek, B.C., to Fairbanks, Alaska. How many round trips, from Dawson to Fairbanks and back, equal the distance from the sun to the Earth?

11. The Lebrun family left Winnipeg at 08:00 on a Saturday morning. They drove to Regina, then Calgary, then Edmonton, and back to Winnipeg. They averaged 90 km/h on the trip and drove for no more than 9 h/day. They spent 2 nights in Regina, 2 nights in Calgary, and 2 nights in Edmonton. They left each city at 08:00, local time.
a) On what day of the week and at about what time did they arrive back in Winnipeg?
b) State any assumptions you made.

12. With a classmate, use your research skills to write an itinerary for a class trip from Montreal to see a Canadian astronaut lift off from the Kennedy Space Center in Florida. Go by bus, averaging 80 km/h and travelling 10 h/day. Plan to spend 3 full days and 4 nights at the Space Center.

13. Newfoundland's time zone is $8\frac{1}{2}$. When it is 12:00 in London, England, it is 08:30 in Newfoundland. Use the Data Bank and your research skills to list other places that have fractional time zones. Compare your list with a classmate's.

14. Use the Data Bank to write a problem. Have a classmate solve your problem.

1.12 Order of Operations

Activity: Study Your ABCs

NATO is an acronym, which is a pronounceable name made from letters or parts of a group of words in a certain order. To land a plane, a pilot follows a certain order of operations.

NATO

Inquire

1. What do the following acronyms mean?

a) NATO   **b)** UNICEF   **c)** GATT   **d)** NASA   **e)** RAM

2. List the order of operations you would follow to get ready to go on a bicycle tour.

To avoid confusion when simplifying mathematical expressions, an order of operations has been agreed upon around the world. The acronym BEDMAS will help you remember the order.

B	E	DM	AS
Do calculations in brackets first.	Simplify all numbers with exponents.	Divide and multiply in order from left to right.	Add and subtract in order from left to right.

Example 1

Simplify $3.6 \times (7 - 2) \div 3^2 + 1.3$.

Solution

$$
\begin{aligned}
&3.6 \times (7 - 2) \div 3^2 + 1.3 && \text{brackets} \\
&= 3.6 \times 5 \div 3^2 + 1.3 && \text{exponents} \\
&= 3.6 \times 5 \div 9 + 1.3 && \text{divide and multiply} \\
&= 2 + 1.3 && \text{add} \\
&= 3.3
\end{aligned}
$$

Example 2

Use a calculator to simplify $24.6 - 3.1 \times 7.4 + 11$.

Solution

Scientific calculators generally follow the order of operations. For other calculators, you can use the memory key.

unicef

Method 1

Use the memory key.

[C] 3 [·] 1 [×] 7 [·] 4 [=] ⎡   22.94 ⎤ [M+]

[C] 24 [·] 6 [−] [MRC] [+] 11

[=] ⎡   12.66 ⎤

The solution is 12.66.

Method 2

Use a scientific calculator that follows the order of operations.

[C] 24 [·] 6 [−] 3 [·] 1 [×] 7 [·] 4 [+] 11

[=] ⎡   12.66 ⎤

The solution is 12.66.

Practice

Simplify.

1. $5 + 7 - 3$

2. $40 - 8 - 4$

3. $3 \times 2 + 5$

4. $7 - 2 \times 3$

5. $5 \times 2 \div 0.1$

6. $5 \div 2 \times 0.1$

7. $7 + 0.8 - 4$

8. $7 - 0.8 \div 4$

*When the word **of** appears in an expression, change it to $\times$. Evaluate these expressions.*

9. $\frac{1}{2}$ of 16

10. $\frac{1}{3}$ of $12 + 7$

11. $12.5 - \frac{1}{4}$ of 8

12. $\frac{1}{2}$ of $(13 - 5)$

Simplify.

13. $4^2 + 1.3$

14. $(5.3 - 4.7) \times 0.2$

15. $6.4 \div 1.6 \times 0.1$

16. $160 \div 2^2 - 5$

17. $(8 - 3)^2 + 18.1$

18. $3.2 + 16.4 \div 4$

Simplify.

19. $8.8 + 7.3 \times 0.1 - 0.46$

20. $9.3 - 7.1 + 3^2 - 0.2 \times 4$

21. $9.4 - 0.5 \div 0.1 + 2^2 - 1$

22. $8.4 \div 2.1 - 0.7 + 6^2$

23. $7.5 \div (2.5 - 1) - (5 - 3)^2$

Simplify. Express your answer to the nearest tenth.

24. $(3.15 + 2.7) \div (5.2 - 1.4)$

25. $6.7 \times (1.2 + 4.9) \div (2.8 + 1.6)$

26. $(3.5 + 2.1) \times (3.5 - 2.1) \div 3^2$

Problems and Applications

Copy each expression. Then, insert a pair of brackets to make the statement true.

27. $7.6 + 5.3 \times 1.2 + 0.7 = 17.67$

28. $7.6 + 5.3 \times 1.2 + 0.7 = 16.18$

29. $3.5 - 1.6 \times 0.4 + 1.2 = 1.96$

30. $3.5 - 1.6 \times 0.4 + 1.2 = 0.94$

Simplify each expression on each side. Then, replace the $\blacklozenge$ with >, <, or = to make each statement true.

31. $6^2 - 3^2 \;\blacklozenge\; (6 - 3)^2$

32. $7^2 + 4^2 \;\blacklozenge\; (7 + 4)^2$

33. $5 \times (8 - 3) - 3 \times 2 \;\blacklozenge\; (15 - 4) \times 6 \div 3$

34. $(12 \times 4) \div (8 + 8) \;\blacklozenge\; (6 \times 2) \div (3 + 1)$

35. Jenna bought two tapes at \$15.68 each and three posters at \$12.95 each. How much did she spend?

36. Max has two part-time jobs. He earns \$7.45/h at the market and \$5.35/h at the bowling alley. Last weekend, he worked 6 h at the market and 5.5 h at the bowling alley. How much did he earn?

37. Write the key sequence to correctly evaluate these expressions on a calculator that does not follow the order of operations.

a) $53.5 + 4.9 \times 5.7 - 1.9$

b) $16.5 \times 11.6 - 9.8 \times 4.7$

CALCULATOR POWER

Some calculators have bracket keys: $\boxed{(}$ and $\boxed{)}$.

To evaluate $42 \times (91 - 53)$, press

$\boxed{C}$ $\boxed{42}$ $\boxed{\times}$ $\boxed{(}$ $\boxed{91}$ $\boxed{-}$ $\boxed{53}$ $\boxed{)}$
$\boxed{=}$ $\boxed{\quad\;\; 1596.}$

1. Write a key sequence for evaluating the above expression on a calculator that does not have bracket keys.

2. Use your calculator to evaluate the following. Check each answer by estimation.

a) $65 \times (49 + 27)$

b) $(98 + 143) \times 56$

c) $215 \div (122 - 36)$

d) $(55 + 99) \div (88 - 32)$

1.13 Sequence the Operations

Global Fitness Centre is open from 06:00 to 22:00 from Monday to Friday, and from 09:00 to 18:00 on Saturday and Sunday. When open, it is staffed by a manager, a receptionist, and 2 instructors. Managers earn $21.75/h, instructors $18.25/h, and receptionists $13.50/h. Two cleaners each work 2 h/day after the centre closes. They each earn $11.15/h. How much does the fitness centre pay in wages each week?

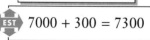

GLOBAL FITNESS CENTRE
OPEN
06:00 22:00
MONDAY TO FRIDAY

Understand the Problem

1. What information are you given?
2. What are you asked to find?
3. Do you need an exact or approximate answer?

Think of a Plan

Find the number of hours the centre is open each week.
Find the total staff pay per hour, then per week.
Find the number of hours of cleaning each week.
Find the total cleaners' pay per hour, then per week.
Find the total paid each week in wages.

Hours of operation

Monday to Friday:	06:00 to 22:00 is 16 h	$5 \times 16 = 80$
Saturday and Sunday:	09:00 to 18:00 is 9 h	$2 \times 9 = 18$
Total hours per week:	$80 + 18 = 98$	

Carry Out the Plan

Staff wages per hour

1 manager: $21.75
2 instructors: $2 \times \$18.25 = \$36.50$
1 receptionist: $13.50   EST $20 + 40 + 10 = 70$
Total: $71.75
Staff wages per week $98 \times \$71.75 = \$7031.50$ EST $100 \times 70 = 7000$

Hours of cleaning per week $7 \times 2 = 14$
Cleaners' wages per hour $2 \times \$11.15 = \$22.30$
Cleaners' wages per week $14 \times \$22.30 = \$312.20$ EST $14 \times 20 = 280$

Total wages per week $\$7031.50 + \$312.20$ EST $7000 + 300 = 7300$
                          $= \$7343.70$

Look Back

The fitness centre pays $7343.70 in wages each week.

Does the answer seem reasonable? Is there another way to solve the problem?

Sequence the Operations

1. List the given facts.
2. Decide on a correct solution sequence.
3. Complete the calculations.
4. Check that your answer is reasonable.

Problems and Applications

1. The football stadium has 32 560 seats. For the last game, 4500 tickets were given away. The rest were sold at $9.50 each. How much money was received from ticket sales?

2. The school library had a used book sale. Paperback books were 25¢ each, and hardcover books were $1.25 each. There were 54 paperbacks and 163 hardcover books sold. How much money did the library raise?

3. Paula repairs swimming pools and earns $14.50/h for the first 35 h she works in a week. For hours over 35 h, she earns 1.5 times as much. If she works 48 h in a week, how much does she earn?

4. Tamara has to go on a business trip. Including taxes, her round trip airfare is $398.60, and her room costs $115.70 per night. The cab fare from the airport to the hotel is $40.00. If Tamara stays for 2 nights, how much does the trip cost, excluding the cost of food?

5. Brazil is the country with the largest number of species of mammals, birds, and reptiles and amphibians. Brazil has 394 species of mammals, 1573 species of birds, and 970 species of reptiles and amphibians. The United States has 346 species of mammals, 650 species of birds, and 122 species of reptiles and amphibians. Altogether, how many more species of mammals, birds, and reptiles and amphibians does Brazil have than the United States?

6. Tides are caused by the sun and moon pulling on the Earth. The greatest tides happen in the Bay of Fundy, where they can rise and fall over 15 m. The ground you walk on also rises and falls, but by only 50 cm a day. What is the difference in the heights of these tides?

7. You can buy a bicycle for $399.95 cash, or pay $34.90/month for 12 months. If you exclude taxes, which price is less and by how much?

8. When he started his job, Terry earned $8.75/h and worked 8 h a week. After 2 months, he got a raise to $9.30/h. How much more a week did he earn? What assumption have you made?

9. Wolfgang Amadeus Mozart started writing music at age 4. He wrote about 1000 pieces of music before he died at age 35. About how many pieces of music was that a year? What assumptions have you made?

10. In 1991, the population of Nova Scotia was 900 000. On the average, the population increased by 4500 per year from 1891 to 1991. What was the population in 1891?

11. Ribbon costs $2.50/m. Find the cost of the ribbon for this present. Allow 80 cm for the bow.

30 cm

40 cm

60 cm

12. Three grade 8 classes decided to raise money for 2 charities by selling boxes of greeting cards. A box of cards cost $3.80 from the supplier and sold for $6.00. One class sold 150 boxes, the second 175, and the third 225. If the proceeds were divided equally between the 2 charities, how much did each receive?

13. Write a problem in which operations must be sequenced. Have a classmate solve your problem.

The Voyageurs

Alexander Mackenzie was a *voyageur* and one of Canada's most famous explorers. The *voyageurs* were fur traders who travelled across the continent by canoe.

Mackenzie was a partner with the North West Company, which had its headquarters in Montreal. He travelled west from Montreal many times. With the help of First Nations guides, Mackenzie's expeditions reached the Arctic Ocean and the coast of British Columbia.

In 1789, Mackenzie's group travelled about 3500 km from Fort Chipewyan, in northern Alberta, down the Big River to its mouth at the Arctic Ocean. This river is now called the Mackenzie River. However, Mackenzie was not looking for the Arctic Ocean. He returned to England in 1791 to go to school and improve his navigational skills. In 1793, Mackenzie led an expedition about 2000 km up the Peace River and over the Rockies to the British Columbia coast.

Two hundred years later, four groups of students from Lakehead University, led by Dr. Jim Smithers, paddled and portaged along Mackenzie's historic 12 000-km route across the country. This adventure took place in four summers from 1989 to 1993.

In each part of the expedition, students spent some days paddling. Other days were spent interacting with local communities and presenting a "Stay in School" program. At full speed, the Lakehead students paddled an average of 54 strokes/min. There were many portages, the longest being the Methye Portage at 19 km and the Grand Portage at 14 km.

Part 1, 1989:

Fort McMurray, Alberta, to Kendall Island, Beaufort Sea

The first part of the expedition started on May 25 in Fort McMurray and ended 3235 km later at Kendall Island on July 27. Dr. Smithers' students paddled for 31 of those days. When Mackenzie travelled this route, he averaged 120 km a day going downstream and 50 km a day going upstream.

Part 2, 1991:

Montreal to Winnipeg

This leg started on May 20 and ended 3400 km later on August 23. The students paddled for 55 days.

Part 3, 1992:

Winnipeg to Peace River, Alberta

In the third summer, the students started on June 5 and ended 3200 km later on August 29. The total number of days spent paddling on this leg was 64.

Part 4, 1993:

Peace River, Alberta, to Bella Coola, British Columbia

The final leg of the expedition started on May 16 and ended 2000 km later on July 22. There were 57 days of paddling. Mackenzie averaged 35 km per day on this part of his trip.

Activity ❶

1. How many days did the students take to complete each part of the expedition?

2. How many days of paddling did it take the students to complete the entire expedition?

3. How many days did the students spend on community interaction and presenting?

4. Draw a double bar graph to show the number of days spent on each part and the number of days paddling.

Activity ❷

1. a) Use the fraction $\frac{\text{kilometres travelled}}{\text{days of paddling}}$ to calculate the average distance travelled per day on each part of the expedition.

b) Calculate the average distance travelled per day for the entire expedition.

2. a) In part 1 of the expedition, along the Mackenzie River, were the students travelling upstream or downstream?

b) Compare the students' rate of travel with Mackenzie's rate of travel for this part of the expedition.

3. Compare the students' and Mackenzie's rates of travel on part 4 of the expedition.

4. Draw a bar graph to show the students' average rate of travel for each part of the expedition.

Activity ❸

1. How many strokes would the paddlers take in 1 h at full speed?

2. The average speed of a canoe was about 7 km/h in still water. How many hours would it take to complete the entire 12 000-km route at this speed?

3. How many strokes of the paddle would be needed to complete the entire route at the average speed?

Activity ❹

1. In your group, decide what you would expect to learn if you were one of the students on the expedition.

2. a) List the things you would bring on the expedition.

b) Identify the 10 most important things and give a reason for including each one.

Review

State whether you will need an exact or an approximate answer.

1. Your friend has asked you to go to Europe in eight months. How much will it cost?

2. In a video game contest, the highest score wins. Who won?

3. At what time does the movie you want to see start?

4. How much food do you need for your camping trip?

Write each number in standard form.

5. $3 \times 1\ 000\ 000 + 8 \times 10\ 000 + 7 \times 100 + 2 \times 1$

6. $5 \times 1 + 2 \times 0.01 + 6 \times 0.001$

Write each number in expanded form.

7. 5627.3   **8.** 0.504   **9.** 988 003

Round each number to the nearest ten, tenth, and hundredth.

10. 34.982   **11.** 12.9087

12. 116.227   **13.** 0.891 435

Estimate, then calculate.

14. $358 + 912 + 289$ **15.** $5.68 + 9.32 + 0.845$

16. $52\ 917 - 7817$ **17.** $47.824 - 6.904$

Calculate mentally.

18. 0.51×100 **19.** $64 \div 10$

20. $188.5 \div 0.1$ **21.** 3.42×0.01

22. 8.37×10 **23.** $25.6 \div 100$

24. $389 \div 0.01$ **25.** 6652×0.1

26. 41.62×1000 **27.** $65 \div 0.001$

28. 155×0.001 **29.** $77.1 \div 1000$

Estimate, then calculate each of the following. Round each answer to the nearest tenth, if necessary.

30. 30×42 **31.** $900 \div 21$

32. $2.3 \times 39 \times 58$ **33.** $200 \div 45 \times 100$

34. $3.2 \div 0.4$ **35.** 41×0.09

36. $4000 \times 0.01 \div 9$ **37.** $21 \times 32 \times 0.6$

38. 2572×455 **39.** 79.84×5.02

40. 7463.2×92.67 **41.** 8225×388

Find the quotient mentally.

42. $\dfrac{25\ 000}{500}$ **43.** $\dfrac{420\ 000}{6000}$ **44.** $\dfrac{125\ 000}{250}$

Divide. Use short division.

45. $4\overline{)1248}$ **46.** $6\overline{)30\ 288}$ **47.** $12\overline{)4572}$

Calculate without your calculator.

48. $32 \div 8 - 2$ **49.** $8 + 4 \times 2$

50. $5 \times (9 - 3) + 3$ **51.** $70 - 3 \times (13 + 7)$

52. $6.7 + 5.3 \times 0.1 + 9$

53. The table gives the number of heartbeats per minute for several animals. Arrange the numbers in order from smallest to largest.

Animal	Heartbeats Per Minute
Chihuahua	122
Gray Whale	8
Shrew	1200
Tasmanian Devil	66
Chicken	220
Elephant	22
Hamster	280
Kangaroo	48

Write the next three numbers of each sequence.

54. 3, 9, 27, ...   **55.** 128, 64, 32, ...

56. 54, 61, 68, 75, ...   **57.** 98, 87, 76, 65, ...

58. The distance across Canada is about 4200 km. How long would it take each of these animals, running at top speed, non-stop, to cross Canada?

Animal	Maximum Speed (km/h)	Time to Cross Canada (h)
Cheetah	114.3	
Ostrich	70	
Cat	48	
Snail	0.04	

59. The table shows the winning throws in the women's shot put at 6 Summer Olympics.

Year	1972	1976	1980	1984	1988	1992
Distance (m)	21.03	21.16	22.41	20.47	22.24	21.06

a) Rank the winning throws from greatest to least.

b) Find the difference between the greatest winning throw and the least.

60. The table shows the areas of the 5 biggest lakes in the Northwest Territories

Lake	Area (km^2)
Great Bear	31 328
Great Slave	28 568
Nettilling	5 542
Dubawnt	3 833
Amadjuak	3 115

Estimate, then calculate the total area of these lakes.

Group Decision Making
The SCAMPER Technique

The mnemonic SCAMPER was first used by the writer B. Eberle to help people expand their thinking when they are brainstorming. It is one way of producing "what if" questions.

S: Substitute — What if a person or a thing takes another's place?

C: Combine — What if you put things together? combine purposes?

A: Adapt: — What if you adjust something? What else can it be?

M: Modify, Magnify, Make Smaller — What if you change the purpose? the size? the colour? the sound? the speed?

P: Put to Other Uses — What are new ways of using something?

E: Eliminate — What if you get rid of a part? a whole?

R: Rearrange — What if you change the order? turn it around? turn it backward? turn it upside down?

1 2 3 4 5	1 2 3 4 5	1 2 3 4 5

Home Groups

1 2 3 4 5	1 2 3 4 5	1 2 3 4 5

1. In your home group, use the SCAMPER technique to design a town. Here are some ideas to get you started.

a) What if you *substitute* parks for parking lots?

b) What if you *combine* parks, schools, zoos, and aquariums?

c) What if you *adapt* sidewalks into moving treadways?

d) What if you *modify* building roofs to become a dome over the town?

e) What if you *put* water in the streets so that boats could use them?

f) What if you *eliminate* cars and trucks, except for emergency vehicles?

g) What if you *rearrange* the buildings so they go down instead of up?

2. Present your design to the class and explain how you used the SCAMPER technique.

Chapter Check

State whether you will need an exact or an approximate answer.

1. How much money do you need to get into the basketball game tonight?

2. How much money do you need to take to sports camp for one week next summer?

Round each number to the stated place value.

3. 83 901   nearest thousand

4. 50.184   nearest tenth

5. 1936.824   nearest one

6. 0.925 782   nearest thousandth

7. Make up three addition questions that all have the sum 3504. Each question must be different.

8. Make up two different subtraction questions whose difference is 5731.

Evaluate mentally.

9. 10×45 **10.** $54 \div 0.01$

11. $20 \times 10 \times 300$ **12.** $82.5 \div 100$

13. 98×0.1 **14.** $1725 \div 0.1$

15. 0.01×5634 **16.** $10.91 \div 10$

17. $0.01 \times 10 \times 0.1 \times 400$

18. $21.6 \div 1000$

Estimate each answer. Use your estimate to decide which of the 3 values given is the correct answer.

19. 35.93×72.3
a) 25.977 390 **b)** 2597.739 **c)** 259.7739

20. 12.842×9.95
a) 127.7779 **b)** 12.777 79 **c)** 1277.779

21. $1494.85 \div 427.1$
a) 3.5 **b)** 0.35 **c)** 350

22. $2.047 \div 0.89$
a) 2300 **b)** 23 **c)** 2.3

Divide. Use short division. State the remainder if there is one.

23. $7\overline{)4361}$ **24.** $5\overline{)43\,920}$

25. $3\overline{)240\,735}$ **26.** $9\overline{)4518}$

27. $6\overline{)3496}$ **28.** $8\overline{)57\,727}$

29. Five of us rented equipment for a fishing expedition. The rental prices were as follows.

Boat	$35.00 plus $15.00/h
Life Jacket	$4.50
Tackle Box	$20.00
Fishing Rod	$10.50

We rented 1 boat for 4 hours, 1 tackle box, and a life jacket and rod for each person. What was the total cost of the equipment?

Calculate.

30. $5 + 4 \times 2$

31. $130 - 12 \times (20 - 15)$

32. $3^2 - 64 \div (4 + 1 + 3)$

33. $209 + 11 - 120 + 7$

34. $(0.1 \times 56 + 2.4) \div 4$

35. $1.5 \times 20 + (29 \times 20)$

36. Write the following word sentence as a numerical sentence and evaluate it. Four times the number 16 is doubled, and then 50 is subtracted.

37. The average adult sleeps for about 8 h a day. How many hours a year is that?

38. Banff and Jasper National Parks are in Alberta. Banff National Park has an area of 6641 km^2. Jasper National Park has an area of 10 878 km^2. Which park is bigger and by how much?

Using the Strategies

1. Look for a pattern and write the next 3 terms.

a) 7, 13, 19, 25, ■ , ■ , ■

b) 1, 2, 4, 8, 16, ■ , ■ , ■

c) 90, 85, 86, 81, 82, ■ , ■ , ■

d) b, d, f, h, ■ , ■ , ■

e) on, tw, th, fo, fi, ■ , ■ , ■

f) 88, 79, 71, 64, 58, ■ , ■ , ■

2. The diagrams show the first 4 triangular numbers.

a) Draw the next 3 triangular numbers.

b) Describe the pattern.

c) Write the first 15 triangular numbers.

d) Add the first 2 triangular numbers. What is the sum? Draw a picture to represent this sum.

e) Add the second and third triangular numbers. Draw a picture to represent this sum.

f) Add the third and fourth triangular numbers.

g) Describe the sequence of numbers you get when you add pairs of triangular numbers.

3. The table gives the sums of odd numbers.

First one	1 = 1
First two	1 + 3 = 4
First three	1 + 3 + 5 = 9
First four	
First five	
First six	

Copy and complete the table. Look for patterns and predict the values of the following sums.

a) 1 + 3 + 5+ ... + 13 + 15

b) 1 + 3 + 5+ ... + 23 + 25

c) 1 + 3 + 5+ ... + 99 + 101

d) 1 + 3 + 5+ ... + 107 + 109

4. A sweatsuit costs $49.95, socks cost $4.59, a headband costs $4.09, and a gym bag costs $24.79. Tia went to a store that was paying all the taxes for the day. She had $80.00. Make 3 lists of possible purchases for Tia. Calculate the change she would get for each list of purchases.

5. A bellhop at a hotel earns $15.25/h for the first 35 h worked in a week and $17.50/h for any hours over 35. Last week, Terry worked 41.5 h. How much did he earn?

6. The expressions show the operation called "trapezoid."

$$7 \diagdown 3 = 12$$
$$9 \diagdown 6 = 9$$
$$4 \diagdown 2 = 6$$

a) State the trapezoid rule.

b) Use the trapezoid rule to complete the expressions.

$$8 \diagdown 1 = ?$$
$$9 \diagdown ? = 21$$
$$? \diagdown 2 = 15$$

7. Bob and Sharon left the highway restaurant and drove in opposite directions. Bob drove at 85 km/h, and Sharon drove at 95 km/h.

a) How far apart were they after 4 h?

b) If they had left the restaurant and driven in the same direction, how far apart would they have been after 4 h?

DATA BANK

Use the Data Bank on pages 470 to 479 to find the information you need.

1. At 6695 km in length, the Nile is the world's longest river. Which 2 Canadian rivers have a combined length that most closely equals the length of the Nile?

2. How long does it take to fly from Edmonton to Ottawa at 800 km/h?

3. Which planet takes about 50 times longer to orbit the sun than Mercury does?

CHAPTER 2

Number Theory

Start with any number, say 12, and write all the divisors.

12: 1, 2, 3, 4, 6, 12

Add all the digits of these numbers to get a new number.

$1 + 2 + 3 + 4 + 6 + 1 + 2 = 19$

Repeat the process for the new number 19.

19: 1, 19

$1 + 1 + 9 = 11$

Repeat the process for 11.

11: 1, 11

$1 + 1 + 1 = 3$

Continue the process for every new number formed.

1. What number eventually keeps repeating?

2. Pick another starting number and repeat the process. Does the number that repeated above always repeat?

3. Write a statement to explain what you discovered. Use mathematical language such as, "The digits of the whole numbers that divide…"

Calendar Magic

Activity ❶ Calendar Patterns

The 3-by-3 squares come from a calendar. Eight dates are missing from each square. Copy and complete the squares.

1.

4	*	*
*	*	*
*	*	*

2.

*	*	*
*	13	*
*	*	*

3.

*	*	11
*	*	*
*	*	*

4.

*	*	*
*	*	*
*	*	30

Activity ❷ Calendar Squares

A square block of 9 dates is outlined on the calendar.

S	M	T	W	T	F	S
		1	2	3	4	5
6	7	8	9	10	11	12
13	14	15	16	17	18	19
20	21	22	23	24	25	26
27	28	29	30			

1. What is the sum of the numbers on each diagonal?

2. What is the sum of the middle row of numbers?

3. What is the sum of the middle column of numbers?

 4. How are the sums in questions 1–3 related to the middle number in the square?

5. Use another set of 9 dates in a square. Repeat questions 1–4. Is the relationship between the sums and the middle number in the square the same?

 6. A magician's trick involves asking someone to choose a square of 9 dates and to state the sum of the middle row. The magician draws the chosen square without seeing the calendar. How is this done?

Activity ❸ Four Corners

S	M	T	W	T	F	S
	1	2	3	4	5	6
7	8	9	10	11	12	13
14	15	16	17	18	19	20
21	22	23	24	25	26	27
28	29	30				

1. What is the sum of the 4 corner numbers in the 3-by-3 square?

2. How is the sum related to the middle number?

3. The sum of the 4 corner numbers in a 3-by-3 square is 76. Draw the piece of the calendar.

Activity ❹ The Whole Square

S	M	T	W	T	F	S
1	2	3	4	5	6	7
8	9	10	11	12	13	14
15	16	17	18	19	20	21
22	23	24	25	26	27	28
29	30					

1. What is the sum of all 9 numbers in the square?

2. How is the sum related to the middle number in the square?

3. Use another set of 9 dates in a square and repeat questions 1 and 2. Is the relationship between the sum of all 9 dates and the middle number in the square the same?

4. The sum of all the numbers on a 3-by-3 square from a calendar is 162. Draw the piece of the calendar.

Activity ➎ Vertical Rectangles

A vertical 3-by-2 rectangle is outlined on the calendar.

S	M	T	W	T	F	S
				1	2	3
4	5	6	7	8	9	10
11	12	13	14	15	16	17
18	19	20	21	22	23	24
25	26	27	28	29	30	31

1. What is the sum of the 6 dates?

2. How is the sum related to the sum of the 2 dates in the middle row?

3. Repeat question 1 for another 3-by-2 vertical rectangle. How is the sum of the 6 dates related to the sum of the 2 dates in the middle row?

4. If the sum of the two dates in the middle row of a vertical 3-by-2 rectangle is 37, what are the other dates in the rectangle?

5. The planet Icon has a calendar with 7 days a week and 70 days in a month. The sum of the 2 dates in the middle row of a 3-by-2 rectangle of this calendar is 99. Draw the rectangle of dates.

Activity ➏ Horizontal Rectangles

A horizontal 2-by-3 rectangle is outlined on the calendar.

S	M	T	W	T	F	S
				1	2	3
4	5	6	7	8	9	10
11	12	13	14	15	16	17
18	19	20	21	22	23	24
25	26	27	28	29	30	31

1. Find the sum of the 6 dates.

2. How is the sum related to the sum of the 2 dates in the middle column?

3. If the sum of the two dates in the middle column of a 2-by-3 rectangle is 27, what are the other dates in the rectangle?

4. Activity 5, question 5, referred to the calendar on the planet Icon. The sum of the 2 dates in the middle column of a 2-by-3 rectangle in the planet Icon's calendar is 99. Draw the rectangle of dates.

Mental Math

Six multiples of 2 are 2, 4, 6, 8, 10, 12. State the following.

1. 8 multiples of 3   **2.** 5 multiples of 5   **3.** 6 multiples of 4   **4.** 6 multiples of 6

5. 7 multiples of 7   **6.** 5 multiples of 8   **7.** 7 multiples of 9   **8.** 6 multiples of 11

State all the divisors of these numbers.

9. 4   **10.** 6   **11.** 7   **12.** 8   **13.** 10   **14.** 20   **15.** 24   **16.** 17   **17.** 16   **18.** 36

Evaluate the powers. Example: $2^3 = 2 \times 2 \times 2 = 8$

19. 3^2 **20.** 4^2 **21.** 6^2 **22.** 3^3 **23.** 2^4 **24.** 1^6 **25.** 10^3 **26.** 5^3

Calculate.

27. $2^2 \times 8$ **28.** $(5-2)^2$ **29.** $2 \times 3 + 4$ **30.** $2 \times (3+4)$ **31.** $4^2 + 2^2$

32. $(4+2)^2$ **33.** $15 \div 3 + 2$ **34.** $15 \div (3+2)$ **35.** $3^2 \div 3$ **36.** $(3 \div 3)^2$

Activity ❶ Rectangles

1. Use a sheet of grid paper. Draw all the rectangles with whole number side lengths and area 12. Summarize your results in a table, like the following.

Area	Length (bottom edge)	Width (side edge)
12	1	12
12	2	6

Your results can be shown on the following graph.

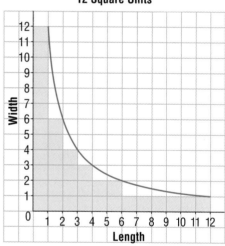

Rectangles of Area 12 Square Units

2. Follow the instructions for step 1 and create graphs for rectangles with the following areas.

a) 8 **b)** 9 **c)** 15 **d)** 16
e) 18 **f)** 24 **g)** 36

3. List the factor pairs for the rectangles whose areas are represented in your graphs. The number 8 is done for you.

$$8 = 1 \times 8$$
$$8 = 2 \times 4$$
$$8 = 4 \times 2$$
$$8 = 8 \times 1$$

4. For each list, indicate the "cutoff" where factors start to repeat. Some cutoffs occur between pairs of factors. Other cutoffs occur at a pair of factors.

$$8 = 1 \times 8$$
$$8 = 2 \times 4$$
$$8 = 4 \times 2 \quad \longleftarrow \text{cutoff}$$
$$8 = 8 \times 1$$

$$4 = 1 \times 4$$
$$4 = 2 \times 2 \quad \longleftarrow \text{cutoff}$$
$$4 = 4 \times 1$$

In each case, the cutoff can be represented by a cutoff point on a graph.

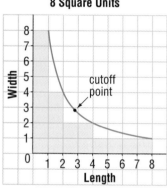

Rectangles of Area 8 Square Units

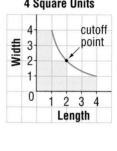

Rectangles of Area 4 Square Units

5. a) Now refer to your graphs in steps 1 and 2. Identify the cutoff point on each grid. Read the number on each scale at this point.
b) For which numbers does the cutoff point occur at a pair of factors?
c) Write the cutoff points for the numbers you listed in part b).
d) How could you use your calculator to find these cutoff points?
e) Find a mathematical name for cutoff points like these.

6. a) Draw factor graphs for these numbers.
20   25   32   49   64

b) Estimate the cutoff points for these numbers. Use a calculator to check your estimates.

c) Write a definition of a perfect square.

7. List the perfect squares between 1 and 150.

Activity ❷ Consecutive Numbers

Consecutive numbers are numbers that differ by 1, such as 2, 3, 4 and 7, 8.

The number 9 can be written as the sum of consecutive numbers in 2 ways.

$$9 = 4 + 5$$
$$9 = 2 + 3 + 4$$

The number 13 can be written as the sum of consecutive numbers in one way.

$$13 = 6 + 7$$

Some numbers cannot be written as the sum of consecutive numbers.

1. Copy the table. Complete it by finding all the ways each number can be written as the sum of consecutive numbers. The greatest number of ways is 3, for just 4 of the numbers.

Number	Sums	Number	Sums	Number	Sums
2		13	6 + 7	24	
3		14		25	
4		15		26	
5		16		27	
6		17		28	
7		18		29	
8		19		30	
9	4 + 5, 2 + 3 + 4	20		31	
10		21		32	
11		22			
12		23			

2. List the numbers that cannot be written as the sum of consecutive numbers. What do the numbers you listed have in common?

3. List the numbers that can be written as the sum of just 2 consecutive numbers. What do the numbers you listed have in common?

4. List the numbers that have 3 consecutive numbers as a solution. What do the numbers you listed have in common?

5. What are the other patterns in the table?

45

2.1 Exponents

All organisms, regardless of how complicated they are, begin with a single cell. This cell splits to form 2 new cells. The 2 new cells split, and the process continues until the organism develops into an adult containing trillions of cells.

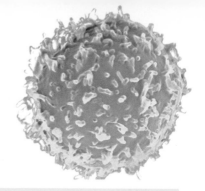

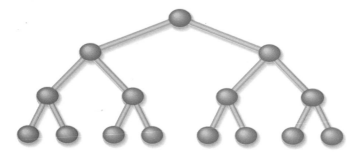

Number of Cells		
Standard Form	Factors	Exponential Form
2	2	2^1
4	2×2	2^2
8	$2 \times 2 \times 2$	2^3
16	$2 \times 2 \times 2 \times 2$	2^4

The product $2 \times 2 \times 2 \times 2$ can be written as 2^4, which is called a **power** of 2. It is read as "2 to the exponent 4" or "2 to the fourth." The **exponent**, 4, is the number of times the **base**, 2, is multiplied.

power ➡ 2^4 ⬅ exponent

base

Activity: Look for the Patterns

Copy and complete the table.

Expression	Factored Form	Exponential Form
$2^3 \times 2^2$	$(2 \times 2 \times 2) \times (2 \times 2)$	2^5
$3^2 \times 3^4$	$(3 \times 3) \times (3 \times 3 \times 3 \times 3)$	
$4^4 \times 4^3$		
$5^6 \times 5^1$		
$3^4 \times 3^4$		
$2^5 \div 2^2$	$\frac{2 \times 2 \times 2 \times 2 \times 2}{2 \times 2}$	2^3
$3^6 \div 3^4$	$\frac{3 \times 3 \times 3 \times 3 \times 3 \times 3}{3 \times 3 \times 3 \times 3}$	
$5^3 \div 5^2$		
$2^3 \div 2^1$		
$4^5 \div 4^3$		

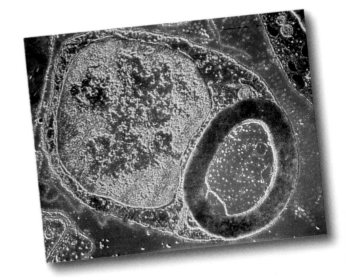

Inquire

1. For the multiplications, how are the exponents in the first column related to the exponents in the last column?

2. For the divisions, how are the exponents in the first column related to the exponents in the last column?

3. Write a rule for multiplying powers with the same base.

4. Write a rule for dividing powers with the same base.

Example 1

Simplify.

a) $3^4 \times 3^2$

b) $4^5 \div 4^2$

Solution

a) To multiply powers with the same base, add the exponents.

$3^4 \times 3^2 = 3^{4+2}$
$\qquad\qquad = 3^6$

b) To divide powers with the same base, subtract the exponents.

$4^5 \div 4^2 = 4^{5-2}$
$\qquad\qquad = 4^3$

Example 2

Evaluate $2^5 \times 2^3$.

Solution

$2^5 \times 2^3 = 2^{5+3}$
$\qquad\qquad = 2^8$ [C] 2 [Yˣ] 8 [=] $\boxed{256.}$
$\qquad\qquad = 256$

Example 3

Evaluate $(2^3)^2$.

Solution

$(2^3)^2 = 2^3 \times 2^3$
$\qquad\quad = 2^{3+3}$
$\qquad\quad = 2^6$
$\qquad\quad = 64$

Practice

Copy and complete the table.

	Power	Base	Exponent	Standard Form
1.	2^5			
2.	4^3			
3.	5^2			
4.	6^1			
5.	7^3			

Write in exponential form.

6. $3 \times 3 \times 3 \times 3 \times 3$

7. $10 \times 10 \times 10 \times 10 \times 10 \times 10 \times 10 \times 10$

8. $(5 \times 5 \times 5) \times (5 \times 5)$

9. $(2 \times 2 \times 2 \times 2 \times 2 \times 2 \times 2) \times (2 \times 2 \times 2)$

Write as a power of 2.

10. 32   **11.** 2   **12.** 128

13. 256   **14.** 1024   **15.** 8

Problems and Applications

Simplify. Leave your answer in exponential form.

16. $2^5 \times 2^2$ **17.** $3^2 \times 3^3$

18. $5^4 \div 5^3$ **19.** $2^7 \div 2^6$

20. $1^4 \times 1^5$ **21.** $1^6 \div 1^3$

22. $5^5 \div 5^2$ **23.** $7^4 \div 7$

Simplify. Leave your answer in exponential form.

24. $5^2 \times 5 \times 5^4$ **25.** $2^8 \times 2^4 \div 2^9$

26. $6^5 \div 6^4 \times 6^3$ **27.** $4^3 \times 4 \times 4^2$

28. $2^2 \times 2^2 \times 2^4$ **29.** $5^4 \times 5 \div 5^2$

30. $4^6 \div 4 \times 4^2$ **31.** $10^2 \times 10^4 \times 10^2$

Evaluate.

32. $(2^2)^2$ **33.** $(3^2)^2$ **34.** $(10^2)^3$

35. $(2^4)^2$ **36.** $(1^5)^6$ **37.** $(3^2)^3$

CONTINUED ➤

38. The mass of Neptune is about 10^{26} kg. The mass of the moon is about 10^{23} kg.
a) About how many times greater is the mass of Neptune than the mass of the moon? Write your answer in standard form.
b) The mass of the sun is about ten million times greater than the mass of the moon. What is the approximate mass of the sun? Write your answer in exponential form.

39. The number of bacteria in a culture doubles every 6 min. Starting with one bacterium, how many bacteria will the culture contain after 1 h?

40. A patch of algae on the surface of a pond doubled in size every day. It took 30 days for the algae to cover the pond. How long did it take the algae to cover half of the pond?

41. A drop of water contains about 10^{21} water molecules. If a billion people could share these molecules equally, how many molecules would each person get? Write your answer in standard form and in words.

42. The expression $3^2 \div 3^2$ can be evaluated in two ways.

$$3^2 \div 3^2 = \frac{3 \times 3}{3 \times 3} \qquad \text{or} \qquad 3^2 \div 3^2 = 3^{2-2}$$
$$= \frac{9}{9} \qquad\qquad\qquad\qquad = 3^0$$
$$= 1$$

What is the value of 3^0?

43. a) Complete each pattern.
1, 3, 9, 27, ■, ■, ■
1, 2, 4, 8, ■, ■, ■
1, 4, 16, ■, ■, ■
1, 10, 100, ■, ■, ■
b) Rewrite each sequence using powers.
c) How will you express the 1 in each sequence as a power?
d) What is the value of any power with exponent zero?

44. a) Take a piece of paper and fold it once. Open it up and count the number of regions formed by the fold lines. Repeat this a second time, then a third, and so on. Complete a chart to keep track of the number of regions you have created after each fold. Continue until you can fold no more.

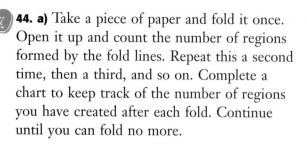

Number of Folds	Number of Regions
0	1
1	2

b) How many times did you fold the paper before you could not physically fold it any more times?
c) Compare your results with a classmate's.

45. Write a problem that requires the use of an exponent. Have a classmate solve your problem.

PATTERN POWER

1. Describe the following pattern in words.
$$2^2 = 3 \times 1 + 1 = 4$$
$$3^2 = 4 \times 2 + 1 = 9$$
$$4^2 = 5 \times 3 + 1 = 16$$
$$5^2 = 6 \times 4 + 1 = 25$$

2. Write the next 3 lines of the pattern.

3. The pattern allows you to use mental math to square some numbers.
$$19^2 = 20 \times 18 + 1$$
$$= 360 + 1$$
$$= 361$$

Use mental math to evaluate the following.
a) 21^2 **b)** 31^2 **c)** 99^2

2.2 Squares and Square Roots

At the Olympic Games in Barcelona, Spain, Jeff Thue from Port Moody, B.C., won a silver medal in the Super Heavyweight division of the wrestling competition.

A wrestling mat is in the shape of a square. The area of the mat is 64 m². The length of each side is 8 m.

Since $8^2 = 64$, 8 is the number whose square is 64. So, 8 is called the **square root** of 64.

Activity: Complete the Table

Mathematicians studied square numbers or perfect squares over 2500 years ago. Square numbers could be shown as squares of pebbles.

They can also be shown as squares on a grid.

Area of Square	Area in Exponential Form	Length of Each Side
1	1^2	1
4	2^2	
9		

Draw squares to represent the next three square numbers. Then, copy and complete the table.

Inquire

1. The length of each side of a square is the square root of its area. What is the square root of each of the areas in the table?

2. How does the exponential form of the area compare to the length of the side and the area of the square?

3. A SCRABBLE® board is a square made up of 225 small squares. What is the square root of 225?

4. The square roots of some numbers are not whole numbers. Which two whole numbers does the square root of 90 lie between? Explain.

CONTINUED ▶

The square root of a number, say 49, is the number that, when multiplied by itself, gives 49. Since $7 \times 7 = 49$, then $\sqrt{49} = 7$.

The symbol $\sqrt{}$ means the positive or **principal square root** of a number.

A number, such as 49, which has a whole number as its principal square root, is called a **perfect square**.

The number 4.41 is not a perfect square, but it does have a square root. Since $2.1 \times 2.1 = 4.41$, then $\sqrt{4.41} = 2.1$.

Example 1

Evaluate.

a) $\sqrt{121}$ **b)** $\sqrt{900}$ **c)** $\sqrt{0.09}$

Solution

a) $11 \times 11 = 121$ **b)** $30 \times 30 = 900$ **c)** $0.3 \times 0.3 = 0.09$
So $\sqrt{121} = 11$ So $\sqrt{900} = 30$ So $\sqrt{0.09} = 0.3$

Some numbers have square roots that are not exact. Suppose a square has an area of 12 cm². Since $3 \times 3 = 9$ and $4 \times 4 = 16$, the square root of 12 is between 3 and 4.

You could measure the length of a side and find that it is about 3.5 cm. So, $\sqrt{12}$ has an approximate value of 3.5. If you check, $3.5 \times 3.5 = 12.25$, which is close to 12.

A calculator also gives approximate values of square roots that are not exact.

12 cm²

Example 2

Estimate. Then, evaluate using a calculator.
Round answers to the nearest tenth.

a) $\sqrt{73}$ **b)** $\sqrt{411}$ **c)** $\sqrt{0.5}$

Solution

a) $\sqrt{73}$ is close to $\sqrt{81}$, which is 9.

C 73 √ ⟨ 8.5440037 ⟩

$\sqrt{73} \doteq 8.5$

b) $\sqrt{411}$ is close to $\sqrt{400}$, which is 20.

C 411 √ ⟨ 20.273135 ⟩

$\sqrt{411} \doteq 20.3$

c) $\sqrt{0.5}$ is close to $\sqrt{0.49}$, which is 0.7.

C 0.5 √ ⟨ 0.7071068 ⟩

$\sqrt{0.5} \doteq 0.7$

Practice

Evaluate.

1. $\sqrt{144}$ **2.** $\sqrt{400}$ **3.** $\sqrt{256}$ **4.** $\sqrt{625}$

5. $\sqrt{4.84}$ **6.** $\sqrt{0.81}$ **7.** $\sqrt{1.69}$ **8.** $\sqrt{0.25}$

Find a number with a square root between the given numbers.

9. 7 and 8   **10.** 11 and 12   **11.** 4 and 5

12. 9 and 10   **13.** 1 and 2   **14.** 3 and 4

Write the two whole numbers closest to each of the following square roots.

15. $\sqrt{60}$ **16.** $\sqrt{30}$ **17.** $\sqrt{20}$

18. $\sqrt{45}$ **19.** $\sqrt{75}$ **20.** $\sqrt{110}$

Estimate. Then, evaluate to the nearest tenth with your calculator.

21. $\sqrt{92}$ **22.** $\sqrt{802}$ **23.** $\sqrt{1000}$

24. $\sqrt{10}$ **25.** $\sqrt{0.8}$ **26.** $\sqrt{0.08}$

Problems and Applications

27. a) List the perfect squares from 1 to 400.
b) Examine the last digit in each perfect square. Write a rule that will help you to identify a perfect square from its last digit.
c) Use your rule to decide which of the following numbers might be perfect squares. Then, use your calculator to check.

1983   551   961   3481   987
2025   3175   1296   1896   1022

28. a) Prince Edward Island is Canada's smallest province. It has an area of 5660 km². If Prince Edward Island were square, what would be the length of each side, to the nearest whole number of kilometres?
b) Canada's largest province, Quebec, has an area of 1 540 680 km². If it were square, what would be the length of each side, to the nearest whole number of kilometres?
c) About how many Prince Edward Island squares could fit into a Quebec square?

29. A square has an area of 81 cm². What is the length of one side? What is the radius of the largest circle you can fit inside it?

30. a) Draw each square on 1-cm grid paper. Count squares to find the area of each figure.

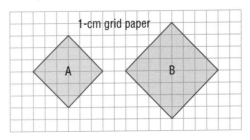

b) Measure the length of a side to find the square root of each area.

31. Is each statement always true, sometimes true, or never true? Explain.
a) The square of a number is larger than the number.
b) The square of an even number is even.
c) The principal square root of an even number is even.
d) The principal square root of a number is half the number.
e) The principal square root of a perfect square is less than 1.

PATTERN POWER

The quotient $96 \div 32 = 3$.
Reverse the digits. $69 \div 23 = 3$

1. Divide $48 \div 24$. Then, reverse the digits and divide again.

2. Describe the pattern in the pairs of digits.

3. Find 2 more pairs of 2-digit numbers with the same property. Do not include pairs of numbers with the same digits, such as 44.

2.3 Solve a Simpler Problem

River

110 m

180 m

Sometimes, you can solve a problem that appears to be difficult by solving a simpler, but similar, problem.

A rectangular campground, 180 m by 110 m, is located on the bank of a river. Evergreen trees are to be planted to form a border on 3 sides of the campground. If the trees are 2 m apart, and there is a tree in each corner of the campground, how many trees are needed?

Understand the Problem

1. What information are you given?

2. What are you asked to find?

3. Do you need an exact or approximate answer?

Think of a Plan

Draw smaller areas and find the number of trees needed for smaller borders. Tabulate the results and look for a pattern.

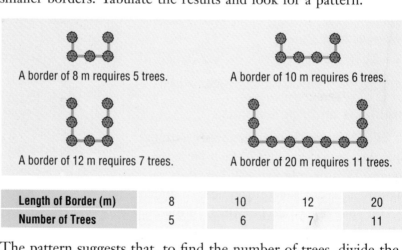

A border of 8 m requires 5 trees.

A border of 10 m requires 6 trees.

Carry Out the Plan

A border of 12 m requires 7 trees.

A border of 20 m requires 11 trees.

Length of Border (m)	8	10	12	20
Number of Trees	5	6	7	11

The pattern suggests that, to find the number of trees, divide the length of the border by 2 and then add 1.

The length of the border is

$$110 + 110 + 180 = 400$$

EST $100 + 100 + 200 = 400$

The number of trees is given by

$$400 \div 2 + 1 = 201$$

So, 201 trees are needed for the campground.

Look Back

How could you check the answer?

Solve a Simpler Problem

1. Break the problem into smaller problems.
2. Solve the problem.
3. Check that your answer is reasonable.

Problems and Applications

1. A horizontal line through the letter N divides the N into a maximum of 4 parts.

Two horizontal lines divide the N into a maximum of 7 parts.

What is the maximum number of parts when 50 horizontal lines divide the N?

2. One horizontal line divides the letter V into a maximum of 3 parts.

Two horizontal lines divide it into a maximum of 5 parts.

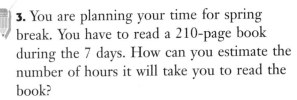

What is the maximum number of parts when 100 horizontal lines divide the V?

3. You are planning your time for spring break. You have to read a 210-page book during the 7 days. How can you estimate the number of hours it will take you to read the book?

4. You are making a schedule for a volleyball league with 10 teams. Every team is to play every other team once. How many games do you have to schedule?

5. There are 12 teams in a hockey league. Every team is to play every other team twice. How many games will be played?

6. A rectangular field measures 620 m by 440 m. The field is to be fenced with fence posts placed 10 m apart and with one post in each corner. How many fence posts will be needed?

7. a) Describe how you would find the approximate number of breaths you take in 1 week. Then, find the number.
b) Your lungs hold about 5.5 L of air. Each time you breathe out, about 1.5 L of air is left in your lungs. About how many litres of air do you breathe in a week?

8. Evaluate $1 \div 200\ 000\ 000$.

9. Describe how you would find the approximate number of cars that pass in front of your school in a month during school hours.

10. The foyer in a building is a 9 m by 17 m rectangle. The floor is to be tiled with square tiles that are 20 cm by 20 cm. How many tiles are needed?

11. The pool area of a hotel is in the shape of a rectangle with the dimensions shown. Two sides of the area are against the hotel. The other two sides are to have shrubs planted along them, with one shrub every metre. Shrubs are to start 1 m from the building. How many shrubs are needed?

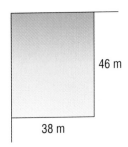

46 m

38 m

12. a) What is the ones digit of the product when one hundred nines are multiplied?
b) What is the ones digit of the product when one hundred threes are multiplied?

13. a) Work with a classmate to determine how much time each step takes when you walk at your normal walking pace. Give your answer to the nearest tenth of a second.
b) Describe the method you used.

2.4 Order of Operations

Activity: Describe the Steps

Some grade 8 students put this sign on a classmate's locker.

HAPPY $\sqrt{4} \times 9 - 16 \div 2^{2}$TH LOUISE

 In what order would you do the calculations?

Inquire

 1. Evaluate the expression and compare your answer with a classmate's.

2. Do $(\sqrt{4} \times 9) - \dfrac{16}{2^2}$ and $\dfrac{(\sqrt{4} \times 9 - 16)}{2^2}$ give the same result? Which result makes more sense for Louise's birthday?

 3. "Two-thirds of $12 plus $9" can have two meanings. What are they? Which amount of money would you rather have?

Recall the order of operations that has been agreed on by mathematicians.

1. Do calculations in brackets first. A division bar acts like a set of brackets. **B**

2. Evaluate exponents. **E**

3. Divide and multiply in order from left to right. **DM**

4. Add and subtract in order from left to right. **AS**

Example 1

Evaluate $8^2 - 5 \times 2$.

Solution

$$8^2 - 5 \times 2$$ exponents
$$= 64 - 5 \times 2$$ multiply
$$= 64 - 10$$ subtract
$$= 54$$

Example 2

Evaluate $\dfrac{10^2 \times 2}{21 - 2^4}$.

Solution

$$\dfrac{10^2 \times 2}{21 - 2^4}$$ division bar acts like brackets

$$= \dfrac{(10^2 \times 2)}{(21 - 2^4)}$$ brackets

$$= \dfrac{200}{5}$$ divide

$$= 40$$

Practice

Evaluate.

1. $7 - 3 + 5$

2. $(7 - 3) + 5$

3. $32 - 4 \times 5$

4. $(32 - 4) \times 5$

5. $8 \times 4 - 15$

6. $5 \times (4 + 3) - 8$

Evaluate.

7. $10 - 2^2$

8. $3^2 - 2^3$

9. $(7 - 3)^2$

10. $(8 - 5)^2$

11. $(3 - 2)^{12}$

12. $8^2 - 3^3 - 2^4$

Evaluate.

13. 6.9×10^2

14. 0.45×10^3

15. $435 \div 10^2$

16. $26\ 783 \div 10^3$

17. $38.2 \div 10 + 0.392 \times 10^2$

The expression $2(5 + 3)$ means
$$2 \times (5 + 3) = 2 \times 8$$
$$= 16$$
Evaluate.

18. $3(7 - 2)$

19. $4(3 + 1) - 7$

20. $2(6 - 4) + 5$

21. $18 + 4(5 + 2)$

22. $23 + 3(5 + 2)$

23. $20 \div 2(6 - 4)$

Evaluate.

24. $(16 - 3)^2 \div 2$

25. $8^2 + (4 \times 8 \div 16)$

26. $\dfrac{24}{8 \times 3 \div 12}$

27. $\dfrac{3^2 + 3 \times 2}{4 \times 5 - 5}$

28. $\dfrac{6 \times 2^3}{15 - 3}$

29. $\dfrac{9^2 - 9}{4^2 - 10}$

Problems and Applications

Replace each ♦ with >, <, or = to make each statement true.

30. $3^2 \;♦\; 4^2$

31. $3^4 \;♦\; 2^4 \div 2^2$

32. $9^2 \;♦\; (5 + 4)^2$

33. $18 \div 3^2 \;♦\; 2^4 \div 8$

34. $3^5 \div 3^2 - 12 \;♦\; 12 - 3^4 \div 3^2$

35. $8^2 \times (3^2 + 1) \;♦\; 3^2 \times (8^2 + 1)$

36. $5 \times (2^2 + 3^2) \;♦\; (5 \times 2^2) + 3^2$

Add brackets to make each statement true.

37. $6 \div 3 + 3 \times 3^2 = 45$

38. $6 \div 3 + 3 \times 3^2 = 9$

39. $6 \div 3 + 3 \times 3^2 = 29$

Write the expressions in order from greatest to least.

40. $6^2,\ 2^6,\ 3^5,\ 5^3$

41. $7^2,\ 2^7,\ (7 - 2)^2,\ (7 + 2)^2$

42. $4.2^3,\ 4.3^2,\ 2.4^3,\ 2.3^4$

43. $(2.5 + 1)^2,\ (2.5 - 1)^3,\ (1.5 + 2)^3,\ (3.5 - 1)^2$

44. a) Write today's date using numbers in the form yy-mm-dd. Use the order of operations and the digits in the date, in the order written, to make a correct number sentence. Include a power, if possible. For example, if today is 99-11-06, you can use 9 9 1 1 0 6, in that order, and the order of operations to make $(9 - 9)^1 = 1 \times 0 \times 6$. If you cannot write a number sentence with today's date, try tomorrow's date, and so on.
b) Compare your number sentence with your classmates'.

CALCULATOR POWER

Some calculators have exponent keys. They look like this. $\boxed{Y^x}$ or $\boxed{x^y}$
To evaluate 5^3, press the following key sequence.

$\boxed{C}\ 5\ \boxed{Y^x}\ 3\ \boxed{=}\ \boxed{\qquad 125.}$

Use your calculator to evaluate each of the following.

1. 6^4

2. 5^4

3. 10^6

4. 11^3

5. 12^4

6. 4^3

2.5 Factors and Divisibility

There are at most 15 white bears in the British Columbia rain forest. They are not albinos, but black bears with unusual colouration. The **factors** of 15 are 1, 3, 5, and 15 because they all divide 15 evenly. The numbers 5 and 3 are factors of 15 because they multiply to give 15. So do 15 and 1. You can also say that 15 *is divisible by* 1, 3, 5, and 15.

Activity: Complete the Table

Use a piece of large grid paper to make a table like the one shown. Write the following test numbers in the left column.

22, 52, 122, 152, 156, 222, 252, 256, 20, 35, 120, 135, 530, 730, 820, 835, 984, 1984, 7984, 321, 333, 999

Decide whether each number is divisible by the number at the top of each column. If it is, shade the rectangle.

Test Number	Divisor							
	2	3	4	5	6	8	9	10
22								
52								
122								

 Inquire

Answer the following questions with a partner. Answer "yes" or "no" and explain each answer.

1. Is every number divisible by 2 also divisible by 4?

2. Is every number divisible by 4 also divisible by 2?

3. Is every number divisible by 3 also divisible by 6?

4. Is every number divisible by 6 also divisible by 2?

5. Is every number divisible by 8 also divisible by 2 and 4?

6. What are the sums of the digits of the numbers divisible by 3?

7. What are the sums of the digits of the numbers divisible by 9?

8. Is every number divisible by 3 also divisible by 9?

9. Is every number divisible by 9 also divisible by 3?

Divisibility Rules

The divisibility rules help to find factors. A number is divisible by:

2 if it ends in 0, 2, 4, 6, or 8
3 if the sum of the digits is divisible by 3
4 if the last two digits are divisible by 4
5 if the number ends in 5 or 0

6 if the number is divisible by 2 and 3
8 if the last three digits are divisible by 8
9 if the sum of the digits is divisible by 9
10 if the number ends in 0

Practice

State the missing factors. There may be more than one correct solution.

1. ■ × ■ = 25   **2.** ■ × ■ = 93

3. ■ × ■ = 50   **4.** ■ × ■ = 24

5. ■ × ■ = 972   **6.** ■ × ■ = 640

Which numbers have 3 as a factor?

7. 3654   **8.** 18 373   **9.** 18 375   **10.** 18 378

Which numbers have 4 as a factor?

11. 348   **12.** 786   **13.** 6536   **14.** 154 732

Which numbers have 6 as a factor?

15. 9225   **16.** 6153   **17.** 9252   **18.** 711 144

Which numbers have 8 as a factor?

19. 7168   **20.** 6586

21. 10 776   **22.** 381 129

Which numbers have 9 as a factor?

23. 3654   **24.** 18 373   **25.** 18 375   **26.** 18 378

List all the factors of each number.

27. 28   **28.** 48   **29.** 85   **30.** 76

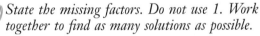 *State the missing factors. Do not use 1. Work together to find as many solutions as possible.*

31. 7 × ■ × ■ = 42   **32.** 6 × ■ × ■ = 360

33. 8 × ■ × ■ = 240   **34.** 9 × ■ × ■ = 108

35. 25 × ■ × ■ = 1800

36. 37 × ■ × ■ = 740

37. 53 × ■ × ■ = 2120

Problems and Applications

What missing digit(s) would make each number divisible by the factor given?

38. ■89; factor 9   **39.** 18■; factor 4

40. 9■08; factor 3   **41.** 56■; factor 2

42. 3■50; factor 6   **43.** 210■; factor 5

44. 48■6; factor 8

45. A marching band has 36 members. What arrangements could they use in order to have equal numbers of players in each row?

46. In the stands at the band concert, the seats in section A are numbered 1 to 250. A door prize will go to everyone whose seat number is a factor of 250. Which seats win prizes?

47. A number's factors, other than itself, are 1, 2, 4, and 8. What is the number?

48. a) The year 2000 has many factors. List some of them.
b) List the factors of the current year.
c) State the next year that will be divisible by 2, 3, 4, 6, 8, and 9; by 2, 3, 4, 6, 8, 9, and 5.

49. Write a divisibility rule for 25 and 100. Test each rule.

50. A number is divisible by 11 if the difference between the sums of alternating digits is divisible by 11. For example, test if 7194 is divisible by 11.
7194: 7 + 9 = 16, 1 + 4 = 5, 16 − 5 = 11
As 11 is divisible by 11, 7194 is divisible by 11. Determine which of these numbers are divisible by 11.
a) 616   **b)** 264   **c)** 4562   **d)** 4596   **e)** 2090

51. Five numbers greater than 50 but less than 80 each have exactly 4 factors (other than 1 and themselves). What are the numbers?

52. The number 10 has 4 factors: 1, 2, 5, and 10. Half the factors are odd and half are even.
a) Find 5 other numbers whose factors are half even and half odd.
b) Write a rule for determining these numbers.

53. Find 4 numbers whose factors, other than 1, are all even.

Networks

Network theory was first developed in the eighteenth century by Leonhard Euler. Today, Euler's theories are used to solve communications and scheduling problems.

 ### Activity ❶

 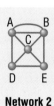 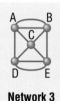 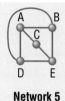 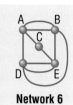

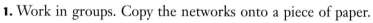

| Network 1 | Network 2 | Network 3 | Network 4 | Network 5 | Network 6 |

1. Work in groups. Copy the networks onto a piece of paper.

2. Determine whether or not each network is *traceable*. This means that you can trace it in one sweep, without raising your pencil from the paper or copying over a line.

3. Label each network using one of the following descriptions.
a) The network is not traceable, no matter where you start.
b) The network is traceable if you start at vertex ■ or ■.
c) The network is traceable, no matter where you start.

4. Classify each vertex as "even" or "odd," depending on whether an even or odd number of line segments meet at that vertex.

Network	Total Number of Vertices	Number of Odd Vertices	Number of Even Vertices
1			
⋮			
6			

5. You can tell if a network is traceable from the number of odd vertices it has. Use your results from steps 3 and 4 to complete each of the following rules by adding "traceable" or "not traceable."
a) A network with more than 2 odd vertices is ■.
b) A network with 2 odd vertices is ■, if you start at an odd vertex.
c) A network with no odd vertices is ■ from any vertex.

6. Test the rules with some networks of your own design.

7. Challenge the members of your group to make one of each of the three kinds of networks described in step 3.

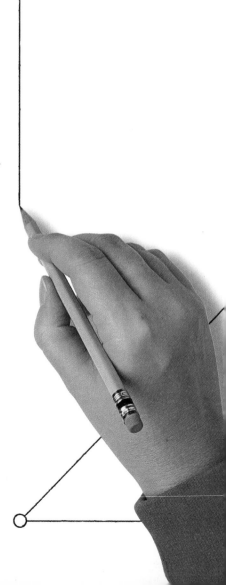

Activity ❷

The following network of communication lines connects computer terminals. The arrows show the ways information can travel.

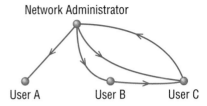

For example, User A can get files or programs from the administrator, but cannot send files to any terminal.

1. Describe what User B can and cannot do.

2. Describe what User C can and cannot do.

3. Describe a way for information to travel from

a) User B to the administrator

b) User C to User B

Activity ❸

The network shows air travel lines between 4 cities.

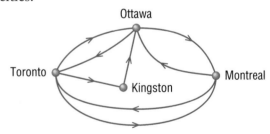

1. List each city and all the places that can be reached with

a) no stopover

b) exactly one stopover. Include return flights to the same city. For example: Toronto to ▮ to Toronto.

2. Can you travel from each city to every other city with no stopovers or, at most, 1 stopover?

3. Matrix 1 shows only some of the information from the network in another way.

Matrix 1: No Stopovers

	T	K	O	M
T	0	1	1	1
K	0	0	1	0
O				
M				

See that, from T on the left, there is 1 flight to K, 1 flight to O, and 1 flight to M. There are 0 ways to go from T to T with no stopover. From K, there is only 1 flight to O. Copy and complete the matrix for flights originating in Ottawa and Montreal.

4. Copy and complete the matrix below to show the number of trips with 1 stopover.

Matrix 2: One Stopover

	T	K	O	M
T	2	0	2	1
K	1	0	0	1
O				
M				

5. Copy and complete the matrix to show the number of trips with, at most, 1 stopover.

Matrix 3: No Stopovers or One Stopover

	T	K	O	M
T	2	1	3	2
K	1	0	1	1
O				
M				

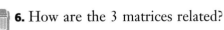 **6.** How are the 3 matrices related?

2.6 Composite and Prime Numbers

Number	Factor Pairs	Different Factors
1		
2		
3		
⋮		
12	$12 \times 1, 4 \times 3, 6 \times 2$	1, 2, 3, 4, 6, 12
⋮		
28		
29		
30		

Activity: Complete the Table

Three pairs of factors that multiply to give 12 are shown in the table. Copy and complete the table for the other numbers.

Inquire

1. A **prime number** is a whole number with exactly two factors: itself and 1. List the prime numbers from 1 to 30.

2. A **composite number** is a whole number with more than 2 factors. List the composite numbers from 1 to 30.

3. List the next 4 prime numbers greater than 30.

4. The number 1 is neither prime nor composite. Explain.

5. How are the primary colours and prime numbers similar?

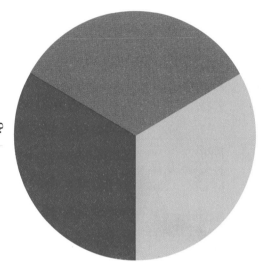

Every composite number can be written as the product of **prime factors**.

Example

Use division to write 60 as a product of its prime factors.

Solution

Divide 60 by prime numbers in increasing order. Start with 2 and keep dividing until 2 no longer divides evenly. Then, divide by the next prime number that divides evenly. Stop when the quotient is 1.

$$60 = 2 \times 2 \times 3 \times 5$$

```
2 | 60
2 | 30
3 | 15
5 |  5
       1
```

Writing a number as the product of its prime factors is called the **prime factorization** of the number.

A factor tree can also be used to write a number as the product of its prime factors.

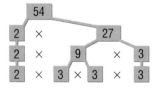

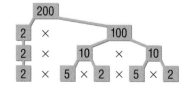

$54 = 2 \times 3 \times 3 \times 3$
$\quad = 2 \times 3^3$

$200 = 2 \times 2 \times 2 \times 5 \times 5$
$\quad\quad = 2^3 \times 5^2$

Practice

Identify each number as prime or composite.

1. 33 **2.** 40 **3.** 47 **4.** 51 **5.** 53

6. 57 **7.** 59 **8.** 3 **9.** 66 **10.** 70

11. 72 **12.** 81 **13.** 83 **14.** 91 **15.** 97

Copy and complete each factor tree.

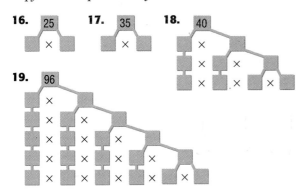

16. 25 **17.** 35 **18.** 40

19. 96

Draw a factor tree for each of these numbers.

20. 20 **21.** 32 **22.** 64 **23.** 88 **24.** 120

25. 378 **26.** 250 **27.** 144 **28.** 300 **29.** 225

Write as the product of prime factors.

30. 28 **31.** 64 **32.** 135 **33.** 165 **34.** 840

35. 256 **36.** 1516 **37.** 1120 **38.** 405 **39.** 567

Problems and Applications

Find the missing prime factor.

40. $504 = 2^3 \times 3^2 \times \blacksquare$

41. $17\ 280 = 2^7 \times 3^3 \times \blacksquare$

42. $77\ 077 = 7^2 \times 11^2 \times \blacksquare$

43. $316\ 875 = \blacksquare \times 5^4 \times 13^2$

44. How do the divisibility rules help you to find out if a number is prime or composite?

45. Every even number greater than 2 can be written as the sum of two prime numbers.
$22 = 3 + 19$ or $22 = 11 + 11$
Write the even numbers from 80 to 96 as the sum of two primes in at least one way.

46. The Sieve of Eratosthenes is a method used to identify prime numbers.

The Sieve of Eratosthenes

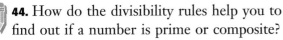

1	2	3	4	5	6	7	8	9	10
11	12	13	...						20
21	22	...							

The method goes like this.

• Make a hundred chart using the pattern shown.

• Cross out 1 because it is not prime (by definition).

• Circle 2 because it is the first prime number (by definition). Cross out all multiples of 2 because they are not prime.

• Circle 3 because it is prime. Cross out all multiples of 3 because they are not prime.

• Continue to circle the next prime number you come to and cross out all multiples of that number.

How many prime numbers are there between 1 and 100?

47. The prime factors of a number are 3, 5, and 7.

a) What is the number?

b) List three other factors of the number that are not prime.

48. a) Find the smallest number with the factors 10, 22, and 55.

b) What are the prime factors of this number?

c) Can you find the largest number with the factors 10, 22, and 55? Explain.

49. How many even prime numbers are there? Explain.

NUMBER POWER

Equal numbers of dollar coins, quarters, nickels, and dimes have a total value of $14. How many of each type of coin are there?

61

2.7 Greatest Common Factor

Activity: Complete the Table

Teresa has 54 hockey cards, 72 baseball cards, and 63 basketball cards. She wants to put them in a binder. Teresa decides that each page of the binder should have cards from a single sport and that there should be the same number of cards on each page. She wants to know the greatest number of cards she can put on a page and how many pages she will need for each sport.

Copy and complete the table by listing all the factors of each number.

Number	Factors
54	
72	
63	

Inquire

1. What factors do 54, 72, and 63 have in common?

2. What is the greatest factor they have in common?

3. What is the greatest number of cards Teresa can put on a page?

4. How many pages of cards will Teresa need for each sport?

The **greatest common factor** (GCF) of two or more numbers is the largest factor they have in common.

Example

A gardener at the botanical gardens has 75 marigolds, 45 impatiens, and 60 daisies. He wants to plant them in groups that have one type of plant in each group and the same number of plants in each group. What is the greatest number of plants he can have in each group? How many groups of each type of plant will he have?

Solution 1

List the factors.
75: 1, 3, 5, 15 , 25, 75
45: 1, 3, 5, 9, 15 , 45
60: 1, 2, 3, 4, 5, 6, 10, 12, 15 , 20, 30, 60
The greatest common factor is 15.

Solution 2

Write each number as a product of its prime factors.

$75 = 3 \times 5 \times 5$
$45 = 3 \times 3 \times 5$
$60 = 2 \times 2 \times 3 \times 5$

Multiply the common factors.

$$GCF = 3 \times 5$$
$$= 15$$

He can put 15 plants in each group. There will be 5 groups of marigolds, 3 groups of impatiens, and 4 groups of daisies.

Draw a plan for the arrangement of flowers he might use.

Practice

Use the prime factorization of each group of numbers to find the numbers and their greatest common factor.

1. $2 \times 3 \times 5 \times 7$
$2 \times 2 \times 5 \times 5$

2. $2 \times 2 \times 2 \times 3 \times 5 \times 7$
$2 \times 2 \times 3 \times 3 \times 5 \times 11$

3. $3 \times 5 \times 7 \times 7$
$2 \times 3 \times 3 \times 5$
$3 \times 3 \times 5 \times 5$

4. $2 \times 3 \times 5 \times 11$
$2 \times 3 \times 3 \times 7$
$2 \times 2 \times 3 \times 5$

Find the greatest common factor of each pair of numbers.

5. 20, 24   **6.** 27, 36   **7.** 54, 81

8. 72, 48   **9.** 64, 96   **10.** 96, 168

11. 15, 27   **12.** 32, 48   **13.** 16, 80

Find the greatest common factor of each group of numbers.

14. 33, 44, 55   **15.** 36, 48, 60

16. 64, 80, 96   **17.** 36, 54, 72

18. 27, 63, 81   **19.** 99, 22, 44

20. 51, 66, 39   **21.** 90, 45, 75

Problems and Applications

22. Jatinder wanted to make a bedcover, 80 cm by 72 cm, with squares of quilted fabric. What were the dimensions of the largest squares she could use?

23. Leo and Annette won ticket voucher packs for a basketball game. The values on the packs were recorded as $69 and $115. If the tickets were all the same price, how many tickets were in each pack?

24. Find 3 numbers with a GCF of 12.

25. The GCF of 2 numbers less than 100 is 32. What are the possible numbers?

26. What is the GCF of 1 and any other number?

27. A pet store has 56 boxes of cat food, 48 boxes of dog food, and 40 boxes of bird seed. They are to be stacked for a display so that each stack has all dog food, all cat food, or all bird seed. Each stack must have the same number of boxes.
a) What is the greatest number of boxes each stack can have?
b) How many stacks of each kind of food will there be?

28. Decide whether each of the following statements can be true for two different whole numbers. In each case, explain your answer and give examples.
a) The GCF can be one of the numbers.
b) The GCF can be greater than either number.
c) The GCF can be less than both numbers.

29. If the GCF of 2 numbers is one of the numbers, what is true about the numbers?

30. Write a problem that can be solved using the GCF. Have a classmate solve your problem.

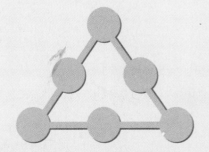

NUMBER POWER

Copy the diagram.

Write the whole numbers from 1 to 6 in the circles so that the sum of each side is a prime number.

63

2.8 Work Backward

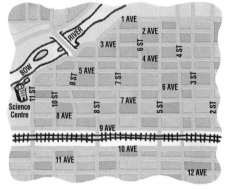

In some problems, you are given the end result and asked to find a fact that gives that result. For these problems, working backward is a useful problem solving strategy.

Kevin visited Calgary and spent a day in the southwest part of the city. The streets and avenues are numbered, as shown on the map. Kevin left his hotel to visit the Alberta Science Centre. He walked 5 blocks west, then 2 blocks south, then 3 blocks west, and finally 1 block south. The Science Centre is at 7th Avenue and 11th Street. Where was Kevin's hotel?

1. What information are you given?

2. What are you asked to find?

3. Do you need an exact or approximate answer?

Understand the Problem

Think of a Plan

Start at the Science Centre and retrace Kevin's walk by working backward.

Kevin's walk had 4 stages. The fourth stage was to walk 1 block south, so walk 1 block north from the Science Centre.

The third stage was 3 blocks west, so walk 3 blocks east.

Carry Out the Plan

The second stage was 2 blocks south, so walk 2 blocks north.

The first stage was 5 blocks west, so walk 5 blocks east.

Kevin's hotel was at 4th Avenue and 3rd Street.

Look Back

Does the answer seem reasonable?
Is there another way to solve the problem?

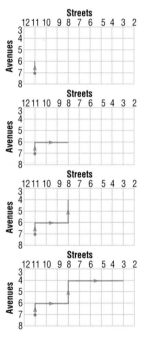

Work Backward	1. Start with what you know.
	2. Work backward to get an answer.
	3. Check that the answer is reasonable.

Problems and Applications

1. A city's streets are numbered and the avenues are lettered, as shown.

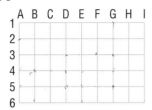

Angelica left the library and walked 4 blocks south, then 3 blocks east, then 1 block north, and finally 2 blocks east to reach the museum. The museum was at the corner of Avenue G and 5th Street. On what corner was the library?

2. An Italian scientist, Guglielmo Marconi, received the first transatlantic radio message in St. John's, Newfoundland. Eighteen years later, the first successful transatlantic flight left St. John's. Thirty years after that, Newfoundland became Canada's tenth province. Newfoundland joined Canada in 1949. In what year did Marconi receive the radio message?

3. The ferry leaves at 08:30. It takes 35 min on the bus from your home to the dock. You should allow 10 min to buy your ferry ticket. You need 45 min to shower and dress. You need another 20 min to eat breakfast and 15 min to walk your dog. For what time should you set your alarm?

4. Sonja had some baseball cards. She gave 7 to her sister and shared the rest equally among herself and two friends. Sonja's share was 13 cards. How many cards did she have originally?

5. The library held a used book sale. Bill went to the mystery section and bought half the books. Jason bought one third of the remaining books. Mark bought the rest of the books. If Mark bought 12 books, how many mystery books were originally on sale?

6. Yasmina said: "If you multiply my age by 2, then add 16, then divide by 3, the result is 20." How old is she?

7. Andy asked Melissa how many teams were in the basketball tournament her team had won. "I'm not sure," Melissa answered. "I do know that all the teams started playing at 08:00, and all the winners played every 2 h. The losers dropped out as soon as they lost, and our team played 4 games." How many teams were in the tournament?

8. Before any taxes were added, a new car had a sticker price of $37 789.60. This included the base price, plus $6345.00 worth of options and $620.00 for the dealer to prepare the car. What was the base price of the car?

9. Ari had $45.67 in his account at the end of the month. During the month, he wrote cheques for $23.80, $19.35, and $167.84. He also withdrew $50.00 at a banking machine and deposited $100.00 from his pay cheque. How much was in his account at the beginning of the month?

10. You are directing the school play. The curtain will go up at 20:15. You want the cast ready 10 min before the play starts. The make-up people need 45 min to do their job. The costume people need 35 min to get the cast ready before make-up. You need a 10-min meeting with the cast when they arrive at the school. At what time should the cast arrive at the school?

11. Money invested at 7% interest per year doubles every 10 years. Cheryl's grandmother invested some money 20 years ago at 7% per year. She now has $100 000. How much did she invest 20 years ago?

 12. Write a problem that can be solved with the work backward strategy. Be creative. Have a classmate solve your problem.

2.9 Multiples and the Lowest Common Multiple

Activity: Use the Data

Jupiter revolves around the sun approximately once every 12 years. It takes Saturn about 30 years. During 1962, Saturn and Jupiter were *in conjunction*, which means they were very close to each other in the night sky. What is the next year this will happen?

Start with 1962. List the next 3 years that Saturn was and will be in its 1962 position. List the years that Jupiter was and will be in its 1962 position. Continue the list for Jupiter until you reach the year when Saturn and Jupiter will be together again.

Inquire

1. When is the next year they will be together in the sky?

2. How many years will have passed since 1962?

3. Is the number you found in question 2 a multiple of 30? of 12?

4. Is there a smaller multiple of both 12 and 30 than the one you found in question 2?

A **multiple** is the product of a given number and any whole number. Five multiples of 3 are 3, 6, 9, 12, and 15. The **lowest common multiple** (LCM) of a set of numbers is the smallest number that is a multiple of each number in the set.

Example

Buses leave downtown for Brownville every 6 min, Orangeville every 12 min, and Greenville every 10 min. The first bus of the day leaves downtown on each route at 06:00. At what time will all 3 buses next leave together?

Solution 1

List the multiples of 6, 12, and 10.
Find the smallest number that is in every list.
Brownville: 6, 12, 18, 24, 30, 36, 42, 48, 54, 60 , 66
Orangeville: 12, 24, 36, 48, 60 , 72, 84, 96
Greenville: 10, 20, 30, 40, 50, 60 , 70, 80, 90

The lowest common multiple is 60, so 3 buses will leave together every 60 min or 1 h.

Three buses will next leave together at 07:00.

Solution 2

Write each number as the product of prime factors. Calculate the smallest number with all the prime factors of each number.

Brownville: $6 = 2 \quad \times 3$
Orangeville: $12 = 2 \times 2 \times 3$
Greenville: $10 = 2 \qquad \times 5$

$2 \times 2 \times 3 \times 5 = 60$

66

Practice

State the missing numbers in each sequence.

1. 5, 10, 15, ▪, ▪   **2.** 12, ▪, 36, 48, ▪

3. ▪, 22, 33, 44, ▪   **4.** 14, 28, ▪, ▪, 70

5. ▪, ▪, 21, 28, 35   **6.** ▪, 70, 105, ▪, 175

Use multiples to find the LCM.

7. 5, 2   **8.** 8, 12   **9.** 10, 15

10. 18, 30   **11.** 14, 28, 35   **12.** 16, 48, 8

Use the prime factorization to find each pair of numbers and their lowest common multiple.

13. $2 \times 2 \times 2 \times 3 \times 5$ **14.** $2 \times 3 \times 5 \times 7$
$2 \times 2 \times 5 \times 7$ $2 \times 2 \times 3 \times 3$

15. $2 \times 3 \times 3 \times 7$ **16.** $3 \times 3 \times 5 \times 5$
$2 \times 2 \times 2 \times 2$ $2 \times 3 \times 5 \times 5$

Use prime factors to find the LCM.

17. 4, 25   **18.** 25, 45

19. 21, 35   **20.** 24, 8

21. 100, 10, 25   **22.** 96, 144, 240

Problems and Applications

23. a) Copy and complete the table.

Numbers	Product	GCF	LCM
2, 4			
6, 12			
3, 5			
4, 6			
8, 12			

b) What is the relationship between the product, the GCF, and the LCM?

c) Is the relationship true for 3 numbers? Use an example to explain your answer.

24. a) Write two numbers such that their LCM is their product.

b) What is the GCF of the 2 numbers?

25. A flat of annuals contains 12 plants, and a flat of perennials contains 16.

a) What is the smallest number of each kind of plant you must buy to have the same number of each kind?

b) How many flats of each kind must you buy?

26. Nadia, Paula, and Anne started jogging on July 1. Nadia then jogged every second day, Paula jogged every third day, and Anne jogged every fifth day.

a) What was the date the next time Nadia and Paula jogged together?

b) What was the date the next time Paula and Anne jogged together?

c) What was the date the next time they all jogged together?

27. At a train station, one gate light flashes every 5 s, another every 8 s, and a third every 12 s. How often will they flash together?

28. The LCM of a number and 18 is 90. What are the possible values of the number?

29. Saturn orbits the sun every 12 years, Jupiter every 30 years, and Uranus every 84 years. In how many years from now will all 3 planets have the same positions in the sky as they do today?

30. Write a problem that can be solved using an LCM. Have a classmate solve your problem.

WORD POWER

The word OTTAWA begins and ends with a vowel. List at least 6 other one-word names of Canadian communities that begin and end with a vowel. Compare your list with a classmate's. Which word has the most letters?

2.10 Make Assumptions

When you leave for school in the morning, you make the assumption that your journey will take about the same length of time as it did the day before. When you solve many problems, you also have to make assumptions.

Lin works Saturdays at the farmers' market. She earns $10.00 if she arrives in time to unload the truck and set up the booth. She also earns $7.25/h for selling vegetables from 06:00 to 16:00, when the market closes. Lin hopes to earn $4000 over the next year. Will she?

1. What information are you given?

Understand the Problem

2. What are you asked to find?

3. What assumptions should you make?

4. Do you need an exact or approximate answer?

Make some assumptions about Lin's work.
• Lin will work 52 Saturdays in the year.
• She will work the same hours every Saturday.

Think of a Plan

• She will always arrive in time to unload the truck and set up the booth.
• She will be paid at the same rate all year.

Then, calculate how much she will earn each Saturday and multiply by 52.

From 06:00 to 16:00 is 10 h.
Earnings for selling: $10 \times \$7.25 = \$72.50$
Earnings for unloading and setting up: $10.00

Carry Out the Plan

Total: $82.50
Earnings in 52 weeks: $52 \times \$82.50 = \$4290.00$

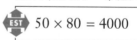
EST $50 \times 80 = 4000$

Lin should earn more than $4000 over the next year.

Does the answer seem reasonable?

Look Back

How could you use division and subtraction to check your answer?

Make Assumptions	1. Decide what assumption(s) to make.
	2. Use your assumption(s) to solve the problem.
	3. Check that your answer is reasonable.

Problems and Applications

1. List some assumptions you make when you
a) leave home to go to a movie
b) sit down to study for a math test

2. Michelle is in grade 8. She called a college and learned that first-year students pay $2000 to attend. She calculated that she must save $400/year for the next 5 years.
a) What assumption did she make?
b) What was wrong with her assumption?

3. Assume that each pattern continues, and write the next 3 terms.
a) 3, 5, 7, 9, ■, ■, ■
b) 22, 18, 14, ■, ■, ■
c) 1, 3, 9, 27, ■, ■, ■
d) 256, 128, 64, ■, ■, ■
e) 1, 2, 4, 7, 11, ■, ■, ■
f) 2, 5, 4, 7, 6, 9, 8, ■, ■, ■
g) a, f, d, i, g, l, ■, ■, ■

4. The distance around an island is 20 km. A patrol boat travels around it at 5 km/h.
a) How many trips can the boat make around the island from 20:00 to 08:00?
b) What assumptions did you make?

5. Jerry scored 10 points in the first basketball game of a 24-game season. He assumed that he would score 240 points altogether.
a) What assumptions did Jerry make?
b) Were his assumptions logical?

6. Thirty students are taking a ski trip. The slopes are 280 km from the school. The bus can travel at 80 km/h.
a) How long will it take to get to the slopes?
b) What assumptions have you made?

7. Five grade 8 students wrapped gifts and put them into 35 holiday baskets for the people in a hospital. The group could make 3 baskets every day before classes started.
a) How long did it take to make the baskets?
b) What assumptions have you made?

8. Frank opened a greeting card store. In the first month, the store sold 8000 cards. Frank calculated it would sell 96 000 cards a year.
a) What assumption did Frank make?
b) What was wrong with his assumption?
c) What are the best months for selling cards?

9. You are the editor of a school newspaper. It is Friday, and all the students have left for the weekend. There are 600 students in grades 6, 7, and 8 in the school. You must have the paper printed on Saturday. You need to know how many students will buy the paper on Monday, so that you can tell the printer how many papers to print.
a) How would you solve the problem?
b) What assumptions would you make?

10. In 1928, the Canadian women's team won the Olympic 4×100-m relay in about 48 s. In 1988, the American women's team won in about 42 s.
a) Predict the approximate winning time in the year 2108.
b) What assumptions have you made?
c) Are your assumptions reasonable?

11. Write 2 problems requiring assumptions. Have a classmate solve your problems.

WORD POWER

Lewis Carroll invented the word game "doublets." You must change one word to another by changing one letter at a time. You must form a real word each time you change a letter. Change the word TOP to the word HAT by changing one letter at a time. Compare your list of words with your classmates'. The best solution has the least steps.

69

Calculators, Computers, and Number Bases

Activity ❶ Base 10

The number 4731 can be rewritten in expanded form as follows:
$$4000 + 700 + 30 + 1 = 4 \times 10^3 + 7 \times 10^2 + 3 \times 10^1 + 1 \times 10^0$$

Numbers such as 4731 are called **base 10** numbers because the digit in each place value is multiplied by a power of 10.

1. Write the following numbers in expanded form using powers of 10.

a) 6   **b)** 41   **c)** 538

d) 8002   **e)** 3973   **f)** 73 692

2. A calculator is helpful in interpreting values or writing numbers in standard form. To write the expanded number
$$4 \times 10^2 + 7 \times 10^1 + 8 \times 10^0$$
in standard form, follow these key strokes.

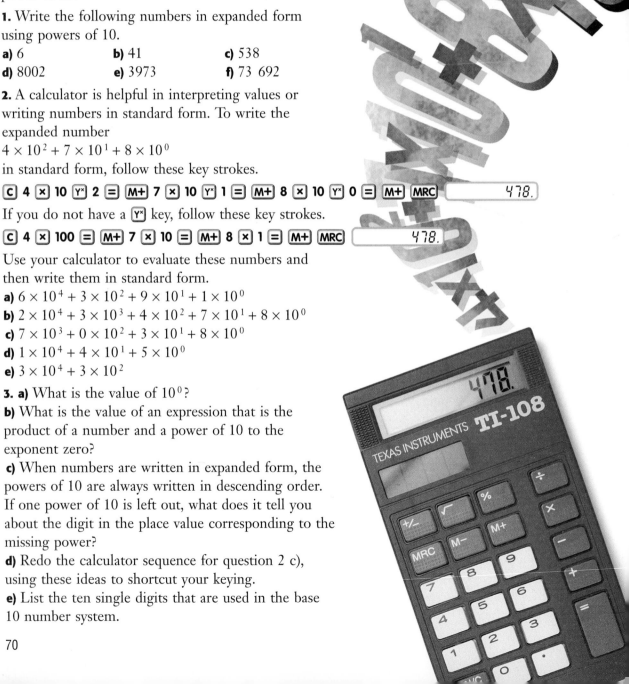

⒞ 4 ⓧ 10 ⒴ˣ 2 ⒠ Ⓜ⁺ 7 ⓧ 10 ⒴ˣ 1 ⒠ Ⓜ⁺ 8 ⓧ 10 ⒴ˣ 0 ⒠ Ⓜ⁺ ⓂⓇⒸ ⟨ 478. ⟩

If you do not have a ⒴ˣ key, follow these key strokes.

⒞ 4 ⓧ 100 ⒠ Ⓜ⁺ 7 ⓧ 10 ⒠ Ⓜ⁺ 8 ⓧ 1 ⒠ Ⓜ⁺ ⓂⓇⒸ ⟨ 478. ⟩

Use your calculator to evaluate these numbers and then write them in standard form.

a) $6 \times 10^4 + 3 \times 10^2 + 9 \times 10^1 + 1 \times 10^0$

b) $2 \times 10^4 + 3 \times 10^3 + 4 \times 10^2 + 7 \times 10^1 + 8 \times 10^0$

c) $7 \times 10^3 + 0 \times 10^2 + 3 \times 10^1 + 8 \times 10^0$

d) $1 \times 10^4 + 4 \times 10^1 + 5 \times 10^0$

e) $3 \times 10^4 + 3 \times 10^2$

 3. a) What is the value of 10^0?

b) What is the value of an expression that is the product of a number and a power of 10 to the exponent zero?

c) When numbers are written in expanded form, the powers of 10 are always written in descending order. If one power of 10 is left out, what does it tell you about the digit in the place value corresponding to the missing power?

d) Redo the calculator sequence for question 2 c), using these ideas to shortcut your keying.

e) List the ten single digits that are used in the base 10 number system.

Activity ❷ Base 2

1. List the sequence of values of the powers of 2 by copying the table and completing 20 rows.

Power of 2	Standard Form
2^0	1
2^1	2
2^2	4
2^3	8
2^4	16

2. With base 10 numbers, you used the digits 0 to 9. In base 2 numbers, you use only two digits. What do you suppose the two digits are?

3. Use your calculator to evaluate these base 2 numbers and to rewrite them as base 10 numbers in standard form.

a) 11111_{two}
$= 1 \times 2^4 + 1 \times 2^3 + 1 \times 2^2 + 1 \times 2^1 + 1 \times 2^0$

b) 1111_{two}
$= 1 \times 2^3 + 1 \times 2^2 + 1 \times 2^1 + 1 \times 2^0$

c) 10101_{two}
$= 1 \times 2^4 + 0 \times 2^3 + 1 \times 2^2 + 0 \times 2^1 + 1 \times 2^0$

d) 10001_{two}
$= 1 \times 2^4 + 0 \times 2^3 + 0 \times 2^2 + 0 \times 2^1 + 1 \times 2^0$

Activity ❸ Binary Numerals

In a computer, binary numerals are used to name all letters and numbers.

1. Copy the table. Use it to complete the list of binary numerals with values from 1 to 31.

Base 10 Numeral	Base 2 Numeral in Expanded Form	Binary Numeral
1	1×2^0	1
2	$1 \times 2^1 + 0 \times 2^0$	10
3	$1 \times 2^1 + 1 \times 2^0$	11
4	$1 \times 2^2 + 0 \times 2^1 + 0 \times 2^0$	100
5	$1 \times 2^2 + 0 \times 2^1 + 1 \times 2^0$	101
6	$1 \times 2^2 + 1 \times 2^1 + 0 \times 2^0$	110

2. With or without your calculator, rewrite these binary numbers as base 10 numbers in standard form.

a) 101_{two}　　　　**b)** 111_{two}
c) 1101_{two}　　　**d)** 1000_{two}
e) 1100_{two}　　　**f)** 1110_{two}
g) 1111_{two}　　　**h)** 10000_{two}

3. The numeral 9 is the highest digit you can use in the base 10 number system. What happens when you add 1 to a base 10 number whose digits are all 9s?

4. The numeral 1 is the highest digit you can use in the base 2 number system. What happens when you add 1 to a base 2 number whose digits are all 1s?

5. Decide with a classmate the similarities and the differences in the results of questions 3 and 4. Explain your results.

Review

Which numbers are divisible by 4? by 8?

1. 34   **2.** 356   **3.** 552   **4.** 808   **5.** 4804

State the missing digit so that the number is divisible by 9. Sometimes there is more than one answer.

6. 12 ▪   **7.** 4 ▪ 0

8. 7 ▪ 83   **9.** 317 4 ▪ 1

10. Write a four-digit number that is divisible by 5 and 10.

11. Write a five-digit number that is divisible by 5, but not by 10.

12. State a number with a square root between 6 and 7.

Evaluate.

13. $\sqrt{121}$ **14.** $\sqrt{0.49}$ **15.** $\sqrt{900}$

16. $\sqrt{0.04}$ **17.** $\sqrt{441}$ **18.** $\sqrt{1.96}$

Estimate. Then, evaluate to the nearest tenth.

19. $\sqrt{150}$ **20.** $\sqrt{8.5}$ **21.** $\sqrt{1700}$

List all the factors of each number.

22. 20   **23.** 35

24. 48   **25.** 60

26. Find a number that has an even number of factors.

27. When you raise 4 to a power, what digits do you always get in the ones position?

Write as a product of prime factors.

28. 28   **29.** 36   **30.** 660

31. Complete the factor tree.

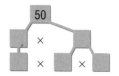

Draw complete factor trees for the following.

32. 45   **33.** 81   **34.** 366

35. Pick at least three perfect squares and make up factor trees to check to see if the following statement is true or false. "Perfect squares always have an even number of prime factors."

Find the greatest common factor of the following sets of numbers.

36. 12 and 18   **37.** 15 and 105

38. 81 and 36   **39.** 16, 48, 64

40. 15, 45, 55   **41.** 49, 28, 210

42. Make up an example to show that the following statement can be true and another example to show that it can also be false. "The greatest common factor of a set of numbers is one of the numbers."

Find the lowest common multiple.

43. 15 and 10   **44.** 4 and 10

45. 64 and 16   **46.** 7, 21, 30

47. 16, 24, 32   **48.** 20, 35, 56

The lowest common multiple is a) the largest number in the set, b) the product of the numbers, or c) between the largest number and the product. Decide which is true for each of the following sets.

49. 4, 6, 8   **50.** 5, 10, 20   **51.** 2, 3, 7

52. Every eighth day, a menu includes broccoli soup. Every sixth day, the menu includes pumpernickel bread. On what days of October are these two served together if they are both on the menu on Tuesday, October 3?

53. Kew's age is a multiple of 7, and Paulo's age is a multiple of 2. They are the same age and both coach their daughters' baseball teams. How old might they be?

The pages of a book are numbered consecutively from 1 to 100. How many pages meet the following requirements?

54. The page number contains a 5 and is also divisible by 5.

55. The page number does not contain a 5 but is divisible by 5.

Write in standard form.

56. $4 \times 2 \times 8$ **57.** 5^4

58. $2 \times 2 \times 2 \times 2 \times 3 \times 3$ **59.** $3^4 \times 5^2$

60. $10 \times 10 \times 10 \times 10$ **61.** 20^3

Write in order from smallest to largest.

62. $3^4, 5^3, 10^2$ **63.** $1^{12}, 4^3, 2^6$

Evaluate.

64. $(3 + 5) \div 2 + 7 \times (8 + 12) \div 10$

65. $3^3 + 3 + 33 \times 3$

66. $\dfrac{(4 + 5) \times (2 + 7) \div (12 - 3)}{(7 - 4)} \times (7 - 4)$

67. $3.45 \times 10^2 + 0.471 \times 10^3$

68. $10^4 - 5^3$ **69.** $5^3 - 5^2$

70. State whether or not each of the following is always true and explain. If the statement is not always true, add a word or two to the condition so that it is always true.
a) "When you triple a number, the new number is always divisible by 3."
b) "When you triple a number, the new number is always divisible by 6."

71. Edmonton is Alberta's biggest city, with an area of 670 km². If you could fit the whole of Edmonton into a square, what would its side length be to the nearest tenth of a kilometre?

72. A light year is the distance that light travels through space in a year. It equals about 10^{13} km. The Milky Way Galaxy is about 10^5 light years across. Express this distance in kilometres.

Group Decision Making
Researching Law Enforcement Careers

1. Brainstorm with the whole class the careers you would like to investigate. They could include such careers as police officer, coast guard crew member, pathologist, judge, forensic scientist, or forensic accountant. Decide as a class on 6 careers.

2. Go to home groups. In your group, decide which career each member will investigate. Also, decide on the questions you want to answer about the careers. Include a question on how math is used in each career.

1 2 3 4 5 6	1 2 3 4 5 6

Home Groups

1 2 3 4 5 6	1 2 3 4 5 6

3. Research your career individually.

4. Form an expert group with students who have researched the same career as you. In your expert group, combine the information you have found.

1 1 1 1	2 2 2 2	3 3 3 3

Expert Groups

4 4 4 4	5 5 5 5	6 6 6 6

5. In your expert group, prepare a report on the career. The report can take any form the group chooses.

6. Present your findings to your home group. Evaluate the process and identify what went well and what you would do differently next time.

Chapter Check

Use these numbers to answer questions 1 to 3.

121 256 834 211   85   81
903 400 186 498 1232 104

1. Which numbers are divisible by 2 and 3?

2. Which numbers are divisible by 3 and 9?

3. Which numbers are divisible by 4 and 8?

List the factors of each of the following numbers.

4. 24   **5.** 38   **6.** 70   **7.** 250

8. List the composite numbers between 20 and 40.

9. List the prime numbers between 80 and 100.

Write as a product of prime factors.

10. 54   **11.** 20   **12.** 68   **13.** 85

Estimate, then evaluate. Round to the nearest tenth, if necessary.

14. $\sqrt{256}$ **15.** $\sqrt{6.4}$ **16.** $\sqrt{88}$ **17.** $\sqrt{0.16}$

Write the greatest common factor of each set.

18. 31, 62   **19.** 12, 8, 44   **20.** 30, 105, 225

Write the lowest common multiple of each set.

21. 3, 4   **22.** 5, 2, 3   **23.** 12, 18, 21

Write as a power and then in standard form.

24. $4 \times 4 \times 4 \times 4 \times 4$

25. $10 \times 10 \times 10 \times 10$

26. $2 \times 2 \times 2 \times 2 \times 2 \times 2 \times 2 \times 2 \times 2$

27. $3 \times 2 \times 3 \times 2$

28. $6 \times 6 \times 6$

Evaluate.

29. $2^5 - 5^2$ **30.** $10^3 - 1$

31. $3 \times (9^2 - 9)$ **32.** $5 \times 2^3 + 6 - 3^2$

33. Every fourth person entering the party gets a free hat and every sixth person gets a noisemaker. Which people will be the first, second, and third to get both a hat and a noisemaker?

34. The number of bacteria in a culture doubles every minute. From each bacterium in the culture, how many bacteria are produced in 6 min?

35. The mass of the Milky Way Galaxy is about 10^{42} kg. The mass of the sun is about 10^{30} kg. About how many times greater is the mass of the Milky Way Galaxy than the mass of the sun?

36. Rosa spent the same amount of money on shorts and T-shirts. A pair of shorts costs $18 and a T-shirt costs $24. What was the smallest amount of money she could have spent on each?

37. Jamil wants to record music from 90-min tapes to 60-min tapes. What combinations of tapes can he use to record complete tapes?

38. Which number is the largest? Write each in standard form to compare.

100^4 1000^3 $10\ 000^2$

"I wouldn't know, sir. Why not count the rings
yourself to see if the bark has been included."

Reprinted by permission: Tribune Media Services

Using the Strategies

Look for a pattern and write the next three terms.

1. 61, 63, 65, …

2. 84, 79, 80, 75, 76, 71, …

3. z, y, x, w, …

4. az, by, cx, dw, …

5. j, f, m, a, m, …

6. Figure 1 has 6 cubes, figure 2 has 11 cubes, and figure 3 has 16 cubes.

  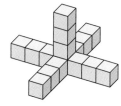

a) How many cubes are there in the fourth figure?

b) How many cubes are there in the 200th figure? the 3000th figure?

7. A tropical fruit salad was being prepared for brunch. The recipe called for twice as many kiwis as pineapples and 4 fewer bananas than kiwis. Twenty-one pieces of fruit were used for the salad. How many pieces of each fruit were used?

8. How would you estimate how long it would take you to complete a 20-km walk-a-thon?

9. The first week Devin cut lawns, he earned $80.

a) How much should he earn in a year?

b) What assumptions did you make?

10. The football stadium has 22 145 seats. On the sides, there are 17 800 seats that cost $23.50 each. The rest of the seats are at the ends and cost $12.25 each. If all the seats are sold for a game, how much money will be collected?

11. Sarah is saving for a telescope that costs $575, including taxes. She has already saved $205. She plans to save the rest in equal amounts for the next 5 months. How much should she save each month?

12. George is 15. He is five times as old as his sister was five years ago. How old is his sister now?

13. a) You have a red bead, a blue bead, and a yellow bead. How many different arrangements of 3 different-coloured beads in a row can you make?

b) Suppose you added a green bead. How many different arrangements of 4 different-coloured beads in a row can you make?

14. Lyndon agreed to train for 2000 h for an upcoming race. He can train for 5 h a day. How long in weeks and days will he have to train to reach his goal?

15. How would you estimate the thickness of one page of a telephone book?

16. What is the sum of the 3 largest prime numbers less than 50?

DATA BANK

1. When it is 03:00 on a Wednesday in Tashkent, Uzbekistan, what time and what day is it in Winnipeg?

2. It is possible to drive from Saskatoon to Vancouver through Edmonton or Calgary. Which route is shorter and by how much?

CHAPTER 3

Geometry

Hampton Court is a palace on the River Thames near London, England. King William III's maze at Hampton Court is one of the oldest hedge mazes in England. The drawing shows that the maze is made up of line segments and angles.

The object is to enter the maze at A, make your way to the centre, B, then come back out at A. This is not a difficult challenge if you can see all of the maze.

To get the feeling of wandering among the hedges, cut out a piece of cardboard about 8 cm by 6 cm. Punch a hole in the middle of it, so that the diameter of the hole is about the same as the thickness of a pencil. Now, place the hole over A. Move the hole to the centre of the maze, B, then move it back out to A.

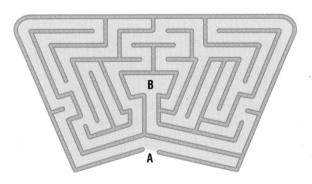

Area on a Grid

The **area** of a figure is the amount of surface it covers. Let each small square on the grid be 1 square unit.

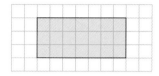

Area of rectangle = 21 square units

Activity ❶ Areas of Rectangles and Squares

Find the area of each figure.

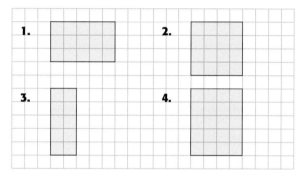

Activity ❷ Areas of Right Triangles

To find the area of a right triangle, draw a rectangle around the triangle and find the area of the rectangle.

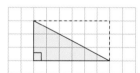

Area of rectangle = 18 square units
Area of triangle = 9 square units

Copy the following triangles onto grid paper and find the area of each.

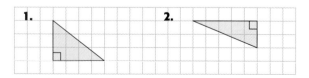

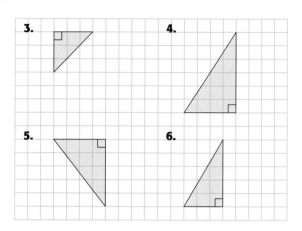

Activity ❸ Areas of Tilted Squares

To calculate the area of a tilted square, divide the square into right triangles. Then, find the sum of the areas of the triangles to find the area of the square.

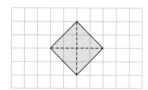

Area of each triangle = 2 square units
Area of square = 8 square units

Copy these squares onto grid paper and find their areas.

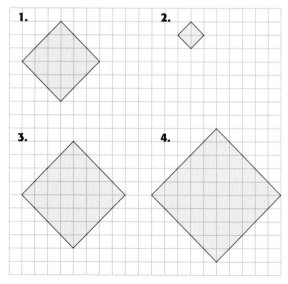

Activity ❹ More Areas of Tilted Squares

To calculate the areas of the tilted squares below, divide each square into right triangles and a square that is not tilted. Then, find the sum of the areas of the triangles and the smaller square.

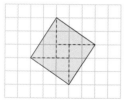

Area of each triangle = 3 square units
Area of small square = 1 square unit
Area of large square = 13 square units

Copy these squares onto grid paper and find their areas.

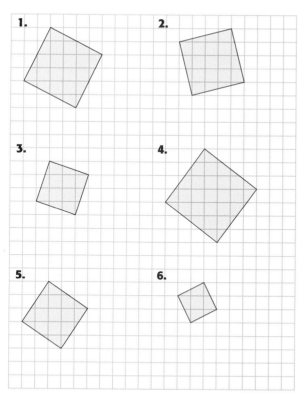

1.
2.
3.
4.
5.
6.

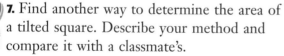

7. Find another way to determine the area of a tilted square. Describe your method and compare it with a classmate's.

Mental Math

Add.

1. 17 + 14	**2.** 27 + 14
3. 36 + 15	**4.** 46 + 15
5. 55 + 16	**6.** 65 + 16
7. 74 + 17	**8.** 84 + 17
9. 93 + 18	**10.** 23 + 18

Subtract.

11. 60 − 11	**12.** 70 − 11
13. 55 − 12	**14.** 35 − 12
15. 46 − 13	**16.** 76 − 13
17. 78 − 14	**18.** 98 − 14
19. 49 − 15	**20.** 79 − 15

Calculate.

21. 34 + 26 − 10	**22.** 43 − 13 + 27
23. 65 − 15 + 8	**24.** 57 − 17 + 15
25. 41 + 19 − 20	**26.** 56 + 24 − 9
27. 33 − 13 + 21	**28.** 61 + 19 − 40
29. 47 + 23 + 5	**30.** 88 − 28 + 14

Multiply.

31. 3×101	**32.** 5×101
33. 4×202	**34.** 7×1001
35. 6×202	**36.** 8×303
37. 2×707	**38.** 3×2002
39. 9×404	**40.** 8×505

Divide.

41. $436 \div 4$	**42.** $535 \div 5$
43. $123 \div 3$	**44.** $186 \div 6$
45. $749 \div 7$	**46.** $856 \div 8$
47. $219 \div 3$	**48.** $287 \div 7$
49. $426 \div 6$	**50.** $945 \div 9$

79

3.1 Terms in Geometry

Here are some important terms used in geometry.

A **point** identifies a position. A point has no size. A dot is used to represent a point, and a capital letter is used to name it.

A **line** is a straight path of points with no endpoints. It extends forever in both directions. A line is named by using any 2 points on the line or with a single lower-case letter.

A **ray** is a part of a line. A ray starts at one endpoint and extends forever in one direction.

A **line segment** is part of a line and has 2 endpoints.

An **angle** is formed by two rays or line segments with a common endpoint, called the **vertex**. The rays or line segments are the **arms** or **sides** of the angle.

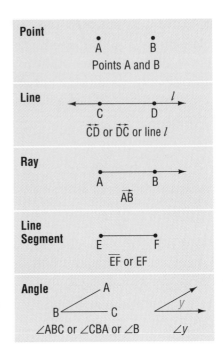

Point	• A • B Points A and B
Line	C D *l* $\overleftrightarrow{CD}$ or $\overleftrightarrow{DC}$ or line *l*
Ray	A B $\overrightarrow{AB}$
Line Segment	E F $\overline{EF}$ or EF
Angle	A, B, C ∠ABC or ∠CBA or ∠B ∠*y*

Activity: Study the Drawing

Leonardo da Vinci (1452–1519) became famous because of his art. His best-known paintings are the *Mona Lisa* and the *Last Supper*. His great contributions to science did not become known until the twentieth century, when his notebooks were found.

Leonardo made this technical drawing of a canal-digging machine in one of his notebooks. He wrote his notes backward, so they could only be read with a mirror.

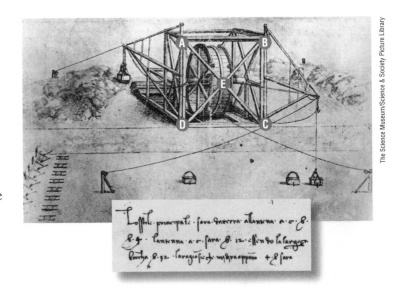

Inquire

1. List 3 points, 3 line segments, and 3 angles found in the drawing.

3. Write the definition of a line segment so that it can be read in a mirror.

 2. Why do you think Leonardo wrote his notes backward?

4. A dot and a point are not exactly the same. How are they different?

Practice

Name each figure.

1. •A   **2.** 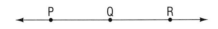   **3.**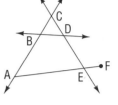

4. 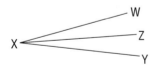   **5.**   **6.** W X Y

Draw each figure.

7. point Q   **8.** line *m*

9. $\overleftrightarrow{DE}$ **10.** GF

11. $\overrightarrow{MN}$ **12.** ∠PQR

13. ∠T   **14.** ∠*b*

15. Points P, Q, and R are on the same line.

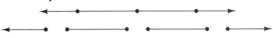

a) Name all the line segments.
b) Name all the rays.

16. Name the angle in 3 ways.

R
S
T

17. Name the 3 angles in the diagram.

W
Z
X
Y

Problems and Applications

18. Name the following in the diagram.
a) all line segments with Q as an endpoint
b) all rays with P as an endpoint
c) 3 different angles with R as the vertex
d) a line

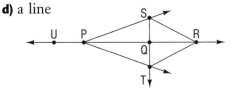

19. Why is ∠A not a good way to name ∠BAC?

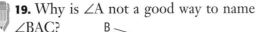

20. Use the figure to name the following.
a) 5 points
b) 3 lines
c) 6 angles
d) 4 rays
e) 5 line segments

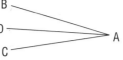

21. If you place 3 points on a line, then separate the parts, you get 2 line segments and 2 rays.

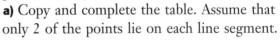

a) Copy and complete the table.

Points	1	2	3	4	5	18	33
Segments			2				
Rays			2				
Total Parts			4				

b) What rule relates the number of points and the total number of parts?

22. If 3 points are not in a straight line, they can be joined to give 3 line segments.
a) Copy and complete the table. Assume that only 2 of the points lie on each line segment.

Points	1	2	3	4	5	6
Line Segments			3			

b) Use the pattern to predict how many line segments can be drawn with 7 points; 8 points; 12 points.

23. Draw 4 points so that you can draw no more than the following numbers of lines through them. Compare your drawings with a classmate's.

a) 1   **b)** 4   **c)** 6

3.2 Measuring, Drawing, and Classifying Angles

Semaphore flags can be used to send messages at sea and on land. Two flags are held at different angles to show different letters.

Angles are commonly measured in degrees. The size of an angle is determined by how much one ray or arm of the angle has been rotated from the other.

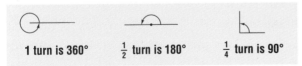

1 turn is 360°   **½ turn is 180°**   **¼ turn is 90°**

Activity: Study the Diagrams

Thirteen semaphore letters are shown. In each case, the angle made by the flags is a multiple of 45°.

Inquire

1. What angle is formed by the flags for
a) R?   **b)** J?   **c)** O?   **d)** K?

2. For which letters do the flags make
a) a 90° angle?   **b)** a 45° angle?

3. What angle do the flags make for
a) M?   **b)** S?   **c)** N?

Angles are classified according to their measures.

acute angle	right angle	obtuse angle	straight angle	reflex angle
less than 90°	90°	between 90° and 180°	180°	between 180° and 360°

A protractor is used to measure and draw angles.

Example

Draw ∠XYZ = 115°.

Solution

Draw YZ. Place the centre of the protractor on Y with the baseline along YZ, so that YZ passes though 0° on the inner scale. Mark X at 115° on the inner scale. Join XY. ∠XYZ = 115°.
Check: Does the drawing show an obtuse angle? Yes.

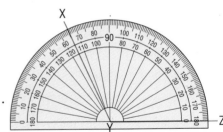

Practice

Write the measures of the following angles shown on the protractor. Classify each angle as acute, right, or obtuse.

1. ∠DXB   **2.** ∠BXF   **3.** ∠GXB

4. ∠JXH   **5.** ∠EXJ   **6.** ∠JXI

7. ∠CXJ   **8.** ∠FXJ   **9.** ∠EXB

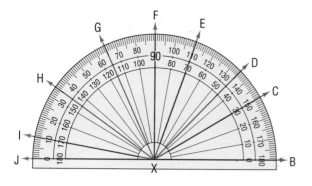

Write the measures of the following angles shown on the protractor. Classify each angle as acute, right, or obtuse.

10. ∠RGW   **11.** ∠NGK   **12.** ∠KGL

13. ∠QGW   **14.** ∠TGK   **15.** ∠MGW

16. ∠NGW   **17.** ∠RGK   **18.** ∠MGK

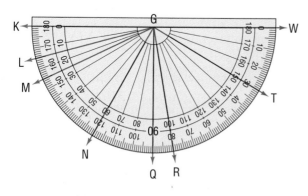

Draw the following angles.

19. 40°   **20.** 75°   **21.** 24°

22. 125°   **23.** 175°   **24.** 220°

25. 265°   **26.** 300°   **27.** 355°

Problems and Applications

Copy the diagram and use it for questions 28–31.

28. Name 3 acute angles.

29. Name 2 right angles.

30. Name 1 obtuse angle.

31. Sketch and name 3 reflex angles.

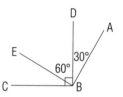

Trace each angle. Estimate its measure, then check your estimate by measuring. To measure, you will need to extend the arms of each angle.

32.   **33.**

34.    **35.**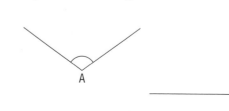

36. List the angles in order from smallest to largest by inspection. Verify your answer by tracing and measuring.

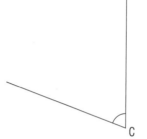

37. Describe how you would use your protractor to measure an angle that is greater than 180°.

83

3.3 Guess and Check

The grade 8 class had a problem solving contest. One group came up with the following problem.

There were 5 bags of dried peas in a row. The total number of peas was 335.

The first bag had 7 fewer peas than the second bag, the second bag had 7 fewer peas than the third bag, and so on.

There was a prize for the first student who correctly guessed the number of peas in the first bag. How many were there?

Understand the Problem

1. What information are you given?

2. What are you asked to find?

3. Do you need an exact or approximate answer?

Think of a Plan

Guess the number of peas in the first bag. Use your guess to write the numbers of peas in the other bags.

Find the total number of peas. If your total is not 335, make another guess at the number of peas in the first bag.

Carry Out the Plan

GUESS						CHECK
Bag 1	Bag 2	Bag 3	Bag 4	Bag 5	Total	Is the total 335?
40	47	54	61	68	270	Too low
60	67	74	81	88	370	Too high
50	57	64	71	78	320	Too low
55	62	69	76	83	345	Too high
52	59	66	73	80	330	Too low
53	60	67	74	81	335	335 = 335

CHECKS!

There were 53 peas in the first bag.

Look Back

Check the answer against the given information.
Does the answer seem reasonable?
Is there another way to solve the problem?

Guess and Check	1. Guess an answer that fits one of the facts.
	2. Check the answer against the other facts.
	3. If necessary, adjust your guess and check again.

Problems and Applications

1. There are 5 bags of dried peas in a row. The second bag has 5 more peas than the first. The third bag has 6 more peas than the second. The fourth bag has 7 more peas than the third. The fifth bag has 8 more peas than the fourth. The total number of peas is 295. How many peas are in the first bag?

2. If you multiply a certain number by 11 and add 76, the result is 208. What is the number?

3. The number in each red square is found by adding the numbers in the small green squares connected to it. Find the numbers in the green squares.

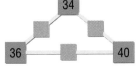

4. Heather scored 21 more points than Justin in a game of SCRABBLE®. Together, they scored a total of 333 points. How many points did each of them score?

In questions 5-8, each letter represents a different digit. Find the value of each letter.

5.
$$\begin{array}{r} I \\ + M \\ \hline M\,E \end{array}$$

6.
$$\begin{array}{r} R\,S \\ \times\ 9 \\ \hline R\,R\,R \end{array}$$

7.
$$\begin{array}{r} A\,8 \\ \times\ \ 3\,B \\ \hline 2\,7\,3\,0 \end{array}$$

8.
$$\begin{array}{r} C\,2\,D \\ 8)\overline{X\,9\,Y} \end{array}$$

9. The length of a rectangle is twice the width, and the area is 112.5 cm². Find the dimensions of this rectangle.

10. Find 4 consecutive whole numbers whose sum is 318.

11. Find 3 consecutive odd whole numbers whose sum is 405.

12. Find 3 consecutive whole numbers such that the sum of their squares is 509.

13. In the number TT5T4, the letter T stands for the same digit. If the number is divisible by 38, find T.

14. Find 2 consecutive whole numbers whose cubes differ by 397.

15. For selling magazine subscriptions, Samira earned $20 a day, plus $4 for every subscription she sold. One day, she earned a total of $232. How many subscriptions did she sell?

16. The cube root of 8 is 2, because 2 × 2 × 2 = 8. Find the cube root of 36, to the nearest tenth.

17. A total 86 of Canada's 295 Members of Parliament (MPs) are elected from the 4 western provinces. Equal numbers of MPs are elected from Saskatchewan and Manitoba. The number elected from Alberta is 12 more than the number elected from Manitoba. The number elected from British Columbia is 18 more than the number elected from Saskatchewan. How many MPs are elected from each of these 4 provinces?

18. Write a problem that can be solved using the guess and check strategy. Have a classmate solve your problem.

LOGIC POWER

One blue cube has the same mass as 3 green cubes. One green cube has the same mass as 4 pink cubes plus 1 red cube. One red cube has the same mass as 2 pink cubes. How many pink cubes have the same mass as 1 blue cube?

3.4 Angle Relationships

Activity: Discover the Relationships

The diagram of Winnipeg International Airport shows the 3 runways and their numbers. Trace the diagram and extend runways 36, 07, 13, 18, and 31. Measure each angle and record each measure.

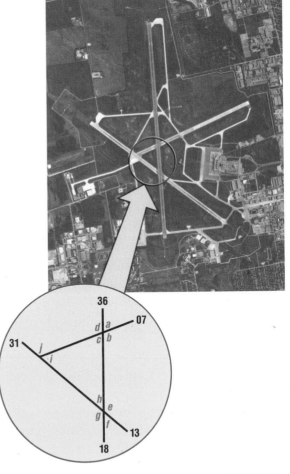

Inquire

1. $\angle a$ and $\angle c$ are called **opposite angles**. Why?

2. Name 3 other pairs of opposite angles.

3. How are the angle measures in a pair of opposite angles related?

4. Two angles whose sum is 180° are called **supplementary angles**. Name the pairs of supplementary angles.

5. Two angles whose sum is 90° are called **complementary angles**. How many pairs of complementary angles are there?

6. Why are the runways numbered in the way they are?

Example

a) Find the measures of the unknown angles.
b) Name a pair of complementary angles.
c) Name a pair of supplementary angles.

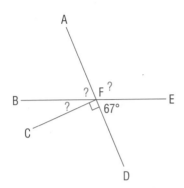

Solution

a) $\angle AFB = \angle EFD$ (opposite angles)
   $\angle AFB = 67°$

$\angle EFD + \angle AFE = 180°$ (straight angle)
   $67° + \angle AFE = 180°$
   $\angle AFE = 113°$

$\angle EFD + \angle CFD + \angle BFC = 180°$ (straight angle)
   $67° + 90° + \angle BFC = 180°$
   $157° + \angle BFC = 180°$
   $\angle BFC = 23°$

b) $\angle AFB + \angle BFC = 67° + 23°$
   $= 90°$
$\angle AFB$ and $\angle BFC$ are complementary angles.

c) $\angle DFE + \angle AFE = 67° + 113°$
   $= 180°$
$\angle DFE$ and $\angle AFE$ are supplementary angles.

Practice

Find the measure of each unknown angle.

1.
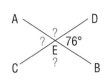

2.

3.

4.

5.

6.

Write the measure of the angle that is complementary to each of the following.

7. $35°$　　　**8.** $56°$　　　**9.** $81°$

Write the measure of the angle that is supplementary to each of the following.

10. $47°$　　　**11.** $106°$　　　**12.** $157°$

State whether each pair of angles is complementary, supplementary, or neither.

13. $34°, 64°$　　　　　**14.** $133°, 47°$

15. $9°, 81°$　　　　　　**16.** $92°, 78°$

Problems and Applications

17. When a ray of light is reflected by a mirror, the angle of incidence, i, equals the angle of reflection, r. If $i = 35°$, what is the measure of

a) the complement of i?
b) r?
c) the complement of r?

 18. The measure of an angle is $40°$ more than the measure of its supplement. What is the measure of each angle?

 19. The measure of an angle is $10°$ more than the measure of its complement. What is the measure of each angle?

 20. If $\angle M$ and $\angle N$ are supplementary angles, and $\angle M$ and $\angle P$ are complementary angles, what is the relationship between $\angle N$ and $\angle P$?

 21. Give examples to show that, when you add the measure of an angle to twice the measure of its complement, the sum is the measure of the angle's supplement.

 22. Give examples to show that, when you add the measure of an angle to three times the measure of its complement, the sum equals the sum of the measures of the angle's complement and supplement.

 23. Use the figure below to name the following angles. Compare your answers with a classmate's.
a) all right angles
b) all pairs of complementary angles
c) all pairs of supplementary angles

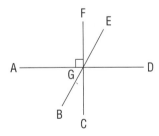

 24. Write a question like one of questions 1 to 6. Have a classmate answer your question.

NUMBER POWER

What is the product of all the integers from $+50$ to -50?

3.5 Parallel and Perpendicular Lines

In mathematics, we often use perpendicular and parallel lines.

Perpendicular lines intersect to form right angles.

Parallel lines are lines in the same plane that do not intersect.

A **transversal** is a line or line segment that crosses 2 or more lines. When a transversal crosses 2 lines, 8 angles are formed. $\angle r$ and $\angle u$ are called **alternate angles**. They form a $\angle$ pattern. $\angle s$ and $\angle t$ are also a pair of alternate angles. They form a $\searrow$ pattern.

$\angle s$ and $\angle w$ are called **corresponding angles**. They form an F pattern. Other pairs of corresponding angles are $\angle r$ and $\angle v$ ($\daleth$ pattern), $\angle q$ and $\angle u$ ($\mathrel{E}$ pattern), and $\angle p$ and $\angle t$ ($\exists$ pattern).

$\angle s$ and $\angle u$ are called **co-interior angles**, which are interior angles on the same side of the transversal. They form a C pattern. $\angle r$ and $\angle t$ are another pair of co-interior angles. They form a $\mathsf{\rfloor}$ pattern.

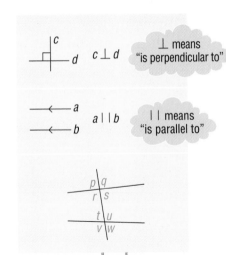

Activity: Complete the Table

Draw 2 parallel lines on grid paper. Draw a transversal and label the 8 angles, as shown. Measure the angles and complete the table.

Inquire

$\angle a =$	$\angle b =$	$\angle c =$	$\angle d =$
$\angle e =$	$\angle f =$	$\angle g =$	$\angle h =$

1. a) Name the 2 pairs of alternate angles.
b) How do the measures in each pair compare?

2. a) Name the 4 pairs of corresponding angles.
b) How do the measures in each pair compare?

3. a) Name the 2 pairs of co-interior angles.
b) What is the sum of the measures in each pair?

4. Repeat the Activity and questions 1 to 3 for a different pair of parallel lines.

5. Copy and complete the following statement. When a transversal crosses 2 parallel lines, the alternate angles are ▆▆▆ , the corresponding angles are ▆▆▆ , and the co-interior angles are ▆▆▆ .

6. The design of the Bank of China building in Hong Kong includes a number of perpendicular and parallel structures. Describe the perpendicular and parallel lines you see in the photo of the Bank of China building.

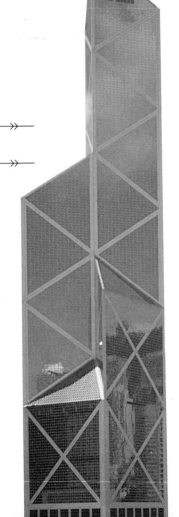

Example

Determine the following angle measures.

a) ∠b   **b)** ∠c   **c)** ∠d

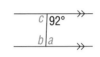

Solution

a) ∠b = ∠a (alternate angles)

∠b = 77°

b) ∠c = ∠a (corresponding angles)

∠c = 77°

c) ∠b + ∠d = 180° (co-interior angles)   or   ∠a + ∠d = 180° (straight angle)

77° + ∠d = 180°   77° + ∠d = 180°

∠d = 103°   ∠d = 103°

Practice

Identify each pair of angles as alternate angles, corresponding angles, co-interior angles, or opposite angles.

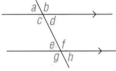

1. ∠a and ∠e   **2.** ∠c and ∠f

3. ∠c and ∠e   **4.** ∠e and ∠h

5. ∠d and ∠h   **6.** ∠f and ∠g

7. ∠d and ∠e   **8.** ∠c and ∠g

9. ∠b and ∠c   **10.** ∠d and ∠f

Problems and Applications

Find the missing angle measures. Give reasons for your answers.

11.

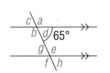

12.

13.

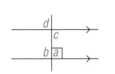

14.

Find the measure of each unknown angle.

15.

16.

17.

18.

19.

20.

21. If the alternate angles created by 2 parallel lines and a transversal are supplementary, what are their measures? Explain.

22. Work with a partner to list sports playing surfaces that have parallel and perpendicular lines on them. Compare your answers with your classmates'.

23. Write a problem like one of questions 11 to 20. Have a classmate solve your problem.

89

3.6 Lines of Symmetry

If you fold the drawing of the hawk along the line shown, one half of the hawk exactly matches the other half. The 2 halves are reflection images of each other. The hawk is said to have a **line of symmetry**. The fold line is the line of symmetry.

A figure can have more than 1 line of symmetry. A starfish has 5.

Activity: Draw the Patterns

In each diagram, the 3-by-3 grid has 3 red squares and 6 white squares. Diagram 1 has 1 line of symmetry, and diagram 2 has 2.

A pattern is **symmetrical** if it has at least 1 line of symmetry. Draw the other symmetrical patterns on a 3-by-3 grid using 3 red squares and 6 white squares. Patterns like those shown to the right are considered to be the same.

Diagram 1   Diagram 2

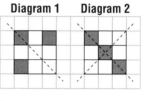

Inquire

1. Compare your patterns with your classmates'. How many different patterns did you find?

2. What is the maximum number of lines of symmetry in any of the patterns?

3. Draw any shape that has 4 lines of symmetry.

4. Draw any shape that has 3 lines of symmetry.

5. Sketch 5 objects in the classroom that have lines of symmetry. Draw the lines of symmetry on your sketches.

Example

How many lines of symmetry does each figure have?

a)

b)

c)
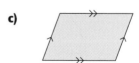

Solution

a) The square has 4.

b) The rectangle has 2.

c) The parallelogram has none. Each diagonal divides it into 2 identical parts, but the parts do not match when the parallelogram is folded along the diagonal.

Practice

Is the red line a line of symmetry? Write "yes" or "no."

1.

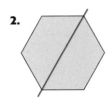

2.

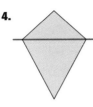

3.

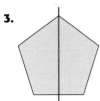

4.

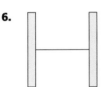

Copy each figure and draw all the lines of symmetry.

5.

6.

7.

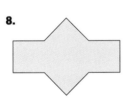

8.

Problems and Applications

Copy each figure onto grid paper. Complete the diagram so that the red line is a line of symmetry.

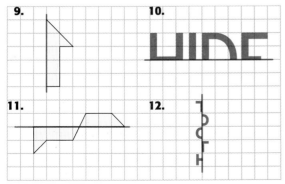

9.

10.

11.

12.

13. Copy each figure onto grid paper. Complete the diagram so that the new figure has
a) 1 line of symmetry **b)** 2 lines of symmetry

The following symbols are used by meteorologists. Copy the symbols and draw the lines of symmetry.

14. Sleet   **15.** Snow   **16.** Haze

17. Overcast   **18.** Hail Showers   **19.** Fog

20. This symbol shows that the wind is calm. How many lines of symmetry does it have? Explain.

21. The diagrams show how 4 squares can be coloured on a 3-by-3 grid to give patterns with 1 line of symmetry and 4 lines of symmetry.

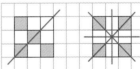

Find how many other ways 4 squares can be shaded on a 3-by-3 grid to give patterns that have lines of symmetry.

22. With a classmate, draw 4 signs, symbols, or logos, each having a different number of lines of symmetry.

23. With a classmate, research the shield of each province and territory.
a) Which shields have a line of symmetry?
b) If you ignored the animals, which of the other shields would have a line of symmetry?

3.7 Draw and Read Graphs

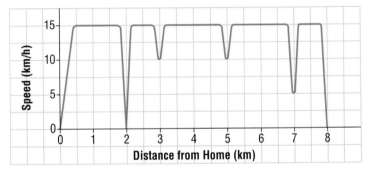

A graph is a useful and attractive way of displaying information. Magazines and newspapers often display information in this way. The ability to draw and interpret graphs is an important life skill.

The diagram shows the route Belen takes to get from her house, H, to the recreation centre, R.

Belen rides her bicycle at 15 km/h. She slows down to make the turns. There is a stop sign, S, 2 km from her house. Sketch a graph of Belen's speed versus the distance from her house.

Understand the Problem

1. What information are you given?

2. What are you asked to do?

Think of a Plan

Draw a horizontal axis to show Belen's distance from her house. Draw a vertical axis to show her speed. Use the map of Belen's route to sketch a graph of her speed at various distances from her house.

Carry Out the Plan

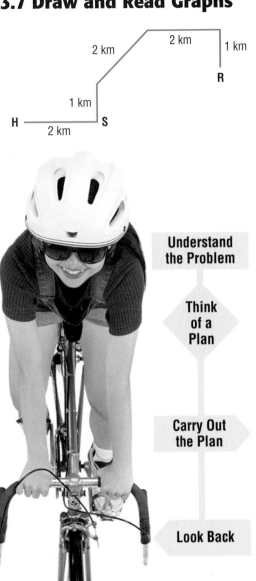

Look Back

Check that the graph agrees with the given facts.

Draw a Graph	1. Draw and label the axes.
	2. Use the data to draw the graph.
	3. Check that the graph is reasonable.

Read a Graph	1. Read the necessary data from the graph.
	2. Use the data to solve the problem.
	3. Check that the answer is reasonable.

Problems and Applications

1. Karen and Isabel live near a lake. They left their house at noon to go for a walk on the beach. The graph shows their distance from home at any one time. Describe what was happening between A and B; B and C; C and D; and D and E.

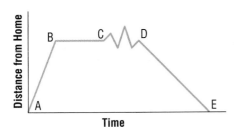

2. Sketch a graph of the number of people in your school on a school day versus the time of day.

3. Sketch a graph of the number of students in a grade 2 classroom on a school day versus the time of day. Assume that the weather is good, so the students can go out for recess.

4. Karl made 5 phone calls to his friends from a pay phone at the airport. The graph shows the friends he called, how long he talked, and the cost of each call.

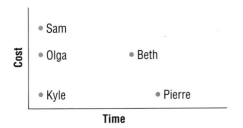

a) Which calls cost the same?
b) Which calls were local?
c) Which calls were long-distance?
d) Which one of Karl's friends lived farthest from the airport?
e) Which of the people he called long-distance lived closest to the airport?

5. Mariko travels to businesses to repair photocopiers. The graph shows her distance from her office on one day. Write a story to describe Mariko's activities for the day.

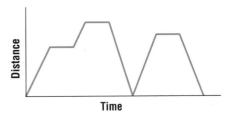

6. The diagram shows Ali's house and the grocery store. Ali drove to the store at 40 km/h along the straight sections of the road and slowed down at the corners.

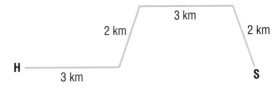

Copy the following axes. Sketch a graph to show the speed of Ali's car from his house to the store.

7. A playground supervisor is pushing a child on a swing. Copy the following axes. Sketch a graph of the child's height above the ground versus time for 3 complete swings.

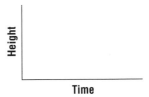

8. Write a problem that requires a sketch of a graph. Have a classmate solve your problem.

3.8 Triangles and Angles

Triangles appear in many designs, including the flag of British Columbia. Triangles are classified by the lengths of their sides and the measures of their angles.

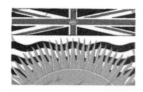

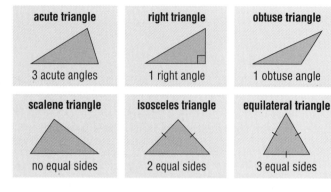

acute triangle	right triangle	obtuse triangle
3 acute angles	1 right angle	1 obtuse angle
scalene triangle	isosceles triangle	equilateral triangle
no equal sides	2 equal sides	3 equal sides

How would you classify the triangles on the flag of British Columbia?

Activity: Use the Definitions

Use a ruler to draw the following triangles. Make each triangle large enough that you can measure its angles with a protractor.

a) a right scalene triangle   **b)** an obtuse isosceles triangle
c) a right isosceles triangle   **d)** an obtuse scalene triangle
e) an acute isosceles triangle

Inquire

1. For each triangle you drew, use a protractor to measure each angle and find the sum of the measures.

2. Draw an acute triangle and cut it out. Tear off the angles and line them up as shown. What is the sum of the measures of the 3 angles?

3. Repeat question 2 for a right triangle and an obtuse triangle.

4. What is the sum of the measures of the interior angles of a triangle?

Example

Calculate the measures of $\angle SRT$ and $\angle WRT$.

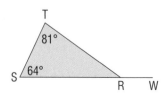

Solution

The sum of the interior angles of a triangle is 180°.

$$\angle S + \angle T + \angle SRT = 180°$$
$$64° + 81° + \angle SRT = 180°$$
$$145° + \angle SRT = 180°$$
$$\angle SRT = 35°$$
$$\angle SRT + \angle WRT = 180° \text{ (straight angle)}$$
$$35° + \angle WRT = 180°$$
$$\angle WRT = 145°$$

Practice

Classify each triangle in 2 ways, by its sides and angles.

1.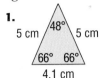

2.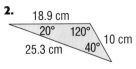

3.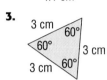

4.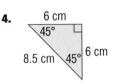

Find the measure of the unknown angle.

5.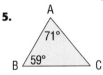

6.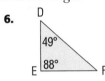

7.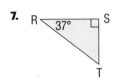

8.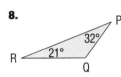

Problems and Applications

Calculate the missing angle measures.

9.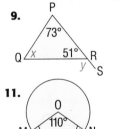

10.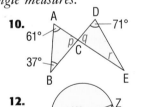

11.

12.

13. On grid paper, draw 2 isosceles triangles like the ones shown.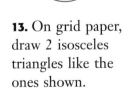

a) Measure the angles. Which angles are equal in each triangle?

b) Describe the relationship between the equal sides and equal angles in each triangle.

14. Find the missing angle measures.

a)

b)

15. An **exterior angle** of a triangle is formed when one side of the triangle is extended. In the diagram, ∠c is an exterior angle, and ∠a and ∠b are the two interior angles opposite to ∠c.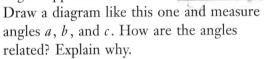
Draw a diagram like this one and measure angles a, b, and c. How are the angles related? Explain why.

16. Triangles can be classified by the number of lines of symmetry they have. How many lines of symmetry do these triangles have?
a) isosceles   **b)** scalene   **c)** equilateral

17. State the maximum number of lines of symmetry the following triangles could have. Show your answer with a diagram.
a) right   **b)** obtuse   **c)** acute

18. A triangle has a perimeter of 12 cm. The length of each side is a whole number of centimetres.
a) How many different triangles can be made?
b) Use the side lengths to classify each triangle.

19. a) Which provinces other than British Columbia have flags that include triangles?
b) With a classmate, find pictures of the flags of the states in the United States. List the flags that include triangles and classify the triangles.

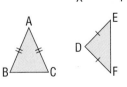
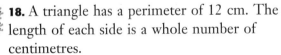
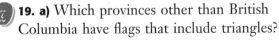

Investigating Quadrilaterals

A **polygon** is a closed figure made from line segments.
A polygon with 4 sides is called a **quadrilateral**. Some
quadrilaterals have special names.

A **trapezoid** is a quadrilateral with exactly 2 parallel sides.	A **parallelogram** is a quadrilateral with opposite sides parallel.	A **kite** is a quadrilateral with 2 pairs of adjacent sides equal.
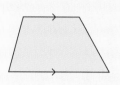	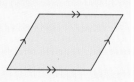	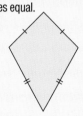

Some parallelograms have special names.

A **rhombus** is a parallelogram with 4 equal sides.	A **rectangle** is a parallelogram with 4 right angles.	A **square** is a parallelogram with 4 equal sides and 4 right angles.
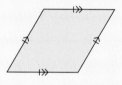	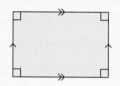	

Activity ❶ Angles and Sides

On grid paper, draw a parallelogram and a rhombus, like the
ones shown. Measure the angles and sides in each figure.

1. How are the opposite angles in a parallelogram related?

2. How are the opposite sides in a parallelogram related?

3. How are the opposite angles in a rhombus related?

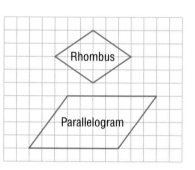

Activity ❷ Lines of Symmetry

Draw the quadrilaterals on grid paper, then draw all the lines
of symmetry for each.

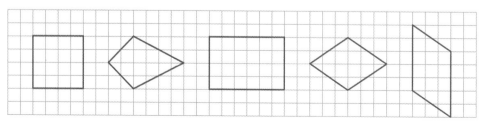

Activity ❸ Diagonals

A **diagonal** is a line segment, other than a side, that joins 2 vertices in a polygon. Copy the figures onto grid paper and draw the diagonals for each.

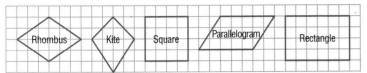

1. Which quadrilaterals have equal diagonals?
2. Which quadrilaterals have diagonals that meet at right angles?
3. Which quadrilaterals have diagonals that bisect each other?

Activity ❹ Missing Measures

Find the missing measures in each figure.

1. Parallelogram

PS = ▨ RS = ▨
∠PSR = ▨ ∠QRS = ▨

2. Square

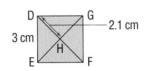

DG = ▨ HF = ▨
GE = ▨ ∠GHF = ▨

3. Kite

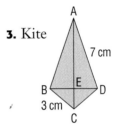

AB = ▨ DC = ▨
∠AED = ▨ ∠DEC = ▨

4. Rectangle

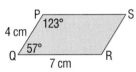

DC = ▨ EC = ▨
AC = ▨ DB = ▨
AD = ▨ BE = ▨

5. Parallelogram

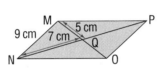

QO = ▨ MO = ▨
PO = ▨ PQ = ▨

6. Rhombus

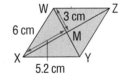

XY = ▨ MY = ▨
XZ = ▨ ∠WMZ = ▨

Activity ❺ Critical Thinking

Decide whether each statement is always true, sometimes true, or never true. Explain.

1. A quadrilateral is a rhombus.
2. A rhombus is a kite.
3. A rectangle is a square.
4. A square is a rectangle.
5. A square is a parallelogram.
6. A square is a rhombus.
7. A trapezoid is a parallelogram.
8. A rectangle is a rhombus.
9. A rhombus is a quadrilateral.
10. A kite is a square.

3.9 Polygons

The front, back, and sides of Sudbury's Big Nickel are made up of polygons. A **polygon** is a closed plane figure made up of 3 or more line segments. A polygon is named according to its number of sides. In a **regular polygon**, all the sides are the same length, and all the angles have the same measure. A **diagonal** joins 2 vertices in a polygon and is not a side.

Activity: Use the Table

Draw the following polygons.

a) a quadrilateral with just 1 right angle

b) a pentagon with just 2 acute angles

c) a hexagon with at least 4 right angles

d) an octagon with at least 1 acute angle, 1 right angle, and 1 obtuse angle

e) a polygon with just 2 diagonals

f) a polygon with just 5 diagonals

Inquire

1. Name the polygons that form the front, back, and sides of Sudbury's Big Nickel. Are the polygons regular? Explain.

2. What is the maximum number of diagonals that can be drawn from 1 vertex of each of the following polygons?

a) quadrilateral   **b)** pentagon   **c)** hexagon

3. Use the pattern from question 2 to find the maximum number of diagonals from 1 vertex of these polygons.

a) octagon   **b)** decagon   **c)** dodecagon

Polygon	Sides
Triangle	3
Quadrilateral	4
Pentagon	5
Hexagon	6
Heptagon	7
Octagon	8
Nonagon	9
Decagon	10
Dodecagon	12

The sum of the measures of the interior angles of a triangle is 180°. To find the sum of the interior angles of other polygons, divide the polygon into triangles using all the diagonals from 1 vertex.

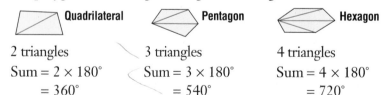

Quadrilateral   Pentagon   Hexagon

2 triangles   3 triangles   4 triangles

Sum = 2 × 180°   Sum = 3 × 180°   Sum = 4 × 180°

= 360°   = 540°   = 720°

The sum of the interior angles of a polygon with n sides is $180° \times (n - 2)$.

Example

Find the measure of each angle in a regular octagon.

Solution

The sum of the interior angles is: $S = 180° \times (8 - 2)$
$$= 180° \times 6$$
$$= 1080°$$

There are 8 equal angles. Each angle is 1080° ÷ 8 or 135°.

Practice

Find the sum of the interior angles in each of the following.

1. heptagon   **2.** nonagon

3. decagon   **4.** dodecagon

Find the measure of the unknown angle in each polygon.

5.

6.

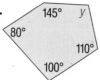

7.

8.

Find the measure of each angle in the following.

9. regular triangle   **10.** regular hexagon

11. regular pentagon   **12.** regular decagon

Problems and Applications

13. What is the common name for a regular quadrilateral?

14. a) How many lines of symmetry are there for a regular hexagon? a regular pentagon?
b) For a regular polygon, how is the number of lines of symmetry related to the number of sides? Test your answer for a regular octagon.

15. Find the measures of the unknown angles in these kites.

a)

b)

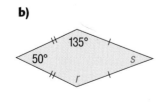

16. An exterior angle of a polygon is formed when one side of the polygon is extended. The diagram shows the 3 exterior angles of an equilateral triangle.

a) What is the measure of each exterior angle?
b) What is the sum of the measures of the 3 exterior angles?
c) Draw any triangle and an exterior angle at each vertex. Measure each exterior angle and find the sum.
d) Draw any quadrilateral and an exterior angle at each vertex. Measure each exterior angle and find the sum.
e) Draw any pentagon and an exterior angle at each vertex. Measure each exterior angle and find the sum.
f) What is the sum of the exterior angles of any polygon?

17. Is it possible for a hexagon to have all 6 sides equal and not be a regular hexagon? Explain.

18. Is it possible for a hexagon to have all 6 angles equal and not be a regular hexagon? Explain.

19. a) If you trace around a one-dollar coin, how many sides does the resulting polygon have?
b) Use your research skills to name a polygon with this number of sides.

20. State an everyday word that has the same prefix as each of the following. Compare your words with your classmates'.
a) triangle   **b)** quadrilateral
c) octagon   **d)** decagon

3.10 Using Angle Relationships

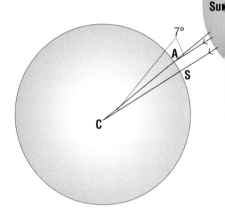

Activity: Study the Diagram

Around 200 B.C., Eratosthenes used an angle relationship to find
the circumference of the Earth. Since the sun is so far away, he
assumed that the sun's rays are parallel lines. When the sun was
directly overhead at Syene (S), the sun's rays made an angle of
about 7° at Alexandria (A), 800 km north of Syene.

A 7° angle is about $\frac{1}{50}$ of a circle. If C is the centre of the Earth,
∠ACS is $\frac{1}{50}$ of a circle because the sun's rays are parallel.

Inquire

1. How do you think that Eratosthenes used the information
to find the Earth's circumference?

2. How close do you think he came to the actual circumference?
Explain.

You have learned the relationships between pairs of lettered
angles in diagrams 1 to 4, below. You have also learned the sums
of the lettered angles in diagrams 5 and 6.

Diagram 1	Diagram 2	Diagram 3	Diagram 4	Diagram 5	Diagram 6

You can apply angle relationships to solve problems.

Example

Find these angle measures and
explain your calculations.

a) ∠CGF   **b)** ∠BFG   **c)** ∠BAC

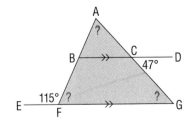

Solution

a) BD || EG, so ∠CGF = ∠DCG (alternate angles)
$$\angle CGF = 47°$$

b) ∠BFG + ∠BFE = 180° (straight angle)
$$\angle BFG + 115° = 180°$$
$$\angle BFG = 65°$$

c) The sum of the interior angles of a triangle is 180°.
$$\angle BAC + \angle BFG + \angle CGF = 180°$$
$$\angle BAC + 65° + 47° = 180°$$
$$\angle BAC + 112° = 180°$$
$$\angle BAC = 68°$$

Practice

Find the unknown angle measures.

1.

2.

3.

4.

5.

6.

Problems and Applications

Find the unknown angle measures.

7.

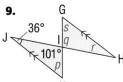

8.

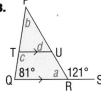

9.

10.

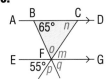

11.

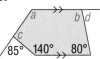

12.

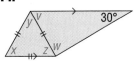

Find the unknown angle measures.

13.

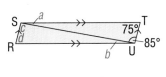

14.

15.

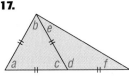

16.

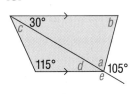

17.

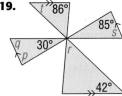

18.

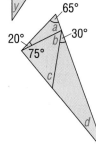

19.

20.

21. When the sun is overhead in Jamaica, it makes an angle of about 26° in Prince Edward Island. To the nearest 100 km, how far apart are the 2 islands? Explain your method. Compare your result with a classmate's.

22. Write a problem that involves finding at least 3 unknown angles. Check that the problem can be solved, then have a classmate solve it.

PATTERN POWER

a) Use a calculator to complete the calculations.

$$19^2 = \blacksquare$$
$$199^2 = \blacksquare$$
$$1999^2 = \blacksquare$$

b) Describe the pattern.

c) Use the pattern to predict $19\ 999^2$ and $199\ 999^2$.

3.11 Use a Diagram

Understand the Problem

Think of a Plan

Carry Out the Plan

Look Back

In some cases, drawing a diagram will help you to solve a problem. This problem solving strategy is used in some careers. Clothing designers start their creations with diagrams. Architects also use diagrams, and so do city planners.

Susan is responsible for setting up 6 refreshment stations for the runners in a marathon. The stations are on one street and are two blocks apart. There are two helpers at each station.

Susan wants to put the main supply of drinks at one of the stations. She wants the total distance walked by the helpers to the main supply to be as short as possible. Where should she put the main supply?

1. What information are you given?

2. What are you asked to find?

3. Do you need an exact or approximate answer?

Draw a diagram of the 6 stations. Choose a location for the main supply at one of the stations.

Calculate the distance from the main supply to each of the other stations and find the sum. Choose other locations for the main supply until you find the smallest sum.

```
      2         2         2         2         2
A---------B---------C---------D---------E---------F
```

Location of Main Supply	Distance to Other Stations	Total Distance
C	A 4; B 2; D 2; E 4; F 6	18
D	A 6; B 4; C 2; E 2; F 4	18
A	B 2; C 4; D 6; E 8; F 10	30
F	A 10; B 8; C 6; D 4; E 2	30
B	A 2; C 2; D 4; E 6; F 8	22
E	A 8; B 6; C 4; D 2; F 2	22

Locations C and D give the smallest sum.
Susan can put the main supply at either of the middle stations.

Were all the calculations necessary?
Does the answer seem reasonable?

Use a Diagram	1. Draw a diagram to represent the situation.
	2. Use the diagram to solve the problem.
	3. Check that the answer is reasonable.

Problems and Applications

1. Four identical squares can be made with 16 toothpicks.

The following diagrams show how 4 identical squares can be made with only 13 toothpicks.

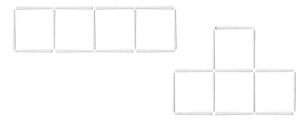

a) What is the smallest number of toothpicks needed to make 4 identical squares? 5 identical squares?

b) What is the maximum number of identical squares you can make with 22 toothpicks?

2. On a sightseeing tour, a bus left the hotel and went 3 blocks due south, 8 blocks due east, 7 blocks due north, 2 blocks due west, and 4 blocks due south. Where was the bus in relation to the hotel?

3. An elevator started on the ground floor, rose 12 floors, rose 3 more floors, descended 5 floors, descended 2 floors, rose 4 floors, and descended 6 floors. Where was the elevator in relation to the ground floor?

4. How many diagonals does a regular hexagon have?

5. Norah needed to fence an 8 m by 12 m yard. She wanted fence posts to be 2 m apart, with a post in each corner. How many posts did she need?

6. Four sticks measure 5 cm, 8 cm, 9 cm, and 13 cm. How many triangles can you make if each triangle has 3 of the sticks as sides?

7. How many isosceles triangles can you draw with a perimeter of 14 cm or less if the lengths of the sides must be whole numbers of centimetres?

8. Mike has 3 containers. One holds 3 L of water, another 5 L, and the third 8 L. How can he use the containers to measure 4 L of water?

9. How can you use 3 sticks that measure 6 cm, 10 cm, and 12 cm to mark off a distance of 8 cm?

10. Each of the 6 teams in a baseball league plays every other team 6 times. How many games are played?

11. How many different-sized squares can you make on a 4-by-4 geoboard?

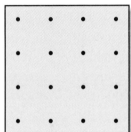

12. A soccer team has 3 different tops, red, white, and blue. There are 2 different shorts, red and blue, and 2 different socks, red and blue. How many different uniforms can the team wear?

13. As the crow flies, the distance from Appletown to Beantown is 40 km. The distance from Appletown to Corntown is 35 km and the distance from Appletown to Dairytown is 36 km. Beantown is 40 km from Corntown and 60 km from Dairytown. Corntown is 24 km from Dairytown. Draw a map that shows the possible locations of the 4 towns. Compare your map with your classmates'.

14. Write a problem that can be solved by drawing a diagram. Have a classmate solve your problem.

3.12 Congruent Polygons

Congruent figures have the same size and shape. A design for space station *Alpha* includes solar panels in the shape of 12 congruent rectangles. A Canadian robot will help to build *Alpha* in space.

Activity: Use the Diagram

The square has been divided into 4 congruent rectangles.

How do you know the figures are rectangles?
How do you know they are congruent?

Inquire

1. Copy the square and divide it into the following.
a) 4 congruent squares
b) 4 congruent isosceles right triangles
c) 4 congruent right triangles different from those in question 2
d) 4 congruent T-shapes
e) 4 congruent L-shapes

2. How many ways are there to divide the square into 2 congruent trapezoids and 2 congruent isosceles triangles? Explain.

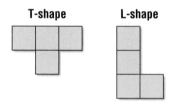

T-shape   L-shape

The 2 triangles, △COT and △NAP, are congruent. A tracing of △NAP fits exactly onto △COT.

△COT ≅ △NAP   ≅ means "is congruent to"

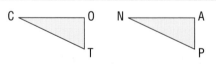

The **corresponding parts** of congruent polygons are also congruent or equal. The marks on the sides and angles indicate which corresponding parts are equal.

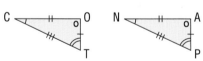

Corresponding Sides	Corresponding Angles
CO = NA	∠C = ∠N
OT = AP	∠O = ∠A
TC = PN	∠T = ∠P

Example

The quadrilaterals PQRS and CDAB are congruent. List and mark the corresponding equal parts.

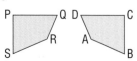

Solution

Corresponding Sides	Corresponding Angles
PQ = CD	∠P = ∠C
QR = DA	∠Q = ∠D
RS = AB	∠R = ∠A
SP = BC	∠S = ∠B

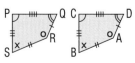

Practice

1. List the pairs of congruent polygons. Give reasons for your answers.

 A

 B

 C

 D

 E

 F

 G

 H

 I

 J

 K

 L

 M

 N

 O

P

Q

R

List the corresponding equal parts in the pairs of congruent polygons.

2.

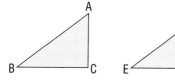

3.

4.

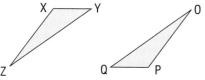

5.

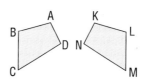

6.

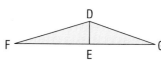

7.

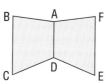

8.

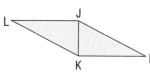

Problems and Applications

9. Draw a pair of triangles on grid paper that have the same shape but not the same size.

10. Draw a pair of quadrilaterals on grid paper that have the same shape but not the same size.

11. Must 2 rectangles be congruent if they have the same perimeter? Explain.

12. Must 2 rectangles be congruent if they have the same area? Explain.

13. Must 2 squares be congruent if they have the same perimeter? Explain.

14. The shape is made up of 4 congruent pieces. Copy the figure onto grid paper and shade each of the 4 congruent pieces a different colour.

15. Write a problem like question 14. Use as many congruent pieces as you wish. Be creative. Have a classmate solve your problem.

Staging Rock Concerts

One of the most exciting aspects of a rock concert is the integration of the music and the lighting. The lights around the stage are held in place by lighting pipes. The process of suspending the lights is known as "flying the pipes."

Before the pipes are flown, the lighting designer must find the proper angles for the lights. To do this, the designer uses a ruler and protractor.

In the following example, the stage has a depth of 8 m. The support for the 3 pipes is to be 1 m from the back of the stage. The 3 pipes, A, B, and C, are to be 9 m, 7 m, and 5 m above the stage floor. To find the angle at which each pipe must be pointed, the designer uses the following steps.

Draw the stage floor, GE, letting 1 cm represent 1 m.

Find $\frac{1}{4}$ of the stage depth. $\frac{1}{4} \times 8 = 2$

Mark the lights' *focal point*, F, $\frac{1}{4}$ of the stage depth or 2 m from the front of the stage.

Mark a point, D, on the pipe support 1 m from the back of the stage.

Draw the pipe support and mark the lighting pipes, A, B, and C, 9 m, 7 m, and 5 m from the stage floor.

Join AF, BF, and CF to make ∠FAD, ∠FBD, and ∠FCD. Measure these 3 angles.

∠FAD = 38°, ∠FBD = 45°, and ∠FCD = 54°.

Lighting technicians set the pipes to these angles on the pipe support before raising the support.

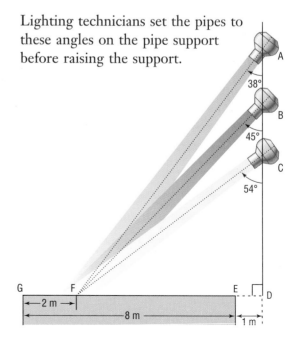

Activity ❶

These questions refer to the example on the opposite page.

1. a) Another way to determine ∠FAD is to measure ∠AFD and use the angle properties of a triangle. What is the relationship between the measures of ∠FAD and ∠AFD? Explain.

b) Why might a designer choose to measure ∠AFD, ∠BFD, and ∠CFD and to calculate ∠FAD, ∠FBD, and ∠FCD from them?

2. The measure of ∠FBD could be determined without the use of a protractor. Explain how.

Activity ❷

The lighting designer adjusts the angles of the lighting pipes for stages of different sizes. Use the table to find the angles needed for pipes A, B, and C at each venue.

Venue	Stage Width (m)	Stage Depth (m)	Pipe Height (m)			Distance of Pipe Support from Stage (m)
			A	B	C	
Maple Leaf Gardens	12	8	11	10	9	3
B.C. Place	16	12	12	10	7	1
O'Keefe Centre	8	6	9	7	6	0
Lansdowne Park	12	10	10	8	6	2

Activity ❸

For some lighting designs, it is important to use the same lighting angles throughout a tour. In these cases, the height of each lighting pipe is the variable that the designer must determine.

1. Choose one of the venues in Activity 2. Use the stage depth and the distance of the pipe support from the stage to determine the heights of the pipes for angles of 35°, 45°, and 50°.

2. Describe how the problem solving process differs from the process used in the example.

Activity ❹

Very few concerts have lighting equipment only behind the performers. For variety and visibility, most designers also hang lighting pipes on both sides of the stage.

1. Using the data from Activity 2, add pipes A, B, and C on stage left, and pipes X, Y, and Z on stage right for one of the venues.

2. How are the triangles you drew for stage left and the triangles you drew for stage right related?

Activity ❺

1. With a partner, choose a performer or group for whom you would like to do a lighting design. Also, choose one of the venues in Activity 2.

2. Decide how many pipes to use
a) at the back of the stage
b) on each side of the stage

3. Decide how far from the stage to place the pipe supports.

4. Choose the colours of the lights.

5. Use the stage dimensions to determine the angles of the lighting pipes.

3.13 The Pythagorean Theorem

Pythagoras was a very famous Greek mathematician who lived in the sixth century B.C. He and his followers, the Pythagoreans, studied many properties of numbers and geometric figures. The most famous discovery made by Pythagoras was the relationship between the side lengths in right triangles.

Activity: Discover the Relationship

In the diagrams, squares have been drawn on the sides of 6 triangles. The sides are labelled a, b, and c, where c is the longest side. Copy the diagrams onto grid paper and find the area of each square. Copy and complete the table.

Triangle	a^2	b^2	c^2	$a^2 + b^2$
1				
2				
3				
4				
5				
6				

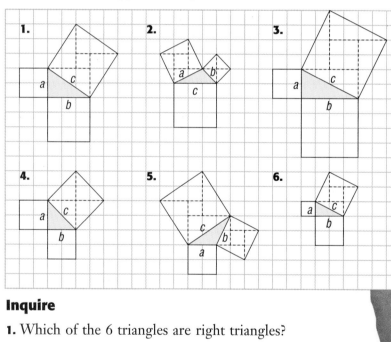

Inquire

1. Which of the 6 triangles are right triangles?

2. In each right triangle, how does the area of the square on the longest side compare with the sum of the areas of the squares on the other 2 sides?

3. Is the relationship you found in question 2 true for the triangles that are not right triangles?

In a right triangle, the longest side is opposite the right angle and is called the **hypotenuse**. The other 2 sides are called **legs**.

Example

Calculate the length of the unknown side.
If necessary, round to the nearest tenth.

a)

b)

Solution

The Pythagorean Theorem states that in any right triangle, if c is the length of the hypotenuse, and a and b are the lengths of the legs, then $a^2 + b^2 = c^2$.

a) In $\triangle ABC$

$$c^2 = a^2 + b^2$$
$$= 4^2 + 3^2$$
$$= 16 + 9$$
$$c^2 = 25$$
$$c = 5$$

[C] 4 [x²] [+] 3 [x²] [=] [√] ⟦ 5. ⟧

b) In $\triangle DEF$

$$e^2 + f^2 = d^2$$
$$6^2 + f^2 = 7^2$$
$$36 + f^2 = 49$$
$$f^2 = 13$$
$$f = \sqrt{13}$$
$$f \doteq 3.6$$
$$f = 3.6 \text{ to the nearest tenth}$$

EST $\sqrt{16} = 4$

$\doteq$ means "approximately equals"

[C] 7 [x²] [−] 6 [x²] [=] [√] ⟦ 3.6055513 ⟧

Practice

Find the length of the unknown side in each right triangle. If necessary, round to the nearest tenth.

1.

5, x, 12

2.
8, x, 6

3.

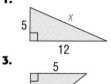
5, 4, x

4.
8, r, 8

Find the length of the unknown side in each triangle. If necessary, round to the nearest tenth.

5.

17, 8, x

6.
9, t, 7

7.

10, x, 26

8.

1, 3, y

Problems and Applications

9. Use the figure to answer the questions.

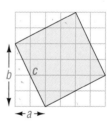

a) What is the area of the large square?
b) What is the area of each triangle?
c) What is the area of the tilted square?
d) What is the relationship between c^2 and $a^2 + b^2$?

10. Which of the following could be the side lengths in a right triangle?
a) 3 cm, 4 cm, 6 cm
b) 15 m, 17 m, 8 m
c) 13 m, 5 m, 12 m
d) 8 cm, 9 cm, 11 cm

3.14 Using the Pythagorean Theorem

Activity: Study the Information

The HMCS *Halifax* left Halifax and sailed east at 25 km/h for 2 h. It then sailed south at 30 km/h for 2 h. The captain wanted to know how far the ship was from Halifax.

Inquire

1. How far did the ship sail east?

2. How far did the ship sail south?

3. Why is ∠HXY a right angle?

4. Write the Pythagorean relationship for △HXY.

5. Find the distance HY to the nearest tenth of a kilometre.

6. a) In questions 3 to 5, what assumption have you made about the surface of the Earth?
b) When is it reasonable to make this assumption?

Example

Galleys sailed the Mediterranean in the fifteenth century. They were 40 m long and 10 m wide. There was a 30-m high mast in the middle of each galley. Support ropes ran from the top of the mast to the front, back, and sides of the ship. Find the lengths of the support ropes, to the nearest tenth of a metre.

Solution

Make a diagram. Because the mast was in the middle of the boat, the front and back support ropes were the same length, and so were the 2 side ropes.

For the front and back ropes

$l^2 = x^2 + y^2$
$\quad = 20^2 + 30^2$
$\quad = 400 + 900$
$l^2 = 1300$
$l \doteq 36.1$

Front and Back Ropes

The front and back support ropes were each 36.1 m long, to the nearest tenth of a metre.

For the side ropes

$s^2 = t^2 + y^2$
$\quad = 5^2 + 30^2$
$\quad = 25 + 900$
$s^2 = 925$
$s \doteq 30.4$

Side Ropes

The side support ropes were each 30.4 m long, to the nearest tenth of a metre.

Practice

Find the length of the third side of each right triangle, to the nearest tenth of a metre.

1.

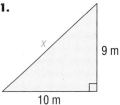

2.

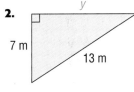

Problems and Applications

3. A 7-m ladder is leaning against a wall of a building. The foot of the ladder is 2 m from the base of the building. How far up the wall is the top of the ladder?

4. A ship left Shippegan, New Brunswick, and sailed east at 20 km/h for 2 h, then south at 25 km/h for 1 h. To the nearest tenth of a kilometre, how far was the ship from Shippegan?

5. A camp swimming race starts from the end of a 30-m long pier. The finish point is on the shore 80 m from the foot of the pier. How long is the race, to the nearest metre?

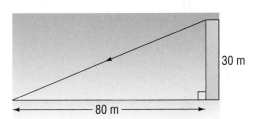

6. Describe how you could use mental math to estimate c.

7. Find x, to the nearest tenth of a centimetre.

8. The base of the Pyramid of Khufu is a square with sides 230 m long. Calculate the length of the diagonal of this square, to the nearest tenth of a metre.

9. An RCMP patrol boat left Long Beach, British Columbia, and sailed west for 2 h at 15 km/h, then north for 2 h at 20 km/h, then east for 1 h at 10 km/h. How far was the patrol boat from Long Beach, to the nearest tenth of a kilometre?

10. Three whole numbers, like 3, 4, and 5, where $3^2 + 4^2 = 5^2$, are called **Pythagorean Triples**. To make Pythagorean Triples, substitute two different whole numbers for x and y in these expressions.

$$a = x^2 - y^2, \ b = 2xy, \ c = x^2 + y^2$$

Use the whole numbers from 1 to 6 to make sets of Pythagorean Triples. Test each triple to see if it satisfies the equation $a^2 + b^2 = c^2$. Compare your triples with your classmates'.

11. A chessboard has diagonals of length 40 cm. What is the length of each side of the board, to the nearest tenth of a centimetre? Explain your reasoning.

12. Write a problem that can be solved using the Pythagorean Theorem. Have a classmate solve your problem.

LOGIC POWER

There are 6 blocks numbered 1 to 6. They must be put into 2 piles with the same height. A higher number must not be above a lower number in either pile. One way is shown. How many other ways are there?

Constructing an Angle Bisector

The **bisector** of an angle divides the angle into 2 equal angles.

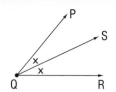

Activity ❶ Paper Folding

The diagrams show how to bisect an angle by paper folding.

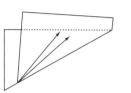

1. Repeat the construction in your notebook for an acute angle.

2. Use a protractor to check your construction.

Activity ❷ Using a Mira

The diagram shows how to bisect an angle using a Mira.

1. Repeat the construction in your notebook for an acute angle and a right angle.

2. Write a description of the steps.

Activity ❸ Ruler and Compasses

The diagrams show how to bisect an angle using a ruler and compasses.

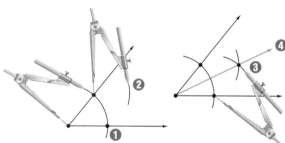

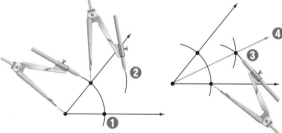

1. Repeat the construction in your notebook for an acute angle and an obtuse angle.

 2. Write a description of the steps.

3. Use a Mira to check your construction.

Activity ❹ Using a Ruler

The diagram shows the first step in bisecting an angle using a ruler. Do the complete construction in your notebook. Use a Mira to check your construction.

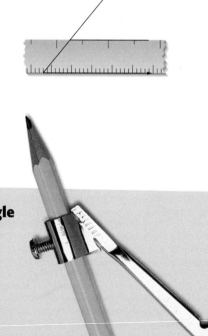

Activity ❺ Constructing Angle Bisectors in a Triangle

1. Draw an acute triangle. Construct the bisector of each angle. If your construction is accurate, the bisectors should intersect at one point.

2. Do the angle bisectors intersect at one point in
a) an obtuse triangle?　　　**b)** a right triangle?

Constructing the Right Bisector of a Line Segment

The **right bisector** of a line segment divides the line segment into 2 equal parts at right angles.

Activity ❶ Using Paper Folding

The diagrams show how to right bisect a line segment by paper folding.

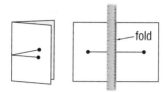

1. Bisect a line segment using this method.

2. Use a protractor and ruler to check your construction.

Activity ❸ Using a Ruler and Compasses

The diagrams show how to right bisect a line segment using a ruler and compasses.

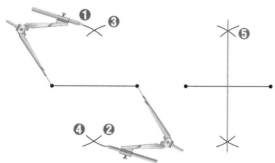

1. Repeat the construction in your notebook for a horizontal line segment and a vertical one.

2. Write a description of the steps.

Activity ❷ Using a Mira

The diagram shows how to right bisect a line segment using a Mira.

1. Repeat the construction in your notebook for a horizontal and a vertical line segment.

2. Write a description of the steps.

3. Check your construction by folding your paper and holding it up to the light.

Activity ❹ Using a Ruler

The diagram shows the first step in right bisecting a line segment using a ruler.

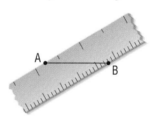

1. Do the complete construction in your notebook.

2. Use a Mira to check your construction.

Activity ❺ Constructing Right Bisectors in a Triangle

1. Draw an acute triangle. Construct the right bisector of each side. If your construction is accurate, the right bisectors should intersect at one point. Repeat for an obtuse triangle and a right triangle.

2. a) Draw an acute triangle and label the vertices A, B, and C.

b) Construct the right bisectors of AB and AC. Label the point where they intersect, D.

c) Draw a circle with centre D and radius AD. Describe the result.

d) Repeat parts a), b), and c) for an obtuse triangle. Describe the result.

Constructing a Perpendicular to a Line

A perpendicular from a point not on a line meets the line at 90°.

Activity ❶ Using Paper Folding

The point P does not lie on the line AB. The diagrams show how to draw a line through P, perpendicular to the line AB, by paper folding.

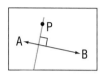

1. Draw a perpendicular by this method.

2. Use a protractor to check your construction.

Activity ❷ Using a Mira

The diagram shows how to draw a perpendicular to a line from a point not on the line using a Mira.

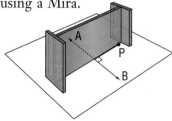

1. Repeat the construction in your notebook.

2. Check your construction by folding your paper and holding it up to the light.

Activity ❸ Using a Ruler and Compasses

The diagrams show how to use a ruler and compasses to construct a perpendicular to a line from a point not on the line.

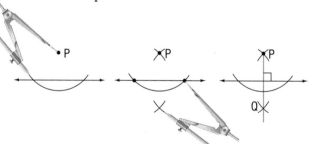

1. Repeat the construction in your notebook.

2. Number each arc in the order you drew it. Write a description of the steps.

3. Check your construction using a Mira.

Activity ❹ Using a Ruler

The diagrams show the steps needed to draw a perpendicular to a line from a point not on the line using a ruler.

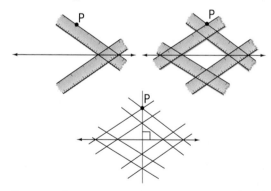

1. Repeat the construction in your notebook.

2. Use a Mira to check your construction.

Activity ❺ Applying a Perpendicular Construction

1. a) Draw an acute triangle ABC.

b) From vertex A, draw a perpendicular to meet BC at D.

c) From vertex B, draw a perpendicular to meet AC at E.

d) From vertex C, draw a perpendicular to meet AB at F.

2. How are the perpendiculars from the three vertices related?

Constructing a Perpendicular at a Point on a Line

A perpendicular at a point on a line meets the line at 90°.

Activity ❶ Using Paper Folding

The point P lies on the line AB. The diagrams show how to draw a line at P, perpendicular to the line AB, by paper folding.

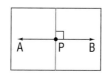

1. Draw a perpendicular at a point on a line by this method.

2. Use a protractor to check your construction.

Activity ❷ Using a Mira

The diagram shows how to draw a perpendicular at a point on a line using a Mira.

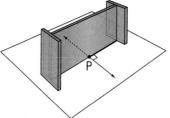

1. Repeat the construction in your notebook.

2. Check your construction by folding your paper and holding it up to the light.

Activity ❸ Using a Ruler and Compasses

The diagrams show how to use a ruler and compasses to construct a perpendicular at a point on a line.

1. Repeat the construction in your notebook.

2. Number each arc in the order you drew it. Write a description of the steps.

3. Check your construction using a Mira.

Activity ❹ Using a Ruler

The diagrams show the steps needed to draw a perpendicular at a point on a line using a ruler.

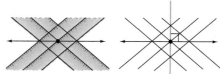

1. Repeat the construction in your notebook.

2. Use a Mira to check your construction.

Activity ❺ Applying a Perpendicular Construction

1. Draw a line segment 5 cm long. Use any of the above methods to construct a square on the line segment.

2. Construct a right triangle with the sides making the right angle each 5 cm long. Measure the third side.

3. How would you construct a perpendicular at the end of a line segment?

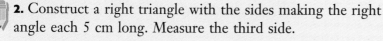

Constructing Parallel Lines

Two lines that never meet are parallel.

Activity ❶ Using a T-square

1. Start with a line and a point not on the line. Use a T-square and the edge of a desk to draw parallel lines. Line up the line on the paper with the T-square, then tape the paper to the desk. Slide the T-square to the point and draw a parallel line through the point.

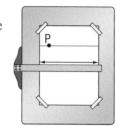

2. Use paper folding to check your construction.

Activity ❷ Using a Mira

1. Use a Mira to draw a line through P perpendicular to the given line. Use a Mira to draw another line through P perpendicular to the second line.

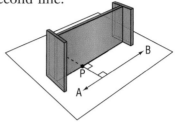

2. Check your construction using paper folding.

Activity ❸ Using a Ruler and Compasses

The diagrams show how to use a ruler and compasses to construct a line parallel to a given line through a point not on the line.

1. Repeat the construction in your notebook.

2. Number each arc in the order you drew it. Write a description of the steps.

3. Check your construction using a Mira.

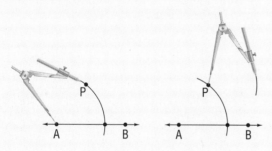

Activity ❹ Applying a Parallel Construction

1. a) Draw an acute triangle ABC.
b) At vertex A, draw a line parallel to BC.
c) At vertex B, draw a line parallel to AC.
d) At vertex C, draw a line parallel to AB.

2. Name the figure formed by the three parallel lines.

3. How is the new figure related to the original triangle ABC?

Geometric Designs I

Activity ❶ Inscribing an Equilateral Triangle in a Circle

Inscribe an equilateral triangle in a circle by following these steps.

1. Draw a circle with centre O and diameter AB.

2. With centre B and radius OB, draw an arc to cut the circle at C and D.

3. Join A, C, and D.

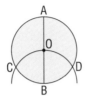 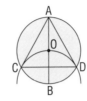

Activity ❷ Inscribing a Regular Hexagon in a Circle

Inscribe a regular hexagon in a circle by following these steps.

1. Draw a circle with centre O and diameter AB.

2. With centre B and radius OB, draw an arc to cut the circle at C and D.

3. With centre A and radius OA, draw an arc to cut the circle at E and F.

4. Join A, E, C, B, D, and F to make the regular hexagon.

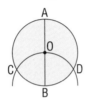 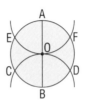

Activity ❸ Constructing a Design

The following designs are based on equilateral triangles and regular hexagons. Construct one of them in your notebook.

Activity ❹ Creating a Design

Create your own design based on equilateral triangles and regular hexagons. Compare your design with your classmates'.

Geometric Designs II

Activity ❶ Inscribing a Square in a Circle

Inscribe a square in a circle by following these steps.

1. Draw a circle with centre O and diameter AB.

2. Construct the right bisector of AB to cut the circle at C and D.

3. Join A, C, B, and D to make the square.

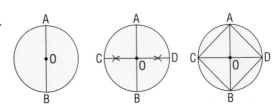

Activity ❷ Inscribing a Regular Octagon in a Circle

Inscribe a regular octagon in a circle by following these steps.

1. Draw a circle with centre O and diameter AB.

2. Construct the right bisector of AB to cut the circle at C and D.

3. Bisect ∠AOC to cut the circle at E.

4. With centre A and radius AE, draw an arc to cut the circle at F.

5. With centre B and radius AE, draw arcs to cut the circle at G and H.

6. Join A, E, C, G, B, H, D, and F to make the octagon.

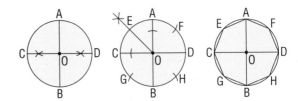

Activity ❸ Constructing a Design

The following designs are based on squares and regular octagons. Construct one of them in your notebook.

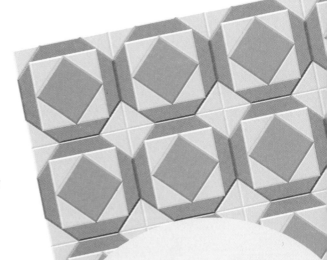

Activity ❹ Creating a Design

Create your own design based on squares and regular octagons. Compare your design with your classmates'.

Geometric Designs III

Activity ❶ Inscribing a Regular Pentagon in a Circle

Inscribe a regular pentagon in a circle by following these steps.

1. Draw a circle with centre O and diameter AB.

2. Construct the right bisector of AB to cut the circle at C and D.

3. Construct the right bisector of CO and label the midpoint X.

4. With centre X and radius XA, draw an arc to cut DO at Y.

5. AY is the length of each side of the pentagon. Start at A and mark 4 arcs on the circle at P, Q, R and S.

6. Join A, P, Q, R, and S to make the regular pentagon.

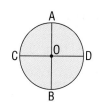

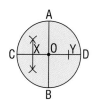

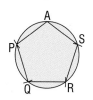

Activity ❷ Inscribing a Regular Decagon in a Circle

1. Start with a regular pentagon in a circle and construct a regular decagon in a circle.

 2. Describe your method.

Activity ❸ Constructing a Design

The following designs are based on regular pentagons and decagons. Construct one of them in your notebook.

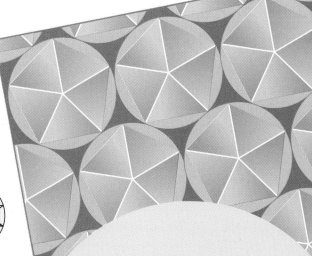

Activity ❹ Creating a Design

Create your own design based on regular pentagons and regular decagons. Compare your design with your classmates'.

Constructing Congruent Triangles

Activity ❶ Side-Side-Side (SSS)

1. Follow these steps to construct △DEF, where DE = 6 cm, EF = 7 cm, and DF = 9 cm.

a) Sketch the triangle and record the given facts on the sketch.

b) Draw line segment DE = 6 cm.

c) Set your compasses to a radius of 9 cm. With D as centre, draw an arc.

d) Set your compasses to a radius of 7 cm. With E as centre, draw an arc to intersect the first arc. Label the point of intersection F.

e) Draw DF and EF.

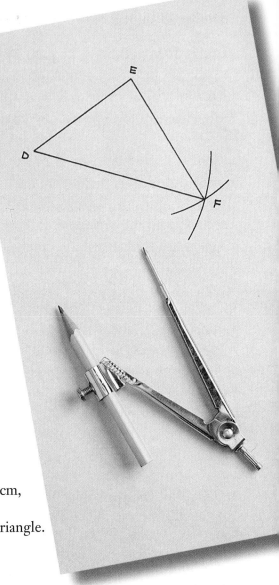

2. Measure the 3 angles in your triangle. Compare the measures with your classmates'. Are all the triangles congruent?

3. a) Construct △RST, where RS = 8 cm, ST = 10 cm, and RT = 9 cm.

b) Measure the 3 angles in your triangle. Compare the measures with your classmates'.

c) Are all the triangles congruent?

4. Are all triangles with the same side lengths congruent?

Activity ❷ Side-Angle-Side (SAS)

1. Follow these steps to construct △ABC, where AB = 8 cm, BC = 7 cm, and ∠ABC = 50°.

a) Sketch the triangle and record the given facts on the triangle.

b) Draw line segment BC = 7 cm.

c) Use a protractor to draw ∠B = 50°.

d) From B, draw AB = 8 cm.

e) Draw AC.

2. Measure AC, ∠C, and ∠A in your triangle. Compare the measures with your classmates'. Are all the triangles congruent?

3. Construct △JKL, where KL = 7.5 cm, JK = 6.5 cm, and ∠JKL = 70°. Measure JL, ∠J, and ∠L in your triangle. Compare the measures with your classmates'. Are all the triangles congruent?

4. Are all triangles with the same 2 side lengths and the same angle between them congruent?

Activity ❸ Angle-Side-Angle (ASA)

1. Follow these steps to construct △CAR, where ∠A = 45°, AR = 8 cm, and ∠R = 65°.

a) Sketch the triangle and record the given facts on the sketch.

b) Draw line segment AR = 8 cm.

c) Use a protractor to draw ∠A = 45° and ∠R = 65°.

d) Extend the arms until they cross at C.

2. a) Measure CA, CR, and ∠C in your triangle. Compare the measures with your classmates'.

b) Are all the triangles congruent?

3. a) Construct △RUN, where UN = 9.5 cm, ∠U = 75°, and ∠N = 50°.

b) Measure RU, RN, and ∠R in your triangle. Compare the measures with your classmates'.

c) Are all the triangles congruent?

4. Are all triangles with the same 2 angles and the same side length between them congruent?

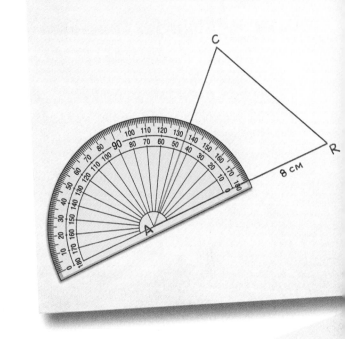

Activity ❹ Other Triangles

1. a) Construct △HAT, so that HA = 7 cm and AT = 9 cm.

b) Is it possible to construct △DIG, with DI = 7 cm and IG = 9 cm, so that the size and shape of △DIG are different from the size and shape of △HAT? Explain.

2. a) Construct △CFL, so that ∠C = 55° and ∠F = 80°.

b) Is it possible to construct △NBA, with ∠N = 55° and ∠B = 80°, so that the size and shape of △NBA are different from the size and shape of △CFL? Explain.

3. a) Construct △WIN, so that ∠W = 55° and WI = 8.5 cm.

b) Is it possible to construct △DOT, with ∠D = 55° and DO = 8.5 cm, so that the size and shape of △DOT are different from the size and shape of △WIN? Explain.

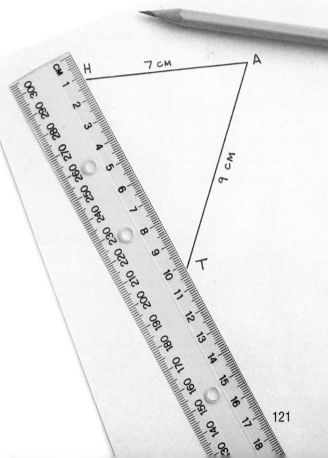

121

3.15 Conditions for Congruent Triangles

The faces of the Great Pyramid of Khufu are 4 triangles measuring 219 m by 219 m by 230 m. The faces are congruent triangles.

It is not necessary to have the 3 angles and 3 sides of one triangle equal to the 3 angles and 3 sides of another triangle before stating that the triangles are congruent.

The chart gives 3 ways to state that two triangles are congruent when 3 parts of one are equal to 3 parts of another.

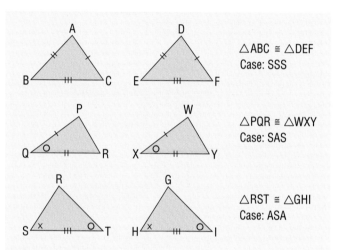

△ABC ≅ △DEF
Case: SSS

△PQR ≅ △WXY
Case: SAS

△RST ≅ △GHI
Case: ASA

Activity: Study the Diagrams

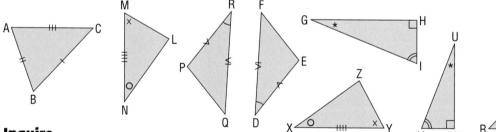

Inquire

1. a) Which two triangles are congruent by SSS?
b) List the equal angles in these congruent triangles.

2. a) Which two triangles are congruent by SAS?
b) List the other equal angles and sides.

3. a) Which two triangles are congruent by ASA?
b) List the other equal sides and angles.

Practice

State whether the triangles are congruent by SSS, SAS, or ASA.

1.

2.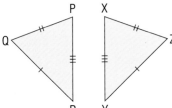

3.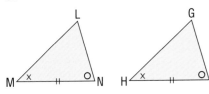

Are the pairs of triangles congruent? If they are, give the case, SSS, SAS, or ASA, and list all the other equal parts.

4.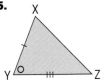

5.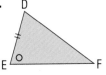

6.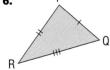

7.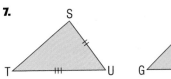

8.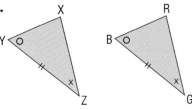

Problems and Applications

9. List the pairs of congruent triangles. State why they are congruent. List the other equal parts.

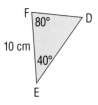

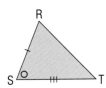

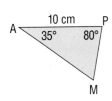

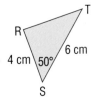

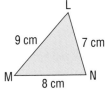

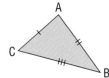

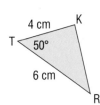

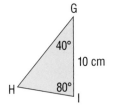

123

Constructing Without a Protractor

Activity ❶ Constructing Angles

The steps show how to construct a 60° angle using a ruler and compasses.

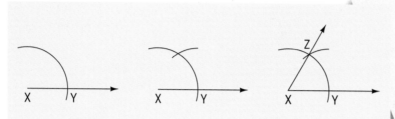

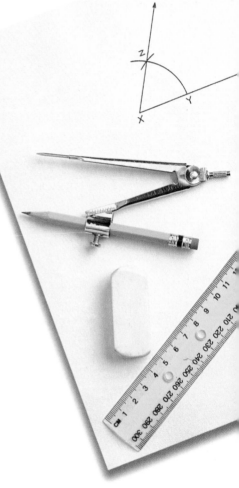

1. a) If you joined YZ, what kind of triangle would be formed?
b) Why is ∠ZXY = 60°?

Complete the following constructions without using a protractor.

2. Construct ∠ABC = 60°.

3. Use ∠ABC to construct angles equal to 30° and 15°.

4. Construct angles equal to 120° and 150°.

5. a) Draw a line segment AB. Mark C on the line segment. Construct a perpendicular to AB at C.
b) Use the diagram from part a) to construct angles equal to 45° and 135°.

6. An angle of 75° can be constructed using a 60° angle and a 15° angle. Construct an angle of 75°. Describe your steps.

7. An angle of 75° can also be constructed using a 45° angle and a 30° angle. Construct an angle of 75°. Describe your steps.

Activity ❷ Constructing Triangles

Construct the following triangles using only a ruler and compasses.

1. Construct △ABC, where BC = 7 cm, ∠B = 60°, and ∠C = 30°.

2. Construct △RST, where ST = 7.5 cm, ∠S = 45°, and ∠T = 60°.

3. Construct △DEF, where EF = 6 cm, ∠DEF = 120°, and DE = 8 cm.

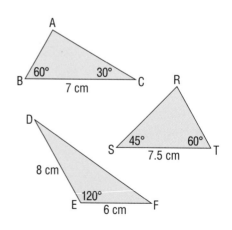

Activity ❸ Constructing Quadrilaterals

Construct the following quadrilaterals using only a ruler and compasses.

1.

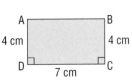

2.

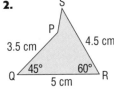

3.

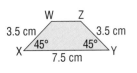

4.

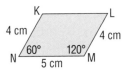

5.

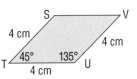

6.

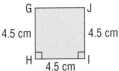

Activity ❹ Finding the Centre of a Circle

1. a) Use a circular object to trace a circle.
b) Draw any chord AB on the circle.
Construct the right bisector of AB.
c) Draw another chord CD, not parallel to AB. Construct the right bisector of CD.
d) Where do the 2 right bisectors intersect? Explain.

2. Use a circular object to trace a circle.
Use paper folding to find the centre of the circle.
Describe your steps.

3. Use a circular object to trace a circle.
Use a Mira to find the centre of the circle.
Describe your steps.

Drawing with LOGO

In the LOGO computer program, a turtle draws on the screen.
These are some LOGO commands.

Command	What the turtle does
FD	Moves forward
FD 50	Moves forward 50 units
BK	Moves backward
BK 30	Moves backward 30 units
RT	Turns right a number of degrees
RT 90	Turns right 90°

Command	What the turtle does
LT	Turns left a number of degrees
PU	Does not draw a line (Pen Up)
PD	Draws a line (Pen Down)
HOME	Goes to the centre of the screen
DRAW	Returns to its home position (DRAW clears the screen.)

For the turtle to draw the picture you want, the commands must
be in the right order. This program draws a rectangle.

FD 30
RT 90
FD 70
RT 90
FD 30
RT 90
FD 70
RT 90

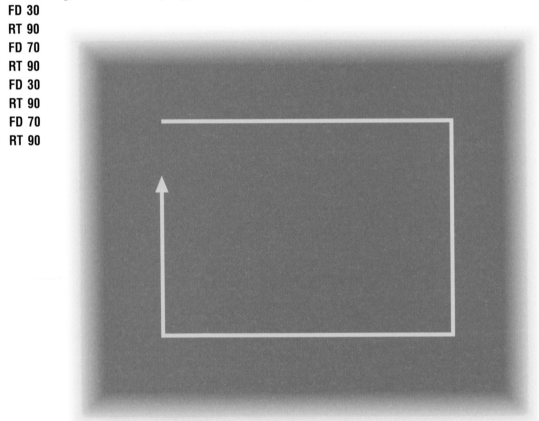

What is the length of the rectangle?

What is the width of the rectangle?

Activity ❶ LOGO Commands

What does the turtle draw with the following commands?

1. FD 60	**2.** RT 60	**3.** LT 30
RT 90	FD 70	FD 40
FD 60	RT 120	LT 60
RT 90	FD 70	FD 60
FD 60	RT 120	LT 120
RT 90	FD 70	FD 40
FD 60	RT 60	LT 60
RT 90		FD 60
		LT 90

Write LOGO commands to draw the following figures.

4. **5.** **6.**

Activity ❸ Joining Figures

Draw what the turtle will draw with these commands.

REPEAT 4[FD 60 RT 90]
RT 90 FD 60 LT 90
REPEAT 4[FD 60 RT 90]
RT 90 FD 60 LT 90
REPEAT 4[FD 60 RT 90]

Write LOGO commands to draw the following figures.

1.

2.

3.

Activity ❷ The REPEAT Command

In question 1 of Activity 1, the commands FD 60 and RT 90 were repeated 4 times. The REPEAT command can be used instead.

REPEAT 4[FD 60 RT 90]

Draw what the turtle will draw with the following commands. Use 1 cm for every 10 turtle units.

1. REPEAT 4[FD 40 LT 90]

2. REPEAT 2[FD 50 LT 90 FD 60 LT 90]

3. REPEAT 4[FD 70 BK 20 RT 90]

4. REPEAT 4[FD 50 BK 50 RT 30]

Write LOGO commands to draw the following figures.

5. 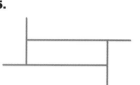 **6.**

7.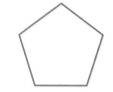

Activity ❹ Designing Figures

Draw your own figure, then write the LOGO commands that draw it.

Review

1. Name the following in the diagram.
a) 4 points
b) 3 lines
c) 5 angles
d) 3 rays
e) 6 line segments

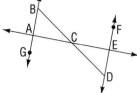

Draw the following angles.

2. 55° **3.** 76° **4.** 135°

5. 156° **6.** 235° **7.** 347°

8. Use the diagram to name the following.

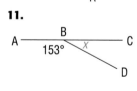

a) 3 acute angles
b) 3 obtuse angles
c) 2 right angles

Find the measure of each unknown angle.

9.
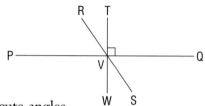
10.

11.
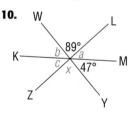
12.
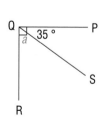

Write the measure of the complementary angle.

13. 35° **14.** 66° **15.** 89°

Write the measure of the supplementary angle.

16. 47° **17.** 102° **18.** 156°

Find the measure of each unknown angle.

19.

20.

21.

22.
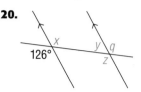

Copy each figure and draw all the lines of symmetry.

23. **24.**

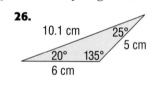

Classify each triangle by sides and by angles.

25. **26.**

Calculate the missing measures.

27.
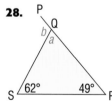
28.

Find the measure of the unknown angle in each polygon.

29.

30.
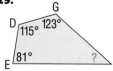

128

Find the measure of each unknown angle.

31.

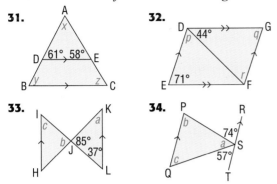

32.

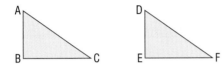

33.

34.

35. List the pairs of congruent parts in the congruent triangles.

36. List the pairs of congruent triangles. State why they are congruent. List the other equal parts.

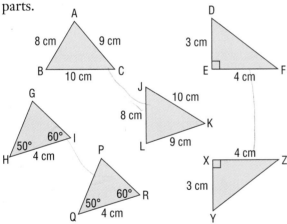

Calculate the length of the unknown side.

37.

38.

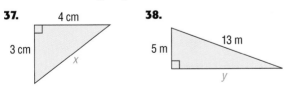

39. A ship left Port Alberni, B.C., and sailed west for 3 h at 15 km/h, then north for 2 h at 20 km/h. To the nearest tenth of a kilometre, how far was the ship from Port Alberni?

Group Decision Making
The Cannonball Run

The Cannonball Run is a famous car rally, which begins and ends in Detroit, Michigan. The course goes through these cities in this order.

Detroit, Michigan	Laredo, Texas
Indianapolis, Indiana	Jackson, Mississippi
Denver, Colorado	Atlanta, Georgia
Las Vegas, Nevada	Darien, Connecticut
Monterey, California	Mansfield, Ohio
Los Angeles, California	Detroit, Michigan
Tucson, Arizona	

1. Work in home groups. Draw a map of the Cannonball Run, using the shortest possible route between cities. Mark the highway numbers on the map.

| 1 | 2 | 3 | 4 | | 1 | 2 | 3 | 4 | | 1 | 2 | 3 | 4 |

Home Groups

| 1 | 2 | 3 | 4 | | 1 | 2 | 3 | 4 | | 1 | 2 | 3 | 4 |

2. Determine the driving distance from Detroit to Indianapolis, from Indianapolis to Denver, and so on. Mark the distances on the map.

3. Find the total driving distance for the Cannonball Run.

4. The speed limit in the rally is 80 km/h. About how many hours would the rally take to complete at this speed?

5. If the rally started at noon on a Saturday, and vehicles were on the road 24 h/day, on what day and at what time would the rally finish?

6. Compare your map and driving times with those of other groups. Account for any differences.

7. Evaluate how effectively the members of your group worked together.

129

Chapter Check

1. Name 3 points, 3 lines, 3 angles, and 3 line segments in the diagram.

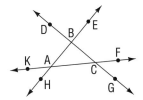

Draw the following angles.

2. 43°   **3.** 156°   **4.** 222°

5. Name 2 acute angles, 2 right angles, and 2 obtuse angles in the diagram.

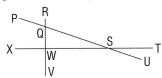

Find the measures of the unknown angles.

6.

7.

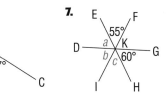

Write the measure of the complementary angle.

8. 44°   **9.** 7°   **10.** 66°

Write the measure of the supplementary angle.

11. 57°   **12.** 101°   **13.** 165°

Copy each figure and draw all the lines of symmetry.

14.

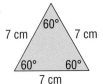

15.

Classify each triangle by sides and by angles.

16.

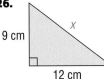

17.

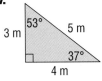

18. What is the measure of each interior angle of a regular dodecagon?

Find the missing measures.

19.

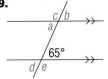

20.

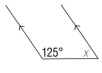

Find the measures of the unknown angles.

21.

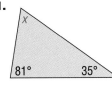

22.

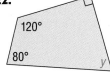

Find the measures of the unknown angles.

23.

24.

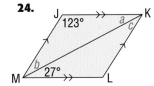

25. State why the triangles are congruent. List the other equal parts.

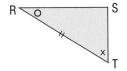

Calculate the length of the unknown side. Round to the nearest tenth, if necessary.

26.

27.

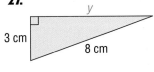

28. A 10-m ladder is leaning against the side of a house. The foot of the ladder is 4 m from the base of the house. How far up the wall is the top of the ladder?

Using the Strategies

1. As you move from the top rung to the bottom rung on this ladder, the length of each rung increases by the same amount.

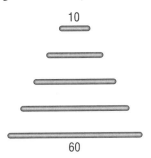

Find the lengths of the middle 3 rungs.

2. Here are 6 towns. What is the smallest number of roads that must be built between towns, so that you can start at any town and get to any other town? Assume that 1 road cannot connect more than 2 towns and that roads cannot cross.

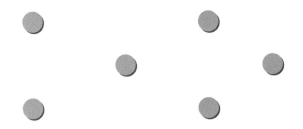

3. Joshua takes the 08:00 bus from Beeton to Carlton. The trip takes 6 h. Buses leave every hour on the hour from Carlton to Beeton. How many buses travelling from Carlton to Beeton will Joshua see on the trip?

4. You must be at work by 08:15. You take 35 min to get there on the bus. Before you leave, you need 20 min to wash and get dressed. You need 25 min to make and eat your breakfast. You have to walk the dog for 15 min before you go. For what time should you set your alarm?

5. Cut out a square and label it as shown.

What figure is formed when you make each of the following folds?
a) W is folded onto Z.
b) W is folded onto Y.
c) W is folded onto Z, then Z is folded onto Y.
d) W is folded onto Y, then Z is folded onto X.

6. The driving distance from Winnipeg to Thunder Bay is 10 km less than from Thunder Bay to Sault Ste. Marie. The driving distance from Thunder Bay to Sault Ste. Marie is 86 km less than from Sault Ste. Marie to Ottawa. The total driving distance from Winnipeg through Thunder Bay and Sault Ste. Marie to Ottawa is 2218 km. What is the driving distance from Sault Ste. Marie to Ottawa?

7. Sketch a graph of the distance you travel versus time on a normal school day, starting when you leave home for school and ending when you get back home.

DATA BANK

1. Jan lives in Windsor, Ontario. She called her friend in Sydney, Australia, at 22:00 on December 31 to wish her a happy New Year. What was the time and date in Sydney when Jan called?

2. If the mouth of the Mackenzie River were at Vancouver, and the river ran along the Canada–U.S. border, where would the river begin?

CHAPTER 4

Perimeter and Area

The tangram puzzle is a square cut into 7 geometric shapes. They are 2 large triangles, 1 medium triangle, 2 small triangles, a square, and a parallelogram.

You can make a square from all 7 tangram pieces, as shown. You can also make slightly larger squares with holes in them from the 7 pieces.

Use the 7 tangram pieces to make squares like the ones shown.

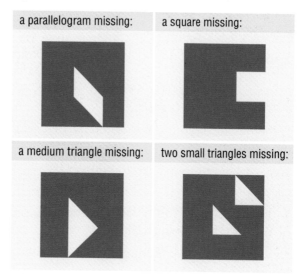

a parallelogram missing:

a square missing:

a medium triangle missing:

two small triangles missing:

The holes do not have to be in the positions shown. Sketch your solutions.

Measuring Length

Activity ❶

1. Copy and complete the statements.

a) 1 m = ▮ mm   **b)** 1 mm = ▮ m

c) 1 m = ▮ cm   **d)** 1 cm = ▮ m

e) 1 m = ▮ km   **f)** 1 km = ▮ m

g) 1 cm = ▮ mm   **h)** 1 mm = ▮ cm

2. Write the meaning of each of the prefixes.

a) centi   **b)** milli   **c)** kilo

Activity ❷

Estimate, then measure the number of each object needed to make 1 m.

1. baseball cards laid end to end

2. quarters laid side by side

3. *MATHPOWER*™ textbooks stacked on top of each other

4. paper clips laid end to end

5. thumbtacks laid side by side

6. new pencils laid end to end

7. hockey pucks stacked on top of each other

8. sticks of chalk laid end to end

Activity ❸

Estimate, then measure to find which distance is greater and by how much.

1. the height of your classroom door or twice its width

2. the distance around the top of the classroom's wastebasket or its height

3. the distance across the face of a dollar coin or the length of a paper clip

4. twice the length of a running shoe or the length of its shoelace

5. the length of the school gymnasium or 3 times the length of your classroom

Activity ❹

Without a ruler, try to draw the length or the width, whichever is stated, of each object. Check your accuracy by measuring.

1. length of a $5.00 bill

2. length of a staple

3. width of a VHS videotape

4. length of a wire coat hanger

5. distance across the face of a dime

6. length of your foot

Activity ❺

Locate a map of your community. If you could walk at a rate of about 6 km/h, how long would it take you to walk from your school to each of the following destinations?

1. the nearest shopping centre

2. the city hall or municipal building

3. the nearest recreation centre

4. the nearest airport

5. the nearest lake or river

6. the nearest bus station

Activity ❻

1. On your school grounds, mark off 100 m.

2. With a group, take turns to count the paces needed to walk 100 m.

3. Calculate the length of the average pace for your group. Using this measurement, estimate, then determine, the following distances.

a) the length of the longest school hallway

b) the width of the gymnasium

c) the distance around the outside of the school building

d) the width of the school's main entrance

e) the distance from your classroom door to the nearest drinking fountain

Warm Up

Write in standard form.

1. four thousand twenty and five tenths

2. sixteen and forty-four hundredths

3. five hundred eighty-seven thousandths

4. six thousand eight hundred thirty-five

5. ninety-two and sixty-three hundredths

Write in words.

6. 112.7 **7.** 2036.08 **8.** 59.006

9. 0.345 **10.** 3.62 **11.** 75 264.9

Round to the given place value.

12. 14.659 to the nearest tenth

13. 425.17 to the nearest one

14. 8.427 to the nearest hundredth

15. 9574.12 to the nearest ten

16. 55.048 to the nearest tenth

Multiply.

17. 5.68×10 **18.** 45.03×100

19. 0.036×1000 **20.** 84.557×10

21. 2.73×0.01 **22.** 18.6×0.1

23. 4652×0.001 **24.** 52.09×0.01

Divide.

25. $2.76 \div 100$ **26.** $38.165 \div 10$

27. $562.19 \div 1000$ **28.** $2.6 \div 100$

29. $7.8 \div 0.01$ **30.** $19.35 \div 0.1$

31. $246.115 \div 0.001$ **32.** $42.06 \div 0.01$

Calculate.

33. $15.73 + 28.04 + 21.98$ **34.** 3×49.56

35. $2 \times 12.3 + 2 \times 16.9$ **36.** 4×9.86

37. $5 \times 16.2 + 8.3 \times 12.5$ **38.** 3.14×12.5

39. $15.4 \times 27.6 - 9.2 \times 10.8$

40. $218.858 \div 3.14$

Mental Math

Express in millimetres.

1. 5 cm **2.** 16 cm **3.** 0.2 cm

4. 2 m **5.** 0.3 m **6.** 1.16 m

Express in centimetres.

7. 4 m **8.** 25 m **9.** 1.7 m

10. 0.8 m **11.** 36 mm **12.** 112 mm

Express in metres.

13. 240 cm **14.** 516 cm **15.** 24 cm

16. 9 cm **17.** 1350 cm **18.** 905 cm

19. 1500 mm **20.** 625 mm **21.** 52 mm

22. 4 km **23.** 0.5 km **24.** 6.3 km

Express in kilometres.

25. 8000 m **26.** 25 700 m **27.** 982 m

28. 46 m **29.** 3405 m **30.** 206 m

Calculate.

31. $2 \times 6 + 2 \times 3$ **32.** $2 \times 9 + 2 \times 4$

33. $2 \times 20 + 2 \times 7$ **34.** $2 \times 8 + 2 \times 2$

35. 4×0.7 **36.** 4×1.2

37. 6×0.8 **38.** 8×0.7

39. 4×0.03 **40.** 4×0.9

Simplify.

41. 8^2 **42.** 3^2 **43.** 9^2

44. 6^2 **45.** 2^3 **46.** 5^3

47. $10^2 - 20$ **48.** $4^2 + 6$ **49.** $7^2 - 2^2$

Calculate.

50. 26×100 **51.** 0.5×10

52. 3.4×1000 **53.** 7.9×100

54. 0.2×1000 **55.** $12 \div 1000$

56. $47 \div 10$ **57.** $326 \div 100$

58. $59.8 \div 100$ **59.** $2.73 \div 10$

4.1 Perimeter

Activity: Think About the Process

Jacob was helping to decorate his room. He chose a wallpaper border to go around the top of the painted walls and also around the middle of the walls.

Inquire

1. What measurements did Jacob need before purchasing the border for the top of the walls?

2. Why did the length of the second border differ from the length of the first?

3. What additional measurements were needed to determine the length of the second border?

 4. Describe a method Jacob may have used to calculate the total length of wallpaper border needed.

The distance around Jacob's room is called the **perimeter**. To calculate the perimeter of a figure, find the sum of the lengths of all the sides.

Example

Calculate the perimeter of the garden.

Solution

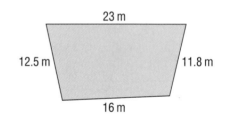

$P = 23 + 11.8 + 16 + 12.5$
$\quad = 63.3$

EST $20 + 10 + 20 + 10 = 60$

The perimeter of the garden is 63.3 m.

Practice

The distance between points on the grid represents 2 cm. Find the perimeter of each figure.

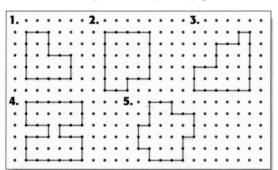

Estimate, then measure each side of the figures. Calculate the perimeter of each figure.

6.

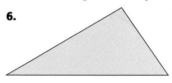

7.

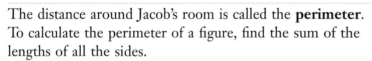

Estimate, then calculate the perimeter of each figure.

8.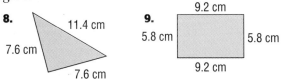

9.

10. **11.**

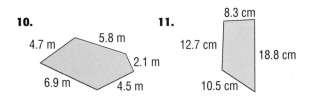

Problems and Applications

Calculate each missing length. Check your answer by measuring.

12. **13.**

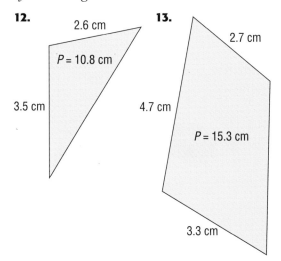

14. Describe the method you used to calculate the missing side of each figure in questions 12 and 13.

15. Shona used adhesive tape to seal the package completely around in 2 directions.

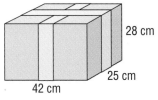

28 cm
25 cm
42 cm

What was the smallest length of tape that Shona could have used?

16. Copy and complete the table.

$P = a + b + c$

a	b	c	P
1.5	1.3	1.2	
2.1	1.6	2.5	
3.7		5.6	14.1
6.9	7.2		19.5
	3.7	4.8	13.5
2.4	4.9	5.3	

17. Copy and complete the table.

$P = a + b + c + d$

a	b	c	d	P
1.7	2.1	3.6	2.9	
2.7	5.6		4.5	17.7
	6.2	5.4	6.7	24.1
1.5	2.5	3.2		10
9.7		8.3	9.5	37.9
3.4	2.6	4.5	2.9	

18. A wallpaper border will be put around the walls of the hallway, at the top of the walls.

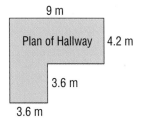

9 m
Plan of Hallway 4.2 m
3.6 m
3.6 m

a) What length of border will be needed?
b) If the border is sold in 6-m rolls, how many rolls must be purchased?
c) What length of border will be left over?

19. The rectangle is made up of 4 different pentominoes. Draw the pentominoes and find the perimeter of each one.

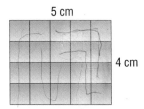

5 cm
4 cm

4.2 Perimeters of Polygons

Activity: Determine a Formula

Andrew is making jewellery for the craft fair. He will use coloured wire for the outer edges of each piece and a variety of decorative stones for the interiors. Andrew planned the pieces of jewellery using 2-cm lengths for the edges.

Inquire

1. How many lengths of wire are needed for the square? What is the total length of wire needed?

2. Using s for the length of a side, determine a formula to calculate the perimeter of a square.

3. Write a formula for the perimeter of an equilateral triangle.

4. Explain why $P = n \times s$ can be used to calculate the perimeter of any polygon with equal sides, when n represents the number of sides.

5. a) What is the length of Andrew's rectangular piece of jewellery?
b) What is its width?
c) What is its perimeter?

6. Write a formula to calculate the perimeter of a rectangle.

Example

Andrew designed a pin composed of 2 pieces, one rectangular and one a regular hexagon. What is the total length of wire he will need for the outer edges of the pin?

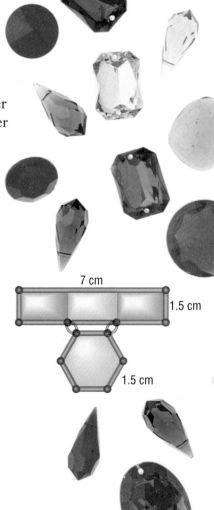

Solution

For the rectangle
$P = 2 \times l + 2 \times w$
$\quad = 2 \times 7 + 2 \times 1.5$
$\quad = 14 + 3$
$\quad = 17$

For the hexagon
$P = 6 \times s$
$\quad = 6 \times 1.5$
$\quad = 9$

$17 + 9 = 26$

The total length of wire he will need is 26 cm.

Practice

Find the perimeter of each regular polygon.

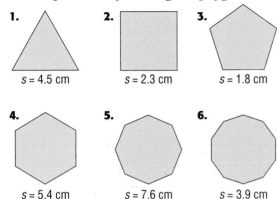

1. s = 4.5 cm

2. s = 2.3 cm

3. s = 1.8 cm

4. s = 5.4 cm

5. s = 7.6 cm

6. s = 3.9 cm

Calculate the perimeter of each rectangle.

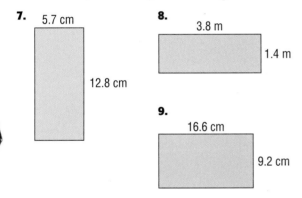

7. 5.7 cm, 12.8 cm

8. 3.8 m, 1.4 m

9. 16.6 cm, 9.2 cm

Problems and Applications

10. Janine's construction company was hired to build a wire fence around the community centre's swimming pool. The pool is 55 m by 30 m, with a 2.5-m paved area around it. What is the total length of fencing needed to enclose the pool area?

Find the length of a side of each regular polygon.

11. pentagon, perimeter 22 cm

12. triangle, perimeter 13.2 cm

13. octagon, perimeter 46.4 cm

14. square, perimeter 2.6 m

15. hexagon, perimeter 58.8 cm

16. Sketch and label 3 different rectangles, each with a perimeter of 80 cm.

17. To warm up before a practice, the soccer coach has the team members run around the field 3 times. The length of the field is 100 m and its width is 73 m. How far does each team member run before a practice?

18. Two gardens in the shape of regular triangles are bordered in decorative tile. What is the total length of the tile?

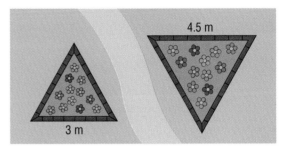

4.5 m

3 m

19. Sketch and label all of the regular polygons whose sides are whole numbers of centimetres greater than 3 cm and whose perimeters are 48 cm.

20. Sketch and label all of the rectangles whose sides are whole numbers of centimetres and whose perimeters are 24 cm.

21. In each of the following pairs of regular polygons, the perimeters are equal. How do the side lengths compare in each pair of polygons?
a) square and octagon
b) triangle and nonagon
c) hexagon and triangle
d) dodecagon and hexagon
e) square and dodecagon
f) pentagon and decagon

22. Write a problem that involves the perimeter of a polygon. Have a classmate solve your problem.

Investigating Geometric Constants

Activity ❶

1. Construct a square with each side 4 cm.

2. Draw a diagonal.

3. Measure the diagonal accurately.

4. Divide the perimeter of the square by the length of the diagonal. Note your result.

$$\frac{\text{perimeter}}{\text{diagonal}} = \blacksquare$$

5. Repeat steps 2 through 4 for four different squares.

6. What do you notice about the results?

7. Approximately how many times greater than the diagonal is the perimeter of a square?

Activity ❷

When very accurate measurements are taken, the value of the perimeter, P, of a square divided by its diagonal, d, is a **constant**, k, equal to approximately 2.83.

1. If $\frac{P}{d} = k$, what is the formula for calculating P?

2. What is the formula for calculating d?

3. If the length of a diagonal of a square is known, how would you find the length of each side, s?

4. Calculate the perimeter and the side of the square for each diagonal. Round answers to the nearest hundredth, if necessary.

a) $d = 10$ cm **b)** $d = 8$ cm **c)** $d = 25$ cm

5. Calculate the length of the diagonal from each side length of a square. Round your answers to the nearest hundredth.

a) $s = 5$ cm **b)** $s = 10$ cm **c)** $s = 12$ cm

Activity ❸

1. Draw an equilateral triangle with each side 5 cm.

2. Mark the midpoint of one side of the triangle and draw a line from this point to the opposite vertex. This line is called the **median** of the triangle.

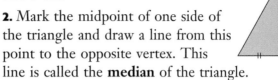

3. Measure the median, m, of the triangle accurately.

4. Divide the perimeter of the triangle by the length of the median. Note your result.

$$\frac{\text{perimeter}}{\text{median}} = \blacksquare$$

5. Repeat steps 2 through 4 for four different equilateral triangles.

6. Does it appear that, in an equilateral triangle, $\frac{P}{m}$ has a constant value? If so, what is that value?

Activity ❹

Investigate geometric constants in other regular polygons.

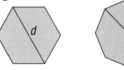

1. Measure the side and the diagonal or median in each of these polygons.

2. Divide the perimeter by the diagonal or median for each type of polygon. Note your results.

3. Construct regular polygons with sides of different lengths. Divide the perimeter by the median or diagonal for different side lengths of each type of polygon.

4. From your results, does it appear that $\frac{P}{m}$ or $\frac{P}{d}$ has a constant value for each type of regular polygon? If so, what is that value?

5. Are the constant values you found in question 4 grouped around any whole number? If so, what is that number?

4.3 Circumference of a Circle

The distance a bicycle travels in one turn of its wheels equals the perimeter or **circumference** of the wheels.

Activity: Discover the Relationship

Draw or trace a circle onto cardboard, then cut it out carefully. Mark a point on the circumference of the circle, then measure the circumference by rolling the circle along a ruler. Fold the circle in half and measure the diameter.

Cut out and measure 4 different circles. Record the measurements in a table. For each set of measurements, divide the circumference by the diameter. Record your answers to the nearest hundredth.

 Compare your answers with those of your classmates.

	Circumference	Diameter	$C \div d$
1.			
2.			
3.			
4.			

Inquire

1. Approximately how many times greater than the diameter is the circumference?

2. The constant that represents $C \div d$ in any circle is represented by the Greek letter π. The value of π is approximately 3.14. How close to π were your results?

3. If $C \div d = \pi$, state the formula that can be used to calculate the circumference when the diameter is known.

4. State the formula that can be used to calculate the diameter when the circumference is known.

 5. Investigate the origin and the development of the value of π. Write a report of the results of your research.

π is spelled "pi" and pronounced "pie."
$\pi = 3.141\ 592\ 653...$
In this book we use $\pi = 3.14$.

Example

The diameter of a Ferris wheel is 55 m. What is its circumference?

Solution

$C = \pi \times d$
$= 3.14 \times 55$
$= 172.7$

EST $3 \times 60 = 180$

The circumference of the Ferris wheel is 172.7 m.

Practice

Round each answer to the nearest hundredth.

Measure each radius or diameter and calculate the circumference of each circle.

1.

2.
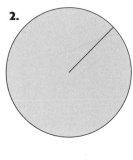

3.
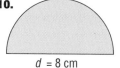

Calculate the circumference of each circle.

4. $r = 5.5$ cm

5. $d = 8.35$ cm

6. $d = 15$ cm

7. $r = 2.8$ m

8. $r = 23$ cm

9. $d = 19.2$ cm

Problems and Applications

Calculate the perimeter of each figure.

10.

$d = 8$ cm

11.
$r = 12.2$ cm

12. How much longer is the circumference of a quarter than the circumference of a dime?

$d = 23.9$ mm

$d = 18$ mm

13. The diameter of the clock face of Big Ben in London, England, is 7.1 m. What is the circumference of the clock face?

14. Penny-farthing bicycles were popular in Victorian times. A penny-farthing had a large front wheel, radius about 65 cm, and a small back wheel, radius about 25 cm.

a) How many times did the back wheel turn for each turn of the front wheel?

b) How many times did the front wheel turn to travel 1 km?

15. What happens to the circumference of a circle in each of these situations? Use examples to explain your answers.

a) The radius is doubled.

b) The diameter is doubled.

Calculate the perimeter of each figure.

16.
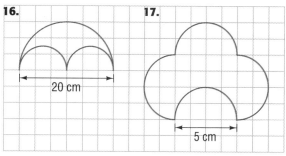
20 cm

17.
5 cm

18. Create a design using circles, semicircles, and quarter circles. Exchange designs with a classmate and calculate the perimeters of each other's designs.

143

4.4 Use a Formula

A formula is an equation that shows how quantities are related. For example, the formula for calculating the perimeter of a rectangle is $P = 2 \times (l + w)$.

Many problems can be solved using formulas.

A person's shoe size depends on the length of the foot. In North America, the sizes of some shoes are given by these 2 formulas.
For males: $S = 1.2 \times f - 22.6$
For females: $S = 1.2 \times f - 20.6$
where S is the shoe size, and f is the length of the foot in centimetres.

The length of one of Bob's feet is 28 cm. The length of one of Susan's feet is 24 cm. What are their shoe sizes?

Understand the Problem

1. What information are you given?

2. What are you asked to find?

3. Do you need an exact or approximate answer?

Think of a Plan

For Bob, use the formula $S = 1.2 \times f - 22.6$ and substitute 28 for f.
For Susan, use the formula $S = 1.2 \times f - 20.6$ and substitute 24 for f.
Use the order of operations to find each value of S.

For Bob

$S = 1.2 \times f - 22.6$
$\quad = 1.2 \times 28 - 22.6$
$\quad = 33.6 - 22.6$
$\quad = 11$

For Susan

$S = 1.2 \times f - 20.6$
$\quad = 1.2 \times 24 - 20.6$
$\quad = 28.8 - 20.6$
$\quad = 8.2$

Carry Out the Plan

Bob's shoe size is 11.
Susan's shoe size is 8.

Look Back

Do the answers seem reasonable?
How could you work backward to check the answers?

Use a Formula	1. Write the formula.
	2. Replace the letters by their values, making sure that you use the proper units.
	3. Complete the calculation.
	4. Check that your answer is reasonable.

Problems and Applications

1. a) The tallest human on record was an American called Robert Wadlow (1918–1940). His feet were about 47 cm long. Use the formula $S = 1.2 \times f - 22.6$ to calculate his shoe size. Round your answer to the nearest whole number.

b) Does one of the formulas on the opposite page work for your shoe size?

2. The formula that relates distance, time, and speed is
$$D = s \times t$$
where D is the distance travelled in kilometres, s is the speed in kilometres per hour, and t is the time in hours. Calculate the distance travelled in each car journey.

a) 3 h at 55 km/h

b) 2.5 h at 80 km/h

3. The formula gives the time, t seconds, an object takes to fall from a height of h metres.
$$t = \sqrt{\frac{h}{4.9}}$$
Calculate the time it takes an object to fall from each of these heights.

a) 19.6 m　　　　**b)** 122.5 m

c) the top of the 92-m high Peace Tower on Canada's Parliament Buildings. Round this answer to the nearest second.

4. The formula can be used to find a dog's age in "dog years," y, from its age in human years, n.
$$y = 21 + 4 \times (n - 1)$$
Find a dog's age in dog years when the dog has the following ages in human years.

a) 1　　**b)** 6　　**c)** 10　　**d)** 15

5. The formula for determining the number of days between water changes in a hot tub is
$$d = \frac{a}{10 \times u}$$
where d is the number of days, a is the volume of water in litres, and u is the average number of people who use the tub each day. If the tub holds 1500 L of water, and an average of 25 people use the tub each day, how many days are there between water changes?

6. Bowling handicaps make competitions fairer among bowlers with different averages. A bowler's handicap is added to the bowler's score in each game. One formula used to calculate a handicap is
$$H = 0.8 \times (200 - a)$$
where H is the bowler's handicap, and a is the bowler's average.

a) Copy the table and calculate each bowler's handicap. Round each answer to the nearest whole number, if necessary.

Bowler	Average	Handicap
Sarah	180	
Paul	155	
Kim	147	
Chung	174	

b) If a bowler's handicap is 44, what is the bowler's average? Describe your method and compare it with a classmate's.

7. State 2 careers in which formulas are used to solve problems. List all the careers suggested by members of your group.

8. Find 4 formulas used to calculate sports statistics. Write the formulas and identify the letters used in each. Write a problem using each formula. Have a classmate solve your problems.

Area

Area is the measure of a surface. Area is expressed in square units.

Activity ❶

Determine the area, in square units, of each figure on the grid.

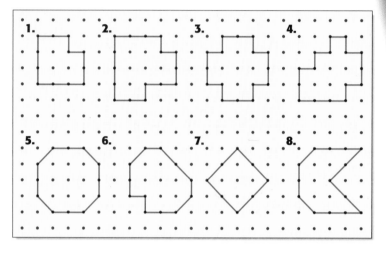

Activity ❷

1. On grid paper, make a region for each of the following.
a) a square with area 16 square units
b) a rectangle with area 18 square units
c) a right triangle with area 6 square units
d) a rectangle with area 12 square units
e) a parallelogram with area 20 square units
f) a right triangle with area 10 square units

2. Compare your results with your classmates'.
a) Which are the same?
b) Which are different?
c) Is it possible to make other regions for the given descriptions?

3. Make all of the possible regions that satisfy each description.

Activity ❸

Use grid paper.

1. a) Make all the rectangles with a perimeter of 24 units and whole-number side lengths. List the measures of the sides and the area for each rectangle.
b) What happens to the area as the rectangles become closer to a square?

2. a) Make all the rectangles with a perimeter of 36 units and whole-number side lengths. List the measures of the sides and the area for each rectangle.
b) What happens to the area as the rectangles become closer to a square?

3. What are the dimensions of the rectangle with a perimeter of 32 units that has the greatest area?

Activity ❹

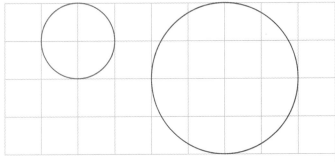

The circles are drawn on centimetre grid paper.

1. What is the radius of each circle?

2. Count squares to estimate the area of each circle. Compare your estimates with the estimates of others in your group. Compare the values given to part squares in your estimates. Decide on a common method.

3. Draw circles with the following radii. Estimate the area of each by counting squares using the group's method. Compare your results with the results of other members of your group.
a) 4 cm   **b)** 1.5 cm   **c)** 6 cm

Activity ❺

When decorating a house, decorators express the areas of walls, windows, and floors in square metres.

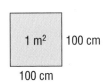

1. How many square centimetres are in 1 m²?

2. Complete each statement.
a) 3 m² = ▨ cm²   **b)** 0.01 m² = ▨ cm²
c) 2500 cm² = ▨ m²   **d)** 450 000 cm² = ▨ m²

3. How many math books are needed to cover approximately 1 m²?

4. How many square metres of carpet would be needed to cover your classroom floor?

5. Decorators recommend that curtain material be 3 times as wide as a window. How many square metres of curtain material would be recommended for your classroom windows?

Activity ❻

Areas of land are measured in hectares or square kilometres.

1 ha   100 m
100 m

1 km²   1000 m
1000 m

1. How many square metres are in 1 ha? 1 km²?

2. The area of a football field is about 0.5 ha. How large is your school playing field, in hectares?

3. How many times would the floor of your school gymnasium fit into 1 ha?

4. Use an almanac to find areas in square kilometres to help you answer the following.
a) How much bigger is the world's largest lake than Canada's smallest province?
b) How many times bigger than Lake Erie is Victoria Island?

4.5 Area of a Rectangle and Square

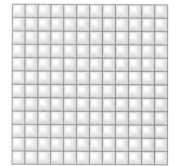

Activity: Discover the Relationship

The rectangular window in the school door is reinforced with wire so that it will not shatter if it is broken. The squares that are formed by the wire each cover 1 cm² of glass.

Inquire

1. The length of the window is 56 cm. How many rows of wire squares are there in the window?

2. The width of the window is 40 cm. How many columns of wire squares are there in the window?

3. What is the total number of squares covering the window?

4. What is the area of the window?

5. If the dimensions of any rectangle are represented by l and w, write a formula for calculating the area of a rectangle.

Activity: Discover the Relationship

There is a small, square window in the door of the boiler room.

Inquire

1. How many rows of wire squares are there in the window?

2. How many columns of wire squares are there?

3. What is the total number of squares covering the window?

4. What is the area of the window?

5. If the side of any square is represented by s, write a formula for calculating the area of a square.

Example

The cost of reinforced window glass is 1.37¢/cm². What is the cost of a window that is 60 cm by 35 cm?

Solution

The window is a rectangle 60 cm by 35 cm.

$A = l \times w$
$\quad = 60 \times 35$
$\quad = 2100$

The area of the window is 2100 cm².
The cost of the glass is 1.37¢/cm².
$1.37 \times 2100 = 2877$¢ or $28.77
The cost of the window is $28.77.

Practice

The diagram illustrates the area of a square with side 2.5 cm. Illustrate the areas of squares with the following sides.

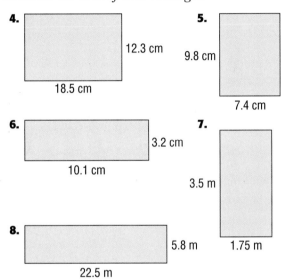

1	1	0.5
1	1	0.5
0.5	0.5	← 0.25

$A = 6.25 \text{ cm}^2$

1. 3.5 cm   **2.** 7.5 cm   **3.** 10.5 cm

Calculate the area of each rectangle.

4. 12.3 cm, 18.5 cm

5. 9.8 cm, 7.4 cm

6. 3.2 cm, 10.1 cm

7. 3.5 m, 1.75 m

8. 5.8 m, 22.5 m

Calculate the area of each square with the following sides.

9. 22 cm   **10.** 4.4 cm   **11.** 14.8 cm

Problems and Applications

12. A garden is twice as long as it is wide. Its length is 15 m. What is its area?

13. The perimeter of a square play area is 33.6 m. What is the area?

14. The area of a pathway is 5.46 m². The width is 78 cm. How long is the pathway?

15. One hectare equals 10 000 m². If the dimensions of a 1-ha area are whole numbers of metres, and all angles are right angles, what are the greatest and smallest perimeters?

16. A tennis court is 23.8 m by 11 m. A tennis club has 3 courts side by side in a fenced area. The courts have 3 m between them and 3 m around the outside.
a) What is the total area of the 3 tennis courts?
b) What are the dimensions of the fenced space?
c) What is the area of the fenced space?

17. Michelle had a valuable stamp mounted and framed. The stamp is 3 cm by 2.5 cm, and the frame is a 9-cm square. What is the area of the background not covered by the stamp?

Stamp reproduced courtesy of Canada Post Corporation

18. The Imperial Palace in Beijing, China, covers a rectangular area 960 m long and 750 m wide. What area, in hectares, does the palace cover?

19. What is the greatest number of 2 cm × 3 cm rectangles that can be cut from a 16 cm × 10 cm rectangle? Make a sketch to show where the cuts would be made. Compare your plan with the plans of some classmates.

LOGIC POWER

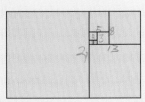

The area of each of the smallest squares is 1 cm². Calculate the area of each of the other squares and the area of the rectangle.

149

4.6 Area of a Parallelogram

The upper and lower rails of the handrail form a
parallelogram with the end posts. Each rail is
the length of the **base** of the parallelogram.
The distance between the rails is the **height**
of the parallelogram.

Activity: Discover the Relationship

Draw a rectangle with length 7 cm and width 5 cm.
Make a non-vertical cut across the rectangle and
fit the 2 pieces together, as shown.

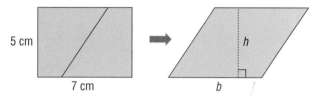

Inquire

1. What figure is formed by the 2 pieces of the rectangle?

2. What is the measure of the base of the figure?

3. What is the measure of the height of the figure?

4. What is the relationship of the area of the new figure to
the area of the rectangle?

5. Write a formula for calculating the area of a parallelogram.

Example

A restaurant sign is a rectangle 2.8 m in length and 0.7 m
in width. The name on the restaurant sign is printed on
a parallelogram. The base of the parallelogram
is 2 m and the height is 0.4 m. What area of
the sign is not covered by the parallelogram?

Solution

The sign is a rectangle.
$$A = l \times w$$
$$= 2.8 \times 0.7$$
$$= 1.96$$

For the parallelogram
$$A = b \times h$$
$$= 2 \times 0.4$$
$$= 0.8$$

$$A_{\text{rectangle}} - A_{\text{parallelogram}} = 1.96 - 0.8$$
$$= 1.16$$

The area of the sign not covered by the parallelogram is 1.16 m^2.

Practice

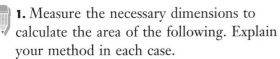

1. Measure the necessary dimensions to calculate the area of the following. Explain your method in each case.

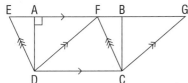

a) rectangle ABCD
b) parallelogram EFCD
c) parallelogram FGCD

Calculate the area of each parallelogram.

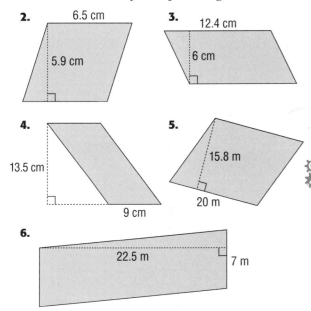

2. 6.5 cm   5.9 cm

3. 12.4 cm   6 cm

4. 13.5 cm   9 cm

5. 15.8 m   20 m

6. 22.5 m   7 m

Problems and Applications

7. The area of a parallelogram is 107.5 cm² and the height is 8.6 cm.
a) Write a formula for calculating the base.
b) Calculate the base.

8. The area of a parallelogram is 22.26 cm² and the base is 5.3 cm.
a) Write a formula for calculating the height.
b) Calculate the height.

9. A wallpaper border on top of the baseboard on a flight of stairs is in the shape of a parallelogram. The bottom of the border is 150 cm and the height is 12 cm. What is the area of the border?

10. In the flag of Trinidad and Tobago, the length of the rectangle is about 4 times the base of the black parallelogram. How do the areas of the rectangle and the parallelogram compare? Explain.

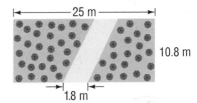

11. The path cuts through a rose garden.

a) What is the area of the path?
b) What area of the garden is planted?

12. a) Copy the trapezoid onto cardboard and cut it out.

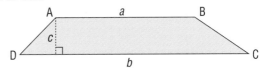

Trace and cut a second identical trapezoid.
b) Fit the 2 figures together along side BC to form a parallelogram. Use a, b, and c to write an expression for the area of the parallelogram.
c) Use a, b, and c to write a formula for the area of the trapezoid.
d) Use your formula to calculate the area of each trapezoid.

151

Seven-Point Geometry

The grid has 7 points, 6 in the shape of a regular hexagon and 1 centre point. Copy the 7-point grid several times in your notebook.

Activity ❶ Drawing Polygons

Three of the 19 different polygons that can be made on the 7-point grid are shown.

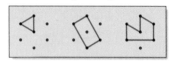

1. Draw the other 16 polygons. Share your answers with your classmates until you have all 16.

2. Number the polygons from 1 to 19. Work together, so that each group numbers the polygons in the same way. You may want to start with the triangles, then the quadrilaterals, and so on.

Activity ❸ Comparing Sides

There are 3 different lengths that can be drawn on the 7-point grid.

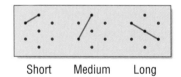

Short   Medium   Long

1. Mark the equal sides on your polygons. Use 1 "tick" for the short length, 2 "ticks" for the medium length, and 3 "ticks" for the long length.

2. Describe each polygon according to the number of equal sides it has. For example:
- All sides have the same length.
- All sides have different lengths.
- Two sides are equal.
- There are two pairs of equal sides.

Activity ❷ Classifying Polygons

1. Name each of the 19 polygons according to the number of sides it has.

2. If you wrap an elastic around a convex polygon, the elastic touches every point of the polygon. If the polygon is concave, the elastic does not touch every point. Classify each of the 19 polygons as either convex or concave.

Activity ❹ Comparing Angles

1. Describe each of your 19 polygons according to the numbers of equal angles it has. For example:
- All angles are equal.
- All angles are different.
- Two angles are equal.
- There are two pairs of equal angles.

2. List the types of angles each polygon contains. For example:
- 3 acute angles
- 2 right angles, 2 acute angles, 1 reflex angle

Activity ❺ Finding Angle Measures

1. Find the measure of each angle.

2. Using the results from question 1, find the measure of each interior angle of each of your 19 polygons. For example, for the figure at the right, the angle measures are 60°, 60°, 60°.

Activity ❻ Finding Lines of Symmetry

When a polygon is folded along a line of symmetry, both parts of the polygon match. The polygon at the right has one line of symmetry.

Sort the 19 polygons according to how many lines of symmetry they have.

Activity ❼ Comparing Areas

Let the small equilateral triangle have an area of 1 square unit.

This triangle also has an area of 1 square unit because it is half of 2 small equilateral triangles.

1. Find the area of each of your 19 polygons.

2. Which polygons have the same area?

3. Which polygon has the largest area?

4.7 Area of a Triangle

The office furnishings store sells a triangular insert that connects a main desk to a computer stand. The amount of additional surface the insert provides is the area of the triangle.

Activity: Determine the Relationship

The polygons are formed by elastics on a geoboard.

More elastics divide each polygon into 2 equal triangles.

    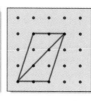

Inquire

1. What is the area in square units of each polygon?

2. Compare each triangle with the polygon from which it is formed.
a) How do their areas compare?
b) How do their bases compare?
c) How do their heights compare?

3. What formula can be used to calculate the area of a triangle?

Example

The sailboat has 2 sails. What is the total area of material in the sails?

Solution

The sails are both triangles.

$$A_1 = \frac{1}{2} \times b \times h \qquad\qquad A_2 = \frac{1}{2} \times b \times h$$
$$= \frac{1}{2} \times 10.8 \times 25 \qquad\qquad = \frac{1}{2} \times 8.5 \times 24$$
$$= 135 \qquad\qquad\qquad\quad = 102$$

$135 + 102 = 237$

The total area of material is 237 m^2.

154

Practice

Determine the area of each shaded triangle.

1.

2.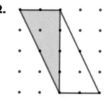

3.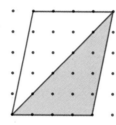

4.

Calculate the area of each triangle.

5. 6.2 cm, 15 cm
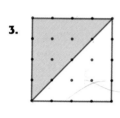

6. 12 cm, 13.6 cm

7. 5.5 cm, 8.6 cm

8. 20 cm, 24 cm
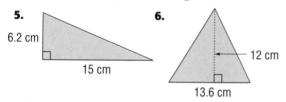

9. 5.9 m, 4.4 m

10. 10.4 m, 6 m
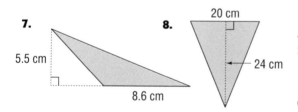

11. 16.5 cm, 18.2 cm

12. 7.7 cm, 32 cm
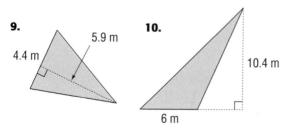

Problems and Applications

Calculate the missing value for each triangle.

	Base	Height	Area
13.		3.8	8.55
14.	12.7		82.55
15.	19	8.4	
16.	4.5		10.35
17.	7.6	10.5	
18.		1.8	5.67

19. This section of a patchwork quilt is a 12-cm square with 5 triangles on it. The base of each triangle is 5.2 cm and the height is 3.6 cm.

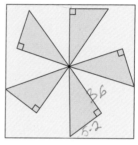

a) What area of fabric is needed for the triangles?

b) What area of the background is visible?

20. What is the area, to the nearest tenth of a square centimetre, of the largest equilateral triangle that can be drawn on a 5-cm square?

21. a) Work with a partner to make a sketch that shows how the largest possible number of pennants can be cut from 1 m of felt with a width of 90 cm.

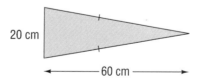

20 cm, 60 cm

b) What area of fabric is used for the pennants?

c) What area of fabric is left over?

4.8 Use Logic

Many problems require no mathematical calculations or no special skills in mathematics. You have to think through the problems logically. Sometimes, it helps to put the information in a table.

Detective Sam Diamond investigated a crime at a mansion. The 4 suspects were Amy, Bob, Colleen, and Domingo. Their jobs at the mansion were secretary, gardener, cook, and driver. Diamond was sure that the cook committed the crime, but the suspects refused to name their jobs. Diamond learned that neither Bob nor Domingo had a driver's licence, Colleen and Domingo did not know where the potatoes were kept, and Colleen worked indoors. Who was the cook?

AMY · BOB · COLLEEN · DOMINGO

Understand the Problem

1. What information are you given?

2. What are you asked to find?

Think of a Plan

Carry Out the Plan

Make a table and fill in the facts from the clues.

Neither Bob nor Domingo was the driver because neither had a licence.

	A	B	C	D
Secretary				
Gardener				
Cook				
Driver		n		n

Since Colleen and Domingo did not know where the potatoes were kept, neither was the cook.

	A	B	C	D
Secretary				
Gardener				
Cook			n	n
Driver		n		n

Colleen worked indoors, so she was not the driver or the gardener. Thus, Colleen was the secretary, and Amy was the driver.

	A	B	C	D
Secretary			y	
Gardener			n	
Cook			n	n
Driver	y	n	n	n

Complete the table.

Bob was the cook.

	A	B	C	D
Secretary	n	n	y	n
Gardener	n	n	n	y
Cook	n	y	n	n
Driver	y	n	n	n

Look Back

Check that the answer agrees with the given facts.

Use Logic

1. Organize the information.

2. Draw conclusions from the information.

3. Check that the answer is reasonable.

Problems and Applications

1. Robert, Peggy, and Jeff study painting, drama, and singing. The singer sang at Peggy's birthday party. Robert and the painter are brothers. Who is the singer?

2. Four students, Ana, Brenda, Carlos, and Devon, wrote a math quiz marked out of 10. Their marks were 8, 7, 6, and 4, but not necessarily in that order. Devon's mark was half of Brenda's. Carlos got a higher mark than Ana. What mark did each student get?

3. Mary, Harminder, and Allison each have one favourite subject. The subjects are math, history, and art. No one likes the subject that begins with the same letter as his or her name. Mary and the student who likes history are cousins. What is the favourite subject of each person?

4. Tessa, Yuri, and Jennifer had 24 books between them. Jennifer gave Tessa 2 books. Then, Tessa gave Yuri 1 book. Finally, Yuri gave Jennifer 1 book. They each ended up with an equal number of books. How many books did each person start with?

5. In a game, 1 orange marker is worth 4 red markers. One red marker is worth 5 yellow markers plus 2 blue markers. One blue marker is worth 3 yellow markers. How many yellow markers is 1 orange marker worth?

6. Francine, Donna, and Shelly finished first, second, and third in a race. Shelly was not third, Francine did not finish first, and Donna was not second. Shelly finished ahead of Donna. In what order did they finish the race?

7. On a history test, Anitha got 4 marks less than Tom. Gino got 5 marks less than Sarah. Tom got 16 marks more than Gino. How many marks more than Sarah did Anitha get?

8. Prince Edward Island, Manitoba, Alberta, and British Columbia became Canadian provinces in different years. Of these 4 provinces, Manitoba did not join second or third. British Columbia did not join first or fourth. Prince Edward Island did not join first or second. Alberta did not join second. Prince Edward Island joined before Alberta. In which order did these provinces join Canada?

9. Aaron, Jessica, Stephanie, and Roberto went to the museum to work on history projects. Each went to a different room — the Egyptian Room, the Dinosaur Room, the Aztec Room, and the Inca Room. Aaron saw Stephanie in the Aztec Room. Roberto did not see the dinosaurs. Roberto and Jessica did not see the Inca exhibit. Which room did each student visit?

10. There are 4 empty seats in the front row of the theatre. Two couples are going to sit in them, but neither couple is willing to be separated. If you were on the stage looking at the 4 people, in how many different ways could they be seated?

11. Write a problem that can be solved using a logic table. Start with a table that shows the correct answers. Then, remove some answers and write clues so that someone else can find the answers. Test the clues to make sure the problem can be solved. Have a classmate solve your problem.

PATTERN POWER

What is the ones digit of the product of one hundred sevens?

4.9 Area of a Circle

Activity: Study the Diagram

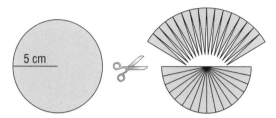

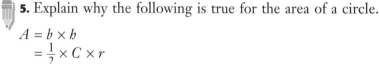

The radius of the circle is 5 cm.
The circumference of the circle is 31.4 cm.

The circle is cut in half, and each half is divided into 16 segments. The segments fit together to form a figure that resembles a parallelogram.

Inquire

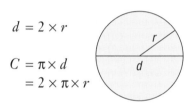

1. The base of the parallelogram is formed by half the circumference of the circle. What is the measure of the base of the parallelogram?

$d = 2 \times r$

$C = \pi \times d$
$\quad = 2 \times \pi \times r$

2. Why is the height of the parallelogram equal to 5 cm?

3. What is the area of the parallelogram?

4. What is the area of the circle?

5. Explain why the following is true for the area of a circle.

$A = b \times h$
$ = \frac{1}{2} \times C \times r$
$ = \frac{1}{2} \times 2 \times \pi \times r \times r$
$ = \pi \times r^2$

Example

The radius of the dart board at the community centre is 23 cm. What area of the wall is covered by the dart board, to the nearest square centimetre?

Solution

$A = \pi \times r^2$
$ = 3.14 \times 23^2$ **EST** $3 \times 500 = 1500$
$ = 3.14 \times 529$
$ = 1661.06$ [C] 3.14 [×] 23 [×] 23 [=] 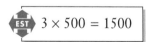

The area of the wall covered by the dart board is 1661 cm^2, to the nearest square centimetre.

Practice

Round each answer to the nearest hundredth.

Measure the radius or diameter of each circle and calculate each area.

1.

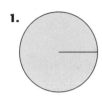

2.

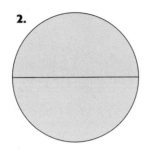

3.

Calculate the area of each circle.

4. $r = 3.8$ cm   **5.** $r = 12$ cm

6. $d = 17$ cm   **7.** $d = 1.2$ m

8. $r = 21$ cm   **9.** $r = 4.6$ m

Problems and Applications

10. The sound waves from a radio station travel approximately 80 km. What is the area of the transmission circle of the station?

11. The world's largest clock face is on a floral clock in Toi, Japan. The clock face is 31 m in diameter. Calculate its area.

Calculate the area of each shaded region.

12.

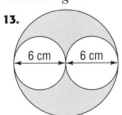

13.

14.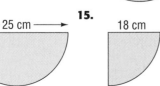

15.

16. A compact disc has a diameter of 12 cm. The hole in the centre has a diameter of 1.5 cm. What is the area
a) including the hole?
b) excluding the hole?

17. A circular window in a door has a diameter of 32 cm. Its frame is 2 cm wide. What is the total area of the window and its frame?

18. Oni wants to draw a circle with an area of about 100 cm². To what distance should she set her compasses?

19. A decorator table has a diameter of 50 cm and a height of 66 cm. Its circular cover hangs to the floor all around. What is the area of the cover?

20. Work in a group to predict what happens to the area of a circle in the following cases. Use examples to check your prediction.
a) The diameter is doubled.
b) The radius is tripled.

LOGIC POWER

Jason decided to design a circular medal with an unusual property. He made its area in square centimetres numerically equal to its circumference in centimetres. What was the diameter of Jason's medal?

159

4.10 Area of Composite Figures

Composite figures are made up of 2 or more distinct regions.

Activity: Use a Diagram

The plan of a garden shows a circular fountain surrounded by a lawn. To find the area of the lawn, subtract the area of the fountain from the area of the whole garden. The garden can be considered as 3 distinct regions.

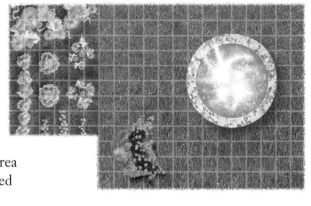

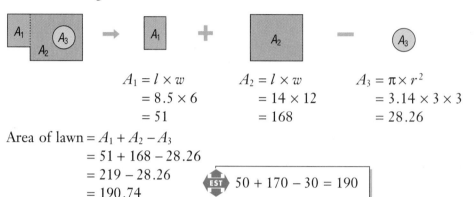

$$A_1 = l \times w \qquad A_2 = l \times w \qquad A_3 = \pi \times r^2$$
$$ = 8.5 \times 6 \qquad = 14 \times 12 \qquad = 3.14 \times 3 \times 3$$
$$ = 51 \qquad = 168 \qquad = 28.26$$

Area of lawn $= A_1 + A_2 - A_3$
$$= 51 + 168 - 28.26$$
$$= 219 - 28.26$$
$$= 190.74$$

EST $50 + 170 - 30 = 190$

The area of the lawn is 190.74 m².

Inquire

1. Copy the diagram. Complete it by adding the dimensions needed to solve the above problem in another way.

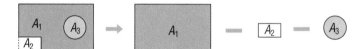

2. Solve the problem using this method.

Example

Calculate the area of the rug.

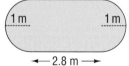

1 m   1 m

←— 2.8 m —→

Solution

The rug can be divided into 3 regions.

A_1 A_2 A_3

$$A_1 = \pi \times r^2 \div 2 \qquad A_2 = l \times w \qquad A_3 = \pi \times r^2 \div 2$$
$$ = 3.14 \times 1 \times 1 \div 2 \qquad = 2.8 \times 2 \qquad = 3.14 \times 1 \times 1 \div 2$$
$$ = 1.57 \qquad = 5.6 \qquad = 1.57$$

Area of rug $= 1.57 + 5.6 + 1.57$
$$= 8.74$$

EST $2 + 6 + 2 = 10$

The area of the rug is 8.74 m².

Practice

Calculate the area of each figure using 2 different methods.

1.

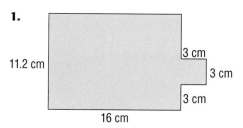

11.2 cm
3 cm
3 cm
3 cm
16 cm

2.

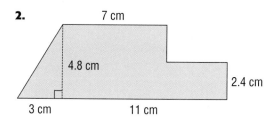

7 cm
4.8 cm
2.4 cm
3 cm
11 cm

Calculate the area of each shaded region.

3.

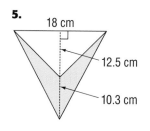

13 m
8 m
15 m

4.

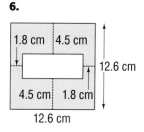

12.5 m
9 m
12.5 m

5.

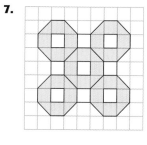

18 cm
12.5 cm
10.3 cm

6.

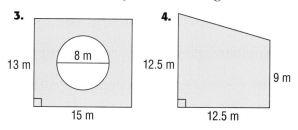

1.8 cm 4.5 cm
12.6 cm
4.5 cm 1.8 cm
12.6 cm

7.

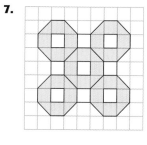

Each square represents 2 cm².

Problems and Applications

8. Calculate the area of paving stone needed for the patio shown.

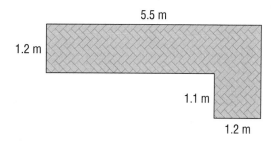

5.5 m
1.2 m
1.1 m
1.2 m

9. Ray's Restaurant has a rectangular patio 15.2 m by 5.1 m. There are 4 small trees on the patio. Each is in a circular pot with a diameter of 1 m. What area of the patio is available for seating?

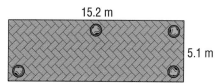

15.2 m
5.1 m

10. What area of carpeting is needed to carpet the rectangular living room?

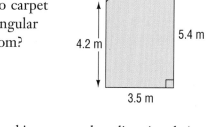

Fireplace
◄2.3 m►
4.2 m
5.4 m
3.5 m

11. The parking garage has directional signs to indicate which way the traffic flows. What is the area of each sign?

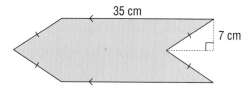

35 cm
7 cm

12. Design a composite figure that includes at least 3 distinct regions. Draw its plan. Ask a classmate to calculate the area of your figure.

4.11 Working with Perimeter and Area

Activity: Solve the Problem

Cans of juice are packed in cases of 24, in 4-by-6 arrays. The diameter of each can is 6.5 cm. The problem is to find how much of the base of the case is not covered by cans.

Inquire

1. If the cans are touching, what is
a) the length of the case?   **b)** the width of the case?

2. What is the area of the base of the case?

3. What is the area of the base of a can?

4. What is the total area of the bases of all the cans?

5. How much of the base of the case is not covered by cans?

Example

Marisa is making a tablecloth for a dining table. The table is 3.2 m long and 1.8 m wide. She wants the cloth to hang 30 cm on all sides.
a) How much material does Marisa need to buy?
b) How much trim will she need to decorate the edges of the cloth?

Solution

Make a diagram.

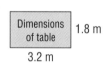

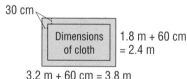

The tablecloth will be a rectangle 3.8 m by 2.4 m.
a) The amount of material needed is the area of the tablecloth.

$A = l \times w$
$\quad = 3.8 \times 2.4$ **EST** $4 \times 2.5 = 10$
$\quad = 9.12$

Marisa needs 9.12 m² of material.
b) The amount of trim needed is the perimeter of the tablecloth.

$P = 2 \times (l + w)$
$\quad = 2 \times (3.8 + 2.4)$ **EST** $4 + 2 = 6$
$\quad = 2 \times 6.2$ $2 \times 6 = 12$
$\quad = 12.4$

Marisa needs 12.4 m of trim.
How could you check the answers?

Recall the steps

Understand
the Problem

Think
of a
Plan

Carry Out
the Plan

Look Back

Problems and Applications

Round your answers to the nearest hundredth, when necessary.

1. The rectangular table has a semicircular leaf at each end.

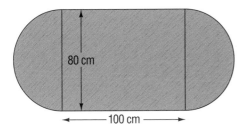

a) What is the total area of the table in square centimetres?

b) Express the area in square metres.

c) What is the total perimeter of the table in centimetres?

d) Express the perimeter in metres.

2. Josh and Brenda made pennants to sell at a fund-raiser for the school basketball team.

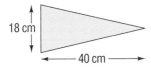

What area of cloth was needed for each pennant?

3. The target is painted on the playground for a game of beanbag toss. The centre circle has a radius of 50 cm. The radius of each circle is 50 cm greater than the one before.

a) Calculate the area and the outside perimeter of each band of colour on the target.

b) If one more band of colour is added, what will be its area?

c) What will be the outside perimeter of the target with the new band of colour?

4. A compact disc has a diameter of 12 cm. It is packaged in a plastic case 14 cm by 12.5 cm.

a) What is the difference between the circumference of the compact disc and the perimeter of the case?

b) What is the difference between the area of the compact disc and the area of the case?

5. The radius of a cylindrical air conditioner in a backyard is 40 cm.

a) What is the length of the sides of the smallest square paving stone that can be used to sit the air conditioner on?

b) What is the area of the paving stone in part a)?

6. A semicircle, with a diameter equal to the side, is drawn on each side of a right triangle.

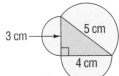

a) Find the area of each semicircle.

b) What relationship do you notice among the 3 areas?

c) Use 2 more examples to check if this relationship is true for all right triangles.

7. In your group, choose a game that is played on a marked playing area. Use centimetre grid paper to draw a plan of your game surface. Investigate to find the placement and dimensions of the playing lines. Mark them on your plan. Use your plan to write 5 questions involving area and perimeter. Exchange questions with another group, and solve each other's questions.

NUMBER POWER

Find 2 right triangles in which the perimeter is the same number of centimetres as the number of square centimetres in the area.

4.12 Use a Table

Charts and tables are efficient ways to organize information. Bus schedules, team standings, and school timetables are 3 examples. Constucting a table is a useful problem solving strategy.

Carla is the business manager of Emerald Lake Park. Ticket sales average 1000 people/day, when the cost of a ticket is $16. People who visit the park spend $4.00 each at the concession stands. Carla has learned that, for every dollar she lowers the price, sales will increase by 100 people/day. For what price should Carla sell tickets to get the greatest total receipts from tickets sales and the concession stands?

Understand the Problem

1. What information are you given?

2. What are you asked to find?

3. Do you need an exact or approximate answer?

Think of a Plan

Set up a table to show the price of a ticket, the number of tickets that will be sold at that price, the receipts from ticket sales, the receipts from concession sales, and the total receipts. Find the ticket price that gives the greatest receipts.

Carry Out the Plan

Ticket Price ($)	Number Sold	Ticket Sales ($)	Concession Sales ($)	Total Receipts ($)
16	1000	16 000	4000	20 000
15	1100	16 500	4400	20 900
14	1200	16 800	4800	21 600
13	1300	16 900	5200	22 100
12	1400	16 800	5600	22 400
11	1500	16 500	6000	**22 500**
10	1600	16 000	6400	22 400

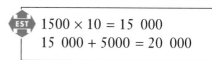

EST $1500 \times 10 = 15\ 000$
$15\ 000 + 5000 = 20\ 000$

A ticket price of $11 gives the greatest total receipts.

Look Back

Check that the receipts are close to the estimate.
How could you use subtraction and division to check your answer?

Use a Table	1. Organize the given information in a table.
	2. Complete the table with the results of your calculations.
	3. Find the answer from the table.
	4. Check that your answer is reasonable.

Problems and Applications

1. The table shows the greatest depths of the Great Lakes.

Lake	Greatest Depth (m)
Erie	64
Huron	229
Michigan	281
Ontario	244
Superior	405

a) How much deeper than Lake Huron is Lake Superior?
b) Which lake is closest to 5 times deeper than Lake Erie?
c) How many times deeper than Lake Ontario is Lake Superior? Round your answer to the nearest hundredth.

2. The toll to cross the Tallahassee Bridge is 75¢ a car. In the lane for drivers with exact change, a driver must toss 75¢ into a hopper, which funnels the coins into a counter. If the total is 75¢, the car is allowed through. The hopper does not accept pennies or 50¢ pieces. Use a table to determine how many different combinations of coins can be used to make the exact change.

Number of Quarters	Number of Dimes	Number of Nickels

3. Water World Aquarium charges $15 admission. There is an average of 150 visitors a day. Researchers have suggested that, for every dollar decrease in price, the number of visitors will increase by 50 a day. Find the admission price that gives the greatest receipts.

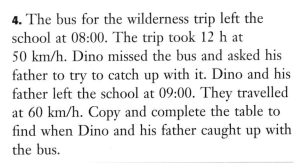

4. The bus for the wilderness trip left the school at 08:00. The trip took 12 h at 50 km/h. Dino missed the bus and asked his father to try to catch up with it. Dino and his father left the school at 09:00. They travelled at 60 km/h. Copy and complete the table to find when Dino and his father caught up with the bus.

Time	Distance Travelled (km)	
	Bus	Car
08:00	0	0
09:00	50	0
10:00	100	60

5. The 3 teams in a soccer league are the Aces, Bisons, and Chargers. Each team has played 4 games. A win is worth 2 points, a tie 1 point. There are no points for a loss. Here is some information about the games played.
• The Bisons have 3 wins and no ties.
• The Chargers have 1 point.

Copy and complete the table to find how many wins, losses, ties, and points each team has.

Team	Won	Lost	Tied	Points

6. A concert promoter can sell 5000 tickets at $30 each. Every $2 decrease in price will result in the sale of another 500 tickets. People attending the concert will spend $10 each at the concession stands. Find the ticket price that will give the greatest total revenue from ticket sales and concessions.

7. Write a problem that can be solved with a table. Have a classmate solve your problem.

Spreadsheets

Activity ❶ Spreadsheet Design

A **spreadsheet** is like a large sheet of paper divided into rows and columns. Each of the rectangles in a spreadsheet is called a **cell**. Three things can be put into cells: numbers, words that tell you what the numbers mean, and arithmetic operations that do calculations.

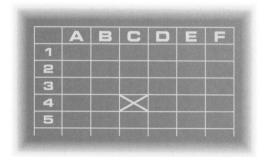

Columns are named across the top of the spreadsheet by capital letters. Rows are named by numbers down the side.

Each cell has its own name. A cell is named using the capital letter of the column the cell is in, followed by the number of the row the cell is in. The cell C4 is in column C and row 4.

1. Name the following cells.

a) 4 columns over and 3 rows down

b) 6 columns over and 2 rows down

c) 2 columns over and 5 rows down

d) 1 column over and 1 row down

2. Find out, and describe, how spreadsheets name columns after the 26 letters of the alphabet have been used.

3. Manual spreadsheets have been used for a long time. Your report card may be like a spreadsheet, if it has cells for words and numbers.

a) List 2 examples of spreadsheets that you see in a newspaper. What are they used for?

b) What are the cells that have words in them used for?

c) What are the cells that have numbers in them used for?

d) Are there any cells that have the result of an arithmetic calculation in them?

Activity ❷ A 3-by-3 Magic Square

The spreadsheet has been set up to make a 3-by-3 magic square. The arithmetic operations are shown in the cells.

On a computer, you would see them at the top of the spreadsheet when you put the cursor in the cell.

	A	B	C	D
1				@SUM(A4,B3,C2)
2	+B2 + 7	1	+B2 + 5	@SUM(A2..C2)
3	+B2 + 2	+B2 + 4	+B2 + 6	@SUM(A3..C3)
4	+B2 + 3	+B2 + 8	+B2 + 1	@SUM(A4..C4)
5	@SUM(A2..A4)	@SUM(B2..B4)	@SUM(C2..C4)	@SUM(A2,B3,C4)

1. What number is in cell B2?

2. What does the instruction in cell A2 tell you to do?

3. Draw a 3-by-3 grid to represent the magic square shown on the spreadsheet. Use the instructions to complete the square.

4. What do the instructions in column D tell you to do? Do the calculations.

5. What do the instructions in row 5 tell you to do? Do the calculations.

6. Why are the numbers in the red box called a magic square?

7. What numbers result in the square when you multiply the entry in cell B2 by 2? by 4? Are the resulting squares magic squares?

Activity ❸ A 4-by-4 Magic Square

1. The arithmetic operations for a 4-by-4 magic square are shown. Copy the spreadsheet and insert the instructions for column E and row 6.

	A	B	C	D	E
1					
2	1	+A2 + 14	+A2 + 13	+A2 + 3	
3	+A2 + 11	+A2 + 5	+A2 + 6	+A2 + 8	
4	+A2 + 7	+A2 + 9	+A2 + 10	+A2 + 4	
5	+A2 + 12	+A2 + 2	+A2 + 1	+A2 + 15	
6					

2. What is the magic number of this square?

How Big Is a Million?

 Use your measurement and estimation skills to decide your answers to the questions about millions. Compare your answers with your classmates' and be prepared to explain your reasoning and the data you had to locate.

Activity ❶

1. How many hours and minutes are in 1 000 000 s?

2. What age were you when you had lived for 1 000 000 min?

3. Can a person live to be 1 000 000 h old?

4. What year was 1 000 000 days ago?

Activity ❷

1. About what distance would 1 000 000 cars stretch if they were parked bumper to bumper ?

2. How many lengths of an Olympic swimming pool equal 1 000 000 m?

3. How many home runs would a baseball player need to run 1 000 000 m?

4. How many new pencils laid end to end measure 1 000 000 mm?

5. A roll of quarters holds 40 coins. How many rolls of quarters laid end to end would stretch 1 000 000 cm?

6. How many times around the equator equal 1 000 000 km?

Activity ❸

1. Does an average household television screen have an area of more or less than 1 000 000 mm^2?

2. How many students could stand in an area of 1 000 000 cm^2?

3. What is the area of a wall built of 1 000 000 bricks?

4. How many school classrooms are needed to equal an area of 1 000 000 m^2?

5. How many times would Prince Edward Island fit into 1 000 000 km^2?

Activity ❹

1. How many pages of a telephone book are needed to hold 1 000 000 names and numbers?

2. Commonwealth Stadium in Edmonton holds the largest crowd for football games in Canada. After how many games would the 1 000 000th spectator attend if the stadium was filled for each game?

3. If you were given 1¢ one day, and the amount you were given was doubled each day after that, on what day would you receive 1 000 000¢?

 4. Make up and answer a problem using 1 000 000. Pin your problem on a classroom bulletin board entitled "How Big Is a Million?" to create a class project.

Activity ❶ The Chicxulub Crater

Something big happened on the Earth 65 million years ago. Species by the hundreds, including the dinosaurs, disappeared.

One theory of their disappearance is that a meteor, about 16 km in diameter, crashed into the Earth, forming a crater with a radius of 160 km. The crater is called the Chicxulub Crater and is located in Mexico's Yucatán Peninsula.

The impact of the meteor caused a huge cloud of dust to be blown into the sky. The dust produced a thick blanket of debris that covered the Earth. The dust was so thick that it blocked out the sun.

The resulting cold, dark conditions might have lasted for months, stopping the most important food-making process—photosynthesis. In this process, plants use the sun's light to grow and to produce oxygen. Plants have produced 99% of the free oxygen added to the atmosphere since the world's beginning.

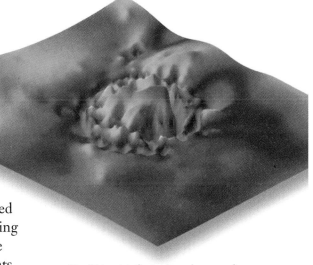

The Chicxulub Crater is underground. In this colour-enhanced computer image, the crater appears in blue to the right of the highest red peak.

1. What is the area of the Chicxulub Crater?

2. What provinces have areas smaller than that of the Chicxulub Crater?

3. Locate the Yucatán Peninsula on a map. What are its latitude and longitude?

4. Why would a huge dust cloud cause hundreds of species to become extinct?

5. What kinds of species would survive? Why?

Activity ❷ Polar Ice

Millions of years ago, the Arctic and Antarctic were rain forests. This meant that the water level on the Earth was about 60 m higher than it is today.

1. Why was the water level higher when the Arctic and the Antarctic were rain forests?

2. List the provincial capitals. Without looking up their elevations, list the ones you think would have been under water when the Arctic and the Antarctic were rain forests.

3. Check your answers to question 2 by locating the elevations of the provincial capitals.

Review

Calculate each perimeter.

1.

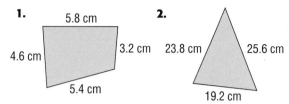

5.8 cm
3.2 cm
4.6 cm
5.4 cm

2.

23.8 cm
25.6 cm
19.2 cm

3.

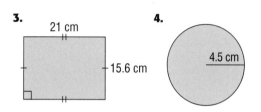

21 cm
15.6 cm

4.

4.5 cm

Calculate the perimeter of each regular polygon.

5. a pentagon with side 8.6 cm

6. a square with side 12.7 cm

7. an octagon with side 3.15 cm

8. a triangle with side 26.9 cm

9. a hexagon with side 6.6 cm

10. a decagon with side 13.45 cm

11. Sketch and label 2 different rectangles with a perimeter of 64 cm.

12. The length of the minute hand on the clock is 11.5 cm. The hour hand is 9 cm long.

a) What is the circumference of the circle traced by the point of the minute hand in 1 h?

b) What is the circumference of the circle traced by the point of the hour hand in one day?

Determine the area of each figure. The pegs are spaced 1 cm apart.

13.

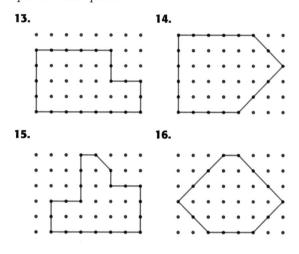

14.

15.

16.

Calculate the area of each figure.

17.

8.4 cm
8.4 cm

18.

2.5 m
6.35 m

19.

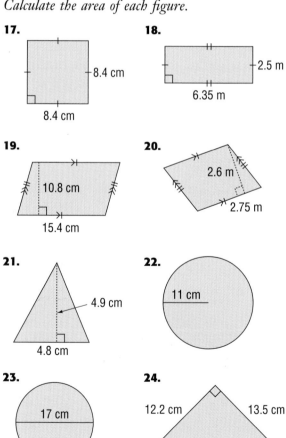

10.8 cm
15.4 cm

20.

2.6 m
2.75 m

21.

4.9 cm
4.8 cm

22.

11 cm

23.

17 cm

24.

12.2 cm
13.5 cm

Calculate the area of each figure.

25.
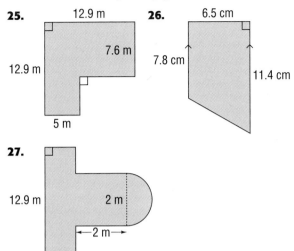
12.9 m
7.6 m
12.9 m
5 m

26.
6.5 cm
7.8 cm
11.4 cm

27.
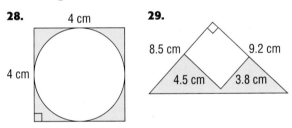
12.9 m
2 m
2 m
1.2 m

In questions 28 and 29, calculate the area of each shaded region.

28.
4 cm
4 cm

29.
8.5 cm
9.2 cm
4.5 cm
3.8 cm

30. a) What is the area of the parking lot?

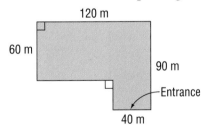
120 m
60 m
90 m
Entrance
40 m

b) How many metres of fencing are needed to surround the parking lot limits, other than the entrance?

31. Find the area of the shape shown at the right.

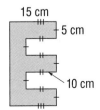
15 cm
5 cm
10 cm

Group Decision Making
Researching Entertainment Careers

1. As a class, list the entertainment careers you would like to investigate. They might include such careers as a disc jockey, television or radio producer, actor, singer, book publisher, song writer, instrumentalist, music publisher, director, theatre or television critic, movie theatre manager, talent agent, or set designer. As a class, select six careers and list the questions you want answered. Include a question on how math is used in each career.

2. Go to home groups. As a group, decide which career each member is going to investigate.

| 1 | 2 | 3 | 4 | 5 | 6 | | 1 | 2 | 3 | 4 | 5 | 6 |

Home Groups

| 1 | 2 | 3 | 4 | 5 | 6 | | 1 | 2 | 3 | 4 | 5 | 6 |

3. Do the research for your career individually.

4. Form an expert group with students who have the same career. Use the results of your research to answer the questions.

| 1 | 1 | 1 | 1 | | 2 | 2 | 2 | 2 | | 3 | 3 | 3 | 3 |

Expert Groups

| 4 | 4 | 4 | 4 | | 5 | 5 | 5 | 5 | | 6 | 6 | 6 | 6 |

5. In your expert group, decide on a format for your report and prepare a report on your assigned career. Include a description of how your career makes use of mathematics.

6. Present your report to the class.

7. Return to your home group and evaluate the group process and the reports.

Chapter Check

Calculate the perimeter of each figure.

1.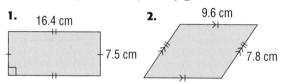
16.4 cm
7.5 cm

2.
9.6 cm
7.8 cm

3.
5.5 cm

4.
10.7 cm
16.5 cm
12.5 cm

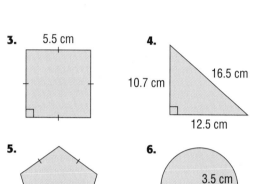

5.
11.8 cm

6.
3.5 cm

Calculate the area of each figure.

7.
8.4 cm
7.5 cm

8.
6.6 m
5.9 m

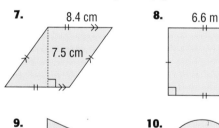

9.
12.5 cm
15.4 cm

10.
7 cm

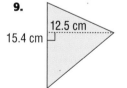

11. Calculate
a) the perimeter of the composite figure
b) the area of the composite figure

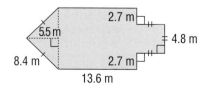

2.7 m
5.5 m
4.8 m
8.4 m
2.7 m
13.6 m

12. The kite is 150 cm long and 90 cm wide. It has a string frame around the outside.

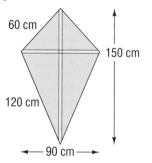

60 cm
150 cm
120 cm
90 cm

a) What is the area of the kite?
b) What is the perimeter of the outside frame?

13. A face-off circle on a hockey rink has a radius of 4.5 m. Calculate the circumference and the area of a face-off circle. Round your answers to the nearest hundredth, if necessary.

14. A soccer goal-mouth is 7.32 m wide and 2.44 m high.

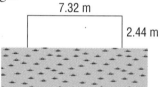

7.32 m
2.44 m

What is the area of the goal-mouth, to the nearest tenth of a square metre?

Using the Strategies

1. Complete the magic square.

9	2	7
5	10	

2. a) What is the area of the triangle?

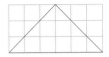

b) Sketch all the different figures that can be made by placing this triangle and an identical triangle together along one side.
c) What is the area of each figure?
d) Sketch all the different figures that can be made by placing the triangle and 3 identical triangles together along complete sides.
e) What is the area of each figure?

3. Use the digits and a decimal point
8 2 5 7 . to complete the following. Do not use the decimal point at the beginning or the end of a number.
a) Write the largest number possible.
b) Write the smallest number possible.
c) Write the number that is closest to 10.
d) Write the number that is closest to 100.
e) Write the number that is closest to 1000.

4. Copy and complete the patterns so that the product of the numbers in the opposite squares is the number in the circle.

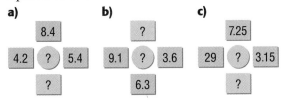

a)

8.4
4.2	?	5.4
?

b)

?
9.1	?	3.6
6.3

c)

7.25
29	?	3.15
?

5. The product of 2 numbers is 972. One number is 3 times the other. What are the numbers?

6. Add the numbers of letters in the names of the cards in a suit of playing cards, from ACE (3) to KING (4). What is significant about the total?

7. Calculate the perimeter of the figure.

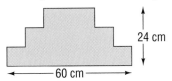

24 cm

60 cm

8. Twelve people can be seated around a table.

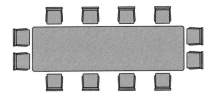

a) Using the same spacing, determine the number of people who could be seated around
• 2 tables joined along the width
• 2 tables joined along the length
• 3 tables joined along the width
• 3 tables joined along the length
b) Predict the number of people who could be seated using 8 tables joined along the width; using 8 tables joined along the length.

9. The pages of a book are numbered from 1 to 200. How many page numbers contain at least one 5?

DATA BANK

1. a) Which provincial capital has the greatest annual precipitation?
b) About how much precipitation does this capital have in September?

2. Use the Data Bank to write a problem. Have a classmate solve your problem.

Chapter 1

List the numbers in order from least to greatest.

1. 15.27, 15.07, 7.152, 1275, 909.0

2. 26 584, 8456, 1 000 001, 25 048, 52 846

Estimate, then evaluate each of the following.

3. $632 + 867 - 295$ **4.** $12.4 - 6.7 + 8.0 - 2.9$

5. $15\ 620 - 3988 - 6482$

Evaluate each of the following mentally.

6. 0.54×100 **7.** $14.72 \div 0.1$

8. $1885.9 \div 0.01$ **9.** 0.0392×1000

10. 147.88×10 **11.** $0.71 \div 100$

12. Round 357 291.8389 to the nearest hundred thousand, ten thousand, thousand, and so on, to the nearest hundredth.

13. Make up two addition questions involving 3 numbers that total 7294. The questions must be different, and the numbers in each question must differ by at least 800.

14. Make up two subtraction questions involving 2 numbers with a difference of 5731. The questions must be different, and each number you use must be greater than 1000.

Calculate.

15. $10 - 8 \times 4$ **16.** $20 - 15 \times (73 - 70)$

17. $2^2 - 24 \div (2 \times 3)$ **18.** $100 \div 25 - 20 \times 2^2$

19. How many 49¢ stamps can you buy for $10.00?

20. Jasper National Park, with an area of 10 878 km², is about 7 times as large as South Moresby National Park, British Columbia. What is the area of South Moresby National Park, to the nearest hundred square kilometres?

Chapter 2

Evaluate. Write your answers in exponential form.

1. $3^2 \times 3^2 \times 3$ **2.** $6^4 \div 6^2$ **3.** $4^5 \div 4^4 \times 4^2$

Evaluate.

4. $(5^2)^2$ **5.** $(2^3)^2$ **6.** $(4^3)^2$

Evaluate.

7. $85 \times 2 - 150$ **8.** $9 - 3 \times (5 - 2)$

9. $3^3 \div 9 + 2^2$ **10.** $(64 \div 2^4)^2$

Which numbers are divisible by 2? by 3? Which numbers are divisible by 2 and 3?

11. 24 **12.** 33 **13.** 72 **14.** 75

15. 672 **16.** 9003 **17.** 8000 **18.** 8400

List all the factors for each.

19. 15 **20.** 28 **21.** 48 **22.** 80

Evaluate.

23. $\sqrt{361}$ **24.** $\sqrt{2.25}$

Draw complete factor trees for the following, showing all prime factors on the bottom row.

25. 24 **26.** 49 **27.** 168 **28.** 256

Find the greatest common factor of each.

29. 24 and 48 **30.** 32 and 48

31. 60 and 84 **32.** 14, 21, and 28

Write the lowest common multiple of each.

33. 6, 5, and 3 **34.** 10, 15 and 18

35. A grade 8 class collects 56 fiction and 72 non-fiction books. It wants to make packs of books for hospital reading rooms. Each pack must have all fiction books or all non-fiction books. There must be the same number of books in each pack.

a) What is the greatest number of books in each pack?

b) If each pack contains the number of books found in part a), how many packs will there be?

Chapter 3

Find the missing measures.

1.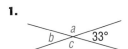

2.

3.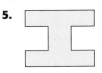

4.

Copy each figure and draw its lines of symmetry.

5.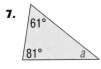

6.

Find the missing measures.

7.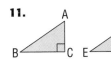

8.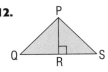

9.

10.

List the corresponding equal parts in the pairs of congruent triangles.

11. 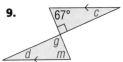 **12.**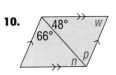

Find the missing length, to the nearest tenth.

13. 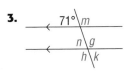 **14.**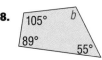

15. Joni has a rectangular garden 20 m by 15 m. She wants to put a single row of paving stones from one corner to the corner diagonally opposite. Each paving stone measures 50 cm by 50 cm. How many paving stones does she need?

Chapter 4

Calculate the perimeter of each figure.

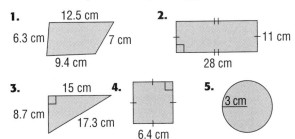

1. 12.5 cm, 6.3 cm, 7 cm, 9.4 cm

2. 11 cm, 28 cm

3. 15 cm, 8.7 cm, 17.3 cm

4. 6.4 cm

5. 3 cm

6. For a figure skating competition, an ice rink had a row of lights installed around the ice surface. The ice surface is 63 m by 32 m. What is the length of the row of lights?

Calculate the area of each figure.

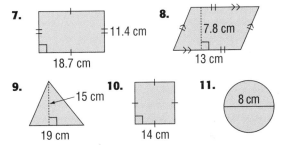

7. 11.4 cm, 18.7 cm

8. 7.8 cm, 13 cm

9. 15 cm, 19 cm

10. 14 cm

11. 8 cm

12. A hockey puck has a diameter of 7.6 cm.
a) What area of the ice does it cover?
b) What distance does the puck travel if it rolls on its side 8 times?

13. Pauline made a square quilt from 64 identical, square pattern pieces. The quilt has an area of 5.76 m². What is the measure of each side of a pattern piece?

14. Find the area of the shaded region.

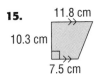

6 cm, 8 cm, 8 cm

Calculate each area.

15.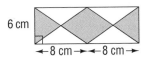

11.8 cm, 10.3 cm, 7.5 cm

16.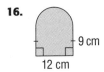

9 cm, 12 cm

CHAPTER 5

Fractions

A sperm whale has the largest brain on Earth. Sperm whales near the Galapagos Islands seem to use clicking sounds to communicate.

Linda Weilgart and Hal Whitehead, Dalhousie University biologists, have found these 23 patterns of clicking sounds the whales use. A vertical line represents a click. A space between two lines gives the time between clicks.

1. Which pattern has the greatest number of clicks?

2. Which patterns have the smallest number of clicks?

3. In which of the patterns are the clicks evenly spaced?

4. Which pattern has the longest length of time between 2 clicks?

5. Which pattern is the longest? About how long does it last?

6. Which pattern is the shortest? About how long does it last?

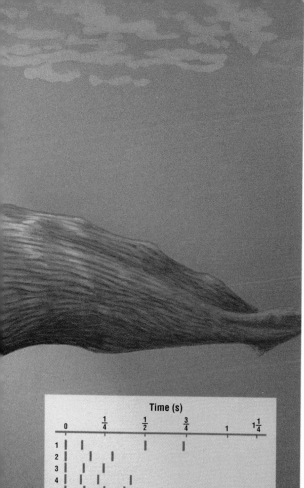

Pattern Blocks

Activity ❶ Shapes

The value of a yellow hexagon is one whole or 1.

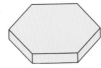

Two red trapezoids cover 1 hexagon.

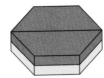

Three blue rhombuses cover 1 hexagon.

Six green triangles cover 1 hexagon.

1. What fraction of a hexagon is covered by 1 triangle?

2. What fraction of a hexagon is covered by 3 triangles? Write the answer in 2 different ways.

3. What shape can be used to replace 3 triangles?

4. What fraction of a hexagon does 1 rhombus cover?

5. What fraction of a hexagon do 2 rhombuses cover?

6. How many triangles are needed to cover 2 rhombuses?

7. What fraction of a hexagon do 4 triangles cover? Write your answer in 2 ways.

Activity ❷ More Shapes

1. Write the fraction of the hexagon that is covered.

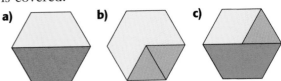

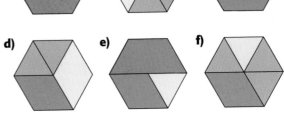

2. How would you use the shapes to show that these statements are true?

a) $\frac{1}{2} = \frac{3}{6}$ **b)** $\frac{1}{3} = \frac{2}{6}$ **c)** $\frac{4}{6} = \frac{2}{3}$

3. What is the total number of hexagons covered in each of the following?

a)

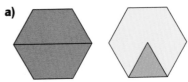

b)

c)

d)

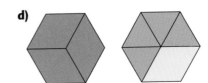

Warm Up

1. Which of the following are divisible by 3?
62, 87, 455, 612, 315, 433, 616

List the prime factors of each number.

2. 35 **3.** 48 **4.** 21

5. 16 **6.** 51 **7.** 144

Find the greatest common factor.

8. 6, 8 **9.** 8, 3 **10.** 5, 10

11. 12, 15 **12.** 8, 24 **13.** 6, 5, 2

14. 18, 12 **15.** 24, 28

List 5 multiples of each number.

16. 8 **17.** 6 **18.** 2 **19.** 4

Find two common multiples for each pair.

20. 3, 4 **21.** 16, 8

Find the lowest common multiple of each group.

22. 4, 6 **23.** 3, 6, 8

24. Name the fractions shown on the number line by the letters.

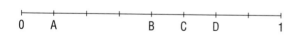

25. Write 8 as a fraction.

26. Which numbers are mixed numbers?
$2\frac{1}{2}$ $\frac{11}{5}$ $1\frac{4}{5}$ $3\frac{1}{4}$ $\frac{5}{6}$ $6\frac{2}{3}$

27. What is an improper fraction? Give an example.

Determine whether each fraction is closest to 0, $\frac{1}{2}$, or 1.

28. $\frac{7}{8}$ **29.** $\frac{3}{5}$ **30.** $\frac{1}{8}$

Round each of the following to the nearest whole number.

31. $\frac{4}{5}$ **32.** $2\frac{1}{8}$ **33.** $3\frac{3}{8}$ **34.** $4\frac{5}{6}$ **35.** $1\frac{1}{4}$

Mental Math

Add.

1. $\frac{1}{2} + \frac{1}{2}$ **2.** $\frac{1}{5} + \frac{3}{5}$

3. $\frac{5}{6} + \frac{1}{6}$ **4.** $\frac{1}{3} + \frac{2}{3}$

5. $2 + 3\frac{1}{4}$ **6.** $1 + 2\frac{1}{2}$

7. $3\frac{2}{5} + 1\frac{1}{5}$ **8.** $2\frac{1}{4} + 1\frac{3}{4}$

Find the remainder.

9. $12 \div 5$ **10.** $8 \div 3$

11. $15 \div 4$ **12.** $16 \div 5$

13. $27 \div 5$ **14.** $32 \div 6$

Subtract.

15. $\frac{2}{3} - \frac{1}{3}$ **16.** $\frac{5}{8} - \frac{1}{8}$

17. $\frac{11}{4} - \frac{7}{4}$ **18.** $\frac{23}{5} - \frac{11}{5}$

19. $2\frac{3}{5} - \frac{1}{5}$ **20.** $1\frac{1}{4} - \frac{3}{4}$

Calculate.

21. $\frac{1}{2}$ of 20 **22.** $\frac{1}{3}$ of 24

23. $\frac{1}{4}$ of 36 **24.** $\frac{1}{2}$ of 16

25. $\frac{1}{5}$ of 25 **26.** $\frac{1}{6}$ of 18

Evaluate.

27. $2 \times 3 + 1$ **28.** $3 \times 4 + 3$

29. $2 \times 5 + 4$ **30.** $2 \times 6 + 5$

31. $3 \times 5 + 2$ **32.** $4 \times 2 + 3$

Evaluate.

33. 2^2 **34.** 3^2 **35.** 2^3

36. 4^2 **37.** 5^2 **38.** 6^2

5.1 Fractions and Mixed Numbers

A **fraction** is used to name part of a whole or part of a group.

Activity: Use the Information

Teams from 4 schools, Northside, Westview, Southmount, and Eastdale, competed in a math contest. Each team had 2 members. Four 8-slice pizzas were delivered after the contest, 3 ham and pineapple and 1 vegetarian. The Northside team ate 7 slices, the Southmount team ate 6 slices, the Westview team ate 5 slices, and the Eastdale team ate 9 slices.

Inquire

1. What fraction of a whole pizza did the Northside team eat?

2. What fraction of a whole pizza did the Westview team eat?

3. What fraction more than a whole pizza did the Eastdale team eat?

4. How much pizza did the Eastdale team eat?

5. What fraction of a whole pizza was not eaten?

6. What fraction of the pizzas were vegetarian? ham and pineapple?

The number $4\frac{2}{3}$ is a **mixed number**. It is the sum of a whole number and a fraction. The number $\frac{17}{4}$ is an **improper fraction**. The numerator is bigger than the denominator.

Example 1

Write $4\frac{2}{3}$ as an improper fraction.

Solution

Multiply the whole number by the denominator. $4 \times 3 = 12$

Add the numerator to the product. $12 + 2 = 14$

Write the sum over the denominator. $\frac{14}{3}$

or $4\frac{2}{3} = \frac{12}{3} + \frac{2}{3}$

$= \frac{14}{3}$

So, $4\frac{2}{3}$ is $\frac{14}{3}$ as an improper fraction.

Example 2

Write $\frac{11}{4}$ as a mixed number.

Solution

Divide the numerator by the denominator to give a whole number and a remainder.

$\begin{array}{r} 2 \leftarrow \text{whole number} \\ 4\overline{)11} \\ \underline{8} \\ 3 \leftarrow \text{remainder} \end{array}$

Write the remainder over the divisor. $\frac{3}{4}$

Add this fraction to the whole number. $2\frac{3}{4}$

So, $\frac{11}{4}$ is $2\frac{3}{4}$ as a mixed number.

Example 3

Identify $1\frac{2}{3}$ on the number line.

Solution

The mixed number $1\frac{2}{3}$ must be between 1 and 2, two-thirds of the distance from 1 to 2.

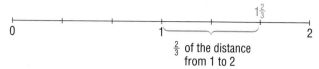

Practice

What fraction is represented by each diagram?

1.

2.

3.

4.

Draw a diagram to represent each fraction or mixed number.

5. $1\frac{1}{2}$ **6.** $\frac{3}{4}$ **7.** $2\frac{2}{3}$

8. $3\frac{3}{10}$ **9.** $1\frac{5}{8}$ **10.** $\frac{3}{5}$

Convert the following to improper fractions. Draw a diagram for each one.

11. $2\frac{1}{2}$ **12.** $3\frac{4}{5}$ **13.** $3\frac{1}{8}$ **14.** $4\frac{3}{4}$

Express as a mixed number.

15. $\frac{7}{2}$ **16.** $\frac{9}{5}$ **17.** $\frac{25}{3}$ **18.** $\frac{17}{6}$

Identify the number represented by each diagram as a mixed number and as an improper fraction.

19.

20.

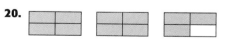

21.

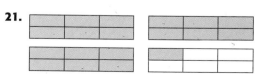

Problems and Applications

22. Draw a diagram to represent the fraction of the provinces of Canada that are west of Manitoba.

23. Jean-Paul has 17 eggs in his refrigerator. How many dozen eggs does he have? Express your answer as an improper fraction and as a mixed number.

24. The population of Montreal is about $\frac{24}{5}$ times the population of Winnipeg. Write this improper fraction as a mixed number.

25. Ramana has 4 pizzas to share equally with 2 other people. Draw the pizzas to show how much each person will get. Write the fraction that each person gets.

26. Show these fractions and mixed numbers on the same number line.

$\frac{3}{4}$ $2\frac{1}{2}$ $3\frac{7}{8}$ $1\frac{1}{4}$ $\frac{3}{8}$

27. The girls' hockey team won 6 games, lost 3 games, and tied 2 games. What fraction of the games did the team win? not win?

28. Write 13 min as a fraction of an hour.

29. Use any digit from 1 to 9 just once in each part of this problem. Write 2 fractions
a) close to 0
b) close to, but not equal to, $\frac{1}{2}$

181

5.2 Equivalent Fractions

Activity: Use the Fraction Bars

The fraction bars show that 1 half covers 2 quarters.
You can write the equality $\frac{2}{4} = \frac{1}{2}$.
You can use fraction bars to write other pairs of equal fractions.

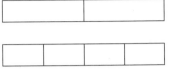

Inquire

1. How many eighths does 1 half cover? Write the equality.

2. How many sixths does 1 half cover? Write the equality.

3. How many eighths does 1 quarter cover? Write the equality.

4. How many eighths do 3 quarters cover? Write the equality.

Fractions that represent the same value are called **equivalent fractions**.

Example 1

Find the missing numerator for $\frac{2}{3} = \frac{\blacksquare}{12}$.

Solution

Using the known denominators, find the factor
that 3 was multiplied by to get 12.
Multiply the numerator by the same factor.

$$\frac{2}{3} = \frac{\blacksquare}{12} \qquad \frac{2}{3} = \frac{8}{12}$$

When the numerator and denominator have no common factors
other than 1, a fraction is in **simplest form** or **lowest terms**.

Example 2

Express $\frac{9}{12}$ in lowest terms.

Solution

Find the greatest common factor of 9 and
12. Divide the numerator and denominator
by the GCF.

$$\frac{9}{12} = \frac{3}{4}$$

The GCF of 9 and 12 is 3.

Example 3

Which is greater, $2\frac{1}{4}$ or $2\frac{1}{3}$?

Solution

The whole numbers are the same. Compare
the fractions by expressing them as equivalent
fractions with a common denominator.

$$\frac{1}{4} = \frac{3}{12} \qquad \frac{1}{3} = \frac{4}{12}$$

The lowest common denominator is 12.

Compare the numerators. $4 > 3$
So, $\frac{4}{12} > \frac{3}{12}$, and $2\frac{4}{12} > 2\frac{3}{12}$.
$2\frac{1}{3}$ is greater than $2\frac{1}{4}$.

Practice

Write the fraction represented by the shaded part of each diagram. Then, write 2 equivalent fractions.

1.

2.

3.

4.

Write 3 fractions equivalent to each of the following.

5. $\frac{1}{2}$ **6.** $\frac{2}{3}$ **7.** $\frac{3}{4}$ **8.** $\frac{4}{5}$

Find the missing value.

9. $\frac{3}{6} = \frac{\blacksquare}{2}$ **10.** $\frac{8}{12} = \frac{4}{\blacksquare}$

11. $\frac{3}{5} = \frac{12}{\blacksquare}$ **12.** $\frac{5}{\blacksquare} = \frac{10}{12}$

Write each fraction in lowest terms.

13. $\frac{9}{12}$ **14.** $\frac{2}{8}$ **15.** $\frac{15}{21}$ **16.** $\frac{6}{24}$

17. $3\frac{6}{9}$ **18.** $\frac{24}{8}$ **19.** $2\frac{15}{18}$ **20.** $\frac{35}{21}$

Replace each ♦ with >, <, or = to make each statement true.

21. $\frac{3}{8}$ ♦ $\frac{1}{2}$ **22.** $\frac{2}{3}$ ♦ $\frac{5}{12}$ **23.** $\frac{5}{6}$ ♦ $\frac{3}{4}$

24. $\frac{7}{8}$ ♦ $\frac{5}{4}$ **25.** $1\frac{1}{2}$ ♦ $\frac{6}{4}$ **26.** $1\frac{3}{4}$ ♦ $\frac{15}{8}$

Order the following from smallest to largest.

27. $\frac{3}{8}, \frac{5}{2}, \frac{7}{4}, \frac{9}{8}, \frac{4}{4}$ **28.** $\frac{1}{2}, \frac{3}{5}, \frac{7}{10}, \frac{3}{10}$

29. $\frac{5}{9}, 1\frac{2}{3}, \frac{7}{6}, 1\frac{4}{9}, \frac{4}{6}$ **30.** $2\frac{3}{4}, \frac{5}{2}, 2, \frac{15}{8}, \frac{7}{4}$

Problems and Applications

31. Ismail scored $\frac{21}{25}$ on a quiz. What was his score out of 100?

One way to convert a number of hours to minutes is to write an equivalent fraction with a denominator of 60. This method is shown in the first line of the table. Copy and complete the table.

	Number of Hours	Equivalent Fractions	Number of Minutes
	$\frac{1}{2}$	$\frac{1}{2} = \frac{30}{60}$	30
32.	$\frac{1}{6}$		
33.	$\frac{2}{3}$		
34.			20
35.	$2\frac{3}{4}$		
36.			75

37. The table shows the fraction of the time that some mammals spend sleeping.

Mammal	Fraction of Time Spent Sleeping
Chimpanzee	$\frac{5}{12}$
Giraffe	$\frac{1}{6}$
Koala	$\frac{11}{12}$
Lemur	$\frac{2}{3}$
Mole	$\frac{1}{3}$
Sheep	$\frac{1}{4}$
Squirrel	$\frac{7}{12}$
Two-toed Sloth	$\frac{5}{6}$

Rank the mammals in order from most sleep to least sleep.

38. a) Which of the fractions in the box are equivalent to $\frac{2}{5}$?

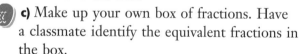

$\frac{3}{8}$	$\frac{10}{30}$	$\frac{8}{20}$	$\frac{3}{9}$	$\frac{15}{25}$	$\frac{12}{30}$
$\frac{4}{10}$	$\frac{15}{40}$	$\frac{10}{50}$	$\frac{18}{30}$	$\frac{5}{15}$	$\frac{16}{40}$

b) Identify 3 other pairs of equivalent fractions in the box.

c) Make up your own box of fractions. Have a classmate identify the equivalent fractions in the box.

5.3 Adding Fractions

Lake Michigan and Lake Huron each cover about $\frac{1}{4}$ of the area of the Great Lakes. Together, Lake Michigan and Lake Huron cover a fraction of the Great Lakes that equals $\frac{1}{4} + \frac{1}{4}$.

To add fractions with the same denominator, add the numerators.

$\frac{1}{4} + \frac{1}{4} = \frac{2}{4}$ or $\frac{1}{2}$

So, Lake Michigan and Lake Huron together cover about $\frac{1}{2}$ of the area of the Great Lakes.

Activity: Use the Diagrams

Two equal-sized pans of lasagna were used for dinner at the camp. The lasagna in one pan was cut into quarters. There was $\frac{1}{4}$ left. The lasagna in the other pan was cut into eighths. There were $\frac{3}{8}$ left. How much lasagna was left?

Inquire

1. Is the amount left closest to $\frac{1}{2}$ a pan, 1 whole pan, or 0?

2. If the pan with $\frac{1}{4}$ left had been cut into eighths, how much lasagna would be left in that pan?

3. What is the total amount left in the 2 pans?

4. Describe a method of adding fractions with different denominators.

5. Use the pictures of the pans to explain why $\frac{1}{4} + \frac{3}{8}$ does not equal $\frac{4}{12}$.

Example

Add.　　**a)** $\frac{2}{3} + \frac{4}{5}$　　**b)** $2\frac{3}{4} + 3\frac{2}{3}$

Solution

To add fractions with different denominators, write equivalent fractions with the lowest common denominator.

a) $\frac{2}{3} + \frac{4}{5}$

$= \frac{10}{15} + \frac{12}{15}$

$= \frac{10 + 12}{15}$

$= \frac{22}{15}$ or $1\frac{7}{15}$

EST $\frac{2}{3} \rightarrow \frac{1}{2}$　$\frac{4}{5} \rightarrow 1$

$\frac{1}{2} + 1 = 1\frac{1}{2}$

b) $2\frac{3}{4} + 3\frac{2}{3}$　← Find the LCD.

$= 2\frac{9}{12} + 3\frac{8}{12}$　← Add the whole numbers.

$= 5 + \frac{9}{12} + \frac{8}{12}$　← Add the fractions.

$= 5\frac{17}{12}$　← Rename.

$= 6\frac{5}{12}$

EST $2\frac{3}{4} \rightarrow 3$　$3\frac{2}{3} \rightarrow 4$

$3 + 4 = 7$

Practice

Express all answers in lowest terms.

Write the addition indicated by each diagram and find the sum.

1.

2.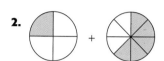

3.

Add.

4. $\frac{2}{5} + \frac{1}{5}$ 5. $\frac{7}{12} + \frac{5}{12}$

6. $\frac{4}{9} + \frac{2}{9}$ 7. $\frac{7}{8} + \frac{5}{8}$

Add.

8. $\frac{3}{4} + \frac{1}{2}$ 9. $\frac{5}{9} + \frac{2}{3}$ 10. $\frac{5}{12} + \frac{1}{4}$

11. $\frac{1}{4} + \frac{2}{3}$ 12. $\frac{1}{6} + \frac{3}{4}$ 13. $\frac{3}{8} + \frac{3}{4}$

Estimate, then add.

14. $2\frac{1}{4} + \frac{1}{4}$ 15. $3\frac{5}{8} + \frac{3}{8}$

16. $4\frac{1}{2} + 1\frac{1}{2}$ 17. $3\frac{3}{5} + 2\frac{4}{5}$

Estimate, then add.

18. $1\frac{1}{2} + \frac{1}{4}$ 19. $2\frac{3}{8} + 1\frac{1}{4}$

20. $2\frac{3}{10} + 1\frac{4}{5}$ 21. $1\frac{1}{2} + 2\frac{1}{3}$

22. $3\frac{2}{3} + 4\frac{3}{5}$ 23. $2\frac{1}{4} + 1\frac{1}{3}$

Estimate, then add.

24. $\frac{5}{8} + \frac{1}{2} + \frac{3}{8}$ 25. $\frac{3}{4} + \frac{1}{2} + \frac{3}{8}$

26. $\frac{3}{7} + \frac{5}{7} + 1\frac{1}{2}$ 27. $1\frac{1}{4} + 2\frac{1}{2} + 3$

Problems and Applications

28. Asia covers about $\frac{3}{10}$ of the area of all the continents, and Africa covers $\frac{1}{5}$. What fraction of the area of the continents do Asia and Africa cover together?

29. In a full set of permanent teeth, $\frac{1}{4}$ of the teeth are incisors, $\frac{1}{4}$ are premolars, and $\frac{3}{8}$ are molars. What fraction of all the teeth are incisors, premolars, or molars?

30. Quebec and Ontario together cover about $\frac{1}{4}$ of the area of Canada. The Territories cover about $\frac{2}{5}$, and the Prairie provinces about $\frac{1}{5}$. What fraction of the area of Canada do these regions cover together?

31. Nada made a snack by combining $\frac{1}{3}$ of a bowl of granola with $\frac{1}{4}$ of a bowl of chopped banana and $\frac{1}{2}$ of a bowl of yogurt. Did one bowl hold all the ingredients at one time? Explain.

32. In his first two hockey games of the season, Kent played about $1\frac{1}{2}$ periods and $1\frac{3}{4}$ periods. About how many periods in all did he play?

33. Write 2 different fractions
    a) with a sum of $\frac{1}{2}$ b) with a sum of $1\frac{1}{2}$

34. Write a problem that involves the addition of fractions or mixed numbers. Have a classmate solve your problem.

5.4 Subtracting Fractions

About $\frac{3}{10}$ of Canadians live in the 4 western provinces.
About $\frac{1}{10}$ of Canadians live in Alberta. The fraction of
Canadians in the other 3 western provinces is $\frac{3}{10} - \frac{1}{10}$.
To subtract 2 fractions with the same denominator,
subtract the numerators.

$\frac{3}{10} - \frac{1}{10} = \frac{2}{10}$ or $\frac{1}{5}$

So, the fraction of Canadians who live in British
Columbia, Saskatchewan, or Manitoba is about $\frac{1}{5}$.

Activity: Use the Information

Before the school picnic, the gauge on the barbecue's
propane tank showed it was $\frac{3}{4}$ full. At the end of the day,
the gauge showed the tank was $\frac{1}{8}$ full.

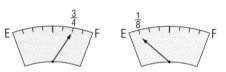

Inquire

1. Read the gauge. What fraction is
equivalent to $\frac{3}{4}$?

2. What fraction of the tank was used at
the picnic?

3. Describe a method of subtracting fractions
with different denominators.

4. Use diagrams to show that $\frac{5}{12} - \frac{1}{4}$ does not
equal $\frac{4}{8}$.

Example

Subtract. **a)** $\frac{4}{5} - \frac{1}{2}$ **b)** $3\frac{1}{2} - 1\frac{2}{3}$

Solution

To subtract fractions with different denominators, write
equivalent fractions with the lowest common denominator.

a) The LCD of 5 and 2 is 10.

$$\overset{\times 2}{\frac{4}{5} = \frac{8}{10}}\underset{\times 2}{} \qquad \overset{\times 5}{\frac{1}{2} = \frac{5}{10}}\underset{\times 5}{}$$

$\frac{4}{5} - \frac{1}{2} = \frac{8}{10} - \frac{5}{10}$ **EST** $1 - \frac{1}{2} = \frac{1}{2}$

$\quad = \frac{8-5}{10}$

$\quad = \frac{3}{10}$

b) The LCD of 2 and 3 is 6.

$3\frac{1}{2} - 1\frac{2}{3}$ **EST** $4 - 2 = 2$

$= 3\frac{3}{6} - 1\frac{4}{6}$ ← $3 < 4$, so rewrite the first mixed number.

$= 2\frac{9}{6} - 1\frac{4}{6}$ ← Subtract whole numbers, then fractions.

$= 1\frac{5}{6}$

Practice

Express all answers in lowest terms.

Find the difference.

1. $\frac{5}{12} - \frac{4}{12}$ *even* **2.** $\frac{3}{4} - \frac{1}{4}$

3. $\frac{7}{9} - \frac{4}{9}$ **4.** $\frac{5}{8} - \frac{3}{8}$

Subtract.

5. $\frac{5}{8} - \frac{1}{2}$ **6.** $\frac{2}{5} - \frac{1}{10}$ **7.** $\frac{5}{6} - \frac{1}{3}$

8. $\frac{2}{3} - \frac{1}{2}$ **9.** $\frac{1}{2} - \frac{1}{6}$ **10.** $\frac{3}{4} - \frac{2}{3}$

Estimate, then subtract.

11. $2\frac{3}{5} - \frac{1}{5}$ **12.** $4\frac{7}{8} - \frac{5}{8}$

13. $5\frac{3}{4} - 1\frac{1}{4}$ **14.** $3\frac{1}{6} - 1\frac{5}{6}$

Estimate, then subtract.

15. $2\frac{3}{4} - \frac{1}{2}$ **16.** $1\frac{3}{8} - \frac{1}{4}$

17. $2\frac{1}{6} - \frac{1}{2}$ **18.** $4\frac{1}{4} - 1\frac{1}{2}$

19. $1\frac{1}{2} - \frac{1}{3}$ **20.** $3\frac{1}{2} - 1\frac{1}{5}$

21. $2\frac{1}{4} - 1\frac{2}{3}$ **22.** $3\frac{1}{6} - 1\frac{1}{4}$

Problems and Applications

23. About $\frac{1}{4}$ of the world's motor vehicles are built in Canada or the United States. About $\frac{1}{5}$ of the world's motor vehicles are built in the United States. What fraction of the world's motor vehicles are built in Canada?

 24. a) Describe how you would find the answer to this problem.
$\frac{2}{3} + \blacksquare = 1\frac{5}{6}$
b) Calculate the answer.

Find the missing value.

25. $\frac{9}{10} - \blacksquare = \frac{1}{2}$ **26.** $\blacksquare - \frac{3}{4} = \frac{2}{3}$

27. $1\frac{3}{4} - \blacksquare = \frac{5}{8}$ **28.** $\blacksquare - \frac{5}{6} = 2\frac{1}{4}$

29. Daniel ran $2\frac{2}{3}$ laps of the track. Carol ran $2\frac{3}{4}$ laps.
a) Who ran farther?
b) How much farther?

30. Interprovincial Pipeline stock prices varied one day from $\$29\frac{3}{4}$ to $\$30\frac{1}{2}$. By how much did the price change?

 31. About $\frac{1}{2}$ of Canada is covered in forest, and about $\frac{1}{12}$ is covered in fresh water. What fraction of Canada is not covered in either forest or fresh water?

 32. Write two fractions
a) with a difference of $\frac{1}{4}$
b) with a difference of $\frac{3}{8}$
c) that have different denominators and a difference of $\frac{1}{2}$

33. Write a problem that involves the subtraction of fractions or mixed numbers. Have a classmate solve your problem.

PATTERN POWER

Look for the pattern, then draw the fourth diagram.

Multiplying Fractions Using Paper Folding

Activity ❶ Folding Fractions

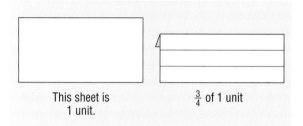

This sheet is
1 unit.

$\frac{3}{4}$ of 1 unit

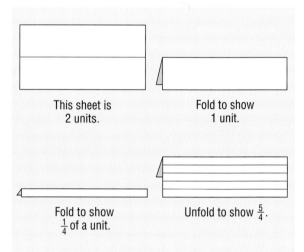

This sheet is
2 units.

Fold to show
1 unit.

Fold to show
$\frac{1}{4}$ of a unit.

Unfold to show $\frac{5}{4}$.

Work with a classmate. Show the following fractions by paper folding.

1. $\frac{2}{3}$ **2.** $\frac{5}{6}$ **3.** $\frac{7}{5}$ **4.** $1\frac{1}{2}$

Activity ❷ Multiplying Fractions Less Than 1

This folding method shows the product of $\frac{1}{3} \times \frac{2}{3}$.

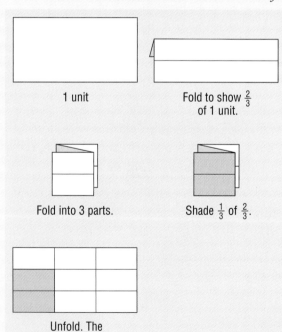

1 unit

Fold to show $\frac{2}{3}$
of 1 unit.

Fold into 3 parts.

Shade $\frac{1}{3}$ of $\frac{2}{3}$.

Unfold. The
product is $\frac{2}{9}$.

Work with a classmate. Find the products by paper folding.

1. $\frac{1}{2} \times \frac{3}{4}$ **2.** $\frac{2}{3} \times \frac{2}{3}$ **3.** $\frac{3}{4} \times \frac{1}{4}$

4. $\frac{1}{4} \times \frac{2}{3}$ **5.** $\frac{1}{6} \times \frac{1}{2}$ **6.** $\frac{2}{3} \times \frac{1}{3}$

7. Use the example and your answer to question 6 to compare the product of $\frac{1}{3} \times \frac{2}{3}$ with the product of $\frac{2}{3} \times \frac{1}{3}$. Does the order of the fractions affect their product?

Activity ❸ Multiplying Fractions Greater Than 1

This folding method shows the product of $\frac{2}{3} \times \frac{5}{4}$.

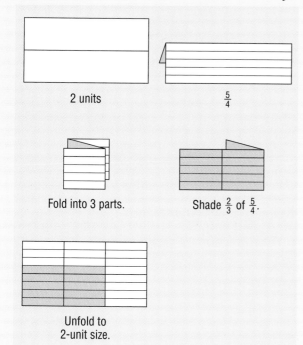

2 units $\frac{5}{4}$

Fold into 3 parts.   Shade $\frac{2}{3}$ of $\frac{5}{4}$.

Unfold to
2-unit size.

In the unfolded result, 10 parts are shaded. There are 12 equal parts *in each unit*. So, the 10 shaded parts represent $\frac{10}{12}$.

$$\frac{2}{3} \times \frac{5}{4} = \frac{10}{12}$$

Work with a classmate. Find the products by paper folding.

1. $\frac{1}{2} \times \frac{4}{3}$ **2.** $\frac{1}{2} \times \frac{3}{2}$ **3.** $\frac{3}{4} \times 1\frac{2}{3}$

Activity ❹ A Special Case

This folding method shows the product of $\frac{1}{2} \times 2$.

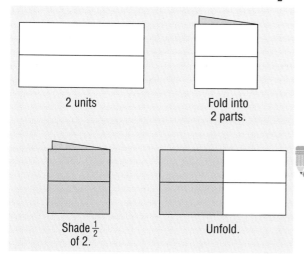

2 units   Fold into
                           2 parts.

Shade $\frac{1}{2}$ Unfold.
of 2.

In the unfolded result, 2 parts are shaded. There are 2 equal parts in each unit. So, the 2 shaded parts represent $\frac{2}{2}$ or 1.

Work with a classmate. Find the products by paper folding.

1. $\frac{1}{3} \times 3$ **2.** $\frac{2}{3} \times \frac{3}{2}$ **3.** $\frac{3}{4} \times \frac{4}{3}$

4. What kinds of fractions give a product of 1?

189

5.5 Multiplying Fractions

The area of Canada is about 10 million square kilometres. The Prairie provinces make up $\frac{1}{5}$ of Canada's area.

$\frac{1}{5}$ of 10 is $\frac{1}{5} \times 10$ or 2. So, the area of the Prairie provinces is about 2 million square kilometres.

Activity: Use the Diagram

The diagram shows the fraction of Canada's area covered by the Northwest Territories. The Northwest Territories are divided into three districts: Franklin, Keewatin, and Mackenzie. The diagram also shows the fraction of the Northwest Territories covered by the Franklin District.

Inquire

1. What fraction of Canada's area do the Northwest Territories cover?

2. What fraction of the Northwest Territories' area does the Franklin District cover?

3. What fraction of Canada's area does the Franklin District cover?

4. What is $\frac{1}{2}$ of $\frac{1}{3}$?

 **5.** Describe a method of multiplying fractions.

Example 1

Multiply.　　**a)** $\frac{3}{4} \times \frac{2}{5}$　　**b)** $1\frac{2}{3} \times 1\frac{1}{5}$

Solution

a) $\frac{3}{4} \times \frac{2}{5}$　← Multiply the numerators. Multiply the denominators.

$= \frac{6}{20}$　← Write the answer in lowest terms.

$= \frac{3}{10}$　**EST** $1 \times \frac{1}{2} = \frac{1}{2}$

b) Write the mixed numbers as improper fractions, then multiply.

$1\frac{2}{3} \times 1\frac{1}{5} = \frac{5}{3} \times \frac{6}{5}$

$= \frac{30}{15}$

$= \frac{2}{1}$ or 2　**EST** $2 \times 1 = 2$

Two numbers whose product is 1 are **reciprocals**.
Since $\frac{3}{4} \times \frac{4}{3}$ is $\frac{12}{12}$ or 1, $\frac{3}{4}$ and $\frac{4}{3}$ are reciprocals.

Example 2

Find the reciprocals.　　**a)** $\frac{2}{3}$　　**b)** 6　　**c)** $2\frac{1}{2}$

Solution

a) The reciprocal is $\frac{3}{2}$, since $\frac{2}{3} \times \frac{3}{2} = 1$.

b) The reciprocal is $\frac{1}{6}$, since $6 \times \frac{1}{6} = 1$.

c) Write $2\frac{1}{2}$ as $\frac{5}{2}$. The reciprocal is $\frac{2}{5}$, since $\frac{5}{2} \times \frac{2}{5} = 1$.

Practice

Write all answers in simplest form.

Multiply.

1. $\frac{1}{4} \times \frac{1}{3}$ **2.** $\frac{2}{3} \times \frac{1}{5}$ **3.** $\frac{1}{2} \times \frac{3}{4}$

4. $\frac{5}{8} \times \frac{2}{3}$ **5.** $\frac{3}{5} \times \frac{5}{6}$ **6.** $\frac{3}{4} \times \frac{5}{6}$

Calculate.

7. $\frac{1}{2}$ of $\frac{1}{4}$ **8.** $\frac{3}{4}$ of $\frac{2}{3}$

9. $\frac{2}{3}$ of 6   **10.** $\frac{3}{5}$ of 15

Estimate, then multiply.

11. $3 \times 1\frac{1}{2}$ **12.** $2\frac{1}{4} \times 4$

13. $3 \times 2\frac{1}{6}$ **14.** $1\frac{2}{3} \times 4$

15. $\frac{1}{4} \times 2\frac{1}{3}$ **16.** $\frac{3}{8} \times 1\frac{1}{2}$

17. $\frac{4}{5} \times 3\frac{3}{4}$ **18.** $2\frac{3}{4} \times 3\frac{1}{3}$

19. $2\frac{1}{2} \times 1\frac{1}{9}$ **20.** $3\frac{1}{6} \times 1\frac{3}{4}$

Multiply.

21. $\frac{2}{3} \times \frac{1}{2} \times \frac{4}{5}$ **22.** $\frac{1}{4} \times 2 \times \frac{5}{6}$

23. $\frac{1}{2} \times 2\frac{1}{3} \times \frac{3}{4}$ **24.** $1\frac{1}{5} \times 2\frac{1}{2} \times 3\frac{2}{3}$

Write the reciprocal.

25. $\frac{1}{4}$ **26.** 3 **27.** $\frac{3}{5}$ **28.** $\frac{5}{4}$

29. $\frac{2}{9}$ **30.** $3\frac{1}{2}$ **31.** $2\frac{1}{3}$ **32.** $1\frac{7}{8}$

Problems and Applications

33. Insects account for about $\frac{5}{6}$ of known animal species. About $\frac{1}{4}$ of insect species are species of beetles. What fraction of all animal species are species of beetles?

34. A marsupial, such as a kangaroo, carries its young in a pouch. About $\frac{1}{25}$ of mammal species are marsupials. About 4250 species of mammals are known. How many species of marsupials are there?

35. Forests once covered $\frac{1}{3}$ of the land on Earth. Two thirds of the forested land has been cleared. What fraction of the land on Earth is now covered in forests?

36. The Bayview Bobcats play an 80-game season. They won $\frac{3}{5}$ of their games in the first half of the season and $\frac{3}{4}$ of their games in the second half of the season. How many games did they win in all?

37. Summerside has $\frac{1}{2}$ as many thunderstorms per year as Edmonton. How many times more thunderstorms per year does Edmonton have than Summerside?

38. Neptune completes $1\frac{1}{2}$ turns about its axis each day. How many turns does it complete in
a) 1 week?   **b)** April?   **c)** 12 h?

39. Can the reciprocal of a mixed number be another mixed number? Explain.

LOGIC POWER

The circle and the square intersect at 2 points.

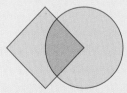

Draw diagrams to show a circle and a square intersecting at 3, 4, and 5 points.

5.6 Dividing Fractions

Kenji buys grapefruit in bags of 4. He eats $\frac{1}{2}$
of a grapefruit with his breakfast each day.
The 4 grapefruit last him 8 days. So, $4 \div \frac{1}{2} = 8$.

Activity: Study the Process

Dividing by fractions uses two ideas you are familiar with.

• Any number divided by 1 gives the number.

$$3 \div 1 = 3 \qquad 2.5 \div 1 = 2.5 \qquad \frac{1}{2} \div 1 = \frac{1}{2}$$

• If the dividend and divisor in a division are multiplied by the
same power of 10, the value of the quotient does not change.

$0.2 \overline{)2.32}$ becomes $0.2 \times 10 \overline{)2.32 \times 10}$, which is $2 \overline{)23.2}$

Now, combine these two ideas to simplify dividing fractions.
Multiply the dividend and divisor by the same fraction to make
the divisor 1.

Copy and complete the table. The first row is done for you.

Division	Multiplication to Make the Divisor 1	New Expression	Answer
$\frac{1}{3} \div \frac{1}{2}$	$\frac{1}{3} \times \frac{2}{1} \div \frac{1}{2} \times \frac{2}{1}$	$\frac{1}{3} \times \frac{2}{1} \div 1$	$\frac{2}{3}$
$\frac{2}{5} \div \frac{1}{3}$			
$\frac{1}{2} \div \frac{1}{4}$			
$\frac{3}{4} \div \frac{2}{3}$			
$\frac{3}{8} \div 2$			
$4 \div \frac{3}{2}$			

Inquire

1. What name is given to the fraction that
multiplies the divisor to make it 1?

 2. In your own words, describe a method
of dividing fractions.

Example

Divide.

a) $\frac{3}{4} \div \frac{2}{5}$

b) $2\frac{2}{3} \div 1\frac{1}{2}$

Solution

To divide by a fraction, multiply by its reciprocal.

a) $\frac{3}{4} \div \frac{2}{5}$ **EST** $1 \div \frac{1}{2} = 2$

$= \frac{3}{4} \times \frac{5}{2}$

$= \frac{15}{8}$ or $1\frac{7}{8}$

b) Write the mixed numbers as
improper fractions, then divide.

$2\frac{2}{3} \div 1\frac{1}{2}$ **EST** $3 \div 2 = \frac{3}{2}$ or $1\frac{1}{2}$

$= \frac{8}{3} \div \frac{3}{2}$

$= \frac{8}{3} \times \frac{2}{3}$

$= \frac{16}{9}$ or $1\frac{7}{9}$

Practice

Write all answers in lowest terms.

Divide.

1. $\frac{1}{2} \div \frac{1}{4}$ **2.** $\frac{3}{8} \div \frac{1}{4}$

3. $\frac{3}{8} \div \frac{1}{2}$ **4.** $\frac{2}{3} \div \frac{3}{5}$

Divide.

5. $3 \div \frac{1}{3}$ **6.** $4 \div \frac{1}{2}$

7. $6 \div \frac{2}{3}$ **8.** $\frac{1}{3} \div 2$

Find the quotient.

9. $2\frac{1}{2} \div \frac{1}{2}$ **10.** $2\frac{3}{4} \div \frac{1}{4}$

11. $\frac{4}{5} \div 1\frac{1}{3}$ **12.** $\frac{3}{4} \div 1\frac{2}{3}$

13. $\frac{5}{9} \div 1\frac{2}{3}$ **14.** $2\frac{1}{4} \div 1\frac{1}{2}$

15. $2\frac{3}{4} \div 1\frac{1}{2}$ **16.** $1\frac{5}{8} \div 2\frac{1}{2}$

Problems and Applications

17. How many people can you serve with 6 pizzas if each person has $\frac{3}{4}$ of a pizza?

18. Nine tenths of a grade 8 class are in the gym. If these students are divided into 3 equal groups, what fraction of the class will be in each group?

19. Michael has a piece of tape that is $7\frac{4}{5}$ units long. If he cuts it into pieces that are each $\frac{3}{5}$ of a unit long, how many pieces will he have?

20. It takes $\frac{3}{4}$ of a minute to do a lap on your bicycle at the velodrome. How many laps could you do in $\frac{1}{2}$ hour?

21. The power used by a light bulb is measured in watts, W. If a light bulb uses $3\frac{3}{4}$ times less power than a 150-W bulb, how much power does it use?

22. The maximum life span of a leopard is 24 years. This life span is $\frac{3}{10}$ of the maximum life span of a salamander. What is the maximum life span of a salamander?

23. Without doing an actual calculation, how would you explain to someone that $6 \div 2\frac{3}{4}$ has an answer closer to 2 than to 3?

24. If you divide a number by a fraction less than 1, is the result larger or smaller than the original number? Explain.

25. a) Work with a classmate to find the quotients for the following problems.

$\frac{2}{3} \div \frac{1}{3}$ $\frac{4}{5} \div \frac{2}{5}$ $\frac{6}{8} \div \frac{3}{8}$

$\frac{2}{10} \div \frac{8}{10}$ $\frac{3}{10} \div \frac{2}{10}$ $\frac{5}{9} \div \frac{4}{9}$ $\frac{2}{5} \div \frac{4}{5}$

b) What do the divisions in part a) have in common?

c) For each division in part a), find the quotient for only the numerators.

d) Write an alternative method for dividing fractions.

e) Test your method on the following divisions.

$\frac{3}{4} \div \frac{1}{2}$ $\frac{5}{6} \div \frac{2}{3}$ $\frac{1}{2} \div \frac{1}{5}$

$2 \div \frac{1}{4}$ $1\frac{1}{4} \div \frac{1}{2}$ $2\frac{1}{2} \div 1\frac{1}{3}$

Patterns in Rectangles

Mathematics is a study of patterns. Once a pattern is found, rules can often be written to describe it.

Activity ❶ 2-by-■ Rectangles

A 2-by-4 rectangle is made up of 8 squares. A diagonal passes through 4 squares.

A 2-by-5 rectangle is made up of 10 squares. A diagonal passes through 6 squares.

Draw the rectangles from 2-by-1 to 2-by-10. Draw a diagonal in each rectangle. Copy and complete the table.

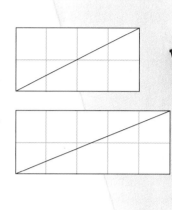

Dimensions	Squares Passed Through
2-by-1	
⋮	
2-by-4	4
2-by-5	6
⋮	
2-by-10	

 1. Describe the pattern in the right-hand column of the table.

2. Extend the table for the next 4 rectangles. Complete the "Squares Passed Through" column without drawing the rectangles and diagonals.

3. How many squares would the diagonal pass through in a 2-by-26 rectangle? a 2-by-31 rectangle?

 4. Write a rule to find the number of squares a diagonal passes through if the second dimension is a multiple of 2.

5. Use your rule to find the number of squares a diagonal passes through in each of these rectangles.
a) 2-by-50   **b)** 2-by-88   **c)** 2-by-2000

 6. Write a rule to find the number of squares a diagonal passes through if the second dimension is not a multiple of 2.

7. Use your rule to find the number of squares a diagonal passes through in each of these rectangles.
a) 2-by-53   **b)** 2-by-99   **c)** 2-by-2013

8. What are the possible values of the second dimension of a rectangle whose diagonal passes through
a) 20 squares?   **b)** 126 squares?   **c)** 210 squares?

Activity ❷ 3-by-■ Rectangles

Draw the rectangles from 3-by-1 to 3-by-9.
Draw a diagonal in each rectangle.

Copy and complete the table.

Dimensions	Squares Passed Through
3-by-1	
:	
3-by-9	

 1. Write a rule to find the number of squares a diagonal passes through if the second dimension is a multiple of 3.

2. Use your rule to find the number of squares a diagonal passes through in each of these rectangles.
a) 3-by-36   **b)** 3-by-45   **c)** 3-by-3000

3. What is the second dimension of a rectangle whose diagonal passes through 333 squares?

 4. Write a rule to find the number of squares a diagonal passes through if the second dimension is not a multiple of 3.

5. Use your rule to find the number of squares a diagonal passes through in each of these rectangles.
a) 3-by-28   **b)** 3-by-44   **c)** 3-by-2000

6. What is the second dimension of a rectangle whose diagonal passes through 79 squares?

Activity ❸ 4-by-■ Rectangles

Draw the rectangles from 4-by-1 to 4-by-8.
Draw a diagonal in each rectangle.

Copy and complete the table.

Dimensions	Squares Passed Through
4-by-1	
:	
4-by-8	

 1. Write rules to find the number of squares a diagonal passes through if you are given the second dimension.

2. Test your rules by drawing the next 4 rectangles and one diagonal for each.

3. Use your rules to find the number of squares a diagonal passes through in each of these rectangles.
a) 4-by-42   **b)** 4-by-55   **c)** 4-by-44

5.7 Fractions and Decimals

A 25-cent piece is called a quarter because it is a quarter of a dollar.

As a fraction, 25¢ is written as $\frac{25}{100}$ of a dollar.

As a decimal, 25¢ is written as 0.25 dollars.

Every fraction can be written as a decimal, and many decimals can be written as fractions.

Activity: Copy and Complete the Tables

Table 1				Table 2		
Decimal	Fraction (Denominator = 10, 100, or 1000)	Fraction in Lowest Terms		Fraction	Division	Decimal
0.6	$\frac{6}{10}$	$\frac{3}{5}$		$\frac{4}{5}$	$4 \div 5$	0.8
0.45				$\frac{3}{4}$		
0.28				$\frac{7}{8}$		
0.375				$\frac{11}{20}$		
0.35				$\frac{2}{3}$		

Inquire

1. Write 1.15 in fraction form. Describe your method.

2. Write $1\frac{1}{8}$ in decimal form. Describe your method.

3. In Table 2, the first 4 decimals are called **terminating decimals**. Explain why.

4. In Table 2, the last decimal is called a **repeating decimal**. Explain why.

Example 1

Write each fraction as a decimal. State whether the decimal is repeating or terminating.

a) $\frac{5}{16}$ **b)** $\frac{3}{11}$

Solution

Use a calculator.

a) [C] 5 [÷] 16 [=] [0.3125]

So, $\frac{5}{16} = 0.3125$.

The calculator display ends at the fourth decimal place. The decimal is terminating.

b) [C] 3 [÷] 11 [=] [0.2727272]

So, $\frac{3}{11} = 0.2727272\ldots$ or $0.\overline{27}$.

> Use a bar to show the digits that repeat.

The decimal does not end. It is repeating.

Example 2

Express $0.\overline{3}$ as a fraction in lowest terms.

Solution

Let $A = 0.\overline{3}$ or $0.3333\ldots$

Multiply by 10. $10A = 3.\overline{3}$

Subtract. $\underline{\quad A = 0.\overline{3}\quad}$

                $9A = 3$

Divide by 9. $\frac{9A}{9} = \frac{3}{9}$

               $A = \frac{3}{9}$ or $\frac{1}{3}$

So, $0.\overline{3} = \frac{1}{3}$.

Check: [C] 1 [÷] 3 [=] [0.3333333]

Practice

Express the following using bar notation.

1. 0.343434...   **2.** 12.727272...

3. 4.5676767...   **4.** 0.2571571...

Find the equivalent fraction, then convert to a decimal.

5. $\dfrac{3}{5} = \dfrac{\blacksquare}{10}$ **6.** $\dfrac{2}{25} = \dfrac{\blacksquare}{100}$

7. $\dfrac{1}{2} = \dfrac{\blacksquare}{10}$ **8.** $\dfrac{3}{20} = \dfrac{\blacksquare}{100}$

9. $\dfrac{3}{200} = \dfrac{\blacksquare}{1000}$ **10.** $\dfrac{7}{500} = \dfrac{\blacksquare}{1000}$

Write as a decimal.

11. $\dfrac{2}{5}$ **12.** $\dfrac{6}{25}$ **13.** $\dfrac{2}{9}$

14. $\dfrac{5}{12}$ **15.** $\dfrac{1}{6}$ **16.** $\dfrac{8}{3}$

17. $1\dfrac{3}{16}$ **18.** $2\dfrac{5}{6}$ **19.** $3\dfrac{1}{9}$

Express as a fraction in lowest terms.

20. 0.777...   **21.** $0.\overline{1}$

22. 0.222...   **23.** $0.\overline{5}$

Express as a mixed number in lowest terms.

24. 1.444...   **25.** 7.666...

Problems and Applications

26. Write the fractions as decimals, then order them from largest to smallest.

$\dfrac{3}{8}$ $\dfrac{2}{5}$ $\dfrac{1}{3}$ $\dfrac{4}{11}$ $\dfrac{3}{10}$

27. Express each number in the following statements as a decimal.

a) Whitehorse gets $3\dfrac{2}{3}$ times as many days of frost a year as Victoria.

b) In January, Iqaluit's precipitation is $\dfrac{2}{9}$ of Charlottetown's precipitation.

c) Dawson's elevation above sea level is $2\dfrac{1}{10}$ times Sault Ste. Marie's.

28. a) Find the decimal equivalents for $\dfrac{1}{11}$, $\dfrac{2}{11}$, $\dfrac{3}{11}$, and $\dfrac{4}{11}$.

b) What pattern do you notice?

c) Use the pattern to predict the decimal equivalents for $\dfrac{5}{11}$ and $\dfrac{8}{11}$.

29. a) Use your calculator to try to find the decimal equivalent of $\dfrac{3}{13}$. Can you tell if the decimal equivalent is terminating or repeating? Explain.

b) Work with a partner to find the decimal equivalent of $\dfrac{3}{13}$ with paper and pencil. How many digits occur before they repeat?

30. Write 0.3434... or $0.\overline{34}$ as a fraction in lowest terms. Describe your method.

PATTERN POWER

The table shows the area, the perimeter, and the quotient $\dfrac{\text{area}}{\text{perimeter}}$ for squares with different side lengths.

Side Length	Area of Square	Perimeter of Square	Area / Perimeter
1	1	4	$\dfrac{1}{4}$
2	4	8	$\dfrac{1}{2}$ or $\dfrac{2}{4}$
3	9	12	$\dfrac{3}{4}$
4	16	16	1 or $\dfrac{4}{4}$

a) Copy the table and complete the next 3 lines of the table.

b) Describe the pattern in the quotients in words.

c) Use the pattern to predict the quotients for side lengths of 10, 50, and 360.

5.8 Order of Operations

When solving problems involving fractions and several operations, use the same order of operations you use with whole numbers and decimals.

B   Do operations in brackets first.
E   Simplify numbers with exponents.
$\left.\begin{array}{l}\textbf{D}\\\textbf{M}\end{array}\right\}$ Divide and multiply in order from left to right.
$\left.\begin{array}{l}\textbf{A}\\\textbf{S}\end{array}\right\}$ Add and subtract in order from left to right.

Activity: Evaluate the Expression

Suppose that the fraction of stars with a planetary system in our galaxy is $\frac{1}{4}$ and that the fraction of the planetary systems with intelligent life is $\frac{1}{10}$. Then, the number of planets supporting intelligent life can be estimated from the following expression.
$4000 \times \frac{1}{4} - 9000 \times \frac{1}{10} - 85$

Inquire

1. If the assumptions are correct, how many planets could support intelligent life?

2. If $\frac{1}{4}$ is changed to $\frac{1}{2}$, how many planets could support intelligent life?

3. If $\frac{1}{4}$ is changed to $\frac{1}{2}$, and $\frac{1}{10}$ to $\frac{1}{9}$, how many planets could support intelligent life?

Example 1

Evaluate $3\frac{1}{2} \times 8 + 4\frac{1}{2} \times 12$.

Solution

Rewrite the mixed numbers as improper fractions. Then, follow the order of operations.

$3\frac{1}{2} \times 8 + 4\frac{1}{2} \times 12$

$= \frac{7}{2} \times 8 + \frac{9}{2} \times 12$ **multiply**

$= \frac{56}{2} + \frac{108}{2}$ **add**

$= \frac{164}{2}$

$= 82$

Example 2

Evaluate $2^2 - \left(\frac{5}{8} + \frac{3}{4}\right) \div \frac{1}{2}$.

Solution

$2^2 - \left(\frac{5}{8} + \frac{3}{4}\right) \div \frac{1}{2}$ **brackets**

$= 2^2 - \frac{11}{8} \div \frac{1}{2}$ **exponent**

$= 4 - \frac{11}{8} \div \frac{1}{2}$ **divide**

$= 4 - \frac{22}{8}$ Write in lowest terms.

$= 4 - \frac{11}{4}$ **subtract**

$= \frac{16}{4} - \frac{11}{4}$

$= \frac{5}{4}$ or $1\frac{1}{4}$

Practice

Write all answers in simplest form.

Copy each problem. Then, underline the part to be calculated first.

1. $\frac{3}{4} - \frac{2}{3} + \frac{1}{2}$

2. $\frac{5}{6} - \frac{1}{2} \times \frac{1}{3}$

3. $\frac{3}{8} + \frac{1}{4} \div \frac{1}{2}$

4. $\frac{1}{2} \times \frac{3}{4} \div \frac{3}{8}$

5. $1\frac{1}{2} \div \frac{1}{4} \times \frac{2}{3}$

6. $2 \times \left(1\frac{1}{2} + 1\frac{1}{5}\right)$

Calculate.

7. $4 \times \frac{2}{3} \div \frac{1}{2}$

8. $\frac{2}{3} \div \frac{3}{4} \div \frac{1}{2}$

9. $1\frac{1}{2} - \frac{1}{2} \times \frac{3}{4}$

10. $3 + 1\frac{1}{2} \times \frac{1}{3}$

11. $3\frac{1}{5} - \left(\frac{7}{10} - \frac{1}{2}\right)$

12. $\left(\frac{1}{2}\right)^2 + \frac{1}{3} \times \frac{1}{4}$

13. $1\frac{1}{5} - \left(\frac{3}{10} \div \frac{1}{3}\right)$

14. $\frac{3}{4} \div \left(\frac{1}{6} + \frac{1}{3}\right)$

 Work with a partner on each question. One partner does the first step, the other does the second step, and so on.

15. $\frac{3}{4} - \frac{2}{3} \times \frac{1}{4}$

16. $\frac{1}{4} + \frac{1}{2} \times \frac{2}{3} \div \frac{1}{3}$

17. $4^2 - 1\frac{1}{2} \times 2 - 3$

18. $\left(\frac{3}{4} - \frac{1}{3}\right) \times \frac{3}{4} \times 4$

Problems and Applications

19. Two thirds of the 132 grade 8s and one half of the 114 grade 9s want to go skiing.
a) Write a mathematical expression to calculate the total number of students who wish to ski.
b) Calculate the total number of students who wish to ski.

20. Kwan spent $1\frac{1}{2}$ hours studying on Monday and $1\frac{2}{3}$ hours studying on Tuesday. If she spent $\frac{1}{4}$ of the total time studying math, for what fraction of an hour did Kwan study math?

21. Add brackets to the left side of the statement to make it true.
$$\frac{3}{4} + \frac{1}{2} - \frac{1}{3} \times 2 = \frac{13}{12}$$

22. Gio bought 120 Domtar shares at $\$6\frac{7}{8}$ each and sold them for $\$7\frac{1}{4}$ each. How much money did he make? Show two ways to make the calculation.

23. One day, the *Greenville Gleaner* newspaper ran 4 advertisements at $\frac{1}{20}$ of a page each, 2 at $\frac{1}{5}$ of a page each, 1 at $\frac{1}{2}$ a page, and 1 at a full page. Did all the advertisements fit onto 2 pages?

24. The average Canadian spends about $\frac{2}{5}$ of the time on leisure activities and $\frac{1}{3}$ of the time sleeping. How many hours a day does the average Canadian spend on leisure activities or sleeping? Write your answer as a mixed number of hours.

25. Simplify.
a) $\dfrac{\frac{1}{2} + \frac{1}{3}}{4 + \frac{1}{2}}$

b) $\dfrac{\frac{2}{3} \div \frac{5}{6}}{3 + 2}$

26. Choose 2 different operations from $+$, $-$, $\times$, and $\div$ to give this expression the largest possible value. $\frac{1}{4} \blacklozenge \frac{1}{2} \blacklozenge \frac{1}{8}$

27. Write an expression involving fractions and the operations $+$, $\times$, and $\div$. Give it to a classmate to evaluate. Then, check that the answer is correct.

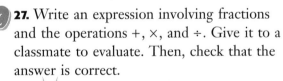

NUMBER POWER

The product of the ages of 3 children is 36. The sum of their ages is a perfect square. How old are the children?

Fractions and Calculators

Activity ❶ Computing in Decimal Form

One way to calculate $1\frac{3}{4} \div \frac{5}{8}$ is to write each fraction as a decimal and to divide the decimals with a calculator.

$$1\frac{3}{4} \div \frac{5}{8} = 1.75 \div 0.625$$
$$= 2.8$$

[C] 1 [.] 75 [÷] 0 [.] 625 [=] [_____ 2.8]

1. Complete the division $1\frac{3}{4} \div \frac{5}{8}$ without writing the fractions as decimals and without using a calculator. Does the answer in fractional form agree with the decimal answer shown above?

2. Complete each of the following calculations in 2 ways. First, leave the numbers in fractional form. Then, repeat the calculation using decimal form and a calculator. In each case, compare your answers and decide which method is faster.

a) $\frac{2}{5} + \frac{1}{4}$

b) $\frac{3}{4} + 1\frac{1}{2}$

c) $\frac{7}{8} - \frac{3}{8}$

d) $1\frac{3}{4} - 1\frac{1}{3}$

e) $\frac{2}{3} \times \frac{1}{2}$

f) $2\frac{1}{4} \times \frac{5}{6}$

g) $\frac{5}{8} \div \frac{3}{4}$

h) $\frac{9}{10} \div \frac{3}{10}$

i) $2\frac{1}{2} \div \frac{1}{4}$

j) $\frac{3}{5} \div 1\frac{1}{5}$

Activity ❷ Using the Order of Operations

1. Activity 1 included the example $1\frac{3}{4} \div \frac{5}{8}$.

a) What answer does your calculator give if you do not write the fractions as decimals and you try to do the calculation all at once? To find out, key in the following sequence.

[C] 1 [+] 3 [÷] 4 [÷] 5 [÷] 8 [=]

b) If your calculator has bracket keys, [(] and [)], work out a way of using them to get the correct answer. Compare your calculator sequence with your classmates' sequences.

c) How can you use the memory keys on your calculator to get the correct answer? Compare your calculator sequence with your classmates' sequences.

2. Use the bracket keys or memory keys on your calculator to evaluate the following. In each case, also complete the calculation with the numbers in fractional form. Compare your answers from each method.

a) $\frac{3}{5} + \frac{1}{4}$

b) $\frac{2}{5} + 1\frac{3}{4}$

c) $1\frac{1}{6} - \frac{2}{3}$

d) $1\frac{1}{2} - \frac{5}{8}$

e) $\frac{1}{3} \times 1\frac{1}{3}$

f) $1\frac{1}{8} \times 3\frac{1}{2}$

g) $2\frac{1}{6} \div \frac{3}{4}$

h) $\frac{1}{2} \div 1\frac{3}{8}$

i) $\frac{5}{9} - \frac{1}{3} \times \frac{3}{4}$

j) $\frac{1}{2} \times \frac{5}{6} + \frac{5}{12}$

Activity ❸ Using Calculators with Fraction Keys

Some calculators have keys that allow numbers to be entered as fractions. These calculators display answers in fractional form. Some calculators use a fraction key showing 〔d/c〕 or 〔ab/c〕 .

On a calculator with an 〔ab/c〕 key, the subtraction $2\frac{3}{4} - 1\frac{1}{8}$ is completed as follows.

〔C〕 2 〔ab/c〕 3 〔ab/c〕 4 〔−〕 1 〔ab/c〕 1 〔ab/c〕 8
〔=〕 [$1 \lrcorner 5 \lrcorner 8$]

Other calculators have a 〔/〕 key for fractions. On this type of calculator, the addition $\frac{2}{3} + \frac{1}{4}$ is completed as follows.

〔C〕 2 〔/〕 3 〔+〕 1 〔/〕 4 〔=〕 [$11/12$]

1. a) How might you enter the mixed number $1\frac{2}{3}$ on a calculator with a 〔/〕 key?

b) Try the addition $1\frac{2}{3} + \frac{1}{4}$ on your calculator.

2. Try the addition $\frac{1}{6} + \frac{1}{3}$ on your calculator. Did it show the answer in simplest form?

3. Try $\frac{5}{6} - \frac{1}{4} \times \frac{1}{3}$. Did the calculator carry out the order of operations correctly?

4. Complete the following calculations on your calculator.

a) $\frac{2}{5} + \frac{1}{2}$ **b)** $1\frac{3}{8} - \frac{2}{3}$ **c)** $\frac{1}{2} \times 2\frac{3}{4}$

d) $8 \div \frac{1}{4}$ **e)** $\frac{3}{4} \div 2\frac{1}{2}$ **f)** $1\frac{2}{3} - \frac{3}{4} \times \frac{1}{2}$

Review

Express all answers in lowest terms.

Express as a mixed number.

1. $\frac{11}{5}$ **2.** $\frac{17}{3}$

Write as an improper fraction.

3. $1\frac{2}{7}$ **4.** $2\frac{1}{3}$

5. Write 3 fractions equivalent to $\frac{3}{4}$.

Find the missing value.

6. $\frac{2}{5} = \frac{8}{\blacksquare}$ **7.** $\frac{\blacksquare}{4} = \frac{15}{12}$ **8.** $\frac{9}{36} = \frac{\blacksquare}{4}$

Replace ◆ with >, <, or = to make the statement true.

9. $\frac{2}{3}$ ◆ $\frac{1}{2}$ **10.** $\frac{3}{4}$ ◆ $\frac{7}{8}$ **11.** $1\frac{1}{2}$ ◆ $1\frac{5}{10}$

12. Order the fractions from largest to smallest. $\frac{3}{4}, \frac{7}{10}, \frac{13}{20}, \frac{4}{5}$

Estimate, then find the sum.

13. $\frac{1}{12} + \frac{5}{12}$ **14.** $\frac{3}{8} + \frac{1}{4}$

15. $1\frac{3}{4} + \frac{5}{6}$ **16.** $2\frac{1}{3} + 4\frac{5}{6}$

Estimate, then subtract.

17. $\frac{5}{6} - \frac{3}{4}$ **18.** $1\frac{1}{3} - \frac{2}{3}$

19. $3\frac{2}{5} - 2\frac{3}{4}$ **20.** $1\frac{3}{8} - 1\frac{1}{4}$

Estimate, then find the product.

21. $\frac{2}{3}$ of 15   **22.** $\frac{1}{4} \times \frac{3}{4}$

23. $2\frac{1}{2} \times \frac{4}{5}$ **24.** $2\frac{2}{3} \times \frac{3}{5} \times \frac{1}{4}$

25. $4 \times \frac{5}{6} \times \frac{1}{3}$ **26.** $3 \times 2\frac{1}{6}$

Write the reciprocal.

27. $\frac{1}{2}$ **28.** $\frac{3}{8}$ **29.** 3   **30.** $5\frac{1}{3}$

Estimate, then divide.

31. $\frac{3}{4} \div \frac{1}{2}$ **32.** $1\frac{1}{10} \div \frac{4}{5}$

33. $2\frac{1}{6} \div 1\frac{1}{3}$ **34.** $1\frac{1}{2} \div 2\frac{3}{4}$

Evaluate.

35. $\frac{1}{2} \times \left(\frac{1}{3} + \frac{3}{4} \right)$ **36.** $1\frac{2}{5} - \frac{1}{2} \times \frac{4}{5}$

37. $\left(\frac{5}{2} \times \frac{4}{5} \right)^2 - \frac{3}{5}$ **38.** $\frac{2}{3} \div \frac{1}{2} \times \frac{6}{7}$

Which of the following are repeating decimals?

39. 0.6 **40.** $\frac{3}{4}$

41. $3.2787878\ldots$ **42.** $\frac{5}{6}$

Write as a decimal.

43. $\frac{3}{5}$ **44.** $\frac{6}{11}$ **45.** $3\frac{7}{8}$ **46.** $1\frac{2}{15}$

Express as a fraction.

47. 0.24 **48.** 0.7 **49.** 1.45 **50.** $0.\overline{4}$

51. Jenise skated for 25 min. For what fraction of an hour did she skate?

52. Tien ran for $\frac{1}{2}$ an hour on Monday, $\frac{3}{4}$ of an hour on Thursday, and $\frac{1}{3}$ of an hour on Saturday. For how many hours did she run?

53. One tenth of Canadians aged 15 and over have a university degree. One fifth of the Canadians with degrees have a degree in education. What fraction of Canadians aged 15 and over have an education degree?

54. Kaitlin ate $\frac{3}{8}$ of a pizza, Michael ate $\frac{3}{4}$ of one, Nicole ate $\frac{1}{4}$, and Rob ate $\frac{1}{2}$ a pizza. There was $\frac{1}{8}$ of a pizza left. How many pizzas were there to begin with?

55. Brad, Kim, and Damian took $1\frac{1}{2}$ hours to cut and trim the lawn. If one of them had done the job alone, how long would it have taken? What assumptions have you made?

56. If $5\frac{1}{4}$ granola bars are shared equally by 6 people, what fraction of a bar does each person receive?

57. Renee ran $3\frac{3}{4}$ laps of a track. Jean ran $4\frac{1}{2}$ laps. How many more laps did Jean run than Renee?

58. Jeremy estimated he used $\frac{2}{3}$ of a tank of gas one day and $\frac{3}{5}$ of a tank the next day. He thought that $\frac{3}{4}$ of the driving he did was on business. What fraction of a tank did he use on business during the 2 days?

59. Of the national parks in Canada or the United States, about $\frac{3}{5}$ are in the United States. What fraction of the national parks are in Canada?

60. The greatest depth of snow on the ground at the Whistler Roundhouse weather station in British Columbia was about $2\frac{1}{2}$ times the greatest depth of snow at the Glenlea station in Manitoba. The greatest depth of snow recorded at Glenlea was about 180 cm. What was the greatest depth of snow at Whistler Roundhouse?

61. The average mass of a grizzly bear is about $\frac{4}{5}$ the average mass of a polar bear. Grizzly bears have a mass of about 340 kg. Find the mass of a polar bear.

62. Is each of the following situations possible? Explain.

a) Farsanah spent $\frac{1}{3}$ of the day sleeping, $\frac{3}{8}$ of the day working, $\frac{1}{12}$ of the day travelling to and from work, and $\frac{1}{4}$ of the day on other activities.

b) About $\frac{4}{5}$ of Canadians live to the east of Alberta. About $\frac{3}{5}$ of Canadians live in Ontario or Quebec.

Group Decision Making
Designing a Classroom Floor Plan

Work in home groups.

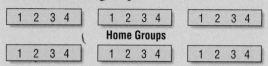

1. Make a rough sketch of the floor area of your classroom. Include fixtures, such as doors, windows, and counters. Do not include movable furniture, such as desks and chairs. Measure the dimensions of the floor and fixtures, and mark them on your sketch.

2. Use grid paper to draw a plan of your classroom floor. Again, include fixtures, but not movable furniture.

3. Measure the movable furniture and make a template for each piece. Use the same type of grid paper as you used for the floor plan. Cut out each template.

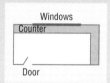

4. Experiment with different arrangements by moving the templates within the floor plan. Consider the effects of each arrangement on such issues as:
• the movement of students and the teacher
• the view of the chalkboard and screen
• the need to keep entrances clear
• the need for access to storage areas

5. Choose the plan you like best. Then, glue the templates onto your floor plan.

6. Display your floor plan with those of other groups. As a class, compare the floor plans and decide on the positive and negative points of each.

Chapter Check

Express all answers in lowest terms.

1. The grade 8 class has 15 boys and 12 girls. What fraction of the class are girls?

2. Express $2\frac{3}{4}$ as an improper fraction.

3. Write 2 fractions equivalent to $\frac{2}{3}$.

4. Find the missing value. $\frac{4}{9} = \frac{20}{\blacksquare}$

5. Replace ♦ with >, <, or = to make the statement true. $\frac{5}{6}$ ♦ $\frac{3}{4}$

6. Order from smallest to largest. $\frac{5}{6}, \frac{1}{2}, \frac{2}{3}, \frac{3}{4}$

Add.

7. $\frac{3}{10} + \frac{9}{10}$

8. $\frac{5}{6} + \frac{1}{2}$

9. $2\frac{5}{6} + \frac{2}{3}$

10. $1\frac{1}{2} + \frac{3}{4}$

Subtract.

11. $\frac{5}{9} - \frac{2}{9}$

12. $\frac{7}{12} - \frac{1}{4}$

13. $2\frac{1}{4} - 1\frac{2}{3}$

14. $5\frac{3}{4} - 3\frac{1}{6}$

Find the product.

15. $\frac{3}{5}$ of 10

16. $\frac{2}{9} \times \frac{3}{4}$

17. $\frac{2}{3} \times \frac{1}{4}$

18. $3\frac{2}{3} \times \frac{1}{2}$

Divide.

19. $\frac{8}{5} \div \frac{4}{5}$

20. $\frac{3}{4} \div \frac{1}{2}$

21. $4 \div \frac{2}{5}$

22. $2\frac{1}{3} \div 1\frac{1}{2}$

Evaluate.

23. $\frac{2}{3} \times \frac{3}{4} - \frac{1}{2}$

24. $\frac{3}{4} + \frac{2}{5} \times 10$

25. What is the reciprocal of $\frac{1}{3}$? $2\frac{1}{5}$?

26. Express the amount shaded in the circle as both a fraction and a decimal.

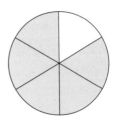

Express as a decimal.

27. $\frac{3}{4}$

28. $2\frac{3}{8}$

29. Convert 0.85 to a fraction.

30. The Desjarlais' yard is $\frac{2}{3}$ lawn and $\frac{1}{3}$ garden.

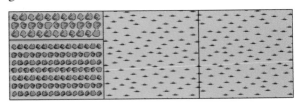

If $\frac{2}{3}$ of the garden is planted with potatoes, what fraction of the yard is planted with potatoes?

31. There were $2\frac{1}{6}$ apple pies and $3\frac{2}{3}$ peach pies left after the bake sale. If $\frac{1}{2}$ of a pie was eaten afterward, how many pies were left?

32. Canada produces about $\frac{2}{3}$ of the world's maple syrup. About $\frac{9}{10}$ of Canada's production comes from Quebec. What fraction of the world's maple syrup comes from Quebec?

33. The average life span of a lynx is $\frac{3}{4}$ of the average life span of a cougar. The average life span of a lynx is 15 years. What is the average life span of a cougar?

Using the Strategies

1. A number is multiplied by 8, increased by 4, and then divided by 3. The result is 12. What is the number?

2. How many different kinds of pizza can be made using toppings of green peppers, mushrooms, and ham if multiple toppings are allowed?

3. Ms. Nguyen wanted to arrange her students in rows, so that each row had the same number of students. She tried 5 in a row, but 1 was left over. She tried 6 in a row, but 3 were left over. Three in a row worked perfectly. What was the smallest possible number of students in the class?

4. Rosalyn went for a walk. From her home, she walked 2 blocks east, 3 blocks south, 1 block west, and 1 block north. What was the shortest route she could take to get home?

5. The graph shows the numbers of blocks from the school to the homes of 4 students and the time it takes for the students to get to school.

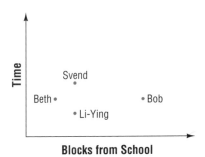

a) Who lives closest to the school?
b) Who lives farthest from the school?
c) Which students live the same distance from the school?
d) Two students walk to school, and two ride bicycles. Which students do you think ride bicycles? Explain.

6. Copy the grid, then join points to make a square with an area of 5 square units.

7. Use each of the digits 1, 2, 3, and 4 once to make the smallest possible sum.

8. Four strips of wood are placed on a table, so that 2 strips are perpendicular to the other 2. Each strip is 10 cm long and 2 cm wide. What area of the table is covered by the strips?

9. Palindromes, such as 777 and 1221, read the same forward and backward. Which perfect squares less than 500 are palindromes?

DATA BANK

1. Write the height of Virginia Falls as a fraction of the height of Chute Montmorency. Express your answer in lowest terms.

2. In which 5 provinces and territories is the total amount of fresh water the same as in Ontario and Quebec combined?

Life History of Nimpkish Island Firs

Fire   Fire   Parents of Present-Day Tall Trees   Potential Future Growth

Height of Trees (m)

Year

1492 Columbus sails to the New World.

Fire destroys all but a few Douglas Firs on Nimpkish Island.

Captain Cook visits Vancouver Island.

CHAPTER 6

Ratio and Rate

The drawing on the opposite page shows the growth of the Douglas firs found in the Nimpkish Island area of British Columbia.

1. About how tall were the trees when Columbus sailed to the New World?

2. a) When Captain Cook visited Vancouver Island, about how much taller than the new trees were the trees that survived the fire?

b) Estimate the height of the new trees as a fraction of the height of the surviving trees when Captain Cook visited Vancouver Island.

3. a) About how many metres did the trees grow between 1300 and 1400?

b) About how many centimetres did they grow between 1300 and 1400?

c) About how many centimetres did they grow each year between 1300 and 1400?

Using Patterns

Activity ❶ Picture Patterns

Draw the next diagram for each of the following.

1.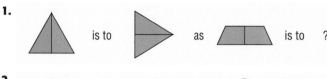

2.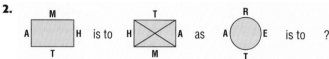

3.

4.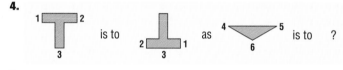

5.

Activity ❷ Analogies

Copy and complete the following analogies.

1. Car is to driver as plane is to ▇.
2. Tree is to bark as orange is to ▇.
3. Horse is to foal as dog is to ▇.
4. TV is to channels as radio is to ▇.
5. Whisper is to yell as walk is to ▇.
6. Moon is to Earth as Earth is to ▇.
7. Boat is to sails as car is to ▇.

Activity ❸ Number Patterns

Copy and complete the following.

1. 3 is to 6 as 4 is to 8 as 5 is to ▇.
2. 20 is to 10 as 8 is to 4 as 12 is to ▇.
3. 3 is to 9 as 4 is to 12 as 5 is to ▇.
4. A is to D as E is to H as I is to ▇.
5. 12 is to 4 as 15 is to 5 as 18 is to ▇.

IS
TO

AS

IS
TO

Warm Up

Copy and complete.

1. In 1 h, you drive 70 km. In 4 h, you drive ▮ km.

2. In 3 h, you walk 12 km. In 1 h, you walk ▮ km.

3. In 5 h, you earn $45. In 1 h, you earn $▮. In 7 h, you earn $▮.

4. In 2 h, you read 40 pages. In 1 h, you read ▮ pages. In 6 h, you read ▮ pages.

5. Three bags have 39 rolls. Four bags have ▮ rolls.

6. Two trucks have 36 wheels. Nine trucks have ▮ wheels.

Express each fraction as a whole number or decimal.

7. $\frac{15}{3}$ **8.** $\frac{49}{7}$ **9.** $\frac{64}{8}$ **10.** $\frac{99}{11}$

11. $\frac{12}{8}$ **12.** $\frac{15}{6}$ **13.** $\frac{5}{10}$ **14.** $\frac{3}{4}$

Express each fraction with a denominator of 100.

15. $\frac{1}{2}$ **16.** $\frac{3}{10}$ **17.** $\frac{7}{10}$ **18.** $\frac{1}{4}$

19. $\frac{3}{50}$ **20.** $\frac{7}{20}$ **21.** $\frac{2}{5}$ **22.** $\frac{3}{25}$

Express each fraction as a decimal.

23. $\frac{3}{10}$ **24.** $\frac{3}{5}$ **25.** $\frac{9}{2}$ **26.** $\frac{15}{8}$

27. $\frac{7}{20}$ **28.** $\frac{11}{4}$ **29.** $\frac{64}{25}$ **30.** $\frac{5}{16}$

Mental Math

Express in lowest terms.

1. $\frac{3}{9}$ **2.** $\frac{2}{6}$ **3.** $\frac{2}{4}$

4. $\frac{5}{10}$ **5.** $\frac{2}{8}$ **6.** $\frac{8}{12}$

7. $\frac{2}{12}$ **8.** $\frac{3}{15}$ **9.** $\frac{4}{16}$

10. $\frac{12}{15}$ **11.** $\frac{10}{15}$ **12.** $\frac{6}{10}$

State an equivalent fraction.

13. $\frac{1}{2}$ **14.** $\frac{1}{3}$ **15.** $\frac{1}{4}$

16. $\frac{2}{3}$ **17.** $\frac{3}{5}$ **18.** $\frac{3}{4}$

19. $\frac{4}{7}$ **20.** $\frac{5}{6}$ **21.** $\frac{3}{8}$

22. $\frac{9}{10}$ **23.** $\frac{2}{9}$ **24.** $\frac{5}{12}$

Multiply.

25. 60×50 **26.** 30×90

27. 70×90 **28.** 14×20

29. 11×30 **30.** 12×40

31. 32×20 **32.** 32×30

Divide.

33. $1400 \div 7$ **34.** $2500 \div 5$

35. $1800 \div 3$ **36.** $3600 \div 4$

37. $1000 \div 20$ **38.** $1500 \div 30$

39. $1600 \div 40$ **40.** $2700 \div 90$

6.1 Ratio

Activity: Use the Diagram

A **ratio** is a comparison of numbers with the same units. The ratio of trumpets to trombones in the symphony orchestra is stated in words as "four to two." In ratio form, the ratio is written 4:2. In fraction form, the ratio is written $\frac{4}{2}$.

As with fractions, ratios can be written in lowest terms or simplest form. The ratio of trumpets to trombones can be written as $\frac{2}{1}$ or 2:1 in lowest terms.

Copy the table. Complete it by writing each ratio in lowest terms.

Instruments	Ratios of Symphony Instruments		
	In Words	In Ratio Form	In Fraction Form
Trumpets to Trombones	two to one	2:1	$\frac{2}{1}$
Oboes to Flutes			
Bassoons to Clarinets			
French Horns to Violas			
First Violins to Violas			
Basses to Second Violins			
French Horns to Trumpets			
Clarinets to First Violins			

Inquire

1. Identify the equal ratios in the table.

2. How is the ratio of oboes to violas related to the ratio of violas to oboes? Explain.

Example

Write each ratio in lowest terms, in ratio form and in fraction form.

a) squares to circles   **b)** circles to triangles
c) triangles to squares

Solution

a) There are 3 squares. There are 4 circles. The ratio is 3:4 or $\frac{3}{4}$.

b) There are 4 circles. There are 6 triangles. The ratio is 4:6 or $\frac{4}{6}$.

$$\frac{4}{6} = \frac{4 \div 2}{6 \div 2}$$
$$= \frac{2}{3} \text{ or } 2:3$$

c) There are 6 triangles. There are 3 squares. The ratio is 6:3 or $\frac{6}{3}$.

$$\frac{6}{3} = \frac{6 \div 3}{3 \div 3}$$
$$= \frac{2}{1} \text{ or } 2:1$$

Practice

Express all ratios in lowest terms.

Use the diagram to express each ratio in 3 ways.

1. yellow circles to blue circles

2. blue circles to yellow circles

3. green circles to all circles

4. all circles to blue circles

Write each ratio in 2 other ways.

5. 9 to 5   **6.** $\frac{2}{3}$ **7.** 6:1

8. $\frac{8}{7}$ **9.** 2:5   **10.** 4 to 11

Write each ratio in lowest terms.

11. 8 to 4   **12.** 10:8   **13.** $\frac{6}{9}$

14. 10:30   **15.** 12 to 15   **16.** $\frac{25}{10}$

17. 16 chairs to 4 tables

18. 8 tripods to 24 legs

19. 6 cars to 30 passengers

20. 36 tourists to 3 tour guides

Problems and Applications

21. There are 22 provinces in China. Write the number of provinces in China to the number of provinces in Canada as a ratio in lowest terms.

22. For every 35 kg of iron within the Earth, there are 30 kg of oxygen and 15 kg of silicon. Express the following ratios in lowest terms.
a) mass of oxygen to mass of silicon
b) mass of silicon to mass of iron
c) mass of iron to mass of oxygen

23. In one year, the Earth averages 2 earthquakes of magnitude 8, 20 earthquakes of magnitude 7, and 100 earthquakes of magnitude 6. Write the following ratios in lowest terms.
a) earthquakes of magnitude 8 to earthquakes of magnitude 7
b) earthquakes of magnitude 6 to earthquakes of magnitude 7
c) earthquakes of magnitude 6 to earthquakes of magnitude 8

24. Find each of the following ratios in lowest terms for the numbers 1, 2, 3,..., 99, and 100.
a) the number of even numbers to the number of odd numbers
b) the number of multiples of 10 to the number of multiples of 5
c) the number of multiples of 2 to the number of multiples of 3
d) the number of multiples of 7 to the number of multiples of 3
e) the number of multiples of 25 to the number of multiples of 50

25. State each ratio by first expressing both quantities in the same unit.
a) 1 cm to 2 m   **b)** 1 min to 1 h
c) 1 m to 1 km   **d)** 1 day to 1 h
e) 1 day to 1 year   **f)** 1 km to 100 m
g) 2 L to 500 mL   **h)** 3.2 kg to 800 g

26. What is the ratio of
a) consonants to vowels in the alphabet?
b) vowels to consonants in the alphabet?
c) vowels to consonants in the name of your school?

CONTINUED ➤

27. The diagram shows a 4-by-4 square divided into smaller squares. Write each of the following ratios in lowest terms.

a) 4-by-4 squares to 1-by-1 squares

b) 1-by-1 squares to 3-by-3 squares

c) 3-by-3 squares to 2-by-2 squares

d) 1-by-1 squares to all squares

28. The number seven can be shown by seven circles.

The ratio of letters to circles is 5:7.

a) For what number is the ratio of letters to circles 1:1?

b) Find 2 numbers that have a ratio of letters to circles of 1:2.

29. Use the smallest possible number of circles, squares, and triangles to draw one diagram that represents these 3 ratios in lowest terms.

3 circles to 4 squares

3 triangles to 8 squares

2 circles to 1 triangle

30. In many cases, it is helpful to use an estimate of a ratio. For example, the ratio of the area of Saskatchewan to the area of British Columbia is 652 330 km² to 947 800 km². To simplify this ratio, we can estimate with compatible numbers. The ratio is about 600 000:900 000 or 2:3. Use your research skills to estimate the following ratios of areas. Your ratios should include no numbers greater than 10. Compare your estimates with a classmate's.

a) New Brunswick to Nova Scotia

b) Quebec to Ontario

c) Manitoba to Saskatchewan

d) British Columbia to Newfoundland

e) Alberta to Quebec

f) Newfoundland to Ontario

LOGIC POWER

Designing a Maze

In the following example, an 8-by-8 grid is used to show you how to design a maze.

1. Mark an entrance and an exit. Now, draw a path of your choice from the entrance to the exit.

2. Draw false paths leading away from your path. There must be a path through every square.

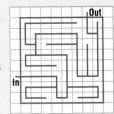

3. Use tracing paper to draw the walls of the maze. The walls are the grid lines that have not been crossed by any path.

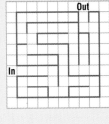

Using the above method, design your own maze. Use grid paper and decide how many squares to use. A 15-by-15 grid is a good place to start. Challenge a classmate to find a way through your maze.

6.2 Three-Term Ratios

Activity: Use the Information

A professional baseball team has 25 players. Some teams have 10 pitchers, 3 catchers, 6 outfielders, and 6 infielders.

Inquire

1. What is the ratio in lowest terms of
a) catchers to outfielders?
b) outfielders to infielders?
c) infielders to catchers?
d) pitchers to all players?

2. What is the ratio in lowest terms of
a) catchers to outfielders to infielders?
b) outfielders to infielders to pitchers?

Example

Write the ratio of dimes to quarters to nickels in lowest terms.

Solution

There are 2 dimes, 4 quarters, and 6 nickels. The ratio is 2:4:6. Divide each number by 2. The ratio in lowest terms is 1:2:3.

Practice

Express all ratios in lowest terms.

Use the diagram to write the following ratios.

1. red squares to black squares to yellow squares

2. yellow squares to red squares to all squares

Write each ratio in lowest terms.

3. 10:25:15   **4.** 35:14:49

5. 16:32:12   **6.** 100:150:225

Problems and Applications

7. State the ratio of AB to BC to AC in △ABC.

A, 15 cm, 9 cm, C, 12 cm, B

8. The annual numbers of days of frost at 3 Canadian airports are as follows.
Quebec City 180, Ottawa 165, Winnipeg 195
Write the ratio of days of frost in Winnipeg to days of frost in Quebec City to days of frost in Ottawa.

9. A cash register contains 12 $2 bills, 10 $5 bills, and 6 $10 bills.
a) What is the ratio of $2 bills to $5 bills to $10 bills?
b) What is the ratio of the value of the $2 bills to the value of the $5 bills to the value of the $10 bills?

 c) Why are the answers to parts a) and b) different?

6.3 Equivalent Ratios and Proportions

Activity: Complete the Table

Copy and complete the table by writing the ratio of the width to the length for each flag. Do not simplify the ratios.

Flag	Ratio
Cuba	
Mongolia	
Nigeria	
Philippines	

Cuba

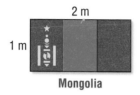

Mongolia

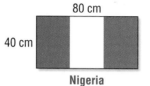

Nigeria

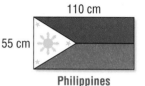

Philippines

Inquire

1. Write the 4 ratios in fraction form.

 2. These ratios are called **equal ratios** or **equivalent ratios**. Why?

3. Write 3 other ratios that are equal to these ratios.

4. Write 3 ratios that are equivalent to 2:3.

 5. Describe a method for finding equal or equivalent ratios.

The table shows the side length, s, of an equilateral triangle and its perimeter, P. The ratios of side length to perimeter are 1:3, 2:6, 3:9, and 4:12. These are equal or equivalent ratios. A statement that 2 ratios are equal, such as $\frac{1}{3} = \frac{2}{6}$, is called a **proportion**.

s (cm)	1	2	3	4
P (cm)	3	6	9	12

Example 1

Find the missing term in each proportion.

a) $\frac{5}{6} = \frac{x}{18}$ **b)** $\frac{12}{20} = \frac{3}{y}$

Solution

a) $\frac{5}{6} = \frac{x}{18}$ Think: $6 \times 3 = 18$ **b)** $\frac{12}{20} = \frac{3}{y}$ Think: $12 \div 4 = 3$

$= \frac{5 \times 3}{6 \times 3}$ $= \frac{12 \div 4}{20 \div 4}$

$= \frac{15}{18}$ $= \frac{3}{5}$

So, the missing term is 15.   So, the missing term is 5.

Example 2

The ratio of width to height for a television screen is 4:3. What is the height of a screen that has a width of 32 cm?

Solution

Let the height of the screen be h. Write the proportion.

$4:3 = 32:h$ or $\frac{4}{3} = \frac{32}{h}$ Think: $4 \times 8 = 32$

$= \frac{4 \times 8}{3 \times 8}$

$= \frac{32}{24}$

So, the height of the screen is 24 cm.

Practice

Write 3 ratios equal to the ratio of circles to squares.

1. 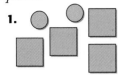 **2.**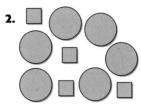

Determine whether the ratios in each pair are equivalent.

3. 2:3 and 4:9   **4.** 1:2 and 2:1

5. 5:8 and 15:32   **6.** 4:1 and 20:5

7. 5:20 and 1:5   **8.** 20:5 and 8:2

9. $\frac{12}{15}$ and $\frac{3}{5}$ **10.** $\frac{48}{16}$ and $\frac{3}{1}$

Find the unknown value in each proportion.

11. $\frac{x}{5} = \frac{4}{20}$ **12.** $\frac{y}{12} = \frac{1}{4}$

13. $\frac{t}{15} = \frac{3}{5}$ **14.** $\frac{w}{25} = \frac{1}{5}$

15. $\frac{15}{x} = \frac{45}{6}$ **16.** $\frac{3}{2} = \frac{15}{a}$

17. $\frac{5}{y} = \frac{50}{30}$ **18.** $\frac{18}{24} = \frac{m}{4}$

Find the unknown value in each proportion.

19. $x:3 = 12:18$ **20.** $y:5 = 15:25$

21. $2:3 = p:12$ **22.** $1:6 = r:24$

23. $n:4 = 3:12$ **24.** $4:c = 12:15$

25. $2:3 = 12:t$ **26.** $x:2 = 2:1$

Problems and Applications

27. At the Winter Olympics in Albertville, France, the ratio of Canada's medals to Austria's medals was 1:3. Austria won 21 medals. How many medals did Canada win?

28. The ratio of the length of the human body to the length of the head is about 8:1. What is the length of the head of a person who is 168 cm tall?

29. The ratio of the length to the width of the Canadian flag is 2:1. What is the width of a 50-cm long Canadian flag?

30. The ratio of the length to the width of the Japanese flag is 3:2. What is the length of a 30-cm wide Japanese flag?

31. In Canadian federal elections, 3 out of 4 voters usually cast their votes. In a riding with 60 000 voters,
a) how many people are expected to vote?
b) how many people are not expected to vote?
c) what is the expected ratio of voters who cast their votes to voters who do not cast their votes?

32. Write a problem that involves a proportion. Have a classmate solve your problem.

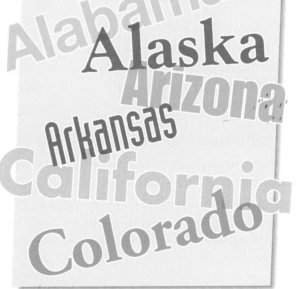

WORD POWER

How many names of the 50 American states contain more vowels than consonants?

215

Estimating with Ratios

Activity ❶ An Experiment with Ratios

Work with a classmate. You will need counters or cubes of 2 different colours, and a box or paper bag. The object is for one person to use ratios to estimate how many counters or cubes of one colour are in the box or bag.

1. Suppose you have red and blue counters, and a paper bag. Together, decide the total number of counters that will be put into the bag. Make it some multiple of 10 and at least 50.

2. Person A puts the agreed number of counters into the bag, without letting Person B see how many are red and how many are blue. Person A then mixes the counters in the bag.

3. Person B now takes a small handful of counters from the bag, and counts the number of blue counters and the total number of counters in this handful. Then, Person B records the results in a table, like the one shown. Person A returns the counters to the bag and mixes them.

Trial	Blue Counters	Total Counters	Ratio (Blue:Total)
1			
2			
3			
4			
5			

4. Repeat step 3 four more times.

5. Use the results in the ratio column to estimate the ratio of blue counters to the total number of counters in the bag. Use a simple ratio, with the second term less than 10.

6. Suppose there were 50 counters in the bag, and the ratio of blue counters to the total number of counters was 1:5. How many blue counters would there be?

7. Use the ratio found in step 5 to estimate the number of blue counters in the bag. Check how close the estimate is to the actual number of blue counters in the bag.

8. Switch roles and repeat the experiment.

Activity ❷ A Capture/Replacement Experiment

You will need counters of 2 different colours, say red and blue, and a box or paper bag. One person will put a number of red counters into the bag. The other person will use the blue counters and ratios to estimate how many red counters were put into the bag.

1. Person A secretly puts a number of red counters greater than 40 into the bag and records the number.

2. Person B takes some red counters from the bag and replaces the red counters with an equal number of blue counters. Person B records the number of blue counters added. Person A then mixes the counters in the bag.

3. Person B picks a small handful of counters from the bag and records the fraction of the counters that are blue.

4. Let the number of red counters in the bag at the start be n. Suppose 10 blue counters were added in step 2. Suppose also that, in step 3, 9 counters were removed, 2 of which were blue. Then,

$$\frac{\text{blue counters removed in step 3}}{\text{total counters removed in step 3}} = \frac{\text{blue counters added to the bag}}{\text{total red counters at the start}}$$

$$\frac{2}{9} = \frac{10}{n}$$

$$\frac{2 \times 5}{9 \times 5} = \frac{10}{n}$$

$$\frac{10}{45} = \frac{10}{n}$$

$$45 = n$$

There were about 45 red counters at the start.

5. Use the results from step 3 to estimate the number of red counters at the start. Check how close the estimate is to the actual number.

6. Switch roles and repeat the experiment.

7. Why is the value of n an estimate?

Activity ❸ Estimating Wildlife Populations

The capture/recapture method, used to estimate the size of wildlife populations, is like the capture/replacement experiment in Activity 2.

1. To estimate the deer population in a park, conservation officers caught and tagged 30 deer. The deer were then released. After the deer had time to mix in the park, another 20 were caught. Of these, 2 had tags.

To estimate the deer population, let n represent the number of deer in the park. Write a proportion.

$$\frac{\text{tagged deer caught}}{\text{total deer caught}} = \frac{\text{total number of tagged deer}}{\text{total number of deer in park}}$$

$$\frac{2}{20} = \frac{30}{n}$$

Find n.

2. To estimate the fish population in a lake, 250 fish were caught, tagged, and released. After sufficient time had passed for the fish to mix in the lake, 100 were caught. Five of these fish had tags. Estimate the fish population in the lake.

3. From a flock of Canada geese, 200 birds were captured and banded. After these birds had mixed with the flock, 300 birds were caught. Eight of them had been banded. Estimate the number of birds in the flock.

6.4 Rate

A ratio is a comparison of numbers with the same units. The ratio 2:4 or 1:2 compares the 2-kg mass of a raven with the 4-kg mass of an eagle owl. In this 2:4 ratio, the numbers are 2 and 4, and the units are kilograms.

A **rate** is a comparison of 2 numbers with different units. A speed of sixty kilometres per hour, or 60 km/h, is a rate. It could be written as 60 km:1 h. The numbers are 60 and 1, and the units are kilometres and hours. A rate is usually written as a **unit rate**, in which the second term is 1.

Activity: Use the Information

British Columbia's Clayoquot Sound rain forest is home to a western red cedar tree that is a celebrity. It is about 1000 years old and has the special name "Hanging Garden Tree." It takes water from the soil and returns it to the atmosphere as water vapour, at about 300 L every 10 h. It is estimated that a large oak tree releases about 2100 L of water vapour every 10 h.

Inquire

1. Write a unit rate, in litres per hour, for water vapour release by the cedar tree.

2. Write a unit rate, in litres per hour, for the oak tree.

3. Write a unit rate, in litres per minute, for
a) the cedar tree **b)** the oak tree

Example 1

Montreal's Nathalie Lambert retired from short-track speed skating as world champion in both the 1000-m and 3000-m events. She won the 1000-m event in 1 min 45.46 s. What was her average speed, to the nearest tenth of a metre per second?

Solution

Divide the distance, in metres, by the time, in seconds, to find the rate in metres per second.

Statement of fact:　　Nathalie skated 1000 m in
　　　　　　　　　　1 min 45.46 s or 105.46 s.

Rate for 1 s:　　　$\frac{1000}{105.46} \doteq 9.5$

EST　$1000 \div 100 = 10$

C 1000 ÷ 105 . 46 = ⌐ 9.4822682

Nathalie's average speed was about 9.5 m/s.
How could you use multiplication to check the answer?

Recall the steps

Understand
the Problem

Think
of a
Plan

Carry Out
the Plan

Look Back

Rate problems can be solved using the "Rule of Three," so called because it involves only 3 steps.

Example 2

Three lemons cost $1.35. What is the cost of 7 lemons?

Solution

Use the Rule of Three.

1. Statement of fact: 3 lemons cost $1.35

2. Rate for 1:   1 lemon costs $\frac{\$1.35}{3} = \$0.45$ ⟵ Divide by 3 to find the cost of 1 lemon.

3. Rate for 7:   7 lemons cost $7 \times \$0.45 = \$3.15$ ⟵ Multiply by 7 to find the cost of 7 lemons.

So, 7 lemons cost $3.15.

Practice

Copy and complete each proportion.

1. $\frac{15}{3} = \frac{\blacksquare}{1}$ **2.** $\frac{21}{7} = \frac{\blacksquare}{1}$ **3.** $\frac{30}{5} = \frac{\blacksquare}{1}$

4. $\frac{88}{11} = \frac{\blacksquare}{1}$ **5.** $\frac{49}{7} = \frac{\blacksquare}{1}$ **6.** $\frac{80}{5} = \frac{\blacksquare}{1}$

Copy and complete each statement.

7. 48 bread rolls in 6 bags = ■ rolls/bag

8. 140 students on 4 buses = ■ students/bus

9. $28 for 4 hours' work = ■/h

10. 300 km in 5 h = ■ km/h

11. one dozen eggs for $1.80 = ■/egg

12. 5 pairs of socks for $25.50 = ■/pair

Write as a unit rate.

13. 1000 paper clips in 10 boxes

14. 60 m in 6 s

15. $2.40 for 6 bagels

16. $1245 for 5 plane tickets

17. 40 slices of apple pie for 20 people

18. earnings of $62.50 for 5 h

Problems and Applications

19. Sumi drove at 75 km/h. How far did she drive in 4 h?

20. Eight bus tickets cost $12. What is the cost of 5 tickets?

21. In 5 years, the average North American eats about 115 kg of fruit. How much fruit does the average North American eat in 7 years?

22. An aircraft flies 4900 km in 7 h. How far will it fly in 4.5 h?

23. The last RCMP Northern Dog Team Patrol left Old Crow in the Yukon on March 11, 1969. The team travelled 804.5 km in 26 days. What was the average rate of travel, to the nearest kilometre per day?

 24. Speed is defined as $\frac{\text{distance}}{\text{time}}$.

a) If you increase the distance you travel in a certain length of time, do you increase or decrease your speed? Explain.

b) If you decrease the time you take to travel a certain distance, do you increase or decrease your speed? Explain.

 25. a) Examine the job section of a newspaper and list 10 jobs that pay by the hour.

b) Rank the jobs from lowest paid to highest paid.

c) What kinds of jobs pay the higher wages?

d) Use your research skills to find the minimum wage for an adult and for a student.

e) Compare the minimum wages with your findings in parts a) and b).

6.5 Comparing Unit Rates and Unit Prices

Activity: Complete the Table

One way to rank hockey players is to compare the rates at which they score points or their "points per game."

The table gives the games played, goals, assists, and points for 5 players in their rookie seasons in the NHL.

Copy the table. Complete it by calculating, to the nearest hundredth, the points per game or $\frac{\text{points}}{\text{game}}$ for each player.

Player	Games Played	Goals	Assists	Points	Points Game
Joe Juneau	84	32	70	102	
Mario Lemieux	73	43	57	100	
Eric Lindros	61	41	34	75	
Joe Nieuwendyk	75	51	41	92	
Teemu Selanne	84	76	56	132	

Inquire

1. Rank the players from first to fifth according to their points per game.

2. Are the 2 players who tied still tied if you round to the nearest thousandth? If not, which one has the higher rank?

3. How does the ranking change if you rank the players by just using
a) points for the season?   **b)** goals for the season?

 4. What do you think is the best way to rank hockey players? Give reasons for your answer.

It is often difficult to know which size of container in a store is the best value. To make a comparison, you must read the mass or volume of the product from the containers. To help consumers decide which size is the best value, some stores show **unit prices**. These unit prices are examples of unit rates.

Example

A 250-mL jar of fruit spread costs $2.90. A 450-mL jar of the same fruit spread costs $5.40. Which size of jar is the better value?

Solution

Use a calculator to find the unit price in cents per millilitre.

Small Size
250 mL cost $2.90 or 290¢.
1 mL costs $\frac{290}{250}$
= 1.16   [C] **290** [÷] **250** [=] | 1.16 |
The unit price is 1.16¢/mL.

Large Size
450 mL cost $5.40 or 540¢.
1 mL costs $\frac{540}{450}$
= 1.2   [C] **540** [÷] **450** [=] | 1.2 |
The unit price is 1.2¢/mL.

Since 1.16 < 1.2, the 250-mL size is the better value.

Practice

Find the unit price.

1. $4.50 for 5 pens

2. $17.80 for 10 floppy disks

3. $6.60 for 4 L of milk

4. 12 bread rolls for $2.88

5. 120 g of tuna for $2.40

6. 14 L of spring water for $12.46

Find the unit price. Round to the nearest tenth of a cent, if necessary.

7. $2.79 for 400 g of breakfast cereal

8. 24 cans of soda for $8.99

9. 10 kg of flour for $5.88

10. $2.49 for 750 g of yogurt

Find the unit rate.

11. keyboarding 520 words in 10 min

12. driving 180 km in 4 h

13. using 200 mL of toothpaste in 8 weeks

14. sharing 6 pizzas among 8 students

Problems and Applications

15. Fruit juice is advertised at $5.99 for 8 packages. Each package contains 3 boxes. What is the unit price per box, to the nearest cent?

Which is the better buy?

16. 8 granola bars for $1.89 or 12 for $2.89

17. $13.00 for 10 bus tokens or $4.50 for 3 tokens

18. $2.19 for 48 tea bags or $3.39 for 72 tea bags

19. 1 L of orange juice for $1.99 or 1.36 L for $2.49

20. $2.75 for 283 g of curry sauce or $3.48 for 380 g

21. 200 sheets of paper for $1.98 or 500 sheets for $4.49

Some stores quote unit prices in terms of 100-g or 100-mL units. Find the price of 100 g or 100 mL of each product. Round to the nearest tenth of a cent, if necessary.

22. pasta at $0.99 for 900 g

23. 1 kg of peanut butter for $3.99

24. $3.24 for 400 mL of salad dressing

25. 500 mL of olive oil for $6.49

26. Athena earned $105.00 for 12 h of cutting lawns. Brad earned $126.75 for 15 h of packing groceries. Who had the higher rate of pay and by how much?

27. In 667 games, Michael Jordan scored 21 541 points. In 1560 games, Kareem Abdul-Jabbar scored 38 387 points. Who scored points at the greater rate per game?

28. Runner Nicki Knapp became Canadian women's 800-m champion in 2 min 4.23 s. Angela Chalmers became the 1500-m champion in 4 min 15.31 s. Who ran faster?

 29. At top speed, an elephant can run at about 40 km/h. The fastest human can run 100 m in about 10 s. Which can run faster, an elephant or a human?

 30. The table shows the prices of frozen pizzas.

Size	Price
35 cm	$5.99
30 cm	$4.99
25 cm	$3.99

Work with a classmate to determine the best buy. Explain your reasoning.

 31. Write a problem that involves the comparison of 2 unit rates. Have a classmate solve your problem.

Computer Spreadsheets and Exchange Rates

Spreadsheets organize data in rows and columns, so that you can work with the data to produce valuable information.

Banks regularly convert from one system of money to another. The formulas in a spreadsheet can be set up to do the calculations that make these conversions.

Activity ❶

You are going to the United States, and you want to know the cost of 100 United States dollars in Canadian dollars.

1. Check a daily newspaper to compare the U.S. dollar with the Canadian dollar. What is the rate of exchange that shows the number of Canadian dollars equal to 1 U.S. dollar?

2. Use the following formula to calculate the cost of 100 U.S. dollars in Canadian dollars.

Canadian dollars = U.S. dollars × rate of exchange

Activity ❷

The following spreadsheet is set up to change foreign currencies to Canadian dollars, and Canadian dollars to foreign currencies. The column "$Cdn Per Unit" gives the exchange rates you multiply by to change from foreign currencies to Canadian dollars. You can also divide by these exchange rates to change from Canadian dollars to foreign currencies.

10 francs

	A	B	C	D	E	F	G
1	Foreign Exchange						
2							
3				Foreign to··········		Canadian to·········	
4				Canadian············		Foreign·············	
5			$Cdn	Foreign	Amount	Amount	Foreign
6	Country	Currency	Per Unit	Units	in $Cdn	in $Cdn	Units
7							
8	Britain	Pound	2.0718		+D8*C8		+F8/C8
9	France	Franc	0.2427		+D9*C9		+F9/C9
10	Germany	Mark	0.8306		+D10*C10		+F10/C10
11	Japan	Yen	0.01319		+D11*C11		+F11/C11
12	Mexico	Peso	0.4132		+D12*C12		+F12/C12
13	U.S.A.	Dollar	1.3738		+D13*C13		+F13/C13

2 pesos

1. What does the formula in each of the following cells calculate?
a) E8   **b)** G10

2. Key in the computer spreadsheet, but replace the values in cells C8 to C13 with the present exchange rates.

3. Use columns D and E to change 100 units of each foreign currency to Canadian dollars.

4. Use columns F and G to change $100 Cdn to each of the foreign currencies.

Activity ❸

This spreadsheet will calculate the cost in Canadian dollars of a purchase made in a foreign currency.

	A	B	C	D	E
1	Foreign Purchases				
2					
3			$Cdn	Value of	Amount
4	Country	Currency	Per Unit	Purchase	in $Cdn
5					
6	Britain	Pound	2.0718		+D6*C6
7	France	Franc	0.2427		+D7*C7
8	Germany	Mark	0.8306		+D8*C8
9	Japan	Yen	0.01319		+D9*C9
10	Mexico	Peso	0.4132		+D10*C10
11	U.S.A.	Dollar	1.3738		+D11*C11

1. Key in the spreadsheet, but replace the values in cells C6 to C11 with the present exchange rates.

2. Find the cost of each of the following purchases in Canadian dollars.
a) a British racing bicycle that cost 2000 pounds
b) a German car that cost 50 000 marks
c) a Japanese computer that cost 95 000 yen
d) a Mexican mango that cost 2 pesos
e) a French croissant that cost 10 francs
f) a ball glove that cost 79.50 U.S. dollars

79.50 U.S. dollars

2000 pounds

223

6.6 Scale Drawings

When it is impossible to draw an object to its actual size, we use a **scale drawing**. Blueprints, maps, and floor plans are examples of scale drawings.

Every scale drawing has a **scale**, which is a ratio of the length of the drawing to the actual length of the real object. If an object measures 2 cm and the scale is 1:1000, the actual length of the object is 1000 × 2 cm or 2000 cm or 20 m.

Activity: Measure the Drawings

Inquire

1. Copy the table. Complete the first row by using the scale of each drawing to calculate the actual height of each object, in metres.

	Eiffel Tower	Washington Monument	Calgary Tower	Tallest Alert Bay Totem Pole
Calculated Height (m)				
Correct Height (m)				

2. Use your research skills to find the correct height of each structure, in metres. Record the values in the second row of the table.

3. Compare the calculated height and the correct height for each object.

 4. Is a scale drawing of any use if the scale is not given? Explain.

Eiffel Tower 1:10 000

Washington Monument 1:6000

Calgary Tower 1:6400

Tallest Alert Bay Totem Pole 1:1700

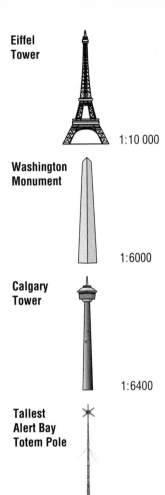

Example

The estuarine or saltwater crocodile from South Asia and Northern Australia is the world's largest crocodile. The scale is 1:60. What is the actual length of the crocodile, in metres?

Solution

The scale is 1:60. This means that 1 cm on the drawing represents 60 cm on the crocodile.

Let l represent the actual length of the crocodile.

$$\text{1 cm on drawing} \longrightarrow \frac{1}{60} = \frac{10}{l} \longleftarrow \text{length of drawing}$$
$$\text{60 cm actual} \qquad\qquad \longleftarrow \text{actual length of crocodile}$$

$$\frac{1}{60} = \frac{1 \times 10}{60 \times 10}$$

$$= \frac{10}{600}$$

$$l = 600$$

The crocodile is 600 cm or 6 m long.

← 10 cm →

Practice

Write each ratio in lowest terms.

1. 4:12 **2.** 5:15 **3.** 10:100

4. 10:1000 **5.** 40:4 **6.** 20:2

7. 0.5:50 **8.** 0.1:1 **9.** 10:0.5

Write each scale as a ratio in lowest terms.

10. 1 cm represents 25 cm

11. 1 cm represents 1 m

12. 1 cm represents 3 m

13. 5 cm represents 50 m

14. 1 cm represents 100 km

15. 2 cm represents 250 km

16. 1 cm represents 0.5 cm

17. 1 cm represents 2 mm

Problems and Applications

18. Find the actual height of the ostrich, in metres.

2.5 cm

Scale 1:100

19. Find the actual length of the beluga whale, in metres.

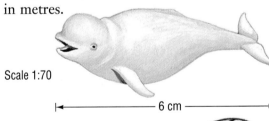

Scale 1:70

|← 6 cm →|

20. Find the actual length of the housefly, in millimetres.

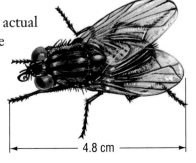

Scale 8:1

|← 4.8 cm →|

21. A Pacific leatherback turtle is about 2 m long. What is the length, in centimetres, of a drawing with a scale of 1:50?

22. A bee hummingbird's egg is 11 mm long. What is the length, in centimetres, of a drawing with a scale of 4:1?

23. Vancouver's Harbour Centre building is 130 m tall. If the height of a drawing is 6.5 cm, what is the scale?

24. The volleyball court is drawn to a scale of 1:300. Use the drawing to determine these lengths, in metres.

a) the length of the court, excluding the service areas

b) the distance between the attack lines

c) the dimensions of each service area

d) the perimeter of the court, excluding the service areas

e) the perimeter of the court, including the service areas

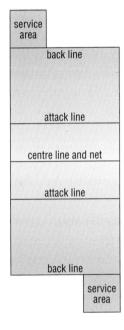

25. If necessary, use your research skills to determine the height of each of the following. Decide on a suitable scale you would use to make a drawing of each in your notebook. Compare your scales with a classmate's.

a) Ottawa's Peace Tower

b) Empire State Building

c) your school

d) yourself

6.7 Maps and Scales

A map is a scale drawing that represents a part of the Earth. The scale of the map is the ratio of a distance on the map to the actual distance on the Earth.

Activity:
Interpret the Map

The map of the Maritimes is drawn to a scale of 1:5 000 000.

Measure the straight-line distance from Moncton to Halifax on the map.

Inquire

1. Use the scale to calculate the actual distance, in kilometres, from Moncton to Halifax.

2. The scale is shown in 2 different ways. Show that they have the same meaning.

3. If the scale was 1:2 500 000, how could you show it in another way?

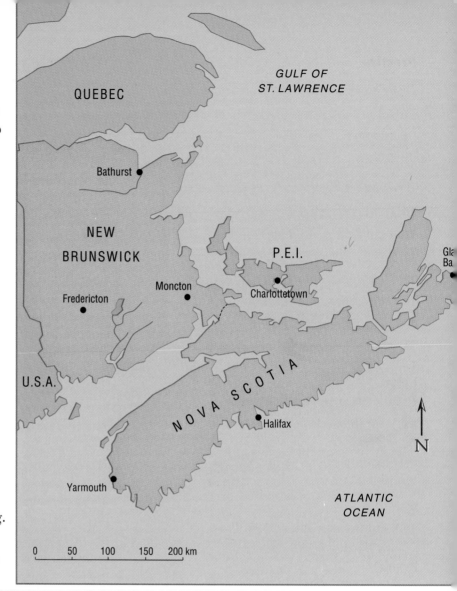

QUEBEC

GULF OF
ST. LAWRENCE

Bathurst

NEW
BRUNSWICK

P.E.I.

Moncton

Fredericton

Charlottetown

Gla
Ba

U.S.A.

N O V A   S C O T I A

Halifax

N

Yarmouth

ATLANTIC
OCEAN

0   50   100   150   200 km

Example

Use the map to find the approximate distance, in kilometres, from Charlottetown to Halifax.

Solution

The distance from Charlottetown to Halifax on the map is about 3.8 cm. On the map, 1 cm represents 50 km on the Earth. Let d represent the distance from Charlottetown to Halifax. Set up and solve a proportion.

1 cm on map ⟶ $\dfrac{1}{50} = \dfrac{3.8}{d}$ ⟵ 3.8 cm on map
50 km actual ⟶ ⟵ actual distance from Charlottetown to Halifax

$$= \frac{1 \times 3.8}{50 \times 3.8}$$

EST $50 \times 4 = 200$

$$= \frac{3.8}{190}$$

$$d = 190$$

The distance from Charlottetown to Halifax is about 190 km.

Practice

Represent each of the following scales in another way.

1. 1:500 000

2. 1:1 000 000

3.

4.

```
0    100   200  300 km        0      25      50    75 km
```

5. On a map with a scale of 1:1 500 000, what actual distance, in kilometres, is represented by 3 cm? 4.8 cm?

6. On a map with a scale of 1:30 000 000, what distance, in centimetres, represents an actual distance of 1500 km?

Problems and Applications

7. On a map, the distance from Montreal to Berlin is 7.5 cm. The scale is 1:80 000 000. Calculate the actual distance, in kilometres, from Montreal to Berlin.

8. Calgary is 520 km from Saskatoon. How far apart are they on a map with a scale of 1:10 000 000?

9. Copy the chart. Use the map of the Maritimes on the opposite page to complete it.

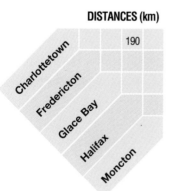

DISTANCES (km)

10. Ostia was an ancient Roman port. When archaeologists excavated the ruins, they found a complex of apartments, shops, and gardens, called the "Garden Houses." A plan of the ground floor is shown below.

The complex included 2 large, rectangular buildings inside a courtyard. Each building had 4 apartments on the ground floor. Around the courtyard were other buildings, containing shops and more apartments. What were the approximate dimensions, in metres, of

a) the courtyard?

b) each building inside the courtyard?

c) each apartment on the ground floor of these buildings?

11. Write a problem based on the plan of the Garden Houses. Have a classmate solve your problem.

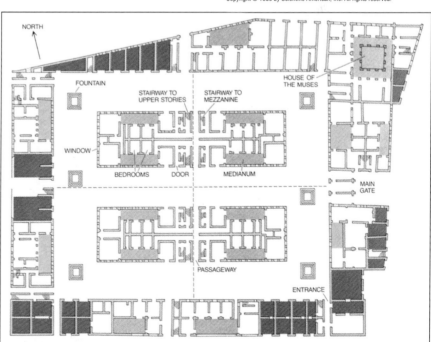

Scale 1:1300

The Footprints at Laetoli

About 3.7 million years ago, a volcano erupted near Laetoli in Tanzania. The volcano left ash deposits on the ground. Mammals and birds walked on the ash and left their footprints. Then, it rained. Because the ash had lime in it, the rain hardened it. More ash from the volcano then covered the ground and protected the footprints from erosion.

The scale diagram below shows some of the footprints discovered by archaeologists in the 1980s.

Activity ❶ Interpreting the Diagram

1. What are the actual length and width of one of the footprints of the elephant?

2. What are the actual length and width of the largest footprint of the rhinoceros?

3. a) What is the actual length of the longest track left by the giraffe?

b) What might have caused the giraffe to make the four long tracks?

4. Make an actual-size drawing of a hyena footprint.

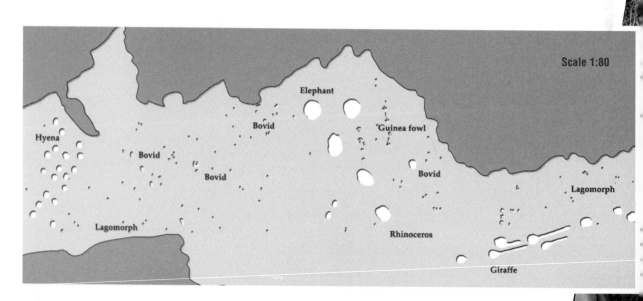

Scale 1:80

Elephant
Bovid
Guinea fowl
Hyena
Bovid
Bovid
Bovid
Lagomorph
Lagomorph
Rhinoceros
Giraffe

Activity ❷ Using Your Research Skills

1. Find out what a guinea fowl is.

2. What is a lagomorph?

3. Locate Tanzania on a map.

4. Use an almanac or encyclopedia to find some interesting data about Tanzania. Share your findings with your classmates.

Review

Express all ratios in lowest terms.

Use the diagrams to express each ratio in 3 ways.

1. yellow squares to red squares

2. red squares to green squares

3. green squares to all squares

4. all squares to yellow squares

5. Make 5 copies of the diagram in your notebook. Colour the small squares red or blue to obtain the following ratios.

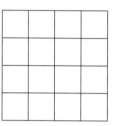

a) red squares to blue squares, 3:1

b) blue squares to red squares, 5:3

c) red squares to blue squares, 7:1

d) blue squares to all small squares, 1:2

e) red squares to all small squares, 1:4

Express in simplest form.

6. 3:9

7. 3:3

8. 4:8

9. 40:5

10. 12:3

11. 50:10

12. 5:45

13. 35:7

14. 5:35

15. 22:11:55

16. 16:24:12

17. 30:15:40

18. The number of wet days per year is 108 in Saskatoon, 120 in Winnipeg, and 156 in Fredericton.

a) Write the ratio of wet days in Saskatoon to wet days in Winnipeg.

b) Write the ratio of wet days in Winnipeg to wet days in Fredericton to wet days in Saskatoon.

Find the unknown value in each proportion.

19. $\dfrac{18}{y} = \dfrac{6}{5}$

20. $\dfrac{n}{50} = \dfrac{7}{10}$

21. $\dfrac{4}{3} = \dfrac{a}{9}$

22. $\dfrac{55}{44} = \dfrac{5}{z}$

23. $m:2 = 5:10$

24. $4:x = 12:15$

25. $8:7 = 32:t$

26. $40:25 = s:5$

27. At the Summer Olympics in Barcelona, Spain, the ratio of Canada's gold medals to Germany's gold medals was 2:11. Canada won 6 gold medals. How many gold medals did Germany win?

28. The ratio of the top speed of a lion to the top speed of a hyena is 5:4. A lion's top speed is 80 km/h. What is a hyena's top speed?

29. Mark Tewksbury broke the Olympic 100-m backstroke record in 53.98 s. What was his average speed, to the nearest hundredth of a metre per second?

30. A car travels 315 km in 3 h. How far would you expect it to travel in 5 h?

31. Don earned $166.50 for 18 h of window washing. Whitney earned $230.40 for 24 h of painting. Who had the higher rate of pay?

32. Measure the height of the diagram of the giraffe. The scale is 1:150. What is the giraffe's actual height, in metres?

Calculate the unit price. Round to the nearest tenth of a cent, if necessary.

33. 10 apples for $5.50

34. $4.50 for 12 sheets of Bristol board

35. 12 m of telephone cable for $4.20

36. $4.98 for 200 vitamin C tablets

Determine the price per 100 g. Round to the nearest tenth of a cent.

37. 550 g of bread for $1.69

38. $3.49 for 2 kg of oranges

Which is the better buy?

39. 2 kg of potatoes for $1.28 or 5 kg for $2.99

40. 3 bagels for $1.29 or 8 bagels for $2.99

41. Use the map of the Maritimes on page 226 to find these distances, in kilometres.
a) Yarmouth to Halifax
b) Bathurst to Glace Bay

42. The scale of a drawing of a building is 1:2500. If the building is 100 m tall, what is the height of the drawing, in centimetres?

43. Fran is charging $100 to mow the lawns and weed the gardens outside an apartment building. How can she make her rate of pay as high as possible?

44. A survey of 1000 people crossing the border into Canada found that 400 came as tourists, 200 came on business, 100 were visiting relatives, and 300 were returning home.
a) Find the ratio of tourists to people visiting relatives.
b) Find the ratio of business visitors to the total number of people crossing.
c) Find the ratio of the total number of people crossing to the people returning home.
d) Why are records kept of people who cross borders?
e) What 5 questions would you ask someone crossing the border if you were a border-crossing guard? Explain your choices.

Group Decision Making
Researching Careers of Your Choice

1. Brainstorm as a class the careers you might like to investigate. They might include such careers as archaeologist, astronaut, professional golfer, movie director, astronomer, television news anchor, hotel chef, or university professor. As a class, decide on 6 careers.

2. As a class, list the questions you want to answer about each career. Include a question on how the career makes use of math.

3. Go to home groups.

1 2 3 4 5 6	1 2 3 4 5 6
Home Groups
| 1 2 3 4 5 6 | 1 2 3 4 5 6 |

As a group, decide on a career for each group member to investigate.

4. Form an expert group with students from other home groups who have the same career to research.

1 1 1 1	2 2 2 2	3 3 3 3
Expert Groups
| 4 4 4 4 | 5 5 5 5 | 6 6 6 6 |

In your expert group, decide how to answer the questions about the career. Then, do the research.

5. In your expert group, prepare a class presentation about the career. Relate the format of the presentation to the career. For example, if you researched the career of an astronaut, your presentation might take the form of a trip to the moon.

6. Return to your home group and evaluate the presentations of the expert groups.

Chapter Check

1. Express the ratio of red tiles to white tiles in lowest terms.

2. Write 3 ratios equivalent to 3:2.

3. There are 6 cities in New Brunswick, 12 cities in Saskatchewan, and 16 cities in Alberta. Write each of the following ratios in lowest terms.
a) cities in Saskatchewan to cities in New Brunswick
b) cities in New Brunswick to cities in Alberta
c) cities in Alberta to cities in Saskatchewan to cities in New Brunswick

Find the value of x.

4. $\dfrac{x}{3} = \dfrac{10}{6}$

5. $\dfrac{8}{3} = \dfrac{24}{x}$

6. The Sharpshooters basketball team won 2 out of every 3 games they played in a season. They played 45 games. How many did they win?

7. Runner Camille Noel became Canadian women's 400-m champion in a time of 52.98 s. What was her average speed, to the nearest hundredth of a metre per second?

8. Darcy ran 8 laps of the track in 12 min. Orly ran 5 laps of the same track in 8 min. Who ran faster?

9. If 250 g of fruit spread cost $3.75, what is the unit price?

10. If 5 apples cost $1.95, how much do 8 apples cost?

11. The height of a blue heron is 96 cm. What is the height of a drawing if the scale is 1:16?

12. Halifax is 880 km from St. John's. If these 2 cities are 4.4 cm apart on a map, what is the scale? Express your answer as a ratio in lowest terms.

Reprinted with permission—The Toronto Star Syndicate.
Copyright: Tribune Media Services.

Using the Strategies

1. Two different types of carnations are growing in the same greenhouse. A plant of one type is 12 cm tall and is growing at 1.5 cm/day. A plant of the other type is 8 cm tall and is growing at 2 cm/day. How long will it take for the two plants to reach the same height?

2. A race car is 1200 m from the finish line. At what speed, in kilometres per hour, must it travel to reach the finish line in 0.4 min?

3. At the produce store, 3 lettuces and 2 cabbages cost $6.75. Two lettuces and 3 cabbages cost $7.00. What is the cost of a cabbage?

4. At 13:00, Kia noticed that her car's odometer reading was 34 614. She drove until 17:00, except for a 1-h rest stop. At 17:00, the odometer reading was 34 899. What was Kia's average speed, excluding the rest stop?

5. Six members of the craft club made 6 bookmarks in 6 min. How many bookmarks could 18 members make in 18 min?

6. a) Draw the next 2 figures.

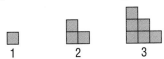

b) Copy and complete the table.

Figure	1	2	3	4	5
Area					
Perimeter					

c) Describe the patterns you see in the table.
d) Extend the table to include figures 6 and 7, without drawing them.

7. In how many ways can you put 25 identical coins into 3 identical bags, so that there is an odd number of coins in each bag, and each bag has more than 1 coin in it?

8. Each of four friends, Amanda, Brittany, Christopher, and Dalil, has a favourite sport. The sports are biking, swimming, jogging, and tennis, but not necessarily in that order. Use the clues to determine each person's favourite sport.
• Amanda and Dalil do not need a racket for their sports.
• Dalil cannot ride a bicycle.
• Dalil and Brittany can participate in their sports on the streets and sidewalks around their homes.

9. The graph describes a pushcart race between Jordan and Justin.

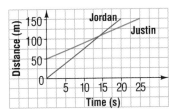

a) How far did Jordan go?
b) How far did Justin go?
c) Who won the race?
d) The lines cross. What does this show?
e) Write a paragraph to describe the race from start to finish.

DATA BANK

1. Which provincial capital is
a) warmest in January?
b) wettest in July?

2. A car uses fuel at a rate of 6.5 L/100 km. How much fuel is needed for each of the following journeys in the car? Round each answer to the nearest litre.
a) Calgary to Vancouver
b) Montreal to Winnipeg
c) Toronto to Regina
d) Halifax to Edmonton

CHAPTER 7

Percent

The flags are used as international signals on ships. Each flag has a different meaning. For example, flag E means: "I am altering my course to starboard." Flag V means: "I require assistance."

All the flags are rectangles, except for flag A and flag B.

1. What fraction of the flags have 2 colours? 3 colours?

2. What colour is used the most? What fraction of the flags have this colour?

3. What colour is used the least? What fraction of the flags have this colour?

4. The length of each flag is greater than the width. There are no squares on the flags. Which flag(s) appear to have squares?

5. List all the geometric shapes you can find on the flags.

6. Which flags have congruent triangles on them?

7. Draw a set of flags to spell the name of your favourite singer or group.

Working with Squares

Activity ❶ Diagonals of Squares

When a square is drawn on a grid, the diagonals of the square cut through the grid squares. In a 2-by-2 square, each small square is cut by 1 diagonal.

In a 3-by-3 square, 4 small squares are cut by 1 diagonal, 1 small square is cut by 2 diagonals, and 4 small squares are not cut by a diagonal.

1. For 4-by-4 to 7-by-7 squares, find the number of small squares cut by 1 diagonal and 2 diagonals, and the number not cut by a diagonal. Copy and complete the table.

Side Length of Square	Number of Small Squares		
	Cut by 1 Diagonal	Cut by 2 Diagonals	Not Cut by a Diagonal
2	4	0	0
3	4	1	4
4			
5			
6			
7			

 2. Describe the patterns you see in the numbers of small squares cut by 1 diagonal and 2 diagonals, and the number of small squares not cut by a diagonal.

3. Use the pattern to predict the next three lines of the table.

4. a) For a 10-by-10 square, what fraction of the small squares are cut by 1 diagonal?

b) For a 10-by-10 square, what fraction of the small squares are not cut by a diagonal?

c) Write the fractions from parts a) and b) in lowest terms.

Activity ❷ Areas of Squares on a Grid

1. The 3-by-3 square has an area of 9 square units. The red square has an area of 5 square units. Its area is $\frac{5}{9}$ of the area of the large square.

There are 3 other different-sized squares you can draw that have intersection points of the grid as vertices, are smaller than the large square, and have whole-number areas. Draw them and express the area of each as a fraction of the area of the large square.

2. The 4-by-4 square has an area of 16 square units. The red square has an area of 2 square units. Its area is $\frac{1}{8}$ of the area of the large square.

There are 6 other different-sized squares you can draw that have intersection points of the grid as vertices, are smaller than the large square, and have whole-number areas. Draw them and express the area of each as a fraction of the area of the large square.

3. The 5-by-5 square has an area of 25 square units.

There are 10 different-sized squares you can draw that have intersection points of the grid as vertices, are smaller than the large square, and have whole-number areas. Draw them and express the area of each as a fraction of the area of the large square.

Warm Up

Estimate, then calculate.

1. $4.80 + $1.65 + $2.99

2. $64.20 + $9.40 + $102.25

3. $6.00 + $17.20 + $1114.28 + $0.72

4. $5.50 + $359.60 + $61.75 + $1.95

Estimate, then calculate.

5. $64.77 − $25.00   **6.** $46.25 − $18.35

7. $224.00 − $69.95   **8.** $75.89 − $36.05

Round to the nearest dollar.

9. $6332.49   **10.** $719.61

11. $99.51   **12.** $354.19

Write as a decimal.

13. twenty-nine thousandths

14. one hundred sixteen and thirty-two hundredths

15. one hundred nine and nine hundredths

16. forty-one and forty-one hundredths

Estimate, then calculate.

17. 6.6×4 **18.** 60.4×12 **19.** 7.5×3.5

Calculate, then round each answer to the nearest hundredth.

20. $1 \div 3$ **21.** $63.9 \div 7$ **22.** $8.2 \div 0.09$

Write as a decimal, then as a fraction in lowest terms.

23. four tenths

24. twenty-five hundredths

25. two hundred fifty thousandths

26. five twenty fifths

Write in lowest terms.

27. $\frac{3}{6}$ **28.** $\frac{32}{50}$ **29.** $\frac{75}{250}$

30. $\frac{12}{8}$ **31.** $\frac{35}{84}$ **32.** $\frac{15}{10}$

Mental Math

Calculate.

1. 16×10 **2.** $16 \div 10$

3. 1.6×100 **4.** $1.6 \div 100$

5. 126×100 **6.** $126 \div 100$

7. 0.82×10 **8.** $0.82 \div 10$

Write as a decimal.

9. $\frac{6}{10}$ **10.** $\frac{2}{25}$ **11.** $\frac{5}{100}$

12. $\frac{8}{16}$ **13.** $\frac{4}{50}$ **14.** $\frac{7}{20}$

15. $\frac{3}{12}$ **16.** $\frac{150}{100}$ **17.** $\frac{4}{5}$

Add.

18. $\frac{1}{2} + \frac{2}{4}$ **19.** $\frac{1}{2} + \frac{3}{4}$ **20.** $\frac{1}{5} + \frac{2}{10}$

21. $\frac{1}{4} + \frac{3}{8}$ **22.** $\frac{1}{2} + \frac{1}{3}$ **23.** $\frac{1}{6} + \frac{1}{3}$

Calculate.

24. $\frac{7}{10} - \frac{2}{5}$ **25.** $\frac{30}{100} - \frac{3}{10}$

26. $\frac{30}{50} - \frac{14}{25}$ **27.** $\frac{75}{100} - \frac{10}{20}$

28. $\frac{3}{5} - \frac{1}{2}$ **29.** $\frac{4}{3} - \frac{1}{6}$

Multiply.

30. $4 \times \frac{1}{2}$ **31.** $6 \times \frac{1}{3}$

32. $10 \times \frac{1}{5}$ **33.** $12 \times \frac{1}{4}$

34. $18 \times \frac{1}{6}$ **35.** $48 \times \frac{1}{8}$

Divide.

36. $1 \div \frac{1}{2}$ **37.** $\frac{1}{2} \div \frac{1}{2}$

38. $6 \div \frac{1}{2}$ **39.** $\frac{1}{2} \div \frac{1}{4}$

40. $\frac{2}{3} \div \frac{1}{6}$ **41.** $3 \div \frac{1}{3}$

Percent

A percent is a useful way to convey information and to make comparisons.

A percent is a ratio that compares a number to 100. Percent means "per hundred," "out of one hundred," or "for every 100."

You can think of a percent as a fraction with a denominator of 100.

So, 45% means $\frac{45}{100}$.

A mark of 21 out of 25 on a test is $\frac{21}{25}$ or $\frac{84}{100}$ or 84%.

Reprinted by permission: Tribune Media Services

Activity ❶ Some Uses of Percent

1. Work with a classmate to list how percent is used in the examples shown on this page.

What Canadians Do for Recreation
(Activities in Previous 12 months)

Sightseeing	Walking	Swimming	Visiting zoos, fairs, amusement parks	Picknicking
46%	53%	53%	50%	48%

NHL Playoff Scoring Leaders			
Player	Shots	Goals Scored	Percent
Ferraro	47	13	27.7
Francis	26	6	23.1
Damphousse	52	11	21.2
Lemieux	40	8	20.0
Gretzky	76	15	19.7

2. Collect examples of how magazines, newspapers, radio and television commercials, and almanacs use percent.

Activity ❷ Percents on a 4-by-4 Grid

Write the fraction of the grid that is shaded in each case.
Then, write each fraction as a percent.

1.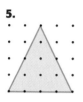

2.

3.

4.

5.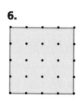

6.

7.

8.

Activity ❸ Percents on Other Grids

Write the fraction of each grid that is shaded. Then, write
each fraction as a percent.

1.

2.

3.

4.

5.

6.

7.

8.

9.

10.

Activity ❹ Percents of Geometric Figures

1. On dot or grid paper draw
5 different geometric figures.
Shade a different percent of
each figure.

2. Exchange figures with a
classmate. Determine the
percents of your classmate's
figures that have been shaded.

7.1 Percents

A **percent** is a fraction with a denominator of 100.

Activity: Study the Information

Wetlands have many benefits. They are flood plains, swamps, or marshes that provide a habitat for wildlife and plants. They also collect sediment that would pollute rivers and streams. Coastal wetlands protect the mainland from damaging waves. Canada has $\frac{1}{4}$ of the world's wetlands. These wetlands cover nearly $\frac{1}{5}$ of the country. At one time, $\frac{7}{25}$ of the world's wetlands were in Canada.

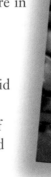

Inquire

1. Write each of the fractions with a denominator of 100.

2. What percent of the world's wetlands are in Canada now?

3. What percent of the country do they cover?

4. What percent of the world's wetlands did Canada once have?

5. What is the difference in the percent of the world's wetlands that Canada once had and the percent that Canada now has?

 6. How does a country lose its wetlands?

Example

About $\frac{1}{25}$ of the United States, $\frac{13}{20}$ of Canada, and $\frac{1}{50}$ of Mexico is wilderness. What percent of each country is wilderness?

Solution

For the United States

$$\frac{1}{25} = \frac{1 \times 4}{25 \times 4}$$
$$= \frac{4}{100}$$
$$= 4\%$$

For Canada

$$\frac{13}{20} = \frac{13 \times 5}{20 \times 5}$$
$$= \frac{65}{100}$$
$$= 65\%$$

For Mexico

$$\frac{1}{50} = \frac{1 \times 2}{50 \times 2}$$
$$= \frac{2}{100}$$
$$= 2\%$$

So, 4% of the United States, 65% of Canada, and 2% of Mexico is wilderness.

Practice

Express the shaded part of each figure as a percent.

1.

2.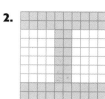

3.

4.

What percent of each figure is shaded?

5.

6.

7.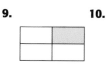

8.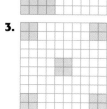

9.

10.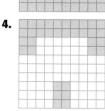

11. What percent of each figure in questions 5–10 is not shaded?

Draw each of the following.

12. a circle with 50% shaded in 2 different ways

13. a square with 25% shaded in 3 different ways

14. a rectangle with 75% shaded in 2 different ways

15. Estimate the percent shaded.

a)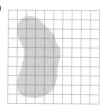

b)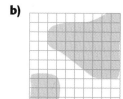

Copy and complete the following.

16. $\frac{3}{20} = \frac{\blacksquare}{100} = \blacksquare\%$ **17.** $\frac{7}{25} = \frac{\blacksquare}{100} = \blacksquare\%$

18. $\frac{\blacksquare}{50} = \frac{\blacksquare}{100} = 88\%$ **19.** $\frac{\blacksquare}{25} = \frac{\blacksquare}{100} = 44\%$

20. $\frac{\blacksquare}{25} = \frac{\blacksquare}{100} = 64\%$ **21.** $\frac{\blacksquare}{20} = \frac{\blacksquare}{100} = 85\%$

Write as a percent.

22. $\frac{7}{10}$ **23.** $\frac{1}{50}$ **24.** $\frac{24}{25}$

25. $\frac{9}{20}$ **26.** $\frac{3}{4}$ **27.** $\frac{1}{20}$

28. $\frac{4}{5}$ **29.** 1   **30.** $\frac{19}{50}$

Write each fraction in lowest terms. Then, write it as a percent.

31. $\frac{12}{15}$ **32.** $\frac{9}{12}$ **33.** $\frac{7}{14}$

34. $\frac{18}{30}$ **35.** $\frac{21}{28}$ **36.** $\frac{7}{35}$

Problems and Applications

37. Around the world, 17 people out of 20 have brown eyes. What percent of the world's population has brown eyes?

38. Did you know that water accounts for about $\frac{3}{5}$ of your body mass? What percent of your body mass does water account for?

39. About $\frac{9}{25}$ of Canada is covered by forests. What percent of Canada is covered by forests?

 40. Explain how the word "percent" can help you remember what it means.

 41. a) Twenty-two out of 25 Canadians put on their right shoe first. What percent of Canadians put on their right shoe first?
b) About what percent of your classmates put on their right shoe first?

42. List the ways percent is used, other than with money. Share your list with your classmates.

241

7.2 Ratios, Fractions, Decimals, and Percents

Activity: Use the Information
In the television and movie industries, a shooting ratio is the ratio of the length of film shot to the length of film used. A well-produced movie has a shooting ratio of 5:1.

Inquire

1. What fraction of the film is used?

2. Write the fraction with a denominator of 100.

3. What percent of the film is used?

4. What percent of the film is not used?

5. Some television commercials have shooting ratios of 50:1. What percent of the film or tape is used?

Example 1

A 30-min television show has 6 min of commercials. What percent of the show is commercials?

Solution

The fraction of the show that is commercials is $\frac{6}{30}$.

Method 1
Express the fraction with a denominator of 100.

$$\overset{\div 6}{\frac{6}{30} = \frac{1}{5}}_{\div 6}$$

$$\frac{1}{5} = \frac{1 \times 20}{5 \times 20}$$
$$= \frac{20}{100}$$
$$= 20\%$$

Method 2
Express the fraction $\frac{6}{30}$ as a decimal.

$$\frac{6}{30} = 6 \div 30$$
$$= 0.2$$
$$= \frac{20}{100}$$
$$= 20\%$$

So, 20% of the show is commercials.

Example 2

Write as percents. **a)** 0.235 **b)** 7:8 **c)** $\frac{2}{3}$

Solution

a) $0.235 = \frac{23.5}{100}$
$= 23.5\%$
or $0.235 = 0.235 \times 100\%$
$= 23.5\%$

b) $7:8 = \frac{7}{8}$
$= 0.875$
$= 0.875 \times 100\%$
$= 87.5\%$

| C | 7 | ÷ | 8 | % | | 87.5 |

c) $\frac{2}{3} = 2 \div 3$
$= 0.667$ (nearest thousandth)
$= 0.667 \times 100\%$
$= 66.7\%$

Example 3

Write as decimals.
a) 7%
b) 43.2%
c) $5\frac{1}{2}\%$

Solution

a) $7\% = \frac{7}{100}$
$= 0.07$

b) $43.2\% = \frac{43.2}{100}$
$= 0.432$

c) $5\frac{1}{2}\% = 5.5\%$
$= \frac{5.5}{100}$
$= 0.055$

Practice

Express as a percent.

1. 0.4   **2.** 1:4   **3.** 3:8

4. $\frac{6}{25}$ **5.** $\frac{19}{20}$ **6.** 9:45

7. 0.125   **8.** $\frac{98}{1000}$ **9.** $\frac{18}{30}$

Express as a percent. Round each answer to the nearest tenth, if necessary.

10. $\frac{1}{3}$ **11.** 2:11   **12.** 0.5

13. $\frac{4}{7}$ **14.** $\frac{11}{12}$ **15.** 5:9

Write as a decimal.

16. 18%   **17.** 85.9%   **18.** $6\frac{3}{4}\%$

19. 3%   **20.** 33.3%   **21.** 5%

Replace each ♦ with >, <, or = to make each statement true.

22. 0.01 ♦ 10%   **23.** $\frac{3}{5}$ ♦ 65%

24. $\frac{35}{50}$ ♦ 35%   **25.** 0.05 ♦ 50%

26. 17:20 ♦ 85%   **27.** 0.8 ♦ 78%

Problems and Applications

28. About $\frac{1}{50}$ of the Earth's water is frozen in ice caps and glaciers. Write this fraction as a percent.

29. The pull of gravity on the surface of Mars is 0.38 of the pull of gravity on the surface of the Earth. Write this decimal as a percent and as a fraction in lowest terms.

The table shows the make-up of the human body, by mass. Copy and complete the table.

	Part	Fraction (lowest terms)	Decimal	Percent
30.	Muscles	$\frac{11}{25}$		
31.	Fat		0.12	
32.	Bones			16%
33.	Internal Organs	$\frac{1}{5}$		
34.	Blood		0.08	

35. The ratio of British Columbians who live in the city of Vancouver to the total number of people in the province is about 1:7.
a) Write this ratio as a decimal.
b) Express the ratio to the nearest percent.

 36. Some schools use a 4-point scale instead of percents for student marks.
a) A grade of 3 on a 4-point scale is $\frac{3}{4} \times 100\%$ or 75%. What percent is a grade of 2? 3.2? 2.4?
b) The following calculation shows how to write 65% as a grade on a 4-point scale.

$$\frac{65}{100} = \frac{n}{4}$$
$$\frac{65 \div 25}{100 \div 25} = \frac{n}{4}$$
$$\frac{2.6}{4} = \frac{n}{4}$$
$$2.6 = n$$

So, 65% is a grade of 2.6.
On a 4-point scale what grade is 25%? 70%? 85%?

7.3 Percent of a Number

Recall that "of" means multiply.

So, $\frac{1}{2}$ of $8 = \frac{1}{2} \times 8$ or 4, and 50% of $8 = 0.5 \times 8$ or 4.

Activity: Calculate the Costs

Feature films can cost anywhere from $500 000 to hundreds of millions of dollars to make. The table gives the motion picture industry's typical breakdown of expenses for a low-budget movie.

Copy the table. Complete it by calculating the cost of each item for a $3 000 000 movie.

Component	Percent	Cost ($)
Screenplay, Producer, Director	10%	
Cast	25%	
Studio Overhead	20%	
Crew and Materials	40%	
Unknowns	5%	

Inquire

1. What is the cost of each component?

2. How would you use addition to check your calculations?

3. Why is there an "unknowns" component when making movies?

Example

Songwriters and song publishers earn royalties when their songs are played on the radio. Radio stations pay 3.25% of their advertising income to a performing rights association. The association pays the writers and publishers. If the money received from advertisers by Canadian radio stations is about $960 000 000 a year, how much does the association receive?

Solution

To find the percent of a number, write the percent as a decimal and then multiply by the number.

$3.25\% = \frac{3.25}{100}$

$\qquad = 0.0325$

3.25% of $\$960\ 000\ 000 = 0.0325 \times \$960\ 000\ 000$

$\qquad\qquad\qquad\qquad = \$31\ 200\ 000$

The association receives $31 200 000.

C 0 · 0325 × 960 000 000
= 3 1200000

EST 0.03 × 1 000 000 000 = 30 000 000

244

Practice

Calculate.

1. 50% of 30

2. 25% of 40

3. 15% of 60

4. 20% of 25

5. 30% of 50

6. 10% of 500

Estimate, then calculate.

7. 12% of 25

8. 14% of 22

9. 8% of 140

10. 95% of 70

11. 55% of 50

12. 14% of 85

Calculate.

13. 2.5% of 120

14. 87.5% of 400

15. 22.5% of 30

16. 6.75% of 1600

17. 66.6% of 45

18. 38.9% of 600

Estimate, then calculate.

19. 13% of 190

20. 48% of 95

21. 26% of 375

22. 62% of 210

23. 51.5% of $126

24. 83% of $565

Replace each ♦ with >, <, or = to make each statement true.

25. 6% of 120 ♦ 60% of 12

26. 25% of 150 ♦ 35% of 120

27. 64% of 3 ♦ 16% of 12

28. 48% of 500 ♦ 73% of 350

Problems and Applications

In questions 29–34, guess the percent and then test with your calculator.

29. ■% of 60 is 30

30. ■% of 44 is 11

31. ■% of 15 is 3.3

32. ■% of 22 is 18.7

33. ■% of 56 is 40.32

34. ■% of 84 is 23.52

35. The area of Lake Winnipeg is about 85% of the area of Great Slave Lake. The area of Great Slave Lake is 28 600 km^2. What is the area of Lake Winnipeg?

36. Many live theatre productions are non-profit. The table shows where the money goes from their ticket sales.

Artists	33%
Promotion	17%
Administration	15%
Production	23%
Theatre	12%

If a ticket costs $40, how much of the $40 goes to each category?

37. A rule of thumb for large commercial theatre productions is that 30% of the cost of a ticket goes to salaries, rent, and production, 30% goes to the investors, and 40% goes to the producer. If a ticket costs $95, how much goes to each category?

38. The table shows how the money you pay for a CD is distributed.

Raw Materials	14%
Record Company Overhead	21%
Royalties to Artist, Composer, Publisher, and Producer	25%
Record Company Profit	8%
Store Markup	32%

Use a current price for a CD and calculate how much goes to each category.

WORD POWER

Change the word WARM to the word COLD by changing one letter at a time. Each time you change a letter, you must form a real word. The best solution has the fewest steps.

Writing and Interpreting Instructions

Activity ❶ Drawing Designs

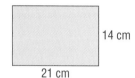

14 cm

21 cm

Work with a classmate.

Use a piece of paper with dimensions about 21 cm by 14 cm, or half the size of a sheet of notepaper. Place the paper on your desk so that the long side is across the top.

Read the instructions and sketch the figures. Read each instruction completely before making the sketch from that instruction. Do not use a ruler or a straight edge. Use your estimation skills to draw the shapes.

1. Mark point A, 6 cm from the left side of the paper and 4 cm from the top.

2. Use A as the centre and draw a circle of radius 3 cm.

3. Draw a square with sides 5 cm, so that the top left vertex of the square is at A. The other sides of the square are parallel to the edges of the paper.

4. Mark point B, 5 cm from the bottom edge of the paper and 5 cm from the right edge.

5. Use point B as the bottom left vertex of a rectangle. The sides of the rectangle are parallel to the edges of the paper. The rectangle has a length of 7 cm and a width of 3 cm. The longer side of the rectangle is parallel to the shorter edge of the paper.

Use a ruler to check how accurate you were in marking A and B. Use a ruler to check the radius of your circle and the dimensions of the square and the rectangle.

Compare your final sketch with the sketches of other pairs.

Activity ❷ Writing Instructions

Write a set of instructions that you would give to a classmate to sketch the design. Each instruction can be given only once.

Check that your instructions would allow someone to sketch the complete design.

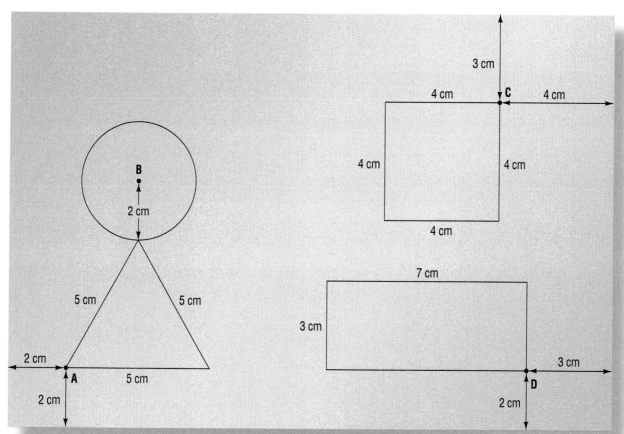

Activity ❸ Making Designs

Make a design of your own, using geometric figures. Write a set of instructions that you would give to classmates, so that they could sketch the design.

Read your instructions to 3 classmates. Have them sketch the design individually, without looking at each other's sketches.

Once you have finished reading the instructions, have the 3 classmates compare their sketches.

How are the sketches the same?

How are they different?

How could you have improved your instructions?

247

7.4 Estimating with Percent: Mental Math

Activity: Use the Information

One way to rate baseball players is to calculate the percent of the time they get on base. The season John Olerud won his first batting championship, he came to the plate 665 times, got 200 hits, and was walked 114 times.

Inquire

1. What was the total number of times he got on base because of hits and walks?

2. What fraction of the times he came to the plate did he get on base?

3. Use this fraction and compatible numbers to estimate a simple fraction.

4. Estimate the percent of the time he got on base.

Example

Fran's bill at a restaurant was $24.75. She wanted to leave a 15% tip. Estimate the tip.

Solution

Think of 15% as 10% + 5%.
$24.75 is about $25.
10% of $25 is $2.50.
5% is $\frac{1}{2}$ of 10%, so $\frac{1}{2}$ of $2.50 is $1.25.
$2.50 + $1.25 = $3.75
The 15% tip was about $3.75.

Practice

Estimate the percent of each area that is shaded.

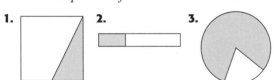

Estimate the percent of each number.

4. 49% of 82   **5.** 11% of 630

6. 9% of $212   **7.** 3% of $308

Estimate the percent for each of these test marks.

8. 46 out of 52   **9.** 15 out of 19

10. 22 out of 33   **11.** 7 out of 16

Problems and Applications

12. Old Glory Mountain in British Columbia has fog 226 days a year. Estimate the percent of the days in a year the mountain has fog.

Estimate the 15% tip for each of these restaurant bills.

13. $39.50   **14.** $16.35   **15.** $9.69

16. $123.42   **17.** $19.43   **18.** $31.56

19. Commonwealth Stadium in Edmonton has a seating capacity of 60 081. Olympic Stadium in Montreal can seat 72.8% of this number. Estimate the seating capacity of Olympic Stadium.

20. The second year the Toronto Blue Jays won the World Series, Joe Carter was at bat 603 times and he got a hit 25.4% of the time. Estimate the number of hits he got.

21. Use your estimation skills to find the approximate percent of the space taken up by advertising in a newspaper or magazine.

7.5 Discount and Sale Price

Activity: Use the Information

To attract people into their stores, some store managers offer discounts on certain items. Other store managers offer a discount on a popular item, such as a CD. A store paid $14.00 for the CD shown. The store can sell 100 copies a week at the list price, or 500 copies a week at the sale price.

Inquire

1. What does the store make
a) on each CD sold at the list price of $20.00?
b) on 100 CDs sold at the list price?

2. Calculate 15% of $20.00.

3. What is the sale price?

4. What does the store make
a) on each CD sold at the sale price?
b) on 500 CDs sold at the sale price?

Example

The regular price of a CD player with an AM/FM receiver is $598.00. What is the sale price after a discount of 25%?

Solution

The discount is 25% of $598.00.
$0.25 \times 598.00 = 149.50$
The discount is $149.50.

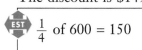

$\boxed{\text{EST} \quad \frac{1}{4} \text{ of } 600 = 150}$

$\boxed{\text{C} \; 598 \; \times \; 25 \; \% \; \text{M+}}$

Sale price = regular price − discount
　　　　 = $598.00 − $149.50
　　　　 = $448.50
The sale price is $448.50.

$\boxed{\text{EST} \quad 600 - 150 = 450}$

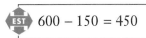

$\boxed{\text{C} \; 598 \; - \; \text{MRC} \; = \quad\quad 448.5}$

Problems and Applications

Estimate, then calculate each discount.

1. 20% off a shirt at $39.95

2. 25% off a blank videocassette at $4.50

3. 40% off perfume at $88.00

4. 60% off designer jeans at $69.95

5. 30% off an exercise bike at $399.95

Estimate, then calculate each sale price.

6. a $2.50 binder at 25% off

7. a $1269 computer at 5% off

8. a $29.95 towel set at 15% off

9. a $449.50 TV set at 20% off

10. Jane says, "A $174.99 personal CD player at 40% off is cheaper than a $149.99 personal CD player at 25% off." Is Jane correct?

11. A Raptors T-shirt that sold for $30 was increased in price by 20%. What was the new price?

12. Write a problem that involves finding a discount or sale price. Have a classmate solve your problem.

249

7.6 PST and GST

Activity: Calculate the Cost

The Goods and Services Tax (GST) is a federal government tax. The rate is the same for all provinces. Each province determines a rate of Provincial Sales Tax (PST).

Inquire

1. What is the rate of GST? your provincial rate of PST?

2. Calculate the GST on the in-line skates.

3. In your province, is the PST calculated on the price of the item, or on the sum of the price and the GST?

4. Calculate the PST on the in-line skates.

5. What is the total cost of the in-line skates?

Example

A mountain bike lists for $550.00. Calculate the total cost if the GST is 7% and the PST is 8%.

Solution 1

(PST on selling price)

$$\text{Selling price} = \$550.00$$
$$\text{GST} = 0.07 \times \$550.00 = \$\ 38.50$$
$$\text{PST} = 0.08 \times \$550.00 = \$\ 44.00$$
$$\text{Total cost} = \$632.50$$

Solution 2

(PST on selling price plus GST)

$$\text{Selling price} = \$550.00$$
$$\text{GST} = 0.07 \times \$550.00 = \$\ 38.50$$
$$\text{Total} = \$588.50$$
$$\text{PST} = 0.08 \times \$588.50 = \$\ 47.08$$
$$\text{Total cost} = \$635.58$$

> **EST** $0.07 \times 600 = 42$
>
> **EST** $0.08 \times 600 = 48$

Problems and Applications

Estimate the GST and PST in your province.

	Item	Price
1.	Radio	$110.00
2.	T-shirt	$18.75
3.	Boat	$31 000.00
4.	Jeans	$55.00

Calculate the total cost, including the GST and PST in your province.

	Item	Price
5.	Portable phone	$99.95
6.	Computer	$2049.00
7.	Sunglasses	$21.75
8.	Pen	$7.90

9. The regular price of a pair of boots is $120.00. The discount is 10%. Calculate the total cost, including the GST and PST in your province.

10. A rowing machine regularly costs $240.00. It is discounted 25%. Calculate the total cost in your province, including all taxes.

11. Cut out of newspapers and magazines the pictures and prices of 6 items that you would like to buy. Glue or tape the pictures into your notebook. Calculate the total cost of each item, including the GST and PST in your province.

 12. List 5 ways your province uses the money it raises from the PST.

7.7 Commission

Some salespeople earn a salary or an hourly wage, plus a **commission** on what they sell. Commission is a percent of the cost of goods sold. Some salespeople work for commission only.

Activity: Calculate the Commission

Lyndsay earns a 4% commission for selling computers. One weekend, she sold 2 at $2200.00 each and 3 at $2600.00 each.

Inquire

1. What were Lyndsay's total sales?

2. What was Lyndsay's commission?

3. What is one advantage of being paid on commission?

4. What is one advantage for an employer to pay on commission?

5. What is one disadvantage for employees? for employers?

6. List 4 jobs for which commission might be all or part of total earnings.

Example	Solution
Carlos sells sports clothes. He earns $9/h, plus 2% commission. How much does he earn for sales of $850 in 7 h?	Commission = 2% of $850 = 0.02 × $850 = $17.00　　EST 0.02 × 1000 = 20 Salary = 7 × $9.00 = $63.00 Earnings = $17.00 + $63.00 = $80.00　　EST 20 + 60 = 80

Problems and Applications

1. Omar sells real estate at 1.5% commission. Calculate his commission on the following sales.

a) $320 000.00 　　**b)** $120 000.00
c) $75 500.00 　　**d)** $93 750.00

2. Elizabeth sells new cars. Her commission is 10% of the profit on each car. Calculate her commission on sales with the following profits.

a) $2000.00 　　**b)** $1550.00
c) $3175.00 　　**d)** $1998.00

3. Marcia works in a clothing store. She earns $12.00/h, plus 2% commission. Calculate her earnings for a 35-h week in which her sales were $4695.00.

4. Ernst works in a computer store. He earns $7.50/h, plus 4% commission. One week he worked 39 h and had sales of $12 456.00. Calculate his earnings for the week.

5. Pat works in a clothing store where he is paid $650.00 a week, plus 2% commission. In the month of May, he had weekly sales of $9367.50, $7123.75, $12 680.25, and $8764.00. Calculate his earnings for the month.

7.8 Finding the Percent

A cube 1 cm long, 1 cm wide, and 1 cm high has a volume of one cubic centimetre (1 cm³). A cube 1 km long, 1 km wide, and 1 km high has a volume of one cubic kilometre (1 km³). Statisticians use cubic kilometres when calculating a country's water supply.

Activity: Use the Information

The amount of water in use in Canada is about 40 km³. Three cubic kilometres are used in agriculture, 32 km³ in industry, and 5 km³ in homes and cities.

Inquire

1. What fraction of the water is used in industry?

2. Write this fraction in lowest terms.

3. Write the fraction with a denominator of 100.

4. What percent of the water is used in industry?

5. What fraction of the water is used in agriculture?

6. Express this fraction as a decimal.

7. Write the decimal as a percent to find the percent of the water used in agriculture.

8. What percent of the water is used in homes and cities?

9. Canada's renewable water supply is 2900 km³. About what percent of the supply is in use?

Example

Commercial breaks in radio broadcasting are called "islands." An island is usually 2.5 min long. Many FM stations have 3 islands every hour. What percent of the time do commercials take up?

Solution

There are 60 min in 1 h.

There are 3×2.5 min or 7.5 min of commercials.

The fraction of commercial time in one hour is $\frac{7.5}{60}$.

$$\frac{7.5}{60} = 0.125 \qquad \boxed{\text{EST} \quad 6 \div 60 = 0.1}$$

$0.125 \times 100\% = 12.5\%$

Commercials take up 12.5% of the time.

Practice

Write each decimal as a percent.

1. 0.8   **2.** 0.57   **3.** 0.515

4. 0.671   **5.** 0.02   **6.** 0.045

7. 0.302   **8.** 0.999   **9.** 0.007

Write as a percent.

10. $\frac{4}{5}$ **11.** $\frac{3}{10}$ **12.** 13:20

13. $\frac{8}{25}$ **14.** $\frac{11}{11}$ **15.** $\frac{18}{72}$

16. 44:200   **17.** $\frac{45}{150}$ **18.** $\frac{24}{64}$

Express as a percent, to the nearest tenth.

19. $\frac{2}{3}$ **20.** $\frac{4}{7}$ **21.** $\frac{5}{9}$

22. 1:6   **23.** $\frac{5}{11}$ **24.** 12:13

Calculate. Round to the nearest tenth, if necessary.

25. 25 is what percent of 200?

26. What percent of 75 is 45?

27. 21 is what percent of 24?

28. 40 is what percent of 45?

29. What percent of 8.6 is 5.9?

30. What percent of 0.8 is 0.12?

Problems and Applications

31. a) Canada's first 6 astronauts were chosen in 1983. The next 4 were chosen in 1992. What percent of Canada's first 10 astronauts were chosen in 1992?

b) The 2 youngest astronauts chosen in 1992 were Julie Payette, aged 28, and Chris Hadfield, aged 32. What percent was Julie's age of Chris's age?

32. In a test on percent applications, Lily answered 28 of the 35 questions correctly. What percent of the questions did Lily
a) answer correctly?   **b)** not answer correctly?

33. Of the 19 events in which Canadians won medals at the Barcelona Olympics, 5 were rowing events, and 4 were swimming events. What percent of the events were rowing or swimming events? Round your answer to the nearest tenth.

34. Agnes Macphail (1890–1954) was the first Canadian woman elected as a Member of Parliament (MP). She was elected in 1921 and served until 1940. For what percent of her life was she an MP? Round your answer to the nearest percent.

35. The price of a pair of sunglasses increased from $120 to $144. By what percent did the price increase?

36. When the Blue Jays won their second World Series, 25 Blue Jays actually played in the 6 World Series games. The Blue Jays gave out 265 championship rings. What percent of the people who received rings did not play in the World Series? Round your answer to the nearest percent.

37. Use your research skills to determine the percent of Canadians who live in each of the following provinces or cities. Round each answer to the nearest tenth of a percent.

a) Alberta   **b)** Prince Edward Island
c) Halifax   **d)** Ontario

NUMBER POWER

Find 5 different digits with a sum of 21 that make the multiplication statement true. ■■ × ■ = ■■

Designing Theatrical Sets

Although drama is classified as a fine art, there is probably more math involved in the theatre than most people realize. For example, a set designer is a technologist who uses math in designing the set for a production.

Long before rehearsals begin or construction starts, the director and the set designer discuss the needs of the play, what shape the set should take, and how the set will relate to the theatre. The set designer listens to the director's ideas, then mentally creates an image of the set. To communicate this image, the designer draws a *ground plan* and a *thumbnail sketch*.

The ground plan shows the physical relationships of the objects in the set, and how they relate to the theatre.

The thumbnail sketch better displays what the audience will actually see.

Activity ❶ A Box Set

Ground Plan (or top view in 2-D)

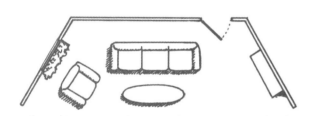

Thumbnail Sketch (or front view in 3-D)

1. The set shown in the above diagrams is known as a box set. Explain why.

2. The front edge of the stage is often called the fourth wall. If the set walls were extended to the fourth wall, what shape would be created
a) in the ground plan?
b) in the thumbnail sketch?

3. You are the set designer for a play that will be performed in a box set. The scene is a dining room. Four people will be seated for dinner. Draw the ground plan and the thumbnail sketch of the set.

254

Activity ❷ A Black-Box Theatre

For more complex sets, the ability to think and draw in both two and three dimensions is more important and more difficult.

Suppose the designer decides to use scaffolds as the major pieces to define the space. The show is performed in a black-box theatre, which has the shape of an empty rectangular prism. In such a theatre, the relationship of the seating to the performing areas is very flexible. The audience may sit on scaffolding around the perimeter, with the actors performing in the centre of the room. The props for the actors may be as simple as boxes.

1. Determine the scaffold from which the designer chose to draw the thumbnail sketch. How would this sketch differ if you sketched the set from

a) the stage left scaffold?

b) the stage right scaffold?

2. The relationship of the ground plan to the thumbnail sketch is very important for showing the designer's image. For example, the ground plan contains the exact height of each scaffold, while the thumbnail sketch shows how many sections high each scaffold is. What other dimensions would you need to know before building the set?

3. The next step in the design process is to combine the information in the diagrams to create a three-dimensional scale model of the set. List other examples of the use of three-dimensional scale models.

4. Design your own black-box theatre. Draw the ground plan and the thumbnail sketch. Include dimensions.

Ground Plan

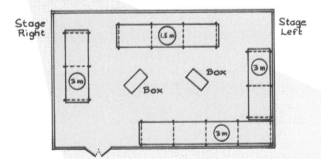

Thumbnail Sketch

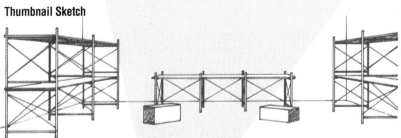

Activity ❸ Using Technology

Activities 1 and 2 could be completed with paper, a pencil, and a ruler. Answer the following questions about how newer technologies might be used.

1. Describe any advantages of using computer graphics to draw the diagrams.

2. How might you use virtual reality to help you design a set?

255

7.9 100% of a Number

Activity: Study the Information

Part of the money you spend on a book goes to the author or authors as royalties. Fernand was part of an author team that wrote a book about the history of Canadian art. He receives a royalty of 1% of sales. His last royalty cheque was for $890.00.

Inquire

1. If 1% of sales was $890.00, how can you find 100% of sales?

2. Calculate 100% of sales.

3. The book publisher gave a total of 10% of sales to the author team as royalties. Calculate 10% of sales.

Example 1

The shooting time for a typical made-for-TV movie is about 40 days. This time accounts for just 20% of the total time needed to make the movie. The rest of the time is used for scripting, preproduction, and postproduction. What is the total number of days needed to make the movie?

Solution 1	Solution 2
20% of the time is 40 days.	Let x represent the total number of days needed. Write a proportion.
1% of the time is $\frac{40}{20}$ or 2 days.	
100% of the time is 100×2 days or 200 days.	$$\frac{20}{100} = \frac{40}{x}$$ $$\frac{20 \times 2}{100 \times 2} = \frac{40}{x}$$ $$\frac{40}{200} = \frac{40}{x}$$ $$200 = x$$

It takes about 200 days to make the movie.

Example 2

If 7% of a number is 8.4, find the number.

Solution 1

7% of the number is 8.4.
1% of the number is $\frac{8.4}{7}$.
100% of the number is
$$100 \times \frac{8.4}{7} = \frac{840}{7}$$
$$= 120$$

The number is 120.

Solution 2

Let x represent the number.
Write a proportion.
$$\frac{7}{100} = \frac{8.4}{x}$$
$$\frac{7 \times 1.2}{100 \times 1.2} = \frac{8.4}{x}$$
$$\frac{8.4}{120} = \frac{8.4}{x}$$
$$120 = x$$

Practice

Copy and complete the statements.

1. 5% of a number is 20.
1% of the number is ■.

2. 20% of a number is 60.
1% of the number is ■.

3. 15% of a number is 30.
1% of the number is ■.

4. 4% of a number is 24.4.
1% of the number is ■.

Find each number.

5. 1% of the number is 5.

6. 1% of the number is 26.

7. 1% of the number is 8.2.

8. 1% of the number is 29.7.

Copy and complete the statements.

9. 5% of a number is 25.
1% of the number is ■.
100% of the number is ■.

10. 15% of a number is 75.
1% of the number is ■.
100% of the number is ■.

11. 12% of a number is 48.
1% of the number is ■.
100% of the number is ■.

Find the value of x.

12. $\frac{40}{100} = \frac{80}{x}$ **13.** $\frac{15}{100} = \frac{45}{x}$

14. $\frac{9}{100} = \frac{54}{x}$ **15.** $\frac{8}{100} = \frac{3.2}{x}$

16. If 10% of a number is 70, find the number.

17. If 20% of a number is 80, find the number.

18. If 9% of a number is 72, find the number.

19. If 6% of a number is 5.4, find the number.

Problems and Applications

20. Susan writes mystery novels. Her royalties are 10% of sales. Her last royalty cheque was for $2300. Calculate the sales.

21. The Earth's surface is about 30% land, and the rest is water. The area of the land is 148 million square kilometres. What is the total area of the Earth, to the nearest million square kilometres?

22. Of all the animal species in North America, 200 are classified as "historic." Scientists know that these species existed at one time and believe that they still survive. Historic species represent 2% of the known North American animal species. How many North American animal species are there?

23. The original price of a camera was reduced by 20%. The selling price was $280. What was the original price?

24. a) $33\frac{1}{3}$% of what number is 20?

b) $66\frac{2}{3}$% of what number is 20?

LOGIC POWER

The 2 train cars are too big to go under the bridge, but the engine can. Either end of the engine can push or pull a car. The engine can also move both cars at once when they are joined together, or it can push one and pull the other. Show how the engine can reverse the positions of the cars and return to its starting position. (Hint: You might use different coins to represent the engine and the cars.)

7.10 Percents Greater Than 100%

Activity: Calculate the Sizes

The first 3 planets detected outside our solar system orbit a star that is 1300 light years from Earth. The diameter of one of the planets is 8% of the Earth's diameter, which is 12 756 km.

$$8\% \text{ of } 12\ 756 = 0.08 \times 12\ 756$$
$$\doteq 1020$$

So, the diameter of this planet is about 1020 km.
The other 2 planets have diameters that are 200% of the Earth's diameter.

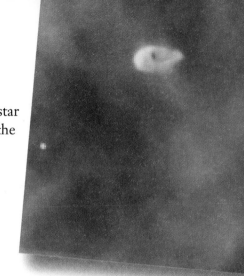

Inquire

1. What is 200% of 12 756 km?

2. What are the diameters of the 2 planets?

3. Make a scale drawing to compare the size of the Earth and the sizes of the 3 new planets.

Percents greater than 100% can be written as fractions or decimals.

$$160\% = \frac{160}{100}$$

Think: $\frac{160}{100} = \frac{160 \div 20}{100 \div 20}$

$$= \frac{8}{5} \text{ or } 1.6$$

Numbers greater than 1 can be written as percents.

$$2\frac{1}{2} = \frac{5}{2}$$

Think: $\frac{5}{2} = \frac{5 \times 50}{2 \times 50}$

$$= \frac{250}{100}$$
$$= 250\%$$

Practice

Write each percent as a decimal.

1. 100%   **2.** 200%   **3.** 1000%

4. 125%   **5.** 4000%   **6.** 225%

Write as a percent.

7. 3   **8.** 1.6   **9.** 1.75   **10.** 15

Express as a percent.

11. $1\frac{1}{2}$ **12.** $\frac{13}{10}$ **13.** $\frac{7}{4}$

14. $1\frac{2}{5}$ **15.** $2\frac{1}{4}$ **16.** $3\frac{1}{10}$

Calculate.

17. 200% of 60   **18.** 300% of 1000

19. 150% of 80   **20.** 1000% of 50

21. 110% of $20   **22.** 107% of $64

Problems and Applications

23. The average Canadian eats about 2.7 kg of breakfast cereal per year. The average American eats 200% of this amount. How much cereal does the average American eat per year?

24. If 1 cm of rain falls as snow, the depth of the snow is 1000% of the depth of the rain. How deep is the snow?

25. Last year, the price of a theatre ticket was $25. This year, it is $30.

a) What is the percent increase over last year's price?

b) What percent of last year's price is this year's price?

26. What percent is the reciprocal of 50%? Explain.

7.11 Simple Interest

When you deposit money in a bank, the bank pays you **interest** for the use of your money. If you borrow money from a bank, you pay interest for the use of the bank's money. The money you deposit or borrow is called the **principal**. The total of the principal and the interest is called the **amount**.

Activity: Calculate the Interest

Francie bought $2000 worth of Canada Savings Bonds. The government paid Francie 7% interest for one year.

Inquire

1. If the interest was 7% of $2000, how much interest did Francie earn?

2. What amount of money did Francie have at the end of one year?

Example

Mark bought a $500 Canada Savings Bond that paid 6.5% interest a year for 5 years.
a) How much interest did Mark earn?
b) What amount of money did Mark have after 5 years?

Solution

a) The formula to calculate simple interest is $I = Prt$, where I is the interest earned, P is the principal, r is the rate of interest, and t is the time in years.

$I = Prt$
$= 500 \times 0.065 \times 5$
$= 162.50$

Mark earned $162.50 in interest.

b) The amount is $500 + $162.50 or $662.50. Mark had $662.50 after 5 years.

Problems and Applications

For each deposit, calculate the interest and the amount.

	Principal	Interest Rate	Time (years)
1.	$800	6%	1
2.	$1000	7%	2
3.	$2000	6.5%	3
4.	$5000	8.2%	0.5

For each loan, calculate the interest and the total amount to be repaid.

	Principal	Rate	Time (years)
5.	$7500	9%	4
6.	$10 000	7.5%	3
7.	$4500	9.2%	3.5
8.	$9000	7.8%	0.5

9. Sofia bought a $1000 Canada Savings Bond. The interest rate was 8% per year. Calculate the amount she had after 9 years.

10. If interest is compounded, the amount at the end of one year becomes the principal for the next year. Copy and complete the table.

Year	Principal	Rate	Interest	Amount
1	$100 000	5%	$5000	$105 000
2	$105 000	5%		
3				
4				
5				

259

Review

What percent of each figure is shaded?

1.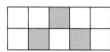

2.

3.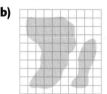

4.

5. Estimate the percent that is shaded.

a) **b)**

Draw each of the following in 2 different ways.

6. a square with 50% shaded

7. a circle with 75% shaded

8. a rectangle with 25% shaded

Express as a decimal.

9. 20%   **10.** 68%   **11.** 35.8%

12. 7%   **13.** 0.5%   **14.** 4.6%

Express as a fraction in lowest terms.

15. 10%   **16.** 60%   **17.** 12.5%

18. 88%   **19.** 36%   **20.** 2%

Write as a percent.

21. $\frac{2}{5}$ **22.** $\frac{11}{20}$ **23.** 24:25

24. 0.83   **25.** 0.015   **26.** $\frac{7}{8}$

Express to the nearest tenth of a percent.

27. $\frac{2}{3}$ **28.** $\frac{4}{9}$ **29.** $0.\overline{54}$

Express as a percent.

30. $\frac{7}{4}$ **31.** 1.32   **32.** 17:10

Estimate the percent of each figure that is shaded.

33.

34.

Estimate.

35. 33% of $190   **36.** 78% of $42

Estimate the 15% tip on these restaurant bills.

37. $15.75   **38.** $73.10

Calculate.

39. 75% of 80   **40.** 25% of 30

41. 60% of $345   **42.** 5% of $68

43. 125% of 50   **44.** 600% of $22.50

45. What percent is 35 of 56?

46. What percent of 50 is 2.5?

47. What percent is 22 of 77, to the nearest tenth of a percent?

48. What percent of 60 is 150?

49. If 15% of a number is 6, what is the number?

50. If 40% of a number is 85, what is the number?

51. Jim has 4 nickels and 6 dimes.
a) What percent of his coins are nickels?
b) What percent of the total value of the coins is the value of the dimes?

52. The elevation of Moose Jaw above sea level is 680% of the elevation of Kingston. The elevation of Kingston is 80 m. What is the elevation of Moose Jaw?

53. Vanessa Monar-Enweani became Canadian women's long jump champion with a leap of 6.42 m. The world record in the women's long jump was then 7.52 m. Calculate the percent that Vanessa's winning jump was of the world record. Round your answer to the nearest tenth of a percent.

54. Mars takes 686 days to orbit the sun. What percent is this of the time it takes the Earth to orbit the sun? Round your answer to the nearest percent.

55. St. John's gets the least sunshine of the provincial capitals. It gets only 1497 h of sunshine a year. There are 4470 h in the year when the sun could shine in St. John's. Estimate, then calculate the percent of the possible time the sun is actually shining. Round your calculated answer to the nearest tenth of a percent.

Calculate the discount and the sale price of each item.

56. $22.50 book at 10% off

57. $159.00 coat at 15% off

58. $79.99 shoes at 25% off

For each item, calculate the GST and the PST in your province.

59. $62.95 watch

60. $95.00 pair of shoes

61. $1299.00 stereo

62. $950.00 bicycle

63. Mario sold a $156 000.00 house for a commission of 1.5%. How much commission did he earn?

64. If you bought $200 worth of Canada Savings Bond at 8.5% interest per year, what amount of money would you have at the end of one year?

Group Decision Making
Important Scientific Discoveries

In this activity, you will choose 6 of the most important scientific discoveries.

1. As a class, decide on the difference between a scientific discovery and an invention. List some branches of science in which important discoveries have been made. Your list might include astronomy, geology, and medicine, for example.

2. In your home group, list 10 important scientific discoveries. Examples might include gravity, the moons of Jupiter, dinosaurs, insulin, and atoms.

1 2 3 4	1 2 3 4	1 2 3 4

Home Groups

1 2 3 4	1 2 3 4	1 2 3 4

3. In your home group, decide how you can rank the discoveries from most important to least important. Then, complete your ranking.

4. Make a presentation to the class. Explain why your group chose each discovery and why you ranked the discoveries in your chosen order.

5. As a class, list the 6 most important scientific discoveries. Choose a different discovery from the list for each home group to research.

6. In your home group, research the discovery and the scientist, or one of the scientists, who made it. Describe how the scientist might have used math to make the discovery. Prepare a report of your findings and present it to the class in a creative way.

7. As a class, evaluate the group decision making process.

Chapter Check

Express as a percent.

1. $\frac{41}{100}$ **2.** 0.5 **3.** 3:5

4. $\frac{1}{4}$ **5.** $\frac{8}{10}$ **6.** 0.095

Express each percent as a decimal and as a fraction in lowest terms.

7. 45% **8.** 62.5% **9.** 120%

What percent is the first number of the second? Round your answer to the nearest tenth, if necessary.

10. 12, 25 **11.** 35, 20 **12.** 4, 22

Calculate.

13. 1% of 300 **14.** 46% of 60

15. Montreal has 16 days of blowing snow a year. Winnipeg has 25 days of blowing snow a year. What percent is the number of days of blowing snow in Montreal of the number of days of blowing snow in Winnipeg?

16. The usual number of bones in the human skeleton is 206. Twenty-nine bones are in the skull. What percent of the bones are in the skull, to the nearest percent?

17. If 5% of a number is 10, what is the number?

18. About a million people live in Saskatchewan. About 20% of these people live in Saskatoon. What is the approximate population of Saskatoon?

19. Estimate the 15% tip on a $65.95 restaurant bill.

20. Manya bought a $500.00 savings bond that earned 8% interest per year. What amount of money did she have at the end of the year?

21. Calculate the total price, including taxes, of a $250.00 CD player in your province.

22. Jacob sold computers for $8.00/h, plus 4% commission on sales. In one 35-h week, he sold $10 500.00 worth of computers. How much did he earn that week?

23. If a coat with a regular price of $199.00 is sold at a 25% discount, what is the sale price?

Using the Strategies

1. Find the 2-digit number that is a perfect square and has exactly 9 whole numbers that will divide it evenly.

2. Starting with one cube, the first figure is made by adding a cube to each face. The first figure has 7 cubes. The second figure is made up of 13 cubes. The third figure is made up of 19 cubes.

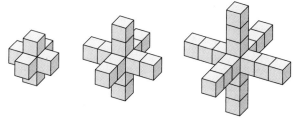

a) How many cubes are in the fourth figure?
b) How many cubes are in the 100th figure? the 3000th figure?

3. The areas of the faces of the box are 20 cm², 15 cm², and 12 cm². What is the volume of the box?

4. Place the digits from 1 to 6 in the squares to make a correct multiplication.

5. A store has some bicycles and some tricycles. There are exactly 27 wheels. List the possible combinations of bicycles and tricycles.

6. Pierre owns 6 dogs. Three cans of dog food feed 2 dogs for one day. How many cans of dog food does Pierre need to buy each week?

7. Assume that a race car must slow down at the curves on the track.

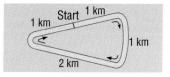

a) Sketch a graph of speed versus distance for 2 laps of the track in the direction shown.

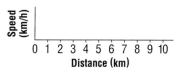

b) Sketch another graph of speed versus distance for 2 laps in the opposite direction.

8. The figure is made up of 6 squares. The total area is 54 m². What is the perimeter of the figure?

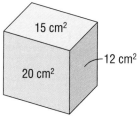

9. Irina left for the ski slopes at 06:00 and drove at 80 km/h. Beth left at 07:00 and followed her. Beth drove at 100 km/h. At what time did Beth catch up with Irina?

10. There are 3 monkeys on one side of a river, and 3 tigers on the other. Each group wants to move to the other side of the river. There is one boat that holds no more than 2 animals. At no time can the tigers outnumber the monkeys on one side of the river. How can they switch sides?

DATA BANK

1. What percent of the flying distance from Vancouver to Ottawa is the driving distance from Vancouver to Ottawa? Round your answer to the nearest percent.

2. a) In which month does Regina have the most precipitation?
b) About how much precipitation does Regina have that month?

CHAPTER 8

Three-Dimensional Geometry

Architects must consider many aspects of a building while they design it. These aspects include the volume of the building and the area of the ground floor.

Let 8 interlocking cubes represent a building of a certain volume. Make 8 models to show buildings with equal volumes but 8 different values for the area of the ground floor. Sketch your models and compare your designs with your classmates'.

If you were asked to design the building with the largest possible area of windows, what shape would you make it? Why?

List the factors that you think can affect the shape of a building.

Building Polygons

Copy each triangle onto cardboard and cut out six of each.
Use the triangles to complete Activities 1 to 4.

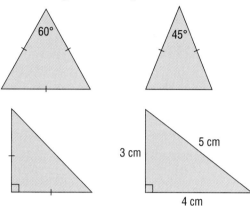

Activity ❶

1. Use equilateral triangles to make each polygon.

a) a rhombus **b)** a parallelogram that is not a rhombus

c) a trapezoid **d)** a hexagon

2. Draw each polygon. Label your drawing to show parallel
lines, congruent line segments, and congruent angles.

Activity ❷

1. Use 45° isosceles triangles to draw a hexagon. Label all
congruent line segments and angles.

2. What regular polygon can you draw using 45° isosceles
triangles? How many triangles do you need?

Activity ❸

1. Use 2 right isosceles triangles to draw 3 different polygons.
Name each polygon.

2. How many different polygons can you make with 4 right
isosceles triangles? Label all perpendicular lines.

3. Is it possible to use the right isosceles triangles to draw a
hexagon? an octagon?

Activity ❹

1. Use right scalene triangles to draw each polygon.

a) a rectangle **b)** a parallelogram that is not a rectangle

c) an isosceles triangle **d)** a trapezoid

2. Calculate the perimeter and the area of each polygon.

Line Symmetry

The following designs were created by Aboriginal peoples of North America in their loom, appliqué, and bead work.

a)

b)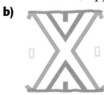

c)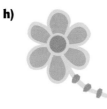

d)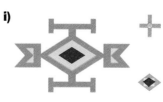

e)

f)

g)

h)

i)

 1. Describe the geometric shapes in each design.

2. What objects from nature are suggested by the designs?

3. Determine the number of lines of symmetry in each design.

Mental Math

Calculate.

1. 2^2 **2.** 4^2 **3.** 2^3 **4.** 5^2 **5.** $3^2 + 4^2$

6. 10^2 **7.** 10^3 **8.** $5^2 - 2^2$ **9.** $6^2 - 4^2$ **10.** $10^2 + 8^2$

Multiply.

11. 3.2×100 **12.** 4.5×10 **13.** 0.16×10 **14.** 0.9×100

15. 2.05×1000 **16.** 1.7×1000 **17.** 8.63×10 **18.** 12.7×100

19. 34.1×1000 **20.** 7.84×10 **21.** 15.6×100 **22.** 0.6×1000

Divide.

23. $24 \div 10$ **24.** $4.8 \div 10$ **25.** $150 \div 100$ **26.** $106 \div 1000$

27. $3.5 \div 100$ **28.** $12.8 \div 100$ **29.** $260 \div 1000$ **30.** $29.5 \div 100$

Write as metres.

31. 216 cm **32.** 48 cm **33.** 5940 cm **34.** 7 cm **35.** 865 cm

Write as centimetres.

36. 2 m **37.** 40 mm **38.** 5.6 m **39.** 675 mm **40.** 0.43 m

Write as millimetres.

41. 25 cm **42.** 3 m **43.** 5.1 cm **44.** 0.72 m **45.** 0.85 cm

8.1 Three-Dimensional Solids

Activity: Study the Shapes

A set of geometric solids includes many different three-dimensional shapes.

 cylinder   cube   rectangular prism   square pyramid   hexagonal prism   pentagonal prism

 triangular prism   triangular pyramid   pentagonal pyramid   sphere cone

Inquire

 1. Sort the solids shown into groups. Share with your classmates the criteria you used for sorting.

2. Sort the solids into groups using different criteria. Which solids are grouped together in both of the ways you sorted? Compare your findings with your classmates'.

 3. In a set of children's building blocks, there are different numbers of each shape. Which shapes should make up the largest number of blocks? the smallest number of blocks? Explain your answers.

Activity: Use the Definition

A **polyhedron** is a three-dimensional figure with faces that are polygons.

A rectangular prism is an example of a polyhedron.

A square pyramid is also a polyhedron.

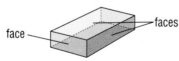
face — faces
face

Inquire

 1. Name the geometric solids at the top of the page that are not polyhedra. Explain why not.

2. List the polyhedra shown at the top of the page. Name the polygons that form the surfaces of each polyhedron and state the number of each polygon needed.

 3. State how prisms and pyramids are the same. State how they are different. Compare your conclusions with your classmates'.

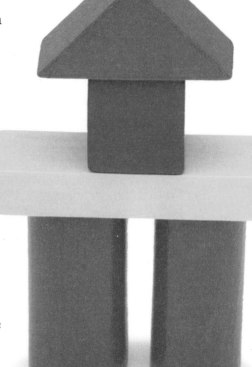

268

Practice

Use the solids shown on the opposite page to list the following.

1. all the solids with more than 4 flat faces

2. all the solids with at least 1 square face

3. all the solids with no flat faces

4. all the solids with no rectangular or square faces

5. all the solids with at least one triangular face

6. The model was built using 3 solids. Name the solids.

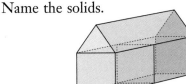

7. Sketch a model of a structure built from at least 3 geometric solids. Name the solids you used.

Problems and Applications

Name the geometric solid suggested by each object.

8.

9.

10.

11.

12.

13.

14. a) From the diagrams on the opposite page, describe how a prism is named.
b) Name the faces on an octagonal prism and state how many faces there are of each type.

15. a) From the diagrams on the opposite page, describe how a pyramid is named.
b) Name the faces on a hexagonal pyramid and state how many faces there are of each type.

16. Describe how a prism is like a cylinder. Describe how they are different.

17. How are a pyramid and a cone alike? How are they different?

18. Is it possible for a three-dimensional solid to have 2 rectangular faces and 4 square faces? Explain.

19. Name the three-dimensional solids that will roll on a flat surface. Predict the path you think each one will trace. Check your prediction with a classmate, then roll each solid to see if you were correct.

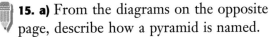

LOGIC POWER

If July 17 falls on a Thursday, on which day of the week will December 31 fall?

269

Exploring Skeletons and Shells

Activity ❶

The children's climbing frame is a **skeleton**. The bars outline the **edges** of the polyhedra that form the structure.

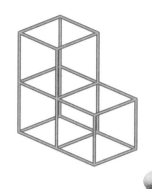

1. Name the polyhedra outlined by the bars of the frame.

2. Name 3 other objects that are skeletons of three-dimensional shapes.

3. Design another children's climbing frame using the skeletons of three-dimensional shapes. Sketch your frame and label it with the names of the three-dimensional shapes.

Activity ❷

The skeletons were constructed from Plasticine and 2 different lengths of sticks.

1. Name each three-dimensional shape.

2. The Plasticine joins the sticks at a **vertex**. How many vertices are there on each skeleton?

3. The sticks form the edges of the polyhedra. How many edges are there on each skeleton?

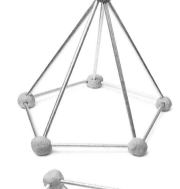

4. Use sticks and Plasticine to construct each polyhedron. State the number of vertices and the number of edges on each one.

a) triangular prism   **b)** cube

c) square pyramid   **d)** hexagonal prism

Activity ❸

A polyhedron can be constructed from pieces of straw joined by pieces of pipe cleaner or wire.

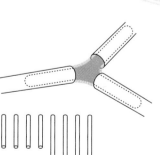

1. Construct and identify each polyhedron.

a)  **b)** **c)**

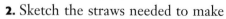

2. Sketch the straws needed to make

a) a pentagonal pyramid

b) a hexagonal prism

Activity ❹

Follow the instructions to construct the **shell** of each polyhedron from cardboard.

1. a) Draw and cut out an equilateral triangle.

b) Fold point A down to the midpoint of BC. The ends of the fold line are called points E and F.

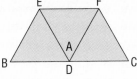

c) Fold point C to point E and point B to point F.

d) Name the polyhedron whose shell can be constructed from the folded triangle.

2. a) Draw a square.

b) Draw congruent squares on each side of the square and cut out the pattern.
c) Cut out and fold the pattern to form the shell of an open cube.
d) Make a sketch to show where you would add a 6th square to the pattern to construct the shell of a closed cube. Check your pattern.

Activity ❺

A pattern that folds to form a polyhedron is called the **net** of the polyhedron.

1. Use solid models of polyhedra. Draw the net of each model by rolling the model on cardboard and tracing the surfaces.

2. a) Compare your nets with your classmates'.
b) Is it possible to have more than one net for a polyhedron?

Activity ❻

1. Which of the nets make the shell of a cylinder?

a) 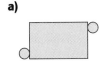   **b)**   **c)**

Trace the surfaces of a cylinder to check your answer.

2. Trace a cone to draw its net.

3. What is the shape of the flat face of a cone?

4. What is the shape of the curved surface?

8.2 Solids, Shells, and Skeletons

Activity: Study the Pictures

The pillars in front of the Parthenon in Athens are solids.

The entrance to the Louvre in Paris is a shell.

A hydro tower is a skeleton.

Inquire

1. How are a solid, a shell, and a skeleton the same? How are they different?

2. With a partner, decide whether each of the following is a solid, a shell, or a skeleton.
a) Aztec pyramid **b)** zoo aviary **c)** SkyDome

3. Write a definition describing the characteristics of
a) a solid **b)** a shell **c)** a skeleton

4. List other structures that are examples of solids, shells, and skeletons.

Activity: Use the Diagrams

One face of a pyramid is called a **base**. What shape are the other faces?

A prism has 2 congruent, parallel bases. What shapes can form the other faces?

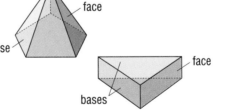

In a shell or solid, the line segment where 2 faces meet is called an **edge**.

In a skeleton, the material used to outline the polyhedron forms the edges.

The point at which edges of a polyhedron meet is called a **vertex**.

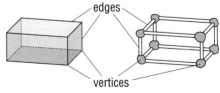

Inquire

1. How many edges does a rectangular prism have?

2. How many vertices does a rectangular prism have?

272

Practice

In questions 1–6, identify each object as a solid, a shell, or a skeleton.

1.

2.

3.

4.

5.

6.

7. a) Sketch the pieces of glass and metal that are needed to construct a fish tank.

b) Is the tank a solid, a shell, or a skeleton?

State the number of each shape of face needed to make the shell of each polyhedron. Identify the shape of the base in each case.

8. cube

9. pentagonal pyramid

10. triangular prism

11. hexagonal prism

12. square pyramid

13. triangular pyramid

Problems and Applications

14. a) Copy and complete the chart for each polyhedron in questions 8–13.

Polyhedron	Number of Vertices, V	Number of Faces, F	Number of Edges, E

b) Which of the following number sentences represents the formula discovered by the Swiss mathematician Leonhard Euler? This formula works for all polyhedra.

$$V = E - F \qquad E + F = V \qquad V + F - E = 2$$

15. Do some research on Euler's life and write a paragraph about him.

In questions 16–19, work in a group to investigate rigidity in polyhedra.

16. Form a triangle and a square using straws and pipe cleaners.

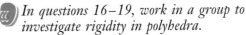

Push down gently on a vertex of the triangle and a vertex of the square. What happens to the shape of each polygon?

17. The triangle is a rigid figure that is used to help to make objects stable.

a) Describe how it is used in each of the following.

b) Name 2 other situations where the triangle is used to provide rigidity.

18. Construct each polyhedron using straws and pipe cleaners. Predict which polyhedra you think are rigid, then test each one by pressing gently on a vertex.

a) pentagonal prism   **b)** cube

c) rectangular prism   **d)** triangular prism

e) square pyramid   **e)** hexagonal prism

19. Add straws with pipe cleaners to make non-rigid polyhedra rigid. Experiment to make sure you add as few pieces as possible. Sketch the polyhedra to show where the extra straws were added.

8.3 Nets of Three-Dimensional Shapes

Activity: Study the Figure

The square pyramid
is constructed from
a building set whose
pieces hinge together
at the sides.

Inquire

1. Which of the following are nets
of the pyramid?

 2. Describe a way to determine whether
or not an arrangement of shapes is a net.

 3. Sketch a different net for the square
pyramid. Exchange sketches with a classmate
and check that each sketch is a net.

Practice

 *In questions 1–3, work with a partner and
use construction pieces or shapes cut from heavy
cardboard to help you. For each polyhedron, state
the number and shape of the base(s) and other
faces, and draw 2 different nets.*

1. triangular prism

2. hexagonal pyramid

3. rectangular prism

Problems and Applications

 4. If you cut out and fold a net to make a
polyhedron, is the result a solid, a shell, or a
skeleton? Explain.

5. a) What polyhedron can be formed from
each net?

b) How many edges must be folded to form
the polyhedron from each net? How many
edges must be sealed?

c) For this polyhedron, is it possible to draw
a net that would need a different number of
folded and sealed edges?

6. The juice container
is a cylinder. Draw the
net of the juice container.

7. The gift box is in the shape of a cone. Draw the net that results when the cone is opened and lying flat.

8. The Wilsons bought a new mailbox for their cottage. Draw its net.

9. The construction pieces have been used to form patterns of 6 squares.

a) Which of the patterns is a net of a cube?
b) For each net, how many edges are folded and how many are sealed to form the cube?
c) A total of 11 patterns of 6 squares can be folded to form a cube. Sketch the patterns that are not shown here.

10. Examine a die to check the numbers of dots on opposite faces. Sketch the net of the die. Mark the dots on the net, so that you could make the die from the net. Compare your net with a classmate's.

11. Tissue boxes come in the shapes of many different rectangular prisms.

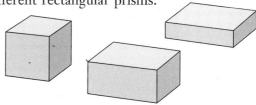

With a classmate, collect several different tissue boxes. Label them A, B, C, and so on. Use a sketch to predict the net for each box. Carefully cut each box and open it to display the net. Compare each of your predictions with the actual net.

LOGIC POWER

A spider is at the vertex S on this wire cube.

The spider wants to walk to vertex F. To get there, it must follow these rules.

1. The spider can walk only along the edges.

2. The spider can walk along an edge only once.

3. The spider can only go down the vertical edges, never up.

4. The spider can visit any vertex except F more than once. When it gets to F, it must stop.

One way for the spider to make the trip is to go from S to A to B to F. In how many other different ways can the spider make the trip?

The Platonic Solids

Ancient Greek scholars thought that mathematics and science could explain many aspects of the universe. A Greek philosopher, Plato, believed that all things are three-dimensional and are made up of atoms in the shapes of regular polyhedra.

In a **regular polyhedron**, all faces are congruent, regular polygons, and the same number of faces meet at each vertex in exactly the same way.

Plato named 4 of the polyhedra for what were then believed to be the 4 elements of the universe. He believed that the fifth polyhedron represented the universe itself. The 5 regular polyhedra he described are now known as the Platonic solids.

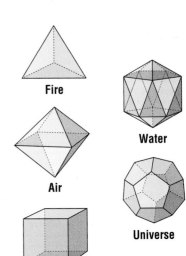

Fire

Water

Air

Universe

Earth

Activity ❶

1. Name the regular polygons that are used to construct each regular polyhedron.

2. Match the correct polyhedron with its name. Find the meaning of each prefix used.

a) cube   **b)** dodecahedron   **c)** tetrahedron
d) icosahedron   **e)** octahedron

3. Suggest another name for the cube, using the appropriate prefix.

4. By what other name do we identify the tetrahedron?

Activity ❷

The following polyhedra have bases that are regular polygons.

 Name and describe each polyhedron and state why it is not regular.

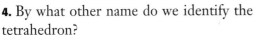

1.   **2.**   **3.**   **4.**

 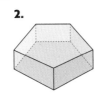 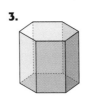 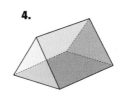

Activity ❸

1. Use grid paper to draw a square. Divide it into 4 smaller squares.

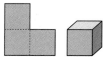

2. Trace the pattern to make 2 copies on stiff cardboard.

3. Cut out one small square from each cardboard piece. Fold each of the resulting shapes so that the cut edges meet. Join the edges with tape.

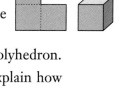

4. Join the two pieces you have made to form a polyhedron.

 5. Name the polyhedron you have constructed. Explain how you know it is regular.

Activity ❹

1. Use triangular dot paper to draw a regular hexagon. Divide it into 6 equilateral triangles.

2. Cut out the hexagon and trace it on stiff cardboard to make 2 copies.

3. For each hexagon, make fold lines on the edges of the triangles. Cut out and discard 2 adjacent triangles. Join the cut edges with tape.

4. How many of these pieces are needed to construct a regular polyhedron?

5. Construct and name the polyhedron.

6. How many triangles meet at a vertex?

7. Describe a way to construct a tetrahedron from these pieces of a hexagon.

Activity ❺

1. The nets of the 5 regular polyhedra are shown. Use dot paper or templates to draw the nets in various sizes. Construct a model of each polyhedron from brightly coloured cardboard.

2. Copy and complete the chart for the 5 Platonic solids.

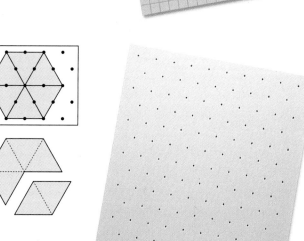

Name	Number of Faces	Shape of Faces	Number of Angles at Each Vertex

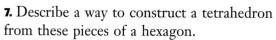

3. Use a set of polyhedra to check whether Euler's formula $V + F = E + 2$ works for each Platonic solid. In this formula, V is the number of vertices, F is the number of faces, and E is the number of edges.

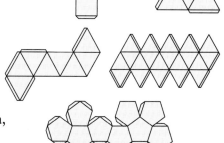

8.4 Points of View

side view   front view   back view

A student standing in the classroom appears different to you, depending on where you are seated.

Objects look very different to us, depending on our **perspective**, or point of view.

Activity: Study the Diagrams

The diagrams show 3 views of a model built with cubes.

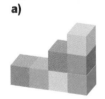 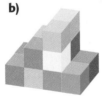 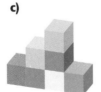

right side view   front view   top view

Inquire

1. How many layers of cubes are there?

2. How many cubes are in each layer?

3. How many cubes are there in the model?

4. Which of these diagrams shows the front right view of the model? Explain.

a) **b)** **c)**

5. Sketch the back view of the model. Compare your sketch with your classmates'.

6. A cube, a square-based prism, and a square pyramid can look alike, depending on your point of view.

a) Which view of each polyhedron do the following diagrams show?

b) How many more views of the polyhedra would you need to name each one?

Practice

Name each object from its side view.

1. **2.** **3.**

4. Sketch the desk as it looks from each point of view.

a) top
b) side
c) front

5. Draw the front view, the side view, and the top view of each object.

a) **b)**

Problems and Applications

 6. The diagrams show 3 views of a model made with cubes.

top view   right side view   front view

a) Which views show the number of layers of cubes?

b) Use cubes to build the model. Sketch the back view of your model. Compare your results with a classmate's. Is there more than one possible model?

c) How many cubes are in your model?

Name each three-dimensional shape and draw the bottom view.

7.

top   front   side

8.

front   side   top

9.

side   front   top

Draw front, side, and top views of each shape.

10.   **11.**

12. An object appears circular from above. From below, it appears as 2 circles with the same centre. From the side, the object seems to be a trapezoid.

a) What might the object be?

b) Draw a sketch and compare it with a classmate's.

13. Have each person in your group sketch 3 views of a building or an object. Exchange sketches and try to draw the original shape. Compare the results and decide if more than one sketch is correct for the views given.

LOGIC POWER

The 8 cubes are numbered identically. Draw the back view, the left view, and the bottom view of the cubes. Is there more than one correct answer?

279

8.5 Sketching Three-Dimensional Shapes

Architects represent various views of buildings they design by drawing them in perspective.

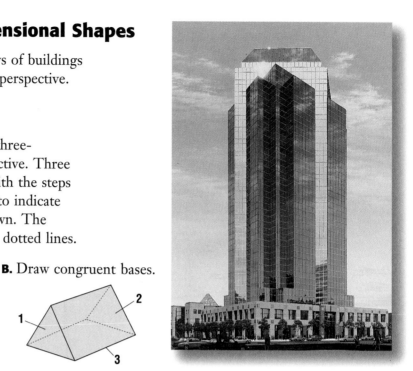

Activity: Study the Diagrams

There are several ways to draw three-dimensional shapes using perspective. Three methods are illustrated below, with the steps marked 1, 2, and 3 in each case to indicate the order in which parts are drawn. The hidden edges are shown as black dotted lines.

A. Use grid or dot paper.

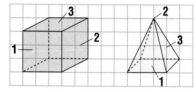

B. Draw congruent bases.

C. Use a vanishing point.

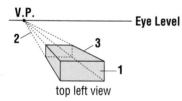

top left view

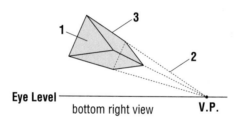

Eye Level

bottom right view

Inquire

1. a) List the steps in each method.

b) In your group, write a paragraph describing each method.

2. The position of the vanishing point determines the view of the object. Where is the vanishing point placed for each of these views?

a)

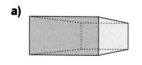

b)

c)

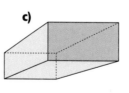

3. a) Draw the bottom left view of a cube by all 3 methods.

b) Which method did you prefer? Why?

c) Describe how the sketch you drew with a vanishing point is different from the other two sketches.

Practice

Draw each three-dimensional shape on grid paper. Name each shape and state the view that is shown.

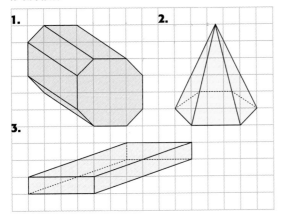

1.

2.

3.

4. Use a vanishing point to redraw the same view of the figure shown in question 3.

Problems and Applications

Copy and complete each figure. Name each one and state the view that is shown.

5.

6.

7.

8.

9. Draw the given views of the die, using the 6 as the front and the 4 as the top.

a) bottom left
b) top right
c) bottom

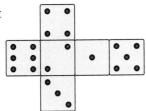

Draw the given view of each figure.

10.

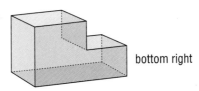

bottom right

11.

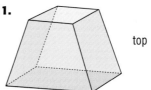

top

12.

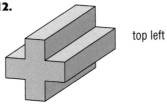

top left

13. The net and the bottom right view of a triangular prism are shown.

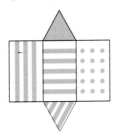

Draw the following views of the prism.
a) top left   **b)** bottom   **c)** right

14. Draw the prism in question 13 to show the top right view from the back. Compare your drawing with a classmate's.

15. Describe the advantages and disadvantages of using one perspective drawing instead of several views of a three-dimensional object. Compare your opinions with your classmates'.

8.6 Planes of Symmetry

Many three-dimensional objects are symmetrical. The left- and right-hand halves of this Canadian aircraft are the same.

Activity: Use the Diagrams

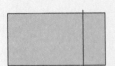

A line cuts a polygon into 2 parts.

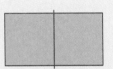

A **line of symmetry** cuts a polygon into 2 congruent parts that are reflection images of each other.

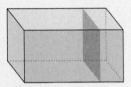

A plane cuts a polyhedron into 2 parts.

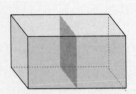

A **plane of symmetry** cuts a polyhedron into 2 congruent parts that are reflection images of each other.

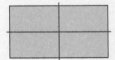

A polygon can have more than one line of symmetry.

A polyhedron can have more than one plane of symmetry.

Inquire

1. How many lines of symmetry does a rectangle have?

2. How many planes of symmetry does a rectangular prism have?

3. Sketch the parts that remain after the rectangular prism is cut by each plane of symmetry.

4. The pyramid has been cut by 2 different planes. Which plane is a plane of symmetry? Sketch the parts that remain after the pyramid is cut by the plane of symmetry.

5. How many planes of symmetry does a square pyramid have?

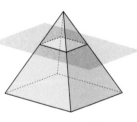

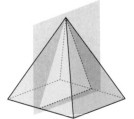

Practice

State whether each plane is a plane of symmetry.

1.

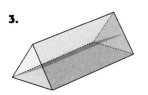

2.

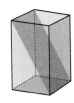

3.

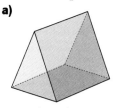

4.

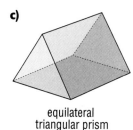

Problems and Applications

5. Determine the number of planes of symmetry in each triangular prism. Then, write a paragraph describing the effect the bases of a triangular prism have on its number of planes of symmetry.

a)

isosceles
triangular prism

b)

right scalene
triangular prism

c)

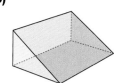

equilateral
triangular prism

6. Use Plasticine or Play-Doh to make a cylinder and a cone. Cut the models into congruent pieces with fine wire.
a) Sketch the shapes of the planes of symmetry of the cylinder.
b) Sketch the shape of the planes of symmetry of the cone.

7. The Eiffel Tower, built from 12 000 pieces of iron, is one of the world's most famous structures. How many planes of symmetry does it have?

8. Work with a group. Use models of three-dimensional shapes.
a) Copy and complete the chart. The first line is completed for you.

Bases of Prism	Lines of Symmetry of Bases	Planes of Symmetry of Prism
Rectangles	2	3
Regular Pentagons		
Regular Hexagons		
Equilateral Triangles		
Regular Octagons		

b) Determine the relationship between the lines of symmetry of the bases and the planes of symmetry of the prisms.
c) Does the relationship hold for a cube? Explain.

9. List 10 objects in your classroom. Find the number of planes of symmetry for each object. Compare your findings with a classmate's.

8.7 Surface Areas of Polyhedra

Activity: Use a Net

Jocelyn designed and built a trinket box. To calculate how much material she needed to make the box, Jocelyn drew its net and calculated the **surface area**.

Inquire

1. a) How many different-sized rectangles did the box have?

b) What were the dimensions of each?

c) How many of each of the rectangles were there?

 2. a) Describe 2 different methods for calculating the surface area of the box.

b) Use both methods to calculate the surface area of the box.

 c) Which method do you prefer? Compare your ideas with your classmates'.

Example

Each edge of the cube is 8 cm. What is the surface area of the cube?

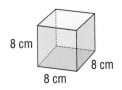

Solution

The cube has 6 square faces.
The area of each face is
$8 \times 8 = 64$

The surface area of the cube is
$6 \times 64 = 384$
The surface area of the cube is 384 cm².

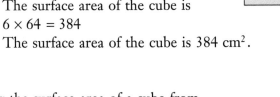

Suggest a formula for calculating the surface area of a cube from the length of an edge.

Practice

Draw the net and calculate the surface area for each polyhedron.

1.

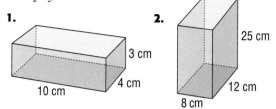
10 cm, 3 cm, 4 cm

2.

25 cm
12 cm
8 cm

3.

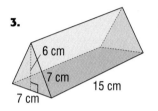
6 cm
7 cm
15 cm
7 cm

4.

12 m
12 m
12 m

5.

15 m
14.4 m 8.6 m
8.6 m

6.

12 cm
7.2 cm
9.6 cm
3 cm

Problems and Applications

7. a) The Chans' television was delivered in a cardboard carton. Calculate the minimum amount of cardboard needed to make the carton. What assumptions have you made?

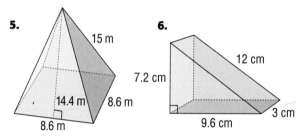
0.6 m
0.8 m   0.7 m

b) Estimate the additional amount of cardboard that would actually be used to make the carton. Explain.

8. A highrise office tower is 165 m tall, 85 m long, and 22 m wide. What is the total surface area of the sides and the roof of the tower?

9. A metal storage building with no floor has the dimensions shown in the diagram. What is the surface area of the building?

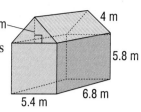
3 m, 4 m, 5.8 m, 6.8 m, 5.4 m

10. The podium used for the medal presentations at swimming competitions is made of wood. The visible surfaces are painted. What area is painted?

60 cm, 60 cm
60 cm, 30 cm
180 cm, 45 cm

11. The surface areas of the rectangular prisms are equal. The missing dimension in each prism is a whole number of centimetres. Find the missing dimensions.

a)
4 cm
4 cm
?

b)
2 cm
10 cm
?

12. a) A rectangular prism is 30 cm by 12 cm by 6 cm. What is its surface area?

b) Predict which pieces have the greatest and least surface areas when the prism is cut by a plane of symmetry.

c) Calculate the surface area of each piece to check your prediction.

8.8 Volumes of Prisms

Many food packages have the shapes of prisms. Different sizes of packages hold different volumes of products.

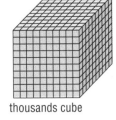

Activity: Explore with Cubes

In a set of place value blocks, each unit cube is 1 cm on every edge. The volume of the unit cube is 1 cm³. The other blocks in the set are:

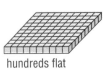

tens rod   hundreds flat   thousands cube

Inquire

1. What are the dimensions of the tens rod? What is its volume?

2. What are the dimensions of the hundreds flat? What is its volume?

3. What are the dimensions of the thousands cube? What is its volume?

4. Suggest a formula that can be used to calculate the volume of a prism. Compare your idea with your classmates'.

5. What is the volume of each of the groups of place value blocks?

a)   **b)** 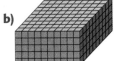   **c)**

Example

Calculate the volume of the triangular prism.

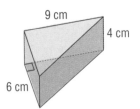

Solution

The volume of a prism is the area of the base multiplied by the height of the prism.

$$\text{Area of base} = \frac{1}{2} \times b \times h$$
$$= \frac{1}{2} \times 9 \times 6$$
$$= 27$$

$$\text{Volume} = \text{area of base} \times \text{height}$$
$$= 27 \times 4$$
$$= 108$$

The volume of the prism is 108 cm³.

Practice

Calculate the volume of each prism.

1.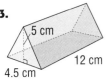
6 cm
6 cm
6 cm

2.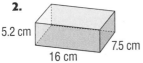
5.2 cm
16 cm
7.5 cm

3.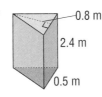
5 cm
12 cm
4.5 cm

4.
18 cm
8 cm
8 cm

5.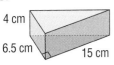
4 cm
6.5 cm
15 cm

6.
0.8 m
2.4 m
0.5 m

Problems and Applications

 7. Calculate the volume of the filing cabinet, in cubic metres.

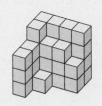
1 m
60 cm
45 cm

 8. a) Measure and determine the total volume of the pages in this book, to the nearest cubic centimetre. Exclude the covers.

b) Compare your answer with a classmate's and account for any differences.

 9. a) How many different rectangular prisms can you make with 24 unit cubes in each one? Sketch each prism and mark its dimensions.

b) What is the volume of each prism?

c) Predict the order of increasing surface area for the prisms. Compare your prediction with a classmate's.

d) Calculate each surface area to check your prediction.

 10. A tent is 4 m long, 3 m wide, and 2 m high.

2 m
3 m
4 m

a) What is the volume of the tent?

b) How many campers could comfortably sleep in the tent? Give reasons for your answer. Compare your answer with your classmates'.

 11. A food company wants to use the smallest amount of material to package a new product. The company is considering 4 possible packages.

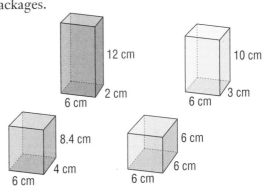
12 cm
6 cm
2 cm

10 cm
6 cm
3 cm

8.4 cm
4 cm
6 cm

6 cm
6 cm
6 cm

a) What is the volume of each package?

b) What is the surface area of each package?

c) Which package is the most economical for the company to use? Explain. Compare your findings with your classmates'.

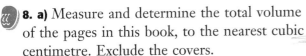

LOGIC POWER

Assume that there are no cubes missing from the back of the stack, and each cube represents 1 cm³.

1. What is the volume of the stack?

2. What is surface area of the stack?

8.9 Surface Area and Volume of a Cylinder

Many objects, including hockey pucks and water heaters, are made in the shape of a cylinder.

Activity: Use a Net

A juice can is made of 2 circular metal bases and a cardboard tube.

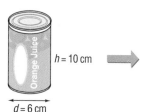

Inquire

1. What measurement of the circle is equal to the length of the cardboard rectangle?

2. Calculate the area of the cardboard rectangle.

3. Calculate the area of each circular base.

4. Calculate the total surface area of the juice can.

 5. State a method for calculating the surface area of a cylinder.

Activity: Use the Relationship

The volume of a cylinder is calculated like the volume of a prism.

$$V = \text{area of base} \times \text{height of cylinder}$$

Inquire

1. What formula is used to calculate the area of the base of a cylinder?

2. Write the number sentence needed to calculate the volume of the above juice can.

3. Calculate the volume of the juice can.

Practice

Round each answer to the nearest tenth of a unit.

Calculate the surface area and the volume of each cylinder. Use $\pi = 3.14$.

 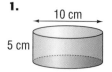 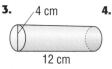 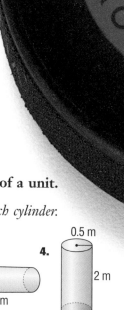

1. 10 cm, 5 cm **2.** 8 cm, 25 cm **3.** 4 cm, 12 cm **4.** 0.5 m, 2 m

Problems and Applications

5. The glue stick has a diameter of 3 cm and a height of 10.5 cm. The glue inside has a diameter of 2.5 cm and a height of 9.5 cm. What is the difference between the volume of the container and the volume of the glue?

6. The Da Silvas installed a cylindrical water heater with a radius of 30 cm and a height of 120 cm.
a) What is the surface area of the water heater?
b) What is the volume of the water heater?

7. a) Describe a method of measuring, with reasonable accuracy, the diameter and the height of a nickel. What are the diameter and the height?
b) What is the volume of a roll of 40 nickels?
c) What is the minimum surface area of the paper needed to roll a stack of nickels?

8. Copy and complete the chart for 4 cylinders.

Height (cm)	10	10	20	20
Diameter (cm)	3	6	3	6
Volume (cm³)				

a) What happens to the volume of a cylinder when the diameter doubles?
b) What happens to the volume of a cylinder when the height doubles?
c) Predict the volume of a cylinder with a height of 10 cm and a diameter of 12 cm. Calculate to check your prediction.
d) Predict the volume of a cylinder with a height of 20 cm and a diameter of 1.5 cm. Calculate to check your prediction.

9. The side length of the base of the square-based prism equals the diameter of the cylinder. The prism and the cylinder have the same height.

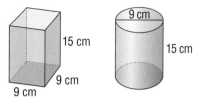

a) Which shape has the greater surface area? By how much is it greater?
b) Which shape has the greater volume? By how much is it greater?

10. The hollow glass tubing used in science laboratories comes in different sizes. A common size has an outer diameter of 8 mm and an inner diameter of 5.8 mm. Calculate the volume of glass in a 100-mm length of this tubing.

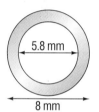

11. Write a problem that requires the calculation of the surface area and volume of a cylinder. Have a classmate solve your problem.

PATTERN POWER

1. Describe the following pattern in words.

$$13^2 = 169$$
$$133^2 = 17\ 689$$
$$1333^2 = 1\ 776\ 889$$
$$13\ 333^2 = \rule{1cm}{0.3cm}$$
$$133\ 333^2 = \rule{1cm}{0.3cm}$$

2. Copy and complete the last 2 lines without using a calculator.

8.10 Mass

Activity: Use the Information

The **mass** of an object is the measure of the amount of matter the object is made up of. The base unit of mass is the gram. Small masses are measured in grams and milligrams. Large masses are measured in kilograms and tonnes.

500 mg   60 g   1 kg

1000 mg = 1 g
1000 g = 1 kg
1000 kg = 1 t

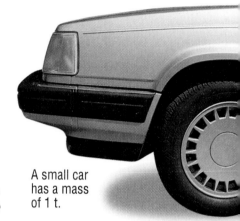

A small car has a mass of 1 t.

Inquire

1. How many vitamin C tablets have the mass of an apple?

2. About how many apples have a mass of 1 kg?

3. The maximum mass of a 10-pin bowling ball is 7248 g. About how many bags of sugar have this mass?

4. A singles luge sled used in the Winter Olympics has a mass of 22 kg. About how many sleds have the mass of a small car?

Practice

Copy and complete.

1. 200 g = ▨ kg   **2.** 45 mg = ▨ g

3. 5600 kg = ▨ t   **4.** 18 300 g = ▨ kg

5. 8 g = ▨ mg   **6.** 2.7 kg = ▨ g

7. 95 kg = ▨ t   **8.** 1.2 t = ▨ kg

Problems and Applications

9. State the unit that would be used to measure the mass of each of the following.

a) a muffin   **b)** an electric iron
c) a pinch of salt   **d)** a watermelon
e) a 747 jet   **f)** a newborn baby
g) a blue jay   **h)** a telephone book
i) a new pencil   **j)** a paving stone

10. The following foods are sold by mass. Give a possible package size for each.

a) box of cereal   **b)** cheese slices
c) sack of potatoes   **d)** lemonade mix
e) instant rice   **f)** box of pepper

11. List 6 more things that may be purchased by mass. Find a possible package size for each.

12. The average female is 3.35 kg at birth and 49 kg at 14 years of age. What is the difference between the 2 average masses?

13. The average male is 3.4 kg at birth and 78.6 kg when fully grown. How many times heavier is the full-grown man than the baby, to the nearest whole number?

14. A family-sized can of iced tea crystals contains 2.2 kg. How many full glasses of iced tea can be made from the can if each full glass needs a 15-g scoop?

15. In 1957, Paul Anderson, a 165-kg weightlifter, raised 2.844 t in a backlift. How many times his own mass did he raise, to the nearest tenth?

8.11 Capacity

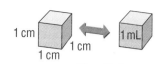

1 cm³ holds 1 mL.

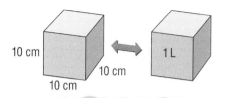

1000 cm³ or 1 dm³ holds 1 L.

Activity: Use the Information

The Stevensons bought a humidifier and a toaster oven for their cottage. The humidifier has a capacity of 13.5 L, and the toaster oven holds a volume of 15 dm³.

Capacity is the greatest volume a container can hold. Capacity is usually measured in litres or millilitres.

Inquire

1. What is the greatest volume of water, in dm³, that the Stevensons' humidifier can hold?

2. What is the capacity of the Stevensons' toaster oven, in litres?

3. Express, in litres, the capacity of a container that is 1 m³ in volume.

4. Large volumes are sometimes measured in kilolitres. If 1 kL equals 1000 L, how many kilolitres equal 1 m³?

Practice

Copy and complete.

1. 1750 mL = ▓ L   **2.** 0.8 L = ▓ mL

3. 4500 L = ▓ kL   **4.** 750 cm³ = ▓ mL

5. 3.8 dm³ = ▓ L   **6.** 6 m³ = ▓ kL

7. 800 L = ▓ cm³   **8.** 10.75 L = ▓ dm³

Problems and Applications

9. The diagrams show the capacities of several common containers.

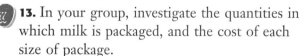

2 mL   175 mL   1 L   600 L

State the capacity unit that would be used to measure each of the following.

a) can of juice   **b)** tube of toothpaste
c) kettle of water   **d)** jug of fabric softener
e) barrel of oil   **f)** drop of food colouring
g) can of paint   **h)** oil truck storage tank

10. A can of lemonade concentrate has a capacity of 355 mL. The concentrate is mixed with 4 cans of water.
a) How much lemonade is made?
b) How many 200-mL glasses can be poured?

11. A waterbed mattress is 2 m long, 1.7 m wide, and 0.2 m deep. How many litres of water are needed to fill it?

12. a) List foods sold in millilitres or litres.
b) What do the foods have in common?
c) Explain your conclusions.
d) Compare your ideas with a classmate's.

13. In your group, investigate the quantities in which milk is packaged, and the cost of each size of package.
a) Calculate the cost per litre for each size.
b) List the sizes according to cost per litre. What do you notice?
c) Suggest why someone might purchase milk in the most costly size.

8.12 Volume, Capacity, and Mass

Activity: Use the Information

Philipe bought a goldfish at the pet store. He brought it home in a plastic bag that held 1 L of water.

The bag has a capacity of 1 L.

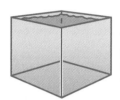

The water would fill a container with a volume of 1000 cm³ or 1 dm³.

The mass of the water is 1 kg.

Inquire

1. There are 1000 mL in 1 L. What is the volume, in cubic centimetres, of a container that holds 1 mL of water? What is the mass, in grams, of 1 mL of water?

2. There are 1000 L in 1 kL. What is the volume, in cubic decimetres, of a container that holds 1 kL of water? What is the mass, in kilograms, of 1 kL of water?

3. What is the volume, in cubic centimetres, of a measuring cup with a capacity of 250 mL? What mass, in grams, of water will it hold?

Example

Philipe emptied his new fish and the water into his fish tank. The tank is 30 cm long, 20 cm wide, and 25 cm deep. Before Philipe added the new fish, the tank was filled to a depth of 20 cm.

a) What is the capacity of Philipe's fish tank?

b) What volume of water was in Philipe's fish tank before he added the new fish?

c) What mass of water was in Philipe's fish tank after he added the new fish?

Solution

a) Total volume $= l \times w \times d$
$$= 30 \times 20 \times 25$$
$$= 15\ 000$$
The capacity of the tank is 15 000 mL or 15 L.

b) Volume of water $= l \times w \times d$
$$= 30 \times 20 \times 20$$
$$= 12\ 000$$
The water had a volume of 12 000 cm³ or 12 dm³.

c) Total volume of water $= 12\ 000 + 1000$
$$= 13\ 000$$
The total volume of water was 13 000 cm³ or 13 dm³. So, the mass of water in the tank was 13 000 g or 13 kg.

Practice

Express each volume in a unit of capacity.

1. 3000 cm³   3L   **2.** 500 cm³ 0·5L

3. 12 000 cm³ 12L   **4.** 250 dm³ 2·5L

5. 2 m³   **6.** 4.5 m³

State the mass of each volume of water.

7. 750 cm³   750g   **8.** 4 dm³ 4kg

9. 12 500 cm³   **10.** 2 m³

11. 5000 cm³   **12.** 36 dm³ 36kg

State the volume of each mass of water.

13. 200 g   **14.** 7 kg

15. 3 t   **16.** 5000 mg

17. 12.4 kg   **18.** 125 g

Problems and Applications

In questions 19–24, what units of measurement are used for each of the following?

19.   **20.**

21.   **22.**

23.    **24.**

25. A swimming pool is 15 m long, 10 m wide, and 2.4 m deep. It is filled to a depth of 1.8 m.
a) What is the capacity of the pool, in kilolitres?
b) What volume of water, in cubic metres, is in it?
c) What is the mass, in tonnes, of the water in the pool?

26. A house safe is 40 cm long, 30 cm wide, and 50 cm high. The walls of the safe are 5 cm thick.
a) What is the outside volume of the safe, in cubic decimetres?
b) What is the capacity of the safe, in litres?

27. An average human adult has 5400 cm³ of blood. Does this account for 54 kg of the adult's mass? Explain your answer.

28. The volume of an object can be measured by dropping the object into a container of water and measuring the volume of water that is displaced. A rock is dropped into a cylinder with a diameter of 8 cm. The water in the cylinder rises 1.6 cm. What is the volume of the rock, to the nearest tenth of a cubic centimetre?

29. An average human breathes about 15 000 L of air each day. Suggest the dimensions of a container that could hold this much air. Compare your answer with a classmate's.

WORD POWER

Change the word GLOW to the word WORM by changing one letter at a time. You must form a real word each time you change a letter. The best solution contains the fewest steps.

Packing a Rock Band's Equipment

You might not expect to hear terms like "spin," "flip," and "rotate" on a rock-and-roll concert tour, but they are used every time the trucks are loaded and unloaded. Some bands can fit all of their equipment into one truck, but most successful bands use 3 trucks or more. For their 1989 *Steel Wheels* tour, the Rolling Stones used 60 tractor-trailers.

Moving the equipment from one concert to the next is the job of a road manager. A band's equipment must usually be set up and taken down in a single day, several times a week. Speed and efficiency are essential. So, a logical plan must be used to pack the trucks with the lighting pipes or "trusses," the speakers, the parts of the set, and the boxes or "road cases" that hold the equipment.

The road manager's task of fitting the equipment into the smallest possible volume is like solving a three-dimensional jigsaw puzzle. The road manager must take into account the safety of the equipment, the ease of loading and unloading, and the order in which the equipment is needed. For example, there is no point in packing the tools first. At the next stop, the entire truck would have to be unloaded to get the tools before assembly work could begin.

To understand the road manager's task, consider a group with 4 instruments, a low budget, and just one truck to carry its equipment.

Activity ❶ Choosing a Truck

The road manager must decide on the size of truck to rent. If the truck is too small, it will not hold all the equipment. If the truck is too big, it will cost more than necessary to rent and operate. Also, the equipment is more likely to be damaged if there is room for it to roll around in transport.

To choose the truck, the road manager lists the equipment, and records the dimensions of the road cases and the equipment that is not packed in cases. The results are shown in the table.

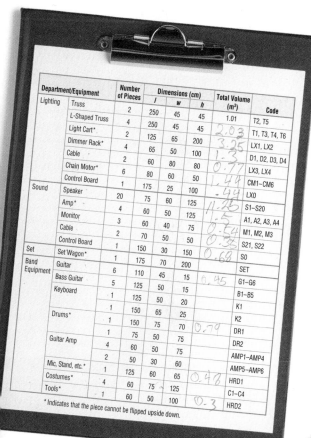

Department/Equipment		Number of Pieces	Dimensions (cm)			Total Volume (m³)	Code
			l	w	h		
Lighting	Truss	2	250	45	45	1.01	T2, T5
	L-Shaped Truss	4	250	45	45	2.03	T1, T3, T4, T6
	Light Cart*	2	125	65	200	3.25	LX1, LX2
	Dimmer Rack*	4	65	50	100	1.3	D1, D2, D3, D4
	Cable	2	60	80	80	0.77	LX3, LX4
	Chain Motor*	6	80	60	50	1.44	CM1–CM6
	Control Board	1	175	25	100	.44	LX0
Sound	Speaker	20	75	60	125	11.25	S1–S20
	Amp*	4	60	50	125	1.5	A1, A2, A3, A4
	Monitor	3	60	40	75	0.54	M1, M2, M3
	Cable	2	70	50	50	0.35	S21, S22
	Control Board	1	150	30	150	0.68	S0
Set	Set Wagon*	1	175	70	200		SET
Band Equipment	Guitar	6	110	45	15	0.45	G1–G6
	Bass Guitar	5	125	50	15		B1–B5
	Keyboard	1	125	50	20		K1
		1	150	65	25		K2
	Drums*	1	150	75	70	0.79	DR1
		1	75	50	75		DR2
	Guitar Amp	4	60	50	75		AMP1–AMP4
		2	50	30	60		AMP5–AMP6
	Mic, Stand, etc.*	1	125	60	65	0.48	HRD1
	Costumes*	4	60	75	125		C1–C4
	Tools*	1	60	50	100	0.3	HRD2

* Indicates that the piece cannot be flipped upside down.

1. a) Copy the table and complete the "Total Volume" column.

b) Add the total volumes to find the volume of equipment that the truck must be able to hold.

2. The table shows the inside dimensions of 3 trucks and the costs of renting from 3 different trucking companies.

Company	Inside Dimensions (m)			Total Volume (m³)	Cost ($/month)
	l	w	h		
A	7	2.5	2.5	43.75	2200.00
B	7.25	2.5	2.75	49.84	2400.00
C	8.25	2.5	2.75	56.72	2950.00

a) Will the equipment fit into each of the trucks?

b) Which truck do you think the equipment will fit into most economically? A

c) The road manager chose to use company B. List some factors, other than volume and cost, that may have influenced this decision.

CONTINUED ▶

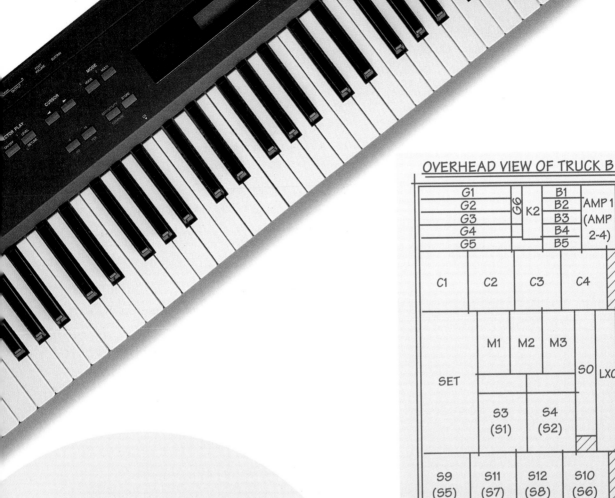

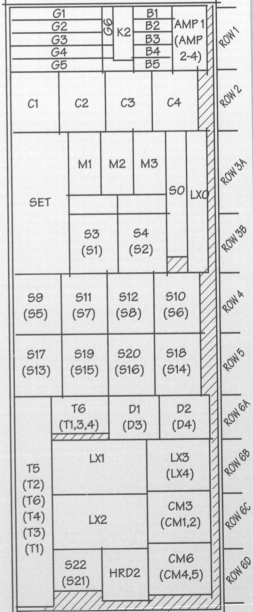

OVERHEAD VIEW OF TRUCK B

G1		B1	AMP 1	ROW 1
G2	G6 K2	B2	(AMP	
G3		B3	2-4)	
G4		B4		
G5		B5		

C1 — C2 — C3 — C4 — ROW 2

SET — M1 M2 M3 — SO LXO — ROW 3A

S3 (S1) — S4 (S2) — ROW 3B

S9 (S5) — S11 (S7) — S12 (S8) — S10 (S6) — ROW 4

S17 (S13) — S19 (S15) — S20 (S16) — S18 (S14) — ROW 5

T6 (T1,3,4) — D1 (D3) — D2 (D4) — ROW 6A

T5 (T2) (T6) (T4) (T3) (T1) — LX1 — LX3 (LX4) — ROW 6B

LX2 — CM3 (CM1,2) — ROW 6C

S22 (S21) — HRD2 — CM6 (CM4,5) — ROW 6D

Activity ❷ Packing the Truck

The road manager now plans how to pack the truck by flipping, rotating, and rearranging pieces of equipment. Instead of wasting time and energy actually packing the equipment on the truck, the road manager figures out the puzzle with paper and pencil or on a computer.

The road manager's plan for packing the truck is shown in the following overhead view and section views. Note that a code shown in brackets indicates an item that is not visible, because it is underneath or behind another item.

296

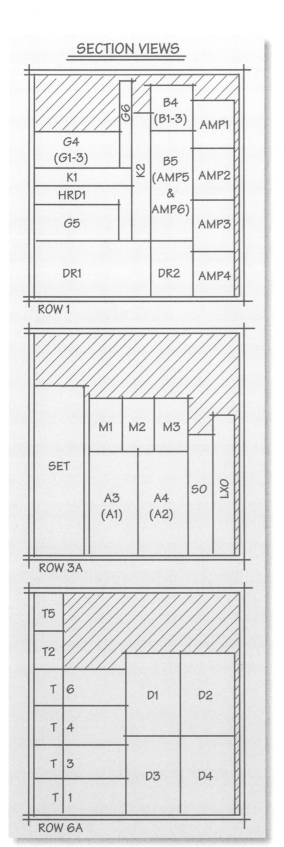

SECTION VIEWS

ROW 1

ROW 3A

ROW 6A

Use the overhead view and section views, and the table you completed in Activity 1, to answer the following questions.

1. How do you know where the back doors of the truck are? *where the loads are*

2. a) List the pieces of equipment in row 1.
b) Where are AMP 5 and AMP 6 in relation to B1 to B5?

3. a) What is in row 2?
b) Why is there no section view for this row?

4. a) Why is row 3 divided into row 3A and row 3B? *barge more space*
b) What is in row 3A?

5. What would the overhead view and section views of row 3A look like if the monitors were removed?

6. Why do you need a section view of row 6A?

7. Draw a three-dimensional representation of the following.
a) lighting truss T5
b) lighting truss T6

8. What area of the truck floor is covered by the speakers? *4.5*

9. What volume of the truck is occupied by the speakers in rows 4 and 5? *9*

10. How far is it from the front of the truck to the front of the row containing the dimmer racks? *4.45*

11. a) How many different types of transformation can be applied to M2? to HRD2?
b) Why is there a difference?

12. What transformation would have to be applied to trusses 1, 3, 4, and 6 if row 6 were loaded with the chain motors on the driver's side?

Review

Name each three-dimensional figure and state the number of faces, edges, and vertices for each one.

1.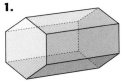

2.

3.

4.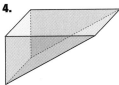

5. Name 3 three-dimensional shapes that are not polyhedra. Explain your answer.

6. Name a three-dimensional solid with each of the following.
a) 2 triangular faces and 3 rectangular faces
b) 4 congruent faces
c) 8 vertices
d) 15 edges

7. Describe how a prism and a pyramid are alike and how they are different.

8. A cylinder contains 1 L of water. Is the cylinder a solid, a shell, or a skeleton? Explain.

9. Draw a net for each of the following containers.

a)

b)

10. The net of a child's cube is shown. Sketch the cube showing
a) the top right view
b) the bottom left view
c) the back view
Use the cat as the front of the cube and the dog as the top.

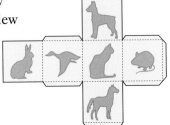

11. Sketch each object and show all the planes of symmetry.

a)

b)

12. The front face and the vanishing point are shown for each prism. Copy and complete each one.

a)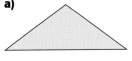

b)

13. For each prism in question 12, state the view that is shown in your completed sketch.

14. Sketch the top view.

a)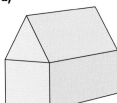

b)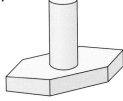

15. Calculate the surface area and the volume.

a)

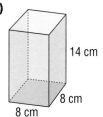

14 cm
8 cm
8 cm

b)

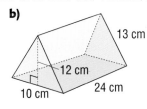

13 cm
12 cm
24 cm
10 cm

c)

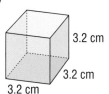

3.2 cm
3.2 cm
3.2 cm

d)

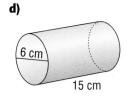

6 cm
15 cm

16. a) The dictionaries are 24 cm high, 18.5 cm wide, and 4.6 cm thick. They are shipped in cartons of 12. What is the smallest possible volume of a carton?

 b) If the dictionaries are each 650 g, what is the mass of each carton of books, to the nearest kilogram? What assumption have you made?

17. A thermos jug is filled with 1250 mL of water. The jug has a mass of 400 g when empty. What is the total mass of the jug and the water, in kilograms?

18. An aquarium is 40 cm long, 25 cm wide, and 30 cm high. It is filled to 4 cm from the top.
a) What is the capacity of the aquarium, in litres?
b) What volume of water, in cubic decimetres, does it contain?

Group Decision Making
Planning a Community

Communities are made up of buildings of many different shapes and sizes. Work in a group to plan and build a model of a community, using your knowledge of three-dimensional shapes.

1 2 3 4	1 2 3 4	1 2 3 4

Home Groups

1 2 3 4	1 2 3 4	1 2 3 4

1. List the buildings that may be found in a community. Include various types of structures from the following categories.

residential	educational
commercial	religious
recreational	governmental
industrial	municipal

2. Work together to plan a small community using a variety of the structures you have listed. Decide which types of buildings you will use and the number of each.

3. On a large piece of cardboard, draw a plan of your community, showing roadways, park areas, and the locations of buildings.

4. Design and build models of your structures using the nets of several three-dimensional shapes.

5. Choose a name for your community and label all the appropriate areas, roadways, and buildings.

6. Compare your community with communities made by other groups. List the three-dimensional structures used in each community.

Chapter Check

Name each polyhedron, and state its number of faces, edges, and vertices.

1.

2.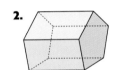

3.

Name the polygons that form the faces of each polyhedron. State the number of each type.

4. hexagonal prism   **5.** cube

Name each three-dimensional shape and draw its net.

6.

7.

Sketch and name the polyhedron made from each net.

8.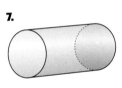

9.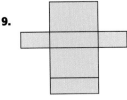

For questions 10 and 11, sketch the top, front, and side views of each three-dimensional shape.

10. cone   **11.** triangular prism

12. Copy and complete the prism, given a base and a vanishing point. Name the prism and state the view that is shown.

 •

13. How many planes of symmetry does this triangular prism have?

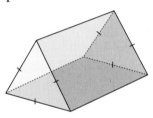

For questions 14–17, calculate the surface area and the volume of each solid.

14.
16 cm
9 cm
9 cm

15.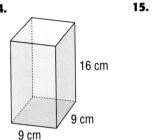
6 cm
14 cm

16.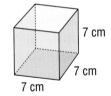
7 cm
7 cm
7 cm

17.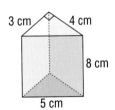
3 cm   4 cm
8 cm
5 cm

18. A cylindrical water jug has a diameter of 15 cm. It is filled to a depth of 24 cm. What mass of water is in the jug

a) in grams?   **b)** in kilograms?

Using the Strategies

1. Six triangles are made from wire. Each side of each triangle is 4.5 cm.

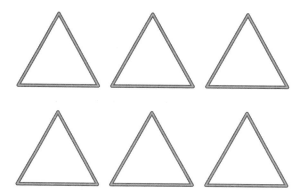

a) What is the perimeter of each triangle?
b) The 6 triangles are used to form a hexagon. What is the perimeter of the hexagon?
c) The 6 triangles are laid side by side to form a parallelogram. Sketch the parallelogram and find its perimeter.
d) Sketch 1 other figure that can be formed from the 6 triangles. Find the perimeter of your figure.

2. What is the smallest whole number that divided by 4 gives a remainder of 3, divided by 3 gives a remainder of 2, and divided by 2 gives a remainder of 1?

3. A pizza ordered by Marc and Pete had a diameter of 30 cm. They ate $\frac{2}{3}$ of the pizza and left 4 pieces. Into how many pieces was the whole pizza cut?

4. The average person uses about 95 L of drinking water each week. How much drinking water is used each week by
a) your family?
b) your class?
c) your school?
d) your community?

5.

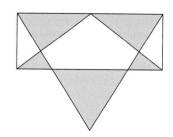

State the number of each polygon that can be found in the diagram.
a) triangles   **b)** rectangles
c) trapezoids   **d)** pentagons
e) other quadrilaterals

6. Mario said to Tara: "Give me $4, so that we will each have the same amount of money." Tara replied to Mario: "No. Give me $4. Then I will have 5 times as much as you." How much money did each of them have?

7. If February 29 falls on a Sunday, on what day of the week will the next February 29 fall?

 8. Julia takes trips to deliver flowers from her store. The graph shows Julia's distance from her store on one trip.

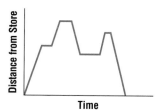

Describe Julia's trip.

DATA BANK

1. How many times larger than Canada's largest island is the world's largest island? Round your answer to the nearest tenth.

2. How many minutes would it take to fly from Victoria to Vancouver at 620 km/h?

Chapter 5

Express all answers in lowest terms.

1. Rank from smallest to greatest.

$\dfrac{9}{10}, \dfrac{1}{2}, \dfrac{4}{5}, \dfrac{3}{5}, \dfrac{7}{10}$

2. Write 3 fractions equivalent to $\dfrac{2}{3}$.

Add.

3. $\dfrac{3}{8} + \dfrac{1}{8}$ **4.** $\dfrac{1}{2} + \dfrac{2}{5}$ **5.** $\dfrac{2}{3} + \dfrac{3}{4}$

6. $2\dfrac{1}{2} + \dfrac{1}{4}$ **7.** $1\dfrac{1}{3} + 1\dfrac{1}{2}$ **8.** $3\dfrac{5}{6} + 1\dfrac{1}{2}$

Subtract.

9. $\dfrac{3}{5} - \dfrac{1}{5}$ **10.** $\dfrac{5}{8} - \dfrac{1}{4}$ **11.** $\dfrac{3}{4} - \dfrac{2}{3}$

12. $1\dfrac{1}{2} - \dfrac{1}{4}$ **13.** $2\dfrac{1}{6} - \dfrac{2}{3}$ **14.** $3\dfrac{1}{2} - 2\dfrac{3}{5}$

Multiply.

15. $\dfrac{1}{2} \times \dfrac{2}{3}$ **16.** $\dfrac{3}{5} \times \dfrac{5}{6}$ **17.** $\dfrac{3}{4} \times \dfrac{1}{2}$

18. $1\dfrac{1}{2} \times \dfrac{1}{4}$ **19.** $1\dfrac{3}{5} \times 2$ **20.** $1\dfrac{1}{3} \times 2\dfrac{1}{2}$

Divide.

21. $3 \div \dfrac{1}{2}$ **22.** $\dfrac{1}{3} \div \dfrac{2}{3}$ **23.** $\dfrac{3}{5} \div \dfrac{1}{4}$

24. $1\dfrac{1}{2} \div 2$ **25.** $1\dfrac{1}{3} \div \dfrac{3}{4}$ **26.** $2\dfrac{1}{2} \div 1\dfrac{1}{5}$

Evaluate.

27. $\dfrac{1}{4} + \dfrac{1}{3} \div \dfrac{1}{2}$ **28.** $\left(\dfrac{7}{8} - \dfrac{1}{2}\right) \times 2^2$

Express as a fraction or mixed number.

29. 0.85   **30.** 3.6   **31.** 0.888...

Express as a decimal.

32. $\dfrac{8}{25}$ **33.** $2\dfrac{3}{4}$ **34.** $\dfrac{5}{6}$

35. About $\dfrac{1}{4}$ of Canada's grizzly bears live in the Northwest Territories (NWT). About 5000 grizzlies live in the NWT. About how many live in Canada?

Chapter 6

Express all answers in lowest terms.

1.

Write the ratio of
a) squares to circles
b) circles to triangles
c) triangles to circles to squares

Express in lowest terms.

2. 16:24   **3.** 40 to 20   **4.** $\dfrac{4}{10}$

5. Write 3 ratios equivalent to 3:5.

Find the unknown value.

6. $\dfrac{3}{2} = \dfrac{x}{8}$ **7.** $\dfrac{6}{y} = \dfrac{12}{10}$ **8.** $\dfrac{32}{8} = \dfrac{8}{n}$

9. Greg drove 300 km in 4 h. Irina drove 400 km in 5 h. Who had the higher average speed?

10. If 7 bananas cost $3.15, what is the cost of 5 bananas?

Find the unit price.

11. $26.00 for 6 L of paint

12. 100 g of grated cheese for $2.20

13. If 175 g of yogurt costs $0.98, and 500 g costs $2.49, which is the better buy?

14. A drawing of a moose is 7 cm long. The scale is 1:40. What is the actual length, in metres, of a moose?

15. Edmonton is 700 km from Regina. How far apart are these cities on a map with a scale of 1:20 000 000?

16. Canada's Marnie McBean and Kathleen Heddle won the women's pairs rowing event at the Barcelona Olympics by rowing 2000 m in 7 min 6.22 s. Find their average speed, to the nearest hundredth of a metre per second.

Chapter 7

Draw in 3 different ways.

1. a rectangle with 50% shaded

2. a square with 75% shaded

Write as a percent.

3. $\frac{23}{50}$ **4.** $\frac{17}{25}$ **5.** 3:5

6. 1:4   **7.** 0.6   **8.** 0.07

Calculate.

9. 13% of 2100   **10.** 21% of 350

11. 4.5% of 80   **12.** 12.6% of 5000

Write as a percent.

13. 0.452   **14.** 3:8   **15.** $\frac{1}{3}$

Write as a decimal.

16. 9%   **17.** 53.6%   **18.** $4\frac{1}{2}$%

19. If 20% of a number is 80, what is the number?

20. If 4% of a number is 2.4, what is the number?

Calculate.

21. 300% of 80   **22.** 200% of 2000

23. 150% of 60   **24.** 110% of 900

25. The regular price of a pair of jeans is $78. What is the sale price after a discount of 20%?

26. Luis sells shoes. He earns $15/h, plus a 5% commission on his sales. One week, he worked for 38 h and had sales of $690. How much did he earn?

27. A sweater sells for $84. Find the total cost, including GST and PST, in your province.

28. Linda bought a $5000 savings bond that paid 7% interest per year. What was the amount after 4 years?

Chapter 8

a) *Name the polyhedron formed from each net.*

b) *Is the polyhedron formed a solid, shell, or skeleton? Explain.*

c) *State the number of faces, edges, and vertices for each polyhedron.*

1.
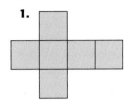
2.
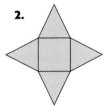

3. Draw the net of a triangular prism.

Sketch the front, side, and top views of each of the following. Assume that each is standing on its base.

4. cylinder   **5.** triangular pyramid

6. Sketch a rectangular prism and show all the planes of symmetry.

Calculate the surface area of each 3-D figure.

7.
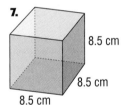
8.5 cm, 8.5 cm, 8.5 cm

8.
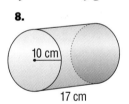
10 cm, 17 cm

Calculate the volume of each 3-D figure.

9.
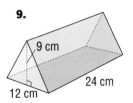
9 cm, 24 cm, 12 cm

10.
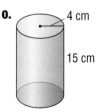
4 cm, 15 cm

11. An aquarium is 75 cm long, 45 cm wide, and 60 cm high. It is filled to a depth of 56 cm.

a) Find the capacity of the aquarium.

b) What volume of water is in the aquarium?

c) What mass of water is in the aquarium?

CHAPTER 9

Statistics and Probability

A *meteor*, or shooting star, is a small piece of rock or metal that burns up in the Earth's atmosphere. A meteor that strikes the Earth is called a *meteorite*. The best time to see meteors is between midnight and dawn.

Astronomers have collected data about the major annual meteor showers we can see. The names of the showers, the constellations from which they seem to come, and their rates are shown in the table.

Name of Shower	Constellation	Date	Rate (number per hour)	
			Average	Maximum
Quadrantids	Draco	January 4	50	100
Lyrids	Lyra	April 21	5	15
Eta Aquarids	Aquarius	May 4	10	20
Capricornids	Capricornus	July 25	15	30
Delta Aquarids	Aquarius	July 27–29	20	35
Perseids	Perseus	August 12	30	70
Orionids	Orion	October 20–22	15	35
Taurids	Taurus	November 1–4	10	15
Leonids	Leo	November 16	15	20
Geminids	Gemini	December 13	50	80
Ursids	Ursa Minor	December 22	10	15

In which season — fall, winter, spring, or summer — can we see the most meteors?

In which month can we see the most meteors?

How would astronomers collect data about meteor showers?

The Paper-and-Pencil Olympics

 Complete the following 4 activities in your group. Decide as a group on the order in which group members will attempt each event. For each event, compare your group's average with the averages of other groups and decide what score best represents your class.

Activity ❶ The 100-m Dash

1. Draw a track with ten 1-cm squares in a row.

2. When it is your turn to be the runner, place a pencil on the start. With your eyes closed, try to put one mark in each square. You score 1 point for each square that contains one and only one mark.

3. Run the race once. Find the average of your group's scores.

Activity ❷ The Hammer Throw

1. Draw a hammer throw area 11 cm long and 1 cm wide, marking every centimetre as shown.

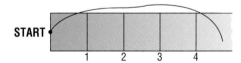

2. When it is your turn to be the thrower, place a pencil on the start and close your eyes. Draw an arc without lifting the pencil. The score on the throw is the farthest score line passed. The score is 0 if the throw does not leave then reenter the hammer throw area.

3. Throw the hammer once. Find the average of your group's scores.

Activity ❸ The Long Jump

1. Draw a jumping pit 13 cm long and 1.5 cm wide, marked every centimetre as shown.

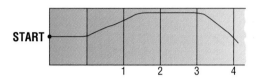

2. When it is your turn to be the jumper, place a pencil on the start and close your eyes. Draw a straight line into the first shaded box, then an arc into the sand pit. The score on a jump is the farthest score line passed. The score is 0 if the jump does not start in the first shaded box or end in the sand pit.

3. Jump twice. Record your better score. Find the average of your group's scores.

Activity ❹ The Javelin

1. Draw a throwing area 11 cm long and 1 cm wide, marking every centimetre as shown.

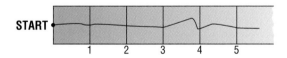

2. When it is your turn to be the thrower, place a pencil on the start and close your eyes. Draw a line, without lifting the pencil. The score on a throw is the farthest score line passed. If any part of the line leaves the throwing area, the score is 0.

3. Take two throws. Record the higher score. Find the average of your group's scores.

Marbles and Tracks

Activity ❶ Predicting Results

1. When a marble is put in the track at X, it will roll down and drop out at A, B, C, or D.

When the marble reaches a point where the track splits, the marble has an equal chance of going either way. If you put 16 marbles in the track at X, how many would you expect to drop out at A, B, C, and D?

2. If 16 marbles were put in the track at X in the following tracks, how many would you expect to drop out at A, B, C, and D?

a)

b)

Activity ❷ Designing Tracks

1. Design a track with each of the following expected drop-outs for 16 marbles.

a)

A	B	C	D
2	3	3	8

b)

A	B	C	D
2	2	6	6

c)

A	B	C	D
2	5	5	4

d)

A	B	C	D
1	1	2	12

 2. Design a track and calculate the expected drop-outs for 16 marbles. Pass the expected drop-outs to a classmate. Have your classmate design a track that gives your expected drop-outs. Compare your track with your classmate's.

Mental Math

Calculate.

1. 50% of 200   **2.** 25% of 80

3. 10% of 10   **4.** 50% of 40

5. 25% of 20   **6.** 75% of 200

7. 1% of 100   **8.** 1% of 500

9. 10% of 80   **10.** 25% of 1000

Calculate. Look for compatible numbers.

11. $37 + 43 + 50$ **12.** $41 - 11 + 16$

13. $78 + 22 - 9$ **14.** $32 + 56 - 16$

15. $21 + 37 + 19$ **16.** $54 + 13 - 24$

17. $47 - 12 - 17$ **18.** $68 + 12 + 4$

19. $74 - 11 - 4$ **20.** $99 - 83 + 1$

Multiply.

21. 4×300 **22.** 0.5×200

23. 5×800 **24.** 7×600

25. 0.2×700 **26.** 0.3×400

27. 0.8×900 **28.** 9×900

29. 4×3000 **30.** 0.2×2000

Simplify.

31. 0.7×100 **32.** 1.3×1000

33. $14 \div 100$ **34.** $0.6 \div 10$

35. 0.12×1000 **36.** 0.005×100

37. $24 \div 1000$ **38.** $8.8 \div 100$

Simplify.

39. $4 \div 0.1$ **40.** 200×0.1

41. 300×0.01 **42.** $100 \div 0.001$

43. 1.2×0.01 **44.** $1.2 \div 0.01$

45. $0.2 \div 0.1$ **46.** 0.2×0.1

9.1 Collecting Data

Statistics is the science of collecting and organizing number facts.

Every 10 years, a **census** is conducted in Canada. A census gathers information from an entire population.

To decide how popular a radio station is, a polling company asks *some* listeners which station they listen to. The people asked are called a **sample.** Their responses are used to represent *all* radio listeners, called the **population**.

Activity: Complete the Survey Sheet

Natalia took a survey to find out which 5 activities would be most popular for the Smithville Winter Carnival. She asked a sample of carnival volunteers to choose one favourite activity each.

Copy and complete the survey sheet by writing the sum of the tallies in the frequency column.

Survey Sheet		
Activity	**Tally**	**Frequency**
Broomball Tournament	ﬀ﬙ ﬀ﬙ ﬀ﬙ IIII	
Cross-Country Skiing	ﬀ﬙ ﬀ﬙ ﬀ﬙	
Scavenger Hunt	ﬀ﬙ ﬀ﬙ II	
Skating Party	ﬀ﬙ ﬀ﬙ ﬀ﬙ ﬀ﬙ ﬀ﬙ III	
Sleigh Ride	ﬀ﬙ ﬀ﬙ ﬀ﬙ ﬀ﬙ ﬀ﬙ ﬀ﬙	
Snow Sculpting	ﬀ﬙ ﬀ﬙ ﬀ﬙ ﬀ﬙ ﬀ﬙ ﬀ﬙ I	
Snowshoeing	ﬀ﬙ ﬀ﬙ ﬀ﬙ IIII	
Snow Snake Competition	ﬀ﬙ ﬀ﬙ ﬀ﬙ ﬀ﬙	
Tobogganing	ﬀ﬙ ﬀ﬙ ﬀ﬙ ﬀ﬙ IIII	

Inquire

1. What were the 5 most popular activities?

2. How else might Natalia have decided on the most popular activities?

3. Why did Natalia survey carnival volunteers, rather than members of the ski club or employees of the skating rink?

A sample for a survey should be a **random sample.** In a random sample, each member of the population has the same chance of being picked. Computers are sometimes used to select random samples.

If each member does not have an equal chance of being picked, the sample is a **biased sample.** A biased sample may give misleading results.

Natalia collected the information by asking people for their opinion. In other words, she conducted a personal survey.

You can also gather information from:
- a telephone survey
- a library
- a mail survey
- an expert
- a data bank
- magazines, books, and newspapers

Name one advantage and one disadvantage of using each method.

Problems and Applications

1. A survey was conducted to see how people like their eggs. Each person was asked to name one favourite type.

How People Like Their Eggs		
Type	**Tally**	**Frequency**
Boiled	‖‖ ‖‖ ‖‖ ‖‖ ||	
Fried	‖‖ ‖‖ ‖‖ ‖‖ ‖‖ |||	
Omelette	||||	
Poached	||	
Scrambled	‖‖ ‖‖ ‖‖ ‖‖ ‖‖ ‖‖ ||||	

a) Copy and complete the tally sheet.
b) How many people liked their eggs poached?
c) Which was the most popular type?
d) How many times more people liked scrambled eggs than liked boiled eggs?
e) How many people were surveyed?

2. Terry used an almanac to list the countries that had won at least 3 gold medals in women's Olympic alpine skiing events, up to, and including, the 1994 Winter Olympics. He recorded his results using these abbreviations: A for Austria, C for Canada, F for France, G for Germany (East and/or West), I for Italy, S for Switzerland, and U for the United States of America.

S U A U U S G S G S C A F F A C F S S U
G C G A S U I G A S S A C I A A G U I S

a) Complete a survey sheet for the data.
b) Order the countries that won at least 3 gold medals from most medals won to least medals won.
c) What was the total number of gold medals awarded to these countries?
d) Use your research skills to name the Canadian women who won gold medals.

3. Would the following information come from a census or a sample? Explain.
a) Eight students in a grade 8 class have dogs for pets.

b) There are 4000 maple trees in the forest.
c) There were 500 000 television sets tuned to the Canadian Figure Skating Championships.
d) The population of Snow Valley is 14 764.

4. Suppose you were asked to find out the favourite restaurant in your town and you decided to survey public opinion.
a) Who would make up the population?
b) How would you select a sample so that it was not biased?
c) Describe a sample that would be biased.
d) Suggest a way of finding out the favourite restaurant without asking people's opinions.

5. Work with a classmate and choose a method to gather data on the following. Give reasons for your choices.
a) the names and heights of the 6 tallest mountains in Canada
b) the most popular television program on Thursday evening in your town
c) the most popular home video game in your school
d) the value of an old coin
e) the least popular newspaper cartoon in your community
f) the weather in Miami in February

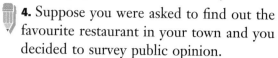

PATTERN POWER

1. Describe this pattern in words.

2. Draw the fourth and fifth figures.

3. Copy the table. Use the pattern to complete it.

Red Tiles	White Tiles	Total
1	5	6
10		
	63	
		87

9.2 Making Predictions

Activity: Study the Information

To predict how much plastic waste was thrown out from lunch during a year, the students from a grade 8 class collected and sorted plastic lunch waste for 5 days. They chose 5 days as a sample to represent the school year.

The table lists the types of waste collected and the number of each item.

Sandwich Bags	937	Juice Containers	379
Straws	174	Pudding Containers	39
Yogurt Containers	29	Spoons	38

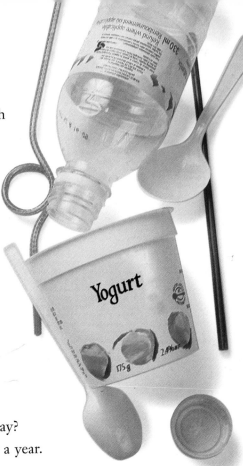

Inquire

1. Calculate the average number of each item that would be thrown out each day.

2. Students eat lunch in school about 180 times in a year. Use your answer to question 1 to predict the number of each item thrown out in a year.

3. Why did the students use 5 days as a sample instead of 1 day?

4. Suggest another way of predicting the amount of waste for a year.

Example

There are about 10 000 people 12 years of age or older in Greensville. Francine conducted a survey to predict how often they go to movies in a year. She chose 50 people for her sample and used a telephone survey. Use the results of Francine's survey to predict how often the people of Greensville go to the movies.

Survey Sheet	
Movies Per Year	**Tally**
0	ⅢⅢ ⅢⅢ ⅢⅢ ⅢⅢ Ⅰ
1 to 4	ⅢⅢ ⅢⅢ ⅢⅢ Ⅰ
5 to 8	ⅢⅢ Ⅰ
9 to 12	ⅢⅠ
13 or more	ⅢⅠ

Solution

Total the tallies for each category. Write each total as a percent of the people surveyed.

Movies Per Year	Tally	Frequency	Fraction	Percent
0	ⅢⅢ ⅢⅢ ⅢⅢ ⅢⅢ Ⅰ	21	$\frac{21}{50}$	42%
1 to 4	ⅢⅢ ⅢⅢ ⅢⅢ Ⅰ	16	$\frac{16}{50}$	32%
5 to 8	ⅢⅢ Ⅰ	6	$\frac{6}{50}$	12%
9 to 12	ⅢⅠ	3	$\frac{3}{50}$	6%
13 or more	ⅢⅠ	4	$\frac{4}{50}$	8%

Apply the percents to the 10 000 people of Greensville.

Movies Per Year	Percent	Number of People
0	42%	42% of 10 000 = 4200
1 to 4	32%	32% of 10 000 = 3200
5 to 8	12%	12% of 10 000 = 1200
9 to 12	6%	6% of 10 000 = 600
13 or more	8%	8% of 10 000 = 800

Francine predicted that 4200 do not go to the movies, 3200 go 1 to 4 times a year, 1200 go 5 to 8 times, 600 go 9 to 12 times, and 800 go 13 or more times.

Problems and Applications

1. A grade 8 class collected the following lunchroom waste over 5 days.

Fruit scraps: 20 kg
Food scraps: 15 kg
Whole fresh fruit: 10 kg
Non-food waste: 5 kg

The students eat lunch in school about 180 times in a year. Predict the amount of waste for each item in a year.

2. There are 30 000 households in Picton. Two hundred households were surveyed to determine people's favourite shopping days. The table gives the results.

Favourite Shopping Days		
Day	Frequency	Percent
Monday	8	
Tuesday	10	
Wednesday	24	
Thursday	26	
Friday	34	
Saturday	58	
Sunday	14	
No Preference	26	

a) Copy and complete the table.
b) Use the percents to predict the number of the 30 000 households in which each day is preferred.
c) In how many households is there no preference?

3. There are about 11 000 000 households in Canada. The table shows how many of every 50 households had certain kinds of juice in the refrigerator.

Juices in Refrigerators		
Juice	Frequency	Percent of Households
Apple	12	
Blended Fruit	9	
Cranberry	6	
Grapefruit	5	
Grape	5	
Orange	28	
Tomato/Vegetable	4	

a) Copy and complete the table.
b) Why do the percents not total 100%?
c) How many Canadian households keep each type of juice in the refrigerator?

4. The table shows some creatures that people fear.

Feared Creatures	
Creature	Percent
Beetles	3%
Mice	38%
Wasps/Bees	45%
Worms	2%
Don't Know	12%

a) Predict how many students in your school fear each type of creature.
b) The population of North America is about 300 000 000. About how many North Americans fear each type of creature?

5. A national survey asked 1200 teens aged 13 to 17 which of the following places or events they had attended in the last year. The table gives the result of the survey.

Events That Teenagers Attended	
Place or Event	Percent Who Attended
Professional Sports	44%
Art Museum	31%
Other Museum	26%
Rock Concert	28%
Symphony Concert	11%

a) How many of the 1200 teens attended each place or event?
b) Why does the percent column total more than 100%?
c) Survey your class to see how many attended these places or events last year. Compare your class results with the national survey and give reasons for any differences.

6. Decide on a strategy for estimating the number of Canadian households that have dogs or cats for pets.

How Much History Do Canadians Know?

The Gallup Corporation, a large polling company, gave the following multiple choice history test to a sample of 1016 Canadian adults. For each question, each adult could choose one of the answers provided or could say "don't know."

1. What was the name of Canada's first Prime Minister?

a) W.L. Mackenzie King   **b)** Sir Wilfrid Laurier

c) Sir John A. Macdonald   **d)** Louis-Joseph Papineau

e) Samuel de Champlain   **f)** Sir Robert Borden

2. Who was Canada's longest serving Prime Minister?

a) Sir John A. Macdonald   **b)** John Diefenbaker

c) Sir Wilfrid Laurier   **d)** Pierre Trudeau

e) W.L. Mackenzie King   **f)** Louis St. Laurent

3. Who was the leader of the North-West Rebellion of 1885?

a) Sir John A. Macdonald   **b)** William Lyon Mackenzie

c) Gabriel Dumont   **d)** Louis-Joseph Papineau

e) Louis Riel   **f)** Sir Charles Tupper

4. What year was Confederation?

a) 1776   **b)** 1865

c) 1812   **d)** 1867

e) 1837   **f)** 1885

5. Who was the leader of the English army at the Battle of the Plains of Abraham?

a) Joseph Howe   **b)** John Durham

c) Edward Cornwallis   **d)** Louis-Joseph de Montcalm

e) James Wolfe   **f)** Sir Isaac Brock

6. Who was the leader of the French army at the Battle of the Plains of Abraham?

a) Louis-Joseph de Montcalm   **b)** Samuel de Champlain

c) Louis-Joseph Papineau   **d)** Jacques Cartier

e) James Wolfe   **f)** Louis de Buade Frontenac

The following are the results of the test.

1. What was the name of Canada's first Prime Minister?
2. Who was Canada's longest serving Prime Minister?
3. Who was the leader of the North-West Rebellion of 1885?
4. What year was Confederation?
5. Who was the leader of the English army at the Battle of the Plains of Abraham?
6. Who was the leader of the French army at the Battle of the Plains of Abraham?

Correct Answer	Other Answer	Don't Know
40%	16%	44%
18%	56%	26%
37%	2%	61%
45%	15%	40%
31%	5%	64%
25%	8%	67%

Activity ❶

Have each member of the class try the test. Record the results in a table like the one above. Compare your class results with the results shown in the table.

Activity ❷

The following table shows how the 1016 Canadian adults did by how many questions they answered correctly.

Number of Questions Answered Correctly	Percent of the Canadian Adults Tested
6	5%
5	9%
4	10%
3	13%
2	15%
1	17%

Complete a similar table for your class. Compare your class results with those of the 1016 Canadian adults who took the test.

Activity ❸

1. If 3 questions correct out of 6 is a pass,
a) what percent of the sample of Canadian adults passed?
b) how many of the sample of Canadian adults passed?
c) what percent of your class passed?

2. a) What percent of the sample of Canadian adults did not get any questions correct?
b) What percent of your class did not get any questions correct?

Activity ❹

Is this 6-question test a good measure of Canadians' knowledge of Canada's history? Compare your conclusion and your reasons with your classmates'.

9.3 Reading and Drawing Bar Graphs

Bar graphs are used to compare things.

Activity: Study the Graph

The double bar graph shows how cats and dogs react around strangers.

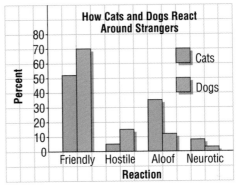

Inquire

1. What does the vertical axis tell you?

2. Is a dog or cat more likely to be friendly to strangers?

3. About what percent of cats are hostile to strangers?

4. About what percent of dogs are aloof from strangers?

5. How might a statistician collect these data?

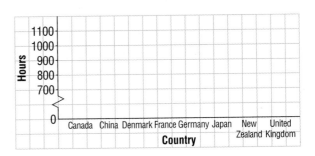

Example

The table gives the average number of hours students spend in class each year in several countries.

Display these data on a bar graph.

Canada	975	China	858
Denmark	1040	France	972
Germany	760	Japan	933
New Zealand	1000	United Kingdom	950

Solution

1. Draw the horizontal axis and decide on the width of the bars. Label the axis.

2. Draw the vertical axis. Since the data go from 760 to 1040, mark the vertical axis from 700 to 1100. Make a break mark at the bottom of the axis to show that the scale between 0 and 700 is not included. Label the axis.

3. Plot the number of hours for each country and draw the bars.

4. Give the graph a title.

Redraw the graph without using a break mark on the vertical axis. Compare the graphs and state the advantages and disadvantages of using the break mark.

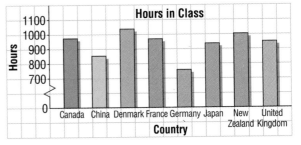

Problems and Applications

1. The horizontal bar graph shows the average distance each person drives a car in a year in each province. To find each figure, the total distance travelled by all the cars in a province is divided by the total population of the province.

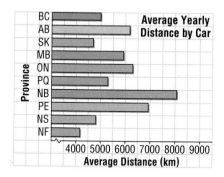

a) In which province is the average distance highest? lowest?

b) About how many more kilometres are driven in Manitoba than in Saskatchewan?

c) In which province is the average distance closest to twice the average distance in Newfoundland?

d) The state of Wyoming has the highest value in North America at 20 600 km per person per year. How much greater is this than the highest value in Canada?

e) List some possible reasons for the differences in the distances.

f) Why are environmentalists interested in these statistics?

2. The table gives the number of people for every automobile in several countries.

Brazil	9.6	Canada	2.2
France	2.4	Japan	3.8
Poland	7.8	Portugal	6.5
U.K.	2.9	U.S.A.	1.7

Display these data on a horizontal bar graph.

3. The table gives percents of the areas of the Great Lakes that lie in Canada and the United States.

Lake	Percent in U.S.A.	Percent in Canada
Erie	50%	50%
Huron	38%	62%
Michigan	100%	0%
Ontario	45%	55%
Superior	65%	35%

Display these data on a double bar graph.

4. The table gives the chief sources of energy for each province by percent of each type used.

Province	Percent of Energy Use		
	Natural Gas	Petroleum	Electricity
BC	31%	42%	25%
AB	49%	33%	16%
SK	48%	36%	14%
MB	37%	38%	23%
ON	36%	33%	21%
PQ	16%	41%	41%
NB	2%	66%	31%
PE	3%	83%	12%
NS	2%	76%	21%
NF	0%	68%	30%

a) Display these data on a triple bar graph.

b) Which provinces use a similar amount and type of energy?

5. With a partner, choose a subject for which you would like to make a comparison. For example, you could choose to compare the favourite rock groups, radio stations, or sports of your classmates.

a) Predict what a bar graph of the comparison will look like.

b) Collect the data and display them on a bar graph.

c) Compare your predicted bar graph with the graph of the data.

9.4 Reading and Drawing Broken-Line Graphs

A broken-line graph is used to show how
something changes over a period of time.

Activity: Study the Graph

The graph shows worldwide whale catches
from 1908 to 1988.

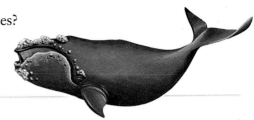

Inquire

1. About how many whales were caught in 1968?

2. In what years were about 10 000 whales caught?

3. In what year do you think the harpoon gun
was invented? Explain.

4. a) In what year was there the greatest number of catches?
b) About how many whales were caught that year?

5. Why did catches drop in 1918 and 1943?

6. Why were there no catches in 1988?

Example

The table gives the areas burned by forest fires in Canada in 7 time periods.

Time Period	1920s	1930s	1940s	1950s	1960s	1970s	1980s
Area (millions of hectares)	13	14	11	9	10	13	24

Display these data on a broken-line graph.

Solution

1. Draw and label the horizontal axis.
Mark the axis from 1920s to 1980s.

2. Draw and label the vertical axis.
Mark the vertical axis from 0 to 24.

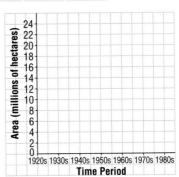

3. Plot the areas burned for different time periods.
Join the points with straight line segments.

4. Give the graph a title.

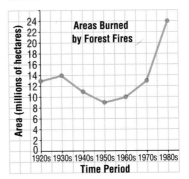

Why did the area burned by forest fires increase
so much in the 1980s?

Problems and Applications

1. The graph shows music sales in Canada, in millions of units by format, over a 20-year period.

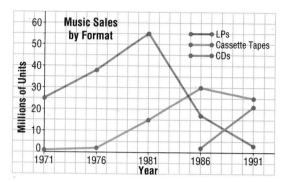

a) About how many LPs were sold in 1981?

b) How many more cassettes than LPs were sold in 1986?

c) What was the difference in CD sales and cassette sales in 1986? in 1991?

d) Which sales showed the greater increase, LPs from 1971 to 1981 or cassettes from 1976 to 1986?

e) Did the total sales of cassettes and CDs in 1991 equal the sales of LPs in 1981? Explain.

2. The table gives the world's population, in billions, from 1900 to 1980 and the United Nation's projected population until 2020.

Year	1900	1920	1940	1960	1980	2000	2020
Population (billions)	1.6	1.9	2.3	3.0	4.4	6.2	7.7

Display these data on a broken-line graph.

3. The table gives the amount of sleep people get each day at different ages.

Age	Newborn	5	10	15
Sleep (h/day)	19	11	8.5	8

Age	20	30	40	50	60
Sleep (h/day)	8	7.5	7	6	5.5

Display these data on a broken-line graph.

4. The table gives the average daily temperature, in degrees Celsius, for each month in Vancouver and Sydney, Australia.

Month	Average Daily Temperature (°C)	
	Vancouver	Sydney
January	2	22
February	3	22
March	5	21
April	9	18
May	12	15
June	15	13
July	18	12
August	17	13
September	13	15
October	9	18
November	5	19
December	2	21

a) Display these data on a double broken-line graph, that is, as two broken-line graphs on the same set of axes.

b) Why might a clothing manufacturer be interested in these data?

5. The table gives the approximate numbers of livestock, in millions, on Canadian farms in different years.

Year	Number of Livestock (millions)		
	Sheep	Cattle	Pigs
1910	3	7	4
1920	3	8	3
1930	4	8	4
1940	2	9	6
1950	2	8	5
1960	1	12	5
1970	1	15	7
1980	1	13	6
1990	2	13	11

Display these data on a triple broken-line graph.

6. With a partner, collect data about the position of a song in the charts over time. Display the data on a broken-line graph.

9.5 Reading and Drawing Circle Graphs

Activity: Study the Graph

Circle graphs are used to show how something is divided. The circle graph at the right shows what people around the world use for eating.

Inquire

1. What is the world's present population to the nearest billion?

2. About how many people in the world use knives, forks, and spoons for eating?

3. About how many people use chopsticks for eating?

4. Do most of the people in the world use a knife?

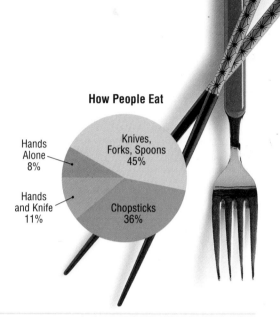

How People Eat

Hands Alone 8%

Knives, Forks, Spoons 45%

Hands and Knife 11%

Chopsticks 36%

Example

A survey asked 500 people at what time they usually get out of bed. The results are shown in the table.

Display this information on a circle graph.

Time	Number
Between 05:00 and 06:00	125
Between 06:00 and 07:00	160
Between 07:00 and 08:00	75
Between 08:00 and 09:00	50
Other	90
Total	500

Solution

1. Write each number as a percent of the total.

Between 05:00 and 06:00 $\frac{125}{500} \times 100\% = 25\%$

Between 06:00 and 07:00 $\frac{160}{500} \times 100\% = 32\%$

Between 07:00 and 08:00 $\frac{75}{500} \times 100\% = 15\%$

Between 08:00 and 09:00 $\frac{50}{500} \times 100\% = 10\%$

Other $\frac{90}{500} \times 100\% = 18\%$

2. A circle has 360°. Calculate each percent of a circle. Round to the nearest degree, if necessary.

25% of 360° = 0.25 × 360° = 90°

32% of 360° = 0.32 × 360° $\doteq$ 115°

15% of 360° = 0.15 × 360° = 54°

10% of 360° = 0.1 × 360° = 36°

18% of 360° = 0.18 × 360° $\doteq$ 65°

3. Draw a circle and measure each angle with a protractor. Label each sector with a name and a percent. Give the graph a title.

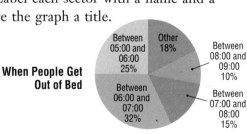

When People Get Out of Bed

Between 05:00 and 06:00 25%

Other 18%

Between 06:00 and 07:00 32%

Between 08:00 and 09:00 10%

Between 07:00 and 08:00 15%

Problems and Applications

1. North Americans eat, on average, 18 L of frozen desserts a year. The circle graph shows the kinds of frozen desserts.

Frozen Dessert Consumption

Ice Cream 63%
Sherbet 3%
Ice Milk 24%
Yogurt 10%

a) How many litres of ice cream does a person eat?
b) How many litres of sherbet does a person eat?
c) How many litres of frozen yogurt?
d) How many litres of ice milk?

2. The circle graphs show the results of a survey of 2000 people. The survey asked how many movies the people watch every month and where they watch them.

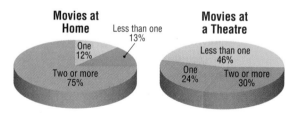

Movies at Home
One 12%
Less than one 13%
Two or more 75%

Movies at a Theatre
Less than one 46%
One 24%
Two or more 30%

a) How many watch 1 movie at home?
b) How many watch 1 movie at a theatre?
c) How many watch 2 or more movies at home?
d) How many watch 2 or more at a theatre?

3. The data show the ways in which our oceans are polluted.

Dumping or from Rivers	54%
Air Pollution	33%
Shipping	12%
Oil, Gas Production	1%

Display these data on a circle graph.

4. The following shows how the average person will spend his or her life.

Activity	Time (years)
Sleeping	24
At Work and School	14
Watching TV	12
Socializing	4
Reading	3
Eating	3
Bathing and Grooming	4
Miscellaneous	11

Display these data on a circle graph.

5. Canada won 6 gold, 6 silver, and 7 bronze medals at the Summer Olympics in Barcelona.
a) Represent these data on a circle graph.
b) Sylvie Frechette won a silver medal for Canada in solo synchronized swimming. A judge's scoring error cost her the gold medal. The error was later corrected, and Sylvie's silver medal was replaced by a gold medal. Correct the data and draw a new circle graph.

6. Choose a subject you would like to display on a circle graph. A possible subject might be: How the broadcast of a sporting event is divided between playing time, announcer talk, and commercials.
a) Predict how the circle graph will look.
b) Collect the data and display them on a circle graph.
c) Compare your graph of the data with your predicted graph.

WORD POWER

Starting with the word PINK, change one letter at a time, forming a new word each time, until you reach the word ROSE. The best solution has the fewest steps.

9.6 Reading and Drawing Pictographs

A graph that uses pictures or symbols to display data is called a pictograph or picture graph.

Activity: Study the Graph

The pictograph shows the number of albums sold for some top-selling Canadian record albums.

Inquire

1. What were the two best-selling albums? About how many albums were sold of each?

2. About how many of Glass Tiger's *The Thin Red Line* album were sold?

3. About how many of Alannah Myles' *Rockinghorse* album were sold?

 4. What is the difference between a pictograph and a bar graph?

5. When would you use a pictograph instead of a bar graph?

Top-Selling Albums

Rockinghorse, Alannah Myles	◎ ◎ (
Reckless, Bryan Adams	◎ ◎ ◎ ◎ ◎ ◎ ◎ ◎ ◎ ◎ ◎ (
Greatest Hits, Anne Murray	◎ ◎ ◎ ◎ ◎ ◎ (
Alien Shores, Platinum Blonde	◎ ◎ ◎ ◎ ◎ (
Boy in the Box, Corey Hart	◎ ◎ ◎ ◎ ◎ ◎ ◎ ◎ ◎ ◎ ◎ (
The Thin Red Line, Glass Tiger	◎ ◎ ◎ ◎ (

Each ◎ represents 100 000 albums.

Example

A few species of plants and animals have survived from prehistoric times. The table lists some of them and the number of years they have been on Earth.

Display these data on a pictograph.

Species	Millions of Years
Giant Redwood	110
Peripatus (worm)	520
Australian Lungfish	230
Duck-billed Platypus	160
Lingula (sea animal)	570
Tuatara (reptile)	190

Solution

Let the symbol 🦫 represent 100 million years. Round each number to the nearest 50 million years, or half a symbol, to find the number of symbols for each prehistoric survivor.

110	1 symbol
520	5 symbols
230	2.5 symbols
160	1.5 symbols
570	5.5 symbols
190	2 symbols

Draw the graph. Include a title. Also include a key to explain what the symbol represents.

Why would you not use each symbol to represent 10 million years? 500 million years?

Prehistoric Survivors

Giant Redwood	🦫
Peripatus	🦫 🦫 🦫 🦫 🦫
Australian Lungfish	🦫 🦫 🦫
Duck-billed Platypus	🦫 🦫
Lingula	🦫 🦫 🦫 🦫 🦫 🦫
Tuatara	🦫 🦫

Each 🦫 represents 100 million years.

Problems and Applications

1. The pictograph shows the water used per person per day in the home in several countries.

Water Use Per Person Per Day	
Germany	🍶🍶🍶
Canada	🍶🍶🍶🍶🍶🍶🍶🍶🍶
China	🍶
Japan	🍶🍶🍶🍶🍶🍶🍶🍶
U.K.	🍶🍶🍶🍶
U.S.A.	🍶🍶🍶🍶🍶🍶🍶🍶🍶🍶🍶
Each 🍶 represents 50 L.	

a) In which country is the most water used?

b) In which country is the least water used?

c) About how many litres of water does a Canadian use every day?

2. The pictograph shows the number of large dams in Canada by province. Large dams are taller than 10 m.

Canada's Large Dams	
Alberta	🪣🪣🪣
British Columbia	🪣🪣🪣🪣🪣🪣
Manitoba	🪣🪣
New Brunswick	🪣
Newfoundland	🪣🪣🪣🪣
Nova Scotia	🪣🪣
Ontario	🪣🪣🪣🪣
P.E.I.	
Quebec	🪣🪣🪣🪣🪣🪣🪣🪣🪣
Saskatchewan	🪣🪣
Each 🪣 represents 20 dams.	

a) Which province has the most large dams? About how many does it have?

b) About how many large dams are there in Alberta?

c) Which provinces have about 50% as many large dams as Newfoundland?

d) About how many more large dams are there in British Columbia than in Manitoba?

 e) Can you be sure from the pictograph that Prince Edward Island has no large dams? Explain.

3. The table gives the length of railway track, in kilometres, for the 5 countries with the greatest length of railway track.

Country	Length of Railway Track (km)
China	50 000
Canada	67 000
U.S.A.	288 000
Former U.S.S.R.	240 000
India	61 000

Display these data on a pictograph.

4. The table gives the mass, in kilograms, of municipal solid waste generated by each person each year in several countries.

Country	Mass of Municipal Solid Waste (kg)
Canada	612
U.S.A.	546
Australia	695
U.K.	364
Japan	331
Italy	248

a) Display these data on a pictograph.

b) Could you display these data on a bar graph? a broken-line graph? a circle graph? Explain.

5. Choose a subject for which you can collect data from your classmates or other sources and can draw a pictograph.

a) Predict how the pictograph will look.

b) Collect the data and display them on a pictograph in a creative way.

c) Compare the pictograph of your data with your prediction.

NUMBER POWER

a) How many darts are needed to score exactly 100 on the dart board?

b) In how many ways could you score 100 on the dart board with this number of darts?

9.7 Mean, Median, and Mode

Activity: Use the Data

The table gives the numbers of gold medals won by Canadians at the Summer and Winter Olympic Games.

Year	1900	1904	1908	1912	1920	1924	1928	1932	1936	1948	1952
Gold Medals	1	5	3	3	1	1	5	3	1	2	2
Year	1956	1960	1964	1968	1972	1976	1980	1984	1988	1992	
Gold Medals	2	2	2	2	0	1	0	12	3	9	

Inquire

1. Arrange the numbers of gold medals in order from smallest to largest.

2. What is the middle number in the new order?

3. What is the number that occurs most often?

4. Find the average number of gold medals.

Three numbers used to describe the centre of a set of data are the mean, median, and mode. They are called **measures of central tendency**.

The **mean**, or average, is found by adding the numbers and dividing by the number of numbers added.

The **median** is the middle number when the numbers are arranged in order. If there are two middle numbers, the median is the mean of the two numbers.

The **mode** is the number that occurs most often. A set of data can have one mode, more than one mode, or no mode.

Example

The Climate Severity Index gives the weather of cities on a scale of 1 to 100. A score of 1 is the least severe climate and a score of 100 is the most severe.
The ratings shown are for the provincial capitals.

Determine the median, mean, and mode of these data.

Charlottetown	48	Edmonton	43
Fredericton	41	Halifax	47
Quebec City	51	Regina	49
St. John's	59	Toronto	36
Victoria	15	Winnipeg	51

Solution

Median: Arrange the data in order from smallest to largest.

15, 36, 41, 43, 47, 48, 49, 51, 51, 59

There are two middle numbers, 47 and 48.

The median is $\frac{47 + 48}{2}$ or 47.5.

Mean: Add the numbers and divide by 10.

$$\frac{15 + 36 + 41 + 43 + 47 + 48 + 49 + 51 + 51 + 59}{10}$$

$$= \frac{440}{10}$$

$$= 44$$

Mode: Since 51 occurs most often, the mode is 51.

So, the median is 47.5, the mean is 44, and the mode is 51.

Practice

Find the mean, median, and mode.

1. 8, 11, 14, 8, 9

2. 18, 14, 18, 14, 18, 17

3. 9, 12, 10, 9, 9, 11, 12, 12

4. 21, 46, 29, 27, 42, 34, 25

5. 9, 8, 9, 8, 9, 8

Problems and Applications

6. List the following.

a) 5 different numbers with a median of 7

b) 5 different numbers with a mean of 8

c) 6 different numbers with a mean of 9

7. The following list shows the number of years each of Canada's first 23 Governors General served. Find the mean, median, and mode.

> 2, 3, 6, 5, 5, 5, 5, 6, 7, 5, 5, 5,
> 5, 4, 5, 6, 6, 7, 8, 6, 6, 4, 6

8. a) What are the mean and median of 61, 57, 55, 60, and 62?

b) Substitute 262 for 62 in the set of data and find the mean and the median.

c) Substitute 5 for 55 in the original set of data and find the mean and the median.

d) Which is affected more by very large or very small numbers, the mean or the median? Explain.

9. The table shows the number of provincial parks in each of Canada's provinces.

Province	Number of Provincial Parks
Newfoundland	93
Prince Edward Island	31
Nova Scotia	122
New Brunswick	48
Quebec	50
Ontario	261
Manitoba	147
Saskatchewan	31
Alberta	115
British Columbia	390

a) Determine the mean, median, and mode.

b) Does the mode give an accurate indication of the centre of these data? Explain.

10. On her first four swimming tests, Mary Lou got marks of 81, 85, 83, and 84. What mark does she need on her next test to have a mean mark of 85?

Which measure of central tendency — the mean, median, or mode — best describes the centre of each of the following sets of data? Explain.

11. the Climate Severity Index found in the example on the previous page

12. the time it takes you to get to school each day

13. the shoe sizes in the class

14. these test marks: 77, 79, 77, 78, 20, 76

15. List the following. Compare your answers with your classmates'.

a) 5 numbers with a mode of 6 and a median of 7

b) 5 numbers with a mode of 4 and a mean of 6

c) 5 different numbers with a median of 8 and a mean of 7

16. Find six numbers so that the mean is 10, the median is less than 10, and the largest of the six numbers is 25. Compare your numbers with your classmates'.

LOGIC POWER

Assume that no cubes are missing from the back of the stack. How many cubes are there?

9.8 Stem-and-Leaf Plots

One way of getting a quick picture of a set of data is to use a stem-and-leaf plot.

Activity: Analyze the Data

The following list shows the numbers of games won by the Calgary Flames in their first 21 seasons in the NHL.

25, 30, 34, 35, 34, 34, 41, 35, 39, 29, 32,
34, 41, 40, 46, 48, 54, 42, 46, 31, 43

The first digit of each piece of data is the **stem**, and the second digit is the **leaf**.

First, list the stems, as shown.		Then, record each leaf next to the proper stem.		Finally, arrange the leaves in order from smallest to largest to give a stem-and-leaf plot.

First, list the stems, as shown.	Then, record each leaf next to the proper stem.	Calgary Flames' Wins
2	2 5 9	2 5 9
3	3 0 4 5 4 4 5 9 2 4 1	3 0 1 2 4 4 4 4 5 5 9
4	4 1 1 0 6 8 2 6 3	4 0 1 1 2 3 6 6 8
5	5 4	5 4

Inquire

1. What is the median of the data?

2. What is the mode?

3. The **range** of a set of data is the difference between the highest value and the lowest value. What is the range of these data?

4. In how many seasons did the team win more than 30 games?

Example

The Hartford Whalers and the Winnipeg Jets entered the NHL in 1979–1980. The data show the numbers of games they won in their first 13 seasons.

Hartford
27, 21, 21, 19, 28, 30, 40,
43, 35, 37, 38, 31, 26

Winnipeg
20, 9, 33, 33, 31, 43, 26,
40, 33, 26, 37, 26, 33

a) Draw a back-to-back stem-and-leaf plot for these data.

b) What was the median number of games won by each team?

c) In how many seasons did each team win less than 30 games?

Solution

a) Write the stems in a middle column and then add the leaves.

Games Won Per Season		
Hartford		Winnipeg
	0	9
9	1	
6 8 1 1 7	2	0 6 6 6
1 8 7 5 0	3	3 3 1 3 7 3
3 0	4	3 0

Arrange the leaves in order, to give a back-to-back stem-and-leaf plot.

Games Won Per Season		
Hartford		Winnipeg
	0	9
9	1	
8 7 6 1 1	2	0 6 6 6
8 7 5 1 0	3	1 3 3 3 3 7
3 0	4	0 3

b) The median number of wins for Hartford was 30. The median number of wins for Winnipeg was 33.

c) Hartford won less than 30 games in 6 seasons. Winnipeg won less than 30 games in 5 seasons.

Problems and Applications

1. The heights of the students in a grade 8 class are shown.

Heights of Students (cm)	
15	6 7 8 8 9 9
16	2 3 4 4 5 6 8 9 9
17	0 2 2 2 4 4 7 8 9
18	0

a) How many students are in the class?
b) What is the median height of the students?
c) What is the mode?
d) What is the range of the data?
e) How many students are taller than 170 cm?

2. The following are the average numbers of days of thunderstorms per year in the provinces and territories.

AB	26	BC	24	MB	26	NB	13
NF	7	NT	12	NS	12	ON	34
PE	11	PQ	27	SK	25	YT	11

a) Display the data on a stem-and-leaf plot.
b) What is the median number of days of thunderstorms?
c) What are the range and the mode?
d) How many provinces or territories have more than 25 days of thunderstorms a year? less than 25?

3. The list shows the numbers of wet days per year for several Canadian cities.

120	137	156	163	166	175	156	148
121	120	162	174	122	143	166	

a) Construct a stem-and-leaf plot.
b) Find the median and the range.
c) How many of the cities have more than 150 wet days a year?
d) How many of the cities have less than 160 wet days a year?

4. The student marks for two first-aid tests are shown.

1st Test	52, 66, 72, 84, 68, 72, 51, 64 54, 81, 84, 67, 70, 73, 60
2nd Test	68, 73, 82, 84, 78, 61, 93, 91 70, 79, 80, 81, 90, 64, 89

a) Display the data on a back-to-back stem-and-leaf plot.
b) How many students wrote each test?
c) What was the median mark for each test?
d) What was the range of marks on each test?
e) How many students scored 70 or higher on the first test? on the second test?
f) How many scored lower than 80 on the first test? on the second test?

9.9 Box-and-Whisker Plots

Activity: Analyze the Data

Listed are the wingspans, in centimetres, of several North American hawks.

Goshawk	106	Broad-winged	83	Red-tailed	121
Cooper's	71	Ferruginous	137	Swainson's	124
Marsh	106	Red-shouldered	101	Sharp-shinned	53
Harlan's	127	Rough-legged	132		

Inquire

1. Arrange the data in order from the smallest wingspan to the largest.

2. What is the lowest value in the data?

3. What is the highest value in the data?

4. What is the median of the data?

5. What is the median of the 5 wingspans whose measures are greater than the median wingspan in question 4? This value is called the **upper quartile.**

6. What is the median of the 5 wingspans whose measures are less than the median wingspan in question 4? This value is called the **lower quartile.**

The five numbers you found in questions 2–6 are called the **five-number summary** for the data. To construct a box-and-whisker plot, plot the numbers on a number line.

Draw a box between the upper and lower quartiles, as shown.

Draw horizontal line segments to the lowest and highest values.

About 50% of the data lie within the box. Each whisker contains about 25% of the data.

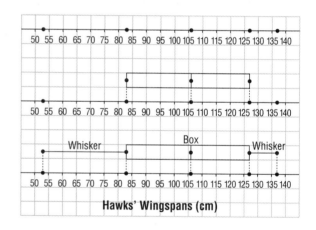

Hawks' Wingspans (cm)

Problems and Applications

1. The masses of 60 deer at a zoo are shown on the box-and-whisker plot.

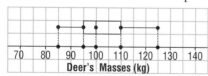

Deer's Masses (kg)

a) What is the median mass of the deer?
b) About how many of the deer have masses greater than 110 kg?

c) About how many deer have masses between 95 kg and 110 kg?

2. The wingspans, in centimetres, of some North American geese are given.

Canada	172	Brant	122
Black Brant	120	Barnacle	142
White-fronted	152	Emperor	134
Blue	147	Snow	149
Ross's	129		

Display the data on a box-and-whisker plot.

Displaying Data

There are many other ways to display data. The following are two examples.

Activity ❶ Range and Average Graphs

The graph shows the length of time, in years, that certain products last.

 1. What does the horizontal axis tell you?

2. What does the vertical axis tell you?

3. a) What is the maximum number of years you can expect a personal computer to last?
b) What is the minimum number of years?
c) What is the average number of years?

4. What product lasts longest if it lasts for its maximum number of years?

5. What products last the least amount of time if they last for their minimum number of years?

6. What product has the longest average lifetime? the shortest?

7. What product has the shortest range?

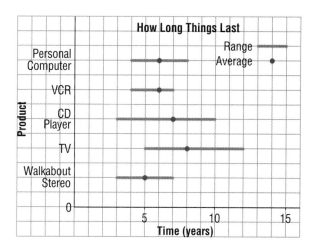

Activity ❷ Histograms

Hurricanes develop in the Atlantic, the Caribbean, and the Gulf of Mexico. The histogram shows the percents of hurricanes that develop at different times of the year.

 1. What does the horizontal axis tell you?

2. What does the vertical axis tell you?

3. How is a histogram like a bar graph?

 4. How is a histogram different from a bar graph?

5. What percent of hurricanes start between June 21 and July 20?

6. What two time periods, together, account for more than 60% of hurricane starts?

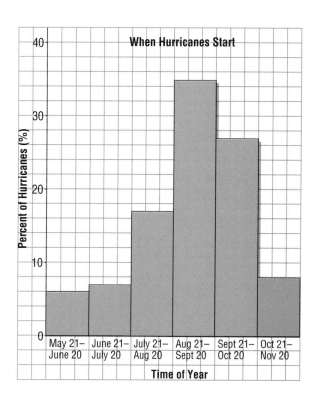

Graphics Software Packages

Microcomputer systems have four parts.

- The hardware consists of the computer, monitor, keyboard, printer, and other devices.
- The software is a program that tells the computer what to do.
- The data are the facts that people input.
- The manuals give the rules to follow when using the hardware, software, and data.

There are many types of software programs: word processing, spreadsheets, database managers, communications, and graphics. Graphics packages display information visually.

Analytical graphics packages display data in line graphs, circle graphs, and bar graphs.

Presentation graphics packages are used by sales people to make presentations. These packages allow the use of colour, pictures, a three-dimensional look, and other methods a graphic artist might use to show data.

A desktop publishing program lets you combine words and graphics to create professional-looking documents like those you see in magazines.

Activity ❶ Television Viewing

A national survey asked 26 000 thirteen-year-olds how many hours a day they spend watching television. The table gives the results.

No time	3%
Up to 1 h	13%
Between 1 h and 2 h	35%
Between 2 h and 3 h	29%
More than 3 h	20%

Use a graphics software package or your own methods to display these data on graphs in different ways. Draw one graph in a creative way, as a graphic artist might.

Activity ❷ Entertainment Spending

The table gives the percent of household entertainment money spent in different ways.

Recreational Equipment, Including Movie Rentals	33%
Electronic Equipment	30%
Admission Fees to Movies, Parks, Concerts	25%
Reading Material	12%

The graph at the right has been drawn using a computer graphics program.

In your group, decide how to display the data in a more appealing and interesting way than the one shown. Draw your graph. Compare your graph with your classmates' graphs.

Activity ❸ Toothbrushes

Survey your class to find out what colour of toothbrush each of your classmates uses. Use a graphics software package or your own methods to display the data in an artistic way.

Activity ❹ Physical Recreational Activities

The table gives the percent of Canadians 10 years old and over who participate in these physical recreational activities.

Skating	22%
Alpine Skiing	20%
Swimming	42%
Bicycling	39%
Home Exercise	30%
Jogging	19%
Dancing	33%

Design and make a one-page document, using graphics and words, to describe the physical recreational activities. In your text, give reasons why some activities are more popular than others. The reasons might include cost, weather, and enjoyment.

Misleading Statistics

Activity ❶ Averages

In baseball, a batting average is calculated by dividing the number of hits by the number of times at bat.

1. Terry and Kelly play for the same baseball team. In the first game of a double-header, Terry had 1 hit, a home run, for 1 at bat. Kelly had 3 hits, all singles, for 4 at bats.

a) What batting average did each have for the first game?

b) Who had the better batting average?

2. In the second game, Terry had 2 hits, a double and a triple, for 5 at bats. Kelly had no hits for 1 at bat.

a) What batting average did each have for the second game?

b) Who had the better batting average?

3. Terry said, "The statistics show that I am a better hitter than Kelly." Kelly said, "The statistics show that I am the better hitter."

a) How many hits did each player have in the two games?

b) Calculate each player's batting average for the two games combined.

c) Who had the better batting average?

d) Is batting average the only way to determine if Kelly or Terry is the better hitter?

 e) Who do you think is the better hitter? Explain.

Activity ❷ Bar Graphs

There are several ways to present data accurately and still mislead people.

The Sherlock's Home bookstore sold 4000 books in December.

The Mystery Place store sold 2000 books in December.

The graphs show two ways of presenting the data.

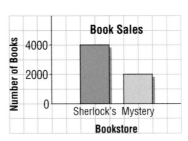

1. Are both graphs presenting the data accurately?

2. How is the graph on the right misleading?

3. The Sherlock's Home bookstore sold twice as many books as the Mystery Place. How many times more sales does the graph on the right suggest?

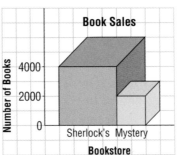

Activity ❸ Polls

Polls are used to get people's opinions. If polls are not random, the results can be misleading.

Suppose the students in your school must decide between a ski trip and a skating trip, and you know that most of them want a skating trip.

1. How could you conduct a poll to show that the students in your school prefer a ski trip?

2. How would you display the results of your poll?

Activity ❹ Line Graphs

The manager of Sherlock's Home bookstore drew this graph to show the owner of the store how sales had increased in 5 weeks.

1. How is the manager trying to mislead the owner with this graph?

2. Draw a broken-line graph to show the increase in sales in a way that is not misleading.

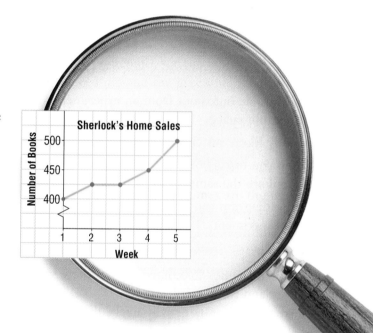

Activity ❺ Advertising

Select two popular products, such as two makes of soft drinks or two makes of shoes. Choose an advertising medium, such as television, radio, or newspapers, where both companies advertise their products.

1. Compare the ways the companies try to get you to buy their products. How are the methods different? How are they the same?

2. Do the companies try to mislead you with their advertisements? If so, how?

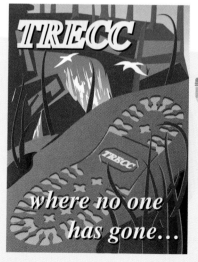

9.11 Probability

Probability is used to study an experiment with several possible outcomes to predict the likelihood of each outcome.

When you toss a coin, there are two possible outcomes. The coin will show a head (H) or a tail (T). If you toss a coin and call "heads," the chance of getting a head is 1 out of 2.

The probability of tossing a head, $P(H) = \frac{1}{2}$

The probability of an event, $P = \dfrac{\text{number of favourable outcomes}}{\text{total number of possible outcomes}}$

Activity: Complete the Tree Diagram

Two lions were born at the zoo each year for two years. Copy and complete the tree diagram to list the possible female (F) and male (M) cubs.

First Year	Second Year	Outcomes
F	F	FF
	M	
M		

Inquire

1. How many possible outcomes are there?

2. What is the probability of getting 2 female cubs?

3. What is the probability of getting just 1 male cub?

4. What is the probability of getting at least 1 female cub?

The probability of an event can be written in lowest terms, just as fractions can be.

Example

Find the probabilities of the following outcomes when you spin the spinner. Write the probabilities as percents.

a) a 3

b) a 5 or a 6

c) an even number

d) a number greater than 7

e) a number from 1 to 10

f) the number 11

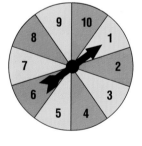

Solution

There are 10 equal sectors on the spinner.

a) $P(3) = \frac{1}{10}$ or 10%

b) $P(5 \text{ or } 6) = \frac{2}{10}$ or $\frac{1}{5}$ or 20%

c) $P(\text{even}) = \frac{5}{10}$ or $\frac{1}{2}$ or 50%

d) $P(\text{greater than } 7) = \frac{3}{10}$ or 30%

e) There are 10 numbers from 1 to 10.
$P(1 \text{ to } 10) = \frac{10}{10}$ or 1 or 100%

f) There is no 11.
$P(11) = \frac{0}{10}$ or 0 or 0%

You can see from the example that an *impossible* outcome has a probability of 0, and a *certain* outcome has a probability of 1. Outcomes that are neither impossible nor certain have probabilities between 0 and 1 or 0% and 100%.

Problems and Applications

In questions 1 to 4, find the probability of each event.

1. Choose 1 cube from the bag.

a) P (red)

b) P (blue)

c) P (yellow)

2. Roll a die.

a) P (6)   **b)** P (3 or 4)   **c)** P (odd number)

d) P (8)   **e)** P (number less than 5)

f) P (number less than 7)

3. Spin the spinner.

a) P (green)

b) P (red or yellow)

c) P (pink, blue, or green)

d) P (white)

4. The names of the provincial capitals are each written on a card and placed in a bag. If you select 1 card from the bag, what is the probability of selecting

a) a city name with exactly 3 vowels?

b) a city name with at least 4 consonants?

c) a city that is on an island?

d) a city in a province that shares a border with the United States?

e) a city in a province whose name has at least 2 words?

5. Use a tree diagram to determine the possible outcomes when a coin is tossed and a die is rolled.

Use your results to find these probabilities.

a) P (H, 3)   **b)** P (T, even number)

c) P (T, 4 or 5)   **d)** P (H or T, 6)

6. Use a tree diagram to show the possible outcomes when you spin the two spinners.

Use your results to find these probabilities. Express the probabilities as percents.

a) P (1, red)   **b)** P (2, green)

c) P (even number, green)

d) P (number less than 4, red)

7. a) List the possible outcomes when you spin the red and blue spinners.

b) How many possible outcomes are there?

c) How many outcomes total 6?

d) What is the probability of spinning a total of 6?

e) What is the probability of spinning a total of 4? 7? 5? 9?

8. a) List the possible outcomes when a red die and a green die are rolled.

b) How many possible outcomes are there?

c) How many outcomes total 9?

d) What is the probability of rolling 9? 7? 12? 10?

 9. Write a probability problem that uses one die and one spinner. Have a classmate solve your problem.

335

Experimental Probability

The probabilities of some outcomes, such as rolling a 5 on a die, can be found mathematically. The probabilities of some other outcomes can be found only by conducting an experiment.

Activity: The Bent Paper Clip

Bend a paper clip like the one shown in the picture.

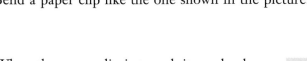

When the paper clip is tossed, it can land in two ways: point up or point down.

1. Estimate the probability of a tossed paper clip landing
a) point up
b) point down

2. Toss a paper clip 20 times and record your results in a table. Use tally marks.

Outcome	Tally
Point Up	
Point Down	

3. Use your results to write the experimental probability of a paper clip landing
a) point up
b) point down

4. Combine your results with those of your classmates. Use the combined results to determine the experimental probability of a paper clip landing
a) point up
b) point down

5. Compare the probabilities found in step 3 and in step 4. Are they different? If they are, explain.

6. Compare the experimental probabilities found in step 4 with the estimated probabilities from step 1.

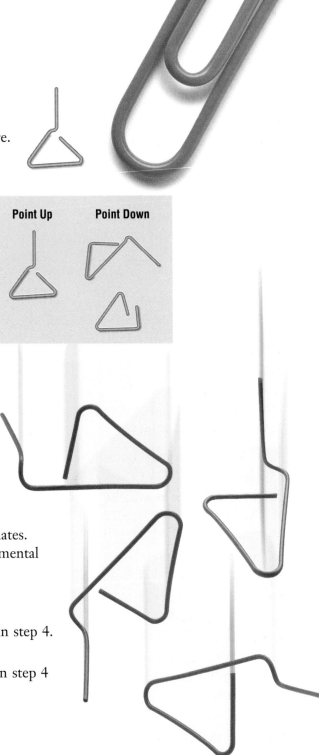

Simulations

Airline pilots train in flight simulators, which act like airplanes.
A **simulation** of an experiment acts like the real experiment.

Activity ❶ A Multiple Choice Test

There are 5 true or false questions on a test.
If you guess at each answer, what is the probability
that you will get 3, 4, or 5 questions correct?

1. Simulate the guesses by tossing 5 coins. A
"head" means a correct answer, and a "tail" means
a wrong answer. Toss the 5 coins 20 times and
record the results in a table, like the one shown.

2. Another way is to use a random number table,
which can be generated by computer. Start
anywhere in the table and use the digits in a
group of 5. Let the digits 0, 2, 4, 6, and 8 mean
a correct answer. Let the digits 1, 3, 5, 7, and
9 mean a wrong answer. Move up or down or
left or right in the table from where you started.
Choose 20 sets of 5 digits. Record your results on
a tally sheet, like the one above.

3. Use your results and the definition of
probability to find the probability of getting 3,
4, or 5 questions correct.

Number Correct	Tally	Frequency
0		
1		
2		
3		
4		
5		

Random Number Table					
29631	69990	01673	08844	61438	23127
30206	84165	05346	80824	23499	56892
26554	60924	88336	20105	77283	43640
80922	95345	31633	87468	23537	94607
03971	37646	23563	52779	46040	69799
18640	80901	03644	77489	22794	86409
12430	52944	29903	01988	44563	32049
80628	88272	06422	75435	85364	43239
55730	74394	68847	69986	39305	58362
56145	10885	02255	67721	83806	72059
58570	39559	14203	17285	58717	51277
81313	84777	79987	24924	13945	80874

Activity ❷ Choosing an Option

A record store has a promotion. If you spend $30 in the store,
you have a chance at grab bags. Half the grab bags are empty,
and half of them contain a voucher for a free tape. There are two
ways to take grab bags from the box.

A. You can pick 3 bags.
B. You can keep picking bags until you get an empty one.

Should you choose A or B?

To solve this problem, simulate option A by repeating Activity 1,
above, with 3 coins instead of 5. Simulate option B by tossing a
coin. A head means the bag has a voucher, and a tail means the
bag is empty. Toss the coin and record the results. They may
look like this.

1. H H T   **2.** T   **3.** H H H T   **4.** H T   **5.** H T   **6.** H H H H T

Carry out the simulation 20 times. Compare the results of the
two experiments to decide what option to choose, A or B.

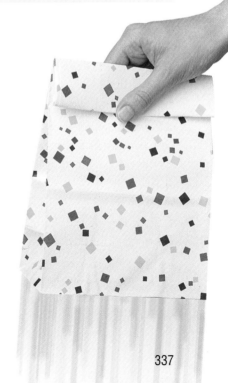

337

9.12 Odds

Probability compares the number of favourable outcomes and the total number of possible outcomes. **Odds** compare the number of favourable outcomes and the number of unfavourable outcomes.

Activity: Use the Definitions

There are 3 blue cubes and 1 red cube in the bag.

The probability of drawing a red cube $= \dfrac{\text{number of favourable outcomes}}{\text{total number of possible outcomes}}$

$= \dfrac{1}{4}$

The **odds in favour of** an event $= \dfrac{\text{number of favourable outcomes}}{\text{number of unfavourable outcomes}}$

The odds in favour of drawing a red cube are $\dfrac{1}{3}$. ← read "1 to 3"

The **odds against** an event $= \dfrac{\text{number of unfavourable outcomes}}{\text{number of favourable outcomes}}$

The odds against drawing a red cube are $\dfrac{3}{1}$. ← read "3 to 1"

Inquire

1. What is the probability of drawing a blue cube?

2. What are the odds in favour of drawing a blue cube?

3. What are the odds against drawing a blue cube?

The odds in favour of, or against, an event can be written in lowest terms in the same way as fractions and probabilities.

Example

Find the odds of the following events when you spin the spinner.
a) the odds in favour of an even number
b) the odds against a 5 or a 6

Solution

a) There are 3 favourable outcomes: 2, 4, and 6.
There are 3 unfavourable outcomes: 1, 3, and 5.
The odds in favour of an even number are $\dfrac{3}{3}$ or $\dfrac{1}{1}$.

b) There are 2 favourable outcomes: 5 and 6.
There are 4 unfavourable outcomes: 1, 2, 3, and 4.
The odds against a 5 or a 6 are $\dfrac{4}{2}$ or $\dfrac{2}{1}$.

338

Problems and Applications

1. There are 2 blue cubes and 3 orange cubes in the bag. One cube is drawn from the bag. State the following.

a) the probability of drawing a blue cube
b) the odds in favour of drawing a blue cube
c) the odds against drawing a blue cube

2. Find each of the following when you spin the spinner.

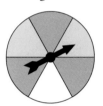

a) the probability of GREEN
b) the odds in favour of GREEN
c) the odds against GREEN
d) the odds in favour of YELLOW
e) the odds against YELLOW
f) the odds in favour of WHITE
g) the odds against WHITE or GREEN

3. The letters of the word MONCTON are written on cards and placed in a bag. One card is then drawn from the bag. State the following.
a) the probability of drawing a C
b) the odds in favour of drawing a C
c) the odds against drawing a C
d) the probability of drawing an O
e) the odds in favour of drawing an O
f) the odds against drawing an O

4. When you spin the spinners, one possible outcome is orange 2, purple 1.

a) How many possible outcomes are there?
b) How many outcomes total 3?
c) What is the probability of spinning a total of 3?
d) What are the odds in favour of a total of 3?
e) What are the odds against a total of 3?

5. The odds in favour of an event are "one to one." What is the probability of the event happening?

6. The odds in favour of drawing a yellow cube from a bag of cubes are $\frac{1}{2}$. What is the probability of drawing a yellow cube from the bag?

7. The odds against drawing a green cube from a bag are $\frac{4}{1}$. What is the probability of drawing a green cube from the bag?

8. The weather report says there is a 50% chance of rain tomorrow.
a) What are the odds in favour of rain?
b) What are the odds against it raining?

GEOGRAPHY POWER

Cities can be located from their coordinates of latitude and longitude.

1. State the parts of the world in which you think cities with the following coordinates are located.
a) 49°N 123°W
b) 39°N 77°W
c) 33°S 73°W

2. Identify the city that is closest to the point with each set of coordinates in question 1.

Review

1. Barry conducted a survey to find out which of the following team nicknames grade 8 students like most: Bears, Lions, Tigers, Eagles, or Wolves. Each student was limited to one choice.

Survey Sheet		
Nickname	**Tally**	**Frequency**
Bears	₩₩ ₩₩ ₩₩ II	
Lions	IIII	
Tigers	₩₩ ₩₩ ₩₩ ₩₩ IIII	
Eagles	₩₩ ₩₩ ₩₩ ₩₩ I	
Wolves	₩₩ ₩₩ IIII	

a) Copy and complete the survey sheet.
b) How many students chose Bears?
c) List the choices from most popular to least popular.
d) How many students were surveyed?

2. The bar graph shows how much hot water is used for activities in the home.

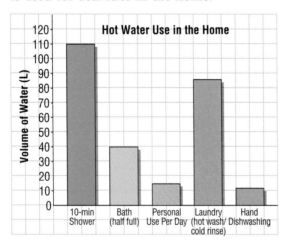

a) About how much hot water is used for a bath if the tub is half full?
b) About how much hot water is used for a 10-min shower? a 2-min shower?
c) Which activity uses about 7 times more hot water than hand dishwashing?

3. The following are the elevations of the world's seven highest cities.

Addis Ababa, Ethiopia	2450 m
Bogotá, Colombia	2639 m
Calgary, Canada	1045 m
Johannesburg, South Africa	1734 m
Mexico City, Mexico	2309 m
Nairobi, Kenya	1820 m
São Paulo, Brazil	776 m

Display these data on a bar graph.

4. The table gives the average daily temperature, in degrees Celsius, for each month in Casablanca, Morocco, and Vienna, Austria.

Average Daily Temperature (°C)					
	Casablanca	**Vienna**		**Casablanca**	**Vienna**
January	12	0	July	22	20
February	13	1	August	23	19
March	14	5	September	22	16
April	16	10	October	20	10
May	18	15	November	16	5
June	20	18	December	13	1

Display these data on a double broken-line graph.

5. The breakdown of residential energy use is as shown.

Space Heating	67%
Water Heating	17%
Appliances	14%
Lighting	2%

Display these data on a circle graph.

6. The following shows what 1 L of gasoline energy provides.

Car	10.5 Passenger-kilometres
City Bus	42 Passenger-kilometres
Boeing 767	5 Passenger-kilometres
Train	30 Passenger-kilometres

Display these data on a pictograph.

7. Find the mean, median, mode, and range of these data: 83, 82, 83, 85, 83, 82.

8. List the following.
a) five different numbers with a median of 8
b) six different numbers with a mean of 7
c) six different numbers with a median of 10

9. The numbers of games won by the Vancouver Canucks in their first 23 seasons are given below.

24	20	22	24	38	33	25	20	25	27	28	30
30	32	25	23	29	25	33	25	28	42	46	

a) Construct a stem-and-leaf plot for these data.
b) Find the median, mode, and range of the data.

10. The wingspans, in centimetres, of 60 large owls and 60 small owls are shown on the box-and-whisker plot.

Owls' Wingspans (cm)

a) What is the median wingspan for each type of owl?
b) How many large owls have wingspans between 100 cm and 130 cm?
c) How many small owls have wingspans between 35 cm and 50 cm?
d) About how many small owls have wingspans less than 35 cm?
e) About how many large owls have wingspans greater than 130 cm?

11. Spin the spinner. Calculate each probability.
a) P (red)
b) P (blue)
c) P (blue or green)
d) P (yellow)
e) P (white)

Group Decision Making
Reducing Waste

Many Canadians are making an effort to reduce waste. The list shows some types of waste and the percent of waste they make up.

Type of Waste	Percent
Mixed Paper (magazines, junk mail, phone books, grocery bags)	20%
Newspaper	15%
Cardboard Boxes	3%
Glass Bottles and Jars	9%
Metals (aluminum cans and foil, tin/steel cans)	5%
Plastic	5%
Yard Waste	25%
Food Scraps	10%

1. Brainstorm as a class the places where waste occurs. Include your school cafeteria, school grounds, home, parks, food stores, and shopping malls.

2. Decide as a class which one of the places each home group will investigate.

3. Go to home groups and list the ways waste can be reduced in your chosen place for four of the categories of waste listed.

1 2 3 4 5 6	1 2 3 4 5 6

Home Groups

1 2 3 4 5 6	1 2 3 4 5 6

4. Prepare a presentation for the class on the ways waste can be reduced. Be creative.

5. As a class, decide what steps you and your classmates can take to reduce waste.

Chapter Check

1. The circle graph shows the population distribution in Canada's four westernmost provinces.

Alberta 32%
Manitoba 14%
Saskatchewan 13%
British Columbia 41%

a) In which two provinces are the populations about equal?

b) Which two provinces, together, account for about three-quarters of the population?

c) The total population of these four provinces is about 8 000 000. About how many people live in Alberta?

2. The table gives the percent of colds that start on each day of the week for teenagers. Display these data on a broken-line graph.

| Sun | 16% | Mon | 17% | Tues | 14% | Wed | 13% |
| Thurs | 12% | Fri | 13% | Sat | 15% | | |

3. Find the mean, median, mode, and range of each set of data.

a) 29, 22, 23, 31, 30, 22, 25
b) 70, 91, 85, 75, 80, 76
c) 7, 10, 9, 7, 10, 9, 1, 9

4. The table gives the percent of Canadians who participate in certain activities while on vacation.

Beaches	64%	Sailing	21%
Fishing	16%	Biking	15%
Skiing	23%	Scuba Diving	16%
Golf	25%	Spectator Sports	14%

Display these data on a bar graph.

5. Marks for a math test are shown.

> 88, 83, 80, 73, 90, 90, 77, 86, 92, 94,
> 73, 80, 89, 93, 85, 82, 78, 91, 88, 92, 89

a) Display the data on a stem-and-leaf plot.
b) What are the median mark and the range of marks?

6. Alice Munro is a famous Canadian writer. Suppose you write each letter of her name on a different card, place the cards in a bag, and draw one card from the bag. Write the following probabilities as percents.

a) P (C)
b) P (M or N)
c) P (vowel)
d) P (consonant)
e) P (L, M, or N)
f) P (not L, M, or N)

Using the Strategies

1. Find the missing number.

1	3	5	7
3	7	15	27
5	15	37	79
7	27	79	?

2. Three points are marked on the circumference of a circle. If you join each point to every other point, you divide the circle into 4 regions.

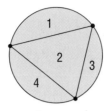

a) Into how many regions do you divide the circle if you start with 4 points?

b) Into how many regions do you divide the circle if you start with 5 points?

3. There are 16 points on the grid. How many squares can be made by joining the points?

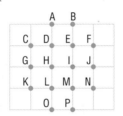

4. Ashir works in the Cookie Loft. A package of oatmeal cookies sells for $1.67, and a package of chocolate chip cookies sells for $1.91. One day, Ashir sold 141 packages of cookies for a total of $255.39. How many packages of each kind of cookie did he sell?

5. If you have 10 coins that total 49¢, what coins do you have?

6. The towns of Acton and Barton are located across from each other on the opposite sides of a lake. Every hour, on the hour, a passenger boat leaves Acton for Barton. It arrives at Barton 1 h later. Sharma left Barton for Acton at 14:15 in her boat. She sailed directly to Acton and arrived at 16:15. How many boats going from Acton to Barton did she meet?

7. One month, John wrote cheques on his bank account for $14.95, $67.80, $21.40, and $114.60. He made one $80.00 withdrawal at the automatic teller. He made two deposits, one for $60.00 and the other for $156.80. At the end of the month, he had $87.88 in his account. How much money was in his account at the start of the month?

8. Maria left the corner grocery store and rode her bicycle 4 blocks north, 3 blocks west, 1 block south, 6 blocks east, 5 blocks south, then 3 blocks east. What is the smallest number of blocks she can ride to get back to the grocery store?

9. Sketch a graph of the number of students in your school gym versus the time of day on a regular Monday.

10. Three students, Tanya, Darrell, and Susan, play in the school band. They play the trumpet, drums, and saxophone. No person's name begins with the same letter as the instrument he or she plays. Susan does not play the trumpet. What instrument does each person play?

DATA BANK

1. Arrange these distances from shortest to longest.

- the driving distance from Edmonton to Victoria
- the length of the South Saskatchewan River
- the flying distance from Toronto to Charlottetown

2. Canada has 9% of the world's fresh water. What percent of the world's fresh water is in Quebec?

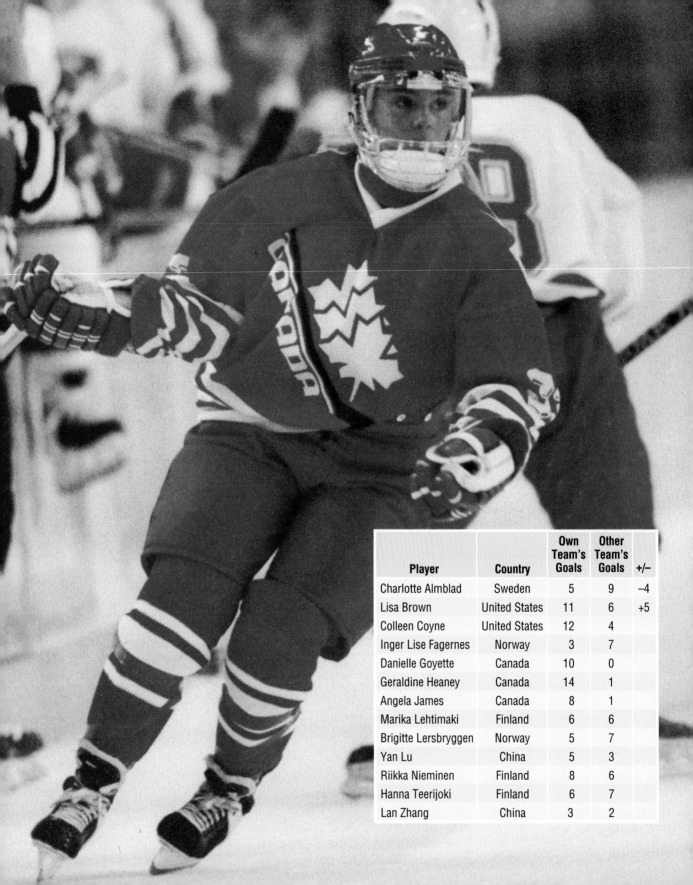

Player	Country	Own Team's Goals	Other Team's Goals	+/−
Charlotte Almblad	Sweden	5	9	−4
Lisa Brown	United States	11	6	+5
Colleen Coyne	United States	12	4	
Inger Lise Fagernes	Norway	3	7	
Danielle Goyette	Canada	10	0	
Geraldine Heaney	Canada	14	1	
Angela James	Canada	8	1	
Marika Lehtimaki	Finland	6	6	
Brigitte Lersbryggen	Norway	5	7	
Yan Lu	China	5	3	
Riikka Nieminen	Finland	8	6	
Hanna Teerijoki	Finland	6	7	
Lan Zhang	China	3	2	

CHAPTER 10

Integers

The plus-minus system is one way of evaluating hockey players. Players, except the goal tender, are each given +1 if they are on the ice when their team scores. They are each given −1 if they are on the ice when the other team scores.

When Canada won the Women's World Hockey Championships in Finland, the Canadian team scored 38 goals in 5 games. Only 3 goals were scored against the Canadian team.

The table lists some of the players who took part in the World Championships and gives the number of times they were on the ice when their team scored and the other team scored. Copy the table and calculate each player's plus-minus record. The first two are completed for you.

How would a hockey coach use plus-minus records to evaluate players? List some other ways that are used to evaluate hockey players.

Activity ❶ Triangle Patterns

Study the triangles to determine the number pattern.

Complete the triangles using the number pattern.

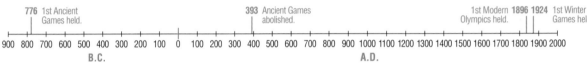

Activity ❷ An Olympic Time Line

776 1st Ancient Games held.   393 Ancient Games abolished.   1st Modern 1896 1924 1st Winter Olympics held. Games held.

900 800 700 600 500 400 300 200 100 0 100 200 300 400 500 600 700 800 900 1000 1100 1200 1300 1400 1500 1600 1700 1800 1900 2000

B.C.   A.D.

The time line shows some significant dates in the history of the Olympic Games.

1. For how many years did the Ancient Games exist?

2. For how many years were no Olympic Games held?

3. How many years were there between the first modern Summer Games and the first Winter Games?

4. In A.D. 67, the Roman emperor Nero fell off his chariot and was unable to finish a race. But he was still declared the winner! How many years was this before the Ancient Games were abolished?

5. How many years after the first Ancient Games were held did each of the following occur?

a) 1908 — The first Canadian National Team participated in the Olympics.

b) 1928 — Women were allowed to participate in track and field for the first time.

c) 1948 — Canada's Barbara Ann Scott won the gold medal in figure skating.

d) 1976 — The Summer Olympics were held in Montreal.

6. The Modern Olympics have been held every 4 years since 1896, except for 1916, 1940, and 1944. Why were the Games cancelled in these years?

Activity ❸ Rolling Dice

The dice are numbered 1 to 6 and 7 to 12. The dice are rolled together.

1. List all the possible totals.

2. List all the possible products.

3. If the smaller number is subtracted from the larger number, list all the possible differences.

4. List all the possible whole number quotients.

5. If the smaller number is used as the numerator and the larger number as the denominator,
a) how many different fractions are possible?
b) how many different fractions in lowest terms are possible?

Warm Up

Replace each ◆ with >, <, or = to make each number sentence true.

1. $9 \times 5 + 8$ ◆ $14 \times 2 + 6$

2. $7 \times 3 - 9$ ◆ $40 - 8 \times 4$

3. $112 \div 4 - 5$ ◆ $62 \div 2 + 1$

4. $3^3 + 10^2$ ◆ $9 + 25 \times 4$

5. $8 \times 7 \div 4$ ◆ $100 - 43 \times 2$

6. $16 - \frac{1}{5}$ of 65 ◆ $\frac{1}{3}$ of 12×2

7. $20 + 6 \times 3$ ◆ $8 \times 4 + 7$

8. $10^3 - 9^2$ ◆ $10^2 \times 3^2$

9. $(12 + 8) \div 5$ ◆ $30 \div (11 - 5)$

10. $\frac{1}{2} \times 6 \times 3 \times 2$ ◆ $3 \times 3 \times 2$

Mental Math

Add.

1. $7 + 8$ **2.** $17 + 8$

3. $37 + 8$ **4.** $67 + 8$

5. $87 + 8$ **6.** $9 + 6$

7. $9 + 16$ **8.** $9 + 36$

9. $9 + 56$ **10.** $9 + 76$

Subtract.

11. $10 - 3$ **12.** $20 - 3$

13. $40 - 3$ **14.** $60 - 3$

15. $80 - 3$ **16.** $13 - 7$

17. $33 - 7$ **18.** $53 - 7$

19. $93 - 7$ **20.** $113 - 7$

Multiply.

21. 4×6 **22.** 14×6

23. 24×6 **24.** 34×6

25. 54×6 **26.** 5×8

27. 5×18 **28.** 5×28

29. 5×48 **30.** 5×68

Divide.

31. $12 \div 4$ **32.** $32 \div 4$

33. $52 \div 4$ **34.** $72 \div 4$

35. $92 \div 4$ **36.** $14 \div 7$

37. $84 \div 7$ **38.** $154 \div 7$

39. $224 \div 7$ **40.** $294 \div 7$

Calculate.

41. $27 + 8 - 13$ **42.** $32 - 17 + 12$

43. $3 \times 5 - 4$ **44.** $32 \div 8 \div 2$

45. $12 \times 4 \div 6$ **46.** $33 \div 11 \times 15$

47. $10 \times 6 - 30$ **48.** $1 + 2 \times 12$

49. $100 \div 10 + 10$ **50.** $25 - 30 \div 3$

10.1 Integers

Activity: Learn About Integers

Integers include positive whole numbers, negative whole numbers, and zero.

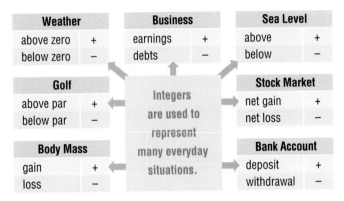

Weather	
above zero	+
below zero	−

Business	
earnings	+
debts	−

Sea Level	
above	+
below	−

Golf	
above par	+
below par	−

Integers are used to represent many everyday situations.

Stock Market	
net gain	+
net loss	−

Body Mass	
gain	+
loss	−

Bank Account	
deposit	+
withdrawal	−

Integers can be represented on a number line.

Negative integers are less than zero.   Zero is neither positive nor negative.   Positive integers are greater than zero.

$$-8 \quad -7 \quad -6 \quad -5 \quad -4 \quad -3 \quad -2 \quad -1 \quad 0 \quad +1 \quad +2 \quad +3 \quad +4 \quad +5 \quad +6 \quad +7 \quad +8$$

−5 and +5 are **opposite integers**.

Inquire

1. Explain the statement: "Each positive integer has an opposite."

2. List activities that involve travelling
a) above sea level
b) below sea level

3. Describe 2 situations in which it is better for numbers to be negative than positive.

Practice

Write in symbols.

1. positive nine

2. negative twelve

3. negative two

4. positive twenty

5. zero

6. negative fifteen

State the opposite of each integer.

7. +3

8. +21

9. −15

10. −6

11. −11

12. +52

13. +1

14. −19

Write as an integer.

15. a gain of five points

16. a ninety-dollar withdrawal

17. six strokes below par

18. ten degrees above zero

19. a profit of three hundred dollars

20. fourteen seconds off the record time

21. five hundred metres above sea level

22. a loss of twelve kilograms

Problems and Applications

23. The floors in the elevator of a large hotel are numbered from −3 to +7, with the street-level lobby represented by L instead of zero. State which floor the elevator stops at after each of the following moves.

	Start	Change
a)	L	up 4
b)	+2	down 3
c)	−3	up 6
d)	+5	down 4
e)	+1	up 5
f)	+7	down 10

24. Corey and Sally used a positive die and a negative die to play a game on a number line. Each player began at zero. They each rolled the positive die, then the negative die. The object of the game was to return to zero after the fewest turns.

a) The table shows what each player rolled. Use a number line to determine who won the game.

	Roll							
	1	**2**	**3**	**4**	**5**	**6**	**7**	**8**
Corey	+4	−5	+2	−6	+3	−1	+4	−1
Sally	+2	−3	+6	−2	+4	−6	+2	−5

b) What roll would bring the other player back to zero?

 25. Sunil used checker pieces to make a concrete model of integers.

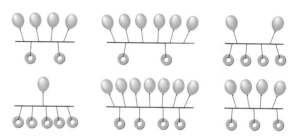

Explain why he used 2 checkers to represent zero.

26. Maria used balloons and metal washers to make a concrete model of integers.

a) State the integer represented by each illustration.

b) Show 2 ways Maria could illustrate zero.

27. Use familiar objects to illustrate integers in a creative, concrete way. Exchange your work with a classmate and interpret each other's ideas.

NUMBER POWER

The number 50 is the smallest whole number that can be written as the sum of 2 squares in 2 ways.

$$50 = 5^2 + 5^2$$
$$50 = 7^2 + 1^2$$

Find the 2 whole numbers between 60 and 90 that can be written as the sum of 2 squares in 2 ways.

Integers on the Thermometer

The temperature scale that is most commonly used was developed by a Swedish scientist named Anders Celsius in 1742. Because he divided the range between the freezing point and the boiling point of water into 100 degrees, the scale was once known as the centigrade scale. It has now been renamed the **Celsius scale** after its originator.

Activity ❶

Several commonly used temperatures are marked on the thermometer at the right. Match each one with the correct item in the list.

human body temperature

boiling point of water

hot tap water

freezing point of water

temperature inside a freezer

a comfortable room

good skating weather

a day when cars will not start

good swimming weather

a high fever

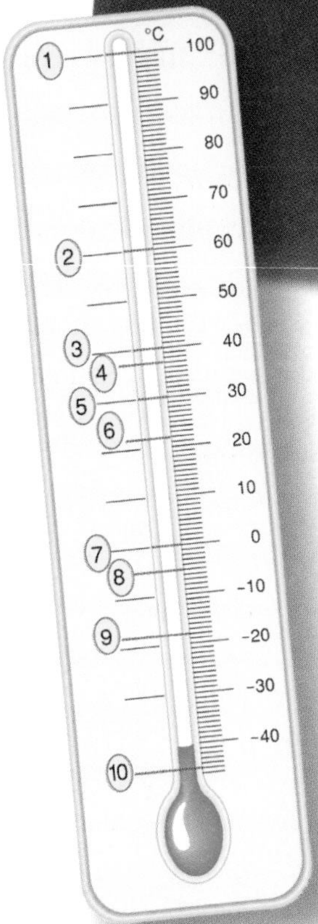

Activity ❷

The table shows the average daily temperatures in January and July for 12 Canadian cities.

City	Average Daily Temperatures (°C)	
	January	July
Winnipeg	−19	20
Calgary	−12	16
Charlottetown	−7	18
Fredericton	−9	19
Whitehorse	−19	14
Montreal	−10	21
Halifax	−5	18
Vancouver	3	16
London	−7	20
Yellowknife	−28	16
St. John's	−4	16
Regina	−17	19

1. Use the thermometer to help you to calculate the difference between the average daily temperature in January and July for each city.

2. Which city has the greatest difference in temperature?

3. Which city has the smallest difference in temperature?

4. Use a map of Canada to locate each of the cities listed. Decide with your classmates which cities you would like to visit and at what time of year.

Activity ❸

1. Look at the approximate ideal body temperatures for each classification of animals. Share your observations with your group.

2. Answer "True" or "False" to each of these statements. Explain your reasoning.

a) The ideal body temperature of warm-blooded animals is higher than that of cold-blooded animals.

b) The larger the animal, the higher is its ideal body temperature.

c) The average ideal body temperature of birds is higher than for the other classifications.

3. Compose 3 statements about warm-blooded or cold-blooded animals. Use your research skills to check whether your statements are true or false.

Activity ❹

The table shows changes in body temperature for 4 warm-blooded animals hibernating in cold weather.

Ideal Body Temperatures

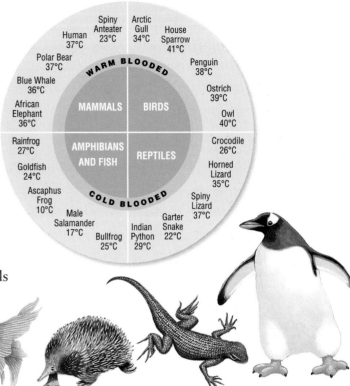

Changes in Body Temperature for Warm-Blooded Animals	
Animal	Temperature Change (°C)
Poorwill	40 to 18
Dormouse	37 to 2
Opossum	35 to 11
Hamster	43 to 6

The table shows the range of body temperatures survived by 4 cold-blooded animals.

Body Temperatures of Cold-Blooded Animals	
Animal	Temperature Range (°C)
Crocodile	23 to 29
Catfish	6 to 34
Salamander	6 to 27
Garter Snake	4 to 39

1. List the hibernating animals, in order, from greatest body temperature change to smallest body temperature change.

2. The extreme body temperatures survived by humans range from about 16°C to 45°C.

a) How many degrees does this range represent?

b) Name the warm-blooded animals that survive over a greater range.

3. Calculate the number of degrees in the body temperature range for each of the cold-blooded animals.

4. Use an almanac or book of records to locate other recorded body temperature ranges and extremes in the animal kingdom. Compare your findings with your classmates'. Decide what is the most interesting or unusual piece of information.

10.2 Comparing and Ordering Integers

Activity: Interpret the Data

Brenda, Aisha, Danny, and Stefan are playing a word game using lettered cards. The players earn points by turning over cards and completing words in a given time. Players lose points if they are unable to complete words with their cards.

Brenda has −15 points, Aisha has 45 points, Danny has −50 points, and Stefan has 30 points.

The scores can be shown on a number line.

Brenda	Aisha	Danny	Stefan
+0	+0	−20	−10
20	25	0	−15
5	30	−15	−5
+0	25	−30	+5
0	35	−40	25
−15	45	−50	30

Inquire

1. Who is winning the game?

2. List the other 3 players and their scores, from greatest to least.

3. How do integers change as you move from right to left along the number line?

4. How do integers change as you move from left to right along the number line?

Example 1

Compare the integers −50 and +30.

Solution 1

An integer to the left of another integer is smaller in value.

Since −50 is located to the left of +30, then −50 is less than +30.

−50 < +30

Solution 2

An integer to the right of another integer is larger in value.

Since +30 is located to the right of −50, then +30 is greater than −50.

+30 > −50

Example 2

Write these integers in order from least to greatest.

−5, +11, −7, −2, +3, −9, +6, +1

Solution

Graph the integers on a number line.

The integers in order from least to greatest are −9, −7, −5, −2, +1, +3, +6, +11.

Practice

Which integer is larger?

1. $+8, +12$ **2.** $-4, -2$

3. $0, -5$ **4.** $-11, -9$

5. $+3, -6$ **6.** $-21, +15$

Which integer is smaller?

7. $+10, +7$ **8.** $-6, -2$

9. $-5, +3$ **10.** $-1, 0$

11. $+14, -20$ **12.** $-4, +8$

Replace ♦ with > or < to make each statement true.

13. $+2$ ♦ $+9$ **14.** -3 ♦ -7

15. 0 ♦ -10 **16.** $+8$ ♦ -5

17. -1 ♦ -10 **18.** -2 ♦ 0

19. -4 ♦ $+1$ **20.** -15 ♦ $+12$

Write the next 4 greater integers.

21. -3 **22.** 0

23. $+2$ **24.** -8

25. -12 **26.** -1

Write the integers between each pair.

27. -4 and $+4$

28. -13 and -8

29. $+5$ and -2

Write the integers from largest to smallest.

30. $+6, -14, +2, -21, 0$

31. $-1, +5, -11, +12, +3$

32. $+7, -1, -8, +3, -15$

Write the integers from smallest to largest.

33. $0, -2, +11, -5, +4$

34. $+3, -1, +6, -4, -8$

35. $+21, -14, -30, +15, -22$

Problems and Applications

36. Arrange the following temperatures from warmest to coldest.

Substance	Change	Temperature (°C)
mercury	freezes	-39
water	boils	100
water	freezes	0
chlorine	freezes	-101
mercury	boils	357
potassium	freezes	64
nitrogen	freezes	-210

37. The bottoms of some Canadian lakes are below sea level, as shown in the table.

Lake	Greatest Depth Below Sea Level (m)
Great Bear	257
Great Slave	458
Huron	53
Ontario	169
Superior	223

Write each measurement as a negative integer. Rank the integers from least to greatest.

38. Write, in increasing order, the integers
a) greater than -5 and less than $+2$
b) less than $+4$ and greater than -3
c) less than zero and greater than -8

Write the next 3 integers.

39. $-7, -4, -1,$ ■, ■, ■

40. $+9, +4, -1,$ ■, ■, ■

41. $-12, -8, -4,$ ■, ■, ■

42. Decide whether each statement is always true, sometimes true, or never true. Explain.
a) Zero is greater than another integer.
b) A negative integer is less than a positive integer.
c) An integer is greater than its opposite.
d) Two integers with different signs are opposites.

Modelling Integer Operations

Because static electricity has positive and negative charges, it can be used as a model for integer operations. Integers include positive and negative whole numbers. In the model, red disks represent positive charges and blue disks represent negative charges.

One red disk represents a charge of +1.

One blue disk represents a charge of −1.

A red disk and a blue disk together represent a charge of zero.

Zero charge

Activity ❶ Naming Charges

Write the charge represented by each group of disks.

Activity ❷ Modelling Charges

The disks show 3 ways of making a charge of +2.

The disks show 3 ways of making a charge of −3.

Use disks or diagrams to show 3 ways of making each charge.

1. +3   **2.** −2   **3.** +1   **4.** −1   **5.** 0

Activity ❸ Adding Integers

Charges can be used to show how integers are added.

The charge is +4.

Add 3 negative charges.

Make and remove zero charges.

The resulting charge is +1.

The addition statement is $(+4) + (-3) = +1$.

Use disks to find each result.

1. $(+6) + (-1) = $ ▪

2. $(+4) + (-6) = $ ▪

3. $(-2) + (-3) = $ ▪

4. $(-4) + (+2) = $ ▪

5. $(+7) + (+5) = $ ▪

6. $(-3) + (+5) = $ ▪

Activity ❹ Subtracting Integers

Charges can be used to show how integers are subtracted.

The charge is –4.

Remove 3 negative charges.

The resulting charge is –1.

The subtraction statement is $(-4) - (-3) = -1$.

If there are not enough charges on the plate of the kind you want to remove, add zero charges to the plate until there are enough. Suppose you want to subtract $(+3)$ in the following.

The charge is –2.

Add zero charges. The charge is –2.

Remove 3 positive charges.

The resulting charge is –5.

The subtraction statement is $(-2) - (+3) = -5$.

Use disks to find each result.

1. $(+4) - (+1) = $ ▪

2. $(+3) - (+4) = $ ▪

3. $(+2) - (-1) = $ ▪

4. $(-3) - (-1) = $ ▪

5. $(-4) - (+2) = $ ▪

6. $(-3) - (-5) = $ ▪

7. $(-1) - (-4) = $ ▪

8. $(+2) - (-4) = $ ▪

9. $0 - (+2) = $ ▪

10. $0 - (-3) = $ ▪

11. $(-2) - (-3) = $ ▪

12. $(+5) - (-6) = $ ▪

10.3 Adding Integers

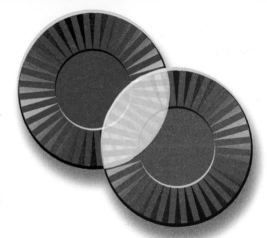

Activity: Use a Model

A model for illustrating integers uses coloured disks.

A red disk represents a positive unit. $(+1)$

A blue disk represents a negative unit. (-1)

When disks are used to illustrate addition,
opposite pairs result in zero value. $(+1) + (-1) = 0$

To add $(+5)$ and (-2)

| The integer is +5 or (+5). | The integer (−2) is added. | Pairs of red and blue disks are removed. | The final integer is +3 or (+3). |

Say: "Positive 5 plus negative 2 equals positive 3."

Write the addition statement: $(+5) + (-2) = +3$.

Addition can also be shown on a number line.
To add $(+4)$ and (-3)

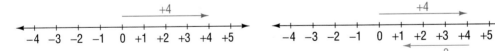

$(+4) + (-3) = +1$

Begin at zero. Move right for positive integers.

Move left for negative integers.

Inquire

1. Illustrate $(+5)$ plus (-2) using a number line.

2. Illustrate $(+4)$ plus (-3) using integer disks.

3. Use integer disks or number lines to complete these addition statements.

a) $(-3) + (+1)$ **b)** $(+6) + (+4)$

c) $(+8) + (-4)$ **d)** $(-5) + (-6)$ **e)** $(+4) + (-4)$

4. Copy and complete each statement.
a) The sum of two positive integers is ▮▮▮ .
b) The sum of two negative integers is ▮▮▮ .
c) The sum of a positive integer and a negative integer is ▮▮▮ .

356

Practice

Write the addition statement.

1.  plus negative three

2.  plus positive one

3.  plus positive eight

4. plus negative five

Write the addition statement.

5.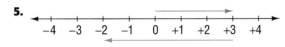
$$-4 \quad -3 \quad -2 \quad -1 \quad 0 \quad +1 \quad +2 \quad +3 \quad +4$$

6.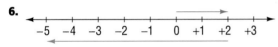
$$-5 \quad -4 \quad -3 \quad -2 \quad -1 \quad 0 \quad +1 \quad +2 \quad +3$$

7.
$$-6 \quad -5 \quad -4 \quad -3 \quad -2 \quad -1 \quad 0 \quad +1 \quad +2$$

8.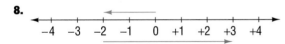
$$-4 \quad -3 \quad -2 \quad -1 \quad 0 \quad +1 \quad +2 \quad +3 \quad +4$$

Illustrate each addition with integer disks. Write each addition statement.

9. $(+2) + (+3)$ **10.** $(-4) + (-5)$

11. $(-6) + (+7)$ **12.** $(+5) + (-8)$

Show each addition on a number line. Write each addition statement.

13. $(+3) + (+5)$ **14.** $(-7) + (+4)$

15. $(-1) + (-3)$ **16.** $(+2) + (-9)$

Add.

17. $(-5) + (-6)$ **18.** $(+2) + (+6)$

19. $(-4) + (+7)$ **20.** $(+8) + (-9)$

21. $(+3) + (-10)$ **22.** $(-6) + (+6)$

Problems and Applications

23. Add.

a) $(-2) + (+1) + (-3)$

b) $(+3) + (-1) + (+2)$

c) $(+4) + (-3) + (+4)$

d) $(-5) + (-4) + (-6)$

24. Find the missing integer.

a) $(+2) + (\blacksquare) = +5$ **b)** $(-3) + (\blacksquare) = -7$

c) $(\blacksquare) + (+4) = -2$ **d)** $(\blacksquare) + (+3) = +1$

25. Patrick borrowed $15.00. He paid $8.00 for lunch tickets and $4.00 for a new notebook. Then, he received his $10.00 allowance. How much more money did Patrick need to repay the $15.00?

26. Use each integer once to copy and complete the addition statements.

$(-7) \quad (-12)$
$(+5) \quad 0$
$(-1) \quad (-2)$
$(+9) \quad (+3)$

$\blacksquare + \blacksquare = (+2)$
$\blacksquare + \blacksquare = (-9)$
$\blacksquare + \blacksquare = (+4)$
$\blacksquare + \blacksquare = (-2)$

27. Augustus, Emperor of Rome, was born in 63 B.C. and died in A.D. 14. How old was he when he died?

28. What is the sum of the integers from

a) (-2) to $(+5)$?   **b)** (-4) to $(+1)$?

c) (-1) to $(+8)$?   **d)** (-7) to 0?

29. Choose an integer from set A and add to it an integer in set B to make 4 consecutive totals. Write each addition statement.

Set A	Set B
(-3) $(+4)$ $(+6)$ (-3)	(-5) (-6) $(+1)$ 0

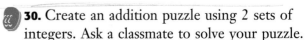 **30.** Create an addition puzzle using 2 sets of integers. Ask a classmate to solve your puzzle.

357

10.4 Subtracting Integers

Activity: Use a Model

Integer disks can be used to model the subtraction of positive integers.

The integer is +3 or (+3).   The integer (+2) is subtracted.   The final integer is +1 or (+1).

    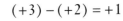 

$$(+3) - (+2) = +1$$

Say: "Positive 3 subtract positive 2 equals positive 1."

The integer is 0.   The integer (+3) is subtracted.   The final integer is –3 or (–3).

$$0 - (+3) = -3$$

Inquire

1. What is the result when a positive integer is subtracted from an integer?

2. The sequence shows the steps for subtracting $(+3) - (+5)$.

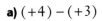 

a) Describe what is happening in each step.   **b)** Write the subtraction statement.

3. Use integer disks to model each subtraction. Write the subtraction statement.

a) $(+4) - (+3)$ **b)** $0 - (+2)$ **c)** $(-1) - (+1)$ **d)** $(+2) - (+5)$

Activity: Use a Model

Integer disks can also be used to model the subtraction of negative integers.

The integer is –3 or (–3).   The integer (–2) is subtracted.   The final integer is –1 or (–1).

$$(-3) - (-2) = -1$$

The integer is 0.   The integer (–3) is subtracted.   The final integer is +3 or (+3).

$$0 - (-3) = +3$$

Inquire

1. What is the result when a negative integer is subtracted from an integer?

2. The sequence shows the steps for subtracting $(-3) - (-5)$.

a) Describe what is happening in each step.   **b)** Write the subtraction statement.

3. Use integer disks to model each subtraction. Write each subtraction statement.

a) $(+2) - (-1)$ **b)** $0 - (-2)$ **c)** $(-3) - (-3)$ **d)** $(-4) - (-6)$

4. Use integer disks to illustrate each pair of calculations. Write each number statement.

a) $(-4)-(-2)$ **b)** $0-(-5)$ **c)** $(+4)-(-2)$ **d)** $(+4)-(+5)$
$(-4)+(+2)$ $0+(+5)$ $(+4)+(+2)$ $(+4)+(-5)$

5. Copy and complete the sentence:
Subtracting an integer gives the same result as ▆▆▆ .

6. Use addition to answer each of the following.

a) $(+2)-(+6)$ **b)** $(-5)-(-8)$ **c)** $(+3)-(-2)$ **d)** $(-7)-(+4)$

Practice

Write the subtraction statement.

1.
minus positive three

2.
minus negative two

3.
minus negative one

4.
minus negative three

Illustrate each subtraction with integer disks. Write each subtraction statement.

5. $(-2)-(-4)$ **6.** $0-(+5)$

7. $(+1)-(-6)$ **8.** $(-2)-(+3)$

9. $(-8)-(-7)$ **10.** $(+1)-(+6)$

Copy and complete each statement.

11. $(-3)-(-2)=(-3)+\blacksquare=\blacksquare$

12. $(+7)-(+3)=(+7)+\blacksquare=\blacksquare$

13. $(-5)-(+4)=(-5)+\blacksquare=\blacksquare$

14. $(+6)-(-8)=(+6)+\blacksquare=\blacksquare$

Write the addition statement and simplify.

15. $(-9)-(-2)$ **16.** $(+5)-(-7)$

17. $(-1)-(-4)$ **18.** $(+3)-(-8)$

19. $(-4)-(+1)$ **20.** $0-(+6)$

Subtract.

21. $(+5)-(+2)$ **22.** $(-7)-(+7)$

23. $(+9)-(-8)$ **24.** $(+1)-(+6)$

25. $(-4)-(-5)$ **26.** $(-3)-(+10)$

Problems and Applications

27. Find the missing integer.

a) $(+6)-(\blacksquare)=+8$ **b)** $(-3)-(\blacksquare)=-7$

c) $(\blacksquare)-(-1)=+3$ **d)** $(\blacksquare)-(+5)=-3$

28. The average early-morning temperature in Churchill, Manitoba, is $-4°C$ in October. In January, it is $27°C$ lower. What is Churchill's average early-morning temperature in January?

29. In a dice game, the red die is positive, and the blue die is negative. Players roll both dice and add the result. They then choose one die to roll and subtract the result. The object is to reach zero. What second roll is needed to make each of these first rolls into a zero score?

a) 5 red **b)** 6 red **c)** 3 red
　2 blue 　1 blue 　6 blue

d) 1 red **e)** 4 red **f)** 2 red
　4 blue 　2 blue 　5 blue

30. Use each integer once to copy and complete the subtraction statements.

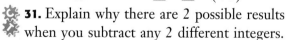

$\blacksquare-\blacksquare=(-7)$
$\blacksquare-\blacksquare=(-6)$
$\blacksquare-\blacksquare=(+5)$
$\blacksquare-\blacksquare=(+1)$

31. Explain why there are 2 possible results when you subtract any 2 different integers.

32. With a partner, find each pair of integers.
a) sum is $+1$; difference is $+7$
b) sum is $+4$; difference is -8
c) sum is -7; difference is $+7$
d) sum is $+3$; difference is -15
e) sum is -5; difference is -11

Adding and Subtracting Integers

Activity ❶ The Alphabet Line

Integers can be represented on an alphabet line.

A B C D E F G H I J K L M N O P Q R S T U V W X Y Z
— — — — — — — — −4 −3 −2 −1 0 +1 +2 +3 +4 — — — — — — — — —

1. Copy and complete the integers on the alphabet line.

2. Write the value of each of the following letters.

a) A **b)** W **c)** T
d) C **e)** Z **f)** M

3. Write the letter that represents the opposite value of each of the following.

a) E **b)** R **c)** G
d) U **e)** Y **f)** H

4. Replace ♦ with > or < to make each statement true.

a) N ♦ H **b)** Y ♦ A **c)** M ♦ G
d) X ♦ Z **e)** S ♦ M **f)** D ♦ E

5. Use the integer represented by each letter to find the total value for each word.

a) ADD **b)** PLUS
c) DIGIT **d)** ANGLE
e) LINE **f)** ZERO
g) NUMBER **h)** INTEGER
i) POSITIVE **j)** NEGATIVE

6. Copy and complete each word so that the integers add to the given total. Compare your words with your classmates'. Is there only one possible answer in each case?

a) R ▆ ▆ T = +10 **b)** B ▆ ▆ T = 0
c) D ▆ ▆ T = −9 **d)** B R ▆ ▆ D = −35
e) B R ▆ ▆ D = −26 **f)** P L A ▆ ▆ = −2
g) T ▆ ▆ ▆ K = −3

7. Add a word to each word below to make a two-syllable word with the given value.

a) C A R ▆ ▆ ▆ = −15
b) ▆ ▆ ▆ S E T = +20
c) O V E R ▆ ▆ ▆ ▆ = +3

8. Find a word with each of the following values. Compare your words with a classmate's.

a) +3 **b)** −8 **c)** −5 **d)** +12

9. Copy and complete each square to make six 3-letter words. Using M = 0 on the alphabet line, calculate each missing value.

a)

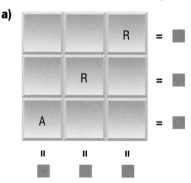

b)

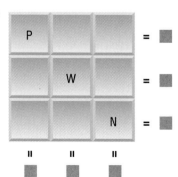

Activity ❷ A Time Line

1. Using this year as 0, state an integer value for each of the following.

a) the year you were born

b) the year you will graduate from high school

c) the year World War II ended

d) the year an astronaut first stepped on the moon

e) the year Canada's first female Prime Minister came to office

f) the year the next Summer Olympics will take place

g) the year we will begin the next century

Activity ❸ Integer Grids

1. Copy and complete each grid using the indicated operations.

a)
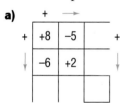

b)

c)
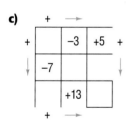

d)
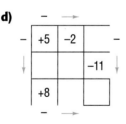

2. Identify the pattern. Then, copy and complete the grid.

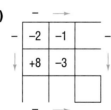

−1			+7		−1	
+3	+2	−4		+5	+8	+3
+4	+8	−5	−3		+9	
+7		−9		+1		+11

Activity ❹ Magic Squares

1. a) Find the sum of each row, column, and diagonal in this magic square.

+4	−3	+2
−1	+1	+3
0	+5	−2

b) Add −2 to each integer in the square. Is the result another magic square?

2. The magic number of the integer square is zero. Copy and complete the magic square.

−16			+10
		+4	−12
+12		+6	
−10	+2		

361

The Information Superhighway

The information superhighway will be a high-speed data network that will link everyone in the country to everyone else. The superhighway will bring information into homes and workplaces on expanded phone lines and cable TV lines.

Among the signals you will be able to receive and send will be sound and three-dimensional pictures. You might choose to dial up a movie and watch digitized images of yourself and your friends in the acting roles. If you wanted, you might even change the script and the ending of the movie!

Videophones, interactive games, electronic newspapers, and 500-plus TV stations will form just a small part of the information superhighway.

Activity ❶ Access to the Superhighway

To get on the superhighway, you will need a tool with extra brain-power. Four types of tools will be:

• a TV set with a box on the top, like a cable TV box today

• a PCTV, which will be a combined computer and TV set

• a screen-based phone

• a personal communicator you can carry with you

1. Which of these tools do you think will be the most popular? Why?

2. Which of these tools would you like to have? Why?

3. What other ways could be used to get onto the superhighway?

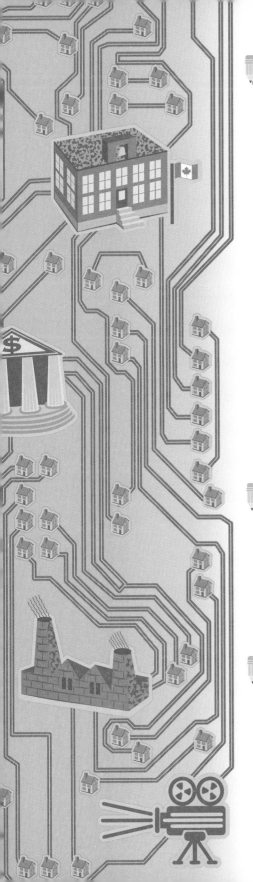

Activity ❷ Superhighway Information

Among the services supplied by the superhighway will be:
- face-to-face phone calls
- access to the world's biggest library
- news and video clips on subjects that interest you
- schools without walls
- round-the-clock pay-per-view movies, concerts, sporting events, and TV show reruns
- shopping and banking

1. What will be the advantages and disadvantages of face-to-face phone calls?

2. What do you think "access to the world's biggest library" means?

3. How do you think schools without walls will work?

4. List some advantages of having access to round-the-clock pay-per-view movies, concerts, sporting events, and TV show reruns. What could be some disadvantages?

5. How do you think shopping and banking will work on the superhighway?

6. What other services would you like to see on the superhighway?

Activity ❸ Environmental Benefits

Some environmentalists say that, once the superhighway is in place, valuable land will be freed up. It might then be restored to its natural state.

1. How might the superhighway free up valuable land?

2. Why might ground and air travel be reduced?

3. How else might the superhighway benefit the environment?

Activity ❹ Security

Concerns about the superhighway include its effects on privacy and security.

1. How could your privacy be invaded by users of the superhighway?

2. Of the information that superhighway users could access, what would you want to be kept secret?

10.5 Multiplying Integers

Activity: Use a Model

Multiplication can be illustrated with arrays of integer disks.

The integer is 0.   Add 3 groups of disks. Each group represents +2.   The final integer is (+6) or +6.

The multiplication statement is $(+3) \times (+2) = +6$.

The integer is 0.   Add 3 groups of disks. Each group represents –2.   The final integer is (–6) or –6.

The multiplication statement is $(+3) \times (-2) = -6$.

The integer is 0.   Remove 3 groups of disks. Each group represents +2.   The final integer is (–6) or –6.

The multiplication statement is $(-3) \times (+2) = -6$.

The integer is 0.   Remove 3 groups of disks. Each group represents –2.   The final integer is (+6) or +6.

The multiplication statement is $(-3) \times (-2) = +6$.

Inquire

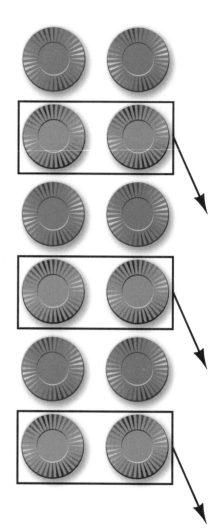

1. The sign rules for multiplying integers are summarized in the chart. In your own words, describe the sign rules for multiplying integers.

×	+	–
+	+	–
–	–	+

2. Use integer disks to model each multiplication. Write each multiplication statement.

a) $(-3) \times (+4)$ **b)** $(+6) \times (-2)$ **c)** $(+5) \times (+2)$

d) $(-1) \times (-7)$ **e)** $(-8) \times (+3)$ **f)** $(+4) \times (-5)$

3. As with multiplying integers, two negatives in written English give a positive effect. Explain this using the sentence "The little boy didn't have nothing in his pocket."

364

Practice

State whether each answer is positive or negative.

1. $(-3) \times (+9) = \blacksquare 27$ **2.** $(-5) \times (-1) = \blacksquare 5$

3. $(+2) \times (+8) = \blacksquare 16$ **4.** $(+4) \times (-3) = \blacksquare 12$

5. $(-6) \times (-3) = \blacksquare 18$ **6.** $(-7) \times (+2) = \blacksquare 14$

Copy and complete the multiplications. Continue each list for 4 more rows.

7. $(+3) \times (+2)$ **8.** $(-5) \times (+3)$
$(+3) \times (+1)$ $(-5) \times (+2)$
$(+3) \times 0$ $(-5) \times (+1)$
$(+3) \times (-1)$ $(-5) \times 0$

Multiply.

9. $(+8) \times (-7)$ **10.** $(-6) \times (-10)$

11. $(-4) \times (+9)$ **12.** $(-11) \times 0$

13. $(+3) \times (+8)$ **14.** $(+12) \times (-5)$

15. $(-7)(-6)$ **16.** $(-9)(+6)$

17. $(+15)(-3)$ **18.** $(-20)(-5)$

Problems and Applications

Copy and complete.

19. $(-2)^2 = (-2) \times (-2) = \blacksquare$

20. $(-2)^3 = (-2) \times (-2) \times (-2) = \blacksquare$

Simplify.

21. $(-3)^3$ **22.** $(-5)^3$ **23.** $(-2)^4$

24. $(-1)^6$ **25.** $(-3)^2$ **26.** $(-2)^5$

27. Use your results from questions 19–26 to make a statement about the positive and negative values of powers of negative integers. Use some examples of your own to support your statement.

28. A bathtub drains 4 L of water in 15 s. How much water will have drained in 2 min?

29. A hot air balloon is descending at a rate of 380 m/min. How much higher was the balloon 6 min ago?

Multiply.

30. $(-2) \times (+4) \times (-1)$ **31.** $(+3) \times (-2) \times (-2)$

32. $(-6) \times (-5) \times (-2)$ **33.** $(+4) \times (+3) \times (-2)$

34. $(+3) \times (-7) \times (+3)$ **35.** $(-1) \times (+9) \times (-5)$

36. Copy and complete the table.

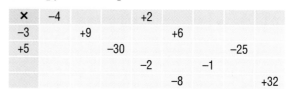

×	−4		+2		
−3	+9		+6		
+5		−30		−25	
		−2	−1		
			−8		+32

37. A small ocean-side hotel makes a profit of $90.00 for each room that is occupied each day and loses $30.00 for each room that is unoccupied. Calculate the profit or loss for each situation in parts a) to c).

a) 25 rooms occupied, 15 unoccupied

b) 16 rooms occupied, 24 unoccupied

c) 35 rooms occupied, 5 unoccupied

d) How many rooms must be occupied for a profit to be made?

38. a) Find the product of each column, row, and diagonal in the magic multiplication square.

b) Multiply each number in the square by -2. Is the result another magic multiplication square?

c) Add $+4$ to each number in the square. Is the result another magic multiplication square?

39. Study the triangles to find the pattern.

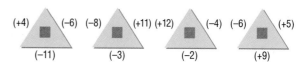

Then, use the pattern to copy and complete these triangles.

365

10.6 Dividing Integers

Activity: Investigate the Relationship

Each multiplication fact has 2 related division facts.

$(+8) \times (+3) = (+24)$
So $(+24) \div (+8) = (+3)$
and $(+24) \div (+3) = (+8)$

$(+8) \times (-3) = (-24)$
So $(-24) \div (+8) = (-3)$
and $(-24) \div (-3) = (+8)$

$(-8) \times (+3) = (-24)$
So $(-24) \div (-8) = (+3)$
and $(-24) \div (+3) = (-8)$

$(-8) \times (-3) = (+24)$
So $(+24) \div (-8) = (-3)$
and $(+24) \div (-3) = (-8)$

Inquire

1. Write two division facts for each multiplication fact.

a) $(+3) \times (-6) = (-18)$

b) $(-5) \times (-4) = (+20)$

c) $(-7) \times (+2) = (-14)$

d) $(+3) \times (+9) = (+27)$

e) $(-8) \times (+6) = (-48)$

f) $(+10) \times (-1) = (-10)$

 2. a) Copy and complete the division sign chart.

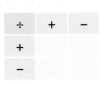

÷	+	−
+		
−		

b) Explain in your own words the sign rules for dividing integers.

3. Is the following statement true or false? Use examples to explain your answer. "The quotient of 2 integers is smaller in value than either of the integers."

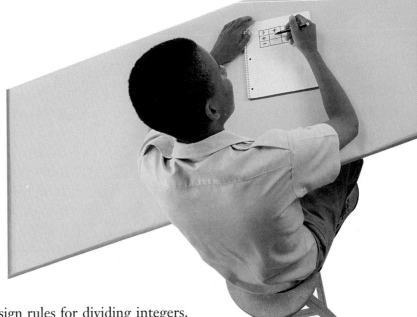

Practice

State whether the answer is positive or negative.

1. $(-12) \div (+3) = \blacksquare 4$

2. $(+25) \div (+5) = \blacksquare 5$

3. $(+36) \div (-4) = \blacksquare 9$

4. $(-16) \div (-2) = \blacksquare 8$

5. $(-56) \div (-8) = \blacksquare 7$

6. $(+36) \div (-6) = \blacksquare 6$

Copy and complete each multiplication fact and write the two related division facts.

7. $(-4) \times (-8)$

8. $(-7) \times (+6)$

9. $(+5) \times (-9)$

10. $(-3) \times (+7)$

11. $(+2) \times (+12)$

12. $(-11) \times (-5)$

Divide.

13. $(-40) \div (-8)$

14. $(+16) \div (-2)$

15. $(+32) \div (-4)$

16. $(-48) \div (+4)$

17. $(-54) \div (+6)$

18. $(+36) \div (-3)$

19. $(+81) \div (+9)$

20. $(-112) \div (+8)$

21. $(-150) \div (-5)$

22. $(-120) \div (+10)$

Divide.

23. $\dfrac{(-48)}{(+2)}$

24. $\dfrac{(+52)}{(+4)}$

25. $\dfrac{(-84)}{(-6)}$

26. $\dfrac{(+48)}{(-12)}$

27. $\dfrac{(-115)}{(+5)}$

28. $\dfrac{(-220)}{(-11)}$

Problems and Applications

29. A tank holds 4500 L of oil. It is being drained at 90 L/min. How long will it take to empty the tank?

30. The normal daily temperatures for the months of January to April in Calgary, Alberta, are $-12°C$, $-7°C$, $-4°C$, and $3°C$. What is the average temperature for the 4 months?

 31. The normal mid-afternoon temperature in Fredericton, New Brunswick, in January is $-4°C$. In July, it is $26°C$. What is the monthly change in the mid-afternoon temperature over this 6-month period? What assumptions have you made?

 32. How many related division facts are there for $(+6) \times 0 = 0$? Explain.

33. Copy and complete the table.

÷	−30		−6		−42
+2		+12		−24	
+3				+6	
−6		−2		−6	

Find the missing integer.

34. $(+12) \div (\blacksquare) = +3$

35. $(\blacksquare) \div (-8) = +9$

36. $(+63) \div (\blacksquare) = -7$

37. $(\blacksquare) \div (+14) = -10$

38. Use each integer once to copy and complete each division statement.

$\blacksquare \div \blacksquare = (+10)$

$\blacksquare \div \blacksquare = (-7)$

$\blacksquare \div \blacksquare = (-12)$

$\blacksquare \div \blacksquare = (+6)$

$\blacksquare \div \blacksquare = (-20)$

(+2) (−40) (−6)
(−5) (−36) (−60)
(+35) (−2) (+5)
(−20)

39. Determine 2 different pairs of integers that satisfy each description.

a) The product is $(+32)$; the quotient is $(+8)$.

b) The product is (-48); the quotient is (-3).

c) The product is $(+72)$; the quotient is $(+2)$.

d) The product is (-100); the quotient is (-4).

e) The product is (-27); the quotient is (-3).

40. Find 5 other product/quotient combinations like those in question 39. Have a classmate solve your puzzle.

PATTERN POWER

a) Describe this pattern in words.

$$1 = 1^2$$
$$1 + 2 + 1 = 2^2$$
$$1 + 2 + 3 + 2 + 1 = 3^2$$

b) Write the next three rows in the pattern.

c) What is the 10th row? the 20th row?

10.7 Integers in Standard Form

Activity: Study the Information

The **sign of quality** indicates whether an integer is positive or negative.
The **sign of operation** tells us to add or subtract.

$$(-8) - (+6) = (-14)$$

sign of quality   sign of operation

For integers in standard form, it is not necessary to write the positive
sign of quality. Negative signs of quality are necessary. Brackets are
used for a negative integer that follows a sign of operation.

$$4 + (-6) = -2 \qquad -4 - 6 = -10 \qquad -4 \times 6 = -24 \qquad 24 \div (-6) = -4$$

Inquire

1. Draw a number line with the integers written in standard form.

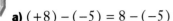

2. Is each statement correctly rewritten in standard form? Explain.

a) $(+8) - (-5) = 8 - (-5)$

b) $(-6) + (-7) = -6 + (-7)$

c) $(+2) - (+4) = 2 - 4$

d) $(-4) \times (+3) = -4 \times 3$

e) $(-15) \div (-3) = -15 \div (-3)$

f) $(+12) - (+8) = 12 - 8$

Practice

Rewrite each number statement in standard form.

1. $(+6) \times (-4) = (-24)$

2. $(-3) + (+7) = (+4)$

3. $(+36) \div (-12) = (-3)$

4. $(-15) - (-4) = (-11)$

5. $(+14) + (+16) = (+30)$

6. $(-40) \div (+10) = (-4)$

7. $(-21) - (+9) = (-30)$

8. $(-4) \times (-8) = (+32)$

9. $(-18) \div (-6) = (+3)$

10. $(+21) + (-14) = (+7)$

Simplify.

11. $-9 \times (-8)$

12. $12 + (-14)$

13. $8 \div (-2)$

14. $-10 - (-6)$

15. $-48 + 52$

16. $-16 \div (-4)$

17. $-6 - 10$

18. $5 \times (-12)$

19. $25 - 18$

20. $-36 \div 9$

Problems and Applications

*Write each of the following in standard form
and simplify.*

21. negative fourteen minus nine

22. positive six times negative ten

23. positive fifty-six divided by negative seven

24. negative nineteen plus four

25. twelve times negative five

*Copy and complete each number statement in
standard form.*

26. $-18 \div \blacksquare = -2$

27. $4 \times \blacksquare = -12$

28. $\blacksquare + (-6) = 13$

29. $\blacksquare - 8 = -4$

30. $64 \div (-8) = \blacksquare$

31. $-33 + \blacksquare = 50$

32. $-20 \times \blacksquare = 60$

33. $-12 - 15 = \blacksquare$

34. $\blacksquare + 27 = 36$

35. $\blacksquare - 19 = -5$

10.8 Integers on a Calculator

Activity: Explore the Sequences

Calculators display integers in standard form. If there is no sign, the integer is positive. The $\boxed{+/-}$ key is used to enter negative numbers.

Enter any number on your calculator and press the $\boxed{+/-}$ key several times. What do you notice?

Inquire

1. Record the display following each of these calculator key sequences.

a) $\boxed{C}$ $\boxed{+/-}$ 8
b) $\boxed{C}$ 8 $\boxed{+/-}$
c) $\boxed{C}$ 8 9 $\boxed{+/-}$

d) $\boxed{C}$ 8 $\boxed{+/-}$ 9
e) $\boxed{C}$ $\boxed{+/-}$ 8 9
f) $\boxed{C}$ 8 $\boxed{+/-}$ 9 $\boxed{+/-}$

2. Determine which calculator sequence can be used to add $-8 + (-9)$.

a) $\boxed{C}$ $\boxed{+/-}$ 8 $\boxed{+}$ $\boxed{+/-}$ 9 $\boxed{=}$
b) $\boxed{C}$ 8 $\boxed{+/-}$ $\boxed{+}$ $\boxed{+/-}$ 9 $\boxed{=}$

c) $\boxed{C}$ 8 $\boxed{+/-}$ $\boxed{+}$ 9 $\boxed{+/-}$ $\boxed{=}$

3. Write the sequence that calculates the correct answer to each of the following.

a) $8 - (-9)$
b) -8×9
c) $-72 \div (-8)$

Practice

Estimate, then use your calculator to add.

1. $28 + (-25)$ **2.** $-62 + 37$

3. $109 + 34$ **4.** $96 + (-58)$

5. $-36 + 81$ **6.** $-129 + (-77)$

7. $141 + (-59)$ **8.** $-200 + 93$

Estimate, then use your calculator to subtract.

9. $54 - 78$ **10.** $60 - (-48)$

11. $-121 - 83$ **12.** $-23 - (-54)$

13. $37 - 19$ **14.** $-110 - 27$

15. $40 - (-34)$ **16.** $-51 - (-85)$

Estimate, then use your calculator to multiply.

17. $20 \times (-14)$ **18.** $-33 \times (-30)$

19. -17×24 **20.** 16×42

21. $-15 \times (-51)$ **22.** -48×19

23. $52 \times (-22)$ **24.** $11 \times (-54)$

25. $41(-18)$ **26.** $(-27)(-21)$

Estimate, then use your calculator to divide.

27. $65 \div (-5)$ **28.** $-180 \div (-12)$

29. $132 \div 11$ **30.** $120 \div (-15)$

31. $182 \div (-7)$ **32.** $-288 \div 9$

33. $-144 \div (-16)$ **34.** $1000 \div (-50)$

35. $299 \div (-13)$ **36.** $-282 \div (-6)$

Problems and Applications

37. To calculate $(-3)^5$, press these keys.

$\boxed{C}$ 3 $\boxed{+/-}$ $\boxed{\times}$ $\boxed{=}$ $\boxed{=}$ $\boxed{=}$ $\boxed{=}$

Write the display for each equal sign.

Evaluate, using the method in question 37.

38. 7^3 **39.** $(-12)^4$ **40.** $(-5)^6$

41. $(-11)^5$ **42.** 4^4 **43.** $(-8)^3$

44. a) Do -2^3 and $(-2)^3$ have the same value? Explain.

b) Do -2^4 and $(-2)^4$ have the same value? Explain.

c) Write and compare calculator sequences to find the values for $(-5)^4$ and -5^4.

10.9 Order of Operations with Integers

Activity: Study the Expressions

In the game Twenty-Four, players are dealt 4 cards, with an integer on each. Each player must combine the numbers in a mathematical expression that equals 24. Muriel and Bushra used their cards to make these expressions.

Muriel's Expression
$6 \times 5 - (-2) \times (-3)$

6 **-2** **-3** **5**

Bushra's Expression
$-3 - 5 \times 6 \div (-2)$

Inquire

1. Explain why Muriel earned points and Bushra did not.

2. Which order of operations rule did Bushra forget?

3. Add brackets to Bushra's expression so that it equals 24.

4. Write the words that are represented by BEDMAS. This acronym helps us remember the correct mathematical order of operations.

5. Which of these expressions would earn points in the game? Give reasons for your answer.

$(-3 + 5) \times (-2) \times 6$ $5 \times (-2) \times (-3) - 6$

Example 1

Simplify $8 + 2 \times (-5) - 6^2$.

Solution

$$
\begin{aligned}
& 8 + 2 \times (-5) - 6^2 && \text{exponent} \\
=\ & 8 + 2 \times (-5) - 36 && \text{multiply} \\
=\ & 8 + (-10) - 36 && \text{add} \\
=\ & -2 - 36 && \text{subtract} \\
=\ & -38
\end{aligned}
$$

Example 2

Simplify $3(6 + (-10)) \div (-2)^2$.

Solution

$$
\begin{aligned}
& 3(6 + (-10)) \div (-2)^2 && \text{brackets} \\
=\ & 3 \times (-4) \div (-2)^2 && \text{exponent} \\
=\ & 3 \times (-4) \div 4 && \text{multiply} \\
=\ & -12 \div 4 && \text{divide} \\
=\ & -3
\end{aligned}
$$

Practice

Simplify.

1. $4 - 3 \times 2$

2. $-7 + 12 \div (-6)$

3. $-5 \times 2 - 10$

4. $36 \div (-4) + 1$

5. $6 \div (-1) - (-3)$

6. $-8 + 5 - (-3)$

7. $20 - 4 \div 4 + (-3)$

8. $10 - 12 + (-6) \times 2$

9. $16 \div (-8) + (-15) \div 5$

10. $-3 \times 4 - 9 \times (-2)$

Simplify.

11. $-5 \times 2^2 - 10$

12. $3^3 \div (-9) + 1$

13. $8 \times (-2) - (-4)^2$

14. $1 + (-2)^3 + 3$

15. $6^2 - 9 \times 3$

16. $(-5)^3 + 10^2$

17. $8 \times 4 + (-2)^4$

18. $7 \times (-3)^2 \div 9$

19. $(-10)^2 \div 2 - 4 \times 3^2$

20. $4^2 - 6^2 + (-2)^3$

Simplify.

21. $5(3 - 6)$

22. $12 - 6(4 - 8)$

23. $24 \div 4(5 - 7)$

24. $2(-6 + 2) \div (-2)$

25. $3(6 - 8) - 4(10 \div 2)$

Calculate.

26. $-3^3 \times 4 \div 9 + (-12)$

27. $5(2 - 8) - 5 \times 4^2$

28. $5 - 13 + 21 \times (-6)$

29. $100 - (-5)^3 \div 5^2$

30. $132 \div (-6) - (-10) \times 5$

Calculate.

31. $\dfrac{-2 \times 4}{-1}$

32. $\dfrac{6 - 5 \times 2}{(-2)^2}$

33. $\dfrac{14 \div 7 \times 3}{2 - 5}$

34. $\dfrac{4 \times (-6)}{3(1 - 5)}$

35. $\dfrac{-2(5 + 7)}{12 - 4}$

36. $\dfrac{-5 + (-7)}{5 - 3^2}$

Problems and Applications

Use any 4 integers in the diagram to write an expression that equals each value.

–6	–5	3
2	10	–4

37. 6

38. –20

39. 14

40. –11

In a game of Twenty-Four, these cards were drawn. Copy each expression and add brackets to make it correct.

41. $-4 - 8 \times 6 \div (-3)$

42. $8 - 6 \times (-3) \times (-4)$

-4	6
8	-3

43. Write two expressions that equal 24 using the integers on these cards. Share your results with your classmates. How many correct expressions can you find?

-10	8	6	-5

44. The sum of negative eighteen and negative six divided by two squared has two meanings.

a) Use integers to write an expression that shows each meaning.

b) Calculate the value of each expression.

c) Work with a classmate to rewrite the statement in words in two ways, so that each meaning is clear.

NUMBER POWER

The expression shows one way of using four -5s and the order of operations to express the value 1.

$$-5 - (-5) + \left(\dfrac{-5}{-5} \right)$$

Use four -5s and the order of operations to write expressions that equal each of these values.

a) 0

b) 2

c) 9

d) 3

e) 7

f) 5

Integer Games

Activity ❶ A Dice Game

| The red die is positive. | The blue die is negative. |

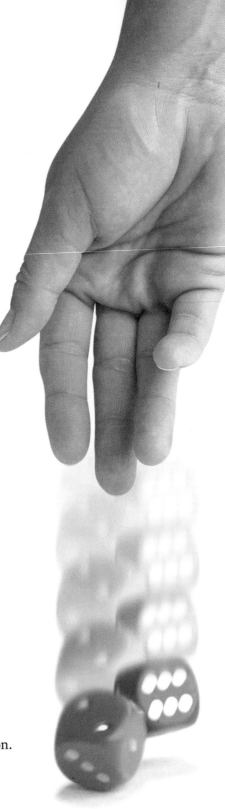

Here are 3 ways of using the numbers on top of the dice:
The numbers are added. $4 + (-2) = 2$
The negative is subtracted from the positive. $4 - (-2) = 6$
The positive is subtracted from the negative. $-2 - 4 = -6$

1. The dice are rolled, and the numbers on top are added.
a) How many possible totals are there?
b) Plot all the possible totals on a number line.

2. The dice are rolled, and the negative is subtracted from the positive.
a) What is the smallest possible difference?
b) What is the largest possible difference?
c) Plot all the possible differences on a number line.

3. The dice are rolled, and the positive is subtracted from the negative.
a) What is the smallest possible difference?
b) What is the largest possible difference?
c) Plot all the possible differences on a number line.

4. Play a game with a partner or in a small group.
a) Decide which operation you will use:
• adding
• subtracting negative from positive
• subtracting positive from negative
b) Have each player draw a number line for the agreed operation.
c) Take turns rolling the dice, performing the operation, and marking the answer on your number line. The first player to mark all the integers on the number line wins the game.

Activity ❷ Hit the Target

1. Each player is dealt 4 cards. The next card is turned up and represents the "target" for the game.

2. Players total their cards. In each of 2 rounds, they can decide to
a) keep their cards as they are, or
b) discard one card and replace it with a card from the leftover pile.

3. After the 2 rounds, players work out their scores by subtracting the total value of their 4 cards from the value of the target card.

The score closest to zero wins.

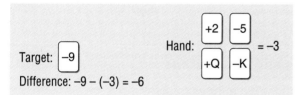

Target: -9
Hand: $+2$ -5 $+Q$ $-K$ $= -3$
Difference: $-9 - (-3) = -6$

Activity ❸ Opposite Pairs

1. Each player is dealt 6 cards. The next card is turned up and placed beside the turned-down leftover pile.

2. Players can set aside any two opposite cards at any time during the game.

3. Taking turns, players have 3 options:
a) Pick up a turned-up card, and then discard one from their hand.
or
b) Pick up a card from the turned-down pile, and then discard one from their hand.
or
c) Pick up a card from the turned-down pile, and then discard it.

4. Play continues until one player has set aside pairs of opposites and has no cards left.

5. Other players add to find their totals. Repeat the game. After a predetermined number of games, the total score closest to zero wins.

> Why should you try to keep your hand as close to zero as possible?

10.10 Scientific Notation: Large Numbers

Activity: Study the Examples

Scientists often deal with very large numbers. To make notation easier, they use a short form that involves decimals and powers of ten. This short form is called **scientific notation.**

Study the numbers in standard form and scientific notation.

a) Cirrocumulus clouds are more than 5000 m high or 5×10^3 m high.

b) The interior temperature of the sun is about 15 000 000°C or 1.5×10^7°C.

c) The area of Hudson Bay is approximately 822 000 km² or 8.22×10^5 km².

 Inquire

1. a) In scientific notation, how many digits are written to the left of the decimal point?

b) What determines the value of the exponent in the power of 10?

2. Write a rule for expressing a large number in scientific notation.

Practice

Write the value of the exponent.

1. $8700 = 8.7 \times 10^{\blacksquare}$

2. $150\ 000 = 1.5 \times 10^{\blacksquare}$

3. $3\ 250\ 000 = 3.25 \times 10^{\blacksquare}$

4. $12\ 600\ 000 = 1.26 \times 10^{\blacksquare}$

5. $75\ 000 = 7.5 \times 10^{\blacksquare}$

6. $4\ 000\ 000 = 4 \times 10^{\blacksquare}$

7. $140\ 000\ 000 = 1.4 \times 10^{\blacksquare}$

Find the value for each $\blacksquare$.

8. $28\ 000 = \blacksquare \times 10^4$

9. $360\ 000 = \blacksquare \times 10^5$

10. $1\ 200\ 000 = \blacksquare \times 10^6$

11. $6300 = \blacksquare \times 10^3$

12. $94\ 500 = \blacksquare \times 10^4$

13. $70\ 000\ 000 = \blacksquare \times 10^7$

14. $5480 = \blacksquare \times 10^3$

Write each number in scientific notation.

15. 43 000   **16.** 825 000   **17.** 1 500 000

18. 9000   **19.** 36 000 000   **20.** 980

21. 8450   **22.** 340 000

Problems and Applications

Write each number in standard form.

23. 5.8×10^4 **24.** 9×10^7

25. 4.25×10^5 **26.** 1.7×10^3

27. 6×10^2 **28.** 2.63×10^8

29. 7.5×10^6 **30.** 3.9×10^4

31. 8.2×10^3 **32.** 5.45×10^9

Express each number in scientific notation.

33. The area of Manitoba is about 650 000 km².

34. The Jurassic period lasted from about 210 000 000 to 140 000 000 years ago.

 35. Find a method of calculating the following. Compare your method with a classmate's.

a) $9 \times 10^3 + 8.2 \times 10^3$ **b)** $6 \times 8.2 \times 10^4$

c) $5 \times 10^5 - 7 \times 10^4$ **d)** $8.1 \times 10^2 \times 7.4 \times 10^6$

10.11 Scientific Notation: Small Numbers

Activity: Study the Examples

Scientific notation is used as a short form for small numbers as well as for large numbers.

Study the small numbers written in standard form and in scientific notation.

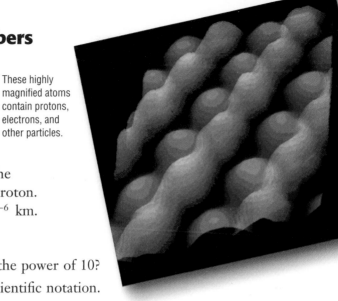

These highly magnified atoms contain protons, electrons, and other particles.

a) The mass of an electron is about 0.000 54 of the mass of a proton or 5.4×10^{-4} of the mass of a proton.

b) One millimetre equals 0.000 001 km or 1×10^{-6} km.

Inquire

1. What determines the value of the exponent in the power of 10?

2. Write a rule for expressing small numbers in scientific notation.

Practice

Write the value of each exponent.

1. $0.027 = 2.7 \times 10^{\blacksquare}$

2. $0.000\ 08 = 8 \times 10^{\blacksquare}$

3. $0.54 = 5.4 \times 10^{\blacksquare}$

4. $0.0037 = 3.7 \times 10^{\blacksquare}$

5. $0.000\ 625 = 6.25 \times 10^{\blacksquare}$

6. $0.000\ 009 = 9 \times 10^{\blacksquare}$

7. $0.000\ 000\ 12 = 1.2 \times 10^{\blacksquare}$

8. $0.0345 = 3.45 \times 10^{\blacksquare}$

9. $0.000\ 69 = 6.9 \times 10^{\blacksquare}$

Find the value for each $\blacksquare$.

10. $0.0046 = \blacksquare \times 10^{-3}$

11. $0.000\ 053 = \blacksquare \times 10^{-5}$

12. $0.024 = \blacksquare \times 10^{-2}$

13. $0.99 = \blacksquare \times 10^{-1}$

14. $0.000\ 000\ 73 = \blacksquare \times 10^{-7}$

15. $0.0004 = \blacksquare \times 10^{-4}$

16. $0.000\ 008\ 7 = \blacksquare \times 10^{-6}$

17. $0.000\ 000\ 012 = \blacksquare \times 10^{-8}$

18. $0.0629 = \blacksquare \times 10^{-2}$

Write each number in scientific notation.

19. 0.000 46

20. 0.000 003

21. 0.0124

22. 0.000 078

23. 0.0001

24. 0.000 000 27

25. 0.0332

26. 0.000 202

Problems and Applications

Write each number in standard form.

27. 5.8×10^{-4}

28. 2.03×10^{-2}

29. 7.96×10^{-9}

30. 4.5×10^{-7}

31. 1.03×10^{-5}

32. 3.45×10^{-3}

33. 8.25×10^{-6}

34. 7.59×10^{-8}

Express each number in scientific notation.

35. The diameter of some cells is 0.005 mm.

36. The percent of neon in dry air at sea level is about 0.0018.

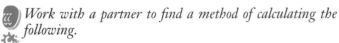

Work with a partner to find a method of calculating the following.

37. $8 \times 4.2 \times 10^{-4}$

38. $2.3 \times 10^{-3} + 5.6 \times 10^{-5}$

39. $9.3 \times 10^{-6} - 7 \times 10^{-8}$

40. $4.6 \times 10^{-2} \times 3.8 \times 10^{-7}$

10.12 Rational Numbers

You have already found the quotient of 2 integers.

$$\frac{8}{2} = 4 \qquad \frac{-6}{3} = -2 \qquad \frac{12}{-4} = -3 \qquad \frac{-18}{-9} = 2$$

The quotient of 2 integers is not always another integer.

$2 \div 5 = \frac{2}{5}$ (a fraction) or 0.4 (a decimal)

Activity: Use a Number Line

The table shows the high temperatures in winter for several Canadian cities. Plot the temperatures on a number line, like the one below.

City	Temperature (°C)
Charlottetown	−3
Halifax	−1.6
London	−2.7
St. John's	−0.5
Toronto	−2.5

Inquire

1. Which 2 integers are closest to the Halifax temperature?

2. Which 2 integers are closest to the Toronto temperature?

3. Here are 2 ways to write the Charlottetown temperature as the quotient of 2 integers.

$$\frac{-6}{2} \qquad\qquad \frac{9}{-3}$$

Give 2 other ways.

4. Write the St. John's temperature as the quotient of 2 integers in 2 ways.

5. Write the Toronto temperature as the quotient of 2 integers in 2 ways.

Rational numbers are numbers that can be written as the quotient of 2 integers, that is, in the form $\frac{a}{b}$, where a is any integer, and b is any integer except 0.

All fractions and mixed numbers are rational numbers. $2\frac{1}{2} = \frac{5}{2}$

All integers are rational numbers. $8 = \frac{8}{1} \quad -4 = \frac{-4}{1}$

All terminating and repeating decimals are rational numbers.
$0.7 = \frac{7}{10} \quad 0.\overline{3} = \frac{1}{3}$

Rational numbers can be written in many equivalent forms.

The rational number −2 can be written as
$\frac{2}{-1}, \frac{-4}{2}, \frac{-2}{1}, -\frac{-2}{-1}$, and so on.

The rational number 3 can be written as
$\frac{3}{1}, \frac{-3}{-1}, \frac{-6}{-2}$, and so on.

376

Example

Write each rational number as the quotient of 2 integers.

a) $3\frac{1}{3}$ **b)** -0.9 **c)** $-1\frac{1}{2}$ **d)** -1.3

Solution

a) $3\frac{1}{3}$
$= \frac{10}{3}$

b) -0.9
$= \frac{-9}{10}$

c) $-1\frac{1}{2}$
$= \frac{-3}{2}$

d) -1.3
$= -1\frac{3}{10}$
$= \frac{-13}{10}$

Practice

Match each rational number to a point on the number line.

1. 2.5 **2.** -3 **3.** $-1\frac{1}{2}$

4. -2.5 **5.** 0.5 **6.** $1\frac{1}{2}$

Express in an equivalent form.

7. 6 **8.** $\frac{-1}{2}$ **9.** $\frac{2}{-3}$

10. $\frac{-4}{-5}$ **11.** -4 **12.** $\frac{2}{7}$

Write each of the following as the quotient of 2 integers in lowest terms.

13. $2\frac{1}{2}$ **14.** -0.4 **15.** $-1\frac{3}{4}$

16. -0.25 **17.** 0.125 **18.** -2.6

Graph the rational numbers on a number line. Then, rewrite the numbers in increasing order.

19. $4, -2, 0, -1, 2, -5$

20. $2.5, -1.5, -3, 1.2, -3.5$

21. $\frac{3}{5}, \frac{-4}{5}, \frac{1}{5}, \frac{-7}{10}, \frac{3}{10}$

Replace each ◆ by <, >, or = to make each statement true.

22. $\frac{1}{2}$ ◆ $\frac{2}{3}$ **23.** $\frac{-1}{4}$ ◆ $\frac{-3}{4}$ **24.** $\frac{-3}{-5}$ ◆ $\frac{3}{5}$

25. $1\frac{1}{3}$ ◆ $\frac{7}{3}$ **26.** $\frac{-1}{2}$ ◆ $\frac{1}{-4}$ **27.** $\frac{7}{12}$ ◆ $\frac{2}{3}$

Problems and Applications

28. Write a rational number for each situation.
a) a loss of 2.5 kg
b) a temperature 3.5°C below zero
c) a price increase of $1.25
d) a loss in value of $12
e) a temperature decrease of 1.2°C

29. The winter high temperature is +5.2°C in Vancouver, and the winter low is −0.2°C. Find the difference between these temperatures.

30. The winter high temperature in Ottawa is −6.4°C, and the winter low is −15.4°C. Find the difference between these temperatures.

LOGIC POWER

Fill in the squares on a 3-by-3 grid with 3 Xs, 3 Ys, and 3 Zs so that the following conditions are met.
- No row from left to right, no column from top to bottom, and no diagonal from top to bottom has the sequence X-Y-Z.
- One Z is directly below a Y and directly to the left of another Z.
- One X is directly below a Y and directly to the left of a Z.
- One Z is directly below an X and directly to the left of a Y.

The Misunderstood Grey Wolf

The grey wolf was once the most widely distributed mammal in the world. It has been relentlessly exterminated wherever humans have settled. It is now found in greatly reduced numbers in a small part of its original range. In some countries where it was once persecuted, there are now protection policies to prevent the wolf's extermination. However, many areas of the world still have vigorous control programs to reduce the number of wolves.

Activity ❶

1. The grey wolf stands about 75 cm at the shoulder. Name 3 objects in your classroom that are this height.

2. The many subspecies of grey wolf found in Canada range from 26 kg to 79 kg in mass. The larger subspecies live in the cold, northern regions. How does the mass of a wolf compare with the mass of an average human adult?

3. Wolves have 42 teeth. The 4 longest teeth are 5 cm long.
a) How many teeth do humans have?
b) Approximately how many times longer than your longest tooth is the wolf's longest tooth?

4. It is common for a pack of wolves to cover 75 km in a day over frozen lakes and through rugged forest. Use a map to locate places that are about 75 km from your home.

5. Wolves are often confused with coyotes, especially in areas where the wolf has disappeared. Locate information about the coyote and compare its size and appearance with those of the wolf.

Activity ❷

The table shows the estimated population of wolves in some parts of Europe and Asia.

1. It is estimated that there are 90 000 wolves left throughout Europe and Asia. What percent of this total is left in each of the countries or areas listed?

2. Approximately 2% of the wolves in Europe and Asia live in India. How many wolves live in India?

3. Researchers believe that about 30% of the wolf population is killed each year. How many wolves might be killed in Europe and Asia each year?

Country/Area	Population
Afghanistan	1000
Greece	500
Iran	1000
Israel	150
Italy	250
Mongolia	10 000
Poland	900
Spain	750
Scandinavia	100
Former U.S.S.R.	70 000

Activity ❸

The map shows the estimated number of wolves living in Canada and Alaska.

Researchers believe there are approximately 1275 wolves in the rest of North America.

1. Estimate the maximum number of wolves living in Canada.

2. What percent of this number lives in each section of Canada?

3. Estimate the maximum number of wolves in North America.

4. What percent of this total lives in Alaska?

5. Between 1600 and 1950, approximately two million wolves were erased from North America. What percent of this number is left?

6. a) Why do you think the number of wolves in the Northwest Territories is so uncertain?

b) What might be the reason that there is no estimated number for Saskatchewan, Manitoba, and Labrador?

Activity ❹

The wolf has been persecuted partly because of fear and misunderstanding. There is a belief that wolves are vicious killers, even though there is no record of a healthy wild wolf attacking a human.

1. Other than fear, why do some hunters and farmers want the wolf exterminated?

2. How do you think the misunderstanding about the wolf's viciousness arose?

3. Look for stories and poems about wolves. What characteristics of wolves are portrayed?

4. Read the story of Romulus and Remus. What characteristics of the wolf are portrayed in this story?

5. Read some accounts about wolves written by researchers and environmentalists. One book you might read is *Never Cry Wolf*, by the Canadian author Farley Mowat. How does the factual evidence compare with the literary images you discovered?

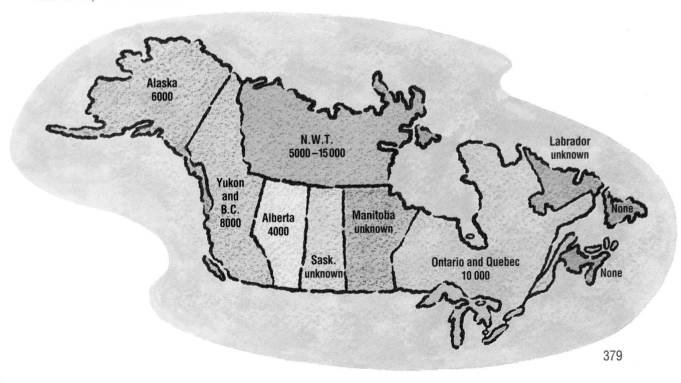

Review

Write as an integer.

1. a profit of eleven dollars

2. a win by six points

3. thirty-five metres below sea level

4. eight degrees below zero

5. a deposit of twenty dollars

Write the opposite of each integer.

6. 9 **7.** -15 **8.** -2 **9.** 4

Replace the ♦ with > or < to make each statement true.

10. $-5 ♦ 0$ **11.** $8 ♦ -2$ **12.** $-3 ♦ 3$

13. $-12 ♦ -10$ **14.** $4 ♦ -6$ **15.** $-14 ♦ 1$

Write the next three integers.

16. $-3, -1, 1,$ ▪ , ▪ , ▪

17. $8, 5, 2,$ ▪ , ▪ , ▪

18. $-11, -7, -3,$ ▪ , ▪ , ▪

19. $9, 6, 3,$ ▪ , ▪ , ▪

Write the integers from least to greatest.

20. $5, -2, 8, 0, 1, -6$

21. $10, -13, 9, 3, -8, -10$

Write the integers from greatest to least.

22. $-5, 4, -2, 11, -9, 1$

23. $16, -12, -3, 5, -18, 7$

Add.

24. $9 + (-4)$ **25.** $-12 + (-5)$

26. $-8 + 0$ **27.** $-6 + 11$

28. $+10 + (-15)$ **29.** $7 - (-7)$

Subtract.

30. $4 - 6$ **31.** $-8 - (-10)$

32. $-2 - 5$ **33.** $3 - (-2)$

34. $0 - (-9)$ **35.** $-7 - (-7)$

Simplify.

36. $4 + (-6) - (-3)$ **37.** $-10 - 5 + (-2)$

38. $8 - 12 + 7$ **39.** $-9 + 1 - (-4) + 2$

Multiply.

40. $-7 \times (-2)$ **41.** -5×6 **42.** $9 \times (-4)$

43. 2×10 **44.** -8×0 **45.** $-3 \times (-11)$

46. -6×6 **47.** $4 \times (-8)$ **48.** 5×7

Divide.

49. $64 \div (-8)$ **50.** $-30 \div (-6)$

51. $-36 \div 9$ **52.** $12 \div 4$

53. $-100 \div (-10)$ **54.** $27 \div (-3)$

55. $\dfrac{20}{-4}$ **56.** $\dfrac{-42}{-7}$

57. $\dfrac{-81}{9}$ **58.** $\dfrac{36}{6}$

Simplify.

59. $24 \div (-4) \times 3$ **60.** $-6 \times (-2) \div (-12)$

61. $10 \times 6 \div (-5)$ **62.** $-4 \times (-9) \div (-3)$

Evaluate.

63. -3^2 **64.** $(-10)^4$ **65.** $(-2)^3$

66. $(-5)^3$ **67.** -4^2 **68.** $-(-3)^4$

Simplify.

69. $(-4 + 6) \times (5 - 8)$

70. $4(6 + (-3) - 9)$

71. $-30 \div 2(-5 + 10)$

72. $16 - 5 \times (-7)$

73. $3(7 + (-9)) \div (-6)$

74. $9 + 6(4 \div (-2))$

75. $5(-12 \div 4) + 6(-9 - (-8))$

Calculate.

76. $\dfrac{5^2 - 6^2}{-3 + 4}$ **77.** $\dfrac{3(-4 + (-5))}{-3^2}$

78. $-5^2 + 4(6 - 8)$ **79.** $11 - 6(-18 \div 2)$

80. $28 \div (-7) + (-42) \div (-6)$

Rewrite each number in scientific notation.

81. 24 000   **82.** 5 800 000

83. 15 600 000 **84.** 360 000

85. 900   **86.** 7500

Rewrite each number in standard form.

87. 2.6×10^4 **88.** 8.31×10^7

89. 4.0×10^3 **90.** 1.7×10^5

91. 9.54×10^6 **92.** 3.6×10^2

Rewrite each number in scientific notation.

93. 0.0063   **94.** 0.000 052

95. 0.000 008 **96.** 0.047

97. 0.0009   **98.** 0.000 000 046

Rewrite each number is standard form.

99. 4.3×10^{-3} **100.** 8.9×10^{-6}

101. 2×10^{-4} **102.** 5.13×10^{-5}

103. 3.3×10^{-8} **104.** 7.15×10^{-7}

105. Between midnight and 01:00, the temperature fell from 2°C to −1°C. It continued to fall at the same rate. What was the temperature at 06:00?

106. The elevation of the highest point in New Orleans, Louisiana, is 5 m above sea level. The lowest point in New Orleans is 6 m lower than the highest point. What is the elevation of the lowest point in relation to sea level?

107. For 5 days in January in Southern Ontario, the high temperatures were listed as −2°C, 4°C, −8°C, −11°C, and −13°C. What was the average high temperature for the 5 days?

108. A microsecond is 0.000 001 s.

a) Write this number in scientific notation.

b) How many microseconds are in 1 min?

c) Write your answer to part b) in scientific notation.

Group Decision Making
Researching Publishing Careers

Publishers have three major products: newspapers, magazines, and books.

1. Brainstorm with the whole class the careers you would like to investigate. They could include reporter, editor, writer, salesperson, photographer, designer, printer, distributor, reviewer, and artist. As a class, select six careers.

2. Go to home groups. As a group, decide which career each group member will research.

1 2 3 4 5 6		1 2 3 4 5 6
Home Groups		
1 2 3 4 5 6		1 2 3 4 5 6

3. Form an expert group with students who have the same career to research. In your expert group, decide what questions you want to answer about the career. Include a question on how math is used. Then, research the answers.

1 1 1 1	2 2 2 2	3 3 3 3
	Expert Groups	
4 4 4 4	5 5 5 5	6 6 6 6

4. In your expert group, prepare a report on your career for the class. As a group, decide what form the report will take. It could be written, acted out, presented as a video, displayed on a poster, or presented in any other appropriate form.

5. Return to your home group and evaluate the process. Identify what worked well and what you could do differently the next time.

Chapter Check

Write as an integer.

1. a gain of seven points

2. six degrees below zero

3. a loss of nine kilograms

4. a profit of twenty dollars

Write the opposite of each integer.

5. -6 6. $+2$ 7. -12

Write the integers between each of these pairs.

8. -5 and $+2$ 9. $+1$ and $+4$

10. -12 and -3 11. -6 and $+6$

Order the integers from least to greatest.

12. $+2, -5, 0, -11, +1, -3$

13. $-1, -12, +5, +2, -8, -10$

Add.

14. $5 + (-8)$ 15. $-9 + 2$

16. $-12 + 15$ 17. $-4 + (-8)$

18. $11 + (-3)$ 19. $-7 + 7$

Subtract.

20. $8 - (-6)$ 21. $-7 - 4$

22. $1 - (-4)$ 23. $-12 - (-8)$

24. $-5 - (-9)$ 25. $3 - (-3)$

Multiply.

26. $5 \times (-4)$ 27. $-6 \times (-2)$

28. -8×3 29. $0 \times (-7)$

30. $2 \times (-1) \times (-7)$ 31. $-3 \times (-2) \times 6$

Evaluate.

32. -2^3 33. $(-2)^3$ 34. $(-5)^2$

35. -4^2 36. $(-10)^5$ 37. $-(-10)^2$

Divide.

38. $24 \div (-4)$ 39. $-40 \div (-5)$

40. $-12 \div 3$ 41. $35 \div (-7)$

42. $\dfrac{-48}{6}$ 43. $\dfrac{-16}{-4}$

Simplify.

44. $4 + (-7) \times (-5)$

45. $-6(4 - 8) \div (-3)$

46. $-2 + 5 - (9 - 11)$

47. $12 - 4(5 - 6) \div 2$

48. $-4^2 - 12 + 6 \times (-4)$

49. $\dfrac{-5 \times (-3)}{7 - 10}$

50. $\dfrac{2(8 \times (-4))}{(-2)^3}$

Write in scientific notation.

51. 52 000   52. 270 000

53. 6 150 000   54. 9600

55. 0.058   56. 0.000 07

57. 0.0094   58. 0.000 103

Write in standard form.

59. 2.7×10^3 60. 7.9×10^4

61. 1.65×10^7 62. 4.38×10^5

63. 3.2×10^{-2} 64. 6.13×10^{-6}

65. 2.8×10^{-5} 66. 5.41×10^{-3}

67. A swimming pool holds 6200 L of water. The water drains at a rate of 20 L/min. How long will the pool take to empty?

68. Travelling at 24 km/h on a snowmobile makes an air temperature of 4°C feel like -6°C because of the wind chill. What is the difference in these temperatures?

69. The largest mammal is the blue whale. It can grow to about 150 000 kg. Write this number in scientific notation.

Using the Strategies

1. What is the smallest number of cubes that can be used to build a tower with 8 layers and a different number of cubes in each layer?

2. What percent of students in your school are in grade 8?

3. The playground is enclosed by a fence with posts 2 m apart. There is a post at each corner.

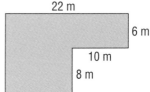

a) What is the total length of the fence?
b) How many posts are there?

4. How many times do you use the digit 3 if you count by tens from 0 to 500?

5. Barry put $\frac{1}{3}$ of his babysitting money into the bank. He spent $\frac{1}{4}$ of it on a cassette tape, and he had $13.00 left. How much did he earn babysitting?

6. The length of a rectangle is 3 times its width. The perimeter is 52 cm.
a) What are the dimensions of the rectangle?
b) What is its area?

7. Petra has the same number of nickels, dimes, and quarters. She has $3.20 altogether. How many of each type of coin does she have?

8. How often does February 29 fall on a Monday?

9. How many diagonals does a regular octagon have?

10. The square of a whole number equals the cube of half the number. What is the number?

11. Straws can be used to represent the sides and a diagonal of a square.

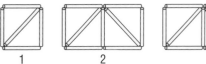
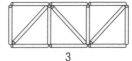

How many straws will be needed for the tenth figure?

12. Alina jogs at a steady pace around an oval track from the starting point shown.

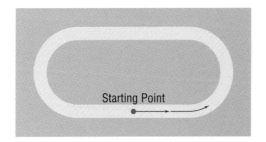

Sketch a graph of her distance from the starting point versus time for one complete circuit of the track.

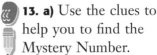

13. a) Use the clues to help you to find the Mystery Number.
b) Make up a set of clues for another Mystery Number. Ask a classmate to find the number.

Mystery Number
1. Between 10^2 and 10^3.
2. Sum of digits 10.
3. Prime factors 5 and 13.
4. All digits prime.

DATA BANK

1. Which Canadian waterfall is closest to one third the height of Della Falls?

2. The lowest wind chill temperature recorded on Prince Edward Island occurred when the air temperature was −32°C and the wind speed was 37 km/h. Estimate the wind chill temperature.

CHAPTER 11

Algebra

Sir Arthur Conan Doyle had Sherlock Holmes crack a stick figure code in a short story, "The Adventure of the Dancing Men." The coded note below was written by Holmes after he cracked the code. Each figure stands for a letter.

1. How many letters are in the note?

2. The note contains 4 words. How is the last letter of each word indicated?

3. The letter E is the most common in the English language. The stick figure used most often in the note represents an E. Draw this stick figure.

4. The next most commonly used letters in the English language are, in order, T, A, O, I, N, S, H, R, D, and L. The letter O is found twice in the note, once in the first half of the first word and once in the first half of the last word. Draw the stick figure for the letter O.

5. Use the following clues to decode the rest of the note.
- The word AT appears in the note.
- The letter C appears twice.
- H, M, N, and R are each used once.

6. Design your own code using stick figures. Write a message with your code and have a classmate try to decipher it.

Patterns

Activity ❶ Illustrating Equations

The balance shows that the mass of 2 cubes equals the mass of 1 cylinder. The mass of each object is a whole number of grams. The total mass of the 3 objects is 12 g.

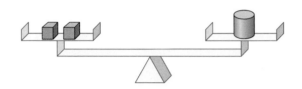

1. Find the mass of

a) a cube   **b)** a cylinder

2. Use your results from part 1 to copy and complete the table.

Number of Cubes	2	3	3	4	4	4	4
Number of Cylinders	1	1	2	1	2	3	4
Total Mass (g)	12						

Activity ❷ Listing All Possibilities

The balance shows that 1 cube, 1 cylinder, and 1 pyramid balance 2 cubes. The mass of each object is a whole number of grams. The total mass of the 5 objects is 20 g. Copy the table and use it to record the possible masses.

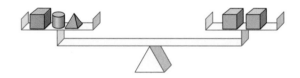

Mass of Cube (g)		
Mass of Cylinder (g)		
Mass of Pyramid (g)		

Activity ❸ Balancing the Scales

1. The balance shows that the mass of 1 cube and 3 pyramids equals the mass of 1 pyramid and 2 cylinders. The mass of each object is a whole number of grams. The total mass of the 7 objects is 20 g. Find the mass of

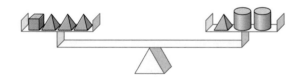

a) a cylinder   **b)** a pyramid   **c)** a cube

2. Design a problem like the one in part 1 of this activity. Have a classmate solve your problem.

Order of Operations

Simplify.

1. $3 \times 2 + 5$ **2.** $3 + 2 \times 5$

3. $3 \times (2 + 5)$ **4.** $(3 + 2) \times 5$

5. $3 + 2 \div 5$ **6.** $(3 + 2) \div 5$

7. $3 \times 2 - 5$ **8.** $3 \times 2 \div 5$

9. $3 \div 2 + 5$ **10.** $3 \div 5 \times 2$

11. $3^2 - 2^2$ **12.** $21 - 2 \times 2^3$

13. $(6 - 4)^2 + 7$ **14.** $4 \times 7 - 3^3$

15. $1^2 + 3^2 + 6^2$ **16.** $98 - 96 \div 3$

Copy the expressions in questions 17–22. Insert one pair of brackets to make each expression equal to 24.

17. $3 + 5 \times 3$ **18.** $2 + 4 \times 4$

19. $12 \times 8 - 6$ **20.** $4 + 5 \times 7 - 3$

21. $2 \times 10 + 2$ **22.** $6 \times 4 + 4 \div 2$

Calculate.

23. $7 \times 2 + 5 \times 2$

24. $6 \times 7 - 2 \times 11$

25. $4 \times 5 - 6 \div 3$

26. $\frac{1}{2}$ of $24 + \frac{1}{3}$ of 24

27. $\frac{1}{2}$ of $(3 + 5) + \frac{1}{4}$ of $(16 - 4)$

28. $15 \div (8 - 5) \times 6$

29. $\frac{1}{3}$ of $12.3 + 8.2 - 2.4$

30. $7 \times 0 + 5 - 0$

31. $(3 + 2) \times (6 - 4) \div (8 - 6) \times (9 - 8)$

32. $28.8 \div 4 + 96.6 \div 3$

Copy the numbers in order. Then, insert $+$, $-$, $\times$, and $\div$ signs so that each expression simplifies to 15.

33. 4   5   2   1   **34.** 3   4   7   4

35. 5   2   6   1   **36.** 36   9   6   5

37. 4   3   4   1   **38.** 6   6   3   3

39. 5   5   3   3   1   **40.** 18   8   3   1   2

Mental Math

Add.

1. $45 + 10$ **2.** $45 + 100$ **3.** $625 + 5$

4. $625 + 25$ **5.** $350 + 50$ **6.** $350 + 150$

7. $350 + 250$ **8.** $350 + 1000$

9. $38 + 12$ **10.** $38 + 102$

Subtract.

11. $125 - 5$ **12.** $125 - 15$ **13.** $125 - 25$

14. $125 - 50$ **15.** $418 - 8$ **16.** $418 - 18$

17. $418 - 108$ **18.** $438 - 28$

19. $147 - 17$ **20.** $147 - 27$

Multiply.

21. 4×12 **22.** 40×12 **23.** 2×25

24. 4×25 **25.** 20×25 **26.** 40×25

27. 47×100 **28.** 47×1000

29. 5×80 **30.** 50×800

Divide.

31. $35 \div 7$ **32.** $3500 \div 7$

33. $3500 \div 70$ **34.** $3500 \div 700$

35. $3500 \div 10$ **36.** $3500 \div 500$

37. $72\ 000 \div 100$ **38.** $72\ 000 \div 12$

39. $72\ 000 \div 72$ **40.** $72\ 000 \div 12\ 000$

State the remainder.

41. $24 \div 5$ **42.** $15 \div 6$ **43.** $45 \div 8$

44. $36 \div 7$ **45.** $36 \div 5$ **46.** $36 \div 10$

47. $50 \div 8$ **48.** $55 \div 9$ **49.** $3002 \div 10$

Simplify.

50. $3.6 + 0.1$ **51.** $4.25 + 0.1$

52. $63.5 - 0.2$ **53.** $63.57 - 0.2$

54. 5.25×0.1 **55.** 5.25×0.01

56. $75.5 \div 0.1$ **57.** $75.5 \div 0.001$

Algebra Tiles

Activity ❶ Expressions with Positive Tiles

Each red tile is a square, with each side 1 unit long.
The area of the square is $1 \times 1 = 1$.
Each red tile represents $+1$.

Each long green tile has a length of x and a width of 1.
The area is $x \times 1 = x$.
Each long green tile represents $+x$ or x.

Each square green tile has a length of x and a width of x.
The area is $x \times x = x^2$.
Each square green tile represents $+x^2$ or x^2.

Groups of tiles represent expressions. Expressions are
made up of terms. Terms are separated by $+$ and $-$.

$3x$ $3x + 2$ $x^2 + 3x + 2$

1. Write the expression represented by each group of tiles.

a)   **b)**   **c)**

d)   **e)**

f)

2. Use algebra tiles or drawings to model
these expressions.

a) $5x$ **b)** $2x + 4$
c) $x^2 + 3x + 7$ **d)** $4x^2 + 2$
e) $2x^2 + x + 1$ **f)** $x + 6$

Activity ❷ Expressions with Negative Tiles

Each white tile represents -1.
Each long white tile represents $-x$.
Each square white tile represents $-x^2$.

-1 $-x$ $-x^2$

1. Write the expression represented by each group of tiles.

a) **b)** **c)** **d)**

2. Use algebra tiles or drawings to model these expressions.
a) $-3x$ **b)** $-x - 3$ **c)** $-2x^2 - 2x - 2$ **d)** $-x^2 - x - 1$

Activity ❸ Simplifying Expressions

Each pair represents zero.

Just as simplifies to $+2$, simplifies to $+2x$.

1. Copy and complete the table. The first row has been done for you.

Tile Display	Simplified Form	Expression
		$x + 3$

2. What is the smallest number of tiles you can add to each group to make zero? Explain.

a)   **b)**  **c)**  **d)**

11.1 Variables and Expressions

A basketball court is 26 m long and 14 m wide. The perimeter of the court is given by $2l + 2w$, where l is the length and w is the width.

$$2l + 2w = 2 \times 26 + 2 \times 14$$
$$= 52 + 28$$
$$= 80$$

A soccer field is 100 m long and 73 m wide.

$$2l + 2w = 2 \times 100 + 2 \times 73$$
$$= 200 + 146$$
$$= 346$$

So, the basketball court has a perimeter of 80 m, and the soccer field has a perimeter of 346 m.

In the **algebraic expression** $2l + 2w$, the **terms** are $2l$ and $2w$. The letters in the expression are called **variables** because they can represent many numbers.

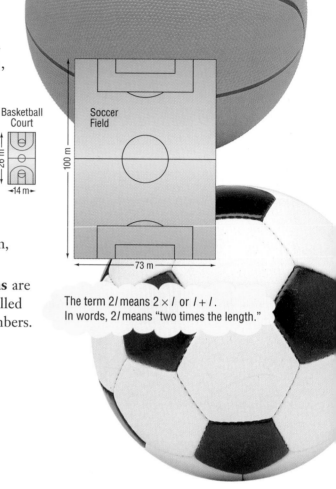

The term $2l$ means $2 \times l$ or $l + l$.
In words, $2l$ means "two times the length."

Activity: Make a Comparison

Arithmetic	Algebra
$5 + 5$	$x + x$
$2(4) - 3$	$2x - 3$
$7(2) + 8(6)$	$7x + 8y$
3^2	x^2

 Inquire

1. How are the expressions $5 + 5$ and $x + x$ alike? How are they different?

2. How are the expressions in each of the other pairs alike? How are they different?

An algebraic expression can have many different values, depending on the numbers assigned to the variables. Replacing a variable by a number is called **substitution**.

Example 1

Evaluate.
a) $2x + 3y$ for $x = 4$ and $y = 5$
b) $x^2 - x$ for $x = 3$

Solution

a) $2x + 3y = 2(4) + 3(5)$
$\qquad\quad = 8 + 15$
$\qquad\quad = 23$

b) $x^2 - x = (3)^2 - 3$
$\qquad\quad = 9 - 3$
$\qquad\quad = 6$

Variables can also be replaced by negative numbers.

Example 2

Evaluate $3t + 5$ for $t = -2$.

Solution

$3t + 5 = 3(-2) + 5$
$\qquad = -6 + 5$
$\qquad = -1$

Practice

Write the words as an algebraic expression.

1. the length plus seven

2. three times the height minus four

3. two times the height plus four times the width

4. five times the number of dogs minus two times the number of cats

Write each expression in words.

5. $2b + 4$ **6.** $3w - 6$

7. $2l + 3w - 1$ **8.** $2d - 3c + 6$

Evaluate.

9. $x + 4$, $x = 2$ **10.** $4y$, $y = 3$

11. $t - 1$, $t = 7$ **12.** $8 - w$, $w = 2$

13. $4m + 2$, $m = 3$ **14.** $6t - 2$, $t = 5$

15. $9 - 2x$, $x = 4$ **16.** $6r + 8$, $r = 7$

Evaluate $4x$ for each value of x.

17. 3 **18.** 7 **19.** 2 **20.** 0

Evaluate $4y + 2$ for each value of y.

21. 1 **22.** 6 **23.** 3 **24.** 5

Evaluate for $x = 2$.

25. $3x$ **26.** $4x + 7$ **27.** $10 - 4x$

28. x^2 **29.** $x^2 - 1$ **30.** $2(x + 1)$

Evaluate for $y = 3$.

31. $4y$ **32.** $8 - y$ **33.** $10 - 3y$

34. $4 + y^2$ **35.** $y^2 - 2$ **36.** $2(y - 2)$

Evaluate for $x = 1$ and $y = 4$.

37. $x + y$ **38.** $2x + y$ **39.** $4x + y + 3$

40. $x + y - 5$ **41.** $2x + 3y - 5$ **42.** $5x - y + 1$

Evaluate for $x = 3.2$ and $y = 1.4$.

43. $x + y$ **44.** $x - y$ **45.** $x + 2y$

46. $3x - 2y$ **47.** $4x + y$ **48.** $2(x + y)$

Evaluate.

49. $2x$, $x = -2$ **50.** $5n$, $n = -1$

51. $y + 6$, $y = -3$ **52.** $4t + 3$, $t = -4$

53. $5 + 3m$, $m = -2$ **54.** $8 - 2n$, $n = -1$

Evaluate for $x = -2$ and $y = -3$.

55. $x + y$ **56.** $2x + 3y$

57. $3x - 2y$ **58.** $5x + 4y + 7$

Problems and Applications

59. The total cost of a banquet, in dollars, is represented by the expression $22n$, where n is the number of people. What is the cost for 37 students?

60. The points total of an NHL team is given by the expression $2w + t$, where w is the number of wins, and t is the number of ties. Copy and complete the table to find the points totals for some Canadian teams in one season.

Team	Wins	Ties	Points
Calgary	43	11	
Edmonton	26	8	
Montreal	48	6	
Ottawa	10	4	
Quebec	47	10	
Toronto	44	11	
Vancouver	46	9	

61. An expression that has 3 terms is called a **trinomial**. The prefix *tri-* means three. Find two other words that start with *tri-*.

62. Evaluate each expression.
a) $(x + 3)^2 + 2y$, $x = 2$, $y = 3$
b) $2(t - 3)^2 - 4s$, $t = 6$, $s = 2$
c) $3(d + 5) - 2e^2$, $d = -3$, $e = -2$

63. Find the whole-number values of x for which the first expression is larger than, or equal to, the second.
a) $2x$, x^2 **b)** $3x$, x^2

11.2 Solving Equations

Activity: Solve the Problem

Memorial School is having a 50-year reunion. Those who attend will receive a commemorative pin. It costs $200 to design the pin, plus $5 to make each pin. The Student Council has budgeted $2200 for pins. If n represents the number of pins made, then the expression for the cost of the pins, in dollars, is $5n + 200$.

Inquire

1. How much does it cost to make
a) 100 pins?   **b)** 200 pins?   **c)** 500 pins?

2. How many pins can be made for $2200?

 3. When you answered question 2, you solved the equation $5n + 200 = 2200$. Explain.

A sentence with an equal sign, =, is called an **equation**. Formulas are examples of equations. Two equations are $P = 2(l + w)$ and $A = bh$. These are also equations: $8 + 4 = 12$ and $4 \times 3 = 12$.

Equations, like other sentences, can be true or false. The equation $7 + 6 = 13$ is true, but $7 - 6 = 2$ is false.

The equation $x + 2 = 5$ contains the variable x. The equation can be either true or false, depending on the number you substitute for the variable. If you replace x by 3, the equation is true. If you replace x by any other number, the equation is false. A number that replaces a variable to make an equation true is called a **solution** of the equation.

Some equations can be solved mentally. This method is called **solving by inspection**.

Example 1

Solve and check $2n - 7 = 1$.

Solution

What number gives 1 when 7 is subtracted from it? Since $8 - 7 = 1$, $2n$ must be 8. If $2n = 8$, then $n = 4$. Substitute $n = 4$ into the left side of the equation. The solution is correct if the value of the left side equals the value of the right side.

Check: **L.S.** $= 2n - 7$ **R.S.** $= 1$
$= 2(4) - 7$
$= 8 - 7$
$= 1$
The solution is $n = 4$.

Example 2

Solve $3x + 13 = 37$.

Solution

Use guess and check. Substitute different numbers for x until you find the solution.

Try $x = 5$.
$$3x + 13 = 3(5) + 13$$
$$= 15 + 13$$
$$= 28 \qquad 3x + 13 \text{ is less than 37.}$$

Try $x = 9$.
$$3x + 13 = 3(9) + 13$$
$$= 27 + 13$$
$$= 40 \qquad 3x + 13 \text{ is greater than 37.}$$

Try $x = 8$.
$$3x + 13 = 3(8) + 13$$
$$= 24 + 13$$
$$= 37 \qquad \text{The solution is } x = 8.$$

Practice

Determine whether the number in brackets is a solution of the equation.

1. $n + 5 = 11$ (6)
2. $4n = 12$ (3)
3. $y - 8 = 12$ (20)
4. $u - 9 = 11$ (20)
5. $\frac{x}{3} = 5$ (8)
6. $\frac{y}{2} = 4$ (8)
7. $4 - n = 1$ (5)
8. $6 + x = 12$ (2)

Solve by inspection.

9. $x + 11 = 15$
10. $z + 7 = 14$
11. $u + 6 = 15$
12. $v + 8 = 13$

Solve by inspection.

13. $n - 10 = 15$
14. $x - 4 = 12$
15. $y - 12 = 0$
16. $u - 0 = 21$

Solve by inspection.

17. $5m = 35$
18. $5n = 45$
19. $2x = 24$
20. $4y = 24$
21. $8x = 56$
22. $9y = 72$

Solve by inspection.

23. $\frac{x}{7} = 7$
24. $\frac{y}{2} = 10$
25. $\frac{m}{2} = 5$
26. $\frac{n}{2} = 20$
27. $\frac{u}{4} = 8$
28. $\frac{v}{6} = 4$

Solve and check.

29. $12 + x = 19$
30. $15 - y = 8$
31. $4m = 28$
32. $\frac{y}{5} = 4$

Solve by guess and check.

33. $5x + 3 = 13$
34. $2n - 1 = 13$
35. $10 - 2n = 2$
36. $3n - 5 = 4$
37. $4 + 3x = 13$
38. $10p + 7 = 67$
39. $8q - 7 = 41$
40. $\frac{x}{3} + 2 = 6$

Problems and Applications

Write an equation in the form shown, replacing the ■ and ▲ with numbers. The solution for x is given in the brackets.

41. $x + \blacksquare = \blacktriangle$ (2)
42. $x + \blacksquare = \blacktriangle$ (3)
43. $\blacksquare x = \blacktriangle$ (5)
44. $\frac{x}{\blacksquare} = \blacktriangle$ (10)

In questions 45 and 46, find the equation that represents the problem and solve it.

45. Five more than a number is 20. What is the number?
a) $n - 20 = 5$
b) $n + 5 = 20$
c) $n - 5 = 20$
d) $5n = 20$

46. There are 150 riders and 30 extra horses. How many horses are there?
a) $n + 30 = 150$
b) $n + 150 = 30$
c) $n - 150 = 30$
d) $30n = 150$

 47. Write 2 equations with the same solution. Have a classmate solve your equations.

393

Seesaws and Number Tiles

Activity ❶ Seesaw Math

Use the clues to find out which objects must replace the question mark to balance the last seesaw. In each case, the object(s) in the left pan of the last seesaw cannot be used in the right pan of the last seesaw.

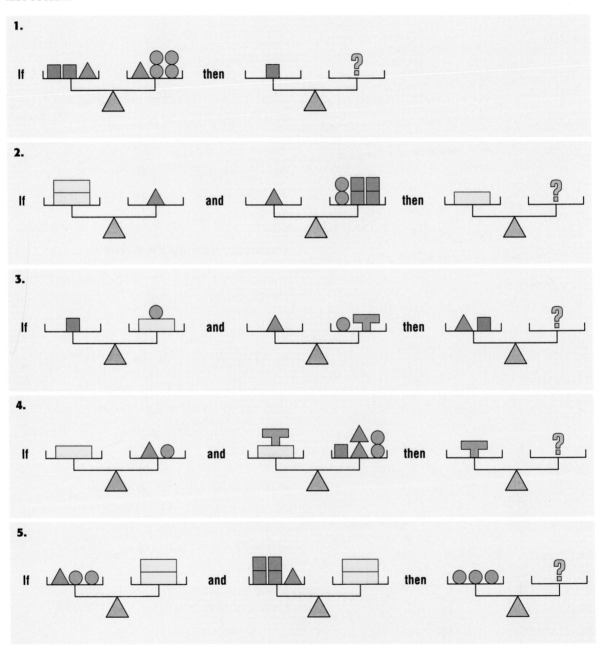

Activity ❷ Number Tiles

Prepare a set of number tiles. You could use small cardboard squares with the numbers from 0 to 9 marked on them.

In each set of 4 equations, you must use each tile just once. Some tiles have been placed for you. The value of the variable in each equation is given to the right of the equation. Copy and complete each equation in each set.

1.

$x - \boxed{} = 2$ $x = 6$

$y - \boxed{} = \boxed{5} - 3$ $y = 4$

$\boxed{6} + t - \boxed{} = \boxed{} - 1$ $t = 4$

$m + \boxed{7} - \boxed{} = \boxed{} + \boxed{0}$ $m = 3$

2.

$x + \boxed{} = 8$ $x = 3$

$y + \boxed{7} = \boxed{} + 7$ $y = 4$

$\boxed{0} + t + \boxed{} = \boxed{} + 12$ $t = 5$

$m - \boxed{} + \boxed{6} = \boxed{} - \boxed{2}$ $m = 4$

3.

$\boxed{}x = 21$ $x = 3$

$\boxed{}y + \boxed{0} = 12$ $y = 4$

$\boxed{4} + \boxed{}t = \boxed{}$ $t = 2$

$\boxed{1} + \boxed{}m = \boxed{9} - \boxed{} + 8$ $m = 2$

4.

$\dfrac{x}{\boxed{}} = 2$ $x = 10$

$\dfrac{y}{\boxed{}} + \boxed{6} = 9$ $y = 12$

$\boxed{1} + \dfrac{t}{\boxed{}} = \boxed{} + 3$ $t = 6$

$\dfrac{m}{\boxed{}} + \boxed{7} = \boxed{9} + \boxed{}$ $m = 20$

11.3 Solving Equations by Addition

Activity: Use Algebra Tiles

Each red tile represents +1, and each white tile represents −1.

A red tile and a white tile together make 0. The long green tile represents the variable +x or x.

The equation $x - 4 = 9$ is shown on the balance scale.

Inquire

1. What is the new equation if you add 4 red tiles to each side of the scale?

2. What is the value of x?

3. What must be added to both sides of $x - 5 = 12$ to solve the equation?

4. What must you add to both sides to solve each of the following equations?
a) $x - 6 = 7$ **b)** $36 = x - 12$ **c)** $-4 + x = 7$

5. Describe a method for solving equations by addition.

Example	Solution

Example

Solve and check $x - 9 = 12$.

Solution

Add 9 to both sides of the equation:

$$x - 9 = 12$$
$$x - 9 + 9 = 12 + 9$$
$$x = 21$$

The solution is $x = 21$.

Check: L.S. $= x - 9$ R.S. $= 12$
$= 21 - 9$
$= 12$

Practice

What number would you add to both sides to solve each equation?

1. $x - 8 = 10$ **2.** $x - 7 = 15$ **3.** $z - 5 = 12$

4. $y - 1 = 2$ **5.** $3 = x - 3$ **6.** $7 = y - 4$

Solve and check.

7. $p - 3 = 6$ **8.** $q - 11 = 22$ **9.** $x - 8 = 2$

10. $y - 5 = 3$ **11.** $x - 12 = 0$ **12.** $z - 10 = 10$

13. $r - 7 = -2$ **14.** $s - 4 = -3$ **15.** $10 = x - 5$

16. $4 = y - 6$ **17.** $-2 + t = 5$ **18.** $-4 + m = 0$

Solve and check.

19. $x - 3 = 5.2$ **20.** $z - 3.5 = 8$

21. $11 = t - 2.2$ **22.** $4.6 = x - 4.5$

23. $m - 3.2 = 4.7$ **24.** $5.1 = s - 0.6$

Problems and Applications

25. Nick spent $9 for a pen. He has $7 left. Solve the equation $x - 9 = 7$ to find how much he had at the start.

26. The average summer high temperature in St. John's, Newfoundland, is 15°C lower than in Calcutta, India. The average summer high in St. John's is 20°C. Solve the equation $x - 15 = 20$ to find the value for Calcutta.

27. Write 2 different equations that have 6 as a solution and can be solved by addition.

28. What is the result when you add 0 to both sides of an equation?

Solve and check.

29. $x - 4 = -7$ **30.** $y - 5 = -9$

31. $t - 8 = -13$ **32.** $m - 7 = -8$

11.4 Solving Equations by Subtraction

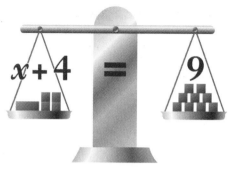

Activity: Use Algebra Tiles

The equation $x + 4 = 9$ is shown on the balance scale with algebra tiles. Recall that each red tile represents $+1$, each white tile represents -1, and the long green tile represents the variable $+x$ or x.

Inquire

1. Add 4 white tiles to both sides of the scale. What is the new equation? What is the value of x?

2. In the original equation, remove 4 red tiles from each side of the scale. What is the new equation? What is the value of x?

3. What must you subtract from both sides of $x + 11 = 35$ to solve it?

4. What number must you subtract from both sides to solve each of the following equations?

a) $x + 7 = 15$ **b)** $9 + x = 24$ **c)** $15 = x + 6$

5. Describe a method for solving equations by subtraction.

Example

Solve and check $x + 17 = 35$.

Solution

Subtract 17 from both sides:

$$x + 17 = 35$$
$$x + 17 - 17 = 35 - 17$$
$$x = 18$$

The solution is $x = 18$.

Check: L.S. $= x + 17$ R.S. $= 35$
$$= 18 + 17$$
$$= 35$$

Practice

What number would you subtract from both sides to solve each equation?

1. $x + 5 = 11$ **2.** $y + 8 = 12$

3. $z + 2 = 23$ **4.** $x + 15 = 45$

5. $32 = y + 7$ **6.** $25 = x + 7$

Solve and check.

7. $y + 9 = 24$ **8.** $x + 12 = 30$

9. $z + 8 = 16$ **10.** $p + 13 = 29$

11. $q + 15 = 34$ **12.** $r + 11 = 15$

13. $5 + x = 18$ **14.** $34 + y = 40$

15. $12 = x + 2$ **16.** $19 = y + 11$

17. $20 = 8 + m$ **18.** $22 = 20 + y$

Solve and check.

19. $z + 4 = 6.7$ **20.** $r + 3 = 8.2$

21. $x + 2.5 = 8$ **22.** $5 = y + 3.7$

23. $s + 7.2 = 10.2$ **24.** $8.1 = m + 5.1$

25. $x + 3.5 = 5.7$ **26.** $0.7 = t + 0.2$

Problems and Applications

27. Montreal's Place Victoria has 15 more storeys than Winnipeg's Richardson Building. Place Victoria has 47 storeys. Solve the equation $x + 15 = 47$ to find how many storeys the Richardson Building has.

28. Write 2 different equations that have 8 as a solution and can be solved by subtraction.

29. What is the result if you subtract zero from both sides of an equation?

Solve and check.

30. $x + 7 = 4$ **31.** $y + 6 = 3$

32. $t + 10 = 6$ **33.** $r + 7 = 6$

11.5 Solving Equations by Division

Activity: Use Algebra Tiles

Recall that 2 long green tiles mean $x + x$ or $2x$. The algebra tiles on the balance scale represent the equation $2x = 6$.

Inquire

1. How many equal parts are there on the left side of the scale?

2. Divide the red tiles into the same number of equal parts. How many red tiles are in each part? What is the value of x?

3. What is the new equation when you divide both sides of the equation $3x = 24$ by 3? What is the value of x?

4. By what number must you divide both sides to solve each equation?
a) $2x = 12$ **b)** $5x = 15$ **c)** $7x = 35$

 5. Describe a method for solving equations by division.

Example

Solve and check
$3x = 18$.

Solution

Divide both sides by 3:

$3x = 18$
$$\frac{3x}{3} = \frac{18}{3}$$
$x = 6$

The solution is $x = 6$.

Check: L.S. $= 3x$ **R.S.** $= 18$
$= 3(6)$
$= 18$

Practice

By what number would you divide both sides to solve each equation?

1. $3x = 6$ **2.** $5x = 10$ **3.** $7z = 42$

4. $4t = 20$ **5.** $9s = 27$ **6.** $10m = 60$

7. $15y = 45$ **8.** $3x = 12$ **9.** $6n = 18$

Solve and check.

10. $4x = 8$ **11.** $9y = 9$ **12.** $2r = 18$

13. $6w = 72$ **14.** $8x = 32$ **15.** $10m = 50$

16. $10 = 5x$ **17.** $24 = 8x$ **18.** $7n = 28$

19. $20 = 5t$ **20.** $25y = 75$ **21.** $60 = 15z$

Solve and check.

22. $2x = 5$ **23.** $4y = 4.8$

24. $5w = 4.5$ **25.** $2 = 4x$

26. $1.2x = 24$ **27.** $8 = 0.2n$

28. $0.4t = 0.8$ **29.** $1.2x = 3.6$

30. $3.6 = 0.6t$ **31.** $20 = 0.1m$

Problems and Applications

32. The height of a great gray owl is 5 times the height of a pygmy owl. A great gray owl can grow to 85 cm in height. Solve the equation $5x = 85$ to find the height of a pygmy owl.

33. Write 2 different equations that have 3 as a solution and that can be solved using division.

 Solve and check.

34. $4x = -8$ **35.** $3x = -12$

36. $2x = -6$ **37.** $-5x = -20$

11.6 Solving Equations by Multiplication

Activity: Interpret the Diagram

The balance scale shows the
equation $\frac{x}{2} = 4$.

Inquire

1. What do you multiply $\frac{x}{2}$ by to
give x?

2. Multiply both sides of the equation by this
number. What is the value of x?

3. By what number must you multiply
both sides to solve each of these equations?

 4. Describe a method for solving equations by
multiplication.

a) $\frac{x}{3} = 6$ **b)** $\frac{x}{5} = 3$ **c)** $\frac{x}{4} = 1$

Example	Solution

Solve and check
$\frac{x}{6} = 2$.

$\frac{x}{6} = 2$ **Check: L.S.** $= \frac{x}{6}$ **R.S.** $= 2$

Multiply both sides by 6: $6 \times \frac{x}{6} = 6 \times 2$ $= \frac{12}{6}$

$x = 12$ $= 2$

The solution is $x = 12$.

Practice

*By what number would you multiply both sides to
solve each equation?*

1. $\frac{x}{3} = 5$ **2.** $\frac{y}{2} = 4$ **3.** $\frac{t}{5} = 7$

4. $\frac{w}{4} = 4$ **5.** $\frac{x}{7} = 9$ **6.** $\frac{m}{6} = 0$

Solve and check.

7. $\frac{x}{4} = 8$ **8.** $\frac{y}{2} = 8$ **9.** $\frac{m}{3} = 6$

10. $\frac{y}{3} = 2$ **11.** $\frac{x}{5} = 5$ **12.** $\frac{y}{2} = 0$

13. $7 = \frac{x}{7}$ **14.** $4 = \frac{y}{2}$ **15.** $9 = \frac{t}{3}$

16. $\frac{x}{2} = 3$ **17.** $\frac{y}{8} = 1$ **18.** $\frac{y}{10} = 0$

Solve and check.

19. $\frac{x}{2} = 3.1$ **20.** $\frac{y}{4} = 0.2$ **21.** $\frac{t}{3} = 1.2$

22. $0.7 = \frac{m}{5}$ **23.** $11.1 = \frac{r}{6}$ **24.** $\frac{s}{9} = 0$

Problems and Applications

25. Chatham, New Brunswick, has blowing
snow on $\frac{1}{4}$ as many days as Churchill,
Manitoba. Chatham has 16 days of blowing
snow a year. Solve the equation $\frac{x}{4} = 16$
to find how many days of blowing snow
Churchill has in a year.

26. Write two different equations that have
7 as a solution and that can be solved using
multiplication.

27. What is the result if you multiply both
sides of an equation by zero?

Solve and check.

28. $\frac{x}{2} = -4$ **29.** $\frac{y}{3} = -1$ **30.** $\frac{m}{-4} = 5$

31. $\frac{n}{-5} = -3$ **32.** $-5 = \frac{w}{2}$ **33.** $-1 = \frac{t}{3}$

Haunts of the Tiger

Tigers are found in Asia. In 1900, even after being hunted for at least 1000 years, there were still about 100 000 tigers remaining in the wild. Today, the tiger is in danger of extinction.

The map shows the names of the subspecies of tigers, an estimate of their current numbers, their former range, and their current range.

Activity ❶

1. What are the names of the known subspecies?

2. How many known subspecies were there?

3. How many subspecies are extinct?

4. What percent of the subspecies are extinct?

400

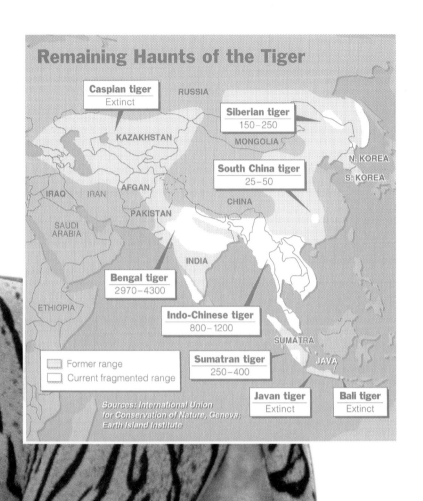

Remaining Haunts of the Tiger

Caspian tiger
Extinct

RUSSIA

KAZAKHSTAN

Siberian tiger
150–250

MONGOLIA

N. KOREA
S. KOREA

South China tiger
25–50

IRAQ   IRAN

AFGAN.

CHINA

PAKISTAN

SAUDI
ARABIA

INDIA

ETHIOPIA

Bengal tiger
2970–4300

Indo-Chinese tiger
800–1200

SUMATRA

Former range
Current fragmented range

Sumatran tiger
250–400

JAVA

Sources: International Union
for Conservation of Nature, Geneva;
Earth Island Institute

Javan tiger
Extinct

Bali tiger
Extinct

Activity ❷

1. Assume that the maximum number of tigers shown for each area is the actual number in that area.

a) About how many tigers are there?

b) What percent of the population in 1900 does this number represent?

c) About what percent of the tigers are Bengal tigers?

2. Assume that the minimum number of tigers shown for each area is the actual number in that area.

a) About how many tigers are there?

b) What percent of the population in 1900 does this number represent?

3. About what percent of its former range does the Sumatran tiger have?

Activity ❸

1. List some reasons why you think tigers are in danger of becoming extinct.

2. Use your research skills to check whether your ideas are reasonable.

401

11.7 Like Terms

Activity: Use Pattern Blocks

The area of the parallelogram is the sum of the areas of the blocks.
The area of each yellow hexagon is h square units.
The area of each blue rhombus is r square units.
The area of each green triangle is t square units.

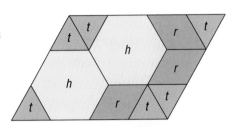

Inquire

1. How many pieces make up the parallelogram?

2. Use each block to write an expression for the area of the parallelogram in terms of h, r, and t.

3. Use the idea that $x + x + x = 3x$ to combine as many terms as possible in the expression you wrote in question 2. What is your new expression?

Terms that have the same variable parts are called **like terms**. The terms $3x$, $4x$, and $6x$ are like terms. The terms $5x$, $2x^2$, and $3y$ are **unlike terms**. They have different variable parts.

Like terms can be combined.
Since $2x$ means $x + x$, and $3x$ means $x + x + x$, then
$$2x + 3x = x + x + x + x + x$$
$$= 5x$$

Example

Simplify $4x + 2y - 2x - 3y$.

Solution

Combine like terms.
$$4x + 2y - 2x - 3y = 4x - 2x + 2y - 3y$$
$$= 2x - y$$

Practice

Simplify.

1. $3x + 5x$

2. $6a - 3a$

3. $2t + 3t + 4t$

4. $7w - 2w + 3w$

5. $9c - 8c - c$

6. $y + 5y - y$

7. $6a + 9 + 7a - 3$

8. $3x + 7x + 4y + 3y$

9. $9 + 6b - b + 4b$

10. $x + y - x - y$

11. $a + b + b + a$

12. $6w - 5w - w + 8y$

Problems and Applications

Simplify, then evaluate for $t = 2$ and $w = 3$.

13. $6t - 3t + 4t + 2w$

14. $5w + 7t - 5t + w$

15. $6t + 4w - 6t - 3w$

16. $3t - 4t + w - 2w$

17. a) Write and simplify an expression for the perimeter of the figure.
b) Find the perimeter if $s = 40$ m and $t = 30$ m.

18. Write two different expressions that simplify to $2x + 3y$. Compare your expressions with your classmates'.

11.8 The Distributive Property

Activity: Use a Diagram

The large rectangle, A, is made up of two smaller rectangles, B and C.

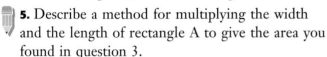

Inquire

1. Write an expression for the area of rectangle B.

2. What is the area of rectangle C?

3. Use the results from questions 1 and 2 to write an expression for the area of rectangle A.

4. For rectangle A, what is the length? the width?

5. Describe a method for multiplying the width and the length of rectangle A to give the area you found in question 3.

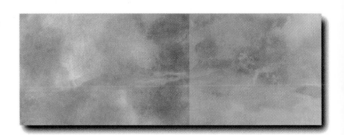

To **expand** an expression with brackets means to remove the brackets by multiplying. This is done using the **distributive property.**

Example

Expand $3(y + 2)$.

Solution

Multiply each term inside the brackets by 3.

$$3(y + 2) = 3(y + 2)$$
$$= 3 \times y + 3 \times 2$$
$$= 3y + 6$$

Practice

Expand.

1. $2(x + 5)$ **2.** $3(b + 3)$ **3.** $6(y - 1)$

4. $5(t - 3)$ **5.** $7(m + 1)$ **6.** $4(a - 7)$

7. $4(4 + m)$ **8.** $8(x - 4)$ **9.** $7(3 + t)$

Expand.

10. $2(3x + 4)$ **11.** $4(2y + 1)$ **12.** $3(4m - 3)$

13. $5(5t - 2)$ **14.** $6(1 + 2x)$ **15.** $7(4w - 7)$

16. $2(3x + 2y)$ **17.** $3(4a + 5b)$

18. $-3(3m - 2n)$ **19.** $-5(3s - t)$

Expand.

20. $3(2x + 4y + 1)$ **21.** $2(a + b + 1)$

22. $4(3c - 2d + 5)$ **23.** $5(x - 3 + 4y)$

24. $-6(2 + 3x + y)$ **25.** $-2(1 - x - y)$

Problems and Applications

Evaluate each expression for $x = 1$ and $y = 1$. Then, expand and evaluate the new expression for $x = 1$ and $y = 1$.

26. $3(5x + 2y + 4)$ **27.** $3(4x - 2y - 1)$

You can use the distributive property to multiply some pairs of numbers without a calculator.

20×38	30×31
$= 20(40 - 2)$	$= 30(30 + 1)$
$= 800 - 40$	$= 900 + 30$
$= 760$	$= 930$

Use this method to multiply the following.

28. 20×19 **29.** 30×28 **30.** 40×37

31. 50×22 **32.** 20×41 **33.** 30×33

11.9 Solving Equations in More Than One Step

Suppose the mass of something was measured in African elephants, instead of kilograms. A sperm whale would have a mass of about 5 elephants.

Let x be the mass of food, in elephants, a person eats in a lifetime. Then, twice this mass minus 3 elephants equals the mass of a sperm whale. This information can be represented by the equation $2x - 3 = 5$.

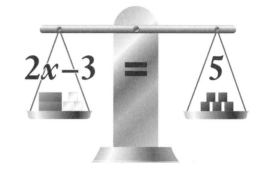

Activity: Use Algebra Tiles

The equation $2x - 3 = 5$ is represented by the balance scale.

Inquire

1. How many red 1-tiles must be added to both sides of the balance so that only the value of the x-tiles remains on the left side?

2. What is the new equation after the red tiles are added?

3. How many red 1-tiles does one green x-tile represent?

4. What mass of food, in elephants, does a person eat in a lifetime?

When you solve equations, the object is to get the variable alone, or to **isolate the variable**, on one side of the equal sign.

Example 1

Solve and check
$4x + 3 = 11$.

Solution

$$4x + 3 = 11$$

Subtract 3 from both sides: $\quad 4x + 3 \;-3 = 11 \;-3$

$$4x = 8$$

Divide both sides by 4: $\qquad \dfrac{4x}{4} = \dfrac{8}{4}$

$$x = 2$$

Check: L.S. $= 4x + 3$ $\qquad$ **R.S.** $= 11$
$$= 4(2) + 3$$
$$= 8 + 3$$
$$= 11$$

The solution is $x = 2$.

You can also use a flow chart to solve equations. Start by isolating the variable on the left side.

START $\longrightarrow$ $4x + 3$ $\longrightarrow$ Subtract 3 $\longrightarrow$ Divide by 4 $\longrightarrow$ x $\longrightarrow$ STOP

Now, apply the same steps to the right side.

START $\longrightarrow$ 11 $\longrightarrow$ Subtract 3 $\longrightarrow$ Divide by 4 $\longrightarrow$ 2 $\longrightarrow$ STOP

Example 2

Solve and check
$3(x-1) = x+5$.

Solution

$$3(x-1) = x+5$$

Remove brackets: $\quad\quad\quad 3x - 3 = x + 5$

Subtract x from both sides: $\quad 3x - x - 3 = x - x + 5$

$$2x - 3 = 5$$

Add 3 to both sides: $\quad\quad\quad 2x - 3 + 3 = 5 + 3$

$$2x = 8$$

Divide both sides by 2: $\quad\quad\quad \dfrac{2x}{2} = \dfrac{8}{2}$

$$x = 4$$

Check: L.S. $= 3(x-1)$ **R.S.** $= x+5$

$\quad\quad\quad\quad = 3(4-1)$ $\quad = 4+5$

$\quad\quad\quad\quad = 3(3)$ $\quad\quad = 9$

$\quad\quad\quad\quad = 9$

The solution is $x = 4$.

Practice

Solve and check.

1. $2x + 1 = 5$ **2.** $3y + 2 = 11$

3. $4t - 3 = 13$ **4.** $5m + 7 = 12$

5. $4 + 2e = 12$ **6.** $16 = 3a + 7$

7. $7z + 1 = 18 - 3$ **8.** $4b + 2 = 6 + 4$

Solve using a flow chart.

9. $5x + 2 = 17$ **10.** $2x + 3 = 9$

Solve and check.

11. $2x - 4 = 2$ **12.** $4n - 3 = 5$

13. $3s - 9 = 6$ **14.** $6r - 2 = 10$

15. $3y - 5 = -2$ **16.** $2b - 9 = -3$

17. $5t - 4 = 22 - 1$ **18.** $4z - 7 = 3 + 10$

Solve and check.

19. $2x + 1.5 = 5.5$ **20.** $3y - 2.6 = 3.4$

21. $4m + 0.9 = 2.5$ **22.** $5t - 1.2 = 4.3$

Solve and check.

23. $\frac{x}{2} + 3 = 4$ **24.** $\frac{n}{3} - 1 = 1$

25. $4 + \frac{z}{2} = 6$ **26.** $2 = \frac{a}{4} - 3$

Solve and check.

27. $3x + 2x = 15$ **28.** $8y - y = 7$

29. $4t - t = 6 + t$ **30.** $3w + 5 = 2w + 7$

31. $4c - 7 = 2c - 1$ **32.** $2z + 4 = 5z - 8$

Solve and check.

33. $2(x + 1) = 6$ **34.** $3(m - 1) = m + 9$

35. $5(y - 3) = y + 1$ **36.** $6 + 4(r - 2) = r + 7$

37. $4 + 2s = 3(s - 2) + 1$

38. $5(g - 3) + 2 = 3(g + 1)$

39. $-3(n - 4) = 6$ **40.** $-3(1 - b) = 2(b + 1)$

Problems and Applications

41. The average mass of a lynx is 16 kg. This mass is 4 kg less than twice the average mass of an otter. Solve the equation $2x - 4 = 16$ to find an otter's mass, in kilograms.

42. Canada has a river named the Mississippi. It is not as long as the Mississippi River in the United States, which is 3780 km long. Solve the equation $18x + 162 = 3780$ to find the length of Canada's Mississippi River.

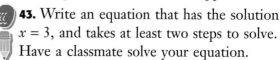 **43.** Write an equation that has the solution $x = 3$, and takes at least two steps to solve. Have a classmate solve your equation.

405

11.10 Writing Equations

Albert Einstein's equation $E = mc^2$ is the most famous in the history of science. This equation allows scientists to understand the energy source of the sun and other stars.

Many problems can be solved by first writing the information as an equation and then solving the equation.

Activity: Use the Information

Heidi has two more fish in her saltwater aquarium than Jerry has. Together they have a total of 18 fish.

Inquire

1. Let n represent the number of fish Jerry has. Write an expression for the number of fish Heidi has.

2. Use numbers and variables to write an equation that gives the information about the fish.

3. Suppose Heidi bought one more fish. What would the new equation be?

Example 1

Write an equation for each sentence.
a) Five more than a number, n, is ten.
b) Six less than a number, x, is five.
c) Five times a number, y, is thirty.
d) When three is added to two times a number, n, the result is nineteen.
e) When five is subtracted from three times a number, t, the result is thirteen.

Solution

a) $n + 5 = 10$
b) $x - 6 = 5$
c) $5y = 30$
d) $2n + 3 = 19$

e) $3t - 5 = 13$

Example 2

There are 110 more species of cuckoos than species of penguins. Together, there is a total of 146 species of these birds. Write an equation to find the number of species of penguins.

Solution

Let n represent the number of species of penguins. Then, the number of species of cuckoos is $n + 110$. The sum of the numbers is 146.

So $\qquad n + n + 110 = 146$
and $\qquad 2n + 110 = 146$

Practice

Write an equation for each sentence.

1. Four more than a number is nineteen.

2. Three less than a number is nine.

3. Four times a number is twelve.

4. Twelve decreased by a number is four.

5. One quarter of a number is three.

6. Six increased by a number is eight.

7. A number multiplied by four, then increased by three, is eleven.

8. A number multiplied by four, then decreased by thirteen, is three.

9. A number increased by three, then multiplied by five, is twenty-three.

10. A number decreased by three, then multiplied by four, is twelve.

11. The sum of a number and five more than the number is fifteen.

12. Four less than twice a number is fifty.

13. The sum of a number and two less than the number is twelve.

Let a letter represent the unknown and write an equation.

14. The length increased by four is eleven.

15. Five times the width is sixty.

16. The perimeter decreased by six is forty.

17. A number divided by six is two.

18. One more than twice a number is seven.

Problems and Applications

Write an equation that could be used to solve each problem.

19. Three years from now, Jenny's age will be sixteen. What is Jenny's age?

20. Julio has fifteen dollars, which is ten dollars less than he needs. How much does Julio need?

21. One Sunday, Angie did math homework for one hour, which was half the total time she spent on homework that day. How much time did she spend on homework?

22. Miki wants to double her present keyboarding rate to 50 words/min. What is her present rate?

Write an equation that could be used to solve each problem.

23. Maria is two years older than Sue, and the sum of their ages is twenty-six. How old is Sue?

24. Vancouver has three times the annual snowfall of Tokyo. Together, they have a total of 80 cm of snow a year. What is Tokyo's annual snowfall?

25. Uranus has three moons less than Saturn. Together, they have thirty-three moons. How many moons does Saturn have?

26. One year, Alberta had 250 forest fires more than Manitoba. The total number of forest fires in these two provinces was 1596 that year. How many forest fires did Manitoba have?

27. Sabi has $2.50 more than Tony. Together, they have $17.50. How much does Tony have?

 Write a word problem that could be solved by each equation. Compare your problems with a classmate's.

28. $x + 3 = 11$

29. $m - 9 = 14$

30. $3y = 18$

31. $\frac{t}{2} = 6$

32. $2x + 1 = 13$

33. $3e - 4 = 17$

34. $2(x + 1) = 6$

35. $3(y - 2) = 9$

11.11 Using Equations to Solve Problems

National parks protect the natural beauty of parts of a
country for its people to see. Both Canada and the United
States have designated certain areas as national parks.

Activity: Solve the Problem

The United States has fifteen more national parks than
Canada. Together they have a total of eighty-nine national
parks. Answer the following questions to find out how
many national parks each country has.

Inquire

1. Let n represent the number of national parks Canada has.
Write an expression for the number of national parks in the
United States.

2. Write an expression for the total number of national parks.

3. Write an equation with your expression from question
2 on one side, and the total number of national parks on
the other.

4. Solve the equation.

5. How many national parks are in

a) Canada?   **b)** the United States?

Example 1

Joanna works in a marina. Boat servicing costs $70.00,
plus $4.50 for each litre of oil. Joanna serviced a boat
and made out a bill for $88.00. How many litres of oil
did she use?

Solution

Let n represent the number of litres of oil she used.
Then, the cost of the oil is $\$4.50 \times n$ or $\$4.50n$.
Write an equation.
Word equation: Basic service $70.00 plus $4.50n$ equals $88.00.

$$70.00 + 4.50n = 88.00$$
$$70.00 - 70.00 + 4.50n = 88.00 - 70.00$$
$$4.50n = 18.00$$
$$\frac{4.50n}{4.50} = \frac{18.00}{4.50}$$
$$n = 4$$

Check:
1 L of oil costs $4.50
4 L of oil cost 4 × $4.50 or $18.00
Basic service $70.00
Total charge $88.00

Joanna used 4 L of oil.

Example 2

The length of a rectangle is 5 m longer than the width. The perimeter of the rectangle is 82 m. Find the length and the width of the rectangle.

Solution

Let w represent the width. Then, the length is $w + 5$.

$$(w + 5) + w + (w + 5) + w = 82$$
$$4w + 10 = 82$$
$$4w + 10 - 10 = 82 - 10$$
$$4w = 72$$
$$\frac{4w}{4} = \frac{72}{4}$$
$$w = 18$$
$$w + 5 = 18 + 5$$
$$= 23$$

Check:
Since $23 - 18 = 5$, the length is 5 m longer than the width.
$$P = 2(l + w)$$
$$= 2(23 + 18)$$
$$= 2(41)$$
$$= 82$$

The length is 23 m and the width is 18 m.

Problems and Applications

1. Mary has 2 CDs more than Jamil. Together, they have 30 CDs. How many CDs does Mary have?

2. A large pizza costs $8.95, plus $0.65 for each additional topping. Remi paid $10.90 for a large pizza. How many additional toppings did he get?

3. Film processing costs $4.95, plus $0.35 for each picture printed. Milan paid $11.95 for processing and printing. How many pictures did he have printed?

4. A store has a total of 108 full-time staff and part-time staff. There are three times as many full-time staff as part-time staff. How many of the staff are in each category?

5. The side lengths in a triangle are three consecutive whole numbers. The perimeter is 24. What is the length of each side?

6. A horse can jump 6 times farther, horizontally, than a lion can. The difference between the distances they can jump is 10 m. How far can each animal jump?

7. Murray works full-time and Earla works part-time at the marina. One week, Murray earned $75.00 more than three times as much as Earla earned. Murray earned $450.00. How much did Earla earn?

8. The sum of three numbers is 39. The second number is 3 times the first. The third number is 4 more than the first. What are the three numbers?

9. Write a problem than can be solved with an equation. Have a classmate solve your problem.

LOGIC POWER

The letter H is made from 17 cubes. If the letter is painted blue, how many cubes will have exactly 4 blue faces?

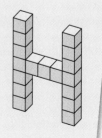

11.12 Developing and Working with Formulas

Activity: Complete the Table

The first figure is made up of one L-shape. It has a perimeter of 12 units. The second figure is made up of 2 connected L-shapes. It has a perimeter of 22 units.

Copy the table. Complete it by finding the perimeters of the figures with the given numbers of L-shapes.

Number of L-Shapes	Perimeter
1	12
2	22
3	
4	
5	

Inquire

1. What is the increase in the perimeter each time an L-shape is added?

2. What is the perimeter of the figure made from
a) 6 L-shapes?   **b)** 7 L-shapes?   **c)** 8 L-shapes?

 3. Describe how you would find the perimeter of a figure made from 80 L-shapes.

4. Write a formula for the perimeter in the form $P = \blacktriangle \times n + \blacksquare$, where n is the number of L-shapes in the figure, and $\blacktriangle$ and $\blacksquare$ represent two different numbers.

5. Use the formula to calculate the perimeter of a figure made from 97 L-shapes.

6. How many L-shapes are in a figure with a perimeter of 272 units?

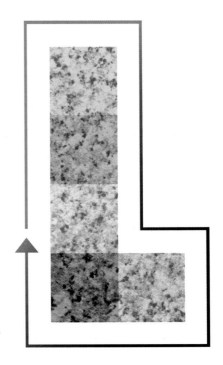

Example

Euler's formula for polyhedra states that the number of vertices plus the number of faces equals the number of edges plus 2, or $V + F = E + 2$. A certain polyhedron has 8 vertices and 12 edges. How many faces does it have?

Solution

Substitute the known values, $V = 8$ and $E = 12$, into the formula and solve for the unknown value.

$$V + F = E + 2$$
$$8 + F = 12 + 2$$
$$8 + F = 14$$
$$8 - 8 + F = 14 - 8$$
$$F = 6$$

Check: L.S. $= V + F$ **R.S.** $= E + 2$
         $= 8 + 6$ $= 12 + 2$
         $= 14$ $= 14$

The polyhedron has 6 faces.

Practice

Copy and complete the table. State a rule for each pattern.

1.

x	1	2	3	4	5	6
y	4	8	12			

2.

s	3	5	7	9	11	13
t	8	10	12			

Copy and complete the table. Then, use the variables to write a formula for each pattern.

3.

Hours (*h*)	1	2	3	4	5	6
Wages (*w*)	9	18	27			

4.

Number of Tickets (*n*)		2	4	6	8
Cost (*c*)			42	84	

5. The formula for the area of a rectangle is $A = l \times w$.
a) Find A when $l = 9$ m and $w = 6$ m.
b) Find l when $A = 30$ m² and $w = 5$ m.
c) Find w when $A = 24$ m² and $l = 8$ m.

6. The formula for the perimeter of a rectangle is $P = 2(l + w)$.
a) Find P when $l = 11$ m and $w = 7$ m.
b) Find w when $P = 80$ m and $l = 23$ m.
c) Find l when $P = 74$ m and $w = 17$ m.

Problems and Applications

7. The first figure is made up of one T-shape. It has a perimeter of 10 units. The second figure is made up of 2 connected T-shapes, and so on.

a) Copy the table. Complete it by finding the perimeters of the figures with the given numbers of T-shapes.

Number of T-Shapes	Perimeter
1	10
⋮	
5	

b) What is the increase in the perimeter each time a T-shape is added?
c) What is the perimeter of the figure made from 6 T-shapes? 7 T-shapes?
d) Write a formula for the perimeter in the form $P = \blacktriangle \times n + \blacksquare$, where n is the number of T-shapes in the figure, and $\blacktriangle$ and $\blacksquare$ represent two different numbers.

8. a) Copy and complete the table.

Number of Triangles	Figure	Perimeter
1	△	3
2	◁▷	4
3	◁▷◁	5
⋮		
6		

b) Write a formula for the perimeter in terms of the number of triangles.
c) What is the perimeter of the figure made from 30 triangles?
d) How many triangles are in the figure with a perimeter of 42 units?

9. a) Copy and complete the table.

Number of L-Shapes	Figure	Perimeter
1		8
2		12
3		16
⋮		
6		

b) Write a formula for the perimeter in terms of the number of L-shapes.
c) What is the perimeter of the figure made from 15 L-shapes?
d) How many L-shapes make a figure with a perimeter of 88 units?

411

11.13 Equations with Integer Solutions

Activity: Use Algebra Tiles

The equation $x - 2 = -7$ is shown on the balance scale. Answer the questions below to find x.

Inquire

1. What is the new equation if you add 2 red tiles to each side of the scale?

2. What is the value of x?

Equations can have negative numbers as solutions. These equations are solved in the same ways as other equations.

Example 1	**Solution**		
Solve and check $x + 5 = 3$.	Subtract 5 from both sides:	$x + 5 = 3$ $x + 5 - 5 = 3 - 5$ $x = -2$	**Check: L.S.** $= x + 5$ $= (-2) + 5$ $= 3$ **R.S.** $= 3$

The solution is $x = -2$.

Example 2	**Solution**
Solve and check $2x - 3 = -9$.	

Add 3 to both sides: $2x - 3 = -9$
$2x - 3 + 3 = -9 + 3$

Divide both sides by 2: $2x = -6$
$$\frac{2x}{2} = \frac{-6}{2}$$
$$x = -3$$

Check: L.S. $= 2x - 3$ **R.S.** $= -9$
$= 2(-3) - 3$
$= -6 - 3$
$= -9$

The solution is $x = -3$.

Example 3

Solve
$4(y - 1) + 3 = 2y - 7$.

Solution

$$4(y - 1) + 3 = 2y - 7$$

Expand: $4y - 4 + 3 = 2y - 7$
$4y - 1 = 2y - 7$

Add 1 to both sides: $4y - 1 + 1 = 2y - 7 + 1$
$4y = 2y - 6$

Subtract $2y$ from both sides: $4y - 2y = 2y - 2y - 6$
$2y = -6$

Divide both sides by 2: $\dfrac{2y}{2} = \dfrac{-6}{2}$
$y = -3$

The solution is $y = -3$.

Practice

Solve and check.

1. $x - 1 = -4$ **2.** $x + 4 = 2$

3. $z - 3 = -7$ **4.** $t + 6 = -1$

5. $4 = m + 9$ **6.** $-5 = y - 2$

7. $6 + r = 3$ **8.** $-2 = 4 + w$

9. $\frac{b}{2} = -6$ **10.** $-7 = \frac{a}{3}$

Solve and check.

11. $2x - 1 = -3$ **12.** $2y + 5 = 1$

13. $4t + 1 = -7$ **14.** $5a - 10 = -30$

15. $7 + 2r = 7$ **16.** $-17 = 6x + 1$

17. $8y - 3 = 13$ **18.** $4w + 4 = 0$

19. $9 + 4x = 1$ **20.** $-4 = 3m + 5$

Solve and check.

21. $3x + 4 = 2x - 3$ **22.** $4m - 7 = 2m - 1$

23. $8 + 4t = 13 - t$ **24.** $6y + 3 = 3y - 7 + y$

25. $3w - 9 = 4 + 7w - 1$

Solve and check.

26. $2(y - 1) = -6$ **27.** $3(m + 2) + 4 = 1$

28. $2t + 3(t - 2) = 4$

29. $5(m + 3) + 2 = 2m + 5$

30. $7x + 4 = 2(x - 3)$

31. $3(w + 2) = 2(w - 1)$

32. $6y + 7 = 3 + 2(y - 4)$

Solve and check.

33. $2(x - 1) + 7 = 4x + 3$

34. $5x - 8x = 3(x + 4)$

35. $6 - 2(m + 3) = 8$

36. $5t - 3t = 5 - 3(t + 5)$

Solve and check.

37. $x + 4.3 = -2.7$ **38.** $t - 1.3 = -5.3$

39. $y - (-1.8) = -4.8$ **40.** $m - (-2.2) = 5.4$

Problems and Applications

 Solve and check.

41. $x^2 + 1 = 5$ **42.** $y^2 - 1 = 8$ **43.** $w^2 + 3 = 28$

44. $m^2 - 6 = 10$ **45.** $\frac{3x}{4} = -6$ **46.** $\frac{2w}{3} = -4$

47. $\frac{w}{6} = \frac{2}{3}$ **48.** $\frac{x}{4} = \frac{1}{2}$ **49.** $\frac{n}{4} = \frac{3}{2}$

50. If you multiply Canada's lowest outside air temperature by 3 and then add 19, you get $-170°$ C. This is the lowest surface temperature on the moon. Write an equation, then solve it to find Canada's lowest outside air temperature.

 51. Write two different equations that have -4 as the solution, and that must be solved using more than 1 step. Have a classmate solve your equations.

LOGIC POWER

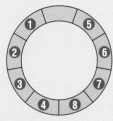

Draw a grid and place 8 markers of 2 different colours on it, as shown. Label the markers, so that you can record your moves.

The object is to switch the positions of the markers in as few moves as possible. A move consists of sliding a marker to an empty space, as in checkers. A marker can jump only another marker of a different colour. The order of the markers at the end does not matter, as long as the blue and red markers exchange places. Making less than 20 moves is good. Making 15 moves is the best.

The 747 Jumbo Jet

The Boeing 747 was the first wide-bodied superjet or jumbo jet. It was built in Seattle and flew for the first time on February 9, 1969.

Activity ❶ Size

The 747 is 70.5 m long and has a wingspan of 59.6 m.

1. In 1903, the Wright brothers' aircraft *Flyer 1* travelled 36.6 m on its first flight. If it had taken off from the tail of a 747, and flown toward the nose, how far short of the nose would it have landed?

2. If you drew a rectangle around a 747, what would be the area of the rectangle?

3. Can you place a 747 on a football field without any parts sticking out?

4. Would a 747 fit inside your school's parking lot?

Activity ❷ Passengers, Costs, and Services

A 747 can carry up to 420 passengers at about 890 km/h. It has a range of about 13 000 km.

1. The circumference of the Earth at the equator is about 40 000 km. In the first 25 years of service, 747s flew the equivalent of 720 000 times around the equator. How many kilometres did they fly in 25 years?

2. Since its first flight, the 747 has carried the equivalent of about one-quarter of the world's population. How many passengers have flown in the 747?

3. The flying distance from London to Tokyo is 9600 km. About how many hours would a non-stop London to Tokyo flight take at 890 km/h?

4. A flight attendant on a 747 walks the length of the aisle about 125 times during a London to Tokyo flight. The length of the aisle is about 64 m. How many kilometres does a flight attendant walk on the flight?

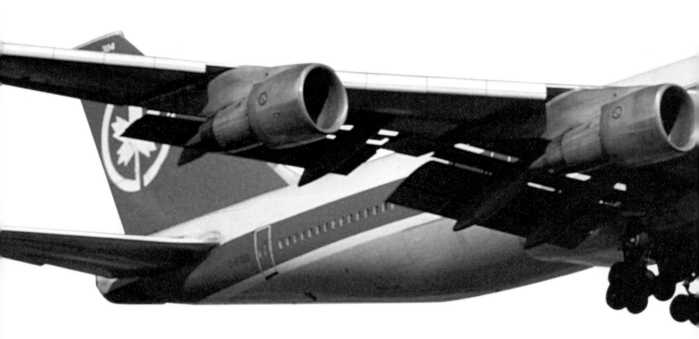

5. The table gives the approximate costs to get a 747 flying.

Item	Cost
Fuel	$35 000
Takeoff Fee	$1990
Food and Accommodations for 20 Crew	$3000
In-flight Catering	$9100
Fuel Taxes	$7600
Terminal Fee	$920
Crew Transportation	$240
Cleaning and Ground Handling	$4000

a) What is the total cost?

b) What is the total cost per passenger if there are 420 passengers on board?

c) A 747 is not painted all over, because paint adds to the mass of the aircraft. In one year, 1 kg of paint would add $30 to the cost of fuel. A 747 would require about 180 kg of paint. What would be the additional fuel cost per year?

11.14 Solving Inequalities

Of all the provincial capitals, Victoria has the least annual snowfall, 50 cm. St. John's has the greatest annual snowfall, 359 cm. The snowfalls for the other provincial capitals can be represented by the inequalities $s > 50$ and $s < 359$. These inequalities show that the snowfalls in the other capitals are greater than 50 cm and less than 359 cm.

Inequalities are mathematical sentences that contain these symbols.

< means "is less than."   ≤ means " is less than or equal to."
> means "is greater than."   ≥ means "is greater than or equal to."

The snowfalls in all the provincial capitals, including Victoria and St. John's, can be represented by the inequalities $s ≥ 50$ and $s ≤ 359$.

An inequality that includes a variable can be true or false, depending on the value you substitute for the variable. The inequality $s > 50$ is true for $s = 51$, but false for $s = 49$.

Activity: Work with Inequalities

Prince Edward Island and Saskatchewan have the smallest numbers of provincial parks. They have 31 each. British Columbia has the greatest number of provincial parks, at 390.

Inquire

1. Write 2 inequalities that represent the numbers of provincial parks in the provinces except B.C. and P.E.I.

2. State a whole-number value of the variable that makes both of your inequalities true.

3. Find the values of x that make each of the following statements true. Assume that x is a whole number.

a) $x + 3 < 9$ **b)** $x - 2 < 7$ **c)** $x + 1 ≤ 6$

Example 1

Solve $x + 2 < 6$ for whole-number values of x.
Graph the solution.

Solution

Find the values of x so that x plus 2 is less than 6.
When $x = 0$, $0 + 2 = 2$, so 0 makes the statement true.
When $x = 1$, $1 + 2 = 3$, so 1 makes the statement true.
When $x = 2$, $2 + 2 = 4$, so 2 makes the statement true.
When $x = 3$, $3 + 2 = 5$, so 3 makes the statement true.
When $x = 4$, $4 + 2 = 6$, so 4 makes the statement false.
The solution is $x = 0$, 1, 2, and 3.
The graph of the solution is as follows.

```
 ●───●───●───●───┼───┼───┼───┼──▶
 0   1   2   3   4   5   6   7
```

Example 2

Solve $x + 3 \geq 11$ for whole-number values of x. Graph the solution.

Solution

To solve the inequality, find the values of x so that x plus 3 is greater than or equal to 11.

When $x = 7$, $7 + 3 = 10$, so 7 makes the statement false.

When $x = 8$, $8 + 3 = 11$, so 8 makes the statement true.

When $x = 9$, $9 + 3 = 12$, so 9 makes the statement true.

Every whole-number value of x greater than 7 makes the statement true.

The solution is $x = 8, 9, 10, \ldots$ The 3 dots mean *and so on*.

The graph of the solution is as follows.

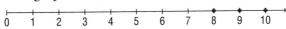

The red arrow means the solution continues without end.

Practice

Solve each inequality for whole-number values of the variable.

1. $x + 1 < 5$ **2.** $3 + t < 8$

3. $y + 2 \leq 5$ **4.** $3t \leq 12$

Solve each inequality for whole-number values of the variable from 0 to 10.

5. $x - 2 > 3$ **6.** $2 + y > 4$

7. $2w \geq 4$ **8.** $z + 1 \leq 8$

Solve each inequality for whole-number values of the variable. Graph the solution.

9. $3x > 5$ **10.** $a + 1 > 3$

11. $t + 4 \geq 9$ **12.** $3 + w < 10$

Problems and Applications

13. Canada's highest waterfall is Della Falls in British Columbia. Della Falls is 440 m high. Canada's tenth highest waterfall is Churchill Falls, Newfoundland, with a height of 75 m.

a) Write 2 inequalities that represent the heights of the other 8 of Canada's 10 highest waterfalls.

b) Write 2 inequalities that represent the heights of all 10 waterfalls.

14. Prince Edward Island is Canada's smallest province, with an area of 5660 km². The largest province is Quebec, with an area of 1 540 680 km². Write 2 inequalities that represent the areas of Canada's other provinces.

15. The elevation, in metres, of Canada's provincial capitals above sea level can be represented by the inequalities $x \geq 9$ and $x \leq 666$. How many times greater is the elevation of the highest capital than the elevation of the lowest capital?

16. Storm-force winds have speeds from 103 km/h to 117 km/h. The inequalities $s \geq 103$ and $s \leq 117$ can be used to represent wind speeds in storms. Use your research skills to find 4 more pieces of information that can be represented by inequalities. Write the inequality in each case.

NUMBER POWER

Suppose you walk the 300 km from Calgary to Edmonton. You cover 1 km the first day, 2 km the second day, 3 km the third day, and so on. How many days do you take to reach Edmonton?

Review

Evaluate for $x = 6$.

1. $x + 5$ **2.** $2x$ **3.** $x - 5$

4. $5 - x$ **5.** $\frac{x}{2}$ **6.** $x^2 - 2$

Evaluate for $x = 2$.

7. $5x$ **8.** $3x - 2$ **9.** x^3

10. $4x + 2$ **11.** $6 - x$ **12.** $2(4x)$

Evaluate for $x = 3$ and $y = 2$.

13. $x + y$ **14.** $2x + y$

15. $x + 2y$ **16.** $2x + 3y$

17. $2(x + y)$ **18.** $x - y$

19. $3x - 2y$ **20.** $2x - 3y$

Evaluate for $x = 2$ and $y = -3$.

21. $x + y$ **22.** $2x + y$

23. $3x + 2y$ **24.** $2x + y + 3$

25. $x - y$ **26.** $2x - y - 1$

Determine whether the number in brackets is a solution of the equation.

27. $x + 3 = 7$ (4)   **28.** $y - 4 = 3$ (1)

29. $\frac{t}{3} = 6$ (2)   **30.** $1 = 4m$ (4)

31. $2s + 1 = 5$ (2)   **32.** $7 = 3n - 2$ (3)

Solve and check.

33. $3x = 12$ **34.** $5n = 20$

35. $\frac{y}{2} = 5$ **36.** $\frac{a}{3} = 2$

37. $x + 5 = 11$ **38.** $b - 3 = 7$

39. $6 = z + 1$ **40.** $2 = t - 5$

Simplify.

41. $5x + 3x$ **42.** $9a - 6a$

43. $2b + 3b - 5$ **44.** $6n + 4 - 3n - 3$

Expand.

45. $4(x + 1)$ **46.** $3(2a - 2)$

47. $2(4m + 3n)$ **48.** $6(2s - t)$

Solve and check.

49. $2m + 1 = 9$ **50.** $5 + 3z = 14$

51. $6r - 3 = 9$ **52.** $6 = 2c - 4$

53. $3x + 2 = 7 + 1$ **54.** $3 + 17 = 8y - 4$

55. $2t - 3.5 = 1.3$ **56.** $4.6 = 3p + 0.7$

Solve and check.

57. $k + 4 = 1$ **58.** $q - 3 = -7$

59. $2x + 9 = 5$ **60.** $-11 = 3y - 2$

61. $2(x + 1) = -4$ **62.** $3 + 1 = 4(y + 2)$

63. $4(a + 1) = 3(a - 1)$

Use the variable x to state the inequality represented by each graph.

64.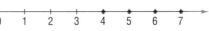

65.

Solve for whole-number values of the variable. Graph the solution.

66. $2a < 8$ **67.** $x + 3 \geq 7$

68. $t - 1 < 6$ **69.** $y - 3 \leq 4$

Write an equation to represent each sentence.

70. If you multiply a number by five, then add two, the result is seventeen.

71. Seven less than twice a number is eleven.

72. Don has $10 less than Donna, and together they have $26.

Solve each problem.

73. One sixth of Canada's planetariums are in Halifax. There are 2 planetariums in Halifax. How many planetariums are there in Canada?

74. At the Winter Olympics in Albertville, Canada and Italy won a total of 21 medals. Italy won twice as many medals as Canada. How many medals did each country win?

75. The average number of days of thunderstorms per year in Windsor, Ontario, is 5 less than 3 times the average number in Fredericton, New Brunswick. Windsor has about 34 days of thunderstorms per year. About how many days of thunderstorms does Fredericton have per year?

76. a) Copy and complete the table.

Number of Pentagons	Figure	Perimeter
1	⬠	5
2	⬠⬠	8
3	⬠⬠⬠	11
⋮		
6		

b) Write a formula for the perimeter in terms of the number of pentagons.
c) What is the perimeter of the figure made from 20 pentagons?
d) How many pentagons make up a figure with a perimeter of 101 units?

77. The highest city in the world is Bogotá, Colombia, with an elevation of 2639 m above sea level. Calgary is the sixth highest city, with an elevation of 1045 m above sea level. Write 2 inequalities that represent the elevations of the other 4 of the 6 highest cities.

Group Decision Making
Designing a Cooperative Game

In cooperative games, players are challenged to work together to achieve a common objective. One example is a game in which a group holds a circular sheet with a small hole in the middle. The objective is to keep a ball moving around on the sheet, without letting the ball fall over the edge or through the hole. Work in your home group to design a cooperative game.

1. Brainstorm to list the characteristics of cooperative games. If necessary, locate source material for ideas.

2. Decide the age group for which your game will be suitable. List the materials that may be used. These might include:

hoops   ropes   mats   chairs   balls   beanbags
balloons   parachutes   beach balls   game boards

3. Decide the objective of the game, the number of students who can safely participate, and the skills involved. Also decide where the game should be played—in the classroom? in a large area, such as a gym? outdoors?

4. Work through your ideas to develop a set of instructions for your game. Remember, all players must participate equally to achieve the objective. Check with your teacher that your game is safe.

5. Teach your game to another group. Evaluate if it has the characteristics of a cooperative game. Make adjustments, if necessary.

6. Write a complete description of your game. Include illustrations, if appropriate.

Chapter Check

Evaluate for $x = 4$.

1. $3x$ **2.** $x + 5$ **3.** x^2

Evaluate for $x = 3$ *and* $y = 5$.

4. $x + 2y$ **5.** $3x - y$ **6.** $2(x + y)$

Solve and check.

7. $3x = 15$ **8.** $\frac{x}{4} = 3$ **9.** $13 = x + 5$

10. $2x + 3 = 11$ **11.** $3x - 5 = 4$

Solve and check.

12. $x + 5 = 1$ **13.** $y - 2 = -6$

Solve and check.

14. $3(x - 2) = 6$ **15.** $6 - 4 = 2(y + 3)$

Solve for whole-number values of x not greater than 10.

16. $x \leq 3$ **17.** $x > 5$ **18.** $2 \leq x$

19. Write an inequality that the graph represents.

Solve each inequality for whole-number values of the variable. Graph the solution.

20. $x + 3 < 9$ **21.** $a - 2 \geq 8$

Simplify.

22. $4y + 2y - y$ **23.** $5t - 7 + 3t + 9$

Expand.

24. $3(n - 2)$ **25.** $2(3x + 4y)$

26. The formula for the perimeter of a rectangle is $P = 2(l + w)$.
a) Find P when $l = 12$ m and $w = 6$ m.
b) Find l when $P = 36$ m and $w = 9$ m.
c) Find w when $P = 42$ m and $l = 14$ m.

27. Canada's highest mountain is Mt. Logan, at 5959 m. The fifth highest mountain is Mt. Steele, at 5067 m. Write 2 inequalities that represent the heights, in metres, of Canada's 5 highest mountains.

28. There are two parts to Niagara Falls. The American Falls are 2 m higher than the Horseshoe Falls. The American Falls are 59 m high. Use this information to write an equation in which the variable represents the height of the Horseshoe Falls.

Solve.

29. Joseph has $2 more than Ghislain. Together they have $32. How much does Joseph have?

30. Hail falls on Cape Scott, British Columbia, on 18 days of the year. This number is 4 more than twice the number of days on which hail falls on Edson, Alberta. On how many days of the year does hail fall on Edson?

Using the Strategies

1. What are the dimensions of a cube that has a volume of 512 cm³?

2. Find three consecutive even numbers whose sum is 144.

3. Find three consecutive odd numbers whose sum is 117.

4. Copy the figure. Show how to divide it into 4 congruent shapes. Each shape must be made up of complete squares.

5. The lengths of 2 sides of a triangle are given. If x is a whole number of centimetres, what are the possible values of x?

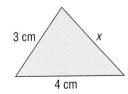

3 cm   x

4 cm

6. Tam has to have a car ready for a customer by 15:00. Tam will take 1 h 30 min to install new tires, 30 min to change the battery, 45 min to install new spark plugs and wires, and 30 min to complete the tune-up. At what time must she start the job in order to have the car ready on time?

7. Barti races mountain bikes. The day she came first and third in two races, she got 13 points. She got 8 points the day she finished second and third. For a first and a second, she got 15 points. How many points are awarded for a first? a second? a third?

8. One afternoon at the riding stable, there were riders and horses in the paddock. Pete counted 50 heads and 164 legs. How many riders and how many horses were there?

9. A shoe box is 30 cm long, 16 cm wide, and 10 cm high. You want to cover the inside walls of the box, but not the base, with one layer of centimetre cubes. How many cubes do you need?

10. Kerri was born on March 29, 1993. Rafhi was born on March 7, 1994. How many days are between their birthdays, not counting their birthdays?

11. The cost price of a ball is $6.00. The cost price is increased by $\frac{1}{2}$ to make the selling price. By what fraction should the selling price be reduced to sell the ball for $6.00?

12. a) Write the names of Canada's provinces. How many names have a ratio of consonants to vowels of 1:1?

b) Repeat part a) for the names of the provincial capitals.

13. A movie theatre is showing a popular movie, once in the afternoon and twice in the evening. Sketch a graph of the number of people in the theatre versus the time of day.

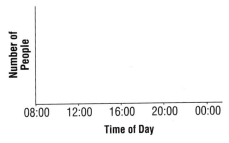

14. Pencils cost $0.50, and erasers cost $0.40. Toivo bought eight items for a total of $3.50. How many of each did he buy?

DATA BANK

1. In January, which provincial capitals have

a) an average low temperature of −8° C?

b) an average high temperature of −8° C?

2. Do New Brunswick, Nova Scotia, and Prince Edward Island have no fresh water at all? Explain.

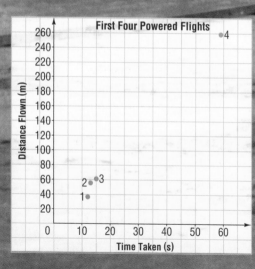

First Four Powered Flights

CHAPTER 12

Relations

The first powered flights took place at Kitty Hawk in North Carolina on December 17, 1903. Wilbur and Orville Wright paved the way for the modern airplane with their pioneer craft, which they called the *Flyer I.* They made 4 flights in one day.

The graph represents data for the 4 flights. It shows that the first flight was about 36 m long and lasted for about 12 s. To calculate the speed, s, of the flight, we can use the formula $s = \frac{d}{t}$, where d is the distance flown, and t is the time taken. For the first flight, the speed was $\frac{36}{12}$ or 3 m/s.

Use the graph to find the distance flown and the time taken for each of the other 3 flights. Use the data to find the speed of each flight. Round to the nearest tenth of a metre per second, if necessary. Give possible reasons why the speeds were not all the same.

Painting Cubes

1. The large cube has dimensions 2-by-2-by-2 and is made from 8 small cubes.

If the outside of the large cube was painted blue, how many of the small cubes would have

a) 3 blue faces? **b)** 2 blue faces?

c) 1 blue face? **d)** 0 blue faces?

2. The large cube is made from 27 small cubes and has dimensions 3-by-3-by-3.

If the outside of the large cube was painted blue, how many of the small cubes would have

a) 3 blue faces? **b)** 2 blue faces?

c) 1 blue face? **d)** 0 blue faces?

3. The large cube is made from 64 small cubes. The dimensions are 4-by-4-by-4.

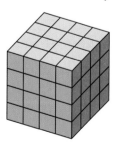

If the outside of the large cube was painted blue, how many of the small cubes would have

a) 3 blue faces? **b)** 2 blue faces?

c) 1 blue face? **d)** 0 blue faces?

4. The large cube is made from 125 small cubes and has dimensions 5-by-5-by-5.

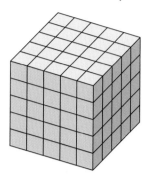

If the outside of the large cube was painted blue, how many of the small cubes would have

a) 3 blue faces? **b)** 2 blue faces?

c) 1 blue face? **d)** 0 blue faces?

5. a) Copy the table. Use the results from questions 1 to 4 to complete it.

Number of Small Cubes	Number of Blue Faces			
	3	2	1	0
8				
27				
64				
125				

b) Use the patterns in the table to complete the next row of the table for a large cube that has dimensions 6-by-6-by-6 and is made from 216 small cubes.

c) Complete the next row of the table for a large cube with dimensions 7-by-7-by-7.

Warm Up

Evaluate.

1. $x + 6$, $x = 3$ **2.** $2y$, $y = 5$

3. $m - 4$, $m = 9$ **4.** $9 - t$, $t = 6$

5. $3s + 4$, $s = 2$ **6.** $5x - 3$, $x = 4$

Evaluate for $x = 2$ and $y = 3$.

7. $x + y$ **8.** $x + 3y$

9. $5x - y$ **10.** $3x + 2y$

11. $x + y - 1$ **12.** $x + 3y - 1$

Evaluate for $x = -2$.

13. $2x$ **14.** $4x$ **15.** $5x + 2$

Evaluate.

16. $2x$, $x = -3$ **17.** $5n$, $n = -1$

18. $y + 6$, $y = -3$ **19.** $4t + 3$, $t = -4$

20. $5 + 3m$, $m = -2$ **21.** $8 - 2n$, $n = -1$

Evaluate for $x = -1$ and $y = -2$.

22. $x + y$ **23.** $x + 2y$

24. $4x - 2y + 5$ **25.** $5x + 2y + 7$

Solve for x.

26. $x + 5 = 7$ **27.** $x - 3 = 4$

28. $2x + 3 = 13$ **29.** $3x - 2 = 16$

Copy and complete each table.

30.

x	2x
5	
4	
3	
2	
1	

31.

x	x + 4
5	
4	
3	
2	
1	

32.

x	x − 2
5	
4	
3	
2	
1	

33.

x	2x + 1
5	
4	
3	
2	
1	

34.

x	x + 2
	3
	5
	7
	9
	11

35.

x	x − 1
	3
	5
	7
	9
	11

Mental Math

If the pattern continues, state the next 3 terms.

1. 1, 3, 5, 7, 9, ...   **2.** 20, 18, 16, 14, ...

3. 1, 4, 7, 10, 13, ...   **4.** 24, 21, 18, 15, ...

5. 1, 2, 4, 7, 11, ...   **6.** 1, 2, 4, 8, 16, ...

7. 3, 6, 9, 12, ...   **8.** 5, 10, 15, 20, ...

9. 3, 5, 8, 12, ...   **10.** 0, 4, 2, 6, 4, 8, ...

11. 10, 8, 13, 11, ...   **12.** 1, 4, 3, 6, 5, 8, ...

Calculate.

13. 200×0.1 **14.** 200×10

15. $200 \div 0.1$ **16.** $200 \div 10$

17. 200×0.01 **18.** $200 \div 0.01$

19. 200×100 **20.** $200 \div 100$

Calculate.

21. $15 + 5$ **22.** $1.5 + 0.5$

23. $20 + 6$ **24.** $2 + 0.6$

25. $205 + 20$ **26.** $20.5 + 2$

27. $320 + 25$ **28.** $32 + 2.5$

29. $125 + 25$ **30.** $1.25 + 0.25$

31. $75 + 25$ **32.** $0.75 + 0.25$

33. $50 + 125$ **34.** $0.5 + 1.25$

35. $150 + 125$ **36.** $1.5 + 1.25$

What is the change from a $2 bill for purchases with each of the following costs?

37. $1.25   **38.** $1.95   **39.** $0.75

40. $1.50   **41.** $0.99   **42.** $1.49

43. $0.49   **44.** $1.35   **45.** $0.89

What is the change from a $5 bill for purchases with each of the following costs?

46. $2.25   **47.** $3.80   **48.** $4.05

49. $3.49   **50.** $2.89   **51.** $3.61

52. $1.89   **53.** $2.77   **54.** $0.69

12.1 Relations as Ordered Pairs

Activity: Complete the Table

A light plane glides when the engine is turned off.
Pilots use the saying "five for one."
This means that the plane will glide 5 m for every
1 m of altitude, or 500 m for every 100 m of altitude.
Copy and complete the table of values.

Altitude (m)	Glide Distance (m)
100	500
200	
600	
1000	
1500	
2000	

Inquire

1. How many metres will a plane glide from an altitude
of 200 m? 600 m? 1500 m?

2. Write the results from the table as **ordered pairs**.
For an altitude of 100 m, the ordered pair is (100, 500),
where the first number is the altitude, and the second
number is the glide distance.

3. Write an equation in the form $d = \blacksquare \times a$ to calculate
the glide distance, d, from the altitude, a.

4. Use your equation to find the glide distance for each
of these altitudes.   **a)** 400 m   **b)** 500 m   **c)** 1250 m

The equation $x + 1 = 4$ has one variable, x.
There is one solution, $x = 3$, that makes the equation true.

There are two variables in the equation $x + y = 7$.
There are many solutions, or values of the variables, that
make the equation true.
One solution is $x = 3$ and $y = 4$, because $3 + 4 = 7$.
This solution can be written as the ordered pair (3, 4).
It is customary to write the x-value first, then the y-value.

A set of ordered pairs is known as a **relation**. A relation can also
be expressed as an equation, as a table of values, or in words.

Example 1

Use the equation $x + y = 4$.
a) Describe the relation in
words.
b) Complete a table of values
for $x = 3, 2, 1, 0, -1$.
c) Write the ordered pairs.

Solution

a) The sum of the x- and y-values is four.
b) Find the y-values. Complete the table of values.

$$x + y = 4$$
$$3 + 1 = 4$$
$$2 + 2 = 4$$
$$1 + 3 = 4$$
$$0 + 4 = 4$$
$$-1 + 5 = 4$$

x	y
3	1
2	2
1	3
0	4
-1	5

c) The ordered pairs are (3, 1), (2, 2), (1, 3), (0, 4), (−1, 5).

Example 2

Use the equation $y = 2x + 3$.
a) Describe the relation in words.
b) Complete a table of values for $x = 2, 1, 0, -1, -2$.
c) Write the ordered pairs.

Solution

a) The value of y is two times the value of x, plus 3.
b) Find the y-values. Complete the table of values.

$y = 2x + 3$
$y = 2(2) + 3 = 7$
$y = 2(1) + 3 = 5$
$y = 2(0) + 3 = 3$
$y = 2(-1) + 3 = 1$
$y = 2(-2) + 3 = -1$

x	y
2	7
1	5
0	3
-1	1
-2	-1

c) The ordered pairs are $(2, 7)$, $(1, 5)$, $(0, 3)$, $(-1, 1)$, and $(-2, -1)$.

Practice

Use each of the following equations.
a) *Describe the relation in words.*
b) *Copy and complete the table of values.*
c) *Write the ordered pairs.*

1. $x + y = 6$

x	y
3	
2	
1	
0	
-1	

2. $x + y = 2$

x	y
2	
1	
0	
-1	
-2	

3. $x - y = 2$

x	y
6	
5	
4	
3	
2	

4. $x - y = 0$

x	y
3	
2	
1	
0	
-1	

5. For the equation $x + y = 9$, find the missing value in each ordered pair.
a) $(3, \blacksquare)$ **b)** $(7, \blacksquare)$
c) $(\blacksquare, 2)$ **d)** $(\blacksquare, 0)$
e) $(-1, \blacksquare)$ **f)** $(-3, \blacksquare)$
g) $(\blacksquare, -2)$ **h)** $(\blacksquare, -7)$

6. For the equation $x - y = 1$, find the missing value in each ordered pair.
a) $(6, \blacksquare)$ **b)** $(2, \blacksquare)$ **c)** $(\blacksquare, 3)$
d) $(\blacksquare, 7)$ **e)** $(-1, \blacksquare)$ **f)** $(\blacksquare, -2)$

Use each of the following equations.
a) *Describe the relation in words.*
b) *Copy and complete the table of values.*
c) *Write the ordered pairs.*

7. $y = x + 3$

x	y
2	
1	
0	
-1	
-2	

8. $y = x - 1$

x	y
3	
2	
1	
0	
-1	

9. $y = 2x + 1$

x	y
2	
1	
0	
-1	
-2	

10. $y = 3x - 2$

x	y
2	
1	
0	
-1	
-2	

11. For the equation $y = x + 2$, find the missing value in each ordered pair.
a) $(2, \blacksquare)$ **b)** $(3, \blacksquare)$ **c)** $(-1, \blacksquare)$
d) $(0, \blacksquare)$ **e)** $(\blacksquare, 5)$ **f)** $(\blacksquare, 0)$

12. For the equation $y = x - 3$, find the missing value in each ordered pair.
a) $(4, \blacksquare)$ **b)** $(6, \blacksquare)$ **c)** $(0, \blacksquare)$
d) $(-1, \blacksquare)$ **e)** $(\blacksquare, 5)$ **f)** $(\blacksquare, 0)$

Write 5 ordered pairs for each relation.
13. $x + y = 5$ **14.** $x - y = 3$
15. $y = x + 4$ **16.** $y = 2x + 2$

CONTINUED ▶

Problems and Applications

Write an equation for each relation.

17.

x	y
1	6
2	5
3	4
4	3
5	2

18.

x	y
8	4
7	3
6	2
5	1
4	0

19.

x	y
4	5
3	4
2	3
1	2
0	1

20.

x	y
6	4
5	3
4	2
3	1
2	0

21. List 5 ordered pairs of a relation for which the y-value is always 4 more than the x-value.

22. List 5 ordered pairs of a relation for which the x-value is always two times the y-value.

23. List 5 ordered pairs of a relation for which the x-value minus the y-value is always 6.

24. Over long distances, the fastest animal on land is the pronghorn. It resembles an antelope and is found in rocky deserts of the western United States. The pronghorn can run at about 15 m/s for 6 min.

a) Copy and complete the table to show the distances a pronghorn can cover in different lengths of time.

Time (s)	Distance (m)
1	15
2	
3	
4	

b) Describe the pattern in the distance column.
c) How far can a pronghorn run in 5 s? 6 s?
d) Write the results from the table as ordered pairs.
e) Describe the relation in words.
f) Let t represent the time. Write an equation of the form $d = \blacksquare \times t$ to find the distance.

g) Use your equation to find the distance a pronghorn can cover in 12 s; 50 s.
h) What distance, in kilometres, can a pronghorn run in 6 min?
i) What is the pronghorn's average speed, in kilometres per hour, over this distance?

25. a) The figures are made up of rows of squares. Copy the table. Complete it by finding the perimeters of the figures.

Figure	Squares	Perimeter
□	1	4
□□	2	6
□□□	3	
□□□□	4	
□□□□□	5	

b) Describe the pattern in the perimeter column.
c) What would the perimeter be for 6 squares? 7 squares?
d) Write the results from the table as ordered pairs.
e) Describe the relation in words.
f) Let n represent the number of squares. Write an equation in the form $P = \blacksquare \times n + ?$ to find the perimeter.
g) Use your equation to find the perimeter of a figure made from 13 squares; 24 squares; 300 squares.

26. Describe each relationship.
a) the speed of a train and the distance it travels
b) the number of daylight hours and the time of year
c) the number of people at the beach and the outside temperature

27. Make up your own table of values like the ones in questions 17 to 20, where there is a relationship between the values of x and y. Have a classmate write an equation for the relation.

12.2 Graphing Ordered Pairs

Activity: Use the Coordinate Grid

A French mathematician, René Descartes, developed a system for plotting ordered pairs on a grid. The horizontal number line is called the **x-axis**. The vertical number line is called the **y-axis**. The two lines meet at a point called the **origin**. For any point on the grid, such as A(2, 4), the first number in the ordered pair is the **x-coordinate**. The second number in the ordered pair is the **y-coordinate**. To plot the point A(2, 4) on the grid, start at the origin, and move 2 units to the right and 4 units up.

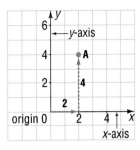

Inquire

1. Name the point that has the following coordinates.
a) (4, 4)　**b)** (8, 3)　**c)** (3, 6)　**d)** (5, 0)　**e)** (0, 6)　**f)** (7, 7)

2. State the coordinates of the following points.
a) C　**b)** L　**c)** H　**d)** M　**e)** G　**f)** I

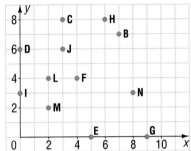

Practice

1. State the coordinates of each point.

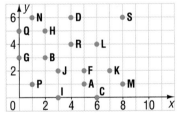

Problems and Applications

In each of the following, identify the closed figure formed by joining the points in the order given, and find the area of the figure.

2. A(1, 1), B(4, 1), C(4, 4)

3. O(0, 0), D(0, 5), E(5, 5), F(5, 0)

4. P(1, 1), Q(1, 5), R(6, 5), S(6, 1)

5. D(1, 1), E(7, 1), F(6, 5), G(2, 5)

6. W(2, 0), X(3, 5), Y(7, 5), Z(6, 0)

7. a) Plot the points P(3, 1), Q(3, 4), R(6, 7), S(9, 4), and T(9, 1) on a grid, and join the points in the order given.
b) Identify the figure and calculate its area.

8. a) Plot the points A(1, 2), B(3, 2), C(3, 5), and D(1, 5) to make a rectangle.
b) Find the perimeter and the area.
c) Multiply each pair of coordinates of the rectangle by 2. So, (1, 2) becomes (2, 4), and so on. Draw the new rectangle. Find the perimeter and the area.
d) How do the perimeter and the area of the new rectangle compare with those of the original rectangle?

9. The points D(8, 2), E(2, 2), and F(2, 5) are 3 vertices of a rectangle.
a) Plot the points on a grid.
b) Find the coordinates of G so that DEFG is a rectangle.
c) Calculate the perimeter and the area of the rectangle.

10. If you join the points (2, 1) and (2, 6) on a grid, you get the letter I.
a) What points would you use to represent the letter A?
b) Use positive coordinates to spell out a word. Have a classmate discover your word.

12.3 Graphing on the Coordinate Plane

For years, a navigator on a ship at sea used a compass, a sextant, and charts to estimate the ship's latitude and longitude. A Canadian company in Vancouver has developed an Electronic Chart Display and Information System (ECDIS). The electronic chart combines radar, satellite, and other data to display the ship's latitude and longitude on a video screen.

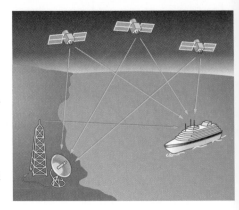

In mathematics, positions of points are given by coordinates on a grid. In this section, the coordinate plane is extended to include integers.

Activity: Study the Grid

The coordinates of point P are (3, −4).
The coordinates of point Q are (−4, −2).

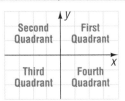

Inquire

1. State the coordinates of the following points.

a) K   **b)** L   **c)** M   **d)** N   **e)** W
f) T   **g)** R   **h)** S   **i)** U   **j)** A

2. The x- and y-axes divide the coordinate plane into 4 quadrants, as shown. In which quadrants are
a) the y-coordinates negative?   **b)** the x-coordinates negative?
c) the signs of the x- and y-coordinates opposite?

Example

a) Plot the points P(1, 2), Q(−4, 2), R(−6, −2), and S(−1, −2) on a grid. Join the points in order.
b) Calculate the area of the figure.

Solution

a) Start at the origin.
For P, move 1 right and 2 up. For Q, move 4 left and 2 up.
For R, move 6 left and 2 down. For S, move 1 left and 2 down.
Join the points P, Q, R, S, P, in order.

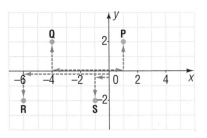

b) The figure is a parallelogram.
If the base is RS, then the length of the base is 5 units.
The distance from Q to RS is the height. The height is 4 units.

$A = b \times h$
$\quad = 5 \times 4$
$\quad = 20$

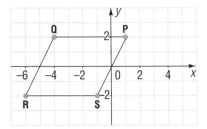

The area of PQRS is 20 square units.

Practice

1. Write the coordinates for each point.

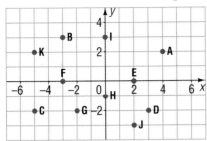

On the following grid, name the points given by these ordered pairs.

2. (2, 3) **3.** (−2, 2) **4.** (−3, −3)

5. (3, −3) **6.** (−4, −1) **7.** (−3, 4)

8. (2, 0) **9.** (0, 4) **10.** (−2, 0)

11. (0, −2) **12.** (−4, 1) **13.** (3, −1)

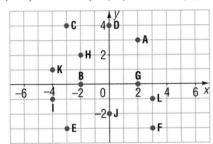

Problems and Applications

14. Plot the ordered pairs to make a word.
a) Join (−3, 0) to (−3, 1), (−3, 0) to (−5, 0), (−5, 2) to (−5, 0), (−5, 2) to (−3, 2), (−3, 1) to (−4, 1).
b) Join (−1, 2) to (1, 2), (−1, 2) to (−1, 0), (1, 1) to (1, 2), (1, 1) to (−1, 1), (1, 0) to (−1, 1).
c) Join (2, 2) to (2, 0).
d) Join (5, 1) to (4, 0), (5, 1) to (4, 2), (3, 0) to (3, 2), (3, 0) to (4, 0), (4, 2) to (3, 2).

Plot the points on a grid and join them in order. Identify each figure and find the area.

15. A(−3, 0), B(−3, 3), C(0, 3), D(0, 0)

16. E(−5, 5), F(−5, −5), G(1, −5), H(1, 5)

17. P(−1, 5), Q(−3, 3), R(−1, 1), S(2, 1), T(2, 5)

18. A(−2, 5), B(−2, −1), C(1, −1), D(1, 2)

19. D(−2, 4), E(−4, 0), F(3, 0), G(5, 4)

20. Plot A(−2, 1) and B(4, 1) on a grid. Find one pair of coordinates for
a) point C so that △ABC is isosceles
b) point E so that △ABE is obtuse
c) point D so that △ABD is a scalene right triangle
d) point F so that △ABF is an isosceles right triangle

21. △ABC has vertices A(−2, 3), B(−2, −1), and C(1, −1).
a) Plot △ABC on a grid.
b) Find the lengths of AB and BC.
c) Use the Pythagorean Theorem to calculate the length of AC.
d) What is the triangle's perimeter? area?

22. a) Points A(1, 1), B(2, 4), and C(6, 4) are 3 vertices of a parallelogram. Plot the points on a grid.
b) Find three different coordinates for point D so that ABCD is a parallelogram.

23. An ant moves from point A on a grid along a straight path determined by the points A(−3, −5), B(−2, −4), and C(−1, −3). An anteater moves from point P on the same grid along a straight path determined by the points P(−2, 6), Q(−1, 5), and R(0, 4). They move at the same speed.
a) Plot the two paths on a grid.
b) What are the coordinates of the point where the paths cross?
c) Does the ant pass in front of the anteater or behind the anteater, or do they meet where their paths cross?
d) Write 3 different ant and anteater problems. In one, have them meeting at a point. In another, have the ant passing in front of the anteater. In another, have the ant passing behind the anteater. Have a classmate solve your problems.

Interpreting Graphs

Activity ❶ Writing Statements

Using the information on the graph, you can write 2 statements about students A and B.

• Student A talked longer on the phone than Student B (or B talked less than A).

• Student B spent more time on homework than Student A (or A spent less time than B).

Write as many statements as you need to describe fully the information on the graphs.

Time Spent by Students

Time on Phone / Time on Homework (A, B)

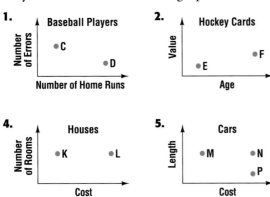

1. Baseball Players — Number of Errors vs Number of Home Runs (C, D)

2. Hockey Cards — Value vs Age (E, F)

3. Dogs — Mass vs Height (G, H)

4. Houses — Number of Rooms vs Cost (K, L)

5. Cars — Length vs Cost (M, N, P)

6. Airplanes — Speed vs Number of Passengers (Q, R, S)

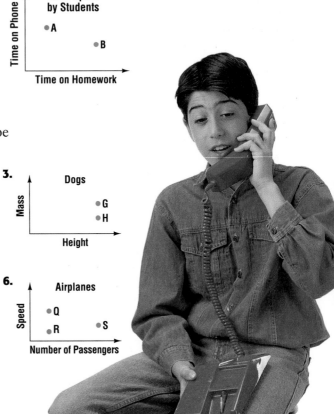

Activity ❷ Interpolating and Extrapolating

Over short distances, a jackrabbit can run at about 20 m/s.

1. Copy and complete the table to show the distances a jackrabbit can cover in different lengths of time.

Time (s)	Distance (m)
1	
2	
3	
4	

2. Draw a grid, like the one shown. Plot the 4 points and join them with a straight line.

3. When you use a graph to find information between the points, the process is called **interpolation**. Use the graph to estimate the following.

a) how far the jackrabbit can run in 2.5 s; 3.8 s

b) how long the jackrabbit will take to run 45 m; 67 m

4. When you extend a graph to find information beyond the points, the process is called **extrapolation**. Extend the graph and use it to estimate the following.

a) how far the jackrabbit can run in 5.5 s; 6.2 s

b) how long the jackrabbit will take to run 95 m; 113 m

432

Programming in BASIC

Activity ❶ Using the Quizmaker

The Quizmaker is a program written in BASIC.

The following version of the program asks for capital cities.

Enter the Quizmaker program and have a classmate take the test.

Program	Explanation
NEW	
10 PRINT	
20 REM QUIZMAKER	
30 PRINT "PROVINCIAL QUIZ"	← Test topic
50 LET N=10	← Number of questions asked
60 LET R=0	← Number of correct answers
70 LET W=0	← Number of incorrect answers
80 DATA "NEWFOUNDLAND","ST. JOHN'S"	
90 DATA "PRINCE EDWARD ISLAND","CHARLOTTETOWN"	
100 DATA "SASKATCHEWAN","REGINA"	
110 DATA "QUEBEC","QUEBEC CITY"	
120 DATA "NEW BRUNSWICK","FREDERICTON"	← Data to give questions and answers
130 DATA "BRITISH COLUMBIA","VICTORIA"	
140 DATA "MANITOBA","WINNIPEG"	
150 DATA "ALBERTA","EDMONTON"	
160 DATA "ONTARIO","TORONTO"	
170 DATA "NOVA SCOTIA","HALIFAX"	
180 FOR I=1 TO N	← Loop to keep asking questions 1 to N
190 READ X$,Y$	← Program reads questions and answers
200 PRINT "WHAT IS THE CAPITAL OF";X$;"?"	← Ask the question
210 INPUT Z$	← Enter the answer
220 IF Y$=Z$ THEN LET R=R+1:PRINT "CORRECT"	← Checking answers
230 IF Y$<>Z$ THEN LET W=W+1:PRINT "INCORRECT"	
240 NEXT I	
250 PRINT "NUMBER OF QUESTIONS ASKED";N	
260 PRINT "NUMBER OF CORRECT ANSWERS";R	← Summary of answers
270 PRINT "NUMBER OF INCORRECT ANSWERS";W	
END	

Activity ❷ Modifying the Quizmaker

1. Modify the program using your own data. Some possibilities are:

Given	Question
Movie name	Who was the male lead in …?
TV show name	Who is the female lead in …?
Rock group name	Who is the lead singer for …?
Country name	What is the capital of …?
Event in history	In what year did … happen?

2. Have a classmate take the new test.

12.4 Graphing Relations

Activity: Complete the Table

Francine has 20 m of fence for a rectangular garden. This means that the sum of the length and the width must be 10 m. There are many possible dimensions for the garden. One possible garden could be 7 m long and 3 m wide. Copy and complete the table for gardens with a perimeter of 20 m and whole-number values of the length and the width.

Length, l	Width, w	Ordered Pair, (l, w)
9		
8		
7	3	(7, 3)
⋮		
1		

Inquire

1. Graph the relation and write the coordinates of each point on the grid.

2. What does the product of each pair of coordinates represent?

3. What are the dimensions of the garden with the largest area?

Example

Graph the relation $y = 3x + 2$ for integer values of the variable.

Solution

Find 5 ordered pairs that satisfy the relation. Graph the ordered pairs.

When $x = 2$, $y = 3(2) + 2$
$= 8$
When $x = 1$, $y = 3(1) + 2$
$= 5$
When $x = 0$, $y = 3(0) + 2$
$= 2$
When $x = -1$, $y = 3(-1) + 2$
$= -1$
When $x = -2$, $y = 3(-2) + 2$
$= -4$

x	y
2	8
1	5
0	2
−1	−1
−2	−4

Many ordered pairs satisfy the relation.
The graph represents part of the graph of $y = 3x + 2$.

434

Practice

Graph each relation and express it in words.

1.	x	y
	3	0
	2	1
	1	2
	0	3
	−1	4

2.	x	y
	5	4
	3	2
	1	0
	−1	−2
	−3	−4

3.	x	y
	3	6
	1	2
	−1	−2
	−3	−6
	−5	−10

Find 5 ordered pairs that satisfy each relation. Draw each graph.

4. $x + y = 7$ **5.** $x + y = 6$ **6.** $x - y = 1$

7. $x - y = 0$ **8.** $x + y = 0$ **9.** $y - x = 2$

Find 5 ordered pairs that satisfy each relation. Draw each graph.

10. $y = x + 4$ **11.** $y = x - 2$

12. $y = 2x + 1$ **13.** $y = 3x - 4$

Problems and Applications

14. The area of a rectangle is 12 cm².
a) Copy the table. Complete it for the possible values of the length and width.

Width, w	Length, l	Ordered Pair, (w, l)
1		
2		
3		
4		
6		
12		

b) Graph the relation and write the coordinates of each point on the grid.
c) For each point, what does the sum of the coordinates represent?
d) What are the whole-number dimensions of a 12-cm² rectangle that has the smallest perimeter?

15. List 5 ordered pairs of a relation for which the *x*-coordinate is always 3 and the *y*-coordinate is an integer. Plot the points on a grid. Describe the result.

16. List 5 ordered pairs of a relation for which the *y*-coordinate is always −3 and the *x*-coordinate is an integer. Plot the points on a grid. Describe the result.

17. Jo-Anna makes ceramic mugs to sell at craft shows. She has two choices to pay for the firing in the kiln.
A: $5 set-up charge, plus $1 per mug
B: $0 set-up charge, and $2 per mug
a) List the ordered pairs for 1 to 10 mugs using choice A.
b) List the ordered pairs for 1 to 10 mugs using choice B.
c) Plot the ordered pairs for each relation on the same grid.
d) Examine the graphs and decide the number of mugs for which
- both choices give the same cost
- choice A gives a lower cost
- choice B gives a lower cost

18. The manager of a supermarket has 24 m of fence available to enclose a rectangular lot for gardening supplies.

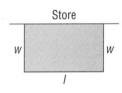

One side of the lot will be against the store wall and will not need fencing.
a) Copy the table. Complete it for the possible whole-number lengths and widths.

Width, w	Length, l	Ordered Pair, (w, l)
1		
2		
⋮		
11		

b) Graph the relation and write the coordinates of each point on the grid.
c) For each point, what does the product of the coordinates represent?
d) What are the whole-number dimensions of the rectangle that has the largest area?

Street Distances

The driving distance or walking distance between two places in a town or city is usually measured in blocks.

The shortest distance between A and B on the street map is 6 blocks.

There are several ways you can walk the 6 blocks from A to B.

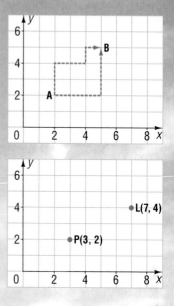

Activity ❶ Locating a Bus Stop

The library is located at (7, 4) and the post office at (3, 2).

1. a) At which corners can a bus stop be located so that the distances from the bus stop to the library and the bus stop to the post office are the same, and the distance to each one is as short as possible?

b) What is the shortest total distance from the bus stop to the library and the bus stop to the post office?

2. At which corners can a bus stop be located so that the shortest distances to the post office and to the library are each 4 blocks?

3. What is the relationship between the shortest total distance found in question 1 b) and the coordinates of the library and the post office?

Activity ❷ Locating a Swimming Pool

An elementary school, a junior high school, and a senior high school are located at E(8, 4), J(3, 2), and S(4, 6).

1. City planners want to build a swimming pool so that the total number of blocks from the pool to each of the schools is as small as possible.

a) What are the coordinates for the location of the pool?

b) What is the distance from the pool to each of the schools?

c) What is the total of the 3 distances in part b)?

d) What is the relationship between the coordinates of the pool found in part a), the coordinates of the 3 schools, and the total distance found in part c)?

2. If the total distance from the pool to the 3 schools can be 10 blocks, what are the coordinates of the possible locations for the pool?

3. a) Find the coordinates of the pool so that the elementary students walk 1 block less than the junior high students, and the junior high students 1 block less than the senior high students.

b) How many blocks is it to each school?

Activity ❸ Travelling Downtown

The theatre is located at T(5, 3), the pool at P(8, 5), the library at L(3, 6), and the record store at R(2, 2).

1. If you get a ride downtown, what are the coordinates of the corners at which you could be dropped off, if you want the pool and the library to be the same number of blocks away and the total walking distance to all 4 places to be as short as possible?

2. If you get a ride downtown, what are the coordinates of the corners at which you could be dropped off, if you want the record store and the theatre to be the same number of blocks away and the total walking distance to all 4 places to be as short as possible?

Review

 1. Describe the relation, in words, between each of the following.

   a) the number of birds and the time of year

   b) a cab fare and the distance travelled

   c) the number of traffic lights and the size of a town

 Use each of the following equations.
a) Describe the relation in words.
b) Copy and complete the table of values.
c) Write the ordered pairs.

2. $x + y = 8$

x	y
4	
3	
2	
1	
0	

3. $x - y = 5$

x	y
8	
7	
6	
5	
4	

4. For the equation $x + y = 5$, find the missing value in each ordered pair.

  a) $(1, \blacksquare)$ **b)** $(5, \blacksquare)$ **c)** $(\blacksquare, 2)$

  d) $(\blacksquare, 0)$ **e)** $(-2, \blacksquare)$ **f)** $(-1, \blacksquare)$

  g) $(\blacksquare, -1)$ **h)** $(\blacksquare, -2)$ **i)** $(0, \blacksquare)$

 Use each of the following equations.
a) Describe the relation in words.
b) Copy and complete the table of values.
c) Write the ordered pairs.

5. $y = x$

x	y
2	
1	
0	
−1	
−2	

6. $y = x + 5$

x	y
2	
1	
0	
−1	
−2	

7. $y = 2x$

x	y
2	
1	
0	
−1	
−2	

8. $y = 2x + 4$

x	y
2	
1	
0	
−1	
−2	

9. For the equation $y = x + 6$, find the missing value in each ordered pair.

  a) $(2, \blacksquare)$ **b)** $(3, \blacksquare)$

  c) $(\blacksquare, 2)$ **d)** $(\blacksquare, 0)$

  e) $(-3, \blacksquare)$ **f)** $(-2, \blacksquare)$

  g) $(\blacksquare, -4)$ **h)** $(\blacksquare, -1)$

Write 5 ordered pairs for each relation.

10. $x + y = 4$ **11.** $x - y = 1$

12. $y = x + 3$ **13.** $y = x - 4$

14. $y = 2x + 5$ **15.** $y = 3x - 1$

Write an equation for each relation.

16.

x	y
1	7
2	6
3	5
4	4
5	3

17.

x	y
5	3
4	2
3	1
2	0
1	−1

18.

x	y
3	5
2	4
1	3
0	2
−1	1

19.

x	y
5	2
4	1
3	0
2	−1
1	−2

20. a) Copy and complete the table for a car travelling at 70 km/h.

Time (h)	Distance (km)
1	70
2	
3	
4	

b) How far would the car travel in 5 h? 6 h?

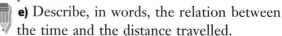 **c)** Describe the pattern in the distance column.

d) Write the results from the table as ordered pairs.

e) Describe, in words, the relation between the time and the distance travelled.

  f) Let t represent the time, in hours. Write an equation in the form $D = \blacksquare \times t$ to find the distance travelled, in kilometres.

g) Use your equation to find the distance travelled in 9 h; 12 h.

Name the points on the grid with the following coordinates.

21. (4, 0) **22.** (3, 2) **23.** (−4, 2)

24. (5, −3) **25.** (−2, −4) **26.** (0, 4)

27. (−3, 0) **28.** (5, 5) **29.** (−5, −1)

30. (0, −5) **31.** (−2, 4) **32.** (1, −3)

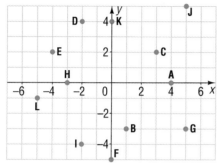

33. a) Plot and join each pair of points to form line segments.

A(−5, −3), B (5, 3)   H(−2, 3), I(2, −3)

D(−3, 4), E(4, −3)   J(−5, 4), K(−4, 5)

F(4, −1), G(−4, 1)   L(−3, 3), M(3, −3)

b) Which line segments pass through (0, 0)?

c) For the line segments that pass through (0, 0), describe any pattern you see in the coordinates of the endpoints.

Plot the points on a grid and join them in order. Identify each figure and find the area.

34. P(1, 4), Q(1, −1), R(4, −1), S(4, 4)

35. A(−1, 1), B(−1, 4), C(−4, 4), D(−4, 1)

36. D(0, −4), E(6, −4), F(4, −2), G(2, −2)

37. I(−8, −5), J(−3, −5), K(−1, −2), L(−6, −2)

38. $\triangle RST$ has vertices R(−3, 4), S(−3, −2), and T(5, −2). Plot $\triangle RST$ on a grid, and find its perimeter and area.

Find 5 ordered pairs that satisfy each relation. Draw each graph.

39. $x + y = 7$ **40.** $x − y = 2$

41. $y = x + 3$ **42.** $y = x − 4$

43. $y = 2x + 3$ **44.** $y = 3x − 1$

Group Decision Making
Writing a Story

1. In your home group, write 6 sentences, each containing the name of an object and a related number, on 6 strips of paper. Two examples are:
"The ring is 10-karat gold."
"The telephone number at the mansion is 555-1234."

2. Have each group put the strips of paper into the same container. Once the strips of paper are mixed, have a member from each group select strips of paper from the container without looking. Each group member should take as many strips as there are home groups.

3. In your home group, choose one strip of paper. Use the information on it to write the first paragraph.

4. Pass your group's first paragraph to another group—group 1 to group 2, group 2 to group 3, and so on.

5. In your group, take one of your other strips of paper. Continue the story you have just received by using the information on the strip to write the second paragraph.

6. Pass the 2 paragraphs to the same group you passed to in step 4. Use a third strip to write the third paragraph of the story your group just received.

7. Continue the process until each group has written as many paragraphs as there are groups. The last paragraph must give the story an ending. Then, pass the stories once more, so that each group gets back the story it started.

8. Meet as a class. Have each group read its story.

Chapter Check

Use each of the following equations.
a) *Describe the relation in words.*
b) *Copy and complete the table of values.*
c) *Write the ordered pairs.*

1. $x + y = 6$

x	y
4	
3	
2	
1	
0	

2. $y = 2x + 5$

x	y
2	
1	
0	
−1	
−2	

Write an equation for each relation.

3.

x	y
1	4
2	3
3	2
4	1
5	0

4.

x	y
3	5
2	4
1	3
0	2
−1	1

5. a) T-shirts at a concert cost $30 each. Copy and complete the table.

Number of T-Shirts	Cost ($)
1	30
2	
3	
4	

b) Describe the pattern in the cost column.

c) What would be the cost of 5 T-shirts? 6 T-shirts?

d) Write the results from the table as ordered pairs.

e) Describe in words the relation between the number of T-shirts and the cost.

f) Let n represent the number of T-shirts. Write an equation in the form $C = \blacksquare \times n$ to find the cost.

g) Use your equation to find the cost of 12 T-shirts; 50 T-shirts.

6. Write the coordinates of each letter on the grid as an ordered pair.

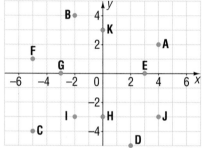

In questions 7 and 8, plot the points on a grid and join them in order. Identify the figure and find its area.

7. A(−2, 1), B(−2, −1), C(4, −1), D(4, 1)

8. E(−3, 1), F(−6, −2), G(4, −2), H(1, 1)

Find 5 ordered pairs that satisfy each relation. Draw each graph.

9. $x + y = 7$ **10.** $y = 2x + 1$

Using the Strategies

 1. The graph shows the distance of an airplane from an airport during an air show. Describe what the plane did.

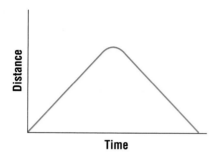

2. Copy the equilateral triangle into your notebook.

How many equilateral triangles can you make by joining points?

3. A mathematician wants to give 10 gold coins to some charities. She decides that a charity should receive only an odd number of coins. One way is to give 9 coins to one charity and 1 coin to another. Or she can give 5 to one, 3 to another, 1 to another, and 1 to another. In how many other ways can she give the coins to charities?

4. Nicole has $2.30 in nickels and quarters. If she has 34 coins, how many of each type of coin does she have?

5. A train is 1 km long and is travelling at a speed of 1 km/min. It passes through a tunnel 1 km long. How much time passes from the time the engine enters the tunnel until the last car leaves the tunnel?

6. Kayla, Phil, Janice, and Serkan line up to get into the theatre. Serkan has to go first because he has the tickets. In how many different ways can they line up?

7. Fifty-one students take a camping trip. Each tent can hold 4 or 5 people. How can the students be divided into groups so that every tent is full, and the number of tents used is less than 12?

8. A skeleton of a cube is made from wire. Each edge is 10 cm long. A fly lands on one vertex of the cube. If the fly walks along the edges and never retraces its steps, what is the greatest distance the fly can walk?

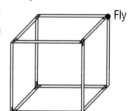

9. Laura, Mary, Hans, and Franco play tennis at the same tennis club. Their cars are red, blue, green, and yellow, but not necessarily in that order. Use the clues to match each person with the colour of his or her car.
- The owner of the yellow car beat Mary and Hans at tennis.
- Hans thinks he is a better player than the owners of the red and blue cars.
- Franco's car is neither blue nor yellow.

DATA BANK

1. The largest structure ever built by humans is the Great Wall of China. It is about 2400 km long. How many times longer is the Great Wall than the Columbia River?

 2. Use information from the Data Bank to write 2 problems. Have a classmate solve your problems.

Chapter 9

1. A recent survey gave the following information on how teenagers describe their environmental education.

Need more: 75%
Need less: 5%
Get the right amount: 20%

Display this information on a circle graph.

2. The following data show where the world's diamonds come from.

Australia   32%   Zaire   25%
Botswana   14%   Former U.S.S.R.   12%
South Africa   11%   Other Countries   6%

Display these data on a bar graph.

3. The table gives the average daily temperature each month for Santiago, Chile, and Boston, Massachusetts.

Month	Temperature (°C) Boston	Santiago
January	0	21
February	0	20
March	3	18
April	9	15
May	15	11
June	20	9
July	23	9
August	22	10
September	19	12
October	13	15
November	7	17
December	1	19

Display these data on a double broken-line graph.

4. Find the mean, median, and mode of each set of data.
a) 15, 12, 20, 21, 13, 12, 19
b) 59, 63, 58, 68, 74, 53
c) 28, 23, 29, 30, 27, 29, 30

5. a) List the possible outcomes when you spin the green and yellow spinners.
b) What is the probability of spinning a total of 4? 6? 7?

Chapter 10

Write as integers.

1. a loss of five points

2. one hundred metres below sea level

3. ten degrees above zero

Write the opposite of each integer.

4. -8 **5.** $+20$ **6.** -1 **7.** $+6$

8. Write the integers from smallest to largest.
$-1, +4, +7, -3, -6, 0, +2$

Add.

9. $(+3) + (-4)$ **10.** $(-2) + (-5)$

11. $(-6) + (+1)$ **12.** $(+10) + (-8)$

Subtract.

13. $(-5) - (+2)$ **14.** $(+1) - (-6)$

15. $(-2) - (-5)$ **16.** $(+8) - (+11)$

Multiply.

17. $(-6) \times (+2)$ **18.** $(+3) \times (+4)$

19. $(-7) \times (-5)$ **20.** $(-9) \times (+3)$

Divide.

21. $(+28) \div (+4)$ **22.** $(-63) \div (-7)$

23. $(+16) \div (-2)$ **24.** $(-48) \div (+6)$

Copy and complete each statement in standard form.

25. $-24 \div \blacksquare = -4$ **26.** $18 \div \blacksquare = -2$

27. $10 \times (-2) = \blacksquare$ **28.** $-14 - \blacksquare = 20$

29. $\blacksquare + 8 = -12$ **30.** $6 \times (-5) = \blacksquare$

Write each number in scientific notation.

31. 28 000 000   **32.** 0.0008

33. 156 000   **34.** 0.000 014

Write each number in standard form.

35. 8.2×10^5 **36.** 2.7×10^{-6}

37. 3.16×10^3 **38.** 5.29×10^{-4}

Chapter 11

Evaluate for $x = 5$.

1. $5 - x$ **2.** $x - 3$ **3.** $x + 5$

4. $x + 1$ **5.** $-3x$ **6.** x^2

Evaluate for $x = -2$.

7. $3x$ **8.** $4x - 1$ **9.** $x^2 + 1$

10. $2x + 1$ **11.** $5 - 2x$ **12.** $3(x + 4)$

Evaluate for $x = 3$ and $y = -2$.

13. $2x + 3y$ **14.** $3(x + y)$ **15.** $x - 2y$

16. $3x + y$ **17.** $5x - 4y$ **18.** $x^2 + y^2$

Determine whether the number in brackets is a solution of the equation.

19. $a - 4 = 3$ (1) **20.** $\frac{s}{3} = 2$ (6)

21. $3m - 2 = 13$ (5) **22.** $2x + 3 = 12$ (4)

Solve and check.

23. $n + 6 = 13$ **24.** $t - 7 = 9$

25. $3y = 15$ **26.** $\frac{x}{4} = 3$

27. $2w + 1 = 13$ **28.** $2(u - 1) = 4$

29. $3y = -9$ **30.** $4d + 6 = 2$

31. $3t + 4 = t - 2$ **32.** $2(g + 1) = -2$

Solve each inequality for whole-number values of the variable. Graph the solution.

33. $y \leq 4$ **34.** $y + 1 < 7$ **35.** $3p \geq 6$

36. a) Copy and complete the table.

Number of Magazines (n)	1	2	3	4
Cost, in Dollars (c)		4	8	

b) Use the variables to write a formula.
c) Use your formula to find the cost of 25 magazines.

37. The average life span of an African elephant is 10 years longer than twice the average life span of a polar bear. The average life span of an African elephant is 60 years. What is the average life span of a polar bear?

Chapter 12

Complete each table of values. Then, write the ordered pairs.

1.

x	$x + 2$
0	
1	
2	
3	
4	
5	

2.

x	$2x + 1$
-2	
-1	
0	
1	
2	
3	

Write 4 ordered pairs for each relation.

3. $x + y = 4$ **4.** $y = 3x + 1$

In each of the following, identify the figure formed by joining the points in the order given. Find the perimeter and the area of each figure.

5. A(2, 1), B(2, −1), C(−2, −1), D(−2, 1)

6. W(2, 2), X(−3, 2), Y(−3, −3), Z(2, −3)

Write an equation for each relation.

7. (1, 3), (2, 2), (3, 1), (4, 0), (5, −1)

8. (4, 1), (3, 0), (2, −1), (1, −2), (0, −3)

Write 5 ordered pairs that satisfy each relation. Draw each graph.

9. $x + y = 2$ **10.** $y = 2x - 1$

11. a) Copy and complete the table for a boat travelling at 15 km/h.

Time (h)	Distance (km)
1	
2	
3	
4	

b) Write the results from the table as ordered pairs.
c) Let t represent the time, in hours. Write an equation in the form $D = \blacksquare \times t$ to find the distance travelled, in kilometres.
d) Use your equation to find the distance travelled in 6 h; 11 h.

CHAPTER 13

Transformations

Copy the diagram onto grid paper.

Now place 6 markers onto the diagram, 3 of each kind, as shown. You could use 6 coins with 3 heads and 3 tails showing.

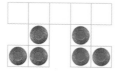

The object is to make a series of moves to reverse the positions of the markers. A move involves sliding a marker vertically, horizontally, or diagonally from its square to another square. The move does not have to be to an adjacent square. A marker cannot jump another marker.

Three first moves are shown. There are many more.

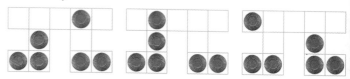

What is the smallest number of moves you can make to reverse the positions of the markers?

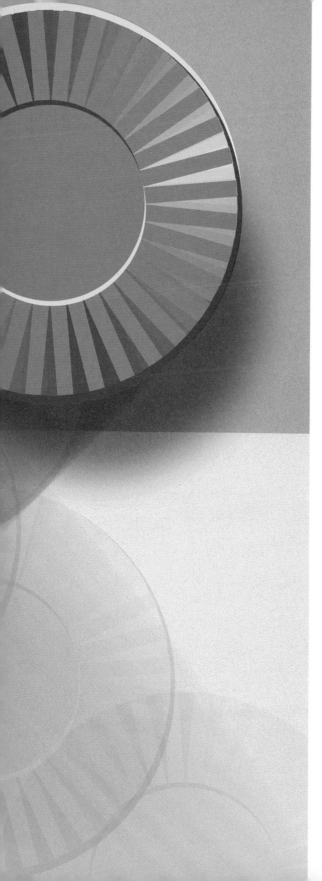

445

Exploring Transformations

Activity ❶ Slides, Flips, and Turns

1. A toboggan slides down a hill. The toboggan at the bottom of the hill is a slide image of the toboggan at the top of the hill.

Draw 2 more examples of slides, and describe why they are slides.

2. The deer reflected in the water is a flip image of the real deer.

Draw 2 more examples of flips, and describe why they are flips.

3. The second hand on a stopwatch turns about the centre. The hand pointing at 15 is a turn image of the hand pointing at 30.

Draw 2 more examples of turns, and describe why they are turns.

Activity ❷ Strip Patterns

You can use geometric shapes, and slides, flips, and turns to make strip patterns. You can find strip patterns around the tops of some buildings. The following are examples of strip patterns.

Slide

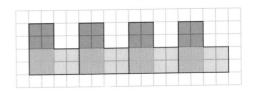

Flip

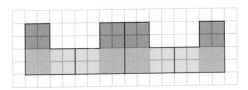

Turn

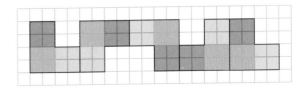

Flip, Then Slide

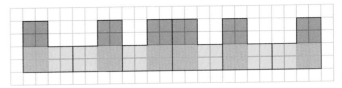

Choose a geometric shape and use it to draw
a) a slide strip pattern
b) a flip strip pattern
c) a turn strip pattern
d) a strip pattern made up of some combination of slides, flips, and turns

Activity ❸ Patterns

Identify each of the following patterns as a slide, a flip, or a turn. If the pattern is a combination, describe how the pattern was formed.

1.

F ⊤ ⅎ ⊔ F ⅎ

2.

P ꟼ P ꟼ P ꟼ

3.

Q Q Q Q Q Q

4.

R ꓤ ꓤ ꓤ R ꓤ

5.

G ꓨ ꓨ ꓨ ꓨ ꓨ

Activity ❹ Tessellations

Patterns that cover a surface without overlapping or leaving gaps are **tiling patterns** or **tessellations**. Two figures have been used to make the tessellation shown.

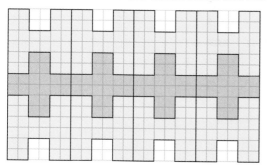

Make your own tessellation using one or more geometric figures. Colour your figures to make an interesting design.

Mental Math

Estimate each amount.

1. $3.70 + $2.99   **2.** $10.42 + $4.98

3. $6.15 + $1.98   **4.** $9.98 + $12.98

5. 2 at $3.95   **6.** 6 at $1.97

7. 3 at $2.95   **8.** 5 at $15.98

Use the numbers in the multiplication table below to help you calculate each of the following.

×	56	93	101	8	37
7	392	651	707	56	259
24	1344	2232	2424	192	888
16	896	1488	1616	128	592

9. 7×560 **10.** 1600×8

11. 80×24 **12.** 700×93

13. 160×80 **14.** 1600×3700

15. 1010×70 **16.** 5600×7000

17. $896 \div 16$ **18.** $2232 \div 93$

Look for compatible factors and multiply.
For example: $2 \times 8 \times 5 \times 9 = (2 \times 5) \times (8 \times 9)$
$$= 10 \times 72$$
$$= 720$$

19. $2 \times 65 \times 5$ **20.** $2 \times 7 \times 6 \times 5$

21. $25 \times 6 \times 4 \times 7$ **22.** $4 \times 8 \times 75$

23. $15 \times 9 \times 2$ **24.** $4 \times 8 \times 15$

25. $7 \times 2 \times 25$ **26.** $6 \times 12 \times 500$

Make compatible factors and multiply mentally.
For example: $36 \times 25 = 9 \times (4 \times 25)$
$$= 9 \times 100$$
$$= 900$$

27. 28×25 **28.** 32×25

29. 14×45 **30.** 25×18

31. 25×40 **32.** 50×22

33. 160×250 **34.** 20×35

13.1 Translations

Speed trials are attempts to achieve world speed records for cars. One place they are held is at the Bonneville Salt Flats in Utah. The tracks are straight and 1.6 km long.

A car travelling along a straight track undergoes a **translation**, which is a motion described by length and direction.

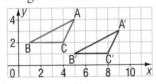

Activity: Study the Diagram

The diagram shows a translation. △A′B′C′ is the translation image of △ABC. The translation is shown by the red arrow.

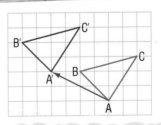

Inquire

1. How many units does △ABC move to the left? move up?

2. Trace △ABC. Then, compare the measures of the sides and the angles of △ABC and △A′B′C′.

3. Are the triangles congruent? Explain.

Say: "A prime," "B prime," "C prime."

A translation arrow describes the distance and direction a figure moves on a plane under a translation.

A translation can also be described by an ordered pair.
[horizontal movement, vertical movement]
The ordered pair [4, −3] describes the translation at the right.
The translation can also be described as a mapping.
$(x, y) \rightarrow (x + 4, y - 3)$

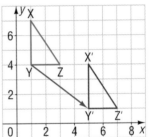

Notice that X, Y, Z and X′, Y′, Z′ read in the same direction, counterclockwise. We say that △XYZ and △X′Y′Z′ have the same **sense**.

Example

Draw the image of △ABC under the translation [4, −1].

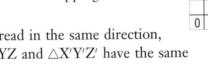

Solution

The ordered pair describes a translation 4 units right and 1 unit down.

Draw △ABC.

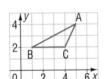

From each vertex, count 4 units right and 1 unit down to locate A′, B′, and C′.

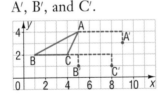

Join A′, B′, and C′.
△A′B′C′ is the translation image of △ABC.

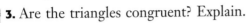

This translation can be written as a mapping. $(x, y) \rightarrow (x + 4, y - 1)$.
So, A(5, 4) → A′(9, 3), B(1, 2) → B′(5, 1), and C(4, 2) → C′(8, 1).

Practice

Draw an arrow on grid or dot paper to represent each translation.

1. 4 units left, 3 units up   **2.** [3, −3]

3. 2 units left, 1 unit down   **4.** [0, −6]

5. 4 units up   **6.** 6 units left   **7.** [4, 0]

8. a) Which quadrilateral is a translation image of quadrilateral HRPQ?

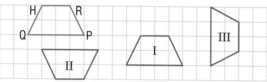

b) Describe the translation in words and in the form [x, y].

Problems and Applications

9. Copy the figure. Use each translation arrow to draw a translation image of the figure.

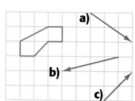

Draw each triangle on grid paper. Then, draw the translation image.

10. X(1, 1), Y(5, 1), Z(4, 3); translation [2, 4]

11. C(5, 2), A(8, 1), T(9, 3); translation [5, −3]

12. A(7, 6), B(4, 6), C(4, 4); $(x, y) \rightarrow (x − 3, y − 3)$

13. △M′N′P′ is the translation image of △MNP.

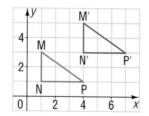

a) What translation maps △MNP onto △M′N′P′?

b) What translation maps △M′N′P′ onto △MNP?

14. A figure is translated [3, −4]. What translation would move the translation image back to its original position?

15. a) Draw △XYZ. Draw its image under the translation [4, −2]. Label the image △X′Y′Z′.

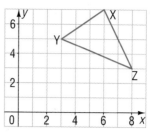

b) Translate △X′Y′Z′ under [2, 3] and label this image △X″Y″Z″.

c) What one translation maps △XYZ onto △X″Y″Z″?

16. The world's longest escalator is at Ocean Park in Hong Kong. Its inclined length is 227 m, and its vertical height is 115 m.

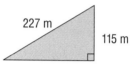

a) Use the Pythagorean Theorem to find the horizontal length of the escalator, to the nearest metre.

b) Write a translation in the form [x, y] to represent a ride from the bottom to the top of the escalator.

17. Copy the figure. Find the image of △SUN under each translation.

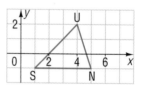

a) [5, −2]   **b)** [−2, −4]

18. State whether each statement is always true, sometimes true, or never true. Explain.

a) The size of a figure remains constant under a translation.

b) The angles of a translation image are twice as large as those of the original figure.

c) The translation image of a figure is vertically above or below the original figure.

19. Is the translation image of a figure congruent to the original figure? Explain.

20. List the properties of a translation. Describe what remains constant and what changes. Compare your list with a classmate's.

449

13.2 Reflections

When you see yourself in a mirror,
you are looking at a reflection of yourself
in the mirror. A **reflection** can be described as
a flip about a **mirror line** or a **reflection line**.

Activity: Study the Diagram

The diagram shows a reflection in the reflection line m.
Quadrilateral P'Q'R'S' is the **reflection image** of quadrilateral
PQRS.

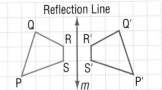

Inquire

1. Copy the diagram onto grid paper. Join PP', QQ', RR', and SS'.
What angles do these line segments make with the reflection line?

2. Measure and compare the distances from the reflection line to
the points in each of the following pairs.
a) P and P'   **b)** Q and Q'   **c)** R and R'   **d)** S and S'

3. How do the measures of the sides of quadrilateral P'Q'R'S'
compare with the measures of the sides of quadrilateral PQRS?

4. Trace quadrilateral PQRS, and compare the measures of the sides and
the angles of PQRS and P'Q'R'S'. Are the quadrilaterals congruent?

5. Do the quadrilaterals have the same sense? Explain.

A reflection is defined by its reflection line. The original figure and
its reflection image are the same distance from the reflection line.

Example

Draw the reflection
image of △ABC in the
reflection line m.

Solution

Draw △ABC and the reflection
line. Locate A' so that the
perpendicular distance from A'
to m is the same as the
perpendicular distance from
A to m. Repeat for B' and C'.

Join A', B', and C'. △A'B'C' is
the reflection image of △ABC
in line m.

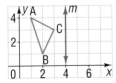
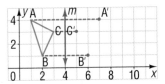
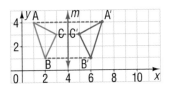

This reflection can be written as a mapping.
A(1, 4) → A'(7, 4), B(2, 1) → B'(6, 1), and C(3, 3) → C'(5, 3).

450

Practice

Each diagram below shows a reflection of a figure in the reflection line m. Name
a) *points that are the same distance from m*
b) *line segments that are perpendicular to m*

1.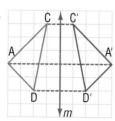

2.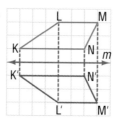

Problems and Applications

Copy each figure and its reflection line onto grid paper. Draw the reflection image. Write the coordinates of corresponding vertices of the figure and its image in the form R(6, 5) → R'(0, 5).

3.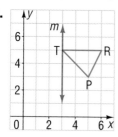

4.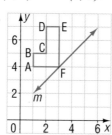

5.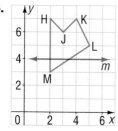

6.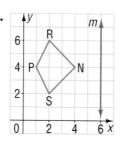

Copy each figure and its reflection image onto grid paper. Draw the reflection line.

7.

8.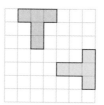

9. Copy △MNP onto grid paper.

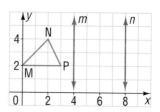

a) Reflect △MNP in *m* to give △M′N′P′. Then, reflect △M′N′P′ in *n* to give △M″N″P″.
b) What translation would map △MNP onto △M″N″P″?
c) Reflect △MNP in *n* to give △M‴N‴P‴. Then, reflect △M‴N‴P‴ in *m* to give △M⁗N⁗P⁗.
d) What translation would map △MNP onto △M⁗N⁗P⁗?

Copy each figure and the reflection line. Draw the reflection image of each figure. Write the coordinates of the vertices of the original figure and its image.

10.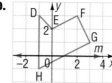

11.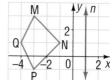

12. State whether each statement is always true, sometimes true, or never true. Explain.
a) The line joining corresponding vertices of a figure and its reflection image is perpendicular to the reflection line.
b) A vertex of a figure is twice as far from the reflection line as the corresponding vertex of its reflection image.
c) A reflection line is vertical or horizontal.

13. Is a figure congruent to its reflection image? Explain.

14. Create a poster showing reflections in photographs, wallpaper, or tilings.

15. List the properties of a reflection. Describe what stays the same and what changes. Compare your list with a classmate's.

451

13.3 Rotations

A wind machine can be used to convert the energy of the wind into electricity. The blades of the machine rotate about a fixed point when the wind catches them.

A **rotation** can be described as a turn about a point. This point is called the **turn centre**.

Activity: Study the Diagram

The diagram shows a rotation.
△D′E′F is the **rotation image** of △DEF.

Inquire

1. Where is the turn centre?

2. How many degrees has △DEF been rotated?

3. Was the rotation clockwise (cw) or counterclockwise (ccw)? Explain.

4. Trace △DEF. Then, compare the measures of the sides and the angles of △DEF and △D′E′F.

5. Are the triangles congruent? Explain.

6. Do the triangles have the same sense?

A rotation of 90° is a $\frac{1}{4}$ turn, a rotation of 180° is a $\frac{1}{2}$ turn, a rotation of 270° is a $\frac{3}{4}$ turn, and a rotation of 360° is a full turn.

Example

Draw the rotation image of ABCD when it is rotated 180° clockwise about S.

Solution

Draw ABCD.
Trace ABCD.

Rotate the tracing 180° clockwise about S. Mark A′, B′, C′, and D′. Complete A′B′C′D′. A′B′C′D′ is the rotation image of ABCD.

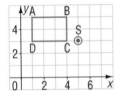
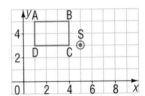
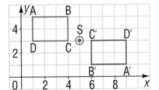

This rotation can be written as a mapping.
A(1, 5) → A′(9, 1), B(4, 5) → B′(6, 1), C(4, 3) → C′(6, 3), and D(1, 3) → D′(9, 3).

Practice

In each diagram, the green flag has been rotated about the turn centre. The purple flag is the image. For each rotation, describe the following.
a) the amount of rotation
b) the direction of the rotation

1. 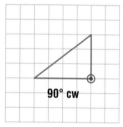 **2.** 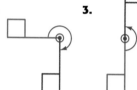 **3.**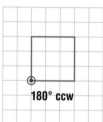

Problems and Applications

Copy each figure onto grid paper. Draw the image after the rotation about the turn centre.

4.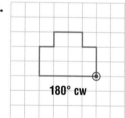

90° cw

5.

180° ccw

6.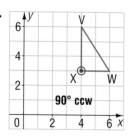

180° cw

7.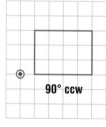

90° ccw

Copy each figure onto grid paper. Draw the rotation image for the given rotation. Then, write the coordinates of the corresponding vertices of each figure and its image as a mapping.

8.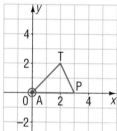

90° ccw

9.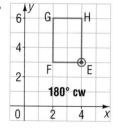

180° cw

Give an amount of rotation and a direction of rotation equal to each of these rotations.

10. 180° counterclockwise

11. 90° clockwise   **12.** 270° clockwise

13. △PQR has vertices P(8, 7), Q(4, 4), and R(8, 4). Find the coordinates of the image of △PQR for each of these rotations.
a) $\frac{1}{4}$ turn cw about R **b)** $\frac{1}{2}$ turn ccw about Q
c) $\frac{1}{2}$ turn cw about P **d)** $\frac{3}{4}$ turn ccw about R

Copy each figure onto grid paper. Draw the rotation images for the following rotations about the origin. Write the coordinates of the corresponding vertices of each figure and its image as a mapping.
a) 180° clockwise
b) 90° counterclockwise
c) 270° counterclockwise

14. 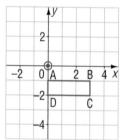 **15.**

16. State whether each of the following is always true, sometimes true, or never true. Explain.
a) The lengths of a side of a figure and the corresponding side of its rotation image are equal.
b) A rotation of 180° clockwise gives the same image as a rotation of 90° counterclockwise.
c) The rotation of a figure moves it from one quadrant to another quadrant.

17. Are a figure and its rotation image congruent? Explain.

18. List the properties of a rotation. Describe what stays the same and what changes. Compare your list with a classmate's.

453

The Drawings of M.C. Escher

A Dutch artist named M.C. Escher made a collection of paintings using tessellations and mathematical transformations.

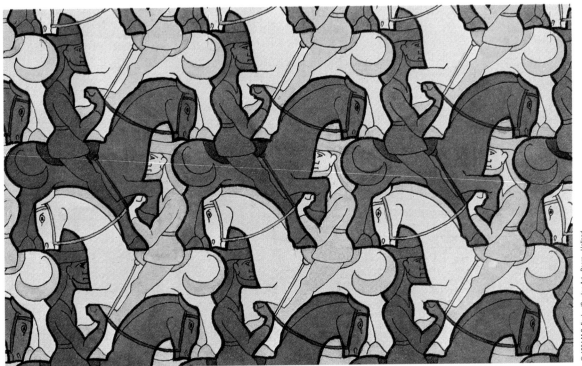

Activity ❶ Tessellating with Translations

1. Take a four-sided shape that tessellates the plane.

2. Make an alteration on one side of the figure.

3. Translate the change to the opposite side of the figure.

4. Show how your new shape tessellates the plane.

Activity ❷ Changing Two Sides

1. Use grid paper.

2. Alter two sides that meet at a vertex.

3. Translate each change to the opposite side.

4. Show how your new shape tessellates the plane.

5. Try the same activity with a rhombus or a rectangle.

454

Activity ❸ Tessellating with Hexagons

1. Alter 3 adjoining sides of a hexagon.

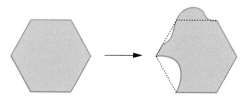

2. Translate each change to the opposite side.

3. Show how your shape tessellates the plane.

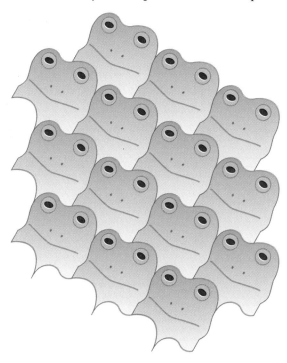

Activity ❹ Tessellating with Rotations

1. Draw a quadrilateral, such as a rectangle. Make a change on one half of one side.

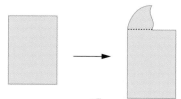

2. Rotate the change about the midpoint of the side.

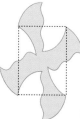

3. Translate the changes on one side to the opposite side.

4. Repeat steps 1, 2, and 3 for the other pair of sides of the rectangle.

5. Show how your shape tessellates the plane.

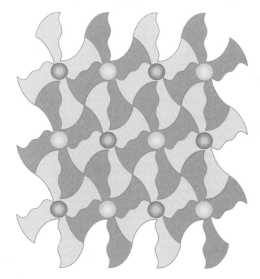

455

Enlargements, Reductions, and Distortions

Activity ❶ Enlargements and Reductions

1. Draw a grid of squares with sides twice as long as in the grid below.

2. Make an enlargement of the whale by copying the contents of each square in the grid below into corresponding squares in the grid from step 1.

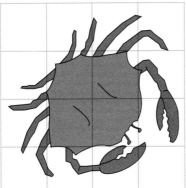

3. Repeat steps 1 and 2 for the crab and the bird, below.

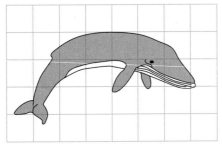

4. Make a reduction of the crab and the bird by using a grid of squares whose side lengths are half as long as in the given grid.

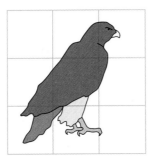

5. a) Draw a grid of 3 cm × 3 cm squares over a picture from a magazine or a newspaper.

b) Draw a grid with 1 cm × 1 cm squares. Use this grid to make a reduction of your picture.

Activity ❷ Enlargements of Cubes

1. Sketch a cube with edges of length 1 unit.

2. Draw an enlargement image of the cube with edges twice the length of the edges of the cube in step 1.

3. Write these ratios.

a) (length of sides in image cube):(length of sides in original cube)

b) (area of one face of image cube):(area of one face of original cube)

c) (total surface area of image cube):(total surface area of original cube)

d) (volume of image cube):(volume of original cube)

4. Repeat steps 1 to 3, but draw the edges of the image cube

a) 3 times longer than the original edges

b) 4 times longer than the original edges

5. Compare the original cube and the 3 image cubes. Copy and complete the following statements.

a) When the edges of a cube are made 2 times longer:
• The surface area is ▇ times greater.
• The volume is ▇ times greater.

b) When the edges of a cube are made 3 times longer:
• The surface area is ▇ times greater.
• The volume is ▇ times greater.

c) When the edges of a cube are made 4 times longer:
• The surface area is ▇ times greater.
• The volume is ▇ times greater.

d) When the edges of a cube are made k times longer:
• The surface area is ▇ times greater.
• The volume is ▇ times greater.

6. An original piece of sculpture required 3 L of clay. Use the relationships you discovered in step 5 to decide the volume of clay a sculptor needs to make a model with lengths 4 times the lengths in the original sculpture.

Activity ❸ Distortions

The diagram below right is a distortion image of the diagram below left.

Distorted grids can be used to draw distortion images. Distorted grids can be constructed from
- curved lines

- radiated lines

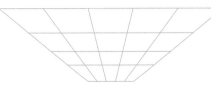

- parallelograms or rectangles

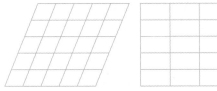

1. Choose two of the distorted grids and copy them onto a piece of paper. Make the sides of each grid unit about twice as large as the sides of the grid units on this page.

2. Choose one of the objects in Activity 1 and use each of your distorted grids to make a distortion image of your chosen object.

3. Construct your own distorted grid and make a distortion image of your chosen object.

Activity ❹ More Transformations

1. Graph the points on a coordinate plane, and join them in the order given. C(1, 3), W(3, 3), R(3, 4), P(4, 4), L(4, 2), T(2, 1), C(1, 3)

2. Perform the transformation described by the mapping $(x, y) \rightarrow (2x, 2y)$. This means that you multiply each coordinate of a point by 2 to get a coordinate of its image. List the ordered pairs for the image points C′, W′, and so on, to T′.

3. Plot the points C′, W′, R′, P′, L′, and T′, and join them in order.

4. List the properties of the transformation. What stays the same and what changes?

5. Repeat steps 2 to 4 for the following transformations.
a) $(x, y) \rightarrow (-x, y)$
b) $(x, y) \rightarrow (-x, -y)$
c) $(x, y) \rightarrow \left(\frac{1}{2}x, \frac{1}{2}y\right)$
d) $(x, y) \rightarrow (-2x, -2y)$

6. For each transformation in step 5, compare the locations of the original figure and its image. Describe the relation between the locations of the original figure and the image figure.

457

13.4 Dilatations

For translations, reflections, and rotations, the original figure and its image are congruent. After a **dilatation**, the original figure and its image have the same shape, but the sizes are different. If the image is larger than the original, the dilatation is an **enlargement**. If the image is smaller than the original, the dilatation is a **reduction**.

The picture of the oil painting *Big Raven*, by the Canadian artist Emily Carr, is a reduction of the original painting.

Activity: Use the Diagram

The diagram shows a dilatation. Rectangle A′B′C′D′ is a **dilatation image** of rectangle ABCD. The coordinates of the vertices of rectangle ABCD are A(2, 4), B(2, 2), C(3, 2), and D(3, 4). Draw the two rectangles on a grid.

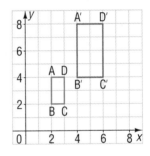

Inquire

1. Write the coordinates of the vertices of rectangle A′B′C′D′.

2. How do the coordinates of A and A′ compare?

3. How do the coordinates of B and B′, C and C′, and D and D′ compare?

4. How do the lengths of the sides of ABCD compare with the corresponding lengths of the sides of A′B′C′D′?

5. How do the ratios of the lengths $\frac{A'B'}{AB}$, $\frac{B'C'}{BC}$, $\frac{C'D'}{CD}$, and $\frac{A'D'}{AD}$ compare?

6. How do the angles of ABCD compare with the corresponding angles of A′B′C′D′?

7. Draw a line from the origin, O, through A, and extend it. Does the line pass through A′?

8. Does a straight line from the origin pass through B and B′? C and C′? D and D′?

9. How do the lengths of OA and OA′ compare? OB and OB′? OC and OC′? OD and OD′?

10. The rectangle ABCD has been enlarged by a dilatation. The **scale factor** is 2, and the **dilatation centre** is (0, 0). Why is the scale factor 2? Why is the dilatation centre (0, 0)?

When a figure is plotted on a coordinate grid, the figure can be dilatated, with dilatation centre (0, 0), by multiplying the coordinates of the vertices of the figure by a scale factor.

A figure can also be dilatated by first connecting each vertex to the dilatation centre with a line segment. The length of each line segment can then be multiplied by the scale factor to locate each vertex of the dilatation image, as shown below.

To reduce the square by a scale factor of $\frac{1}{2}$, with the given dilatation centre O:

1. Join each of the 4 vertices to the dilatation centre O.

2. Multiply the lengths of OA, OB, OC, and OD by $\frac{1}{2}$ to locate A', B', C', and D'.

3. Join A', B', C', and D'. A'B'C'D' is the dilatation image of ABCD.

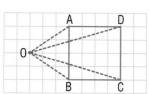
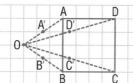
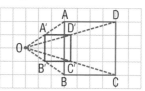

This dilatation can be written as a mapping. $(x, y) \rightarrow \left(\frac{1}{2}x, \frac{1}{2}y\right)$

Problems and Applications

1. Enlarge each figure by a scale factor of 2, with the dilatation centre (0, 0). Write the coordinates of the vertices of each image.

a)
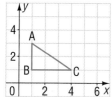

b)
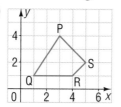

2. Repeat question 1 for a scale factor of 3.

3. Reduce each figure by a scale factor of $\frac{1}{2}$, with the dilatation centre (0, 0). Write the coordinates of the vertices of each image.

a)
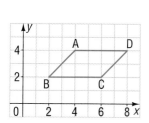

b)
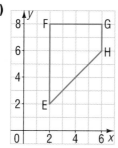

Copy each figure onto grid paper. Draw the dilatation image, given the dilatation centre and the scale factor.

4. scale factor 3

5. scale factor 2
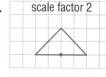

6.

scale factor 2

7.
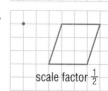
scale factor $\frac{1}{2}$

8. A photographer processed a negative film with dimensions 4 cm × 5 cm into a photograph of dimensions 20 cm × 25 cm. What was the scale factor?

9. a) Are maps examples of dilatations? Explain.
b) Investigate 5 different maps. Find the scale factor of each map.
c) Write another name for the scale factor of a map.

10. Write the coordinates of the vertices of the dilatation image of PQRS for each scale factor. The dilatation centre is (0, 0).
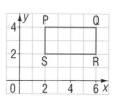

a) −2   **b)** −$\frac{1}{2}$

459

13.5 Similar Figures

Similar figures have the same shape, but not necessarily the same size.

Activity: Discover the Relationship

△TNE is similar to △CFA. Copy the figures onto grid paper.
Use a protractor to measure the angles of each figure.

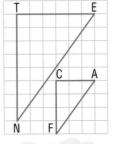

In △TNE   ∠T = ⬛   ∠N = ⬛   ∠E = ⬛
In △CFA   ∠C = ⬛   ∠F = ⬛   ∠A = ⬛

Use a ruler to measure the lengths of corresponding sides.

In △TNE   TN = ⬛   NE = ⬛   TE = ⬛
In △CFA   CF = ⬛   FA = ⬛   CA = ⬛

Corresponding sides are opposite equal angles.

Inquire

1. How are the measures of the corresponding angles related?

2. Write the following ratios in lowest terms.
$$\frac{TN}{CF} \qquad \frac{NE}{FA} \qquad \frac{TE}{CA}$$

3. How are the ratios of the lengths of corresponding sides related?

4. Write a statement involving the measures of corresponding angles and the ratios of the lengths of corresponding sides in similar triangles.

5. Similar figures are dilatation images of each other. What scale factor is used to transform

a) △TNE into △CFA?   **b)** △CFA into △TNE?

Triangles GHI and XYZ are similar.
The similarity statement is: △GHI ~ △XYZ.
The order of the letters shows the corresponding equal angles and indicates the corresponding sides.

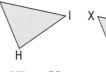

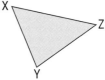

∠G = ∠X, ∠H = ∠Y, ∠I = ∠Z, and $\dfrac{GH}{XY} = \dfrac{HI}{YZ} = \dfrac{GI}{XZ}$

Example

△ABC and △PQR are similar.

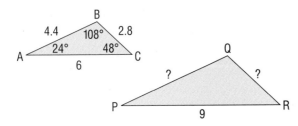

a) Find the measures of ∠P, ∠Q, and ∠R.
b) Find the lengths of PQ and QR.

Solution

a) For similar triangles, corresponding angles are equal. ∠A = ∠P = 24°, ∠B = ∠Q = 108°, ∠C = ∠R = 48°.

b) For similar triangles, the ratios of corresponding sides are equal.

$$\frac{PQ}{AB} = \frac{QR}{BC} = \frac{RP}{CA}, \text{ and } \frac{RP}{CA} = \frac{9}{6} \text{ or } \frac{3}{2}$$

$$\frac{PQ}{AB} = \frac{PQ}{4.4} = \frac{3}{2} \qquad\qquad \frac{QR}{BC} = \frac{QR}{2.8} = \frac{3}{2}$$

$$4.4 \times \frac{PQ}{4.4} = 4.4 \times \frac{3}{2} \qquad 2.8 \times \frac{QR}{2.8} = 2.8 \times \frac{3}{2}$$

$$PQ = \frac{4.4 \times 3}{2} \qquad\qquad QR = \frac{2.8 \times 3}{2}$$

$$PQ = 6.6 \qquad\qquad QR = 4.2$$

Practice

Each pair of triangles is similar.
a) *Name the equal angles.*
b) *Write the proportion for the sides.*
c) *Write a similarity statement.*

1.

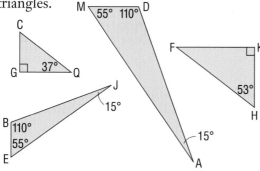

2.

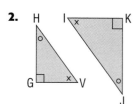

3.

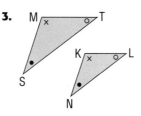

4. Decide which triangles are similar. Write similarity statements for pairs of similar triangles.

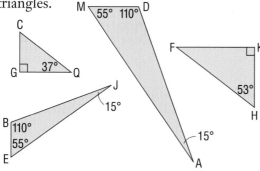

5. The overlapping triangles, △ABC and △AYZ, can be separated into 2 triangles.

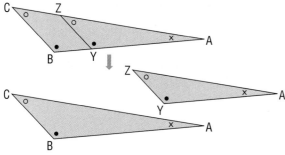

a) Name the equal angles.
b) Write the proportion for the sides.
c) Write a similarity statement.

Problems and Applications

6. △SPD ~ △SKN.
The ratio of corresponding sides $\frac{SK}{SP}$ is $\frac{1}{3}$.
Find these lengths.
a) SP   **b)** PD
c) DS   **d)** KP

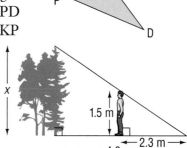

7. Find the height of the tree.

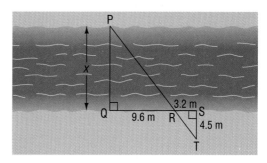

8. a) Which triangles are similar?

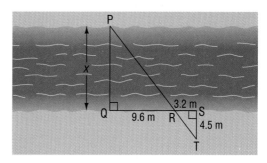

b) Calculate the value of the ratio of corresponding sides.
c) Find the width of the river.

9. Congruent triangles are always similar, but similar triangles are not always congruent. Explain.

10. a) Draw a rectangle. Find its perimeter and area.
b) Draw a second rectangle whose sides are twice the sides of your original rectangle. Find the perimeter and the area of the second rectangle.
c) Compare your results from parts a) and b).
d) Describe how the perimeter and the area of a rectangle increase when the side lengths increase by a factor of k.

Transformations on a Spreadsheet

Activity ❶

1. Use grid paper to set up a coordinate plane with 4 quadrants. Label the axes x and y.

2. Plot the following points and join them in alphabetical order to make an airplane.
M(8, 7), N(6, 6), P(4, 8), Q(4, 6), R(5, 5), S(3, 3), T(2, 1), V(4, 2), W(6, 4), X(7, 3), Y(9, 3), Z(7, 5), then back to M.

Activity ❷

1. Use a computer spreadsheet, or a table in your notebook, to set up the ordered pairs (x, y). Put the letter that names the point in column A. Put the x-coordinates in column B and the y-coordinates in column C. A partial table is shown.

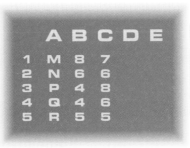

	A	B	C	D	E
1	M	8	7		
2	N	6	6		
3	P	4	8		
4	Q	4	6		
5	R	5	5		

2. Apply the transformation $(x, y) \rightarrow (x + 3, y - 5)$ to the coordinates of the airplane to make an image of the airplane. To add 3 to all the values in column B, go to cell D1, type +B1+3, and hit the enter key. Use the copy function to copy the formula to cells D2 to D13, so that 3 is added to each x-coordinate in column B.

To subtract 5 from all the values in column C, go to cell E1, type +C1−5, and hit the enter key. Use the copy function to copy the formula to cells E2 to E13, so that 5 is subtracted from each y-coordinate in column C.

Use the new x-coordinates from column D and the new y-coordinates from column E to plot your new airplane on grid paper. Describe the transformation.

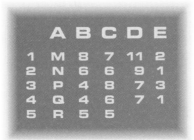

	A	B	C	D	E
1	M	8	7	11	2
2	N	6	6	9	1
3	P	4	8	7	3
4	Q	4	6	7	1
5	R	5	5		

Activity ❸

Use your spreadsheet to transform your original airplane under the mapping $(x, y) \rightarrow (-x, -y)$. To multiply all the values in column B by -1, go to cell D1, type $+B1*(-1)$, and hit the enter key. Use the copy function to copy the formula to cells D2 to D13, so that each x-coordinate in column B is multiplied by -1.

To multiply all the values in column C by -1, go to cell E1, type $+C1*(-1)$, and hit the enter key. Use the copy function to copy the formula to cells E2 to E13, so that each y-coordinate in column C is multiplied by -1.

	A	B	C	D	E
1	M	8	7	-8	-7
2	N	6	6	-6	-6
3	P	4	8	-4	-8
4	Q	4	6	-4	-6
5	R	5	5	-5	-5

Use the new x-coordinates from column D and the new y-coordinates from column E to plot your new airplane on grid paper. Describe this transformation.

Activity ❹

Draw the image of your airplane under each of these transformations. Describe what each transformation does to the original airplane.

1. $(x, y) \rightarrow (2x, 2y)$
2. $(x, y) \rightarrow (-x, y)$
3. $(x, y) \rightarrow (x, -y)$

Activity ❺

Write a transformation of your own. Predict what the transformation will do to the airplane. Using your transformation, draw the image of the airplane.

Symmetry

Activity ❶ Line and Rotational Symmetry

1. A line of symmetry is a mirror line that reflects an object onto itself. The Jamaican flag has two lines of symmetry. Copy the Jamaican flag into your notebook and draw the lines of symmetry.

2. The Jamaican flag has **rotational symmetry**, or turn symmetry, of order 2. Trace your copy of the Jamaican flag. Put the tracing on top of your copy. Put a pencil point on the centre of the tracing. Turn the tracing. Count the number of times the tracing matches your copy of the flag when you turn the tracing 360°.

3. An equilateral triangle has rotational symmetry of order 3. Copy the equilateral triangle into your notebook. Make a tracing of the triangle. Rotate the tracing about the centre. Count the number of times the tracing matches the copy when you turn the tracing 360°.

4. A scalene triangle does not have rotational symmetry. Copy the scalene triangle into your notebook. Make a tracing of the triangle. Rotate the tracing about the centre. Count the number of times the tracing matches the copy when you turn the tracing 360°.

5. Write a definition of rotational symmetry.

Activity ❷ Chladni Patterns

A metal plate is sprinkled with sand and supported at its centre. If you draw a bowstring across an edge of the plate, the sand forms geometric designs on the plate. These designs are called Chladni patterns. Nine Chladni patterns are shown.

1. Copy the patterns into your notebook.

2. Determine the number of lines of symmetry each pattern has.

3. Determine the order of rotational symmetry for each pattern.

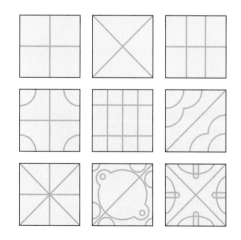

Activity ❸ Symmetry in Designs

The T-shaped mosaic was designed to advertise the Tile Store. Refer to the squares in the design as follows.

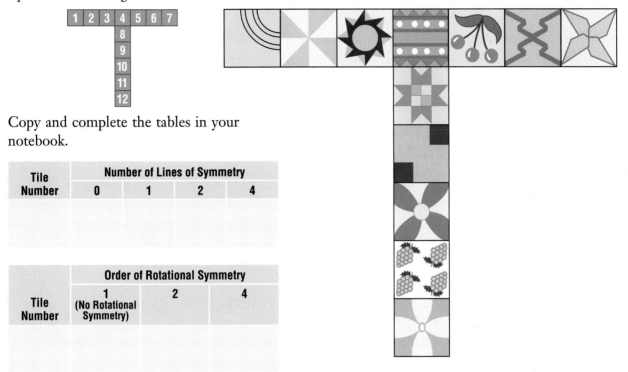

Copy and complete the tables in your notebook.

Tile Number	Number of Lines of Symmetry			
	0	1	2	4

Tile Number	Order of Rotational Symmetry		
	1 (No Rotational Symmetry)	2	4

Activity ❹ Symmetry in Logos

1. The symbols shown represent services provided by hotels and bed-and-breakfast establishments.

a) Identify any lines of symmetry that each symbol may have.

b) Describe any rotational symmetry each symbol may have.

c) Use your research skills to find out what service each symbol represents.

2. Many logos are used in business. Collect logos of businesses from newspapers and magazines. Make a poster to show rotational symmetry of orders 2, 3, 4, and 5.

3. Why do you think designers use symmetry when they design logos?

Review

Match the transformation to its related action.

1. translate   **a)** shrink or stretch

2. rotate   **b)** slide

3. reflect   **c)** turn

4. dilatate   **d)** flip

Describe each translation in words.

5.

6. [5, 0]

7. Copy the figure onto grid paper.

a) Draw the image of SBMN translated 3 units right and 1 unit down.

b) Draw the image of SBMN under the translation [1, −4].

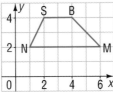

8. Draw △HKT and the image of △HKT after it has been reflected in the line *m*.

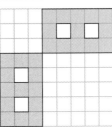

9. A figure 8 has been reflected in a line to give a second figure 8. Copy the diagram and draw the line of reflection.

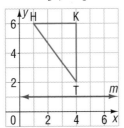

10. Copy the diagram.

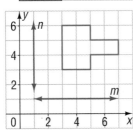

a) Draw the image of the figure after it has been reflected in the line *n*.

b) Reflect the image figure in the line *m*.

c) What transformation is equivalent to the double reflection?

11. Copy each figure onto grid paper. Draw the image after a rotation about the turn centre. Write the coordinates of the vertices of the image.

a)

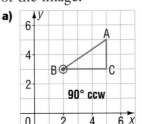

b)

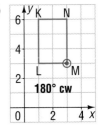

Name another rotation equivalent to each of the following.

12. $\frac{1}{4}$ turn clockwise

13. 180° clockwise

14. $\frac{3}{4}$ turn counterclockwise

15. 90° counterclockwise

Identify each of the following as a translation, a reflection, or a rotation. Copy and continue the pattern, repeating the image 4 more times.

16.

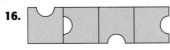

17.

18.

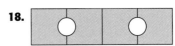

19. Copy the figure onto grid paper. Use each of the scale factors to draw a dilatation image for the given dilatation centre.

a) 2   **b)** $\frac{1}{2}$

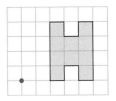

20. The triangles are similar.

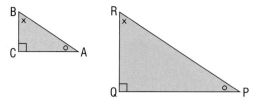

a) Name the equal angles.
b) Write the proportion for the sides.
c) Write a similarity statement.

The pairs of figures are similar. Find the unknown sides.

21.

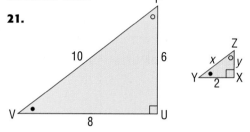

22.

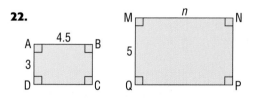

23.

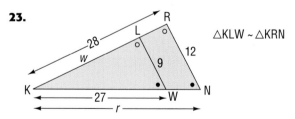

△KLW ~ △KRN

24. Copy and complete the following table. Write an S for properties that remain the same, and C for properties that change under each transformation.

Transformation	Size	Shape	Sense
Translation			
Reflection			
Rotation			
Dilatation			

Group Decision Making
Making Important Decisions

The science teacher has just given the class a list of 7 questions to study for a test. The teacher said that 4 of the 7 questions will be on the test. Students will be asked to answer any 2 questions.

1. As a class, make sure everyone understands the situation. Your task will be to work in groups to answer the following 4 questions.
a) If you studied answers to 3 of the questions, would you be ready to answer the 2 questions on the test?
b) What is the minimum number of questions you need to study?
c) How would you convince the rest of the class that your answer to question b) is correct?
d) Do you think you should study all 7 questions? Justify your answer.

2. Break into pairs for a 5-min discussion on questions a) and b).

3. Join pairs to make groups of 4.

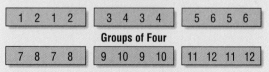

4. In your group of 4, come to an agreement on the answers to questions a) and b).

5. In your group of 4, discuss possible answers to questions c) and d). Present some answers to the class and post others on the board.

Chapter Check

Identify each pattern as a translation, a reflection, or a rotation. Draw the next two figures in each pattern.

1.

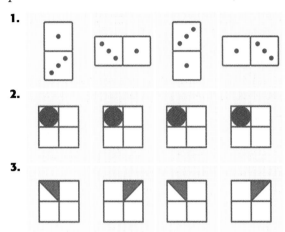

2.

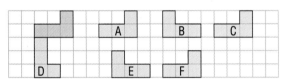

3.

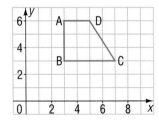

4. a) Which labelled figure(s) are translation images of the original figure?

b) Name each translation in the form $[x, y]$.
c) Which labelled figure(s) are rotation images of the original figure?
d) Which labelled figure(s) are reflection images of the original figure?

5. Copy the figure onto grid paper.

a) Draw the image of ABCD translated 2 units left and 3 units down.
b) Draw the image of ABCD under the translation $[2, 1]$.

6. Copy each figure onto grid paper. Then, draw the reflection image in line m.

a)   **b)**   **c)**

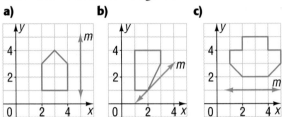

7. Copy the figure onto grid paper. Draw the image of the figure after a rotation about the turn centre.

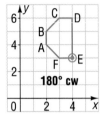

180° cw

8. Copy the figure and the dilatation centre onto grid paper. Draw a dilatation image of the figure, using these scale factors.

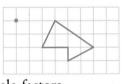

a) 3   **b)** $\frac{1}{2}$

9. Find the missing lengths in the similar triangles.

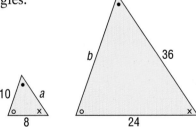

10. Figures A and B are dilatation images of the original figure. The dilatation centre is C. What is the scale factor for each dilatation?

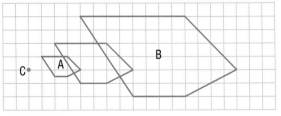

468

Using the Strategies

1. What comes next in the pattern?

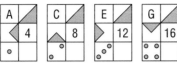

2. Each small square is to be coloured red or blue. Each row, column, and diagonal must contain exactly 2 small squares of each colour. Copy the diagram and use the rules to identify the colour of each small square.

The information in each sentence below refers only to that row or column.

1: No 2 adjacent squares are the same colour.
2: Each red is immediately to the left of a blue.
3: The 2 blues are not together.
4: Each blue is immediately to the left of a red.
A: 1 blue is above a red, and 1 blue is below the other red.
B: The blues are between the reds.
C: 1 red is below a blue, and 1 red is above the other blue.
D: The order of the colours is the same from top to bottom as it is from bottom to top.

3. a) Put a penny on the table. How many other pennies can you fit around the first penny if they must all touch?
b) Repeat the activity for quarters and for dimes.
c) How do your answers compare for each type of coin?

4. A board is 2 m in length. It is cut into 2 pieces. One piece is 18 cm longer than the other piece. How long is each piece of board?

5. A rectangular field is twice as long as it is wide. It is surrounded by a fence. The fence posts are 4 m apart. There is a post at each corner of the field. There are 30 posts. What are the dimensions of the field?

6. The school newspaper will be printed double-sided on 22 cm × 36 cm paper, and folded and stapled to make a booklet 22 cm × 18 cm. There is enough copy to fill 24 booklet pages.
a) How many pieces of paper are needed to print 1 booklet?
b) There are 458 people in the school, including the staff. How many pieces of paper are required to print a booklet for each person?
c) If the paper to be used sells for $4.99 for 500 sheets, how much will the paper to print all the booklets cost?
d) Calculate the final price of the paper if you add 15% for taxes.

7. Maria and Tony left home together to walk to school. If they had walked the whole way, they would have been late. One of them ran for a while, then walked the rest of the way. The other walked and then ran. Use the graph to answer the following. Explain your reasoning.
a) Who walked and then ran?
b) Who arrived at the school first?

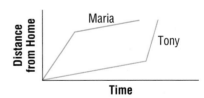

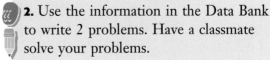

1. a) What is the lowest average annual temperature for a provincial capital?
b) How many provincial capitals have this average annual temperature?

2. Use the information in the Data Bank to write 2 problems. Have a classmate solve your problems.

FLYING DISTANCES BETWEEN CANADIAN CITIES

From	To	(km)
Calgary	Edmonton	248
	Montreal	3003
	Ottawa	2877
	Regina	661
	Saskatoon	520
	Toronto	2686
	Vancouver	685
	Victoria	725
	Winnipeg	1191
Charlottetown	Ottawa	976
	Toronto	1326
Edmonton	Calgary	248
	Ottawa	2848
	Regina	698
	Saskatoon	484
	Toronto	2687
	Vancouver	826
	Winnipeg	1187
Halifax	Montreal	803
	Ottawa	958
	Saint John	192
	St. John's	880
	Sydney	306
	Toronto	1287
Montreal	Calgary	3003
	Fredericton	562
	Halifax	803
	Moncton	707
	Ottawa	151
	Saint John	614
	St. John's	1618
	Toronto	508
	Vancouver	3679
	Winnipeg	1816

From	To	(km)
Ottawa	Calgary	2877
	Charlottetown	976
	Edmonton	2848
	Halifax	958
	Montreal	151
	Toronto	363
	Vancouver	3550
	Winnipeg	1687
Regina	Calgary	661
	Edmonton	698
	Saskatoon	239
	Toronto	2026
	Vancouver	1330
	Winnipeg	533
St. John's	Halifax	880
	Montreal	1618
	Toronto	2122
Toronto	Calgary	2686
	Charlottetown	1326
	Edmonton	2687
	Halifax	1287
	Montreal	508
	Ottawa	363
	Regina	2026
	St. John's	2122
	Vancouver	3342
	Windsor	314
	Winnipeg	1502
Victoria	Calgary	725
	Vancouver	62
Windsor	Toronto	314
Winnipeg	Calgary	1191
	Edmonton	1187
	Montreal	1816
	Ottawa	1687
	Regina	533
	Saskatoon	707
	Toronto	1502
	Vancouver	1862

DRIVING DISTANCES BETWEEN CANADIAN CITIES (km)

From \ To	Edmonton	Halifax	Montreal	Ottawa	Quebec City	Regina	Saint John	St. John's	Saskatoon	Toronto	Vancouver	Victoria	Whitehorse	Winnipeg
Calgary	299	4973	3743	3553	4014	764	4664	6334	620	3434	1057	1162	2385	1336
Edmonton		5013	3764	3574	4035	785	4704	6367	528	3455	1244	1349	2086	1357
Halifax			1249	1439	982	4228	309	1503	4485	1788	6050	6154	7099	3656
Montreal				190	270	2979	940	2602	3236	539	4801	4905	5850	2408
Ottawa					460	2789	1130	2792	3046	399	4611	4715	5660	2218
Quebec City						3249	673	2363	3507	809	5071	5176	6120	2678
Regina							3919	5581	257	2670	1822	1926	2871	571
Saint John								1727	4176	1479	5741	5845	6790	3347
St. John's									5839	3141	7403	7775	8452	5010
Saskatoon										2927	1677	1782	2614	829
Toronto											4492	4596	5528	2099
Vancouver												105	2697	2232
Victoria													2802	2337
Whitehorse														3524

PLANETS: DISTANCES, ORBITS, MOONS

Mercury
Distance from the sun: 58 000 000 km

Time to orbit sun: 88 d

Number of moons: 0

Venus
Distance from the sun: 108 000 000 km

Time to orbit sun: 225 d

Number of moons: 0

Earth
Distance from the sun: 150 000 000 km

Time to orbit sun: 1 year

Number of moons: 1

Mars
Distance from the sun: 228 000 000 km

Time to orbit sun: 687 d

Number of moons: 2

Jupiter
Distance from the sun: 779 000 000 km

Time to orbit sun: 12 years

Number of moons: 16

Saturn
Distance from the sun: 1 425 000 000 km

Time to orbit sun: 29.5 years

Number of moons: 18

Uranus
Distance from the sun: 2 870 000 000 km

Time to orbit sun: 84 years

Number of moons: 15

Neptune
Distance from the sun: 4 497 000 000 km

Time to orbit sun: 165 years

Number of moons: 8

Pluto
Distance from the sun: 5 866 000 000 km

Time to orbit sun: 248 years

Number of moons: 1

WIND CHILL CHART

Wind Speed	Thermometer Reading (degrees Celsius)					Cold			Very Cold			Bitterly Cold			Extremely Cold
	4	2	−1	−4	−7	−9	−12	−15	−18	−21	−23	−26	−29	−32	−34
Calm	4	2	−1	−4	−7	−9	−12	−15	−18	−21	−23	−26	−29	−32	−34
8 km/h	3	1	−3	−6	−9	−11	−14	−17	−21	−24	−26	−29	−32	−36	−37
16 km/h	−2	−6	−9	−13	−17	−19	−23	−26	−30	−33	−36	−39	−43	−47	−50
24 km/h	−6	−9	−12	−17	−21	−24	−28	−32	−36	−40	−43	−46	−51	−54	−57
32 km/h	−8	−11	−16	−20	−23	−27	−31	−36	−40	−43	−47	−51	−56	−60	−63
40 km/h	−9	−14	−18	−22	−26	−30	−34	−38	−43	−47	−50	−55	−59	−64	−67
48 km/h	−11	−15	−19	−24	−28	−32	−36	−41	−45	−49	−53	−57	−61	−66	−70
56 km/h	−12	−16	−20	−25	−29	−33	−37	−42	−47	−51	−55	−58	−64	−68	−72
64 km/h	−13	−17	−21	−26	−30	−34	−38	−43	−48	−52	−56	−60	−66	−70	−74

CANADA'S LONGEST RIVERS

River	Length (km)
Mackenzie	4241
Yukon	3185
St. Lawrence	3058
Nelson	2575
Columbia	2000
Saskatchewan	1939
Peace	1923
Churchill (Manitoba)	1609
South Saskatchewan	1392
Fraser	1370

WORLD'S LARGEST ISLANDS

Island	Area (km²)
Greenland	2 175 600
New Guinea	792 540
Borneo	725 459
Madagascar	587 044
Baffin	507 454
Sumatra	427 350
Honshu	227 415
Great Britain	218 078
Victoria	217 291
Ellesmere	196 237

CANADA'S FRESH WATER

Province/ Territory	Percent of Canada's Fresh Water (nearest percent)
Alberta	2%
British Columbia	2%
Manitoba	13%
New Brunswick	0%
Newfoundland	5%
Northwest Territories	18%
Nova Scotia	0%
Ontario	24%
Prince Edward Island	0%
Quebec	24%
Saskatchewan	11%
Yukon Territory	1%

CANADA'S TALLEST WATERFALLS

Waterfall	Vertical Drop (m)
Della Falls	440
Takakkaw Falls	254
Hunlen Falls	253
Panther Falls	183
Helmcken Falls	137
Bridal Veil Falls	122
Virginia Falls	90
Chute Montmorency	84
Chute Ouiatchouan	79
Churchill Falls	75

CANADIAN WEATHER DATA

Average Monthly High and Low Temperatures

The temperature is represented by a vertical bar. The top of the bar represents the average daily high temperature for that month. The bottom of the bar represents the average daily low temperature for that month. The horizontal line represents the average annual temperature.

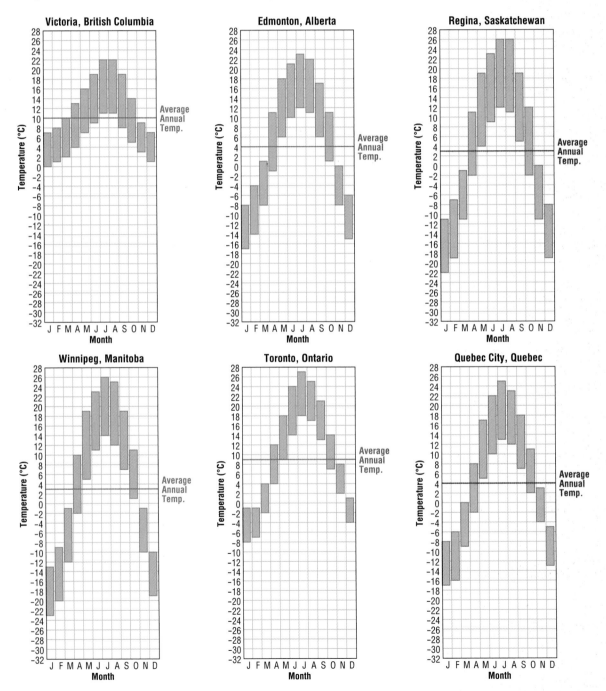

476

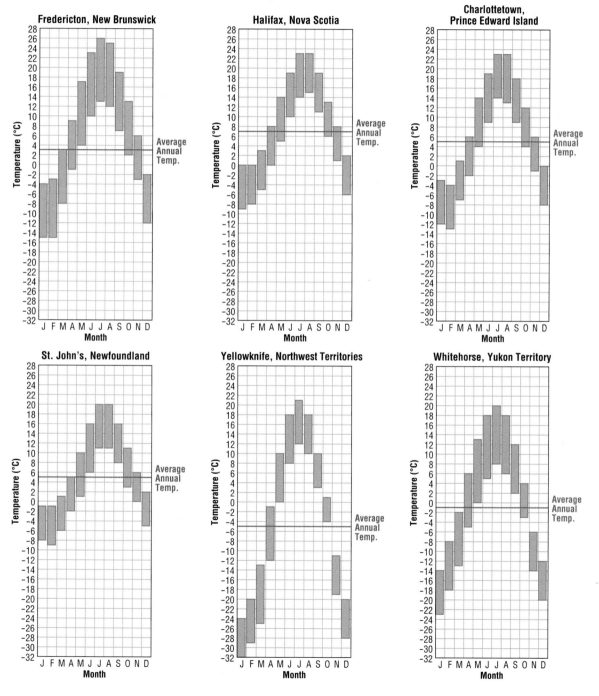

CANADIAN WEATHER DATA

Average Monthly Precipitation

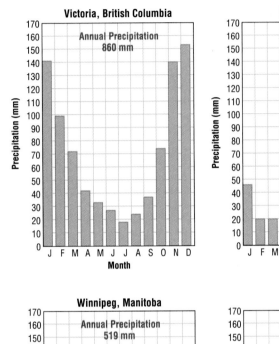

Victoria, British Columbia

Annual Precipitation
860 mm

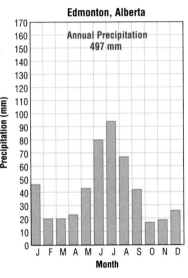

Edmonton, Alberta

Annual Precipitation
497 mm

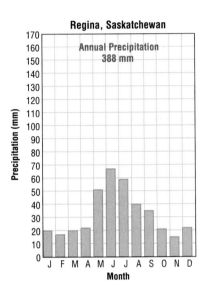

Regina, Saskatchewan

Annual Precipitation
388 mm

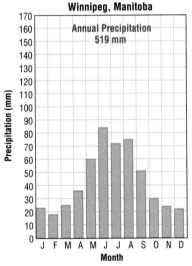

Winnipeg, Manitoba

Annual Precipitation
519 mm

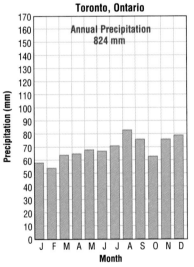

Toronto, Ontario

Annual Precipitation
824 mm

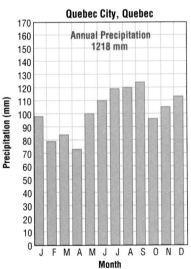

Quebec City, Quebec

Annual Precipitation
1218 mm

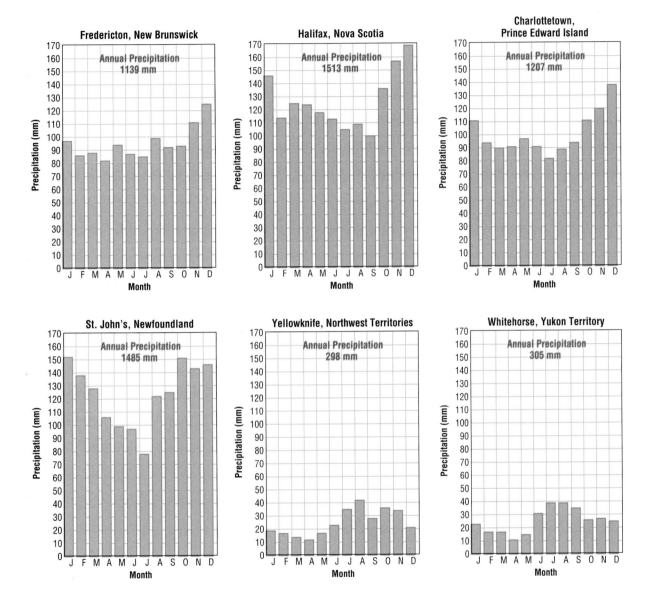

Fredericton, New Brunswick
Annual Precipitation 1139 mm

Halifax, Nova Scotia
Annual Precipitation 1513 mm

Charlottetown, Prince Edward Island
Annual Precipitation 1207 mm

St. John's, Newfoundland
Annual Precipitation 1485 mm

Yellowknife, Northwest Territories
Annual Precipitation 298 mm

Whitehorse, Yukon Territory
Annual Precipitation 305 mm

Glossary

A

Acute Angle An angle whose measure is less than 90°.

Acute Triangle A triangle with all 3 angles less than 90°.

Alternate Angles Two angles formed by two lines and a transversal. The angles are on opposite sides of the transversal in a Z or $\rotatebox[origin=c]{180}{Z}$ pattern.

Amount The total of the principal and the interest for a deposit or loan.

Angle The figure formed by 2 rays or 2 line segments with a common endpoint.

Angle Bisector A line that divides an angle into 2 equal parts.

Arc A part of the circumference of a circle.

Area The number of square units needed to cover a surface.

Average The mean of a set of numbers, found by dividing the sum of the numbers by the number of numbers.

Axes The intersecting number lines on a graph.

B

Bar Graph A graph that uses bars to represent data visually.

Base (of a polygon) Any side of a polygon.

Base (of a power) The number used as a factor for repeated multiplication. In 6^3, the base is 6.

Biased Sample A sample in which each member of the population does not have an equal chance of being selected.

Binary System The number system that consists of the two digits 0 and 1.

Broken-Line Graph A graph that represents data with line segments joined end to end.

C

Capacity The greatest volume that a container can hold, usually measured in litres or millilitres.

Census A survey in which data are collected from every member of a population.

Chord A line segment that joins 2 points on the circumference of a circle.

Circle Graph A graph that uses sectors of a circle to show how data are divided into parts.

Circumference The perimeter of a circle.

Co-interior Angles Two angles formed by 2 lines and a tranversal. Co-interior angles are on the same side of the transversal in a $\sqsubset$ or $\sqsupset$ pattern.

Common Denominator A number that is a common multiple of the denominators of a set of fractions. The common denominator of $\frac{1}{2}$ and $\frac{1}{3}$ is 6.

Common Factor A number that is a factor of two or more numbers. The common factor of 6 and 9 is 3.

Common Multiple A number that is a multiple of two or more numbers. Common multiples of 6 and 10 are 30, 60, 90, and so on.

Complementary Angles Two angles whose sum is 90°.

Composite Number A number that has more than 2 different factors. $6 = 1 \times 2 \times 3$

Computer Spreadsheet A computer program that stores information in cells and uses formulas to perform a variety of computations.

Congruent Figures Figures with the same size and shape.

Consecutive Numbers Numbers that differ by 1. Examples are 7, 8, and 9.

Coordinate Plane The 2-dimensional or (x, y) plane. Also known as the Cartesian plane.

Coordinates An ordered pair, (x, y), that locates a point on a coordinate plane.

Corresponding Angles Angles that have the same relative positions in geometric figures.

Corresponding Angles (from 2 lines and a transversal) Two angles that form an $\vdash$, $\dashv$, $\vdash$, or $\dashv$ pattern.

Corresponding Sides Sides that have the same relative positions in geometric figures.

Cube A polyhedron with 6 congruent square faces.

Data Facts or information.

Database An organized and sorted list of information.

Decagon A polygon with 10 sides.

Degree The unit for measuring angles. $1° = \frac{1}{360}$ of a complete turn.

Denominator The number of equal parts in a whole or a group. In $\frac{3}{4}$, the denominator is 4.

Diagonal A line segment joining 2 nonadjacent vertices in a polygon.

Diameter A chord that passes through the centre of a circle.

Dilatation A transformation that changes the size of an object.

Discount An amount deducted from the price of an item.

Divisible A number is divisible by another number when the remainder is zero.

Dodecagon A polygon with 12 sides.

Edge The straight line formed where 2 faces of a polyhedron meet.

Enlargement A dilatation for which the image is larger than the original figure.

Equation A number sentence that contains the symbol $=$.

Equilateral Triangle A triangle with all sides equal.

Equivalent Fractions Fractions, such as $\frac{1}{3}$, $\frac{2}{6}$, and $\frac{3}{9}$, that represent the same part of a whole or a group.

Equivalent Ratios Ratios, such as 1:3, 2:6, and 3:9, that represent the same fractional number or amount.

Event Any possible outcome of an experiment in probability.

Expanded Form The way in which numbers are written to show the total value of each digit. $235 = 2 \times 100 + 3 \times 10 + 5 \times 1$

Exponent The raised number used in a power to show the number of repeated multiplications of the base. In 4^2, the exponent is 2.

Exponential Form A shorthand method for writing numbers expressed as repeated multiplications. $81 = 3 \times 3 \times 3 \times 3 = 3^4$

Expression A mathematical phrase made up of numbers and variables, connected by operators.

Exterior Angle of a Polygon An angle formed by one extended side of a polygon and the other side at the same vertex.

Face A plane surface of a polyhedron.

Factors The numbers multiplied to give a specific product.

Factor Tree A diagram used to factor a number into its prime factors.

Flow Chart An organized diagram that displays the steps in the solution to a problem.

Fraction A number that describes part of a whole or part of a group.

Frequency The number of times an item or event occurs.

Frequency Table A table that uses tallies to count data.

Graph A representation of data in a pictorial form.

Greatest Common Factor (GCF) The largest factor that two or more numbers have in common. The GCF of 8, 12, and 24 is 4.

Grid A pattern of dots or lines.

Height The perpendicular distance from a vertex of a polygon to the opposite side.

Heptagon A polygon with 7 sides.

Hexagon A polygon with 6 sides.

Histogram A type of bar graph used to summarize and display a large set of data.

Hypotenuse The side opposite the right angle in a right triangle.

Image The figure produced by a transformation.

Improper Fraction A fraction whose numerator is greater than its denominator.

Included Angle An angle whose rays contain 2 sides of a triangle.

Inequality The statement that one expression is greater than, less than, or not equal to another expression.

Integers Numbers in the sequence $\ldots, -3, -2, -1, 0, 1, 2, 3, \ldots$.

Intersecting Lines Two lines that cross each other at 1 point.

Isosceles Triangle A triangle with 2 equal sides.

Key Digit The digit to the right of the place value to which a number is being rounded.

Kite A quadrilateral with 2 pairs of adjacent sides equal.

Like Terms Terms such as x and $4x$ with the same variable.

Line A set of points that contains no endpoints.

Line of Symmetry A mirror line that reflects an object onto itself.

Line Segment A part of a line. A line segment has 2 endpoints.

Lowest Common Denominator (LCD)
The lowest multiple shared by two or more denominators. The LCD of $\frac{1}{8}$ and $\frac{1}{6}$ is 24.

Lowest Common Multiple (LCM) The lowest multiple shared by two or more numbers. The LCM of 5, 10, and 15 is 30.

Lowest Terms A way of writing a fraction so that the numerator and denominator have no common factors other than 1.

M

Mapping A correspondence of points between an object and its image.

Mass The amount of matter in an object. Mass is usually measured in grams or kilograms.

Mean The sum of the numbers divided by the number of numbers in a set.

Median The middle number in a set of numbers arranged in order. If there is an even number of numbers, the median is the average of the 2 middle numbers.

Midpoint The point that divides a line segment into 2 equal parts.

Mixed Number A number that is the sum of a whole number and a fraction. An example is $3\frac{1}{2}$.

Mode The number that occurs most frequently in a set of data. In 1, 2, 2, 6, 6, 6, the mode is 6.

Multiples Repeated additions within a group. For example, 5, 10, 15, and 20 are multiples of 5.

N

Net A pattern used to construct a polyhedron.

Nonagon A polygon with 9 sides.

Numerator The number of equal parts being considered in a whole or a group. In the fraction $\frac{3}{4}$, the numerator is 3.

O

Obtuse Angle An angle whose measure is more than 90° but less than 180°.

Obtuse Triangle A triangle with 1 obtuse angle.

Octagon A polygon with 8 sides.

Odds Against (an event) The ratio of the number of unfavourable outcomes to the number of favourable outcomes.

Odds in Favour (of an event) The ratio of the number of favourable outcomes to the number of unfavourable outcomes.

Opposite Angles The equal angles formed by 2 intersecting lines.

Order of Operations The rules to be followed when simplifying expressions: **B**rackets, **E**xponents, **D**ivision and **M**ultiplication, **A**ddition and **S**ubtraction.

Ordered Pair A pair of numbers, (x, y), indicating the x- and y-coordinates of a point on a coordinate plane.

Origin The intersection of the horizontal and vertical axes on a graph. The origin has coordinates (0, 0).

Outcome The result of an experiment.

P

Parallel Lines Lines in the same plane that never meet.

Parallelogram A quadrilateral with opposite sides parallel and equal in length.

Pentagon A polygon with 5 sides.

Percent A fraction or ratio in which the denominator is 100.

Perfect Square A number that has a whole number as its principal square root.

Perimeter The distance around a polygon.

Periods Groups of 3 digits separated by spaces in numbers with more than 4 digits. There are 3 periods in 123 456 789.

Perpendicular Bisector The line that cuts a line segment into 2 equal parts at right angles.

Perpendicular Lines Two lines that intersect at a 90° angle.

Perspective The different views of an object, for example, top, bottom, side, front.

Pi (π) The quotient that results when the circumference of a circle is divided by its diameter.

Pictograph A graph that uses pictures or symbols to represent similar data.

Platonic Solids All the regular polyhedra.

Polygon A closed figure formed by 3 or more line segments.

Polyhedron A 3-dimensional figure with polygons as faces.

Population The entire set of items from which data can be taken.

Power A number, such as 3^4, written in exponential form.

Prime Factorization A composite number expressed as a product of its prime factors. $30 = 2 \times 3 \times 5$

Prime Number A number with exactly 2 different factors, 1 and itself. $3 = 1 \times 3$

Principal Square Root The positive square root of a number.

Prism A polyhedron with 2 parallel and congruent bases in the shape of polygons. The other faces are parallelograms.

Probability The ratio of the number of ways an outcome can occur to the total number of possible outcomes.

Program A set of instructions that a computer carries out in order.

Proper Fraction A fraction whose numerator is smaller that its denominator.

Proportion An equation, such as $\frac{3}{4} = \frac{6}{8}$, which states that 2 ratios are equal.

Pyramid A polyhedron with 1 base and the same number of triangular faces as there are sides on the base.

Pythagorean Theorem The area of the square drawn on the hypotenuse of a right triangle is equal to the sum of the areas of the squares drawn on the other 2 sides.

Quadrant One of the 4 regions formed in the coordinate plane by the intersection of the x-axis and the y-axis.

Quadrilateral A polygon with 4 sides.

Quotient A number resulting from a division.

Radius The length of the line segment that joins the centre of a circle and a point on the circumference.

Random Sample A sample in which each member of the population has an equal chance of being selected.

Range The difference between the highest and lowest numbers in a set.

Rate A comparison of 2 measurements with different units, such as $\frac{9\,m}{2\,s}$.

Ratio A comparison of numbers, such as 4:5 or $\frac{4}{5}$.

Rational Number A number that can be expressed as the quotient of 2 integers.

Ray A part of a line. A ray contains 1 endpoint.

Reciprocals Two numbers whose product is 1.

Rectangle A quadrilateral with opposite sides parallel and equal in length, and with four 90° angles.

Rectangular Prism A prism whose bases are congruent rectangles.

Reduction A dilatation for which the image is smaller than the original figure.

Reflection A flip transformation of an object in a mirror line or reflection line.

Reflex Angle An angle whose measure is more than 180° but less than 360°.

Regular Polygon A closed figure with all sides equal and all angles equal.

Regular Polyhedron A 3-dimensional figure with identical regular polygons as faces.

Relation A set of ordered pairs.

Repeating Decimal A decimal in which a digit or digits repeat without end.
$\frac{9}{11} = 0.818181\ldots$ or $0.\overline{81}$

Rhombus A quadrilateral with opposite sides parallel and all 4 sides equal.

Right Angle An angle whose measure is 90°.

Right Bisector A line that divides another line into 2 congruent segments at a 90° angle.

Right Triangle A triangle with 1 right angle.

Rotation A turn tranformation of an object about a fixed point or turn centre.

Rotational Symmetry A figure has rotational symmetry if it maps onto itself more than once in a complete turn.

Sample A selection from a population.

Sample Space The possible outcomes from an experiment.

Scale Drawing An accurate drawing that is either an enlargement or a reduction of an actual object.

Scalene Triangle A triangle with no sides equal.

Shell A 3-dimensional object whose interior is empty.

Similar Figures Figures that have the same shape but not always the same size.

Simplest Form The form of a fraction in which the numerator and the denominator have no common factors other than 1.

Skeleton A representation of the edges of a polyhedron.

Solid A 3-dimensional object whose interior is completely filled.

Solution A number that replaces a variable to make an equation true.

Square A quadrilateral with 4 equal sides and 4 right angles.

Square Root of a Number A number that multiplies itself to give the number.
$8 \times 8 = 64$, so 8 is a square root of 64.

Standard Form The way in which numbers are usually written. Examples are 2.345 and 678 000.

Stem-and-Leaf Plot Numbers tabulated so that the last digit is the leaf, and the digit or digits in front of it are the stem.

Straight Angle An angle whose measure is 180°.

Substitution The replacement of a variable with a number.

Supplementary Angles Two angles whose sum is 180°.

Surface Area The sum of the areas of the faces of a 3-dimensional figure.

Survey A sampling of information.

Terminating Decimal A decimal, such as 3.154, whose digits terminate.

Tessellation A repeated pattern of geometric figures that will completely cover a surface.

Transformation A mapping of points of a plane onto points of the same plane.

Translation A slide transformation of an object.

Transversal A line that intersects 2 lines in the same plane in 2 distinct points.

Trapezoid A quadrilateral with exactly 2 parallel sides.

Tree Diagram A diagram that shows the possible outcomes of consecutive events.

Triangle A polygon with 3 sides.

Unit Rate A comparison of 2 measurements in which the second term is 1, for example, $\frac{3m}{1s}$ or 3 m/s.

Unlike Terms Terms, such as $2x$, $3x^2$, and $2y$, with different variables.

Variable A letter or symbol used to represent a number.

Vertex The common endpoint of 2 rays or line segments.

Volume The number of cubic units contained in a space.

Whole Numbers Numbers in the sequence 0, 1, 2, 3, 4, 5, ….

***x*-axis** The horizontal number line in the Cartesian coordinate system.

***y*-axis** The vertical number line in the Cartesian coordinate system.

Index

exchange. *See* Exchange rate
ratio, 207–229
unit, 218, 220
Ratio, 210
equal, 214
equivalent, 214
estimation, 216–217
fraction form, 210
lowest terms, 210
percent, 242
rate, 207–229
ratio form, 210
scale drawing, 224
simplest form, 210
three-term, 213
Rational number, 376
integer, 376
Ray, 80
Reciprocals, 190
Rectangles, 44, 96
area, 78, 148
diagonals, 194–195
Rectangular prism, 268
Reductions, 456
dilatations, 458
Reflections, 450
mirror line, 450
reflection image, 450
reflection line, 450
sense, 450
Reflex angle, 82
Regular polygon, 98
Regular polyhedron, 276
Relations, 423–437
graph, 434
ordered pairs, 426
Repeating decimals, 196
Rhombus, 96
Right angle, 82
Right bisector, 113
Right triangle, 94, 108
area, 78
hypotenuse, 108
legs, 108
Roots. *See* Square roots
Rotational symmetry, 464–465
Rotations, 452

rotation image, 452
tessellations, 455
turn centre, 452
Rounding, 10, 14. *See also*
Estimation
key digit, 10
products, 22
quotients, 22

S

Sale price, 249
Sample, 308
biased, 308
random, 308
Sample space, 332
Scale, 224
maps, 226
Scale drawing, 224
maps, 226
Scalene triangle, 94
SCAMPER technique, 37
Scientific notation, 374
large numbers, 374
small numbers, 375
Seesaw math, 394
Sequence the operations, 32
Sequences, 369
Shell, 270–271, 272
edge, 272
Sides, 80
angle, 80
corresponding, 104
quadrilaterals, 96
Sieve of Eratosthenes, 61
Sign of operation, 368
Sign of quality, 368
Similar figures, 460
Simple interest, 259
Simplest form, 182
ratio, 210
Simulations, 337
Skeleton, 270, 272
Slides, 446
patterns, 447
strip patterns, 446
Small numbers, 375

scientific notation, 375
Solid, 272
Platonic, 276–277
three-dimensional, 268, 272
Sphere, 268
Spreadsheets, 166–167
cell, 166
column, 166
exchange rate, 222–223
magic square, 167
manual, 166
row, 166
transformations, 462–463
Square pyramid, 268
Square roots, 49
principal, 50
Squares, 49, 96
area, 78–79, 148, 236
diagonals, 236
in a circle, 118
magic, 167
perfect, 50
Standard form
integers, 368
number, 8
number system, 8
powers of ten, 20
Statistics, xxii, 305–343
averages, 330
measures of central tendency.
See Measures of central
tendency
misleading, 330
predictions, 310
probability, xxiii, 334–339
Stem, 324
Stem-and-leaf plots, 324
Straight angle, 82
Strip patterns, 446
flips, 446
slides, 446
turns, 446
Substitution
expression, 390
variable, 390
Subtraction, 16. *See also*
Differences

Text Credit

312 Gallup Canada

Photo Credits

Stone Worldwide, **422–423** The Bettmann Archive, **424** Susan Ashukian, **426** Barrett & MacKay/Masterfile, **432** Ian Crysler, **434** Dan Paul, **446 bottom** Dan Paul, **448** UPI/Bettmann, **450** Susan Ashukian, **452** J.A. Kraulis/Masterfile, **457 right** Todd Powell/Tony Stone Images, **458 top left** Canapress Photo Service, **462 top** Air Canada, **462 bottom** Ian Crysler (photo manipulation by Jun Park).

Illustration Credits

xiii Michael Herman, **xiv left** Margo Davies Leclair/Visual Sense Illustration, **xxiii** Michael Herman, **xxiv top right** © 1994 M.C. Escher/Cordon Art - Baarn - Holland. All Rights Reserved, **xxiv bottom right** Canadian Olympic Association, **4** Michael Herman, **10** Bernadette Lau, **17** Stephen Harris, **18–19** Ian Phillips, **20** Michael Herman, **25** Margo Davies Leclair/Visual Sense Illustration, **26** Dave Whamond, **28** Jun Park, **34 left** Stephen Harris, **43** Dave Whamond, **45** Michael Herman, **49 right** Jun Park, **64 top** Stephen Harris, **70 top, 71** Michael Herman, **74** Reprinted by permission: Tribune Media Services, **80** The Science Museum/Science & Society Picture Library, **82** Margo Davies Leclair/Visual Sense Illustration, **90 top** Bernadette Lau, **104, 106 bottom, 117–119** Margo Davies Leclair/Visual Sense Illustration, **149** Stamp reproduced courtesy of Canada Post Corporation, **156** Bill Suddick, **160** Michael Herman, **168 top** Pronk&Associates, **176–177** Margo Stahl, **177 left** The Globe and Mail, **184, 186** Stephen Harris, **190** Pronk&Associates, **193** Bernadette Lau, **198** Michael Herman, **200 left, 201 right** Pronk&Associates, **204** Bernadette Lau, **206 inset** © John Bianchi, **208, 210** Pronk&Associates, **211** Stephen Harris, **215** Pronk&Associates, **224 top right** Margo Davies Leclair/Visual Sense Illustration, **224 bottom, 225** Bernadette Lau, **226** Margo Davies Leclair/Visual Sense Illustration, **227** From "A Roman Apartment Complex," by Donald J. Watts and Carol Martin Watts. Copyright © 1986 by Scientific American, Inc. All rights reserved, **228 bottom** From © Oxford University Press, Leakey and Harris. *Laetoli*, 1987. Reprinted by permission of Oxford University Press, **230** Bernadette Lau, **232** Reprinted with permission — The Toronto Star Syndicate. Copyright: Tribune Media Services, **238 top right** Reprinted by permission: Tribune Media Services, **252 top** Ted Nasmith, **252 bottom** Michel Garneau, **254, 255** Ted Nasmith, **262** Reprinted by permission of United Feature Syndicate, **267, 269 bottom left, 273 bottom right, 274 top left and bottom right** Margo Davies Leclair/Visual Sense Illustration, **280 right** Ted Nasmith, **285 bottom left, 288 top left, 291 left, 292 top, 293 left** Margo Davies Leclair/Visual Sense Illustration, **294** Martha Newbigging, **296 right, 297** Margo Davies Leclair/Visual Sense Illustration, **304–305** Ted Nasmith, **308** Michael Herman, **312 top** Pronk&Associates, **314** Michel Garneau, **316** Bernadette Lau, **318 bottom** Michel Garneau, **326** Bernadette Lau, **328 top** Margo Davies Leclair/Visual Sense Illustration, **328 bottom** Pronk&Associates, **329 bottom right** Michel Garneau, **330** Dave McKay, **331 top right** Michel Garneau, **331 bottom left** Dave McKay, **342 bottom** Reprinted with permission — The Toronto Star Syndicate. Copyright: Tribune Media Services, **350 bottom** Margo Davies Leclair/Visual Sense Illustration, **351** Bernadette Lau, **362–363** Ian Phillips, **379** Stephen Harris, **392, 396–399** Margo Davies Leclair/Visual Sense Illustration, **401 top left** Copyright © 1994 by The New York Times Company. Reprinted by permission, **402, 403, 410 bottom** Michael Herman, **420** Reprinted with permission — The Toronto Star Syndicate. Copyright: Tribune Media Services, **430** Margo Davies Leclair/Visual Sense Illustration, **436–437** Michael Herman, **440** Reprinted with permission — The Toronto Star Syndicate. Copyright: Tribune Media Services, **444–445** Jun Park, **446 top and centre, 447 bottom** Margo Davies Leclair/Visual Sense Illustration, **454 top** © 1994 M.C. Escher/Cordon Art - Baarn - Holland. All Rights Reserved, **454 bottom, 455, 456, 457 left** Margo Davies Leclair/Visual Sense Illustration, **458 right** Collection: Vancouver Art Gallery, Emily Carr Trust, **464** Jun Park, **465** Margo Davies Leclair/Visual Sense Illustration.